Criminal Justice Policy

Criminal Justice Policy

Stacy L. Mallicoat
California State University, Fullerton

Christine L. Gardiner
California State University, Fullerton

Los Angeles | London | New Delhi
Singapore | Washington DC

Los Angeles | London | New Delhi
Singapore | Washington DC

FOR INFORMATION:

SAGE Publications, Inc.
2455 Teller Road
Thousand Oaks, California 91320
E-mail: order@sagepub.com

SAGE Publications Ltd.
1 Oliver's Yard
55 City Road
London, EC1Y 1SP
United Kingdom

SAGE Publications India Pvt. Ltd.
B 1/I 1 Mohan Cooperative Industrial Area
Mathura Road, New Delhi 110 044
India

SAGE Publications Asia-Pacific Pte. Ltd.
3 Church Street
#10-04 Samsung Hub
Singapore 049483

Acquisitions Editor: Jerry Westby
Assistant Editor: Rachael Leblond
Publishing Associate: MaryAnn Vail
Production Editor: Stephanie Palermini
Copy Editor: Janet Ford
Typesetter: Hurix Systems Pvt Ltd.
Proofreader: Dennis W. Webb
Indexer: Judy Hunt
Cover Designer: Anupama Krishnan
Marketing Manager: Terra Schultz

Printed in the United States of America

Library of Congress Cataloging-in-Publication Data

Criminal justice policy / Stacy L. Mallicoat, California State University, Fullerton; Christine L. Gardiner, California State University, Fullerton.

pages cm

Includes bibliographical references and index.

ISBN 978-1-4522-4224-8 (pbk. : alk. paper)
– ISBN 978-1-4833-1181-4 (web pdf)

1. Criminal justice, Administration of–United States.
I. Mallicoat, Stacy L., editor of compilation.
II. Gardiner, Christine, editor of compilation.

HV9950.C74319 2014

364.973–dc23

2013021329

This book is printed on acid-free paper.

13 14 15 16 17 10 9 8 7 6 5 4 3 2 1

Brief Contents

Preface   xvii
Stacy L. Mallicoat and Christine L. Gardiner

Section I: The Foundations of Criminal Justice Policy

Chapter 1: The Politics of Crime and the Policy Making Process   1
Stacy L. Mallicoat

**Chapter 2: The Influence of Research and Evidence-Based Practices on
Criminal Justice Policy**   15
Christine L. Gardiner

Chapter 3: Street-Level Bureaucracy: From Policy to Practice   37
Shelly Arsneault

Section II: Criminal Justice Policy in Action

Chapter 4: Policing High-Risk Places   53
William Sousa

Chapter 5: Homeland Security: A New Criminal Justice Mandate   67
Larry K. Gaines

Chapter 6: Immigrants and Crime   87
Nicole Palasz and Katherine Fennelly

Chapter 7: Mandatory Arrest and Intimate Partner Violence   101
Alesha Durfee

**Chapter 8: From "Just Say No!" to "Well, Maybe"—The War on
Drugs and Sensible Alternatives**   121
Clayton J. Mosher and Scott Akins

Chapter 9: Controlling the Sexual Offender   145
Chrysanthi Leon and Ashley Kilmer

Chapter 10: Public Policy and White-Collar and Corporate Crime   159
   Henry N. Pontell and Gilbert Geis

**Chapter 11: America's "War on Gangs": Response to a Real Threat
   or a Moral Panic?**   175
   John Hagedorn and Meda Chesney Lind

Chapter 12: Juvenile Waiver Policies   191
   Aaron Kupchik and Megan Gosse

Chapter 13: Criminal Justice Responses to the Mentally Ill   201
   Henry F. Fradella and Rebecca Smith-Casey

Chapter 14: Gender Responsive Practices   225
   Barbara Koons-Witt and Courtney Crittenden

Chapter 15: Restorative Justice   241
   Donna Decker Morris

**Chapter 16: Three Strikes: Passage, Implementation,
   Evaluation, and Reform**   261
   Elsa Chen

Chapter 17: The Supermax: Issues and Challenges   275
   Brett Garland, H. Daniel Butler, and Benjamin Steiner

Chapter 18: Capital Punishment   293
   Robert M. Bohm

**Chapter 19: Reentry and Rehabilitation: Generating
   Successful Outcomes During Challenging Times**   309
   Faith E. Lutze and Roger L. Schaefer

Section III: Future Directions

Chapter 20: Emerging Issues in Criminal Justice Policy   325
   Christine L. Gardiner and Stacy L. Mallicoat

References   341
Index   385
About the Editors and Contributors   419

Detailed Contents

Preface   **xvii**

Stacy L. Mallicoat and Christine L. Gardiner

The Foundations of Criminal Justice Policy   xvii

Criminal Justice Policy in Action   xvii

Future Directions in Criminal Justice Policy   xx

Ancillaries   xx

Acknowledgments   xx

Section I: The Foundations of Criminal Justice Policy

Chapter 1: The Politics of Crime and the Policy Making Process   **1**

Stacy L. Mallicoat

What Is Policy?   1

    The Need for Criminal Justice Policy   2

The Development of Criminal Justice Policy   5

    Politics and Criminal Justice Policy   7

    Politics and the Models of Criminal Justice   10

The Role of Fear and the Media on Criminal Justice Policies   10

Conclusion   13

Key Terms   13

Discussion Questions   14

Websites for Additional Research   14

Chapter 2: The Influence of Research and Evidence-Based Practices on Criminal Justice Policy   **15**

Christine L. Gardiner

The Commencement of Criminal Justice Research   16

What We Know about Crime and Delinquency that Policy Should Consider   19

    Biological and Psychological Risk Factors   20

    Family Risk Factors   21

    Social Risk Factors   22

    Environmental Risk Factors   23

Current State of Knowledge 24
  What Works 25
  What Doesn't Work 31
  Available Resources on Evidence-Based Practices 32
Conclusion 33
Key Terms 34
Discussion Questions 35
Websites for Additional Research 35

Chapter 3: Street-Level Bureaucracy: From Policy to Practice 37
Shelly Arsneault
What is Bureaucracy? 38
Street-Level Bureaucracy 39
  Rules, Regulations, and Professional Norms 41
  Discretion 42
  Autonomy 45
  Accountability 47
Implications for the Criminal Justice System 49
Key Terms 50
Discussion Questions 50
Websites for Additional Research 51

Section II: Criminal Justice Policy in Action

Chapter 4: Policing High-Risk Places 53
William H. Sousa
The Back Story 54
  Early History of Policing Problem Places 54
  "Hazards" and Random Preventive Patrol 54
  Theoretical Developments and the Emergence of the "Hot Spots" Concept 55
The Current State of the Policy: Practice and Research 57
  The Identification of Problem Locations 57
  Understanding Problem-Prone Locations: What Makes a Place a Concern? 57
  Police Innovations at Problem Places 59
Race, Gender, and Class Implications 62
  The Complexities of Policing Nuisance Locations 62
How Do We Fix It? Problems at High-Risk Locations 64
Key Terms 65
Discussion Questions 65
Websites for Additional Research 65

Chapter 5: Homeland Security: A New Criminal Justice Mandate 67
Larry K. Gaines
The Back Story: What is Homeland Security? 68
The Current State of Homeland Security 69

The U.S.A. PATRIOT Act   69
Weapons of Mass Destruction   70
Critical Infrastructure and Key Resources   71
Challenges of Homeland Security: The Homeland Security Apparatuses   72
Problems in Administering the DHS   72
The Current Status of Homeland Security   73
Transportation   73
Border Protection   73
Immigration Enforcement   74
Financial and Identification Crime   75
Cybersecurity   76
Terrorist Financing and Money Laundering   77
Responding to Terrorist Attacks and Other Critical Events   79
National Response Framework   79
National Incident Management System   80
The Police and Homeland Security   81
Conclusion   83
Key Terms   84
Discussion Questions   85
Websites for Additional Research   85

Chapter 6: Immigrants and Crime   87
Nicole Palasz and Katherine Fennelly

The Back Story: Immigration and the Law   88
The Current State of the Policy   89
Federal Policies   89
Federal-State Immigration Partnerships   92
State and Local Initiatives   93
What Research has Taught Us about Immigrants and Crime   94
Unintended Consequences of the Enforcement Policies   96
How Do We Fix It? Suggestions for Policy Reform   98
Expand Community-Based Alternatives to Detention   99
Scrutinize the Role of the Prison Industry   99
Pass Comprehensive Immigration Reform   99
Key Terms   99
Discussion Questions   100
Websites for Additional Research   100

Chapter 7: Mandatory Arrest Policies and Intimate Partner Violence   101
Alesha Durfee

The Back Story: The Creation of Mandatory Arrest Policies in the United States   103
The Current State of the Policy   106
What Research Has Taught Us: Extant Research on Mandatory Arrest Policies   108
Gender, Race, Ethnicity, Class, Sexuality, and Immigration Status Implications   109
Gender   109

Race and Ethnicity 111
Class 112
Sexuality 113
Immigration Status 114
How Do We Fix It? Suggestions for Policy Reform 115
Implement "Mandatory Action" Policies Instead of Mandatory Arrest Policies 115
Make "Mandatory Action" Policies Part of a "Coordinated Community Response" to IPV 116
Incorporate Primary Aggressor Statutes into Mandatory Action Policies 116
Increase Formal Sanctions for IPV When an Arrest Is Made 117
Conclusion 117
Key Terms 118
Discussion Questions 118
Websites for Additional Research 119

Chapter 8: From "Just Say No!" to "Well, Maybe"—The War on Drugs and Sensible Alternatives **121**
Clayton J. Mosher and Scott Akins
The Back Story: The History of Drug Laws in the United States 121
The Current State of Drug Policies in the United States 126
Specific (and Ancillary) Drug Policies 128
Race, Gender, and Class Implications of Drug Policies in the United States 134
Unintended Consequences of U.S. Drug Criminalization Policies 135
What Research Has Taught Us: Outcomes Associated with Less Punitive Drug Policies 137
How Do We Fix It? Recent Developments in United States Drug Policies 141
Treatment in Lieu of Incarceration Laws 141
Sentencing Reductions 141
Conclusion 143
Key Terms 143
Discussion Questions 144
Websites for Additional Research 144

Chapter 9: Controlling the Sexual Offender **145**
Chrysanthi Leon and Ashley Kilmer
The Back Story on Sexual Offenders 145
The Current State of the Policy 147
What Research has Taught Us 150
Sex Offenders and Repeat Crimes (Recidivism) 150
The Impact of Laws on Known and Unknown Offenders 153
Race, Gender, and Class Implications of the Policy 155
Sex Offenses Committed by Youths 155
How Do We Fix It? Suggestions for Policy Reform 156
Key Terms 157
Discussion Questions 157
Websites for Additional Research 157

Chapter 10: Public Policy and White-Collar and Corporate Crime   159
Henry N. Pontell and Gilbert Geis

The Back Story   160
    The FDA, Thalidomide, and RUR-426   161
The Current State of the Policy   163
    Broken Windows and White-Collar Crime   164
What Research Has Taught Us   165
    The Savings and Loan Debacle   165
    Enron, Arthur Andersen, and Others   166
Consequences of White-Collar and Corporate Crimes: The Monstrous Meltdown   166
    Bear Stearns   167
    The American International Group (AIG)   167
    Lehman Brothers Holdings   167
    Dodd-Frank Remedial Legislation   168
    What Took Place Thereafter   169
    The CREW Report   169
    Fraud in the World of Medicine   170
Race, Class, and Gender Implications of the Policy   170
How Do We Fix It?   170
    Corporations and Criminal Law   171
    Attorneys and White-Collar and Corporate Crime   171
Key Terms   173
Discussion Questions   173
Websites for Additional Research   174

Chapter 11: America's "War on Gangs": Response to a Real Threat or a Moral Panic?   175
John Hagedorn and Meda Chesney-Lind

The Back Story   177
    Media and the Framing of Crime and Gangs   178
The Current State of the Policy   178
Race, Class, and Gender Implications of the Policy   180
Unintended Consequences of the Policy: The Fallacy of Increasing Gang Violence   181
What Research Has Taught Us About Gangs   183
    Gangs, Chicago, and Homicide   185
How Do We Fix It? Suggestions for Policy Reform   187
Key Terms   189
Discussion Questions   189
Websites for Additional Research   189

Chapter 12: Juvenile Waiver Policies   191
Aaron Kupchik and Megan Gosse

The Back Story   191
The Current State of the Policy   193

What Research Has Taught Us: Outcomes of Waiver Laws 195
Race, Class, and Gender Implications 196
Unintended Consequences of Juvenile Waiver Policies 197
How Do We Fix It? Suggestions for Policy Reform 198
Key Terms 199
Discussion Questions 200
Websites for Additional Research 200

Chapter 13: Criminal Justice Responses to the Mentally Ill **201**
Henry F. Fradella and Rebecca Smith-Casey
    The Back Story: Historical Foundations 202
        First-Wave Reform Efforts: From Jails and Prisons to Asylums 203
        Second-Wave Reform Efforts: The Rise of Psychiatry and Psychology 204
        Third-Wave Reform Efforts: The Community Mental Health Movement 204
    The Current State of the Policy 207
        Estimates of Mentally Ill Inmates 207
        Explanations for the High Prevalence of Inmates with SMIs 208
        The Mentally Ill Offender Treatment and Crime Reduction Act of 2004 211
    What Research Has Taught Us 212
        Mental Health Courts 212
        Specialty Mental Health Probation 214
        Prisoner Reentry and Aftercare Programs 214
    Differences Involving Race, Ethnicity, Gender, and Class 215
        Race and Ethnicity 215
        Gender 216
        Socioeconomic Status 217
    Unintended Consequences of the Policy 217
    How Do We Fix It? Suggestions for Policy Reform 219
        Legislative Changes to Address Financial Problems 219
        Increased Diversion Efforts by Expanding the Number and Scope of
            Mental Health Courts 219
        Reform Civil Commitment Laws 220
        Improve Services for the Mentally Ill Within and Beyond the Criminal
            Justice System 221
    Key Terms 223
    Discussion Questions 223
    Websites for Additional Research 223

Chapter 14: Gender Responsive Practices **225**
Barbara Koons-Witt and Courtney Crittenden
    The Back Story: The Need for Gender-Responsive Practices 225
        Brief Profile of Women Offenders 226
        Historical Perspective of Treatment and Programming 226
    The Current State of Gender-Responsive Practices and Research 228

        Assessment of Risk and Needs   228
        Correctional Programming   230
    Considerations of Race/Ethnicity and Class in Gender-Responsive Practices   237
    How Do We Fix It? The Future and Gender-Responsive Practices   238
    Key Terms   240
    Discussion Questions   240
    Websites for Additional Research   240

Chapter 15: Restorative Justice   241
Donna Decker Morris
    The Back Story: Historical Perspectives on Restorative Justice   241
        Community Justice   243
        Victims' Rights Movement   244
        First Nation Peoples and Village-Based Cultural Philosophies   245
        Faith-Based Influences   247
        Common Themes in Restorative Justice Programming   247
    The Current State of the Policy   247
    What Research Has Taught Us   251
    Race, Gender, and Class Implications   253
    How Do We Fix It? Suggestions for Reform   255
    Key Terms   259
    Discussion Questions   260
    Websites for Additional Research   260

Chapter 16: Three Strikes: Passage, Implementation,
Evaluation, and Reform   261
Elsa Chen
    The Back Story: How the Idea Became Reality   262
    The Current State of the Implementation of Three Strikes   264
    What Research Has Taught Us: The Effects of Three Strikes   264
    Race, Class, and Gender Implications of the Policy   266
    How Do We Fix It? Efforts to Reform Three Strikes   267
    Future Directions: What Lies Ahead for Three Strikes in California?   270
    Conclusion   273
    Key Terms   274
    Discussion Questions   274
    Websites for Additional Research   274

Chapter 17: The Supermax: Issues and Challenges   275
Brett Garland, H. Daniel Butler, and Benjamin Steiner
    The Back Story: The Rise of Supermax Confinement   276
    The Current State of the Policy: Is the Supermax a "Good" Correctional Practice?   277
        Incapacitation   278
        Deterrence   280

What Research Has Taught Us: The Impact of Supermax Prisons   281
Race, Class, and Gender Implications   282
Implications of the Policy   284
    Financial Costs   284
    Legal Issues   285
How Do We Fix It? The Future of the Supermax   287
Conclusion   291
Key Terms   291
Discussion Questions   291
Websites for Additional Research   292

Chapter 18: Capital Punishment   **293**
Robert M. Bohm

The Back Story   293
The Current State of the Policy   294
What Research Has Taught Us   295
Arbitrary Application   296
    Cost   296
General Deterrence   297
Race, Gender, and Class Implications of the Policy   298
    Class   298
    Gender   299
    Race   300
How Do We Fix It? Suggestions for Reform   302
    Good Defense Attorneys Can Make a Difference   302
    Punish the Misconduct of Defense Attorneys   303
    Improve Police Investigations, Interrogations, and the Handling of Evidence   303
    Improve Eyewitness Identification Techniques and Procedures   303
    Punish Police Misconduct   304
    Improve the Work and Credibility of Crime Lab Technicians   304
    Require DNA Testing   304
    Set Rigorous Standards for Jailhouse Snitches/Informants   304
    Guide Prosecutors' Decisions to Seek the Death Penalty 304
    Improve Disclosure Requirements   305
    Punish Prosecutor Misconduct   305
    Better Training and Certification of Trial Judges in Capital Cases   305
    Give Trial Judges Veto Power   305
    Eliminate Time Limits and Other Constraints on Claims of Actual Innocence   305
    Improve the Clemency Process   305
    Moratorium   306
Conclusion   306
Key Terms   306
Discussion Questions   306
Websites for Additional Research   307

Chapter 19: Reentry and Rehabilitation: Generating Successful Outcomes During Challenging Times   **309**
Faith E. Lutze and Roger L. Schaefer

The Back Story: The Political, Economic, and Social Context of Community Corrections   310
The Current State of Prison Reentry   312
Race, Gender, and Class Implications of the Policy   313
What Research Has Taught Us: Evidence-Based Practices and Reentry   314
    What Works to Enhance Success in Community Corrections   314
    Coordinated Responses to Reentry and a Continuum of Care   317
Challenges of Reentry: The Importance of Implementation   318
    Preparing for Innovation   319
    Managing Organizational Success   319
    Community Supervision Practices   320
How Do We Fix It? Policy Recommendations for Reentry and Rehabilitation   321
Key Terms   323
Discussion Questions   323
Websites for Additional Research   323

Section III: Future Directions

Chapter 20: Emerging Issues in Criminal Justice Policy   **325**
Christine L. Gardiner and Stacy L. Mallicoat

Incarceration and Realignment: The Case of California   325
Zero Tolerance and Tough on Crime: Rolling Back on Juvenile Offending   328
Gun Control Policy: A Renewed Interest in the Second Amendment   330
    Why Is Gun Policy So Contentious?   332
Search and Seizure in the 21st century   334
    Drones   334
    DNA   336
    Other Emerging Technologies   337
Conclusion   338
Key Terms   338
Discussion Questions   338
Websites for Additional Research   339

References   **341**

Index   **385**

About the Editors and Contributors   **419**

Preface

The discussion of criminal justice policy is a key issue in understanding the functions and operations of the criminal justice system. Scholars, practitioners, and politicians debate the value of these policies in their evaluations of the criminal justice system. The nature of this subject involves a host of concerns, including politics, public sentiment, research, and practice. Throughout this book, you'll be exposed to a thematic overview of criminal justice policy and its relationship to the American criminal justice system. Containing original chapters written by experts and scholars in the field, this manuscript highlights the current debates about criminal justice policy and discusses the implications for the system and society at large.

The book is divided into three thematic areas: (a) the foundations of criminal justice policy; (b) criminal justice policy in action; and (c) future directions.

The Foundations of Criminal Justice Policy

The introductory section of this book highlights the current state of crime and the nature of criminal justice policy in the United States today. The first chapter begins with a definition of what is public policy, explanations of how public policy is developed, and the theoretical foundations of policy making. Following this discussion, you learn about the role of politics in the development and implementation of criminal justice policy, and how the media and fears about crime can influence this process. Chapter 2 discusses the influence of social science research and evidence-based practices on the development of criminal justice policy. It describes the federal government's role in creating and disseminating criminal justice research as well as what we know about crime, criminals, and intervention programs. Finally, this chapter explores what, if any, effect such understanding can (or should) have on criminal justice policy. The third chapter highlights the role of bureaucracy, particularly how street-level bureaucracy influences the implementation and effectiveness of criminal justice policies.

Criminal Justice Policy in Action

The second section, which comprises the bulk of the book provides substantive discussions on criminal justice policies. Each chapter in this section focuses on a particular example of criminal justice policy. Written by researchers and scholars who are experts in their field, this section is designed to expose students to the realities of criminal justice policy and the effects of these examples for the system. Each chapter follows a similar framework that covers the following themes: (a) The backstory: historical foundations of the policy; (b) The current state of the policy; (c) What research has taught us (what works, what doesn't work, and what don't we know); (d) Race, gender, and class implications of the policy; and (e) How do we fix it? Suggestions for reform. Several of the chapters also include discussions about the implications of the policy, unintended consequences of the policy, or discussions about particular issues facing the implementations of these policies, or the future directions.

Chapter 4 highlights the policies that transformed modern day policing. This chapter traces the history of policing and the implementation of practices, such as hot spots policing, community oriented policing, problem oriented policing, and order maintenance policing, in an effort to understand policing strategies focused on managing crime-prone communities.

Chapter 5 focuses on the nature of homeland security as a new criminal justice mandate. In light of the September 11, 2001, attacks by foreign terrorists on American soil, homeland security and combating terrorism are now national priorities. While the risk of these offenses is low, the emphasis on the development and implementation of a national security and prevention effort dominates the political landscape. As the defenders against such attacks, criminal justice agencies at both the national and local levels have seen new policies that impact their daily lives. This chapter traces the development of homeland security, from the organization of national level objections to the effects for local agents as first responders.

Chapter 6 provides insight to a recent phenomenon in the American criminal justice system: the role of immigration and its links to criminal activity and organizations. The perception that illegal immigrants engage in illegal activities is used to support the rise of punitive policies toward members of immigrant communities. This chapter explores the current state of federal and state-level policies toward immigration enforcement and its implications for the criminal justice system.

Chapter 7 presents a discussion on the use of mandatory arrest policies in cases of intimate partner violence. There is significant debate about whether mandatory arrest policies are helpful or harmful. This chapter provides an overview of the development of mandatory arrest policies, reviews the efficacy of such practices, and discusses some of the consequences of these policies, including how the status characteristics of victims and abusers (such as gender, race, ethnicity, class, sexuality, and immigration status) influences how cases of intimate partner violence are treated by agents of the criminal justice system.

Chapter 8 highlights how the abuse of illegal substances and related harms has transformed our criminal justice system. The chapter examines the economic and social costs of drug policies and how mandatory minimum sentencing policies have a disproportionately negative impact on the poor and people of color. The chapter concludes with a review of alternative approaches to drug regulation around the world as well as recent changes in the response to illegal drugs in the United States at the state and federal levels.

Chapter 9 focuses on policies related to the control of sexual offenders in the community. Despite the increase in policies like Megan's Law, which provides for community notification of convicted sexual offenders and residency requirements, the majority of sex offenders are not held accountable by the criminal justice system due to the low reporting rates for these crimes. This chapter traces the history of sexual offender legislation to the modern day implementation of a "one size fits all" model of strict supervision.

Chapter 10 provides a review of the background and current context within which white-collar crimes and corporate offenses take place. From the savings and loan scandal to Enron, these crimes have a significant impact on society. Contrary to public opinion, the effects of white-collar and corporate crimes have a greater detrimental effect than the crimes of violence that dominate our media reports. Despite the negative consequences of these crimes, the laws regarding white-collar and corporate offenses are both inadequate and favor the interests of the offender. This chapter highlights some of these issues and presents suggestions for reform.

Chapter 11 examines common criminal justice policy responses toward gangs as well as media's role in constructing the modern gang problem. This chapter provides an overview of the gang problem in the United States as well as an assessment of policies generated to prevent, intervene, and suppress gang membership. Despite best intentions, many of the efforts to curb gang violence are shown to be ineffective or counterproductive in communities where gangs dominate. Within the criminal justice system, gangs serve as a key factor in the "get tough on crime" movement toward increased penalties.

Chapter 12 continues the discussion of increased penalties for juvenile offenders with a dialogue about juvenile waiver penalties. While the juvenile court was first founded on the philosophy of "the best interests of the child," recent trends in the punishment of juveniles move away from the rehabilitative focus of the juvenile court with policies that send the message of "do the adult crime, do the adult time." This chapter describes how the use of juvenile waiver policies has expanded in recent years and the effect of these policies.

Chapter 13 highlights how issues of mental illness are now a significant part of our criminal justice system. This chapter traces the roots of mental health reform and how society has failed this population. Not only are police more likely to arrest the mentally ill for "nuisance" crimes, but the lack of mental health alternatives leads to the incarceration of offenders, ultimately turning our prisons into the new asylums. This chapter highlights the issues that mentally ill offenders face and an analysis of effective programs and reforms for the system.

Chapter 14 focuses on the issues of gender responsive practices. These practices acknowledge that there are gendered pathways to crime and that programs and policies need to be geared toward women's unique needs in order to be successful in negotiating reentry from an incarcerated environment. This chapter highlights some of the gender responsive practices that are used throughout the criminal justice system, and discusses the future of these policies and the implications for the criminal justice system.

Chapter 15 provides a review of restorative justice practices that are in use in justice systems worldwide. Restorative justice represents a paradigmatic shift in society's response to crime by expanding beyond a two-party structure of the state (government) as the "victim," and the defendant as the offender. Rather, restorative justice considers much broader questions involving who was harmed by the crime, what is the nature of the harm, and how the harm can be repaired. This chapter presents a review of restorative justice practices both nationally and internationally. Together, these examples provide insight to a new way of looking at criminal justice issues.

Chapter 16 presents a discussion of California's Three Strikes law as an example of habitual sentencing laws that appeared nationwide throughout the 1990s in an effort to respond to rising crime rates and failures in the rehabilitative attempts throughout the criminal justice system. The chapter follows the implementation of the law, the consequences that arose as a result of loopholes in the law, and efforts to reform the law. The chapter concludes with some thoughts about the future of three strikes in California.

Chapter 17 highlights the unique features of the supermax prison environment. This chapter describes the rise of the supermax from its early beginnings at Alcatraz and Marion federal prisons. Following a critical examination of the justifications for supermax confinement, the chapter explores the financial and legal implications for this practice within the criminal justice system. The chapter concludes with recommendations for improving supermax policy and guiding research on this controversial practice.

Chapter 18 focuses on the controversial use of the ultimate criminal justice punishment: the death penalty. This chapter presents a modern history of capital punishment in the United States and follows the path to its abolition in 1972 and subsequent reinstatement in 1976. While new provisions were seen as a way to fix a system that was arbitrary and discriminatory, there are significant questions about whether these new procedures have eliminated or significantly reduced the problems with the administration of capital punishment. The chapter concludes with policy suggestions about what can be done to fix the problems that remain.

Chapter 19 provides a review of community correctional practices related to prisoner reentry. The chapter discusses some of the research on effective strategies to reduce recidivism and achieve reintegration at both the individual level of intervention and at the agency level of operation. The chapter concludes with recommended strategies that can be implemented by policy makers as they take responsibility for supporting and intelligently guiding the future of community corrections.

Future Directions

The concluding chapter of this book focuses on emerging issues within criminal justice policy. In this chapter, we highlight four prominent themes: (a) criminal justice realignment as a policy response to violations of inmates' constitutional rights, (b) juvenile justice policy modifications in response to the U.S. Supreme Court's changing view of juveniles, (c) a renewed debate about gun control policies in response to high profile incidents and recent 2nd Amendment decisions, and (d) 4th Amendment protections in the new digital age. Two of these topics are particularly pertinent because they represent criminal justice policies born as a response to specific constitutional concerns raised by the courts, while the other two represent especially interesting and complex constitutional issues that the courts will have to grapple with in the very near future.

Ancillaries

A password-protected Instructor Teaching Site is available at **www.sagepub.com/mallicoatcjp**. This site features resources that have been designed to help instructors plan and teach their courses. It includes an extensive test bank in both Word and Respondus formats, chapter-specific PowerPoint presentations, and links to SAGE journal articles.

Acknowledgements

Stacy L. Mallicoat

First and foremost, I give my appreciation and thanks to Jerry Westby for his support and encouragement to write about issues in criminal justice that I am passionate about. Special thanks to the many amazing scholars who agreed to contribute to this book and share your knowledge with students and members of the criminal justice community. Appreciation goes out to the reviewers of this text and support staff at SAGE Publications for your insightful commentary and suggestions that helped bring this book into print. Many thanks to the friends and colleagues that helped me along the way and provided immeasurable support for my many endeavors. Additional gratitude goes to the many mentors that I learned from throughout my career—Denise Paquette Boots, Allison Cotton, Hillary Potter, Joanne Belknap, Hank Fradella, Anthony Peguero, Lorenzo "L-bunny" Boyd, Kareem Jordan, Kenethia Fuller, Cassandra Bullers Reyes, and

Jill Rosenbaum. I also want to acknowledge my colleagues in the Division of Politics, Administration and Justice at California State University for the laughter in the halls and camaraderie in the day-to-day life. Special thanks to my coauthor and coeditor, Christie Gardiner, for your support, care, and collaboration as we embarked on this journey together. Finally, I am deeply indebted to my husband Jeff, my son Keegan and extended family and friends for their love, support, and care, and their endless encouragement for my adventures in academia and beyond.

Christine L. Gardiner

Thanks to my mentor, colleague, coauthor/coeditor, and friend, Stacy Mallicoat, for inviting me onto this project and having immense patience as I learned the trade and juggled a few too many tasks. Thanks also to Jerry Westby for his support and faith in this project and in us. Thank you to our incredibly talented and wonderful chapter authors who contributed their immense knowledge and sacred time to this project. Also, thank you to the many reviewers who gave us their honest and helpful feedback to improve the book, and to the staff at SAGE who continued improving the book, even after we thought it was done. Thanks to my many colleagues and mentors who have sharpened my intellect and challenged me in unexpected ways. A special shout out to Elliott Currie as well as Susan Turner, Ron Huff, Frank Zimring, Joan Petersilia, Cheryl Maxson, and Bryan Vila for guiding, supporting, and shaping me into the scholar that I am today. Also to my CSUF colleagues who make my job thoroughly enjoyable. Finally, gigantic thanks to Steve, Allie, Mackenzie, and my extended family for your unending love and support. You are the light of my life and the reason for my perseverance.

The Politics of Crime and the Policy Making Process

Stacy L. Mallicoat

Throughout the past century, debates about criminal justice policies dominated our political landscape. Indeed, government agencies and their representatives spend their days in cities, states, and the nation's capital lobbying for protection, intervention, and processes to advocate and protect individual and group interests. This chapter focuses on the development of criminal justice policy and begins with a review of policy as a general issue as well as a discussion on the need for policy within the criminal justice arena. Following a discussion of crime rates, this chapter reviews the role of politics in discussions about crime and criminal justice policy and the roles of political actors in this process. The chapter concludes with a discussion on the effect of fear about crime and the media in the policy making process.

What Is Policy?

If one consults the Merriam-Webster Dictionary, the term "*policy*" includes definitions, such as the "prudence or wisdom in the management of affairs" and "a definite course or method of action selected from among alternatives and in light of given conditions to guide and determine present and future decisions" (Merriam-Webster, n.d.). Policies are utilized throughout governments and organizations to facilitate and regulate action, guide the decision-making process and provide direction as the policy is implemented. While there have been a number of different theories and discussions about the policy development process, we can generally organize this process into six stages: (a) problem identification, (b) policy demands, (c) agenda formation, (d) policy adoption, (e) policy implementation, and (f) policy evaluation. Figure 1.1 showcases how these six stages work together in the development of policy. Before a policy can be developed, there must be an issue at hand. Issues can be identified by concerned citizens, the media, and advocacy groups, as well as by politicians. Issues in criminal justice might include rising crime rates, the need for drug and alcohol counseling in prisons, or concerns about the residency requirements for convicted sex offenders in the community.

Once an issue is identified, there can be significant debate over the demands of the policy. What is the goal or objective of the policy? Is it to increase punishments? Is it to increase community safety? It is during this stage that the intent of the policy is put forward. Once this is decided, the agenda formation process begins. This is perhaps one of the most politicized stages in policy development as it involves a variety of different voices—from government officials to special interest groups and individuals who ultimately are affected by the policy—all of whom want to be heard. The next stage involves the adoption of the policy. Depending on the nature of the policy, this could involve the passage of new laws or the signing of executive orders. Upon completion of this stage, the cycle moves to policy implementation. Implementation is all about spending money—from hiring more officers, to increasing police presence in particular regions, to allocating funds to supervise offenders in the community. The ways in which a policy is implemented may differ significantly from the original intention of the authors of a policy. This can present significant challenges—perhaps the law as it was written was too vague, or there isn't enough funding to effectively implement the policy, or there may be challenges to the policy that may stall or halt the implementation. Finally, the evaluation stage looks at the efficacy of the policy. Did the policy accomplish what it set out to do? What impact does the policy have (Cochran, Mayer, Carr, Cayer, & McKenzie, 2011)? Policy evaluation can be divided into two general categories: process evaluation and outcome evaluation. ***Process evaluation*** involves looking at the progression of the policy development experience. Are there areas where these methods could be improved or streamlined? If the implementation of the policy differs from the original intent (positively or negatively), how might this be resolved? In contrast, an ***outcome evaluation*** looks at the changes that occur as a result of the policy. For example, does the implementation of early intervention programming in elementary schools reduce the number of youth who are adjudicated delinquent in the juvenile court? It is important that both process and outcome evaluations are conducted in order to identify whether the policy produced a change (outcome) and why the change did or did not occur (process). Evaluation is perhaps the most important stage of policy development, but one that many suggest is overlooked and under-emphasized.

The Need for Criminal Justice Policy

Changes in criminal justice policy generally occur in response to a need or issue that faces the criminal justice system and society as a whole. Much of these needs are rooted in discussions about the levels of crime in society. Here, policy is seen as a way to deal with the presence of crime and the handling of offenders. The federal government has been an active player in the creation of crime control policies. Table 1.1 highlights some of the significant pieces of Federal legislation implemented by Congress over the past five decades. Throughout this text, you are exposed to several of these different pieces of legislation and how the implementation of these policies affected the management of our criminal justice system. Given the high level of policy implementation related to criminal justice issues, one might be led to believe that crime rates have spiraled out of control. After all, we have more police officers on the streets, our prisons are overcrowded, and we spend billions of dollars nationwide supporting the enterprise of criminal justice. In 2012, the Department of Justice's budget included 28.2 billion dollars in discretionary funding (U.S. Department of Justice, 2012).

Yet with all these policies designed to respond to crime and punish offenders, what impact has this had on our crime rates? A review of the FBI's Uniform Crime Report finds that crime across the nation decreased over the past twenty years. In 1992, the violent crime rate was 757.7 per 100,000 individuals. In 2011, the crime rate was 386.3, a 49% decrease. In 1992, the property crime rate was 4,903.7 compared to 2,908.7 in 2011 (FBI, 2012). It is certainly possible that the criminal justice

| Figure 1.1 | Incarcerated Americans 1920–2006 |

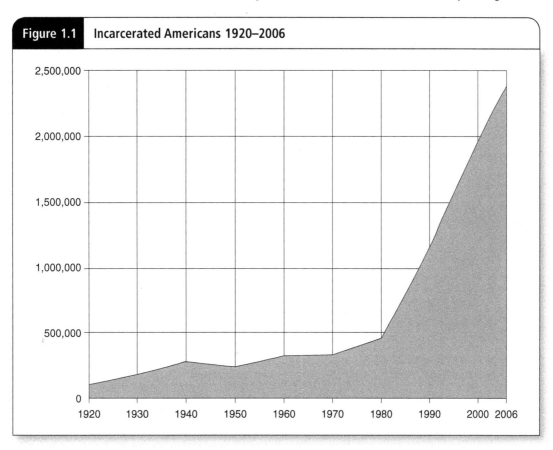

Sources: Justice Policy Institute Report: The Punishing Decade, & U.S. Bureau of Justice Statistics Bulletin NCJ 219416 - Prisoners in 2006.

policies implemented over the past twenty years may have contributed to these lower crime rates. After all, such policies created interventions for at-risk and low level offenders, increased screening tools for risk assessment, provided funds for more officers on the streets, and increased prison capacities. Despite the fact that the rate of crimes known to law enforcement significantly decreased, our prison population has increased over 500% nationwide[1] since the 1980's (which is when many of the "tough on crime" policies were first passed). Figure 1.2 demonstrates this trend. For example, the federal incarceration rate in 2000 was 44 (per 100,000 residents) and increased to 63 by 2010 (an average of 3% increase annually). State prisons also increased, though not at such a dramatic rate (426 per 100,000 in 2000, compared to 429 per 100,000 in 2010, an average of 0.3% increase annually) (Carson & Sabol, 2012). The impact of many of these policies had detrimental effects for certain populations. Drug offenders make up the majority of the incarcerated population

---

[1] Includes data on state and federal prison populations.

Table 1.1	**Examples of Federal Criminal Justice Policies**
• Controlled Substances Act (Comprehensive Drug Abuse Prevention and Control Act of 1970) – Regulated the manufacturing, importation, possession, and use of controlled substances (both legal and illegal).
• Combat Methamphetamine Epidemic Act of 2005 – Regulates the over-the-counter sale of medicinal products containing ephedrine, pseudoephedrine and phenylpropanolamine (products typically found in cold medications and used to manufacture methamphetamine).
• Anti-Drug Abuse Act of 1986 – Enacted mandatory minimum sentences for drug possession.
• Fair Sentencing Act of 2010 – Changed the sentencing ratio between crack cocaine and powder cocaine to 1 to 18 (previously a 1 to 100 ratio).
• Sentencing Reform Act of 1984 (Comprehensive Crime Control Act) – Created sentencing structure for Federal offenses, established the U.S. Sentencing Commission, and abolished Federal parole.
• Sex Offender (Jacob Wetterling) Act of 1994 – Requires convicted sex offenders to notify policy of changes to residency and employment status.
• Adam Walsh Child Protection and Safety Act of 2006 – Organizes sex offenders into a 3-tier system and mandates timelines for registration based on tier. Creates a national sex offender registry and provides for the civil commitment for sexually dangerous persons.
• U.S. Patriot Act (2001) – Expanded the power of police agencies to gather intelligence data on terrorism suspects, and broadened discretionary powers to detain and deport immigrants suspected of terrorism.
• Fraud Enforcement and Recovery Act of 2009 – Enhanced criminal punishments for Federal fraud laws, including mortgage fraud, securities fraud, commodities fraud, and fraud by financial institutions.
• Juvenile Justice and Delinquency Prevention Act of 1974 – Deinstitutionalized status offenders, provided for separation from youth and adult inmates, and required the states to review disproportionate minority confinement. Created the Office of Juvenile Justice and Delinquency Prevention (OJJDP) and the National Institute for Juvenile Justice and Delinquency Prevention (NIJJDP). Reauthorized six times (1977, 1980, 1984, 1988, 1992, and 2002) with additional provisions, such as addressing gender bias, an emphasis on prevention and treatment, family strengthening, graduate sanctions, risk and needs assessments, and funding provisions.
• Violent Crime Control and Law Enforcement Act of 1994 – Largest crime bill in history. Includes: o Federal Assault Weapons Ban of 1994 (banned the manufacturing of all fully automatic firearms and selected semi-automatic firearms, as well as high capacity ammunition magazines) o Federal Death Penalty Act of 1994 (increased the number of federal crimes that are eligible for the death penalty) o Violence Against Women Act of 1994 (provided funding for the prosecution of offenders of crimes of domestic violence, imposed mandatory restitution, and created opportunities for civil remedies for victims. Reauthorized in 2000 and 2005) o Community Oriented Policing Services (COPS) program of 2000 (provided funding to implement community policing programs in jurisdictions nationwide)

in Federal prisons and their length of sentences for these crimes accounted for one-third of the prison growth between 1998 and 2010 (Mallik-Kane, Parthasarathy, & Adams, 2012). Much of this growth can be associated with the use of mandatory minimum sentencing for drugs, which you learn more about in Chapter 8 of this text. Trends in the disproportionate minority confinement are also present, as the rate of white male incarceration in 2011 was 478 (per 100,000), while the rate of African American male incarceration was 3,023, and the rate for Hispanic males was 1,238. Similar patterns exist for female incarceration rates where 51 (per 100,000) of incarcerated women are white, compared to rates of African American (129) and Hispanic (71) females, respectfully (Carson & Sabol, 2012).

The Development of Criminal Justice Policy

When it comes to developing criminal justice policy, there are several key players involved. Political figures, such as a congressional member of a state government or a member of the U.S. Congress, may sponsor a bill that affects the criminal justice system. Following a period of debate and discussion about the proposed

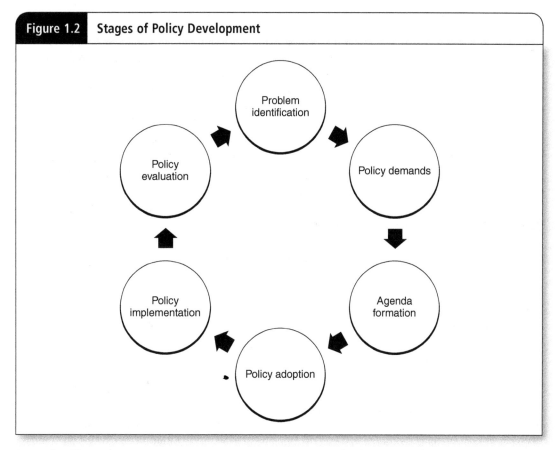

Figure 1.2   Stages of Policy Development

Source: Adapted from Cochran, C. E., Mayer, L. C., Carr, T. R., Cayer, N. J., & McKenzie, M. (2011). *American Public Policy: An Introduction.* Boston, MA: Wadsworth.

policy, the bill is voted on by the members of the governing body and is then signed into law by either the state's Governor or the President of the United States (depending on whether it is a state or federal policy that is being enacted). For many states, this is the primary way that new policies are developed and implemented. However, some states have an alternative method of creating new laws and policies. Under the practice of **direct democracy**, citizens in 17 states are empowered to make law through an **initiative** process. The initiative process begins with a petition for a new law. If a minimum number of signatures from registered voters are obtained, the measure is placed on the ballot for the citizenry to vote on. In states like California, if a measure receives a majority of the votes, it is enacted into law. What makes the process of direct democracy unique is that it completely bypasses the traditional structures of lawmaking—that is, it does not require the support of elected officials in order to pass new laws. In addition, a policy enacted through the process of direct democracy does not necessarily endure the same rigorous process of vetting the budget in terms of implementing such a policy (Stambough, 2012). Many of California's most famous criminal justice policies were created through the citizen initiative process: the habitual offender Three Strikes law (Proposition 184, 1994, later amended through Proposition 36 in 2012); Jessica's Law (Proposition 83, 2006), which created new regulations for sexual offenders; and the diversion of low-level drug offenders from prison to drug treatment (Proposition 36, 2000).

In many cases, criminal justice policies are implemented to change the way that offenders are processed by the criminal justice system. A review of recent history demonstrates that many of these policies are designed to be tougher on crime by increasing the penalties for various crimes and restricting the movement of offenders in the community. Despite the continued push toward retributive punishments, we do find examples of policies that seek to change the definitions of criminal behavior and the responses by police agencies to crime. In recent years, many states have either attempted to legalize the use of marijuana for medical purposes or to decriminalize marijuana use in general. For example in 2010, California citizens introduced an initiative to legalize marijuana. While California's measure ultimately failed at the ballot box, other states have been successful in changing their state laws. In 2012, voters legalized the use of marijuana in both Washington and Colorado. Washington state voters approved the possession of up to an ounce of marijuana for individuals over the age of 21. While the sale of marijuana remains illegal, the state is making plans to set up a system of state-approved growers (similar to having state-licensed liquor stores) within the year, a plan that could bring in hundreds of millions of dollars to the state budget (Johnson, 2012). A similar law passed in Colorado with 55% of voters in support (Wyatt, 2012).

Attempts like these highlighted the fiscal concerns of states, as many are struggling to maintain the growing incarcerated populations stemming from the implementation of the "tough on crime" initiatives that dominated the criminal justice landscape in recent times. However, the legalization of marijuana is not the only topic up for debate in this deliberation about dollars and cents. For example, the SAFE Act (Savings, Accountability and Full Enforcement Act) of California (2012) highlighted the fiscal concerns of maintaining the death penalty. While public polling data indicated that many California voters were in support of this initiative, it ultimately failed with only 48% of the votes in favor of the measure (SAFE, 2012). In Maryland, legislators sought to introduce a graduated sanctions program for technical parole violators. Rather than return these offenders back to prison, this program allowed for nonincarceration forms of punishment in cases like missing a meeting with a parole officer or failing to complete community service hours. This change in policy would have made available some of the one-billion dollars that the state spends on its correctional system. The implementation of the program was scaled back to only three counties instead of a state-wide effort, due to the high start-up costs of the program versus a focus on its long-term savings (Chettiar, 2012).

Victims of crime also influence criminal justice politics. As the victim rights' movement began to gain speed, there was a significant increase in the number of pieces of legislation aimed at increasing the surveillance and punishment of offenders in the hopes of reducing future victimizations. Here, individual tragedies led to changes for the general population. For example, Megan's Law is named after Megan Kanka, a 7-year-old girl from New Jersey who was raped and murdered in 1994 by a convicted sex offender who was residing in her neighborhood. At the time, there were no widespread programs for community notifications when a sexual offender was released. Today, Megan's Laws have been adopted in all 50 states and provides resources for not only alerting members of the community about offenders living in their area, but it also provides restrictions on where offenders can live in terms of proximity to children (such as distances from schools and playgrounds) as well as requirements to register with local police authorities on an annual basis (http://www.meganslaw.com). Another example of crime policy legislation aimed at providing services for victims is the Campus Sexual Assault Victims' Bill of Rights, which requires institutions of higher education to provide victims with physical protections from their abuser (such as the right to transfer housing accommodations, or class schedules) as well as counseling (Campus Sexual Assault Victims' Bill of Rights, 1992).

Despite best intentions, criminal justice policies can also be used in ways that legislators and the public never intended. Consider Florida's "stand your ground" law. Initially designed as a measure to protect citizens from prosecution in cases of self-defense, the "stand your ground" law requires that the police and courts only consider three basic criteria: (a) Was the individual entitled to be present, (b) Was the individual engaged in a law-abiding activity, and (c) Could the individual reasonably believe that he or she was at risk for significant bodily harm or injury? If an individual claims self-defense under the "stand your ground" law, they can request a hearing where they are only required to prove their claim under the "preponderance of the evidence" standard of proof standard, not the "beyond a reasonable doubt" standard. As a result, many criminal offenders have successfully used the "stand your ground" law to avoid prosecution. The law recently came under public debate following the death of 17-year-old Trayvon Martin. Martin was walking in his gated neighborhood community following a trip to a local convenience store. George Zimmerman, head of the neighborhood watch, contacted the police to report a suspicious individual (Martin) walking in the neighborhood. Zimmerman followed Martin and confronted him. While the details of what happened are somewhat murky, Zimmerman alleges that Martin attacked him. In response, Zimmerman pulled out a gun and shot Martin, who died from his injuries. The public outcry for the case stretched across the United States as citizens demanded the arrest of George Zimmerman. While some had questioned whether Zimmerman's case would draw upon Florida's "stand your ground" law, his lawyers ultimately argued that Zimmerman shot and killed Trayvon Martin in self-defense. In July 2013, Zimmerman was found not guilty of 2nd degree murder (Clark, 2013).

Politics and Criminal Justice Policy

When we think about politics, we can generally divide beliefs into two separate camps: ***liberals*** and ***conservatives***. Liberal politics tend to focus on the importance of due process, individual freedoms, and constitutional rights. Liberals also look to the government to help create equality in society and to solve problems. Socially, liberals believe that the government should help support those individuals who may suffer from various disadvantages in society. In terms of crime related issues, liberals believe that society should fight against the racist, gendered, and classist disparities that exist in the system. When it comes to the punishment of offenders, liberals tend to lean toward a more rehabilitative focus.

In contrast, conservative politics lean toward less intervention by the government and focus on traditional values. "Conservatism also refers to a belief that existing economic and political inequalities are justified and that the existing order is about as close as is practically attainable to an ideal order" (Shelden, n.d.). On crime, conservatives see the actions of criminals as part of a rational choice process whereby the offender makes a cognitive decision to participate in criminal activity. Conservatives follow more of a "law and order" philosophy and generally cite retributive values or "eye for an eye" perspective on punishing offenders.

Given these different philosophical foundations, it is not surprising that liberals and conservatives think differently about criminal justice policies. One example is Arizona's immigration law (called the Support our Law Enforcement and Safe Neighborhoods Act, or **SB 1070**). Since the law was adopted in 2010, it has been debated by politicians and the public and challenged in the legal arena. One of the more controversial issues within the law calls for police officers to determine whether an individual is a legal U.S. citizen during "lawful stop, detention or arrest," or any other form of "lawful contact" where there is reasonable suspicion that the person is an illegal immigrant. Supporters of SB 1070 (most of whom are conservative policy makers) argued that the Federal government failed to adequately police the issue of illegal immigration. For these conservatives, SB 1070 served to protect its communities from rising crime rates and other social issues (such as strains on educational resources, and the state welfare system) that they perceived were directly related to illegal immigrants. However, opponents of the law (who generally identify as more liberal on the political spectrum) argued that Arizona's law was unconstitutional on the grounds that the implementation of SB 1070 diverted important resources away from fighting violent crimes (Gorman & Riccardi, 2010). Ultimately, the U.S. Supreme Court held that the investigation of immigration status in cases of lawful stops, detention and arrest is permissible (*Arizona v. United States*, 2012).

Even examples of crime policy that traditionally represented bipartisan efforts to protect the interests of victims can be subjected to political controversy. Consider the most recent reauthorization efforts in 2012 of the Violence Against Women Act. First passed in 1994, the Violence Against Women Act (VAWA) provided victims of intimate partner violence support through the allocation of federal funds for prosecuting offenders, coordinated services for victims, and established the Office of Violence Against Women within the Department of Justice. Reauthorized with support from both sides of the political aisle in 2000 and 2005, VAWA continued to expand the rights of victims in these cases. However, the 2012 attempts to reauthorize the bill were filled with partisan debates over the protections of victims of intimate partner violence (IPV) for specific populations, such as same-sex victims, immigrants, and Native Americans. What had once been joint collegial effort between Democrats and Republicans transformed into a hotly contested political debate. Regrettably, conservatives and liberal representatives were unable to find a compromise on the issues prior to the end of the 2012 congressional session (Eichelberger, 2013). The issue was once again raised at the onset of the 2013 congressional session. Despite holding a majority political representation in the House, the GOP version of the bill that advocated for narrower protections for certain population groups, ultimately failed. This paved the way for the House to pass the Senate's version of the bill in February 2013, which ensured that LGBT, Native American, and immigrant victims have access to federally funded programs and resources (Cohen, 2013).

Regardless of values and ideologies, criminal justice issues are a hot topic for the body politic, including the White House. A focus on policing first began back in the 1930s with the creation of the Wickersham Commission (by President Hoover) and continued into the 1960s with research by groups like the President's Commission on Law Enforcement and President Johnson's the Kerner Commission (Gardiner, 2012).

However, it wasn't until the 1970s that crime became a key component of a presidential platform when then-President Richard Nixon declared a war on crime. During the 1980s, President Ronald Reagan's emphasis on drugs and drug-related crimes was represented by the slogan "just say no." The shift toward being tough on crime hit a turning point during the 1988 presidential elections when the Democratic candidate for president, Massachusetts Governor Michael Dukakis, was heavily criticized by Republican candidate, George Bush, for Dukakis's support of weekend furlough releases for convicted offenders. The weekend furlough program was used by the Massachusetts State Prison as part of the State's rehabilitation program for offenders. While Willie Horton was a convicted murder who had received a sentence of life without the possibility of parole for his crime, he was still permitted to participate in the program. Unfortunately, Horton never returned from his furlough and traveled to Maryland, where he robbed a local couple, physically assaulted the male, and raped the woman (Bidinotto, 1988). As governor, Dukakis was held politically responsible for Horton's release (which led to these crimes) and declared to be "soft on crime," a position that ultimately contributed to his loss in the election (Benson, 2012). As a result of growing public concerns about crime, it seems that virtually every election discussion on crime issues results in a candidate presenting a "tough on crime" stance in their attempts to garner public support.

As the leader of our nation's government structure, the president has surprisingly little power when it comes to making policy. While each president enters the office with ideas for reforming policies like health care, education, and social welfare, any eventual success of enacting these reforms is dependent on the actions of the House and the Senate. While it is up to the president to sign these acts of legislation into law, even this practice can be overruled by a two-thirds vote. In the United States, presidents have no direct ability to pass legislation; rather their goal is to persuade members of Congress to introduce items that are consistent with their interests.[2]

Given that criminal justice issues have been a part of presidential policy agendas for the past five decades, it begs the question of how much influence any president has over Congress's ability to introduce legislation on crime-related issues. Research by Oliver (2003) documents that between 1946 and 1996, a total of 3,373 congressional hearings were held on crime-related issues, such as drug abuse and drug trafficking, juvenile crime, white-collar crime, and court administration. In comparing these data with the number of presidential speeches and conferences on crime-related issues, Oliver found that the president had little influence over the actions of Congress when it comes to crime policy. In investigating this relationship, he controlled for media exposure, public opinion, whether it was an election year (where increases in crime-related policy statements might increase as part of the political campaigning process), crime rates, congressional control (who's in power in Congress), and presidential party affiliation. In looking at these variables, Oliver's findings determined that the only variables that appeared to influence crime policy discussions in Congress were the crime rate and whether it was an election year. Specifically, as the crime rate increased, the number of congressional hearings on crime-related issues increased. In addition, the number of congressional hearings on crime dropped significantly during an election year. While presidential politics don't appear to impact congressional activity during that same year, it does appear to have an influence on the actions on Congress in the following year. Oliver's findings reinforce that it can take time to raise awareness of an issue among Congress and to effect behavioral changes.

---

[2] At the state level, similar processes occur between the governor and the state senators and representatives.

Politics and the Models of Criminal Justice

In thinking about the functions of the criminal justice system, the perspectives of liberalism and conservatism can be linked to the criminal justice models of due process and crime control. In his 1968 book *The Limits of the Criminal Sanction,* Herbert Packer, a law professor from Stanford University, identified how the fight between these two models forms the basis of our criminal justice system. The *crime control model* asserts that the most important function of the criminal justice system is to suppress and control criminal behavior as a function of public order in society. This philosophy is often aligned with a more conservative perspective. The crime control model focuses on a criminal justice system that processes criminals in an efficient, consistent manner. Packer suggested that justice under the crime control model resembled an "assembly-line." Under the crime control model, the plea bargain is an essential tool as it allows the wheels of justice to continue to move; alternatively trials take up excessive time in the system, which slows down the efficiency of the "factory." Here, the focus is on swift and severe punishments for offenders. For example, supporters of a crime control model argue that the identification and detention of enemy combatants following the 9/11 terror attacks was a good policy to control against future terrorist threats. Any risk of violating individual liberties was considered secondary to the need to protect and ensure the safety of the community.

In contrast, the *due process model* believes that the protection of individual rights and freedoms is of upmost importance. The due process model embodies more of a liberal perspective compared to the crime control model. One could argue under the due process model that it is better for the guilty to go free than to risk incarcerating or executing the innocent. In contrast to his identification of the crime control model as an "assembly-line," Parker suggested that the due process model resembles an "obstacle course," consisting of a variety of legal challenges that must be satisfied throughout the criminal justice process in order to hold someone accountable for a criminal action (and therefore, to punish them for said action). Indeed, the due process model emphasizes the formalized legal practices of the criminal justice process and requires that each stage of the criminal justice system represent a fair and equitable treatment of all cases and all offenders. Drawing from the 9/11 example above, supporters of the due process model argued that individuals identified as enemy combatants following the 9/11 terror attacks were denied their due process rights and were therefore detained by the United States government illegally. Under the due process model, it is not acceptable to engage in such practices just to suppress the risk for potential harm. While liberals argue that the crime control model infringes on the rights of individuals, conservatives fear that the due process model ignores crime victims and gives criminals too much leeway to escape "justice."

The Role of Fear and the Media on Criminal Justice Policies

The majority of Americans have limited direct experience with the criminal justice system. As a result, much of the fear about crime comes not from personal victimization, but perhaps the victimization of others known to them (peers and family members), or within the general community. Much of the research on the fear of crime is gendered—women experience fear at different levels, and for different reasons than men. For women, the fear of being a victim of a crime is often related to feelings of vulnerability (Young, 1992). Some research suggests that "a loss of control over the situation and a perceived inadequate capacity to resist the direct and indirect consequences of victimization" contributes to the feelings that women have about crime (Cops & Pleysier, 2011, p. 59). For example, women are more likely to experience fear in certain environments that they perceive increase the risk of victimization, such as poorly lit parking lots and groups loitering in public spaces (Fisher & May, 2009). Despite engaging in measures to increase their safety (e.g., by avoiding these types of environments), women's fears about being victimized (particularly by sex-based crimes) appear to increase rather than decrease (Lane, Gover, & Dahod, 2009). As De Groof (2008) explains, "fear of crime is, in other words, partly a result of feelings of personal discomfort and uncertainty, which are projected onto the threat of crime and victimization" (p. 281).

The mass media also have significant power in shaping individual perceptions of crime and justice, which can also contribute to citizens' fears about crime (Dowler, 2003; Garofalo, 1981; Surette, 2010). The scope of the media is extensive, as it includes "mechanisms for public presentations of entertainment, propaganda, and nonfiction information" (Garofalo, 1981, p. 319). Research indicates that as individuals increase their consumption of local and national television news, their fears about crime increase, regardless of actual crime rates, gender, or a personal history of victimization (Chiricos, Padgett, & Gertz, 2000). Indeed regarding the world we live in, media outlets are a primary method of socialization. While research by Boos (1997) indicates that individuals watch an average of four hours of television programming each day, and are exposed to over eleven hours of media exposure, other research indicates that the viewing of local news alone can rise up to 140 hours over a two-week period (Nellis & Savage, 2012). With the inclusion of social media sites, such as Facebook and the viewing of news stories via the Internet, the consumption of information is extensive.

More important than the levels of media consumption is how the information is interpreted (Ditton, Chadee, Farrall, Gilchrist, & Bannister, 2004). Since the majority of Americans have limited direct experience with the criminal justice system, most are left with the images generated by the media regarding crime and criminal justice, much of which is internalized as "facts" about the world we live in (Boos, 1997). "The public's perception of victims, criminals, deviants and law enforcement officials is largely determined by their portrayal in the mass media" (Dowler, 2003, p.109). However, the content and prevalence of stories relating to crime presents a distorted view of the realities of the criminal justice system. The popular expression "if it bleeds, it leads" represents the prevalent position of crime stories for media outlets. While stories about violent crime make up almost one-third of all news time, such is not the reality of crime in society (Klite, Bardwell, & Salzman, 1997). Additionally, news stories are more likely to reflect incidents of violent crime rather than property crime (Maguire, 1988). These exaggerations have a direct relationship on the understanding of the realities of crime in society. Adding to this equation are findings that individuals tend to retain the content of these stories, only affirming any negative notions regarding crime, criminals, and criminal justice (Graber, 1980). For example, fears about terrorism since the events of September 11th, 2001 have significantly increased, with one in three individuals fearing that they, or a family member, will be a victim of a terrorist act (Carlson, 2004). Interestingly, people are less likely to fear their own victimization by an act of terrorism, but indicate greater levels of fear for their family member. This fear about their loved ones is significantly related to their exposure to television news programming—the more one watches the news, the greater their fears (Nellis & Savage, 2012).

In addition to the portrayal of crime within the news, stories of crime, criminals, and criminal justice are a major staple of television entertainment programming. Also, these images present a distorted view of the reality of crime, as they generally present crime as graphic, random, and violent incidents (Gerbner, Gross, Morgan, & Signorielli, 1980). Entertainment television about crime covers a variety of topics, including policing, courtroom portrayals, forensic investigations, and corrections. For example, the number of different installations of the Law and Order series (Criminal Minds, Special Victims Unit (SVU), etc.) covers all aspects of the criminal justice system from offenders to the police and investigators, to the court process and its actors. These crime dramas have such an impact on individuals that criminologists have begun to study what is called the "CSI Effect." This is a reference to the popular crime drama *CSI: Crime Scene Investigation*, where crimes are solved in a single episode using sophisticated techniques of crime analysis that aren't readily available or utilized in a typical criminal case. Crime is also present in "reality-TV" programming. From *COPS* to *Forensic Files*, viewers are afforded the opportunity to see the criminal justice system in action. In addition, networks like A&E, the Discovery Channel, TruTV, and the History Channel include documentaries about crime and justice as a major component of their programming.

While there is documentation that the saturation of crime stories on the news impacts viewers' opinions of crime, how does crime as "entertainment" influence fears about crime and victimization? In general, crimes of murder and violence are overemphasized in television entertainment (Estep & MacDonald, 1984). For example, the victimization of women is often portrayed by "movie of the week" outlets, such as Lifetime TV that showcase storylines of women being sexually assaulted, stalked, or otherwise injured by a stranger. Unfortunately, these popular culture references paint a false picture of the realities of crime because most women are not maltreated by strangers (as portrayed in these storylines), but are victimized by people known to them (Black et al., 2011). While the enjoyment of reality-based crime programming is related to punitive attitudes on crime, such an effect is not found for viewers of fictional-based crime dramas (Oliver & Armstrong, 1995). However, Kort-Butler and Sittner Hartshorn (2011) found that viewers of nonfiction television shows (e.g., the documentary series *The First 48*) show an increase in fears about crime. Soulliere (2003) posits why these themes may have a different effect compared to news programming:

> It is important to keep in mind that producers of television crime dramas, including reality-based crime shows, have a very different goal than scientific and public consumption. Above all, the primary purpose of the crime drama is to entertain. In order to appeal to the entertainment senses of its consumers, crime drama content is likely to focus on unusual and/or exaggerated images and events. After all, the routine and mundane are the stuff of everyday life, not drama. (p. 14)

While the public's concern about crime may be very real, it can also be inflamed by inaccurate data on crime rates, or a misunderstanding about the community supervision of offenders and recidivism rates. Indeed, a fear about crime, coupled with the public's perception about rising crime rates, contributes to a lack of faith by citizens in the efficacy of the criminal justice system (Kort-Butler & Sittner Hartshorn, 2011). Watching television news programs also contributes to this perception, as the increased viewing of local news is associated with punitive beliefs in the punishment of offenders (Trautman, 2004). Together, these factors can influence a rise in the public dialogue about crime, which can lead to changes in criminal justice policies. Agents of criminal justice can respond to a community's fear of crime by increasing police patrols, while district attorneys pursue tough-on-crime stances in their prosecution of criminal cases. Politicians respond to community concerns about violent crime by creating and implementing tough-on-crime legislation, such as habitual sentencing laws like "three strikes," and targeting perceived crimes of danger, such as the "war on drugs." Unfortunately, as Frost and Phillips (2011) argue, "public policy is influenced more by media misinformation and sensationalized high profile cases than by careful or thoughtful analysis" (p. 88).

The use of the public's fear about crime as momentum for generating crime control policies can be a dangerous incentive. Indeed, many of our criminal justice policies (refer back to Table 1.1 on p. 4) have been named after crime victims or high profile events that helped inspire or influence the development and passage of such legislation. Given that much of the public's fear about crime is generated not from their personal experiences, it is important to remain aware of the role of the media in generating fear (and consequently, crime control policies). "Even if information coming through the media causes fear, first amendment protections for freedom of the press have to be respected and many follow the credo that the public has a right to know regardless of the outcome" (Nellis & Savage, 2012, p. 765).

While high profile events may lead to "knee-jerk reactions" in the creation of criminal justice policy, they can also open important dialogue for areas in need of reform. Consider the recent tragic events on December 14, 2012, at Sandy Hook Elementary School, where Adam Landa killed twenty children and six teachers before turning the gun on himself. While previous incidents of school violence, such as Columbine and Virginia Tech, inspired "zero-tolerance" policies toward violence and antibullying curricula (Regoli, Hewitt, & DeLisi, 2009), the Sandy Hook tragedy (as well as other recent incidents of mass gun violence) has inspired significant debates surrounding the issues of gun control. Chapter 20 highlights some of the key debates within this policy discussion. While some have called for stricter regulation of guns, the National Rifle Association and others object to the development of legislation that places limits on the Second Amendment rights of American citizens. While many applauded President Obama's attempts to make gun control and violence prevention a key piece of his agenda during his second term, the success of these efforts depends largely on the ability of members of Congress to introduce and pass legislation that addresses these issues.

Conclusion

From elected officials who utilize criminal justice issues as key components of their political platform to citizens who issue demands for safer communities and increased punishments for offenders, discussions about criminal justice policy invoke a variety of emotions across the ranks. Throughout this book, you learn about a variety of criminal justice politics. Each of these policies relied on political influence to pass and implement these practices. While politicians aim to reflect the values and ideals of their constituency, agents of the media can inflame the "threats" that criminal activity can represent.

Despite the best intentions of the authors of such policies, the implementation of criminal justice policies has the potential for unintended consequences. In Chapter 2, you learn about evidence-based research and its role in the development of criminal justice policy, while Chapter 3 highlights the role of street bureaucracy in the implementation of such policies. Regardless of the backstory or history of each of these policies, it is important that we develop an understanding from social science research about "what works," and "what doesn't work," or the failures of a policy. Together, this information can be utilized in determining the future of criminal justice policy.

KEY TERMS

Conservative	Initiative	Process evaluation
Crime control model	Liberal	SB 1070
Direct democracy	Outcome evaluation	
Due process model	Policy	

DISCUSSION QUESTIONS

1. How does fear about crime influence criminal justice policy decisions?

2. Review the six stages of policy development. Pick a criminal justice policy and discuss how your example developed through each of these stages.

3. How have criminal justice policies led to unintended consequences for individuals and the larger system?

4. How might a criminal justice policy or practice be compromised or challenged due to political differences?

WEBSITES FOR ADDITIONAL RESEARCH

White House: http://www.whitehouse.gov/

Federal Bureau of Investigation: http://www.fbi.gov

Urban Institute Research Center: http://www.urban.org/justice/

Center for Evidence Based Crime Policy: http://gemini.gmu.edu/cebcp/criminaljusticepolicy.html

Center for Research on Direct Democracy: http://c2d.ch/

Initiative & Referendum Institute: http://www.iandrinstitute.org/

CHAPTER

II

The Influence of Research and Evidence-Based Practices on Criminal Justice Policy

Christine L. Gardiner

How is crime policy made? How is it decided which crime prevention strategies or programs get funded? Do politicians sit around a large table discussing the most current and rigorous research on the topic? Or, do they create policy by doing what seems logical? How much do policy makers know about the correlates of crime or theories about why people commit crime? How much influence does research have on policy? Unfortunately, policy makers do not usually know as much about the causes of crime as we expect, and research does not inform policy as much as it should. While there are certainly examples of agencies, municipalities, and even states that carefully consider research when creating or changing policy—these are the exceptions rather than the rule. Thankfully, this story is changing, albeit slowly; research is now better (and there is more of it), and researchers are doing a better job disseminating it to practitioners and policy makers.

This chapter is divided into three sections and explains the context of research and its nexus to policy. The first section chronicles the evolution of criminal justice research, specifically the federal government's role in creating and disseminating criminal justice research. The second section explains what we know about crime and delinquency, including the known *risk factors* that should be taken into account when implementing policies or programs. Finally, the third section discusses the current state of knowledge on evidence-based programs and describes the resources available to practitioners, policy makers, students, and others.

The Commencement of Criminal Justice Research

The first efforts to produce and fund wide-scale research on criminal justice came in 1968 with the passage of the Omnibus Crime Control and Safe Streets Act (OCCSSA). This act established the ***Law Enforcement Assistance Agency (LEAA),*** and within it the National Institute of Law Enforcement and Criminal Justice (NILECJ). LEAA, the lead agency, provided grants to law enforcement agencies to improve public safety (most often to purchase new equipment and personnel) while NILECJ was the research center of the LEAA.

As the criminal justice research arm of the federal government, the NILECJ (since renamed the ***National Institute of Justice [NIJ]***) was created to "advance scientific research, development, and evaluation to enhance the administration of justice and public safety" (Wellford, Chemers, & Schuck, 2010, p.14). It accomplishes this mandate by awarding federal grants and contracts to universities, public agencies, and private institutions engaged in research and demonstration projects that expand our knowledge of "what works" in preventing and controlling crime, and by disseminating those findings to researchers and practitioners. It may be surprising to learn that prior to the establishment of the NILECJ in 1968, there was no national agency encouraging, conducting, or disseminating criminal justice research. Research was conducted by a few small, independent agencies (such as California Institute for the Study of Crime and Delinquency, National Council on Crime and Delinquency, and the Vera Institute), but there was no unified research agenda nor concerted effort to organize or circulate the findings (Wellford et al., 2010).

This changed when Congress passed the ***Omnibus Crime Control and Safe Streets Act of 1968*** to provide federal monies to research criminal justice issues and to "provide more accurate information on the causes of crime and the effectiveness of various means of preventing crime" (Wellsford et al., 2010, p. 27). As a result of this funding, we expanded our knowledge about crime control strategies and learned a great deal about policing practices, and a few things about prison alternatives, drug treatment programs, and other programs thought to prevent crime. Some of the well-known studies that you may be familiar with that were funded as a result of this act include: the Kansas City Preventative Patrol Experiment, the Newark and Flint Foot Patrol Experiments, as well as many other studies on police response time, neighborhood watch programs, team policing strategies, crime prevention through environmental design, fingerprinting, investigations, habitual criminals, and plea bargaining (LEAA, 1978).

Only a few of the funded studies were methodologically rigorous by today's standards. Still, this was the first time that federal grant money was made available on a wide-scale for criminal justice research, and the legislation was vitally important for the avenues of inquiry it initiated. The legislation is also highly important for having instigated the creation of criminal justice as a discipline, separate and distinct from sociology. Unfortunately, the money spent on criminal justice programs (and research) did not have any effect on the rising crime rates at the time; so much of the grant money disappeared. Some of the early programs funded by the 1968 OCCSSA are still in existence today (Barker, 2010). Incidentally, many researchers made a name for themselves on these research projects and went on to have long, successful research careers as a result.

One of the first efforts to disseminate research findings came 40 years ago with the passage of the Crime Control Act of 1973, which established NILECJ as the first clearinghouse of criminal justice information. There are now many federal agencies that fund or disseminate research (e.g., Office of Justice Programs, Office of Juvenile Justice and Delinquency Prevention, Community Oriented Policing Services, Office on Violence Against Women); each plays an important role in criminal justice research and policy in the United States. There are also numerous private (partisan and nonpartisan) foundations and organizations that fund, conduct, and/or disseminate criminal justice research and which have been integral in our quest to understand, control, and prevent crime and ascertain the benefits and consequences of criminal justice related policies.

Although the Omnibus Crime Control and Safe Streets Act of 1968 provided considerable federal monies to local agencies to implement new programs and conduct research, it did not *require* research of funded programs right away.[1] There were a few instances in which Congress required program evaluations, but for the most part these directives went unfulfilled due to budget and resource constraints (Sherman et al., 1997). More recently in 1996, Congress mandated that crime prevention programs funded by the federal government be evaluated for effectiveness. It stipulated that the evaluations be "independent," "employ rigorous and scientifically recognized standards and methodologies," and focus on the correlates of juvenile crime and the effectiveness of the programs to address known correlates (Sherman et al., 1997). As a result of this mandate, University of Maryland scholars, led by Lawrence Sherman, were commissioned by the National Institute of Justice in 1996 to conduct an independent review of the 500+ program evaluations that constituted the relevant scientific literature at the time. This was a "state of the science report on what [was] known—and what [was] not—about the effectiveness of local crime prevention programs and practices" (Sherman et al., 1997, p. 1–1).

The report examined more than 500 studies of crime prevention programs in seven institutional settings: communities, families, schools, places, labor markets, police agencies, and other criminal justice agencies. Using established scientific standards for inferring causation, researchers placed programs into one of four classifications (what works, what doesn't, what's promising, and what's unknown) for each crime prevention category. Each study was rated on rigor of scientific methods and program effectiveness on a scale of 1 to 5 (1 was the lowest, 5 was the highest, 3 was considered "moderately strong").

Of the 500+ studies evaluated, 14 programs had at least two moderately strong studies (scientific methods score of 3 or higher) that demonstrated program effectiveness and received the "what works" label; 23 programs had at least two moderately strong studies that demonstrated program ineffectiveness, and were classified in the "what doesn't work" category; and 30 programs were catalogued as "promising" because they had at least one moderately strong research study that suggested the program was effective. All other programs were classified as "what's unknown" (Sherman et al., 1997). See Table 2.1 for a list of programs in each classification.

Table 2.1   University of Maryland Report: What Works, What's Promising, and What Doesn't Work

What Works	
Home visiting programs for moms	Preschool with home visits by teacher
Teaching competency skills in schools	Family therapy & parent training
Coaching high-risk youth in thinking skills	Vocational training for male ex-offenders
Schools that communicate & reinforce clear, consistent norms	Therapeutic community treatment for substance users in prison
Nuisance abatement action on landlords of rental housing with drug dealing	On-scene arrests for domestic abusers
Rehabilitation programs with risk-focused treatment	Monitoring high-risk repeat offenders by specialized police units
Incarcerating high-risk repeat offenders	Extra police patrols in high crime hotspots

(Continued)

[1] In 1972, the law was amended to require evaluations of programs funded by local assistance grants (Sherman et al., 1997).

Table 2.1 **(Continued)**

What's Promising	
Improved classroom management & instructional techniques	"Thinking skills" training for high-risk youth
Community-based mentoring by Big Brothers/Big Sisters of America	Community-based after-school recreation programs
Gang member monitoring by community members, police, probation	Job Corps residential training programs for at-risk youth
"Schools within schools" that group students into smaller units	Building school capacity through organizational development
Community policing with meetings to set priorities	Police showing greater respect to arrested offenders
Polite field interrogations of suspicious persons	Higher numbers of police officers
Mailing arrest warrants to domestic violence suspects who leave before police arrive	Proactive drunk driving arrests with breath testing
Battered women's shelters	Enterprise zones
Two store clerks in already-robbed convenience stores	Improved training & management of bar staff
Redesigned layout of retail stores	Metal detectors
Street closures, barricades, & rerouting	Target hardening
Problem solving analysis unique to the crime situation	Proactive arrests for carrying concealed weapons
Drug courts	Fines for criminal acts
Drug treatment in jails followed by urine testing in the community	Intensive supervision and aftercare of juvenile offenders
Prison-based vocational education programs for adult inmates	Moving urban public housing residents to suburban homes
What Doesn't Work	
Gun buy-back programs	Arrests of juveniles for minor offenses
Drug Abuse Resistance Education (D.A.R.E.)	Drug prevention classes focused on fear or self-esteem
School-based, leisure-time enrichment programs	Counseling and peer counseling of students in schools
Short-term, nonresidential training programs for at-risk youth	Summer jobs or subsidized work programs for at-risk youth
Diversion from court to job training as a condition of case management	Community mobilization against crime in high-crime poverty areas
Police organized neighborhood watch programs	Police newsletter with local crime information
Police counseling visits to couples days after a domestic violence incident	Arrests of unemployed suspects for domestic assault
Increased arrests or raids on drug markets	Storefront police offices
Correctional boot camps using traditional military basic training	"Scared Straight" programs in which juveniles visit adult programs
Shock probation, shock parole, and split sentences adding jail time to probation/parole	Residential programs for juvenile offenders using challenging experiences in rural settings

Table 2.1	(Continued)
What Doesn't Work	
Rehabilitation programs using vague, unstructured counseling	Intensive supervision parole or probation (ISP)
Home detention with electronic monitoring	

Source: Adapted from Sherman, Gottfredson, MacKenzie, Eck, Reuter, & Bushway (1998).

This report was a first of its kind in the criminal justice arena and sparked a new interest in summative studies. Unfortunately, however, the authors concluded that the "number and strength of available evaluations [was] insufficient for providing adequate guidance to the national effort to reduce serious crime" (Sherman et al., 1997, p. vi); and further, limited funding did not allow "the nation to learn **why** some innovations work[ed], exactly **what** was done, and **how** [programs/practices could] be successfully adapted in other cities" (emphasis in original, p. xi). In other words, we needed better (more scientifically rigorous) studies that could adequately guide replication efforts. Unfortunately, federal money invested in criminal justice research continues to lag far behind money invested in research on other social issues. On a brighter note, the federal grant money devoted to criminal justice research has improved over time, and research on crime prevention programs has significantly advanced since this 1997 report. Our commitment to research has evolved to the point where federal grant seekers are now required to incorporate best practices as well as methodologically rigorous evaluations of the proposed programs into their applications for funding.

What We Know About Crime and Delinquency That Policy Should Consider

Research has taught us some important "facts" about crime and delinquency that should be taken into account when developing criminal justice responses and policy. To begin, *crime is disproportionally committed by young people, specifically adolescents and young adults.* Self-report studies reveal that more than 90% of juveniles admit to committing some minor delinquency (Agnew & Brezina, 2012; Regoli, Hewitt, & DeLisi, 2011). While many people engage in minor delinquency during their youth, the vast majority of people desist by their early to mid-20s (on their own, without any criminal justice intervention) (Shader, 2003). Many scholars theorize why antisocial behavior peaks during adolescence and propose that it may result from individual characteristics (such as a latent trait or biological vulnerabilities), social and environmental experiences, and/or other significant changes during the life course (graduation, marriage, birth of a child). Recent brain imaging research that indicates that the brain is not fully developed until early adulthood is also part of the explanation.

While persons who dabble in illegal behaviors during their youth account for the bulk of delinquents, they do not commit the majority of crimes. *A small percent of individuals, sometimes called* ***career criminals****, commit a large proportion of crimes.* So, while a lot of people commit a little crime for a short period of time, a small number of individuals start their "criminal careers" early, and continue to offend at a high rate for a long period of time (decades or more); the former are referred to as low-rate, minor, or ***adolescent-limited offenders*** while the latter are referred to as high-rate, serious, chronic, or ***life-course-persistent offenders*** (Moffitt, 1993). Another fact is that *males commit more crime and delinquency than females.* Approximately 70% of juveniles arrested are male, while approximately 30%

are female (this gap used to be much larger) (Chesney-Lind, Morash, & Stevens, 2008). Although both genders commit a broad array of crimes, males commit more serious delinquency than females and females commit more larceny/theft offenses than males (Agnew & Brezina, 2012; Shader (OJJDP), 2006).

There are also some crime differences by race and class. Specifically, some research indicates that the rate of involvement in minor crime is consistent between juveniles of different races and social classes, but African American and lower class youths are more likely to engage in serious delinquency. This correlation exists because there are more high-rate offenders in lower class communities than in middle class communities and more high-rate offenders of African American descent than any other race (Agnew & Brezina, 2012). The question is: why?

We now know that some people are at greater risk of becoming delinquent than others—these individuals often have certain traits or life circumstances in common. These traits, which increase the risk of a person committing delinquent/criminal acts, are known as risk factors and include biological and psychological risk factors, family risk factors, social risk factors (e.g., the schools they attend, or their peer associates), and environmental risk factors (their residential community). It is also believed that there are some traits, known as **protective factors,** which decrease the likelihood of delinquency. Each of these contributes to an individual's risk profile and is discussed below.[2]

Risk factors are often clustered in people and places. Life-course-persistent offenders tend to have the most risk factors, but there is not a single "key" risk factor that means someone is going to be a criminal. Rather, it is the accumulation of risk factors that increases the *likelihood* of a person engaging in antisocial/criminal behavior. Similarly, neighborhoods of **concentrated disadvantage** can "activate" risk factors that might remain dormant if the child lived in a middle-class neighborhood (possibly due to the increased presence of delinquent peers and/or opportunities for crime in disadvantaged communities) (Wikström & Loeber, 2000).

Biological and Psychological Risk Factors

The nature-nurture debate has captivated humans for hundreds of years. Scientists have learned that while half of the variance in antisocial behavior is influenced by genes (nature), environment (nurture) can and does play an important role in determining whether, and to what degree, a person engages in antisocial behaviors (Moffitt, Ross, & Raine, 2011). For example, the MAOA gene, which is associated with moderating the effect of childhood maltreatment on violence, is affected by environmental factors. Thus, two people who have the MAOA gene and have experienced childhood maltreatment may be more (or less) affected by the childhood maltreatment based on how the MAOA gene interacts with environmental and other factors unique to the person and his or her life (Moffitt et al., 2011).

We know that many antisocial individuals are *chronically underaroused* (as indicated by low resting heart rate, slow EEG, and minimal sweating). There is also strong evidence that *impaired communication between the frontal lobes of the brain* (which regulate self-control) *and the temporal lobes of the brain* (which regulate emotions) can result in higher risk-seeking behavior and criminality (Moffitt et al., 2011). This finding is consistent with, and helps explain, the elevated offending levels found in youth around the globe, and the standard decline in offending during early adulthood (once the brain is fully

[2] This chapter only addresses the correlates of delinquency because other chapters in this volume concentrate on other important rehabilitation and crime prevention strategies and policies. For example, see Chapter 19 to learn about correctional rehabilitation programs, Chapter 4 for policing strategies, Chapter 8 for substance abuse prevention, and Chapter 9 for sex offender programs.

developed). Other consistent individual risk factors that have a biological basis are *low intelligence* (verbal IQ), *lack of empathy* (the ability to understand and relate to another person's thoughts/feelings), and *irritability* (having a heightened sensitivity to stressors, a tendency to overreact and blame others for personal misfortune, and exhibiting overtly antagonistic behavior).

People who are considered chronic, life-course-persistent offenders tend to have multiple "biological vulnerabilities" (risk factors).[3] These biological vulnerabilities affect people living in criminogenic environments more powerfully than they affect people living in stable, healthy environments. Some of these biological influences can be counteracted through proper nutrition, healthy living, and the presence of protective factors. One important note: biological influences *predispose* a person to antisocial behavior; they do not predetermine who will or will not be antisocial or criminal (just as a near-sighted mother predisposes her children to poor vision).

What should we do with this knowledge? Does this evidence mean that criminals are born, and therefore not responsible for their actions? Should criminals with specific genes be sentenced less severely than criminals without these same genes? Should all people get tested to ascertain whether they have any "criminal genes"? This information has significant implications for criminal justice policy.

As importantly, what does research mean for crime prevention policies? The evidence that biological vulnerabilities can be switched on/off (or at least turned up/down) by the environment tells us that money spent to create and/or expand healthy environments (families, schools, communities) is likely to decrease criminality, especially in communities that experience concentrated disadvantage. At the very least, programs and policies that help women (from all socioeconomic backgrounds and healthcare insurance statuses) have healthy pregnancies, that allow children and adolescents to obtain proper nutrition and to grow up in toxin-free neighborhoods, and that decrease the number and severity of traumatic brain injuries should be incorporated into our national criminal justice policy agenda because they help prevent delinquency, along with a host of other issues (cancer, obesity, and suicide, for example).

Family Risk Factors

Crime is concentrated in families; in other words, a small percentage of families account for a large proportion of offenders (Farrington, Barnes, & Lambert, 1996; Loeber & Southhamer-Loeber, 1986). There are several possible reasons for this observation. First, it is possible that parents pass on criminogenic predispositions through shared genes that incline their offspring to antisocial behavior. Second, parents may role-model antisocial behavior and thought processes. Third, parents and children may be exposed to similar, multiple risk factors across generations that repeat and increase the likelihood of offending (such as poverty, abuse, or teenage parenthood). Finally, antisocial parents may be ineffective parents and raise antisocial children. Having *antisocial parents* (picture drug users, alcoholics, and individuals engaged in other antisocial or criminal behavior) is one of many major risk factors for delinquency; *large family size, poor child rearing methods, and high conflict homes* are others.

Research consistently confirms that having a *large number of siblings* is correlated with delinquency. Although researchers are still debating the reasons for this correlation, a favorite among academics is that

[3] This is a common pattern and one that is repeated in both family and community risk factors.

the amount of parental supervision each child receives decreases as the number of children in a family increases, and supervision is tightly tied to delinquency. It is also held that families with many children may be highly stressful environments due to resource strain and personal space challenges (overcrowding). West and Farrington (1973) found that families that were less crowded (had more rooms than children) had fewer delinquent children.

Poor child rearing methods is another major family risk factor for delinquency. Specifically, parents who use *harsh and/or erratic discipline, do not properly supervise their children, do not have a warm relationship with their children,* and/or *are not involved in their children's lives* are more likely to raise delinquent children. The most important aspect of child rearing from a delinquency prevention standpoint is parental supervision, as it is the risk factor that most strongly and consistently predicts future offending. Researchers found that juveniles are twice as likely to offend if their parent(s) do not conscientiously and consistently monitor their activities (Farrington & Welsh, 2007). Likewise, physical punishment of elementary school age and older children (not spanking toddlers), predicts later offending as does unpredictable and inconsistent discipline. While cold and rejecting parents increase the likelihood of delinquency, warm and caring parents decrease the amount of offending and may serve as a protective factor against the effects of harsh discipline (Farrington & Welsh, 2007). For example, McCord (1997) found that boys with a cold, physically punishing mother were 2.5 times more likely to be convicted of delinquency than boys with a warm, physically punishing mother (she noted a similar effect for fathers). Although most physically abused or neglected children do not go on to become delinquents, they are more likely to become offenders than are children who were not physically abused or neglected (Maxfield & Widom, 1996).

The quality of home life is also very important, as *high conflict families* produce more than their representative share of delinquents. It is often popular to blame "broken homes" for delinquency; the truth is that the amount of conflict within the family unit is much more important than the number of "parents" who reside in the house (Farrington & Welsh, 2007; McCord, 1982). According to research, the best parenting style is authoritative, which is a style that is both warm and firm (also defined as "firm but fair").

Given these findings, policy should focus on funding cost-effective programs that improve parenting practices. Also, while it would be unethical to dictate how many children a family may have, policy could be used to ensure that all families (large families included) have access to the necessary resources (adequate child care, appropriate housing, proper nutrition, etc.) to ensure the healthiest childhood and family situation possible.

Social Risk Factors

The main social risk factor for delinquency is having *delinquent friends.* Unlike adults who offend alone, juveniles tend to co-offend in small groups (usually 2–3 youth). For most youth, this means shoplifting, vandalizing property, or being involved in a schoolyard fight. However, for some it can include much more serious crimes, such as robbery, carjacking, or homicide. In particular, youth who are gang members commit a lot more crimes and more serious crimes than do juveniles who are not in a gang. Further, there is a large increase in a person's pattern of offending while the person is active in a gang, and a large decrease in offending after he or she leaves the gang. Only a small percent of youth join gangs (between 6% and 30%), but those in gangs commit a disproportionate amount of crime, especially violent crimes (Maxson, 2011).

This means that gangs are a ripe target for policy intervention. If we can decrease the number of juveniles who join gangs, or reduce the amount of time they spend in a gang, we can reduce crime, particularly violent crime. Unfortunately, as research demonstrates, successful gang prevention and intervention programs and policies have been particularly difficult to achieve.[4]

Schools are also correlated with delinquency; however, it is usually through factors that may not be easily influenced by school administrators, staff, or faculty. For example, the *rate of delinquents who attend a school* increases the likelihood of others engaging in crime. *Dropping out of school* is also a school-related risk factor, as are behaviors like *habitual tardiness, school misbehavior, low attachment to school, poor relations with teachers, little school involvement,* and *having low educational/occupational goals* (Agnew & Brezina, 2012). Research suggests that schools with lower than expected delinquency rates have some characteristics in common—these characteristics might be thought of as protective factors. For example, they have *clear rules that are consistently enforced,* have *high expectations for students, praise student achievement* and *offer opportunities for school success,* have *strong community involvement* and *adequate resources,* and are *pleasant places to learn* (Agnew & Brezina, 2012).

These findings suggest that school policies that encourage or incentivize administrators and faculty to identify and intervene with students recognized as chronically truant and at-risk for dropping out could have a significant impact on delinquency (as well as on students' self-efficacy and future lifetime achievements). Also, providing a variety of opportunities and funding for students to participate in extracurricular activities (such as sports, drama, music, art, and academic programs) allows students to develop competencies in those areas as well as increasing connections to the school and their prosocial peers. Finally, policies also should focus on creating school environments that have been shown to reduce delinquency rates.

Environmental Risk Factors

There is considerable research evidence that validates the negative effects that *concentrated disadvantage* has on both children and adults. Concentrated disadvantage is a term used to describe ethnic minority communities that have high rates of poverty, unemployment, and family disruption. The neighborhoods themselves frequently (though not always) have high crime rates with a high proportion of probationers and parolees as residents. Among other things, children who grow up in these communities are at risk for delinquency/criminality, teenage parenthood, child neglect and maltreatment, and school failure (Sampson, Morenoff, & Gannon-Rowley, 2002).

Not all poor, minority neighborhoods have high rates of crime and criminal justice intervention, however. Some neighborhoods, those with high levels of **collective efficacy** (high residential stability combined with high connectivity [mutual trust] between residents, and high levels of informal social control), have low crime rates.[5] For example, research finds that the delinquency rate of a neighborhood is correlated with the neighborhood's ability to maintain social control, the proportion of residents engaged in "neighboring activities" (borrowing items, helping one another, having lunch, etc.), and the level of organizational participation (belonging to organizations with other community members) in the neighborhood (Sampson, 2011).

Communities represent a key opportunity to focus comprehensive prevention programs on a large group of at-risk individuals at a single time. Though some of these neighborhoods pose numerous and

---

[4] See Chapter 11 for a more thorough discussion of gang prevention and intervention programs.
[5] Collective efficacy can be equated to a protective factor.

significant challenges, there is a strong financial incentive to change the way we approach high crime and high criminal justice expenditure communities ("million dollar blocks"). These neighborhoods are very costly—both in terms of current criminal justice related costs (police, courts, probation, parole, incarceration, and loss to victims), other social costs (Temporary Assistance for Needy Families (TANF), welfare, etc.), but also future lost productivity, wages, and tax earnings.

Research suggests that, to prevent crime, policy should attempt to create and foster collective efficacy and informal social control in neighborhoods, especially in those communities that are at a tipping point. Sampson (2011) contends that increasing positive connections between youth and adults in the community is the key to accomplishing this collective efficacy. Additionally, reducing social and physical disorder (e.g., broken windows, trash, panhandlers, graffiti, and prostitution) is important, as these have been shown to increase fear of crime (Skogan, 1990), possibly serious crime, and may influence neighborhood sustainability by inciting law-abiding people and businesses to move out of the area (Sampson & Raudenbush, 1999). Of course, the ultimate answer is to increase human capital interventions for children in these neighborhoods in order to decrease the individual and family-level risk factors that are more often found in children living in concentrated disadvantage. A view confirmed by Wikström and Loeber (2000) who found that boys with balanced risk/protective scores or high protective scores only became delinquent when living in disadvantaged public housing areas (in comparison to boys with high risk scores who became delinquent regardless of where they lived).

Current State of Knowledge

Just as research about delinquency has exploded over the past forty years, so has research on effective prevention programs. Before declaring which prevention strategies and programs are the most effective, it is useful for students to understand that prevention programs are categorized by the general target population. While definitions vary slightly by definer, there are typically three levels of prevention/intervention: universal (primary), selective (secondary), and indicated (tertiary). **Universal prevention** programs (also referred to as primary prevention) *target an entire population without discerning which individuals are at elevated risk.* Public service messages and general education programs/seminars are examples. For instance, the now-infamous drug prevention commercial from the 1980s of an egg being cracked into a frying pan with a commentator stating "This is your brain—and this is your brain on drugs;" antiplagiarism posters hung throughout a college campus; a bullying prevention program given to all third graders in an elementary school; and a parenting seminar offered by a local community group to all parents in a low-crime neighborhood are good examples of universal prevention efforts. Universal prevention programs are not highly effective, but they are generally very cost effective and often relatively easy to administer.

Selective (or secondary) prevention programs *target those at elevated risk for anti-social behavior or delinquency.* Individuals are identified by their risk profiles (the number and nature of risk factors in comparison to the number and nature of protective factors). Those with elevated risk profiles (for a specific behavior, such as gang joining, school dropout, or substance abuse) are targeted for participation in programs intended to discourage the unwanted behavior. A gang prevention program for youth in a gang neighborhood, a preschool program for low-income children, a home visiting program for young at-risk moms, and high school graduation incentives for dropouts and teen parents are all examples of selective prevention programs. Some scholars and practitioners also include early intervention programs for youth caught committing minor crimes, or status offenses in this category. For example, in an effort to curb unwanted behavior before it escalates into something more serious, a youth caught smoking might be allowed (encouraged) to participate in a tobacco information program in lieu of being petitioned in court. The costs of programs in this category vary tremendously, with some very cost effective (i.e., education classes or graduation incentives) and others very expensive (home visiting programs for at-risk moms for example). Regardless of the cost-per-participant, prevention programs in this category are usually more effective than primary prevention programs.

Finally, **indicated (or tertiary) prevention** programs *are intervention programs for those already engaged in repeated or serious delinquency.* Here, the targeted population is usually identified by school administrators, police officers, or court personnel. These programs may take place in the community or within a correctional setting. Examples of indicated programs include: multisystemic therapy, functional family therapy, and multidimensional treatment foster care. These are typically the most expensive programs to administer because the programs are usually multifaceted and intensive, address multiple risk factors and social units associated with each involved youth, and are rather lengthy (in comparison to selective programs).

What Works

So, what programs/policies are endorsed by research? While it is beyond the scope of this chapter to detail every crime prevention/intervention program shown to be effective;[6] in general, there is significant research support that the following strategies reduce delinquency (Farrington & Welsh, 2007; Greenwood & Turner, 2011):[7,8]

- *Academic skills enhancement*—one-on-one and group tutoring sessions to improve subject mastery or passing the GED equivalency exam
- *Behavioral programs*—teaching school-age children appropriate behavior by rewarding selected behaviors
- *Case management*—case manager provides services and connects youth and his or her family to other needed resources
- *Community-based mentoring*—prosocial volunteers spend time with and mentor at-risk children and youth
- *Counseling*—individual, family, and group counseling
- *Cognitive behavioral therapy*—method of teaching/counseling that involves challenging a person's thought processes or behavior, modeling new thoughts and behaviors, and practicing new thinking and behavior
- *Home visiting programs for young moms*—prevention program administered by health or social work professionals in the home; aimed at improving prenatal care and parenting skills of at-risk mothers
- *Parent management training programs*—teaching parents good parenting skills; programs use a variety of methods

---

[6] A list of 442 federal and privately rated programs is available at: http://www.blueprintsprograms.com/resources.php.

[7] This list is restricted to delinquency prevention programs because other chapters in this volume comprehensively address other relevant crime prevention programs and policy choices.

[8] Unless otherwise stated, programs may be for prevention or intervention purposes.

- *Preschool enrichment for low income 3- and 4-year-olds*—prevention; high quality education for at-risk children; one goal is to improve school readiness
- *Restorative justice for low-risk offenders*—intervention for youth who commit minor offenses; involves victim-offender mediation and restitution (mediation only and restitution only are also effective)
- *Social skills training*—teaching school-age children appropriate social behavior; programs use a variety of methods
- *Teen court*—intervention for juveniles who commit minor offenses; court process and sentence administered by peers

In addition to the proven *strategies* above, Blueprints, a project of the Center for the Study and Prevention of Violence (CSPV), University of Colorado Boulder, identified several specific proven *programs,* which are listed in Table 2.2 below. Programs are essentially name-brand strategies. Whereas strategies are a general technique or practice; programs are an entire "package" that includes curriculum and course materials for a specified population, training for program facilitators, specific instructions for course delivery and dosage, as well as other program and facilitator requirements.

Table 2.2 **Blueprints Model and Promising Programs (as of 2/2013)**

Name	Description[9]
Model Programs	
Brief Alcohol Screening and Intervention for College Students (BASICS)	BASICS is a brief motivational intervention designed to reduce heavy drinking and its adverse consequences among high-risk college students by enhancing motivation to change, promoting healthier choices, providing accurate information about alcohol, and teaching coping skills for harm reduction.
Functional Family Therapy (FFT)	FFT is a family therapy intervention designed to assess family behaviors that maintain delinquent behavior, modify dysfunctional family communication, train family members to negotiate effectively, set clear rules about privileges and responsibilities, and generalize changes to community contexts and relationships.
LifeSkills Training (LST)	LST is a 3-year middle school classroom curriculum to prevent adolescent tobacco, alcohol, and marijuana use. LST also targets reduction of violence and other risk behaviors. Program components teach students personal self-management skills, social skills, and drug information and resistance skills.
Multidimensional Treatment Foster Care (MTFC)	MTFC maintains chronic delinquents in alternative family homes in the community with the ultimate goals of reuniting the families, reducing delinquent behavior, and increasing participation in prosocial activities. The program promotes the use of close supervision, fair and consistent limits, predictable consequences for rule breaking, a supportive relationship with at least one mentoring adult, and reduced exposure to delinquent peers.

[9] All descriptions are directly quoted from the Blueprints website (http://www.blueprintsprograms.com/allPrograms.php)

Table 2.2 **(Continued)**

Name	Description
Multisystemic Therapy (MST)	MST provides intensive family therapy with the goal to improve the real-world functioning of youth by changing their natural settings— home, school, and neighborhood—in ways that promote prosocial behavior while decreasing antisocial behavior.
Nurse-Family Partnerships (NFP)	NFP utilizes nurses to work with first-time pregnant mothers in their homes to: 1) improve maternal and fetal health during pregnancy; 2) improve the health and development of the child by helping parents to become more competent caregivers; and 3) enhance parents' personal development by helping them plan future pregnancies, continue their education, and find work.
Project Toward No Drug Abuse (TND)	Project Toward No Drug Abuse (TND) is a high school prevention curriculum taught by teachers designed to prevent cigarette, alcohol, marijuana, and hard drug use.
Promoting Alternative Thinking Strategies (PATHS)	PATHS strives to reduce aggression and behavior problems by promoting the development of social and emotional competencies in children during the elementary school age years.
Promising Programs	
Adolescent Coping with Depression	A therapeutic group intervention that seeks to reduce and prevent major depression or dysthymia among adolescents.
Athletes Training and Learning to Avoid Steroids (ATLAS)	ATLAS is a drug prevention and health promotion program that deters substance use among high school adolescents in school-sponsored athletics by educating youth on the harms of anabolic steroids, alcohol, and other drug use, and by promoting sports nutrition and exercise.
Be Proud! Be Responsible!	The program goal is to reduce risky sexual behavior (unprotected sex) leading to potential HIV/STD contraction among adolescents. It aims to teach new skills and provide information to reach these goals. This is usually accomplished through one or more 2- to 8-hour sessions.
Behavioral Monitoring and Reinforcement Program	A middle school two-year intervention that uses small group meetings designed to reduce adolescent drug abuse by enhancing the incompatible behaviors of school attendance, promptness, achievement, and discipline among high-risk adolescents.
Big Brothers Big Sisters of America (BBBSA)	BBBSA is a mentoring program that works with at-risk adolescents to delay or reduce antisocial behaviors, improve academic performance, attitudes and behaviors, improve peer and family relationships, strengthen self-concept, and provide social and cultural enrichment.
Bright Bodies	The program uses nutrition education, behavior modification, and exercise to positively affect body composition, weight, blood pressure and lipid profiles, and reduce metabolic complications in ethnically diverse, overweight children.

(Continued)

Table 2.2 **(Continued)**

Name	Description
Cognitive Behavioral Intervention for Trauma in Schools (CBITS)	Mental health professionals provide a 10-session group intervention to reduce children's symptoms of PTSD, depression and anxiety resulting from exposure to violence. Also included are 1 to3 individual child sessions, 2 optional parent sessions, and a teacher educational session.
Communities That Care (CTC)	Communities That Care (CTC) is a prevention system designed to reduce levels of adolescent delinquency and substance use through the selection and use of effective preventive interventions tailored to a community's specific profile of risk and protection.
Coping Power	Coping Power has a parent and child focus to prevent substance abuse and reduce aggressive attitudes and behaviors among high-risk children.
Early Literacy and Learning Model	The Early Literacy and Learning Model is a literacy-focused curriculum and support system designed for young children from low-income families. The program is designed to enhance existing classroom curricula by specifically focusing on improving children's early literacy skills and knowledge.
Effekt	EFFEKT seeks to reduce teenage use of alcohol primarily by providing information to parents delivered through the schools.
Familias Unidas	A family-based intervention to promote protection against, and reduce risk for behavior problems, illicit drug use, cigarette use, and unsafe sexual behavior in Hispanic youth and adolescents.
Good Behavior Game (GBG)	GBG is a classroom-based behavior management strategy designed to reduce individual aggressive, disruptive behavior, particularly among highly aggressive, disruptive children, and thereby create an effective classroom learning environment supportive of all children being able to learn.
Guiding Good Choices	A family competency training program to enhance parenting behaviors and skills, to enhance effective child management behaviors and parent-child interactions and bonding, to teach children skills to resist peer influence, and to reduce adolescent problem behaviors.
Highscope Preschool	HighScope is implemented in preschools and aims to build cognitive skills and attitudes to succeed in school by increasing opportunities for active learning. In the long term, it aims to prevent adolescent delinquency and school dropout among "high risk" children, and improve their lives as adults.
Incredible Years – Child Treatment (IY)	Therapists work with small groups of children in weekly sessions for 18 to 19 weeks to reduce conduct problems and enhance children's school behaviors, promote social competence and positive peer interactions, develop appropriate conflict management strategies, communicate feelings (emotional literacy), and manage anger.

Table 2.2   **(Continued)**

Name	Description
Incredible Years – Parent (IY)	IY Parent has three goals: 1) to provide a cost-effective, early intervention parent program to promote young children's social, emotional, and academic competence, and prevent the development of behavior problems; 2) to provide interventions that target treating and reducing the early onset of child conduct problems; and 3) to provide parent training aimed at reducing negative and promoting positive parenting.
Incredible Years – Teacher Classroom Management (IY)	The Incredible Years (IY) Teacher Classroom Management Program provides teachers with classroom management strategies to manage difficult and inappropriate child behavior problems, while also promoting social, emotional, and academic competence. The program goals aim to increase the students' motivation and joy for learning through the effective use of positive and proactive teaching techniques, positive teacher-student relationships, and supportive teacher-parent relationships.
InShape	InShape is a brief multiple behavior program that includes a Fitness Behavior Screen, one-on-one consultation, and a one-page goal plan. The program is designed to reduce drug abuse while increasing positive mental and physical health outcomes among college students age 18 to21.
Olweus Bullying Prevention Program	To reduce and prevent schools' bully/victim problems by restructuring the existing school environment to reduce opportunities and rewards for bullying behavior.
Parent-Child Interaction Therapy (PCIT)	PCIT, through 12 weekly, one-half hour parent-child sessions, aims to decrease child disruptive behavior and abusive parenting by improving parent-child relationships, teaching effective parenting techniques, and encouraging effective discipline.
Peer Assisted Learning Strategies (PALS)	PALS main goal is to improve reading and mathematics skills of students through guided peer-assisted learning strategies.
Positive Family Support-Family Check Up	Positive Family Support-Family Check-Up is a family-based, 3-tiered intervention that targets adolescent problem behavior at the universal, selected, and indicated levels. Goals are to reduce problem behavior and risk for substance abuse and depression, improve family management practices and communication skills as well as adolescents' self-regulation skills and prosocial behaviors.
Project Northland	Provides comprehensive programming at the school, peer, parent, and community levels to reduce adolescent alcohol use, improve parent-child communication about alcohol use, increase students' self-efficacy to resist alcohol and understanding of alcohol use norms, decrease peer influences to drink, and reduce students' ease of access to alcohol in their communities.
Quick Reads	Quick Reads is a repeated reading program designed to build fluency and comprehension by utilizing grade-level, high-frequency words that reflect appropriate phonics and syllable patterns. The program is targeted to elementary students with below-grade reading skills.

(Continued)

Table 2.2 (Continued)	
Name	**Description**
Raising Healthy Children	Raising Healthy Children is a preventive intervention with teacher, parent, and child components, designed to promote positive youth development by enhancing protective factors, reducing identified risk factors, and preventing adolescent problem behaviors and academic failure.
Safe Dates	Safe Dates is a 10-session dating abuse prevention program to raise students' awareness of what constitutes healthy and abusive dating relationships, as well as the causes and consequences of dating abuse. It helps change adolescent norms about dating violence, equips students with skills and resources to develop healthy dating relationships, positive communication, anger management, and conflict resolution.
Sport	SPORT is a health promotion program that seeks to reduce the use of alcohol, tobacco, and drug use by high school students in addition to improving their overall physical health.
Steps to Respect	Steps to Respect has three main goals: (1) reducing bullying and destructive bystander behaviors; (2) increasing prosocial beliefs related to bullying; and (3) increasing social-emotional skills.
Story-Talk – Interactive Book Reading Program	Interactive book reading is a reading strategy intended to promote the development of language and literacy skills in young children from low-income families.
Strengthening Families 10-14 (SF10-14)	SF10-14 is a 7-session parenting and youth skills program, designed to improve parenting and family management skills, with the long-term goal of a reducing aggressive and hostile behavior, substance abuse, and other problem behaviors of young adolescents.
Strong African American Families Program	A 7-week interactive educational program for African American parents and their early adolescent children that strives to reduce adolescent substance use, conduct problems, and sexual involvement. Goals are achieved by enhancing parents'/caregivers' skill set for disciplining and guiding youth, helping youth develop a healthy future orientation and increased acceptance of parental guidance, and teaching youth skills for dealing with peer pressure to be involved with risky behavior.
Success for All	Success for All establishes school-wide reform which includes a basic literacy program that ensures that every child reaches the 3rd grade on time with the adequate reading skills and builds on those skills throughout elementary school.
Targeted Reading Intervention	Individualized instruction by classroom teachers takes the form of 15-minute sessions for a struggling reader in kindergarten and first grade until the child makes rapid progress in reading.
Triple P System	Triple P System uses a public health approach to reach all parents in a community to enhance parental competence and prevent or alter dysfunctional parenting practices, thereby reducing family risk factors both for child maltreatment and for children's behavioral and emotional problems.

Table 2.2 (Continued)	
Name	**Description**
Wyman's Teen Outreach Program	The Teen Outreach Program® seeks to reduce rates of teen pregnancy, course failure, and academic suspension by providing community volunteer experiences and enhancing general adolescent developmental skills, such as understanding selves, understanding relationships to others, managing conflict and stress, making good decisions, and setting goals.

Program fidelity is extremely important. Fidelity means implementing the program the way that researchers intended for it to be implemented. The California Healthy Kids Resource Center identified seven dimensions of fidelity: delivery, dosage, setting, target population, materials, provider qualifications, and provider training (http://www.californiahealthykids.org/fidelity). *Delivery* refers to the instructional strategies employed to deliver the material (for example didactic lecture, Socratic method, modeling, participant practice, and social reinforcement). *Dosage* refers to the number, length, and frequency of sessions in the program. How many sessions do participants attend (one, five, nine . . .)? How long are the sessions (one hour, four hours, etc.)? How often are the sessions (daily, weekly, monthly)? *Setting* refers to where the program takes place (classroom, community center, etc.). *Target population* refers to the intended participants (gender, age, specific characteristics or risk factors, prior history of exhibiting behavior). *Materials* include all the written and audiovisual modules included in the program curriculum. *Provider qualifications* are the credentials or qualifications required of program providers (Marriage and Family Therapist (M.F.T.), Master of Social Work (M.S.W.), health specialist, teacher, etc.). Finally, *provider training* is the nature and length of training required to become a program provider.

If any of the above components are not delivered exactly as intended, the program is unlikely to achieve the desired results. Reducing the measured quantity, altering the delivery, or substituting and/or removing parts of the curriculum are almost guaranteed to reduce, if not completely eliminate, positive outcomes. For example, researchers found no measurable effect of the Life Skills Training program (a model Blueprints program) when less than 60% of the curriculum was delivered (Botvin, Baker, Dusenbury, Botvin, & Diaz, 1995). Similarly, programs intended for one population, but given to another may not work. A universal program intended for all adolescents in a community that is given to adolescents with severe behavioral problems is not going to achieve the same results. Moreover, researchers have found that programs designed for boys often do not work effectively for girls (Chesney-Lind et al., 2008).

In general, research reveals that the most effective programs include: a focus on high-risk youth (as opposed to low risk); are intensive (have a high dosage) and focus on multiple risk factors (specifically the ones that cause the delinquency in the group being treated); start early in life; are community-based (not institutional); and have an authoritative ("firm but fair") relationship between counselors and juveniles. Finally, it is important to remember that crime prevention does not occur in a vacuum, but rather within society, and a program or policy that works in one community may not work in another community (even if the program is implemented with strong fidelity).

What Doesn't Work

In addition to knowing what does work, we also know that a few (popular) crime prevention/intervention strategies do not work. In some cases, these strategies simply do not reduce the unwanted behavior;

for example D.A.R.E. (Drug Abuse Resistance Education),[10] boot camps, court supervision, and intensive supervision probation or parole. In other cases, such as Scared Straight, the program *increases* the unwanted behavior. Policy makers and practitioners should avoid these programs completely.

Available Resources on Evidence-Based Practices

The best programs, the ones that have proven effective (and on which policy should be based), can be found in the academic literature as well as several websites maintained by academic research centers, think tanks, foundations, nonprofits, and governmental agencies. While there are several websites purporting to highlight effective programs, some of these are simply company websites attempting to promote their product(s). The very best resources for evidence-based practices are the following (all are nonpartisan and wholly focused on providing research findings to decision makers):

Blueprints

The Center for the Study and Prevention of Violence (CSPV) at University of Colorado, Boulder, established in 1996, is one of the most well respected authorities on violence prevention programs in the world. The center evaluates programs that promote healthy youth development. It also provides information on scientifically tested "Blueprints" programs, and trains practitioners in implementation (http://www.colorado.edu/cspv/blueprints/). In the past 16 years, the center has reviewed more than 1,100 programs. Of these, only 8 (less than 1%) met their extremely stringent criteria and earned the title "model" program, and 36 (3%) were deemed "promising" (Blueprints). See Table 2.2 (pp. 26–31) for a current list of programs.

Campbell Collaboration

The Campbell Collaboration is an international organization of researchers that exists to "help people make well-informed decisions by preparing, maintaining, and disseminating systematic reviews in education, criminal justice, and social welfare" (www.cambellcollaboration.org/). Since 2005, it has published more than 75 systematic reviews on varied criminal justice policy-relevant topics using meta-analysis, a technique that allows researchers to summarize the results of multiple studies on a topic. Unlike Blueprints, which only highlights programs proven to be effective, Campbell reviews provide information on the relevant knowledge of what does and does not work.

Washington State Institute for Public Policy (WSIPP)

Washington State Institute for Public Policy (WSIPP) was created in 1983 to "carry out practical, nonpartisan research—at legislative direction—on issues of importance to Washington State" (www.wsip.wa.gov). Since the early 1990s, WSIPP has used meta-analysis and cost-benefit analysis to study a variety of criminal justice policies and programs. It does not conduct program evaluations, but is well known and respected for its research, especially its cost-benefit analyses. It is a very good example of policy makers requesting (and using) research to inform significant policy questions, and may be one of the reasons that Washington state is often considered at the forefront of juvenile and criminal justice policy.

---

[10] While DARE does not decease substance use among teens, it has been shown to positively impact participants view of police officers (Lucas, 2008).

OJJDP Model Programs

The Office of Juvenile Justice and Delinquency Prevention (OJJDP) maintains a database of more than 200 evidence-based youth programs for practitioners, policy makers, and researchers (http://www.ojjdp .gov). The database includes programs at every stage of the juvenile justice process, including prevention, immediate sanctions, intermediate sanctions, residential, and reentry. Programs are rated as exemplary, effective, or promising based on research results.

Crimesolutions.gov

Crimesolutions.gov is a relatively new website, created in 2012 by the U.S. Department of Justice to make it easy for practitioners and researchers to identify "what works" in criminal justice, juvenile justice, and crime victim services. It covers a much wider range of topics than Blueprints, but is not as selective as Blueprints. To date, 253 programs in 8 categories have been reviewed; 72 (28%) are classified as "effective," and 157 (61%) are classified as "promising."[11]

A similar "what works" website for education (http://whatworks.ed.gov) is also very useful and contains programs that can reduce delinquency by targeting school risk factors, such as student behavior and dropout prevention. There is also a "what works" website for Problem Oriented Policing (www.popcenter.org/) and for substance abuse prevention (http://www.nrepp.samhsa.gov/).

Coalition for Evidence-Based Policy

The Coalition for Evidence-Based Policy is a nonprofit, nonpartisan organization devoted to providing information about "social interventions shown in rigorous studies to produce sizable, sustained benefits to participants and/or society" (http://evidencebasedprograms.org/). The organization's purpose is to help policy officials identify the few truly effective social interventions (those backed by randomized control experiments) from the many programs that claim to be effective (but are not backed by rigorous research). It is much broader than the other websites mentioned and includes research on homelessness, mental health, obesity, teen pregnancy, employment, and a host of other social issues in addition to crime and justice, but it only considers programs supported by a randomized control experimental design (few programs in criminal justice are of this design). It ranks strategies as "top tier" or "near top tier." Thus far, 10 strategies earned the "top tier" ranking and 7 earned the "near top tier" ranking.

Conclusion

Historically, crime policy was formed by instinct and political ideology alone. For much of our country's history, we knew little about the causes of crime or about how to control/prevent crime. This situation has begun to change and much has been learned about preventing and reducing crime and delinquency since that first watershed report by University of Maryland scholars in 1997. As new research becomes available on "what works," some institutions and states are beginning to look for scientific, not just anecdotal, evidence that crime policies are likely to succeed and that public monies are spent wisely. Fifteen years ago, the major impediment to offering effective prevention programs was a dearth of rigorous research; today

---

[11] There is most certainly a selection bias effect here, as only researchers with significant (usually positive) findings submit their research for inclusion on the website.

the problem is funding (Greenwood & Turner, 2011). If there is one good thing that came out of the economic downturn (recession) which began in 2008, it is that many practitioners and policy makers are earnestly seeking cost-effective, evidence-based practices and policies to replace the arcane, cost-prohibitive incarceration-based strategies that have been the mainstay of criminal justice systems around the nation for the past 30 to 40 years. Nevertheless, though we have made much progress, we are far from the point where criminal justice policy is guided primarily by solid research rather than politics.

Still, the big question that criminologists, criminal justice practitioners, and policy makers want to answer is: How do we reduce crime? There are essentially two paths from which to choose. We can decrease the recidivism rate of convicted offenders, or we can prevent would-be-offenders from entering the criminal justice system in the first place. Whichever option we choose (this chapter focuses primarily on the second option), research should guide our solutions. If we are serious about preventing crime, our solutions should (a) be theory driven, (b) focus on the known risk factors of criminality, and (c) be appropriate for the targeted population. In other words, our policies and programs should take into account what we know about crime and criminals—*who* commits crime and *why* they commit crime—and focus on reducing the causal mechanisms that lead to criminal behavior.

Fortunately, we now know a lot about the causes and correlates of delinquency as well as how to prevent crime and reduce reoffending in a variety of arenas. For example, research continually affirms that "programs that emphasize family interactions are the most successful" (Greenwood & Turner, 2011, p. 121); they are also very cost effective. However, despite enormous benefits and 18 years of child-rearing duties, few parents ever take a parenting class. Curiously, in comparison, it is commonplace (if not customary) for first-time parents in the United States to attend 20 to 40 hours of birthing classes prior to their expected due date in hopes of having a positive delivery experience (in spite of the fact that the active phases of childbirth typically last fewer than 5 hours). Imagine the positive benefits we could achieve if parents were offered (and participated in) low-cost or free parenting classes in their community, with childcare provided, on a semi-regular (or as needed) basis as their children aged and entered new developmental stages (infant, toddler, child, preteenager, teenager). It can be done easily and inexpensively by working with schools, community groups, and faith-based organizations.

Good research should guide policy; it should not determine policy. Best policy choices should be made using a variety of criteria, including research findings. For example, research supports the efficacy of high-quality preschool programs for many young children, but providing free high-quality preschool for all children in the United States would be very costly. While it may be good policy to provide free high-quality preschool to all children, it may be cost prohibitive. We must consider the social costs and future productivity benefits as well as the delinquency reducing benefits when deciding if something is "good policy" or not.

KEY TERMS

Adolescent-limited offenders

Blueprints model and promising programs

Career criminals

Collective efficacy

Concentrated disadvantage

Indicated prevention (aka tertiary prevention)

Law Enforcement Assistance Agency (LEAA)

Life-course-persistent offenders

National Institute of Justice (NIJ)

Omnibus Crime Control and Safe Streets Act of 1968

Program fidelity

Protective factors

Risk factors

Selective prevention (aka secondary prevention)

Universal prevention (aka primary prevention

DISCUSSION QUESTIONS

1. What was the federal government's role in creating and disseminating criminal justice research?

2. What are the known facts concerning crime and delinquency? How should these facts be incorporated into criminal justice policy?

3. What are the known risk factors of delinquency? Which do you find most compelling? What are the implications for criminal justice policy?

4. The mayor of your city asks for your thoughts about crime prevention (or intervention) strategies/programs that can be used in your city. What do you tell her or him? Which strategies are most effective? Where can she or he go to find more information?

WEBSITES FOR ADDITIONAL RESEARCH

University of Colorado Blueprints: http://www.colorado.edu/cspv/blueprints/

Campbell Collaboration: http://www.cambellcollaboration.org/

Washington State Institute of Public Policy: http://www.wsip.wa.gov

Office of Juvenile Justice and Delinquency Prevention: http://www.ojjdp.gov

Crime Solutions: http://www.crimesolutions.gov

U.S. Department of Education, What Works Database: http://whatworks.ed.gov

Problem Oriented Policing Center: http://www.popcenter.org/

U.S. Substance Abuse & Mental Health Services Administration National Registry of Evidence-based Programs and Practices: http://www.nrepp.samhsa.gov/

Coalition for Evidence-Based Policy: http://evidencebasedprograms.org/

National Institute of Justice: http://www.nij.gov/

CHAPTER

III

Street-Level Bureaucracy: From Policy to Practice

Shelly Arsneault

Public policy includes all actions taken by government to address public needs, and it comes in a variety of forms. Policy can be the result of a piece of legislation passed at the state level, as in Arizona's SB 1070 that authorizes police officers to check the immigration status of anyone legally detained whom they suspect is in the United States illegally. It can be the result of judicial action, such as the 1985 *Tennessee v. Garner* case in which the federal Supreme Court limited the use of deadly force by officers to cases in which a life is threatened. Or, public policy can simply be an internal agency policy that requires paperwork to be processed in a certain manner. Within the areas of criminal justice, the policy actions we are concerned with in this chapter are typically undertaken by public servants, such as police, probation, and court and corrections officers. These are the **street-level bureaucrats** of the criminal justice system; the people at the front lines of public service who put policy into action. In other words, they are responsible for criminal justice **policy implementation.**

We begin this chapter with a well-known secret: Without someone to implement it, policy is nothing more than words on a page. Furthermore, what is written as policy is often more theory than reality, because implementing a policy at the street-level is seldom as neat and clean as it appears on the page—this phenomenon is described as the "**law-on-the-books**" versus the "**law-in-action**" (Jenness & Grattet, 2005). You learned a bit about this concept in Chapter 1 with the example of Florida's "Stand Your Ground Law." Another example of this, mentioned above, is the federal Supreme Court's ruling on the constitutionality of Arizona's SB 1070. In June 2012, the Court struck down three parts of SB 1070, but allowed the "show me your papers" provision, which authorizes checking the immigration status of detainees. However, the Court added an important caveat: While the "show me your papers" provision is not unconstitutional as written, the justices warned that if implemented by police officers through racial profiling, harassment, or discrimination, it could easily face constitutional challenge. This is just one example of the ways in which a public policy as written might differ dramatically from the reality of that policy when implemented.

Chapter 3 is structured to first look at the criminal justice system, the **bureaucracy**, then move to the characteristics of street-level bureaucrats and how those characteristics impact the way criminal justice policies are implemented, and concludes with some of the implications these influences have for our system of justice. As you read this chapter, remember that the term bureaucrat is meant to describe not to disparage. Whether we call them public servants or street-level bureaucrats, these are the people at the front lines, carrying out the difficult, often dangerous work of the justice system.

◩   What Is Bureaucracy?

The study of modern organizations is usually traced back to Max Weber's work on bureaucracy at the turn of the 20th century. Bureaucracy can be defined as the structure and rules that allow large organizations to pursue their missions and goals, and is indicative of any sizable organization—from the Walt Disney Corporation, to the university, to government agencies. Weber was writing as the industrial revolution was underway, and he recognized that all organizations would grow in size and become more formally structured as society became more complex; not surprisingly, public organizations like police agencies, corrections departments, and the court system all exhibit this formalization and complexity (Weber, 1964). While the study of bureaucracy has advanced well beyond Weber, many of the basic characteristics that he identified nearly 100 years ago remain important components of modern organizational structures, including specialization and division of labor, hierarchy, formal rules and neutrality.

In criminal justice agencies, specialization and division of labor are obvious. The courts have judges, prosecuting and defense attorneys, and bailiffs; all these positions necessitating specific education, training, and experience requirements, and each plays a very different role in the courtroom. Police departments have officers, detectives, police captains and chiefs of police, and while all may have had to go through the police academy at one point, their titles connote a clear division of labor within their departments. The example of a police department also illustrates the hierarchical nature of bureaucracy with police officers stationed at the lowest ranks, followed by detectives, sergeants, lieutenants, captains, and chiefs. As with many bureaucratic organizations, in a police department there are distinct career ranks that one may attain over the course of a career. These characteristics are important for the maintenance of professionalism and discipline as street-level bureaucrats carry out public policy. Of course, there are many formal rules which dictate operations of employees of the criminal justice system, including those guaranteeing rights to citizens by the U.S. and state constitutions as well as federal and state statutes and agency specific requirements. For example, parole and probation officers operate under a host of regulations regarding their legal and procedural duties when implementing their agency's policies. Under the protocols found in Megan's Laws (specifically, those regarding sex offenders released from incarceration), parole officers in many states have experienced an expansion of responsibilities for monitoring and supervising parolees, for life.

Finally, while the courts and probation and parole offices are fairly standard public sector bureaucracies, police agencies and corrections departments have the distinction of being **quasi-military organizations**, which affects the way their officers implement policy. These agencies are characterized by fairly rigid hierarchies and authoritarian command structures designed to ensure that strict discipline is maintained in emergency situations where rapid mobilization is required. For example, the academy experience for police and corrections officers is designed to socialize them to accept this hierarchical structure and instill in them a loyalty and dedication to their profession (Jermier & Berkes, 1979).

On the other hand, the nature of street-level bureaucracy is such that formal bureaucratic structures are infused with informal **organizational cultures** (Brehm & Gates, 1997; Jenness & Grattet, 2005; Jermier, Slocum, Fry, & Gaines, 1991). Culture in an organization describes all of the characteristics that help the organization to function—from uniforms and oaths, to celebrations and rites of passage; organizational culture is often described as "how we do things around here." A high level of loyalty to one another and to their profession is a unique aspect of policing, and is considered an important part of the *police culture* as loyalty helps officers maneuver through the complex, often dangerous landscape of police work (Carlson, 2005). As explained by Robert Jackall (2005),

> Police guard a social order that they had little hand in forming. Even when they give voice to the plight of victims who can no longer speak for themselves, or rush into ugliness and danger from which others flee, their efforts become subject to an endless, concerted public acrimony over what kind of social order shall prevail. Their beleaguerment helps shape a remarkable occupational solidarity that binds them one to another. (p. 19)

These same aspects of the police culture can produce problems, when their loyalty to one another leads them to ignore instances of misconduct or citizen abuse, an issue taken up later in this chapter (Carlson, 2005; Greene, 2007).

Another pertinent characteristic of bureaucracy that Max Weber described is its *impersonal nature*. The size and complexity of modern society and organizations make it impractical for bureaucrats to become closely tied to the people they serve; thus, as they implement public policies they are supposed to be neutral toward citizens. This is particularly important with criminal justice policy because our system expects fairness and equal treatment under the law. Of course, in practice this means that a couple celebrating with champagne their 25th wedding anniversary in the park where they were married is equally at risk of being fined for an "open alcohol" violation as a homeless person drinking a bottle of Boone's Farm from a paper bag in that same park (Carlson, 2005). As we know, however, law enforcement is often implemented with a fair degree of bureaucratic **discretion** and while equally engaged in illegal behavior, the individuals in the two scenarios just described may experience different treatment from the police. This high level of discretion over policies implemented by street-level bureaucrats is a factor that becomes increasingly important as we examine work at the front lines of the criminal justice system (Jermier et al., 1991; Lipsky, 2010; Maynard-Moody & Musheno, 2003).

Street-Level Bureaucracy

In 1980, Michael Lipsky coined the phrase street-level bureaucrat, which he defined as "Public service workers who interact directly with citizens in the course of their jobs, and who have substantial discretion in the execution of their work" (Lipsky, 2010, p. 3). Lipsky argued that beyond simply implementing public policy, bureaucrats *make* policy at the street level in two ways. First, they exercise wide discretion when interacting with citizens, and second, when individual actions of street-level bureaucrats are taken together, they have the effect of becoming agency policy. The two keys to their policy-making role are their bureaucratic discretion and their autonomy from the authority of their agency hierarchy. These two characteristics of the street-level bureaucrat are discussed in more detail below, as are the implications of street-level policy making in a democracy.

In addition to the commonalities of direct citizen interaction, bureaucratic discretion, and relative autonomy, Lipsky noted that street-level bureaucrats typically experience five additional factors that shape the way they implement policy. First, they are faced with chronically inadequate resources to perform their tasks. For example, public defenders' offices are consistently underfunded in the United States, with average spending just $10 per defendant; for comparison, data indicate that in the United Kingdom spending is $34 per defendant (The Sentencing Project, 2007). Underfunding leads directly to understaffing, which affords the average public defender very little time to interview clients before going into the courtroom (Mounts, 1982; The Sentencing Project, 2007; Weitzer, 1996). The Bureau of Justice Statistics reported that in 18% of state court cases, the defendant did not speak to a public defender before the day of trial; among defendants with private attorneys, this was 5.4% (Harlow, 2000). The result is that public defenders are often less familiar with the details of the clients and cases that they represent, and therefore have strong incentives to seek plea bargains in order to quickly process their clients through the system. This can have very serious negative consequences for defendants who rely on public defenders. Studies indicate that these clients are less likely to be given pretrial release, are far more likely to accept plea bargains, and are much less likely to have their cases dismissed than defendants with private attorneys (Champion, 1989; Harlow, 2000). This example is not unique; inadequate public budgets are commonplace for street-level bureaucracies, thus they often lack essential resources and sufficient numbers of staff to appropriately attend to the needs of their clients.

Second, the demand for the services provided by street-level bureaucrats has a tendency to increase to meet the supply; therefore, even if more resources are provided the demand increases to exceed those resources. In the criminal justice bureaucracy, two examples are the introduction of 911 emergency services and public defenders to provide legal aid to the poor. In both cases, the needs for these public services far outweighed the supply—even before policies and programs were created—therefore both programs were initially inundated by citizens desirous of services, and regardless of the growth of these programs, they continue to experience more demand than they can meet (Gorman, 2012; Lipsky, 2010).

A third common characteristic of **street-level policy implementation** is that work goals are typically vague, often ambiguous, and sometimes contradictory. Consider the example of a public defender, a position that frequently involves role ambiguity: Is the primary goal to get an innocent verdict for the client?; is it to do what is in the best interest of the client, such as negotiate a plea agreement that provides the client with much needed drug treatment?; or is it to ensure that justice is served? A complex example of contradictory goals for street-level bureaucrats comes from the trend over the past 30 years to move away from rehabilitation of prisoners and toward stricter punishment, prevention, and deterrence of crime (Pizarro, Stenius & Pratt, 2006). While this trend corresponds with the current "tough on crime" attitude of policy makers and the public, it also runs counter to the goal of reducing prison overcrowding, an important problem in most states. Therefore, legislatures that require felony prosecutions in certain drug cases, or impose determinate sentencing laws, leave prosecutors and judges with little of the discretion that allows them to seek alternatives to incarceration that could curb the growth of the prison population (Miller & Sloan, 1994).

Related to this ambiguity and contradiction is the fourth facet of street-level bureaucracy: Performance toward goal expectations is difficult if not impossible to objectively measure (Lipsky, 2010). Consider a police agency with goals to ensure citizen safety and reduce levels of crime. Although crime statistics are collected, analyzed, and retained, it is impossible to assess the impact of a single officer on community crime rates. In fact, given the nature of crime (often dependent on many extraneous variables, including the state of the economy, the unemployment rate, and regional demographics like age), it is typically difficult to assess the impact of an entire police force on the relative crime rate.

The fifth characteristic experienced by street-level bureaucrats, especially those in the criminal justice system, is that clients are often not voluntarily involved in services. No one chooses to be victimized, offenders do not want to be imprisoned, those driving while under the influence do not volunteer to take Breathalyzer tests. Most people who find themselves interacting with officers of the law or the court system are forced to do so, and this has important, often negative, implications for the tenor of their interactions with street-level bureaucrats.

A final characteristic of importance to policy implementation at the street-level is *public accountability*. In a representative democracy like the U.S. system, citizens are granted the right to elect the representatives that they believe best reflect their interests on public funds expenditures, policy decision making, and important pieces of legislation. We do not elect bureaucrats. Instead, based on education, training, and scores on civil service exams, public servants are hired by the state to implement the policies enacted by elected officials. It is this point—the power of the street-level bureaucrat to implement and make public policy as well as to profoundly affect the lives of individual citizens—that makes the maintenance of public accountability imperative. Their use of public funds and other taxpayer-provided resources; the fact that they represent the government in hundreds of millions of face-to-face interactions with citizens each day; and, especially for those in the criminal justice system, their coercive power, including the right to kill, make accountability of crucial importance for street-level bureaucracy.

These six factors have important consequences for the way in which those at the front lines of the criminal justice system perform their duties. Attempting to carry out the mandates of public policy while faced with inadequate resources, ever-increasing demands for services, work goals that are vague and difficult to objectively measure, and clients that do not want to be involved with the system while being held accountable to the public creates an extremely difficult set of tasks for those implementing criminal justice policies. In order to best serve and remain accountable to the public, street-level bureaucrats are governed by many rules and regulations as they implement public policy. At the same time, because of the difficult conditions under which public servants operate, they seek to maintain and enhance their own levels of discretion and autonomy.

Rules, Regulations, and Professional Norms

As discussed above, every public bureaucracy is filled with rules, regulations, and standard operating procedures to ensure that policies are implemented uniformly, public money is spent wisely, and citizens are treated equally. These rules begin with the laws, statutes, and programs implemented, all of which are public record, and the specifics of which are typically contained in manuals and standardized forms. The public accessibility of laws, rules, and procedures, known as ***transparency,*** allows both street-level bureaucrats and their clients to understand the policies and procedures and helps to ensure that they apply equally to everyone. For example, when making an arrest there are standard protocols and paperwork that must be filed by officers to ensure due process; charges can be dropped against a defendant, or a case can be thrown out of court if officers fail to follow proper procedures. In the courts, legislatures have created determinate sentencing laws that require judges to impose mandatory prison sentences for certain classes of criminals, lengthening the time they serve (Kessler & Piehl, 1998). In addition to facilitating fair and transparent implementation of public policies, these regulations and procedures are a way to manage large workloads and to limit the discretion of street-level bureaucrats.

Beyond the rules and regulations imposed by policy makers and supervisors, there are a host of occupational, professional, and community norms under which public servants operate. Street-level bureaucrats typically consider themselves professionals whose discretion should be trusted and whose professional training and associations often dictate rules on administrative behavior (Hupe & Hill, 2007). Minimum standards of professional behavior, for example, codes of conduct and ethics, oaths of loyalty, and state-sanctioned licenses and certifications are common for those working in the criminal justice system. While professional norms and licensing act as constraints on bureaucratic behavior, they also promote an aura of expertise that street-level bureaucrats fully embrace. Further, by virtue of their direct interaction with citizens, those at the front lines of public service gain a great deal of experience and a level of mastery over their duties that cannot be learned from books or in training. For instance, studies show that experienced police officers often learn how to detect cues of suspicion that lead them to successful discovery of contraband during discretionary citizen searches (Tillyer & Klahm, 2011; Tillyer, Klahm, & Engel, 2012). This hint of suspicion was referred to as "occupational common sense" by Grimshaw and Jefferson (1987), or "***street-level realism***" (Maynard-Moody & Musheno, 2003), and it can often be at odds with the rules and regulations set down by elected officials, agencies, and managers.

In practice, the street-level bureaucrat uses both realism and rules by dividing work into job parts: one part where decisions can be made using occupational common sense, and another part where decisions are made through regulations and standard operating procedures. A police officer has "an obligation to uphold the law in his area, yet due to finite knowledge, time and resources cannot possibly do so absolutely, a process of *selective* law enforcement is inevitable" (Grimshaw & Jefferson, 1987, p. 292). For example, an officer could not write a ticket or make an arrest for every infraction he observes in the course of a day, which is why it is likely that you have exceeded the speed limit at least once and yet been passed by a highway patrol officer without being pulled over. By necessity, street-level bureaucrats rely on both formal rules, which "specify the duties and obligations of officials," and bureaucratic discretion which "allows them freedom of action" (Hupe & Hill, 2007, p. 281). It is the important element of discretion to which we now turn.

Discretion

Bureaucratic discretion involves using one's own judgments, opinions, or reasoning to make decisions in the course of carrying out public policies. No policy, rule, or law can execute itself, and those tasked with policy implementation often face situations in which the formal rules are ambiguous, contradictory, or nonexistent. In these cases, street-level bureaucrats use their discretion—based on their training, education, experience, community norms, and moral judgments—to carry out policy. Discretion is evidently in play when a prosecutor decides to file charges against a 16-year-old as an adult versus a juvenile, or when a judge sentences someone to the minimum rather than the maximum term in prison. Discretion occurs when prison guards "file injurious reports on inmates whom they judge to be guilty of 'silent insolence.' Clearly what does or does not constitute a dirty look is a matter of some subjectivity" (Lipsky, 2010, p. 14).

The use of discretion by street-level bureaucrats is a complex and sometimes controversial phenomenon. In their study, *Cops, Teachers, Counselors, Stories from the Front Lines of Public Service,* Steven Maynard-Moody and Michael Musheno (2003) discuss two narratives of the street-level bureaucrat: the ***state-agent narrative,*** which assumes that public policies are carried out through abidance to the laws, regulations, and standard operating procedures of the bureaucratic agency and the bureaucrat's profession; and the ***citizen-agent narrative,*** which involves the judgments that street-level bureaucrats make about the characters, motives, and identities of the citizens with whom they come into contact. Maynard-Moody and Musheno note that both of these narratives, the law abidance of the state-agent and the cultural abidance of the citizen-agent, occur within every street-level bureaucrat at different times. As they note, there are many situations in which "law, public policy, and agency procedures provide a good match with the street-level workers' views of the people they encounter," but at other times, law, policy, and procedure may be "ill matched to the workers' views of fairness and appropriate action" at which point "street-level work smolders with conflict over what is the right decision and what is the right thing to do" (Maynard-Moody & Musheno, 2003, p. 9).

In their study, Maynard-Moody and Musheno (2003) illustrate the use of the state-agent versus citizen-agent model in a case that involved two small-time drug dealers who turned a gun on their former partner, Francisco. In the course of the fight that ensued, Francisco managed to grab the gun and pursue the other two on foot. During the pursuit, he fired at the pair, hitting one, but also lodging several bullets into a neighboring home. The police officer in the case, relying on his judgments about each of the drug dealers decided not to file any charges against Francisco. On the other hand, the first two dealers were charged, convicted, and served time in prison. The officer explained that he gave Francisco a second chance because he was otherwise hardworking and "he had come clean with us" (p. 101). The other two dealers were judged more harshly by the officer; he described them as trouble-makers, who never did "anything that was aboveboard" (Maynard-Moody & Musheno, 2003, p. 99). In this and other cases, police officers use their discretion to make important judgments about the citizens with whom they interact and to whom public services are delivered.

The example of Francisco and the two drug dealers begs a few important questions about how judgments are made and when discretion is used to benefit rather than hinder citizens. In his discussion of these street-level interactions, Lipsky (2010) focuses on factors like control over clients and rationing of services, but introduces the other side of bureaucratic discretion which involves giving citizens the benefit of the doubt, cutting them a break, or not charging them with violations they clearly committed, as in the case of Francisco. These two facets of judgment are often based on the perceived worthiness of the citizen in question (Lipsky, 2010; Maynard-Moody & Musheno, 2003). Maynard-Moody and Musheno note that there are four ways in which street-level bureaucrats typically respond to their clients: (a) in some cases, bureaucrats offer "the normal, routine bureaucratic treatment" which "is good treatment" (p. 94) in most cases; (b) other times, when citizens are deemed particularly worthy, the street-level bureaucrat may provide extraordinary treatment to clients, going beyond the rules to secure the best outcome for someone perceived as deserving special treatment; (c) sometimes, particularly in the criminal justice system in which officers must gain the compliance or cooperation of citizens, bureaucratic response is about making the most practical decision rather than the ideal; and (d) in some situations, citizens are deemed unworthy by street-level bureaucrats and they respond to those clients with strict adherence to the rules, providing nothing more than a minimal, "by-the-book" response.

Perceived worthiness is clearly an important factor in bureaucratic treatment of clients and citizens. In the eyes of most street-level bureaucrats, worthy clients have several characteristics: first, the client is deserving of help and has not caused their own trouble; second, an assessment that the client, with help, will be successful; third, the client is respectful and appreciative of the bureaucratic intervention; fourth, the client is contrite, apologetic, repentant, and/or expresses sorrow for his or her transgressions; finally, clients are more likely to be deemed worthy when the street-level bureaucrat can personally identify with them (Maynard-Moody & Musheno, 2003). In Francisco's case, the officer considered him worthy for many reasons: he admitted that both he and his wife had jobs, but he began dealing drugs when his family started having trouble making financial ends meet; the officer also believed that Francisco was afraid that his former partners were going to kill him, thus he only pursued and shot at them out of self-defense;

additionally, the damage to his neighbor's house was viewed as purely accidental. The officer in this case identified with Francisco whom he considered to be a hardworking husband and father, and whom he believed would stay on the straight and narrow after this incident, if only given the chance.

Street-level bureaucrats make these assessments about citizens every day. While most of the time the normal, routine bureaucratic response is warranted, sometimes the client is deemed worthy of the benefit of the doubt, as in Francisco's case. Certainly, in other cases the client may be deemed unworthy by display-ing characteristics opposite to those of the worthy: they are disrespectful and challenge the authority of the street-level bureaucrat; they are considered "bad" people who are not likely to change their behavior; the street-level bureaucrat cannot identify with their immoral and different behaviors; they are often consid-ered irresponsible or lazy, and therefore the cause of their own problems; finally, even if given a chance, the street-level bureaucrat does not believe this client will ever make good (Maynard-Moody & Musheno, 2003).

When clients are judged unworthy, those working on the front lines often see themselves as enforcers of moral codes, not just rules and regulations. In these cases, citizens "may receive minimal, even harsh, treatment and, when available, severe punishment" (Maynard-Moody & Musheno, 2003, p. 144). This is evident in another case detailed by Maynard-Moody and Musheno where two 17-year-old girls used a stolen credit card to go on a spending spree at local boutiques and restaurants, racking up $12,000 in charges. While both girls initially denied any knowledge of the crime, the parents of one of the girls even-tually convinced her to go with them to the police station and confess; the second girl continued to deny any involvement. At this point, the officer on the case began to view the girls differently, judging the first to be worthy, and the second unworthy. He described the first girl as repentant and changed; her parents, a married couple, were described as "so cooperative" with the police. The second girl's parents were divorced, causing the officer to "always have to see them separately;" the girl was judged to have "really no sense of right and wrong" (2003, p. 109). In the end, the officer recommended juvenile court for the first girl, but adult court for the second. Although they were partners in the same crime, being deemed worthy meant that the first girl's juvenile record remained permanently sealed, she went off to college, "and was doing really well" (p. 109). Neither the second girl, nor her uncooperative, divorced parents ever admitted her guilt; she ended up with a felony police record, and never graduated from high school (Maynard-Moody & Musheno, 2003).

It is situations like this, where two equally guilty teenagers are treated so *un*equally, that create con-troversy over bureaucratic discretion. When police, prosecutors, judges, and corrections and parole officers have such power over the lives of citizens, especially in the criminal justice system, discretion can be seen as discriminatory, unfair, and even political. In an early study of California's Three Strikes Law, for example, it was found that district attorneys and judges at the local level played an important role in imple-mentation of the law, as they were granted a fair amount of discretion over how prior "strike" violations were treated. Consequently, in politically liberal regions of the state in which voters were less supportive of Three Strikes, such as the San Francisco Bay area, there were lower levels of compliance with the law than in more politically conservative areas (Gerber, Lupia, McCubbins, & Kiewiet, 2001). Some would argue that differing rates of compliance based on political ideology is a clear misuse of bureaucratic discretion.

Although discretion can lead to inequities in policy implementation, and fears that laws enacted by elected officials are being thwarted by bureaucrats, those at the street level are granted discretion for a variety of reasons. First, as discussed earlier, in complex work situations where programmed decisions are simply inadequate, discretion allows bureaucrats the freedom to take action to carry out their duties and obligations (Hupe & Hill, 2007; Lipsky, 2010). Detailed instructions to a police officer on how to deal with a suicidal individual or a domestic violence case are fruitless, and as Lipsky points out, if required to use strict operating procedures, most officers "would refuse to intervene in potentially dangerous situations" (2010, p. 15). Rather, street-level policy implementation often requires the sensitive observations and judgments about individuals detailed in the Maynard-Moody and Musheno (2003) study.

Further, discretion is a key to the legitimacy of the individual street-level bureaucrat; because the state has entrusted this person with authority and discretion over citizens, they are perceived as a legitimate agent of the state. Finally, it is important to note that while statutes, legislation, and regulations are often lengthy, they are also typically vague. Members of federal, state, and local legislative bodies are not experts on all matters. Instead, they and their supporters have ideas about the direction they wish for society, and write legislation and policies to reflect those preferences; the details are left to be determined during implementation, which often translates to the street-level through agency or individual decisions. Therefore, gaps between the "law-on-the-books" and the "law-in-action" abound in the criminal justice system (Jenness & Grattet, 2005).

Autonomy

In addition to discretion, street-level bureaucracy is characterized by fairly high levels of autonomy as a result of little direct supervision. Prosecutors and public defenders do not interview clients and witnesses or build their cases while being constantly monitored; police officers are frequently in the field, far from supervisory control; parole officers often meet their clients outside of an office setting, away from direct monitoring. Street-level bureaucrats use their autonomy in conjunction with their discretion as a way to carry out their work under the constraints of public service, which include large caseloads, inadequate resources, public scrutiny, and vague, often unachievable goals. They do this by using both the rules and regulations of their occupations and agencies and their bureaucratic discretion. Street-level bureaucrats, therefore, work to protect and expand their autonomy. Indeed, because they consider themselves professionals with vast amounts of direct client experience, those on the front lines often view managers and policy makers as out-of-touch with the reality of street-level bureaucracy and see efforts to dictate the parameters of service delivery as illegitimate or overbearing (Lipsky, 2010; Maynard-Moody & Musheno, 2003). Studies indicate that implementation of law enforcement innovation, for example, has a varied record of success. Innovative polices have been ignored, delayed, or selectively enforced because officers and the agencies for which they work often see "the flood of innovative policies as a reflection of political whims, the politicization of law enforcement, and a distraction from basic 'good police work'" (Jenness & Grattet, 2005, p. 337).

Another aspect of the high level of autonomy exercised by street-level bureaucrats is their potential to avoid their duties rather than work—the classic image is of the police officer killing time in the donut shop rather than working in the field keeping the streets safe. Social scientists looked at this problem from the perspective of ***principal-agent theory***, which refers to the relationship between the actor that creates the work (the principal) and the actor that carries out the work (the agent). In the classic conceptualization, the principal must use a series of strategies, including rule setting, monitoring, and evaluation, to ensure that the agent is carrying out the work of the principal as expected and not engaging in opportunistic behavior like wasting time or abusing the power of their positions. In the language of principal-agent theory, principals (supervisors and elected officials) must find ways to ensure that their agents (street-level bureaucrats), whose autonomy precludes close monitoring, are not engaged in either ***shirking***—hanging out in the donut shop—or ***sabotage***—undermining criminal justice policy objectives.

It is probably obvious that principal-agent theory assumes a model of conflict between superiors and subordinates where both supervisors and elected officials need to impose ever more rules and monitoring strategies to ensure that bureaucrats appropriately implement public policies. In addition to rules, regulations, and standard operating procedures that help to ensure compliance with policy mandates, supervisors use other tools to encourage working rather than shirking or sabotage. These inducements include both rewards like better shift assignments and sanctions, such as assigning a patrol officer to desk duty. Lipsky (2010) notes that although under civil service and union rules, managers have the ability to demote or fire, the costs of using these sanctions, such as prolonged periods of arbitration, are often greater than supervisors are willing to bear. In these cases, managers are more likely to use their ability to define the work environment—shift assignments, including geographic areas, and their influence over promotions and transfers—to control street-level bureaucrats in the field.

Brehm & Gates (1997) examined the principal-agent model in police departments using data from field observations and attitudinal surveys of officers. They analyzed the tendencies for officers to use their autonomy to shirk rather than work by examining police relationships with peers and supervisors, their level of professionalism, and the organizational cultures of individual police departments. As expected, they found that when officers and their departments are more professional, they are more likely to work than shirk; that operating within networks of hard-working peers encourages working over shirking, and that officers who like their jobs are far less likely to shirk. These results comport nicely with the concept of *public service motivation,* which posits that people seek occupations in fields like criminal justice out of an affinity for their public missions and a desire to serve the public interest (Perry & Recascino Wise, 1990). Public service motivation is an intrinsic factor that attracts people to public service professions, and individuals with high levels of public service motivation work harder in organizations that meet public needs (Frank & Lewis, 2000; Wright, 2007). These findings are consistent with Brehm & Gates' conclusion that police officers are "highly professional and strongly influenced by principles that cohere to the mission of their organizations" (1997, p. 202).

In a second study that looks beyond shirking behavior, Brehm & Gates (1997) examined instances of sabotage of agency policies by police officers, specifically, police brutality, including threats, ridicule, unnecessary searches, and use of excessive force against citizens. Importantly, the data indicate that most officers do not abuse their autonomy and power and that incidents of misconduct are most likely to occur only when an officer is predisposed to such behavior. Further, these forms of police brutality are rare, occurring in about 7% of encounters with citizens; the most egregious, excessive force, occurred in just over 1% of encounters. Interestingly, officers investigating violent crimes were 8% more likely to defect from stated agency policies and engage in one or more of these forms of brutality (Brehm & Gates, 1997). This finding coincides with the idea that street-level bureaucrats treat citizens differently depending on their judgments of them; in these cases, police officers appear to judge violent offenders as less worthy of standard methods of policing (Lipsky, 2010; Maynard-Moody & Musheno, 2003). Similar to their findings on shirking, Brehm and Gates (1997) concluded that factors that restrain police brutality are officer professionalism, liking one's job, and working in a departmental culture in which misconduct is less tolerated. Finally, they found that incidents of police brutality increased when there were more officers at a scene. They offer two possible explanations for this result: (a) officers may feel pressured toward brutality by the presence of other officers, and/or (b) the nature of the situation in which a large number of officers are present is unusual in itself, facilitating the use of tactics outside the normal parameters of law enforcement (Brehm & Gates, 1997).

Both incidences of shirking and sabotage can occur in the work of street-level bureaucrats because of their high levels of autonomy. Police officers on patrol are among the best examples of both shirking and sabotage behaviors because while in the field they are far from direct supervision. Although police logs are kept, cameras are often placed in patrol cars, and the number of tickets issued or arrests made are monitored by managers, most of the decisions made by bureaucrats in the criminal justice system are made outside of public view and are therefore subject to evaluation only after the fact. In this way, street-level bureaucrats are not simply agents carrying out policy mandates, but are part of a process in which policy is made both from the top down and the bottom up (Lipksy, 2010).

Accountability

In addition to the problems with discretion and autonomy, a variety of other factors make accountability vitally important to the work of street-level bureaucrats. First is the fact that street-level bureaucrats earn their livings and carry out their duties using tax dollars; second is their power to implement and make public policy which can profoundly affect the lives of individual citizens; third, for those in the criminal justice system, such as police, corrections, parole and probation officers, the coercive power of the state requires monitoring of bureaucratic activities to ensure due process and equal treatment of citizens; finally, and fairly unique to the criminal justice bureaucracy, the right to take a life, either in the course of ensuring public safety or in the ability to seek, impose, or carry out the death penalty, requires a very high level of public accountability.

Accountability is often considered to be a top-down exercise, as when viewed through the lens of principal-agent theory; however, accountability is actually much broader and includes both ***professional accountability*** and participatory/citizen accountability (Hupe & Hill, 2007; Lipsky, 2010). Professional accountability is horizontal in nature, including both the behaviors that are shaped by one's peers and the ethical norms of one's profession. Brehm and Gates (1997) found that police officers in departments in which other officers disapproved of shirking were less likely to shirk themselves. In the court system, public defenders, prosecutors, and judges are all bound to the same ethical dictates of the legal profession and can be removed and even disbarred for transgressions.

Participatory accountability is from the bottom up and involves clients and other members of the public using their citizenship responsibilities to influence the behavior of street-level bureaucrats (Hupe & Hill, 2007). This accountability is evident in the existence of citizen oversight committees assigned to monitor police agencies. On the other hand, especially for those in the criminal justice system, certain paradoxes are created for street-level bureaucrats when responsiveness to the public is part of accountability (Lipsky, 2010). For example, it is difficult to reconcile the protection of privacy and anonymity for victims of violent crimes while maintaining public accountability through a transparent criminal justice system. Similarly, while the general public and those within the justice system wish to see batterers prosecuted, women in violent relationships are sometimes reluctant to press charges against their partners because they fear the effects that incarceration will have on both their children and their family's economic stability (Hart, 1993). These conflicts between differing yet legitimate public concerns can complicate determinations of accountability and leave policy makers and street-level bureaucrats in the difficult position of prioritizing some public values over others as they formulate and carry out public policy.

Finally, there is top-down or ***political accountability***, which is considered the essential link between bureaucracy and our representative system of democracy (Lipsky, 2010; Hupe & Hill, 2007). Public servants are hired by the state to implement the policies enacted by elected officials, and while there are rules and procedures to follow, the unavoidable discretion and autonomy afforded street-level bureaucrats means that they must be held accountable for their day-to-day work. Particularly in recent years, managers seek objective, quantitative measures of individual performance as a tool for keeping bureaucrats accountable. Street-level work, however, is often not amenable to this kind of accounting; remember the vague and difficult to measure goals of the street-level bureaucrat. Keeping track of the amount of time a parole officer spends with clients tells us nothing about the quality of those interactions, and asking a parolee to evaluate officer performance might be useful, but would have to be regarded with some amount of skepticism. In addition, quantitative assessments can actually lead employees *away* from agency goals. For example, if the performance of a patrol officer is evaluated based on traffic tickets, it follows that the officer increases his efforts to write traffic tickets, which in turn can become a serious problem if he increases those efforts at the expense of other aspects of his job. This is not to imply that street-level bureaucrats should not be held accountable for their work, but simply to point out that performance assessment is a complicated matter.

As noted earlier, elected officials have to know that the laws they create are implemented as intended; therefore, another aspect of top-down accountability is linking bureaucracy to democracy by holding bureaucrats responsible for compliance with policy directives. Maynard-Moody and Musheno's (2005) characterization of the state-agent versus the citizen-agent narrative is important here. In the state-agent narrative, accountability is about carrying out public policies through abidance to the laws, regulations, and the standard operating procedures of elected officials and agencies. When these are breached, the desire to control bureaucratic behavior and ensure stricter compliance typically results in the enactment of more rules. On the other hand, in the citizen-agent narrative, street-level bureaucrats make judgments about the characters, motives, and identities of citizens, often with the view that strict rules and supervisors can impede doing what is right and fair for citizens (Maynard-Moody & Musheno, 2005). These are the cases in which Lipsky (2010) notes that frontline public servants should be open to the possibility that every new client may present a case unique enough to warrant a flexible, innovative approach. His suggestion is that street-level bureaucrats should be considered accountable to their clients as well as to their agencies and policy makers.

As is true of so much of street-level bureaucracy, accountability is a complicated issue. While complying with the laws, court directives, and policies promulgated by elected officials, policy makers, and their managers, delivering services to citizens through the criminal justice system often requires far more complex and nuanced decision making than anticipated by those making the rules. This can and does lead to abuse in some cases. Instances of violence and charges of excessive force at the hands of prison guards or police officers are not uncommon, nor are examples of discrimination or racial profiling. Too often the "code of silence" among police officers still protects those who engage in misconduct (Carlson, 2005; Greene, 2007). Two well-known examples of such abuse are the videotaped beating of Rodney King by Los Angeles Police Department officers in 1991 and the shooting death of Amadou Diallo in 1999 by four members of the New York Police Department. After such incidents of misconduct, calls for greater accountability and policy reform come from both the bottom up and the top down. Members of the public and elected officials typically seek to check the power of the police through such mechanisms as creation of citizen oversight committees, introduction of new training procedures, and increased hiring of minority officers (Weitzer, 2002).

It is important to remember that accountability for those serving in the criminal justice system involves being accountable to many different groups: to the victims of crime who expect justice to be served, to the felons in their care; to their fellow officers, and the professional associations to which they belong; to the elected officials who write the laws, and their supervisors who review their personnel files. As discussed, members of these groups may have different and contradictory views about what successful implementation of criminal justice policy means. In the end, discretion and autonomy must exist, side-by-side with rules and accountability in order for street-level bureaucrats to best serve the public.

✕ Implications for the Criminal Justice System

Policy implementation is never easy. Laws are often vague, goals can be difficult to reach and may conflict with one another, resources are usually insufficient to meet public need, and success is often in the eye of the beholder as public values are prioritized differently by different constituencies. In the policy area of criminal justice, these difficulties can be magnified. Policy implementation in the criminal justice system is frequently mundane, as when performing the routine procedures of every day administration; policy implementation is often difficult; for example, in no other policy area is it more important to ensure due process and equal protection under the law. And policy implementation is occasionally dangerous, serving clients that often exist at the margins of society. Jackall writes that the police agencies, district attorneys' offices, and courthouses of the criminal justice system are "a world of splintered jurisdictions and scattered information, intense competition for prestige, vying hierarchies, and arcane, hair-splitting distinctions. These bureaucratic behemoths fracture authority and knowledge and make absurdity the constant bedfellow of rationality" (2005, p. 18). The street-level bureaucrats of the criminal justice system navigate this difficult environment by relying on standard rules and procedures, but the unique circumstances of individual citizens often require making judgments, exercising discretion, and developing shortcuts in order to process their large, complex workloads (Lipsky, 2010).

While some worry that street-level bureaucrats simply use their autonomy and discretion to wield excessive power over defenseless citizens, flouting agency procedures, and ignoring policy mandates at will, it must be remembered that there are a number of constraints on bureaucratic misbehavior. These include basic rules and procedures that must be followed, supervisor evaluations of performance, and sanctions for underperformance. Constraints also exist in the form of oversight from legislative committees and the courts. As discussed at the start of this chapter, even though the Supreme Court ruled that "show me your papers" is constitutional, they left open the possibility that if the ruling is implemented by police in a manner that violates civil rights, then the court could take another look at the law's constitutionality. Client feedback is another source of bureaucratic restraint and citizen complaints can be taken very seriously, especially when agencies have formal grievance procedures. Similarly, civilian oversight commissions are growing in popularity as a way to hold police agencies accountable to the public, and while not perfect, represent an important step forward in shedding light on the often insular practices of police work (Greene, 2007; Wells & Schafer, 2007). The media and other watchdog groups also act to constrain misconduct in the criminal justice field. One such example is The Sentencing Project, a nonprofit organization founded in 1986 to provide training to defense attorneys and to help reduce incarceration rates in the United States. Since that time, the organization has become a strong voice for research and advocacy to create a more just and fair criminal justice system.

Other factors constraining bureaucratic behavior are the professional norms and codes of conduct for those working in the field of criminal justice. Attorneys and judges who fail to uphold appropriate legal standards or who engage in unethical behavior can be disbarred from the profession, for example. Appropriate peer behavior and a positive organizational culture are also important in keeping street-level bureaucrats accountable to their agencies and the public, as evidenced in Brehm and Gates' (1997) work. Finally, public service motivation, which attracts individuals to the public sector in the first place, often leads street-level bureaucrats to view public service as a noble calling and to dedicate themselves to it, thereby reducing the odds of either shirking or sabotage.

Given the wide range of difficulties inherent in the work of street-level bureaucracy, and beyond the rules and monitoring, an intrinsic feeling of professionalism and dedication to public service drive most of those employed in the courts, prisons, and parole and police departments to implement public policy to the best of their abilities. As Brehm and Gates (1997) concluded, street-level bureaucracy does not work because of principal-agent relationships, rather, bureaucracy works because public servants act as "principled agents" as they implement the public policies for which they are responsible.

KEY TERMS

Bureaucracy	Policy implementation	State-agent narrative
Citizen-agent narrative	Political accountability	Street-level bureaucrats
Discretion	Principal-agent theory	Street-level policy implementation
Law-in-action	Professional accountability	Street-level realism
Law-on-the-books	Quasi-military organization	Transparency
Organizational cultures	Sabotage	
Participatory accountability	Shirking	

DISCUSSION QUESTIONS

1. Street-level bureaucrats in the criminal justice system share a variety of characteristics, including direct citizen interaction, bureaucratic discretion, autonomy, inadequate resources, excessive demand for services, vague and difficult to measure work goals, clients who are involuntary involved with the system, and work that is subject to public accountability. How do these characteristics affect the work of those on the front lines of the criminal justice system, both for better and for worse?

2. Many aspects of bureaucracy constrain the work of those in the criminal justice system, including specialization, division of labor, formal rules, regulations and the law: what is known as the "state-agent narrative." At the same time, other aspects of their work, including professional experience, autonomy, and agency culture allow workers a greater degree of discretion: the "citizen-agent narrative." Discuss the tensions between these two narratives. Is it more appropriate for these officials to follow the state-agent or the citizen-agent narrative when carrying out their work in the criminal justice system?

3. Accountability manifests itself in different ways for those working in the criminal justice system. The criminal justice worker is accountable to whom and why? Discuss the differences between top-down and bottom-up accountability. Which, in your opinion, is more important for street-level bureaucrats implementing policy in the criminal justice system?

WEBSITES FOR ADDITIONAL RESEARCH

History of Social Work: http://www.historyofsocialwork.org/eng/details.php?cps=17

RAND: http://www.rand.org/research_areas.html

American Society for Public Administration: http://www.aspanet.org/public/

NASPAA (National Schools of Public Affairs and Administration) Public Service Careers: http://www.publicservicecareers.org/

Partnership for Public Service: http://www.ourpublicservice.org/OPS/

Governing Magazine Online: http://www.governing.com/

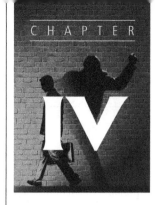

CHAPTER

IV

Policing High-Risk Places

William H. Sousa

The association between crime and place is well documented in the fields of sociology and criminology. Criminal activity often varies significantly from neighborhood to neighborhood within an urban environment, and serious crime often concentrates in particular communities (Reiss & Tonry, 1986). Moreover, the significance of place is not limited to serious crime. Minor disorders, quality of life offenses, neighborhood disorganization, fear of crime, and other community problems are also linked to specific places.

Mindful of the connection between place and community problems, police often direct resources to specific neighborhoods that are known to have troubled histories with crime and disorder. But, while knowing where to direct resources is clearly a concern, utilizing proper tactics to identify and address community problems at those locations is essential. Improper tactics may be ineffective at resolving community problems, waste valuable criminal justice resources, and potentially damage relationships between police and citizens.

The methods used by police to manage problems at crime-prone locations vary considerably. Contemporary practices such as hot spots policing, problem-oriented policing, and order maintenance policing are products of decades of reform. An understanding of the history of policing at places is necessary to appreciate these current tactics. Therefore, this chapter begins with a presentation of the evolution of policing at crime-prone locations. The current state of police practice at problem locations is then discussed, along with relevant evaluation research. The chapter concludes with some of the complexities and controversies that may arise as police attempt to address problems in high-crime settings.

The Back Story

Early History of Policing Problem Places

The idea that police should focus resources at specific, ***problem locations*** is as old as modern policing itself. Indeed, it can be argued that the first regular professional police force in London was created as a response to "hot spots" of criminal activity. Writing about the history of policing in England, Critchley (1972) notes that during the late 1700s and early 1800s, the dockyards in London offered particular incentives for crime. Critchley draws on the observations of Patrick Colquhoun, a British politician and strong advocate for crime control during the late 18th and early 19th centuries who lamented the extent of theft and prostitution on the docks along the Thames River. These disorderly locations served as motivation to create a preventive police force to patrol the riverside. Although initially financed by private merchants to protect their shipping interests, the Thames River police eventually became a public police force under the administration of the British Home Secretary. Their orientation toward crime prevention was the guiding principle for the establishment of later public police organizations in England, including the London Metropolitan Police in 1829.

The strategy of preventive patrol in high-risk areas carried over into American policing as well. Leonhard Fuld (1971), an early commentator on American policing, placed a special emphasis on the prevention of crime. Fuld wrote in the early 1900s when foot patrol was the norm and argued that patrol officers should be held accountable for the crime and disorder that occurred on their beats. As such, a patrol officer's principle duty was to develop an intimate knowledge of the people and locations on his post. Patrol officers should then be encouraged (and expected) to cover their entire post each shift; however, to enhance their efficiency and preventive capacity, they should concentrate their efforts by walking in the most important locations. Fuld's observations implied that crime and disorder could best be managed when police are proactive at problem-prone locations.

"Hazards" and Random Preventive Patrol

The significance of police action in high-risk areas moved into the mid-1900s in the form of "hazards" patrols. O. W. Wilson, a prominent police chief in the mid-20th century who authored many influential works on police administration, regarded hazards as situations that have a high risk of accidents or criminal activity. Influenced by the work of his mentor, August Vollmer (who was himself a leading reformer and important figure in American policing), Wilson advocated for police to pinpoint hazards like high-risk property and places. According to Wilson, the identification and inspection of crime hazards was essential to the successful performance of patrol duty. The use of motorized, preventive patrol at these locations was considered particularly useful at reducing hazard factors, and Wilson criticized the practice of distributing the patrol force evenly over equal areas (see Wilson & McLaren, 1972). For optimum performance, preventive patrol should be deployed according to hourly and geographical concentrations of crime.

For much of the history of policing, determining the geographical boundaries of high-risk areas was inexact. Police administrators and officers relied on their memory and experience to estimate the amount of crime in an area. Only then could they determine the most efficient routes of preventive patrol. As Wilson and McLaren (1972) indicate, however, this began to change with the appearance of pin maps in police organizations. By using pin (or spot) maps, police could chart the distribution of offenses in a city or district. Spot maps essentially became the start of the systematic process for determining patrol allocation at problematic locations (Wilson & McLaren, 1972). What followed were attempts to use more sophisticated statistical methods to plot patrol procedures according to the geography of crime. Larson (1972), for example, describes preventive patrol formulas based on the weighting of hazards in a given area. Elliot (1973) describes deployment formulas following an "interception" patrol model. He notes that based on past history, certain street segments in different sections of cities are more susceptible to crime than others. Elliot takes into account factors such as the probability of crime reoccurring in these crime-prone areas, the time it takes to commit an offense, and the speed of patrol. Based on these factors, a patrol route could be designed that theoretically had a better chance of either preventing an offense or intercepting a crime in progress.

Hazards-oriented patrol and interception models that targeted high-crime areas were widely recognized, accepted, and utilized for years. Police periodically used "sweeps" or "crackdown" tactics that placed a high emphasis on arrests and citations, but the primary tactic that police employed in hazard-prone places was ***random preventive patrol*** in automobiles. Police administrators argued that officers could provide a sense of omnipresence in communities by driving by problem-prone locations and through high-risk areas in a random fashion. Criminals, aware of this omnipresence and sensing that police may be nearby, would be deterred from committing unlawful acts for fear of detection and quick apprehension.

These methods made intuitive sense to police—and police administrators successfully marketed tactics associated with hazards models and random preventive patrol to politicians and to citizens. Nevertheless, several challenges to these practices emerged during the 1970s. In some cases, concerns focused on the methodologies used to plot hazards and patrol patterns, including the ability of statistical models to predict crime and properly allocate workload (Larson, 1972). However, the more serious concerns focused on the specific tactics that police employed once they were at high-risk locations. The Kansas City Preventive Patrol Experiment provided what was perhaps the most significant challenge to preventive patrol tactics. In the Kansas City experiment, researchers essentially found that neither increasing nor decreasing the amount of random motorized patrol in an area—regardless of its initial level of crime—had any substantial impact on criminal activity (Kelling, Pate, Dieckman, & Brown, 1974).

It is important to note that the Kansas City experiment did not say that patrol officers could not be effective. The results were instead a commentary on the ineffectiveness of the specific tactic of random preventive patrol at deterring crime.[1] Nevertheless, the study's findings defied conventional police wisdom. Police administrators adamantly defended the practice of random preventive patrol in automobiles as a method of crime suppression. As a result, random motorized patrol remained the dominant standard operating procedure for police agencies into the latter part of the 20th century.

Theoretical Developments and the Emergence of the "Hot Spots" Concept

By the 1980s, interest in the policing of problem places gained momentum, sparked (at least in part) by increasingly cooperative efforts between academics and practitioners. Several factors contributed to the renewed interest in the policing of high-risk areas. One of these factors involved the

---

[1] Research conducted around the same time period revealed that other methods of patrol were of value. The Newark Foot Patrol Experiment (Kelling, Pate, Ferrara, Utne, & Brown, 1981), for example, demonstrated that officers on walking beats were more effective than officers in automobiles at reducing citizens' fear of crime. Chaiken, Lawless, and Stevenson (1974) demonstrated that saturating a crime-prone location (in this case, the New York subway) with police presence decreased a number of minor crimes and reduced felonies. Similarly, Pate, Bowers, and Parks (1976) found that a location-oriented approach involving overt and covert surveillance by police was more promising than standard, random patrol.

recognition of crime "hot spots"—the notion that a small number of specific locations generate a disproportionately large number of calls for service to police (Pierce, Spaar, & Briggs, 1986; Sherman, Gartin, & Buerger, 1989; Sherman, 1989). For example, Sherman et al. (1989) discovered that 50% of calls for service to the Minneapolis police in a one-year period came from only 3% of the addresses and intersections in the city, whereas most addresses generated no calls at all. Additionally, the researchers found that the more calls to police a location generated, the more likely it was to produce repeat calls.[2]

The emphasis on hot spots triggered further empirical research that highlighted the importance of focusing on specific crime-prone locations. Academics who compared criminal histories of locations to criminal careers of offenders demonstrated that location-oriented interventions could be more effective than perpetrator-oriented tactics (Spelman & Eck, 1989). Spelman (1995) also determined that the risk of future criminal activity at locations was relatively stable over time, allowing him to conclude that it was prudent for police to focus on problem-solving techniques at locations. Sherman (1995), drawing on his previous research (Sherman et al., 1989) and the work of Wolfgang, Figlio, and Sellin (1972), estimated that future crime might be six times more predictable by the location of the occurrence than by the identity of the perpetrator. These estimates prompted Sherman to argue that police should focus more specifically on "wheredunit rather than just whodunit" (1995, p. 37).

The hot spots concept also coincided with theoretical developments in academia that illustrated the importance of crime and place. These theoretical advances included the rational choice perspective (Cornish & Clarke, 1986), which describes offenders as rational decision makers who take advantage of crime opportunities; the routine activities approach (Cohen & Felson, 1979), which explains how crime opportunities emerge where the routine activities of potential offenders and victims converge in time and place; and crime pattern theory (Brantingham & Brantingham, 1991), which argues that crime can be patterned by considering environmental characteristics and constraints while studying the movement and decisions of offenders. Braga and Weisburd (2010) argue that these theories help to explain the relationship between crime and place, with crime pattern theory blending rational choice and routine activities to describe how crime is distributed spatially: "[u]nderstanding the characteristics of places . . . is important as these attributes give rise to the opportunities that rational offenders will encounter during their routine activities" (p. 75).

Thus, theoretical developments and empirical research demonstrating the specificity of hot spots caused police and researchers to begin to rethink the manner in which they viewed problem locations. Although police and citizens had long realized that crime concentrates in particular places, the tendency had always been to consider crime as randomly distributed in those places (Sherman et al., 1989). In other words, people are inclined to look at general problem areas rather than at the specific problem locations. Thus, we perceive "violent" neighborhoods, or "dangerous" streets, when in actuality, most places in those neighborhoods and most parts of those streets are relatively safe and problem free. This understanding of crime and place helped to influence how police manage problems at nuisance-prone locations.

---

[2] The concept of hot spots relates closely to the notion of repeat victimization. Early research on repeat victims, carried out primarily in the United Kingdom, demonstrated that a small percentage of all victims accounts for a relatively large portion of all victimizations (see Farrell (1995) for a review). Farrell and Sousa (2001) discuss the potential overlap between hot spots and repeat victims, suggesting, for example, that addressing repeat victimization may automatically place resources in hot spots.

The Current State of the Policy: Practice and Research

The Identification of Problem Locations

The past several decades have seen advances in the policing of problem locations. These advances include improvements in methods of identifying nuisance locations, progress in our understanding of problems at these locations, and innovations in terms of resolving those problems. Technological improvements, especially in the area of geographic information systems (GIS), have enhanced the ability to identify and understand at-risk locations. GIS software links a jurisdiction's geographic files with databases that contain information on incident addresses (i.e., calls-for-service data, arrest reports, etc.). As a result, police analysts can pinpoint event locations and generate visual representations of crime patterns without relying strictly on officers' experiential knowledge, or pin maps. Given the proper data and application criteria, GIS analyses can identify specific problems within geographic areas, determine if those problems cluster together in time and place, examine whether those problems are related to other community concerns that may also exist in those areas, and detect changes in those problems over time. Furthermore, by analyzing historical trends, GIS applications can essentially be used to predict the risk of problems occurring at given locations in the future—a process known as risk terrain modeling (see Caplan & Kennedy, 2010).

The use of GIS for crime mapping purposes has become common practice among police departments in the United States. As of 2007, nearly all local police departments serving populations over 500,000 used computers for crime mapping and hot spot identification purposes (Reaves, 2010). The proliferation of scholarship in the field, including the introduction of academic outlets tailored for GIS applications to crime (such as *Crime Mapping: A Journal of Research and Practice*), also demonstrates the importance of GIS as a tool for researchers who seek to study crime trends and test environmentally based theories.

Despite its importance to the identification of problem places, like all analytic tools, GIS is limited by the nature of its source data. Part of the challenge of understanding nuisance locations is in recognizing the proper factors that make a place problematic. In order to determine the factors that create a problem location, one must examine the variety of concerns people have while going about their daily activities in public places.

Understanding Problem-Prone Locations: What Makes a Place a Concern?

A metric that is often used to gauge the level or degree of "problem" at a location is its concentration of "serious" crime. Criminal justice agencies generally use the number or rate of FBI index offense reports as a measure of serious criminal activity.[3] Several factors contribute to the reason why index offenses are considered to be a determinant of risk at a location. First, the threat of being a victim of a felonious offense is clearly a concern of citizens. Although results vary by demographics, research generally demonstrates that one's perception of the level of serious crime in their neighborhood, as well as prior personal victimizations,

---

[3] The FBI Part 1 index offenses include murder, rape, serious assault, robbery, burglary, grand larceny, and auto theft. Police agencies often group murder, rape, serious assault, and robbery together as a general measure of violent crime, while burglary, grand larceny, and auto theft are combined to form a measure of property crime. Arson is the eighth Part 1 index offense, although in practice it is often not included in aggregate measures of serious criminal activity.

contribute to one's sense of fear of crime (Moore & Trojanowicz, 1988). Second, serious ***index crimes***—such as high profile murders, commercial robberies, or a string of auto thefts—are likely to be reported by the media, which focuses the public's attention on the importance of these offenses. Third, since the adoption of the index offenses, they serve as a type of performance measure for the police: Police agencies are often assessed by their ability to prevent or reduce index offenses; police officers are often evaluated based (at least in part) on the number of arrests they make of serious offenders; police detectives are often judged by their ability to clear serious crimes off their caseloads. Given the degree of significance placed on the index offenses by agencies, a fair amount of information about these crimes is recorded by police, including both reports of their occurrence and arrests of perpetrators. Thus, if someone is looking for a measure of community problems, the most reliable information the police have is likely to come in the form of the serious index offenses.

The concentration of index offenses is therefore often used to identify problem locations, yet there are several difficulties with this measure. For example, index offenses represent only some felonies and do not capture all serious offenses that concern citizens. Most people would agree, for instance, that drug dealing is a serious criminal offense that can cause major distress in neighborhoods. However, while police certainly record arrests for drug dealing, data on incident reports for this type of activity are often much less reliable.

Perhaps more importantly, research over the past several decades shows that serious community problems do not necessarily stem from the threat of "serious" crimes. Minor crimes and disorderly offenses can also be of concern to citizens and be indicators of problem locations. Researchers identified two types of community disorders: social disorder (e.g., street prostitution, public alcohol and drug use, public urination and defecation, obstreperous youth, aggressive panhandlers and street vendors, etc.) and physical disorder (e.g., graffiti, discarded drug paraphernalia, abandoned vehicles and buildings, trash and litter, etc.) (Skogan, 1990; Taylor, 2001). These disorders do not necessarily refer to illegal activities, but they can nevertheless represent intimidating behavior or conditions that negatively impact the quality of life in communities. Studies indicate that minor disorders are connected to citizen fear (Ross & Jang, 2000; Skogan & Maxfield, 1981). Additionally, research suggests that disorders like these may indeed give rise to more serious offenses (Wilson & Kelling, 1982).

Unfortunately, methods to systematically record information on disorderly activities are lacking in most police departments. Agencies may track arrests or citations for minor offenses, but procedures for recording these incidents of occurrence are generally less consistent. As a result, GIS and other software are restricted in their ability to utilize minor offenses as a source of information to identify or analyze community problems. Put simply, official data from police records can only tell part of the story—thus police should not rely on these data alone to understand complex problems in communities.

The limits of police data point to the significance of communication with citizens regarding their opinions of problems in neighborhoods. While analytic tools provide a snapshot of problem places, they lack important elements of context. GIS and predictive analyses can help point police in the right direction, but citizen input—along with experiential knowledge from beat officers—is necessary to understand the nature of problems at locations.[4] Furthermore, citizen input can help inform the tactics that police use to help resolve problems at nuisance locations.

---

[4] Understanding problem places is further complicated by the varying capacities of locations to "absorb" crime and disorder. A fair amount of disorder at a location does not necessarily mean that the location is a major problem. For example, consider Las Vegas Boulevard (the "Strip") in Las Vegas, Nevada. The Strip is a place with a considerable amount of disorder, ranging from public alcohol use to aggressive panhandlers and street peddlers. Yet, most of the Strip's patrons do not consider it to be a problematic place—the amount of life in the area is able to absorb many disorders and minor offenses, making them relatively innocuous to passersby. If those disorders manifested themselves in a quiet residential neighborhood, however, the result may be quite different.

Police Innovations at Problem Places

Police strategies designed to manage problems at crime-prone locations have evolved considerably since the early research on patrol tactics conducted during the 1970s. Much of this evolution is the result of research and theoretical developments on "hot spots" as well as research findings that examine the relationship between fear, crime, and disorder in neighborhoods. Additionally, the 1970s and 1980s are generally identified as the beginning of the community-policing era of American policing. This era is associated with increased police accountability to the public and a greater willingness of police to work with citizens on neighborhood problems (see Kelling & Moore, 1988). Importantly, community policing tactics are commonly recognized as more proactive than those associated with previous paradigms of police work, which tended to be reactive in terms of responding to the needs of citizens.

Hot Spots Policing

Related to this proactive approach, it is now common practice for police agencies to experiment with patrol tactics directed at specific problem locations. Often referred to as "***hot spots policing***," these methods differ from the patrol tactics that characterized much of police history during the 1900s. Rather than driving through or past high-risk areas at random times, hot spots policing involves a more directed approach where officers focus on times and specific locations that have been precisely identified by crime analysis and computer mapping (Sherman & Eck, 2002). Early evaluations of hot spots policing demonstrated its potential at deterring criminal activity (see Sherman & Weisburd, 1995). In a more recent systematic review of evaluations of hot spots policing, Braga, Papachristos, and Hureau (2012) find that most studies show an overall crime-reduction benefit when police focus their efforts and resources at specific, problem-prone locations (see also Braga & Weisburd, 2010). Therefore in general, proactive patrols directed at hot spots are promising in terms of managing locations that are at high risk of criminal activity.

Despite potential benefits, the notion of hot spots policing is somewhat limited in terms of its utility to police departments. The analytic tools associated with hot spots can help guide police in a number of ways, including where to focus resources; what types of activities are likely to occur at specific locations; when those activities are likely to occur; and the types of actors (offenders and victims) officers may encounter at those locations. Hot spots analyses, however, do not necessarily advise police on what officers should do once they arrive at problem locations (if they should do anything at all). In other words, hot spots policing can tell police where to place their resources, but the tactic by itself does little to help manage resources at those hot spots (see Rosenbaum, 2006). Complicating matters, scholars who study location-based police strategies do not always adequately document or describe specific tactics implemented by officers. As a result, it is often difficult to determine the policy relevance of the tactics employed by officers performing hot spots policing.[5]

Problem-Oriented Policing

Accordingly, a question of critical importance concerns the types of activities that should be performed by officers while at problem places. Police scholars agree that ***problem-oriented policing*** strategies offer great potential for dealing with nuisance locations (Eck, 2006; Braga, 2008; Weisburd & Eck, 2004).

---

[5] See Eck (2010) for an interesting discussion of how the lack of clarity in program descriptions can lead to misinterpretation in terms of policy implementation as well as a disconnect between academics and practitioners.

Herman Goldstein (1979), the originator of the problem-oriented policing concept, argues that police can fall into a pattern of responding to individual incidents of crime rather than addressing the source of those incidents. Without addressing the source, a response to a single incident is only a short-term solution because the problem itself could remain and may well generate more incidents in the future. Goldstein recommends that police should instead focus on the underlying source of problems—by doing so, they are better able to prevent future incidents from occurring.

The principles of problem-oriented policing suggest that officer presence by itself may not be enough to resolve the fundamental issues that give rise to problems at hot spots. Simply placing officers at specific locations without further direction, therefore, is likely to have only a limited impact. Police may indeed serve a deterrent purpose while at nuisance places—and officer presence may lead to citations or arrests of wrongdoers—but such activity may not have long-term effects on the problems at those locations.

To be effective, problem-oriented policing requires a detailed analysis to understand the source of problems at a given location. This examination must go beyond the usual hot spots analyses that are produced by police agencies, which generally lack the depth necessary to inform the nature of the problem (see Braga, 2008; Goldstein, 1979). When analyzing problems at a specific location, for example, police should consider the type of location (industrial, residential, commercial, etc.), the motivations of offenders at the location, the nature of victims, the history and magnitude of the problems as reported by citizens, the suitability of past police responses, and other environmental and social factors that allow the problem to continue (Goldstein, 1979).

A detailed analysis helps to define problems with greater precision. With this knowledge, police can develop a response that is designed to address the specific problem at the identified location. Since tactics are tailored to the specific locale, problem-oriented responses tend to be more nuanced and innovative than traditional police tactics—such as "crackdowns"—that rely heavily on arrests and citations of offenders. Researchers have identified a range of problem-oriented tactics utilized in hot spots, including community outreach and social service interventions, interventions designed to change the physical environment of the hot spot, and other enforcement efforts (Braga, Hureau, & Papachristos, 2012). A number of proactive strategies support problem-oriented policing at hot spots. Among these, situational crime prevention, "pulling levers" initiatives, and order maintenance policing are especially relevant to place-based policing tactics.

Situational crime prevention (SCP) refers to a branch of criminology that seeks to deter crime problems by altering the criminal opportunity structure (Clarke, 1997). SCP assumes that regardless of motivation, criminals must be presented with the proper opportunity in order to commit a criminal act. Thus, by eliminating opportunities for criminal activity, police can reduce and manage larger community problems. SCP attempts to change the environment by reducing crime opportunities through five broad categories of intervention: increasing the effort it takes to commit the act (e.g., target hardening), increasing risks (e.g., improved street lighting to assist natural surveillance), reducing rewards (e.g., ink tags on merchandise to reduce the benefits of theft), reducing potential provocations, and removing excuses (Cornish & Clarke, 2003).[6] The principles of SCP have long supported the strategy of problem-oriented policing (Braga, 2008), and the SCP focus on reducing specific crimes by altering local environments supports place-based initiatives in particular.

---

[6] Cornish and Clarke (2003) discuss 25 total techniques of situational crime prevention that fall under these five broad categories.

Because some SCP techniques call for heightened surveillance and increased target hardening, SCP has been criticized in the past for promoting a "Big Brother" or "fortress" society (Clarke, 1997). Citizens, however, tend to accept SCP techniques as they are often unobtrusive and generally confined to specific locations. Numerous studies have demonstrated the effectiveness of SCP tactics. For example, SCP initiatives have been associated with efforts as varied as reducing street prostitution in red light districts (Mathews, 1997), managing violence associated with crowds in public places (Madensen & Knutsson, 2011), reducing crime and disorder within public transportation systems (Clarke, 1996; Sloan-Howitt & Kelling, 1997), and preventing problems at gang and drug hot spots (Lasley, 1998).

"Pulling levers" is a deterrence strategy focused on identifying high-risk, chronic offenders, and preventing their future criminal activity (Kennedy, 1998; 2006). The term "pulling levers" is a reference to the variety of options available to criminal justice agencies that, when combined and focused on a small group of individuals, can be effective at deterring crime and violence. Pulling levers strategies involve creating a mechanism (typically an interagency working group) that can identify high-risk individuals, communicate the message of deterrence directly to those individuals, notify them of the various enforcement consequences (or "levers") if they do not change their behavior, and offer social services and community support to assist in their transition away from a high-risk lifestyle (Kennedy, 1998; 2006). Although pulling levers can be classified as an offender-based rather than a place-based strategy, it can be highly effective when the identified problems at specific locations are associated with small groups of individuals (see, for example, Kennedy, Braga, & Piehl, 2001).[7]

The design of pulling levers interventions is dependent on the nature of the violence problem, the relationships between key stakeholders, and the political and social culture of a particular place. As such, it is difficult to replicate a pulling levers intervention from one location to the next (Braga & Winship, 2006). Furthermore, the nature of the intervention is often not conducive to rigorous scientific methods of evaluation (Braga & Winship, 2006; Kennedy, 2006). However, pulling levers tactics have been implemented in a number of cities in the United States and demonstrated success at reducing youth and gun violence (e.g., Braga, Kennedy, Waring, & Piehl, 2001; McGarrell & Chermak, 2004).

Order maintenance policing refers to a police tactic that focuses on managing minor offenses and community disorders. Order maintenance is an operational strategy associated with the "broken windows" hypothesis developed by James Q. Wilson and George Kelling in 1982. In brief, "broken windows" suggests that minor offenses are linked to more serious community problems in a developmental sequence.[8] The authors contend that minor offenses, if left unmanaged, can potentially send signals indicating that community controls are compromised in that neighborhood. Although not inevitable, weak community controls can result in even more minor offenses, citizen fear, and possibly in serious criminal activity at that location. The policy implication of broken windows (i.e., order maintenance policing) is that if police and citizens can manage minor offenses (through formal or informal means), they can reduce fear and possibly reduce serious crime. Additionally, to the extent that disorders and minor offenses are themselves identified as major problems in a particular community, order maintenance policing has intrinsic value as a mechanism for reducing that source of citizen concern (Sousa & Kelling, 2006; Thacher, 2004). Many projects that focus on place-based initiatives identify order maintenance activities

---

[7] As part of their description of "Operation Ceasefire," Kennedy et al. (2001) demonstrate the relationship between violence and gang territory in Boston (see also Braga, 2008).

[8] The term "broken windows" is a metaphor. The authors suggest that one broken window in a building, left unrepaired, can send a signal that no one cares. As a result, people who believe that such behavior is acceptable may well break more windows in the building.

as a component to their problem-oriented policing strategy (Braga et al.,1999; Braga & Bond, 2008; Braga et al., 2012; Kelling & Coles, 1996; Sousa & Kelling, 2010).

Order maintenance tactics as implemented by some police departments have been criticized as overly aggressive and potentially detrimental to police legitimacy, although evidence of this is controversial.[9] Rigorous evaluations of order maintenance tactics are also limited, although studies suggest the value of order maintenance practices. Order maintenance tactics have indeed been linked to reductions in crime and disorder in public parks (Sousa and Kelling, 2010), public transportation systems (Kelling & Coles, 1996), problem hot spots (Braga & Bond, 2008), and residential neighborhoods (Kelling & Sousa, 2001).

Race, Gender, and Class Implications

The Complexities of Policing Nuisance Locations

Methods to identify hot spots, combined with proactive, problem-oriented strategies involving such tactics as situational crime prevention, pulling levers, and order maintenance can be effective at reducing problems at nuisance locations. These methods, however, are not without their critics. One argument is that police activities at nuisance locations have a limited effect because crime may be displaced to other locations. Others are concerned with the moral and ethical complexities of police methods in hot spots as they relate to community acceptance of those tactics.

Crime Displacement

An issue of concern for many proactive police initiatives—particularly those directed at specific places—is the potential problem of ***crime displacement***. Displacement occurs when offenders react to police tactics by altering their behavior so as to circumvent police activities. Theoretically, offenders can move to a different location (i.e., spatial displacement), offend at a time when officers are not present (i.e., temporal displacement), modify their *modus operandi* so as to more easily avoid detection (i.e., tactical displacement), select different targets or victims that are not as well guarded (i.e., target displacement), or choose to commit other types of crimes that are not the focus of police activity (i.e., offense displacement) (Eck, 1993; Repetto, 1976).[10] The positive benefits of a hot spot initiative are thus limited—or even negated—if crime and disorder are simply displaced.

Although it is a common criticism of place-based police initiatives, recent studies that examine displacement find little evidence that it happens to any great degree (see Braga and Weisburd, 2010). When evidence is found, the overall effect is often minimal and can be relatively benign (e.g., if displacement results in offenses that are less serious or less impactful on the community) (Guerette, 2009). Furthermore, research suggests that problem-solving efforts that focus on high-risk locations may actually have a benefit

---

[9] The term 'order maintenance' is often erroneously associated with the term 'zero tolerance.' Order maintenance policing emphasizes the proper use of police discretion when managing minor offenses (Kelling, 1999; Sousa & Kelling, 2006). Formal police procedures—such as arrest or citation—are options, but informal means of resolving problems are equal possibilities (Sousa, 2010). ***"Zero tolerance"*** emphasizes the use of formal enforcement while minimizing officer discretion.

[10] Researchers may also look for offender displacement—the process by which new offenders begin operating in an area after old offenders have been removed by police actions (Eck, 1993).

beyond the targeted locations—a phenomenon known as "diffusion of benefits" (Clarke & Weisburd, 1994). Indeed, a recent review of hot-spots initiatives found that diffusion of crime control benefits rather than displacement, were more likely the result (Braga et al., 2012).

Community Acceptance of Police Practices at Problem Locations

A more important question relates to community acceptance of police tactics in hot spots. The perceived legitimacy of police activities in problem locations is imperative. Regardless of their impact on crime and disorder, officer actions that are viewed as improper, excessively punitive, or abusive could damage relations between police and citizens. This is particularly an issue in some poor, urban, often minority communities that have historically had fragile relationships with police.

One of the criticisms of aggressive police tactics at problem places is that they have a disproportionate impact on young, minority males living in economically disadvantaged neighborhoods. Studies conducted in New York City, for example, suggest that stop and frisk practices associated with police order maintenance activities are linked to demographic and socioeconomic conditions in largely minority communities (Fagan, Geller, Davies, & West, 2010) and that arrest practices for minor offenses disproportionately impact minorities in relation to their representation in the population (Harcourt & Ludwig, 2007). While these studies suggest a potential racial bias in police practice, they themselves have become somewhat controversial. Other research, for example, finds minimal evidence of racial bias in New York's stop and frisk practices after controlling for neighborhood crime levels (Ridgeway, 2007), causing some commentators to challenge the objectivity of researchers who examine these issues (see Baker & Rivera, 2010).

Critics of police tactics at problem places have a point, however. Clumsy police "sweeps," and overly aggressive "crackdowns" that rely heavily on stop and frisk procedures and arrest practices, may achieve short-term success in terms of crime reduction, but these tactics can potentially alienate citizens, infringe on civil rights, and ultimately minimize any crime-prevention benefits that are achieved. Furthermore, aggressive policing could increase fear among citizens by giving residents the perception that they live in dangerous neighborhoods (Hinkle & Weisburd, 2008). This points to the importance of police communicating with citizens regarding the specific locations that will be the focus, the problems that will be addressed, and the activities that officers will perform.

To be sure, police methods in high-risk locations must be legally appropriate. Additionally, to achieve and maintain strong relationships with citizens, police practice at those locations must be morally justified. Critics of proactive policing properly note the ethical obligations of police and call attention to the moral complexities of policing problem places (see Rosenbaum, 2006). Indeed, while proactive policing may benefit a high-risk location as a whole, caution is needed to maintain a balance between community interests and the rights of individual citizens (Wilson & Kelling, 1982).

Although proactive policing at high-risk locations must be properly managed, it should be noted that some of the strongest supporters of proactive policing are the residents who live in the areas most affected (Rosenbaum, 2006). Citizens who live near hot spots are often confronted with disorderly conditions on a routine basis. Consequently, they have high demands for police to "do something" about problems at these locations (see Skogan, 1990). Furthermore, research suggests that citizens do not perceive aggressive police tactics as harmful to police legitimacy (Weisburd, Hinkle, Famega, & Ready, 2011).

It should also be noted that while critics properly point out the moral complexities of aggressive enforcement, few provide substantial evidence of widespread or systematic abuse by police. Many academic critics, for example, claim objectivity, but base their assumptions and analyses on dramatized media accounts, political statements, and ideological viewpoints (Beck, Bratton, & Kelling, 2011; Sousa &

Kelling, 2006). Like all police tools, hot spots policing and its associated problem-oriented tactics can be misapplied and misused. However, basing criticisms on flawed or ideological assumptions makes assessing the value of proactive policing methods difficult.

⊠ How Do We Fix It? Problems at High-Risk Locations

Police practice as it relates to managing problems at high-risk locations has evolved considerably, both in terms of identifying problem locations and in terms of addressing community concerns at those locations. Police once relied on experiential knowledge and pin maps to identify problem places, and then relied on random patrol and the occasional "crackdown" to manage issues of crime and disorder. These practices yielded few long-term successes and, in some cases, contributed to poor relationships between police and citizens. In contrast, contemporary methods involve more sophisticated procedures for identifying problem locations, more systematic ways of assessing the level and type of problems at those places, and more effective means of addressing crime and disorder through proactive strategies.

While departments have become more scientific in terms of pinpointing high-risk places, police can still improve their methods of identifying and diagnosing problems at specific locations. Rather than relying primarily on measures of serious crime, police should also consider measures of social and physical disorder, citizen fear of crime, and citizen perceptions of neighborhood problems. These factors are often not readily available to police, yet they contribute substantially to what citizens believe are important community issues that officers should help to address.

The specific identification of a high-risk place is an important step in reducing crime and disorder. Nevertheless, the identification of a problem place is only an early step in the longer process of managing problems at specific locations. Hot spots analyses can tell officers where to go, but they do not necessarily inform police in terms of what should be done once they arrive at problem locations. To be sure, contemporary practices that involve proactive problem solving—such as order maintenance policing, pulling levers strategies, and situational crime prevention—have established their potential, but the suitability of these methods depends on a detailed understanding of the nature of the problem at a given location.

The appropriateness of police tactics at problem locations also depends on citizen support of those tactics. Communication with citizens who live near high-risk places can help identify the nature of problems, determine the proper approach to managing those problems, and garner support for police strategies. Communication with neighborhood residents can also enhance police legitimacy in the eyes of citizens, particularly in areas that have had problematic relationships with police in the past.

While police should strive to communicate with citizens regarding tactics, more needs to be done within the scientific community to describe police methods at hot spots. Black box evaluations that provide only a cursory description of hot spots initiatives can help determine the effectiveness of interventions, but they do little in terms of informing best practices. Furthermore, cursory descriptions invite confusion and misinterpretation over the applications and goals of proactive police activities.

KEY TERMS

Crime displacement

Hot spots policing

Index crimes

Order maintenance policing

Problem locations

Problem-oriented policing

Pulling levers

Random preventive patrol

Situational crime prevention

Zero tolerance

DISCUSSION QUESTIONS

1. How do rational choice theory, routine activities theory, and broken windows theory support the idea of police focusing resources on problem places?

2. How does problem-oriented policing differ from hot spots policing and order maintenance policing?

3. There are concerns that broken windows policing often becomes aggressive zero-tolerance policing in practice. What are the concerns? What are the consequences of zero-tolerance policing (or overly aggressive police tactics)? What can police officers and agencies do to encourage community acceptance for police practices at problem locations?

WEBSITES FOR ADDITIONAL RESEARCH

Center for Problem-Oriented Policing: http://www.popcenter.org/

Community Oriented Policing Services: http://www.cops.usdoj.gov/default.asp?item=36

RAND Center for Quality Policing: http://www.rand.org/jie/centers/quality-policing.html

Link to the original Broken Windows Article by Wilson and Kelling in The Atlantic Monthly: http://www.rand.org/jie/centers/quality-policing.html

Police Executive Research Forum: http://www.policeforum.org/

Police Foundation: http://www.policefoundation.org/

Scottish Institute of Policing Research: http://www.sipr.ac.uk/

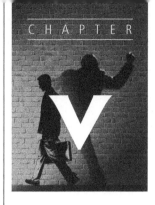

CHAPTER V

Homeland Security: A New Criminal Justice Mandate

Larry K. Gaines

Although various forms of terrorism have existed for centuries (see Burgess, 2003), it did not become a national priority in the United States until the September 11, 2001, attacks on the World Trade Center in New York City and the Pentagon in northern Virginia. The attacks resulted in over 3,000 deaths and billions of dollars lost in the American economy. Previously, there had been other terrorist attacks on Americans and American interests, but the magnitude and brazenness of the 9/11 attacks by foreign terrorists shocked the American people. Homeland security and combating terrorism immediately became national priorities.

The attacks had a profound effect on the American populace. For example, in 2007, six years after the attacks, a survey on the fear of crime found that 36% of the population feared being a victim of a terrorist attack (University of Albany, 2007). The only fears that ranked higher in the survey were being a victim of a burglary and auto larceny. Crimes such as being a victim in a homicide and being sexually assaulted ranked lower in the survey, even though there are many more of these crimes reported. Even though the fear of being victimized by a terrorist attack has subsided, its residual effects remain. In 2011, ten years after 9/11, 30% of respondents in the fear of crime survey stated that they were fearful of being a victim of terrorism (University of Albany, 2012). The 9/11 attacks profoundly changed America. The most evident change has been the implementation of homeland security and its accompanying government apparatus.

Many believe that homeland security is exclusively a national imperative; however, it affects federal, state, and local criminal justice agencies. If a terrorist attack or event occurs, it is going to occur in a local community. As Carter (2004) notes, we must think globally, but act locally. When an event occurs, it involves local and state public safety personnel. They will be the first responders. The 9/11 attacks and the recognition that homeland security is a priority have thrust local criminal justice agencies into the mix. They must be prepared to respond and be adept at gathering terrorist-related intelligence to help prevent attacks. Local agencies represent the first-line defense and response for any event, whether it is a terrorist attack or a natural disaster.

✄ The Back Story: What Is Homeland Security?

The Department of Homeland Security (DHS) is the federal department that is primarily responsible for the security of our homeland. As such, the DHS (2010) identified five core homeland security mission areas, and these mission areas serve as a template for all agencies involved in homeland security. The first is preventing terrorism and enhancing security. There are internal and external terrorist **threats** to the United States. They are ideological, political, and religiously based. All terrorist threats must be identified and actions taken to ensure that terrorists do not mount an attack on the United States or on American interests overseas. This means that an elaborate security apparatus must be developed and implemented. Second, we must secure and manage our rather porous borders. They must be controlled to ensure that terrorists, and other illegal immigrants, do not enter. Third, we must enforce and administer our immigration laws. The *al Qaeda* terrorists who perpetrated the 9/11 attacks slipped into the United States, but did so legally. They essentially remained here and were free to travel as a result of lax enforcement of immigration laws. In the past, the United States did a poor job of monitoring those who had visitor, work, or student visas. Our immigration policies and enforcement must be strengthened. Fourth, we must safeguard and secure cyberspace. Today, almost every facet of life involves cyberspace: banking, energy, industry, utilities, transportation, business, and leisure activities. Billions of dollars flow daily through the Internet. The Internet is used to control all sorts of industrial and public utility operations. Disruptions to these processes can have dire economic consequences, and in some cases result in loss of life or injuries to citizens. Finally, we must ensure our resilience to disasters. Whereas the DHS's first core mission is to prevent terrorist attacks, this core mission refers to withstanding an attack and contains two primary dimensions: First, we must have a system where we rapidly and effectively respond to some type of event, which means having first responders and others properly trained and equipped; and second, it infers that we must be able to mobilize assets in a timely basis to minimize damage and disruption. We must have comprehensive operational response plans. The DHS elaborated a comprehensive plan for homeland security that maximizes protection and response.

Although the DHS core mission statements are straightforward, their implementation has not been consistent. Bellavita (2008) examined the homeland security literature and found a variety of definitions. They included seven:

1. *Terrorism*—the prevention, response, and mitigation of terrorist acts by federal, state, and local governments.

2. *All Hazards*—prevent attacks, protect against natural and human-made disasters, and respond and recover from such incidents.

3. *Terrorism and Catastrophes*—efforts by the DHS and other agencies to respond to terrorist and catastrophes that affect security.

4. *Jurisdictional Hazards*—each political jurisdiction in the United States has homeland security priorities that focus on assets in a particular jurisdiction.

5. *Meta Hazards*—efforts to deal with threats to the American way of life, including global warming, shortages of water, shortages of petroleum, and so on.

6. *National Security*—efforts to protect the homeland, population, and critical infrastructure.

7. *Security Uber Alles*—justification by government officials to curtail American civil liberties with an emphasis on processes rather than outcomes.

The literature on homeland security shows substantial variation in its role, and to some extent, its ultimate implementation. The literature focuses on terrorism, disasters, and other catastrophes; global problems, such as energy; and changes in procedural law. These definitions demonstrate that homeland security has become rather expansive with bureaucrats sometimes socially constructing it to meet the needs of the bureaucracy and political ideology.

Government actions and policies should be based on some theoretical perspective. For example, Tibbetts (2012) defined theory "as a set of concepts linked together by a series of statements to explain why an event or phenomenon occurs" (p. 2). Curran and Renzetti (1994) define a theory as "a set of interconnected statements or propositions that explain how two or more events or factors are related to one another" (p. 2). In essence, theory focuses on an event or activity and attempts to identify the underlying causal factors. It guides responses.

Using Bellavita's definitions, homeland security is not grounded in theory. It essentially is reactive with government developing policies that target all possible alternatives or conditions, ranging from terrorist attacks to disasters or catastrophes. This is a shotgun approach where all strategies and tactics are implemented without regard to strategic importance, economy, or effectiveness. Moreover, this approach is opportunistic because all programs are implemented regardless of their utility or where they fit into a matrix of strategies. Implementation is based on available funding, which historically has been plentiful, resulting in duplication of target area and ineffectiveness.

Although homeland security is not grounded in theory as it is currently implemented, there is a potential for theory to guide its advancement. Threats are not equally distributed across the United States. First, terrorists are more likely to attack cities like New York City, Washington, DC, or Los Angeles as compared to cities, such as Wichita, Akron, or Birmingham. Second, some targets are more attractive to terrorists, and some targets are more amenable to certain types of attacks as compared to others. A hierarchy of targets can be estimated. Third, since the greatest terrorist threat to America today comes from Middle-Eastern communities, these terrorists need a significant Muslim community to blend into and remain inconspicuous. This identifies areas with a higher probability of attack or areas from which some terrorist attacks may emanate. Fourth, we can limit the size of the target population by examining terrorist attacks in the United States and other countries to identify the types of targets that terrorists attack and their modus operandi. There certainly are other factors which help limit targets for terrorists, but the point is, we can begin to develop probability tables that theoretically rank potential targets. Although still broad in terms of potential targets, this process can help to better focus homeland security efforts and contribute to a theoretical foundation for such efforts.

The Current State of Homeland Security

The USA PATRIOT Act

The **USA PATRIOT Act** was passed in 2001 in response to the 9/11 attacks. It was designed to strengthen America's ability to combat terrorism and other threats like transnational organized crime. The Act was fairly comprehensive addressing a number of areas, and as such, it amended a number of other federal statutes, ranging from the Bank Holding Act of 1956, to the Violent Crime Control and Law Enforcement Act of 1994. Its comprehensiveness provided law enforcement and homeland security officers expanded authority to investigate and intervene in potential terrorist plots.

Some of the key provisions of the Act included providing agents with more latitude in collecting intelligence. A critical part of the intelligence collection provisions was the extension of surveillance to

U.S. citizens with the procurement of a Federal Intelligence Surveillance court order. The Act also provided new powers to control money laundering. This provision was aimed at reducing terrorists' access to funds. The Act also provided funding and enhanced border security by increasing funding to those agencies responsible for securing our borders (Doyle, 2002). The most controversial of the USA PATRIOT Act's provisions is the enhanced surveillance of American citizens. Since the Act was signed into law, thousands of surveillance warrants have been issued. Many civil libertarians assert that this surveillance violates American citizens' right to privacy.

Weapons of Mass Destruction

Even though homeland security involves an "all hazards" approach where all sorts of catastrophes and disasters require a DHS response, the primary concern is *weapons of mass destruction (WMD)*. They include biological, chemical, and radiological or nuclear weapons. *Biological weapons* consist of bacteria, viruses, and biological toxins. Bacteria of most concern include anthrax and the plague. Although bacteria are prevalent on the human body and in the environment, the vast majority do not pose a health risk. Viruses include diseases, such as Ebola, HIV, hepatitis, smallpox, avian influenza or H5N1 bird flu, and SARS. They are the most dangerous since they can pass from one person to another. For example, if smallpox were introduced to a large crowd of people it potentially could spread throughout a large population. Also, scientists report that the H5N1 influenza has mutated and can rapidly contaminate humans. Viruses pose a significant health problem, and if used as a weapon of mass destruction, could cause large numbers of deaths and illnesses.

Chemical weapons consist of a number of toxic chemicals that may be released on a large number of people. Various blood agents, choking agents, and nerve agents could be used. The DHS regulates security at high-risk chemical facilities to reduce the possibility that terrorists can obtain the chemicals necessary for a chemical WMD. As an example, the ammonium nitrate security program regulates ammonium nitrate, the chemical used to construct a bomb in the Oklahoma City bombing in 1995. Nonetheless, since some chemical weapons can be easily constructed using a variety of chemicals, the current levels of security are of concern.

Finally, *radiological weapons* entail the use of nuclear or radiological materials by terrorists. These materials are highly restricted. Most American nuclear facilities have highly enhanced security, but small amounts of nuclear materials at university laboratories and other research facilities do not have this level of security. Storage facilities with spent nuclear materials also have less stringent security. If terrorists build a nuclear bomb, and attempt to bring the materials into the United States, it would be difficult since DHS has nuclear sensors placed at ports of entry and in some cities. For example, the New York Police Department has equipped patrolling officers with personal radiological sensors, and the department has purchased a helicopter equipped with radiological sensing devices. Conceivably, terrorists could construct a dirty bomb and use a conventional explosion to spread nuclear materials over a large area, but again, access to the nuclear materials would be difficult.

Although weapons of mass destruction present a significant danger, the probability of them being deployed is at a minimum because of the complicated process to develop and deploy these weapons. Gaines and Kappeler (2012) elaborate this intricate process: (a) have or obtain expertise to build a weapon, (b) acquire the materials, (c) develop a logistics and support network, (d) recruit a deployment team, (e) develop the weapon, (f) develop a delivery system, (g) test weapon for functionality, (h) transport weapon and deployment team to target site, and (i) deploy the weapon. This is a complicated process where mistakes, such as biological or chemical spills, could occur during transportation and prior to deployment.

The weapon must be transported over an extended distance, increasing the probability of detection especially considering that American and international intelligence agencies are constantly monitoring for such weapons and dozens of countries have deployed electronic sensors in an attempt to locate these weapons. Given this complicated and dangerous process, it is likely that terrorists will continue to resort to conventional bombs and improvised explosive devices, such as the ones used by alleged Boston Marathon Bombing suspects Tamerlan Tsarnaev and Dzhokhar Tsarnaev on April 15, 2013.

Critical Infrastructure and Key Resources

The most significant homeland security concern on American soil is our critical infrastructure and key assets. The DHS (2006b) in its *National Infrastructure Protection Plan* issued a plan for protecting our critical infrastructure and key resources (CI/KR). CI/KR consists of infrastructure that is vital to the safety and security of the United States, including assets that are of critical economic interest. The *Plan* identified three major categories of CI/KR, comprising physical, human, and cyber.

Critical infrastructure assets were defined in the U.S.A. PATRIOT Act as, "Systems and assets . . . so vital to the United States that the incapacity or destruction of such systems and assets would have a debilitating impact on security, national economy security, national public health and safety, or any combination of those matters" (U.S.A. PATRIOT Act, 2001). The list of these assets is expansive and includes assets such as telecommunications, chemicals, transportation, emergency services, shipping services, agriculture, water, energy, banking, national monuments and icons, and the defense industrial complex. This listing obviously includes thousands of facilities across the country. Priorities for securing facilities are based on the consequences of their destruction. For example, securing a nuclear facility has a much higher priority than for a public water facility in rural America.

Human assets essentially refer to large congregations of people. This includes dense population centers, shopping malls, and other similar venues where large numbers of people congregate, such as special and sporting events. An explosive device, or the introduction of a biological or chemical weapon on a large congregation of people, could result in hundreds, if not thousands, of casualties.

Finally, *cyber assets* refer to the hardware, software, Internet, and other platforms that facilitate cyber communications. The cyber world today is inseparable from the real world. It goes well beyond talking on cell phones, texting, or surfing the Internet; all walks of life are now affected or controlled through cyber assets and include activities such as banking, business, medicine, education, and so on. The destruction or disabling of these assets can cause millions of dollars in economic losses, and in some cases, deaths and injuries. The problem goes well beyond identity theft or fraud. In 2010, the cyber worm "Stuxnet" was released targeting Iranian computers used in their nuclear development program. The worm eventually affected over 60,000 computers worldwide with more than half of them in Iran (Farwell & Rohozinski, 2011). It effectively set the Iranian nuclear program back several years as it destroyed computers and approximately 1,000 centrifuges. What is interesting about Stuxnet is that it was designed only to attack Iranian computers that were used in its nuclear development program. In 2012, it was made public that President Obama authorized the attack (Sanger, 2012). There have been other instances of cyberwar (see Gaines & Kappeler, 2012), but this was the most significant, and it likely was a prelude to future devastating attacks both by countries and on countries across the globe.

The DHS attempted to compile a database of critical infrastructure assets by querying industries and the states, but it proved to be a daunting experience. The DHS did try to provide guidelines, such as list refineries with a capacity of 225,000 barrels of oil per day, commercial centers with the potential loss of

$10 billion, or population gatherings of 35,000 or more. These DHS guidelines provided little structure in reality. For example, Indiana had more assets than California, Texas, or New York, which are much larger in terms of infrastructure. North Dakota submitted more banking facilities as compared to New York (Moteff, 2007). Our identification of these critical assets must be refined. Strides have been made in airline security and to a much lesser extent, other types of transportation. DHS and the Department of Energy have strict security standards for nuclear facilities, and the DHS has issued guidelines for chemical facilities. Nonetheless, much of America's infrastructure remains unprotected and without federal security guidelines.

⊠ Challenges of Homeland Security: The Homeland Security Apparatuses

There are a number of agencies involved in homeland security. The most prominent agency is the DHS. The DHS was created in the wake of the 9/11 attacks by moving 22 agencies from other federal departments into the DHS. Some of the agencies moved to DHS include the secret service, customs and border protection (CBP), immigration and customs enforcement (ICE), transportation security administration (TSA), federal emergency management (FEMA), and U.S. Coast Guard. After the DHS was created, it became the third largest department in the federal government with 180,000 employees (DHS, 2008a), with a diverse workforce and organizational mission. The 2012 budget for the DHS was $57 billion (DHS, 2012).

Problems in Administering the DHS

There is substantial criticism of the initial setup, organization, and operation of the DHS. For example, Shapiro (2007) argues

> Policy discussions of homeland security issues are driven not by rigorous analysis but by fear, perceptions of past mistakes, pork-barrel politics, and insistence on an invulnerability that cannot possibly be achieved. It is time for a more analytic, threat-based approach, grounded in concepts of sufficiency, prioritization, and measured effectiveness.... homeland security should evolve from a set of emergency measures into a permanent field of important government policy that, like any other, must justify its allocation of taxpayer funds through solid analysis. (pp. 1–2)

Gaines and Kappeler (2012) point out that many of the agencies within the DHS suffered from mission distortion; specifically, referring to the fact that prior to the reorganization, they had a number of responsibilities. When they were moved to the DHS, counterterrorism objectives were added to existing responsibilities. Many of these agencies did not receive additional personnel to perform these new duties, and it was unclear as to which of these tasks should receive the highest priority. For some agencies, this problem still exists today. Some agencies likely focus on their traditional responsibilities and perhaps neglect some of the new ones since officers assigned to these agencies seldom encounter anything relating to terrorist activities.

FEMA deserves special consideration here. As Bellavita (2008) noted the response to disasters and catastrophes appears in a number of the operational definitions for homeland security, and it is one of the core mission areas within the DHS. This largely is due to FEMA being a part of the DHS. FEMA responds to terrorist events, a part of the DHS's mandate, but it also is the primary federal agency for providing assistance when there is any other type of disaster or catastrophe in the United States. For example, in 2011, FEMA responded to 99 major disaster declarations, 29 emergency declarations, and 114 fire management assistance declarations (FEMA, 2012). The presence of FEMA in the DHS contributes to additional mission distortion. Some have suggested that FEMA be removed from the DHS, noting that it would clarify both the DHS and FEMA's mission objectives (Perrow, 2002).

Another problem with the DHS and homeland security in general is that there are approximately 80 different committees and subcommittees in Congress that oversee various aspects of homeland security. The committees have overlapping authority over homeland security, often resulting in the interjection of politics into policy decisions. Frequently, committee chairs are unwilling to defer to the decisions and dictates of other committees, and hearings and decisions are not coordinated. The White House is also involved in formulating policy for the DHS. Again, some initiatives and priorities are driven by politics, which further complicates the homeland security enterprise.

The Current Status of Homeland Security

As noted, the DHS is involved in a number of activities, and in some cases works with agencies outside the department. An overview of these various activities is provided here.

Transportation

The ***Transportation Security Administration (TSA)*** is the agency primarily responsible for safeguarding America's transportation system. The TSA's activities are most evident in airports where TSA officers screen passengers for weapons and contraband. In terms of airport security, the TSA is also responsible for screening checked luggage and packages that are shipped using commercial aircraft. This mandate generally is accomplished by x-raying luggage and packages. The TSA also attempts to ensure that flights are secure by providing flight crew members with self-defense training and through the U.S. air marshals' program where armed air marshals are randomly placed on flights.

Additionally, the TSA is responsible for rail, pipelines, subway, bus transportation, and highway and trucking security. In other words, as terrorist actions are not limited to airplanes, the TSA is responsible for safeguarding our transportation system beyond air travel. In 2007, terrorists in London detonated a bomb on a bus killing 13 people. The DHS provides grants to bus companies to improve security. The rail and trucking industries carry substantial quantities of hazardous materials. Security and tracking systems are being implemented to enhance the security of these materials. Passengers using some of our subway systems are now subject to searches and screening, and over time, more of these security measures will be implemented. These areas are provided security through partnerships with other law enforcement agencies, and TSA officers, in order to ensure security, also provide random inspection of facilities and the people who work or use these transportation facilities.

Border Protection

There are two DHS agencies involved in protecting our borders. First, the U.S. Coast Guard is the nation's primary maritime law enforcement agency. It has a number of responsibilities, including protecting U.S. fishing interests, drug and other contraband interdiction, and enforcing immigration law at sea.

The coast guard's authority extends to our shores and includes intercostal waterways. The coast guard interdicts contraband and illegal immigrants before they reach our shores, which generally is accomplished by monitoring and inspecting ships and boats in U.S. waters.

The *Customs and Border Protection Agency (CBP)* has the responsibility of securing our borders and ports of entry. The agency has officers stationed on our northern and southern borders as well as our ports of entry, including international airports and maritime ports of entry. These agents screen people and goods and materials coming into the United States. They ensure that people entering the United States have proper immigration papers and visas, and they inspect goods to collect federal taxes and to interdict drugs and other contraband, such as counterfeit merchandise. On a typical day, the agency processes 932,456 people at entry points, processes 64,483 truck, rail, and sea containers, makes 932 arrests, and seizes 13,717 pounds of drugs (U.S. CBP, 2012). These agents also deploy sensors at ports of entry and border crossings to screen for nuclear materials being smuggled into the United States.

During the 1990s, border security tactics were altered. Officers were placed as close to the border as possible to prevent illegal immigrants from entering the United States. This change ultimately resulted in fewer apprehensions, which brought swift criticism from conservatives who viewed the reduction in apprehensions as lax border enforcement (Bach, 2005). Politicians evaluated border security by numbers of apprehensions, an inaccurate methodology. This criticism resulted in border patrol agents being stationed further from the border even though prevention as opposed to apprehension was a more effective tactic in reducing the number of illegal immigrants coming to the United States. However, today border security is being pushed back closer to the border in some cases to reduce the number of illegal entries. The recession in the 2010 decade resulted in almost zero net illegal entries, because fewer people attempted to enter the United States unlawfully, and many returned south of the border because of a lack of employment opportunities.

In 2006, the CBP awarded a contract to the Boeing Company to construct the first phase of the Secure Border Initiative (SBInet) on the Arizona Mexican border. As planned, the SBInet consisted of an integrated system of radar, sensors, and video to monitor the border for illegal immigrants crossing the border. An electronic barrier was seen as more economical as opposed to human staffing in these expansive areas. Although Boeing installed hundreds of miles of fences and numerous vehicle barriers, and after spending over $3.7 billion, the company was not able to integrate the equipment in an effective manner. The program constantly suffered cost overruns and missed deadlines. The project was cancelled in 2011. The failed program demonstrates the difficulty in devising effective border security measures. Today, human resources and fencing are the primary immigration security measures being used.

Immigration Enforcement

Whereas the coast guard and customs and border agency protect and safeguard the borders, the *Immigration and Customs Enforcement Agency (ICE)* is responsible for immigration enforcement in the interior of the United States. These agents apprehend and deport illegal immigrants from the United States. In 2011, ICE removed 180,699 people. Of that total, 77,830 were repeat immigration violators and 18,699 were fugitives (ICE, 2012a). The number of repeat immigration violators indicates that large numbers of illegal immigrants who are removed subsequently return. The numbers also show that ICE is removing a significant number of immigrant criminals. Even though ICE agents removed over 180,000 people in 2011, the Pew Hispanic Center estimates that there are approximately 11 million illegal immigrants in the United States (Bahrampour, 2010).

There is substantial controversy surrounding ICE's operations. Some parties complain that ICE officers apprehend working immigrants with families instead of concentrating on criminal immigrants. In some cases, this criticism intensifies when anchor babies (i.e., children born in the United States to immigrant parents) and children are involved; parents are deported, resulting in American citizens having to leave the country or remain in the United States without their parents. In other cases, young children, adolescents, and young adults have been deported who were brought to America by their parents when they were very young and lived here for most of their lives. A second controversy involves state and local law enforcement. Several states passed anti-immigration laws where police officers are directed to check the status of persons who appear to be in this country illegally. One result of these laws, affecting primarily Hispanic persons, is racial profiling, even though there are large numbers of other ethnic groups in the United States illegally. Another result of these laws is the harassment of many Hispanic citizens by the police.

A growing problem within ICE's purview is human trafficking. Human trafficking is not only an international problem, but it is increasing in the United States. Some recent examples of ICE investigations include 15 members of a trafficking organization that were charged with forcing at least 17 young Mexican women into prostitution in New York, and 34 members of a Somali gang were charged with sex trafficking seven young girls in Minnesota and Tennessee (ICE, 2012b). Raymond and Hughes (2001) estimated that 50,000 women and children are trafficked in the United States each year. Many of them end up in the sex business as street prostitutes or working at massage parlors, after-hours clubs, and escort services and in immigrant worker camp brothels. It is interesting to note that a study of confirmed cases found that 83% of the victims in sex trafficking cases were American citizens (Banks & Kyckelhahn, 2011). This is a growing problem, and it should have a higher priority within ICE and other law enforcement agencies.

Although the federal government provides funding to a variety of entities, including law enforcement and victim advocacy groups to help combat the problem, it appears that the investigation of human trafficking for sexual purposes has received a low priority. Banks and Kyckelhahn (2011) advise that state and local police agencies are the lead agencies in 92% of human sex trafficking cases and only seven percent of the cases were opened by federal agents, specifically ICE officers. Federal agents were more likely to open cases for labor-related human trafficking. Given that human trafficking is a growing problem and it falls within the authority of ICE, it is apparent that ICE officers should expend more effort to investigate and prosecute these types of cases. Human traffickers are dangerous criminals and as such should receive a high priority status within ICE.

Financial and Identification Crime

Financial crime and identity theft, although a problem before the 9/11 attacks, became a major homeland security issue because of the possibility of terrorist financing though financial crimes and the use of identity theft for fraudulent purposes and for illegal entry into the United States. The agency primarily responsible for investigating financial fraud is the U.S. Secret Service. Its other primary responsibility is executive protection.

One area of great concern is counterfeiting. The American dollar is the world standard in terms of currency; commodities across the globe are traded in U.S. dollars. According to the Federal Reserve Bank of San Francisco (2004) there is about $667 billion in currency in circulation with 60% of that amount held overseas. The bank estimates that 0.01% or $6.67 billion is counterfeit. Counterfeiting by individuals and organized crime groups is a problem since there are sophisticated photocopier machines that can copy detail and in color. However, this is not the primary problem. For example, in 2004, FBI and Secret Service agents began operations on the east and west coasts of the United States that resulted in the seizure of several million dollars in counterfeit $100 bills. The money was counterfeited by the North Korean government (Mihm, 2006). The United States is not the only country with a counterfeit money problem. Rama Lakshmi (2012) reported that counterfeit money in India increased 400% in one year. The fake money was produced in Pakistan, and the Indian government has accused the Pakistani government with complicity in the problem. Indian officials see the counterfeit bills as a terrorist attack and economic sabotage. Sums of counterfeit money have been found in the hands of several terrorist groups in India. It is difficult for criminals and organized crime to counterfeit today's money given the watermarks, composition of the paper, special ink, and other special unique characteristics. However, many nations have the capacity to produce high quality counterfeit bills from other counties, and this is now becoming a form of state-sponsored terrorism.

Identity theft is a major homeland security issue. Terrorists attempt to obtain false identities to avoid travel watch lists, obscure their locations, and gain unauthorized access to other countries. If terrorists can assume new identities, it can lead to catastrophic problems. They can move from one country to another without detection, and thus possibly perpetrate terrorist acts.

One way terrorists and criminals gain new identities is through the use of breeder documents. A breeder document is a form of identification used to obtain other forms of identity. The more common breeder documents include social security cards, drivers' licenses, passports, and birth certificates. Once one of these documents is obtained, it can be used to secure other documents with the new identity. Congress passed the Real ID Act that requires drivers' licenses to contain certain information like photo IDs and requires certain identification documentation prior to issuance, but several states failed to comply because of the costs associated with the new drivers' licenses. This failure makes it easier for terrorists and criminals to procure false identification.

Identity fraud has become a monumental problem. ***Identity fraud*** is where a false identity has been assumed, typically to fraudulently obtain money, access resources, or obtain credit and other benefits. This crime is now much more prevalent with the increased commerce conducted on the Internet. In 2011, the Consumer Sentinel Network of the Federal Trade Commission (2012) received over seven million complaints for fraud (55%), identity theft (15%), and other types of complaints (30%). The most common form of identity theft was government documents and benefits fraud. Kane and Wall (2005) examined possible terrorist connections to fraud and found that terrorist groups were using a variety of fraudulent activities to avoid detection or identification and to procure funds. In some cases, they obtained welfare and unemployment benefits and attempted to procure many other types of government benefits.

Cybersecurity

President Obama noted that "cyber threats is one of the most serious economic and national security challenges we face as a nation" and "America's economic prosperity in the 21st century will depend on cybersecurity" (White House, 2009). As discussed above, there are numerous types of threats to our cybersecurity, including cyberwarfare, fraud, identity theft, and malicious hacking. Most problematic are the attacks that can disable our cyber infrastructure or steal critical military or industrial secrets.

The Comprehensive National Cybersecurity Initiative is the policy that provides structure to our cybersecurity. It attempts to merge U.S. government systems into one system with limited and secure access. It also deploys sensors to detect unauthorized intrusions and the deployment of intrusion prevention systems. The Initiative essentially centralizes the federal government's efforts to secure its cybersystems. As a result of this Initiative, the Einstein program was deployed to monitor the system for intrusions and to disable them when detected. For example, Bullock, Haddow, and Coppola (2013) report that Einstein sensors registered 5.4 million attempted intrusions in 2010. This illustrates the magnitude of the attacks on our government's cybersystems. Most of these efforts focused on the federal government's computer systems.

Intrusions into private computer systems, such as industry, banking, public utilities, and so on, were not included in these numbers. All of these systems have not received the needed security attention since intrusions into some of these systems can have catastrophic results. Congress continues to debate mandated legislative computer system security requirements for the private sector. However, such requirements have not been enacted due to resistance from the business community. The private sector remains a prime target for domestic terrorism, and more importantly, these systems often contain critical classified information that should not fall into the hands of terrorists or other governments.

There are a number of federal agencies involved in cybersecurity. First, the DHS, through its National Cybersecurity and Communications Integration Center, monitors cyber operations for malicious intrusions. It is responsible for warnings or alerts about intrusions and coordinating response. The U.S. Cyber Command is under the aegis of the Department of Defense and is responsible for protecting cyberspace in terms of security and cyberwar. The Cyber Command researches and implements defenses for the Department's cyber networks. It also works with the DHS and the private sector to support cyber critical infrastructure. Finally, the Federal Bureau of Investigation is responsible for investigating cyberattacks perpetrated against the public. This is accomplished through a two-pronged approach: the Bureau's Cyber Action Teams travel around the world to respond to cyberattacks, and its Computer Crimes Task Forces are responsible for investigating Internet scams and fraud:

Terrorist Financing and Money Laundering

Terrorist financing is a critical component in combating terrorist threats. One control approach is to "starve the beast." Since acts of terrorism consume large amounts of money, and if that money is eliminated or restricted, then it reduces a terrorist groups' options or ability to conduct terrorist acts. Another approach is to follow the movement of money. In some cases, this is a successful way to identify terrorist groups and plots by tracking the funding. Conspicuously, terrorist money laundering and corruption can undermine the foundation of government in countries. The International Monetary Fund (2012) summarizes the caustic nature of terrorist funds as it applies to countries:

> Money laundering and terrorist financing activities can undermine the integrity and stability of financial institutions and systems, discourage foreign investment, and distort international capital flows. They may have negative consequences for a country's financial stability and macroeconomic performance, resulting in welfare losses, draining resources from more productive economic activities, and even having destabilizing spillover effects on the economies of other countries. In an increasingly interconnected world, the problems presented by these activities are global, as are the links between financial stability and financial integrity. (p.1)

The U.S.A. PATRIOT Act amended the Bank Secrecy Act after the 9/11 attacks. Essentially, the PATRIOT Act required financial institutions to institute measures that facilitate the prevention, detection, and prosecution of international money laundering and terrorist financing. Some of the provisions required the reporting of suspicious activities, the reporting of all transactions in excess of $10,000 in currency, verifying the identity of customers, and the gathering of information on international transactions. These provisions facilitated the gathering of information about terrorist financing, and they helped to thwart the flow of monies to terrorist groups.

It is important to control the flow of funds to terrorist organizations. If a terrorist group does not have the financing, it cannot conduct a terrorist attack, or at the least must scale back the magnitude and number of attacks. Terrorist attacks, by themselves, are fairly inexpensive. For example, it is estimated that the 9/11 attacks cost between $400,000 and $500,000 (National Commission on Terrorist Attacks Upon the United States, 2004). Other attacks were conducted without great expense (e.g., London transportation system attacks, GBP £8,000, Madrid train bombings, $10,000, USS Cole attack, $10,000, and the East Africa embassy bombings, $50,000; Financial Action Task Force, 2008).

Even though these attacks were conducted without substantial costs; the costs behind any terrorist attack are significant. In other words, an enormous amount of capital is required to maintain terrorist organizations that perpetrate attacks. Terrorists have to pay their leaders and fighters' salaries, including when they are inactive; terrorists and their families must have shelter and food. The logistics of maintaining and operating multiple training camps are momentous and expensive, not to mention the travel costs as well as the costs to purchase false documentation to ensure safety and unobtrusiveness. Additionally, there are the expenses required to purchase weapons, ammunition, and explosives. In some cases, bribes to government officials to allow them to operate unfettered must be included. Irrefutably, to some extent terrorist organizations are bureaucratic with substantial expenses beyond the expenses associated with conducting terrorist attacks.

Terrorists use a variety of methods to raise funds. A number of terrorists resort to common criminality to raise funds for their terrorist cell. These crimes include robbery, burglary, extortion, and kidnapping. For example, in 1996, a number of Saudis met in Paris to conspire to bribe *al Qaeda,* and Osama bin Laden by paying them to not mount attacks in Saudi Arabia (Lee, 2002). Drug trafficking is considered to be the most lucrative source of money for some terrorist groups. Many speculate that *al Qaeda* and the Taliban, as well as other terrorist groups, raise funds through drug trafficking. The FBI (2002) maintained that *al Qaeda* raised millions of dollars smuggling heroin through central Asian countries to countries in East Africa. In 2007, the DEA arrested Mohammad Essa for conspiring to import $25 million worth of heroin to the United States from Afghanistan and Pakistan. His trafficking organization was loosely affiliated with the Taliban (MacKinzie-Mulvey, 2007). In another report, Hutchinson (2001) states that 70% of the world's heroin now comes from Afghanistan, with much of it under the control of the Taliban and other terrorist groups.

Some of the crimes committed by terrorists to raise money are fairly mundane. Horwitz (2004) reported that the Bureau of Alcohol, Tobacco, Firearms, and Explosives had 300 open cases involving cigarette smuggling with many cases associated with *Hezbollah* and *al Qaeda.* The smugglers bought cigarettes in states like North Carolina and Virginia where the taxes are low, and then smuggled them into states like Michigan, Maryland, New York, and New Jersey and sold them without paying the higher tax. The smuggling operations reaped millions of dollars for terrorist organizations.

A principle method used by terrorist groups to receive funding is through donations to charities. One of the five pillars of Islam is almsgiving or *zakat,* and as such, all Muslims are obligated to donate. Although a substantial amount of charitable giving goes to the needy, some of this money is siphoned off to terrorist groups. When the Federal Bureau of Investigation and Treasury agents were investigating the Dallas-based Holy Land Foundation, they found that it funneled money to the terrorist group *Hamas.* It was estimated that in the year 2000 alone, the organization raised $13 million in the United States for Palestinian relief (Looney, 2006). Many charities in the Middle East and throughout the world raise millions of dollars each year in support of terrorist groups.

In some cases, terrorist groups are involved in legitimate businesses. Miller and Gerth (2001) found that *al Qaeda* had been involved in mining, diamonds, trading firms, construction companies, agriculture, and honey exports. Such businesses not only make money for the terrorists, but they also provide fronts for them to move money from one location to another. It is important for terrorist groups to move money to their terrorist training camps, fund operational cells, and fund ongoing terrorist conspiracies. They also use diamonds, gold, and works of art as a way to transmit and launder money.

Terrorist financing is a complicated, multipronged process making it difficult for authorities to intercede. Nonetheless, it is important to stem the flow of money to terrorist groups, since intervention weakens these groups and ultimately reduces the number and magnitude of terrorist attacks. Whereas this section examined some of the primary responsibilities under the homeland security umbrella, the following section details the response to terrorist attacks and other critical incidents.

✍ Responding to Terrorist Attacks and Other Critical Events

One of the core missions for homeland security is to ensure our resilience to disasters; whether from terrorist attacks, or natural or man-made disasters, such as hurricanes or explosions at chemical plants or oil refineries (DHS, 2010). Resilience infers two critical activities, prevention and mitigation. In terms of prevention, we must develop systems that prevent attacks on our critical infrastructure, and we must also deploy systems that enable them to better withstand any kind of attack or disaster. When there is some sort of an event, mitigation is enhanced when there is a rapid and effective response. In order to increase the likelihood of an effective response, the DHS developed the National Response Framework (Department of Homeland Security, 2008b) and the National Incident Management System (Department of Homeland Security, 2008c).

National Response Framework

The National Response Framework represents a layered response to critical incidents. All incidents, whether they are a terrorist attack or a natural disaster, occur in a local jurisdiction. This means that local first responders initially attend to the situation. When local communities cannot handle the situation, state resources are called, and if the state and local resources are unable to mitigate the incident, federal resources are summoned to the scene. Local resources include law enforcement, public health, medical facilities and personnel, fire, local disaster relief, waste management, and so on.

Federal assistance to an incident is dictated by the Stafford Act. The Stafford Act essentially directs that federal assistance can come only after presidential approval. The governor in the affected state requests assistance from the state's *Federal Emergency Management Agency (FEMA)* who advises FEMA's administrator, who notifies the president of the incident. If the incident and the resulting damage are significant, the president issues a declaration of emergency and federal resources are mobilized. The primary federal disaster response agency is FEMA, but other federal agencies may also be placed in service, depending on the nature of the emergency. For example, in 2005, when Hurricane Katrina hit the Gulf Coast, President George W. Bush dispatched 20,000 active military personnel to assist local authorities.

The National Response Framework establishes that agencies must prepare for disasters. This includes comprehensive planning across all agencies involved in a response. Their roles and responsibilities must be identified. Second, personnel must be organized, trained, and equipped. The DHS makes a number of grants available to the states for equipment and training. Third, they must exercise and practice their response plans. They must use mock drills to test all agency responses in order to fulfill planned expectations. Finally, the drills must be evaluated and, where applicable, responses must be improved. These preparations are intended as a continuous process.

Once an incident occurs, there are a number of immediate actions that must be taken to enhance safety and mitigate the situation. The Framework identifies them as

- Those injured must be evacuated.
- People in convalescent homes and hospitals must also be evacuated.
- Safe shelters for victims and those who are evacuated from the affected area must be identified and made ready.
- Arrangements for food and water must be made.
- Search and rescue operations must commence immediately to reduce the incidence of injuries and fatalities.
- Treatment facilities for the injured must be established.
- Hazards, such as fires or contamination, must be contained.
- In some cases, quarantines must be established and maintained.
- Arrangements must be made to ensure the safety and health of the first responders.
- Information must be provided to the public.

In terms of recovery after a situation, both short-term goals as well as long-term goals must be identified. Immediate needs include the restoration of transportation, food and water, shelter, and government programs. Long-term goals refer to the complete restoration of social functioning of the affected community. Agencies at all levels must be prepared to take action to mitigate the problem.

National Incident Management System

Whereas the National Response Framework provided guidelines for preparing to respond to an incident, the *National Incident Management System (NIMS)* provides information on the structure of the response. Essentially, the NIMS standardizes responses so when an agency becomes involved, its personnel follow this standard routine. The NIMS ensures that everyone knows their responsibilities and roles.

The first step is to administer communications and management. This is usually accomplished by establishing a command center or emergency operations center where the commanders of all the agencies involved in the response coordinate the agencies' activities. Once established, all activities emanate from the center. This is to ensure that all activities and personnel are coordinated. The command center warrants that all actions as identified in the National Response Framework are addressed. Responses are less chaotic when the command center is used.

Once an incident occurs, responders must acquire equipment and materials used in the recovery, resource management. The flow of activities for resource management is (a) identify requirements, (b) order and acquire equipment and materials, (c) mobilize resources, (d) track and report activities and expenditures, (e) recover and demobilize, (f) reimburse for expenditures, and (g) inventory remaining materials. All sorts of materials must be acquired, e.g., heavy equipment like bulldozers, food and water, construction materials, temporary shelter for displaced victims as well as those working the disaster site, electrical generators, and so on. The required materials are based on the nature and scope of the disaster, and they must be purchased and there must be an accounting of the costs.

If the incident is significant in size, the command center has several functional supervisors. The incident commander makes all decisions relative to the response, takes command of all resources, and coordinates the activities of all the agencies involved in the recovery. This involves working with the agency commanders. A public information officer is responsible for providing information to the public. This not only includes the news media, but this official is responsible for providing information and guidance to victims. During Hurricane Katrina, if people had been provided with information about when and where to evacuate, there would have been fewer deaths. Providing information to citizens about what they should do is critical. The command center has a safety officer who is responsible for ensuring that responders use safe work habits to reduce injuries to victims and responders. A liaison officer maintains communications among the commanders and supervisors of the agencies involved in the response. This officer attempts to ensure there is maximum cooperation and coordination among the agencies. Often, there are also operations section chiefs. If an incident is substantial in size, it may be divided into parts or geographical areas, with teams responsible for each part or section. The section chiefs supervise the activities in these parts or sections. A planning section chief plans the response or provides a roadmap for each of the operations section's activities. A logistics section chief ensures that victims and responders have the equipment and materials needed for an effective response. Finally, a finance/administration section chief provides an accounting of the materials and costs of the recovery efforts; at some point, the bills must be paid requiring an accurate accounting.

This discussion centers on FEMA and other emergency responders. However, there are specialized disaster response units that are also important. First, the National Disaster Medical System is designed to have outside medical personnel at a scene within 12 to 24 hours (Knouss, 2001). Disasters, especially those involving weapons of mass destruction, can quickly outstrip the capacity of local medical facilities. The National Disaster Medical System can mobilize disaster medical assistance teams, national medical response teams, burn teams, pediatric teams, crush medicine teams, international medical-surgical teams, mental health teams, veterinary medical assistance teams, and disaster mortuary teams. Additionally, the military and other federal agencies provide teams available to respond to radiological, biological, or chemical incidents. These teams monitor the magnitude of the affected area, assist with evaluation, help treat victims, and assist in mitigating the problem.

The National Response Framework and the National Incident Management System are key tools in responding to threats of homeland security. These two official documents provide primary guidance when there is a significant incident by establishing procedures for ensuring that a response is rapid and effective.

The Police and Homeland Security

The police play a vital role in homeland security. Generally, they are the first to arrive at the scene of an incident, and as first responders, police officers coordinate initial actions to mitigate problems associated with the incident. As such, police officers must be properly equipped and trained to respond to a variety of disasters whether they are terrorist attacks, natural disasters, or man-made disasters. Unfortunately, most police officers are often not prepared to respond to these types of disasters. The problem lies in the nature of police work. Police officers have a multitude of tasks and responsibilities that inherently require an immediate response; consequently, preparing for incidents or disasters often becomes neglected as a result of resource and time constraints.

A second issue is that even though numerous departments provide officers with emergency response training, the acquired skills become stale over time, and a measure of effectiveness is inevitably lost. This can be partially overcome through exercising or mock disaster drills, but large scale exercises are expensive, and few departments have the resources to conduct them with any frequency. This remains a problem without a workable solution. Perhaps the best solution is to ensure that federal and state disaster relief personnel arrive as quickly as possible.

Identifying essential key infrastructures remains a critical homeland security task for local police departments. They must survey their jurisdictions and identify potential terrorist targets. Once potential targets have been identified, officials must develop emergency response plans for each potential target. If one of the targets is attacked, or a critical incident occurs at a site, departments require a response plan ready to implement. These plans should include all agencies with expected involvement in a first response. This reduces confusion and increases response effectiveness.

One way to better secure critical infrastructure is to develop partnerships with local private security firms. Many critical infrastructures employ private security to safeguard assets. Because these firms generally concentrate on access control, their security personnel can observe activities in and around the facilities. A working relationship can result in police notification when there are any incidents of suspicious persons or activities. This is important since much of this infrastructure is viewed as prime targets for terrorists. As an example, the Las Vegas Police Department has monthly meetings with security personnel to discuss problems or unusual activities (Morabito & Greenberg, 2005). These partnerships increase the police presence. Responding to incidents is not the only role played by law enforcement in homeland security. Police officers are also an important source of intelligence. Police officers patrol, investigate crimes, and work with citizens throughout a jurisdiction to solve problems and to respond to crimes and disorder. Consequently, they are in a position to gather information about suspicious activities and persons. Since terrorists attempt to blend into a community, positive working relationships with the public increase the probability that officers discover suspicious persons and activities or plots. For example, the New York City Police Department sponsored a cricket league to develop better relations with some Middle Eastern groups. A number of police departments now have programs designed to foster better relations with Arab communities (see Lyon, 2002). Moreover, some significant terrorist cases have been solved by citizens providing information to the police. Some examples of cases solved with the public's assistance include: the John Allen Muhammad and John Lee Malvo random shooting spree in the Washington, DC, area was solved by information provided by citizens (Brown, 2007); the Times Square bomber was captured as a result of citizen information (Newman & Moynihan, 2010); and a conspiracy by Muslims to attack soldiers at Fort Dix was cleared through citizen information (Russakoff & Eggen, 2007). After the 9/11 attacks, there was some discussion in the policing arena that officers should abandon community policing and move back to more of a law enforcement orientation in order to ferret out terrorists. However, working relationships with the community often result in the police gaining more intelligence information that can assist in a terrorist investigation.

When police officers collect intelligence about possible terrorist activities, it is of little value if it is not used. To ensure that intelligence is used and shared with all the concerned agencies, a number of police departments now are involved in fusion centers. **Fusion centers** serve as focal points within the state and local environment for the receipt, analysis, gathering, and sharing of threat-related information between the federal government and state, local, tribal, territorial, and private sector partners. They centers normally are headed by FBI agents with local, state, and other federal law enforcement officials participating. In addition to law enforcement, other partners include public health, hospital personnel, security and others representing critical infrastructure, fire services, and homeland security. The fusion center acquires information from all of these entities in an effort to determine if terrorist activities are occurring in the community. For example, public health officials are included since they may see an increase in diseases possibly caused by a biological weapon. Fire officials are included since they may encounter suspicious fires or chemicals in the community. The fusion centers attempt to collect all sorts of information, collate it, and determine if terrorist activities are occurring.

The fusion centers in turn coordinate with the FBI's Joint Terrorism Task Force (JTTF). The JTTFs are organized regionally across the country. They are composed of representatives from federal law enforcement and intelligence agencies as well as local law enforcement. Their purpose is to coordinate intelligence among the various agencies. They receive intelligence from all agencies, including the fusion centers. In turn, when a JTTF receives information about a threat in a local community, the fusion center or local law enforcement is notified. The matrix of JTTFs and fusion centers represents a network where intelligence is shared with all agencies potentially involved in investigating or responding to a terrorist attack.

The fusion centers are not without criticism; Monahan and Palmer (2009) identified a number of problems associated with them. First, they are ineffective considering the costs and improbability of a terrorist attack. Moreover, they consume substantial local resources as local personnel are necessarily included. Second, there is the potential for mission creep. Since terrorist attacks and encounters with possible terrorists is a very low probability, fusion centers may expand their purview into other areas, and in the process neglect homeland security and terrorism. Finally, they note that some activities performed by fusion centers may violate civil liberties, and fusion center personnel may spy on ordinary Americans who are not deemed a security threat.

Conclusion

This chapter provides an overview of homeland security. It identifies the principle players or agencies, their primary responsibilities, and some of the problems associated with homeland security today. As noted, there is some confusion about the DHS's mission since FEMA, one of DHS's primary agencies, is involved in responding to natural and manmade disasters as well as responding to terrorist attacks. The merging of a number of agencies from different federal departments into the DHS initially caused mission distortion. These agencies retained a number of nonhomeland security responsibilities, and there were growing pains as these agencies assimilated their new homeland security responsibilities. Today, the DHS is the third largest department in the federal government.

The DHS has a number of primary responsibilities directly pertaining to homeland security. First, the DHS is responsible for security of the nation's critical infrastructure. The most obvious evidence of this responsibility is the TSA, which is charged with safeguarding air travel. This agency is also responsible for other travel-related infrastructure, such as buses, subways, trains, and energy pipelines. In many cases, policies are promulgated requiring security measures. The DHS has three primary agencies involved in border security. They include CBP, U.S. Coast Guard, and ICE. These agencies attempt to secure our borders keeping illegal immigrants and terrorists from entering the United States. ICE is also responsible for deporting illegal immigrants. Another responsibility of the DHS is the investigation of financial crimes and identity theft. These are important areas for homeland security since financial crimes and identity theft are used by terrorists: the former to fund their activities, and the latter to remain undiscovered when attempting to carry out a terrorist act. Cybersecurity is an important DHS objective as intrusions into our cyber networks can result in catastrophic problems within the economy and cause serious physical damage to our critical infrastructure. Along with a number of other federal agencies, the DHS is responsible for combating terrorist money laundering. We can adversely affect terrorist organizations if we can limit their access to resources.

The DHS developed two major protocols for responding to terrorist attacks and other disasters. The first is the National Response Framework. The Framework establishes protocols for responding to events. The second is the National Incident Management System. These two planning documents outline how agencies at all levels are to cooperate and respond to a disaster. By providing a measure of uniformity, these documents help ensure that responses are timely, organized, and effective.

Finally, the police play a key role in homeland security. Since they operate in most jurisdictions on a 24-hour basis, come into contact with large numbers of people, and are first responders when an event occurs, they are in position to gather information about terrorists and suspicious activities in a community. Moreover, by engaging in community policing and developing good relations with citizens, police officers are in a better position to receive intelligence information about suspicious persons or activities. In this sense, the police play a key role in intelligence. Many departments participate in fusion centers, which in turn work with joint terrorism task forces to ensure that information is shared across agencies.

Finally, as mentioned above, there is a need for theory development in the homeland security arena. Theory would not only result in more measured decision making, but it also would result in cost reductions as resources are expended for programming that provides more utility and makes us safer. We currently spend an astronomical amount on homeland security. Mueller and Stewart (2011) point out that the federal budget for homeland security has increased by $360 billion since the 9/11 attacks; state and local governments and the private sector have increased their homeland security budgets by $100 billion; and we are spending $110 billion more in intelligence to combat terrorism. Spending more money on homeland security does not necessarily make America safer. We must identify those programs that fulfill homeland security needs and requirements. This means that expenditures must be grounded in theory and we must begin to prioritize needs and implement programs that effectively satisfy those identified needs. This means developing theories that explain how the homeland is best protected.

KEY TERMS

All hazards	Human assets	Radiological weapons
Biological weapons	Identity fraud	Security *uber alles*
Chemical weapons	Identity theft	Terrorism
Critical infrastructure	Immigration and Customs Enforcement Agency (ICE)	Threats
Customs and Border Protection Agency (CBP)	Jurisdictional hazards	Transportation Security Administration (TSA)
Cyber assets	Meta hazards	U.S.A. PATRIOT Act
Federal Emergency Management Agency (FEMA)	National Incident Management System (NIMS)	Weapons of mass destruction
Fusion Centers	National security	

DISCUSSION QUESTIONS

1. What is homeland security? Do you think the Department of Homeland Security effectively addresses the many threats to homeland security?

2. There are various categories of critical infrastructure. Which types of infrastructure should receive the most attention as we attempt to prevent terrorist attacks?

3. Border security is a critical part of homeland security. How should border security affect immigration policies?

4. What is the relationship between drug trafficking and terrorism?

WEBSITES FOR ADDITIONAL RESEARCH

Department of Homeland Security: http://www.dhs.gov/

Immigration and Customs Enforcement: http://www.ice.gov/

Text of the Homeland Security Act of 2002: http://www.house.gov/legcoun/Comps/HSA02.PDF

PBS: http://www.pbs.org/newshour/indepth_coverage/terrorism/homeland/securityact.html

Text of the U.S. PATRIOT Act of 2001: http://www.gpo.gov/fdsys/pkg/PLAW-107pub156/pdf/PLAW-107pub156.pdf

National Public Radio (NPR): http://www.npr.org/news/specials/patriotact/patriotactprovisions.html

American Civil Liberties Union: http://www.aclu.org/

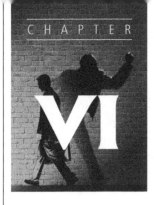

Immigrants and Crime

Nicole Palasz and Katherine Fennelly

I n recent years, immigrants are increasingly caught up in the criminal justice system as the federal government expands detention and deportation efforts and partners with local law enforcement officials to enforce immigration laws. One significant consequence of these actions is to perpetuate the notion that immigration, and particularly so-called 'illegal immigration,' is associated with increased criminality. This perception, in turn, is used to justify ever more punitive policies, in spite of the fact that many of those detained and deported are individuals whose only 'crime' is to be present in the United States without authorization.

Contrary to public perceptions of immigrant criminality, there is abundant research that demonstrates that foreign-born residents actually have *lower* crime rates than the native-born, and that communities with large immigrant populations tend to experience less crime. In fact, some researchers hypothesize that the presence of immigrants may actually *reduce* criminal activity and that increases in the foreign-born population may explain much of the decrease in crime rates in metropolitan areas across the country over the past few decades (Stowell, Messner, McGeever, & Raffalovich, 2009; Wadsworth, 2010).

In this chapter, we begin with a historical overview of immigrant surveillance and detention. Next, we explore the current state of immigration policy as it relates to criminal detention and law enforcement, including the expanding role for local and state governments. We also examine the evidence linking immigration and crime rates and highlight some of the impacts of immigration enforcement trends on immigrants, families, and host communities. We conclude this chapter with some policy recommendations on this issue.

⬛ The Back Story: Immigration and the Law

Immigrants have been the target of government surveillance, detention, and persecution throughout U.S. history, particularly during periods of economic crisis and times of war. Many of these reactions reflect an underlying assumption that immigrants lack loyalty to the United States and may represent a threat to national security. For example, dating back to 1798, the Alien and Sedition Acts specifically targeted the foreign-born, "subjecting aliens and their American associates to government surveillance, as well as criminalizing certain forms of political protest" (Zolberg, 2006, p. 87).

In the 1880s, American unions were upset with European immigrants for taking what they perceived to be their union jobs. As a result, the Anti-Alien Contract Labor Law was passed in 1885, making it illegal to hire a worker with a prearranged contract. Also highly significant was the Chinese Exclusion Act signed into law in 1882, which prohibited the immigration of Chinese workers and made it impossible for foreign-born Chinese residents to become U.S. citizens (Lee, 2006). It was intended to last for 10 years, but the Geary Act of 1892 strengthened and extended the ban until the Chinese Exclusion Act was finally repealed in 1943 (60 years after it was passed). The impetus for both of these laws (and many others) was heightened nativism, or anti-immigration sentiment, instigated by concerns that immigrants were taking good jobs away from American citizens (Calavita, 1993).

Following World War I, as workers organized strikes across the country, fears of communism grew and the government cracked down on communist sympathizers. In 1920, the Attorney General ordered the arrest of approximately "6,000 allegedly seditious men and women, most of them immigrants, of whom many were subsequently deported" (Zolberg, 2006, p. 248). This presaged policies during the Cold War that "barred all aliens who had been Communist Party members and deported those already in the United States" (Lee, 2006, p. 17).

At various points in U.S. history, specific immigrant groups have been the target of restrictive policies. For example, the Second World War provided the justification for some of the most punitive policies in U.S. history. Following the attack on Pearl Harbor, and entry of the United States into World War II, President Franklin Roosevelt issued Executive Order 9066. Citing military necessity, the order authorized the mass removal of 112,000 Japanese Americans, including U.S. citizens, from the West Coast to temporary assembly centers, and subsequently to remote confinement camps in the interior of the country for the duration of the war (Robinson, 2009). During this same period, the President was authorized to deport any "alien whose removal was 'in the interest of the United States.'" (Lee, 2006, p. 16).

The stated goal of the Immigration Reform and Control Act of 1986 (IRCA) was to restrict immigration, decrease undocumented workers, and "regain control of our borders," thus making it illegal to hire illegal immigrants and also to provide paths to citizenship for agricultural workers and others (Calavita, 1993). California's Proposition 187, passed in 1994 despite containing unconstitutional provisions, barred undocumented immigrants from receiving health care from public health clinics and barred the children of undocumented immigrants from attending school. These laws, like many others, were passed at a time when nativism was high, jobs were few, and there was a large budget deficit (Calavita, 1996). Once again, immigrants were an ideal scapegoat for our economic ills.

Immigrants caught up in restrictive policies typically have few avenues for recourse. Immigrant detainees have long been denied access to the same protections as criminal defendants. As early as the 1890s, the Supreme Court ruled that detention and deportation represented an administrative rather than criminal process, and therefore immigrant detainees were not subject to the same rights as those held under suspicion of criminal activity (Hernández, 2009).

The Current State of the Policy

In 2010, there were nearly 40 million foreign-born residents in the United States, representing 12.5% of the U.S. population (U.S. Census Bureau, 2012). Immigrants come from all corners of the globe, and include both the most educated and the least educated among us. Most arrived in the country after 1965 during an era of mass immigration, particularly from the global south. During this same period, the United States vastly expanded its prison system and increased incarceration rates for crimes of all kinds (Rumbaut, 2008).

Since 9/11, "immigration" and "crime" are increasingly conflated in the public mind, in tandem with increasingly harsh federal immigration laws. The pressure to prevent future terrorist attacks, combined with growing anti-immigrant rhetoric, resulted in a significant expansion of immigration enforcement efforts and legislation at federal, state, and local levels.

Immigration offenses include both civil and criminal violations, and the distinctions are complex and confusing. Presence in the country without authorization is a civil rather than a criminal offense, and illegal entry is a petty misdemeanor; but reentry after deportation or failure to depart after an order of removal is a criminal offense—if the government can show that an individual "willfully" failed to leave the country (National Immigration Forum, 2007). However, if an individual is unaware of a removal order, the same offense is a civil violation. These overlapping definitions result in a blurring of distinctions between "undocumented immigrants" and criminals. Another result is that immigration violations account for a very large percentage of new federal criminal prosecutions—almost half (47%) in the first half of FY 2011 and 59% in October of that year (TRAC, 2011; 2012a).

Furthermore, concerns over national security and terrorism led to a proliferation of strict security measures at national and local levels. Sweeping changes were put into effect in the months and years following the September 11, 2001, attacks, after it was revealed that several of the hijackers had overstayed their visas and were residing in the United States without authorization.

The subsequent *War on Terror* provided a pretext for surveillance of all immigrants and for the large-scale detention and deportation of thousands of undocumented residents in federal, state, county, and private facilities. Detainees included undocumented immigrants arrested for minor traffic violations or other nonviolent offenses; individuals seeking asylum; and others convicted of a felony or aggravated felony, or who completed their sentences for more serious violations only to be turned over to ICE, Immigration and Customs Enforcement (Lejeune, 2009). While the majority of detainees were from Mexico and Central America, they represented over 170 countries (Amnesty International, 2009; Kerwin & Yi-Ying Lin, 2009).

Federal Policies

After the September 11 attacks, the war on terror was used as a rationale for the extension of federal power into the use of domestic and border surveillance and the criminal prosecution of many foreign nationals who were interrogated, detained, and deported. In 2003, opportunities to identify and arrest so-called "criminal aliens" were enhanced by the merger of 22 government agencies to create the Department of Homeland Security (DHS)—the largest federal reorganization effort since the creation of the Department of Defense after the Second World War (McCabe & Meissner, 2010). Immediately after 9/11, the Immigration and Naturalization Service (INS) was charged with bolstering policing of the U.S. border, and development of an increased capacity to arrest and deport undocumented aliens already in the United States. These efforts accelerated after 2003, when the newly constituted Department of Homeland Security

(2006a) expanded its immigration enforcement capabilities inside the United States and created the Immigration and Custom Enforcement agency (ICE), a successor to the INS.

Following the attacks, Muslim and Arab American communities in the United States were subjected to increased surveillance and detention. A National Security Entry-Exit Registration System (NSEERS) was implemented, requiring men from certain predominantly Muslim countries to register their names and fingerprints with the government (Golash-Boza, 2012). Approximately 80,000 individuals were registered through this process; none of whom were convicted of any crimes. Over 5,000 foreign-born individuals from Muslim countries were also detained (Tirman, 2010).

In 2005, the Department of Homeland Security announced the **Secure Border Initiative (SBI)**, a plan to secure American borders and decrease unauthorized migration. The first phase of SBI expanded personnel and the use of technology on the border (as had other initiatives before it) and restructured the system for the detention and removal of unauthorized immigrants already in the country (DHS, 2005). The second phase of SBI focused on immigration enforcement in the interior of the country. On April 20, 2006, ICE issued a press release stating that the primary objective of its new interior enforcement strategy was "to reverse the tolerance of illegal employment and illegal immigration in the United States" (DHS, 2006a). Among the ICE programs highlighted in the press release were the identification and removal of immigration violators, and building worksite enforcement and compliance programs to deter the employment of undocumented aliens by employers (DHS, 2006a). ICE undertook a series of workplace raids, and workplace arrests continued to increase steadily. From fiscal year 2002 to 2008, workplace arrests increased annually from 510 to 6,287 (Jones-Correa, 2012).

Arrests by 'fugitive operations teams' also expanded. The **National Fugitive Operations Program (NFOP)** was created to locate and deport "dangerous fugitive aliens as part of a new funding initiative." Between 2003 and 2009, funding for the program increased 23 fold, from $9 million to $218 million, with a 1300% percent increase in personnel (Mendelson, Strom, & Wishnae, 2009). Ninety-six thousand individuals were deported under NFOP during that same period; 73% of them had no criminal convictions.

While less visible than ICE workplace raids, 'fugitive operation' arrests affected many more individuals and communities. Arrests of 'fugitive' undocumented immigrants increased from 1,900 in 2003 to over 34,000 in 2008 and over 40,000 in 2011 (ICE, 2012a). Deportations also accelerated. Since the beginning of the Obama administration, over 1.1 million individuals have been deported (Preston, 2012). Many of those arrested were "ordinary status violators"—individuals who are believed to be unauthorized, or in violation of immigration laws, but who have not been charged with a crime. There were a record 400,000 deportations in 2011, and although Secretary Napolitano reported that 55% had criminal convictions, this included misdemeanors, as well as felonies (Gavett, 2011). According to a 2009 report by the Migration Policy Institute, the program has netted fewer violent criminals, and arrested greater numbers of unauthorized immigrants with no criminal histories. In 2011, the Obama administration announced it would ease deportations of undocumented immigrants without criminal convictions and review all pending cases, and deportation filings declined in 2012 (Transactional Records Access Clearinghouse, TRAC, 2012b).

Nonetheless, human rights organizations continue to voice concerns about the conditions facing immigrants in detention under the Obama administration. While detainees who are held on civil immigration violations are supposed to be held in separate facilities from convicted criminals, in many cases immigrants are housed in prisons with individuals convicted of criminal violations (Amnesty International, 2009). Many detainees' experienced long detentions with multiple transfers to locations far from their families, making legal representation more difficult to secure (Human Rights Watch, 2011). There are also cases of lengthy detentions of a year or more (Kerwin and Yi-Ying Lin, 2009). Unlike other prisoners in the U.S. criminal justice system, many immigrants are subject to "mandatory detention" even if they have not committed violent crimes and are ineligible for bond hearings to assess their flight risks (Human Rights Watch, 2010).

The *U.S.A. PATRIOT Act* extended historical legislation of individuals suspected of terrorism (Siskin, 2012); therefore many more individuals are now eligible for mandatory detention than in the past. The 1952 *Immigration and Nationality Act* authorized the Attorney General to detain noncitizens while they await deportation hearings (Hernández, 2009). The 1996 *Illegal Immigrant Reform and Immigrant Responsibility Act (IIRIRA)* expanded the number of offenses that allowed legal permanent residents to be eligible for deportation, and several different groups of immigrants are subject to possible detention without bond review (American Civil Liberties Union, 2009). These include individuals who may be legal residents of the United States and who have criminal convictions, even if they are for minor offenses or took place prior to the law's enactment. Individuals awaiting review of their removal orders may also be detained. Detainees also include individuals apprehended on arrival to the United States, such as asylum seekers who maintain they are unable to return to their countries for fear of persecution.

Overall, between 2002 and 2010 there was a rapid rise in immigrant detentions (Mittelstadt, Speaker, Meissner, & Chishti, 2011). In fact, immigrants represent the fastest growing population in the prison system. About half of the more than 30,000 immigrants in detention on a daily basis are held in just 17 prison facilities across the country, many of which are administered by private contractors (Kerwin & Yi-Ying Lin, 2009). While private prisons house approximately 8% of inmates overall, they account for half of the federal immigration detainees (Hartney & Glesmann, 2012; National Immigration Forum, 2011). This means that private prison corporations have a vested interest in maintaining and expanding restrictive immigration enforcement measures. Indeed, private corporations attempted to influence state and federal legislation pertaining to criminal immigrant detention. Federal lobbying by private prison corporations, such as the Corrections Corporation of America (CCA), increased significantly following the creation of ICE in 2003; prison companies also made political contributions at the state level (Mason, 2012). Since 2000, contributions by the three largest private prison contractors, CCA, Geo Group, and Cornell Industries, totaled approximately $835,000 for federal candidates and well over $6 million to politicians at the state level. The companies also employ teams of lobbyists who weigh in on immigration-related matters, including ICE appropriations for detention and restrictive state policies, such as Arizona's SB 1070, which expands local law enforcement's role in cracking down on undocumented immigration (Justice Policy Institute, 2011b).

With the dramatic expansion in immigrant detention in recent years, the costs to state, local, and federal governments have also risen. It costs over $150 per person per day to detain migrants (National Immigration Forum, 2011). This is significantly more expensive than alternatives to detention, such as electronic monitoring, reporting requirements, or curfews, which can cost as little as $12 per day. Moreover, ICE acknowledges that the alternative programs have very high compliance rates. It administers three such programs, the *Intensive Supervision Appearance Program (ISAP)*, *Enhanced Supervision Reporting (ESR),* and *Electronic Monitoring (EM) initiative.* The percentage of participants in these programs who appeared at their final removal hearings was 87%, 96%, and 96%, respectively (American Bar Association Commission on Immigration, 2010). Many individuals view alternatives to detention as more humane and less costly options for dealing with individuals in violation of immigration laws, but these alternatives have also garnered criticism. A report by the Rutgers School of Law—Newark Immigrant Rights Clinic and American Friends Service Committee (2012) found that many immigrants subjected to surveillance and monitoring through alternatives to detention were either previously released or were unlikely ever to be deported. The report also found that the implementation of these programs was arbitrary and caused economic, emotional, and physical hardships on immigrants who were not involved in any criminal activity.

ICE officials expressed a commitment to reduce its reliance on the local and state prison system for detained migrants, but detention remains the primary approach to dealing with immigration violations. In 2011, the Obama administration acknowledged an overreliance on prisons and issued a new blueprint for "Building a 21st Century Immigration System" that included the expansion of alternatives to detention (White House, 2011).

Federal-State Immigration Partnerships

The federal government relies increasingly on states to enforce immigration regulations. The ***287(g) federal-state partnership program***, enacted as part of the 1996 *Illegal Immigration Reform and Immigrant Responsibility Act (IIRIRA)*, allows the federal government to shift immigration enforcement efforts to state and local law enforcement (Mittelstadt et al., 2011). The deputization of state and local law enforcement officers under *IIRIRA* authorizes them to perform the roles of federal immigration agents and to enter into agreements with ICE to take on a variety of immigration-related tasks, including "screening inmates at local jails and state prisons for immigration status, arresting and detaining individuals for immigration violations, investigating immigration cases, and working with ICE on task forces to address immigration-related crimes" (Rodríguez, Chishti, Capps, & St. John, 2010). Once a 287(g) Memorandum of Understanding is signed with ICE, local and state law enforcement officials receive training and federal certification to perform immigration-related functions (Mitnik & Halpern-Finnerty, 2010). Though they have been on the books since 1996, these collaborative 287(g) agreements between ICE and local and state law enforcement agencies expanded significantly after 2006 (ICE, 2005). As of 2009, there were 66 active memoranda of understanding between ICE and various local and state law enforcement agencies for the joint apprehension of undocumented immigrants; of these, before 2006, only four existed (ICE, 2009).

In 2008, the Department of Homeland Security initiated a new "Secure Communities" program. Secure Communities allows local law enforcement agencies across the United States to cross-check fingerprints of individuals booked in local jails with national databases to identify individuals who may have violated immigration laws. The information is then shared with federal officials who make a determination as to whether the individual should be detained on immigration charges (Mittelstadt et al., 2011). ICE's ***Criminal Alien Program*** helps secure removal orders for immigrants who are being held in local, state, or federal prisons prior to their release. As of June 2012, Secure Communities was operating in 97% of U.S. jurisdictions and in all 50 states; it will be fully operational in 2013 (ICE, 2012b). Secure Communities has been promoted as a way to capture and deport "dangerous criminals," but there is evidence that it has had more far-reaching impacts. The National Day Labor Organizing Network, Center for Constitutional Rights, and Cardozo Immigration Justice Clinic filed a Freedom of Information Act suit to secure information regarding the implementation of the Secure Communities program in California. Emails released in July 2012 from the FBI and ICE indicated that the agencies advised state officials that individuals without proper identification at drivers' license checkpoints could be deported through Secure Communities (National Day Laborer Organizing Network, 2012).

The rapid expansion of this program and absence of clarity and coordination of efforts has led to numerous errors. A 2011 report by the UC-Berkeley Warren Institute found that 2% of individuals apprehended by ICE through the Secure Communities program were U.S. citizens (Kohli, Markowitz, & Chavez, 2011). More recently, the Congressional Research Service (2012) discovered over 1,800 cases of individuals rearrested after ICE failed to detain individuals who had committed serious offenses and may have been eligible for deportation. Meanwhile, the report identified 48,660 U.S. citizens who were released after matches were found within the Secure Communities system. As of this writing, a U.S. citizen computer specialist was suing the FBI and the DHS for his arrest and detention in a maximum security prison after being misidentified as an undocumented immigrant under Secure Communities program (Bennett, 2012).

By promoting 287(g) cooperation agreements between ICE and local law enforcement authorities, and partnerships like the Secure Communities program, the distinctive roles of city and county police and federal agents have become blurred. In some cases, the federal government has taken on state functions, such as the denial of driver's licenses for unauthorized immigrants under the REAL ID Act of 2005 (McCabe & Meissner, 2010).

State and Local Initiatives

Immigration policy and enforcement is the responsibility of the federal government. However, in the absence of federal immigration reform, states and localities around the country attempt to devise their own laws to impose criminal penalties on undocumented immigrants. In 2010, and in the first quarter of 2011, local legislators in the 50 states and Puerto Rico introduced 1,538 bills and resolutions relating to immigrants and refugees—a 30% increase over the first quarter of 2010 (National Conference of State Legislatures, 2011). The majority were measures that *expanded* recognition or services to immigrants, but others included highly restrictive enforcement measures, such as notorious bills in Alabama and Arizona that require local law enforcement officials to identify and apprehend undocumented immigrants for immigration offenses.

For example, Arizona's 2010 law, SB 1070, prohibits law enforcement from limiting enforcement of federal immigration laws and requires law enforcement officers to check the immigration status of individuals questioned during a lawful stop, detention, or arrest. It also adds penalties for trespassing, seeking and engaging in unauthorized employment, and failing to carry registration documents verifying their status. In addition, SB 1070 authorizes warrantless arrests if law enforcement officials suspect an individual committed an offense that could result in removal from the country (Federation for American Immigration Reform, 2012; National Conference of State Legislatures, 2010). Several harsh provisions of the Arizona law were struck down by the Supreme Court in July of 2012, including

- authorization of warrantless arrests for undocumented immigrants,
- misdemeanor offense and penalties for the failure to "complete or carry an alien registration document," and
- criminalization of undocumented immigrants who seek or engage in unauthorized employment (Gilbert, 2012; National Conference of State Legislatures, 2012).

The decision reaffirmed federal jurisdiction over immigration laws. In *Arizona v. United States* (2012), Justice Anthony Kennedy, writing for the majority, stated: "By authorizing state and local officers to make warrantless arrests of certain aliens suspected of being removable [The Arizona law] too creates an obstacle to federal law. As a general rule, it is not a crime for a removable alien to remain in the United

States." However, the Court let stand the "show me your papers" provision requiring state law enforcement officials to determine the immigration status of anyone they stop or arrest if they suspect that the individual is undocumented, as long as it is during the course of an "otherwise legitimate stop or arrest" (Gilbert, 2012).

What Research Has Taught Us About Immigrants and Crime

Since 9/11, undocumented immigrants have been vilified as criminals by growing numbers of Americans. Attacks in the media frequently employ language and images that present immigrants as threats. However, the narrative of the "criminal alien" is hardly new; it was a common motif of the Know Nothing Party of the 1850s. Just before 9/11, the label was evident in legislative debates on the 1996 *Illegal Immigration Reform and Immigrant Responsibility Act* that depicted immigrants as inherently criminal and reinforced the notion that illegal immigrants have, by definition, broken the law (Newton, 2005). After 9/11, the frame of "illegal aliens" as a threat to American sovereignty was taken up with relish by conservative radio and television commentators. In 2006 and 2007, national media attention reached a fever pitch, with restrictionists coalescing in opposition to Congressional proposals for the legalization of undocumented immigrants—they labeled this legalization as "amnesty" for criminals. These efforts were effective; polls consistently show that a majority of Americans believe that immigration increases crime rates. For example, in a national poll taken in 2000[1], 73% of adults agreed that immigration is "very" or "somewhat" likely to cause increases in crime. A 2007 Gallup poll found that 58% of respondents thought immigrants to the United States degrade the crime situation in the country (Newport, 2007) While some of these views may be attributed to concerns about crime and terrorism, broader anxiety about immigration is also influenced by a sense of economic insecurity as well as the scope and diversity of immigration to the United States in recent years, particularly in communities that traditionally had not received large influxes of immigrants (Jones-Correa, 2012).

Without looking at the research data, there are several reasons to expect that immigration might be associated with higher crime rates. Many immigrants move into economically disadvantaged neighborhoods where crime is prevalent, which could increase the likelihood that they become involved in criminal behavior. Large percentages of immigrants are young adults—an age group that is more likely to engage in criminal behavior than younger or older individuals. When arriving in a new country and community, immigrants may experience less attachment to the neighborhoods in which they reside, which could lead to a decline in neighborhood quality of life, and thus drive up crime rates. As newcomers, immigrants may also be socially isolated and vulnerable to exploitation from criminal elements already in the community, leading to increases in overall crime (Davies & Fagan, 2012).

Surprisingly, the opposite appears to be the case. Research consistently shows that immigrants commit crimes at lower rates than the native-born population, even in areas with higher rates of crime and unemployment (Butcher & Piehl, 1998; Morenoff & Astor, 2006; Sampson, Morenoff, & Raudenbush, 2005). Furthermore, population centers that received the largest influxes of immigrants experienced the most precipitous *declines* in crime rates over time (Butcher & Piehl, 2008; MacDonald & Saunders, 2012; Wadsworth, 2010). Stowell et al. (2009) used data from diverse geographic regions in the United States and determined that violent crimes decreased dramatically across metropolitan areas over the course of the

---

[1] National Opinion Research Center, 2000. General Social Survey

past two decades, particularly in communities with high concentrations of immigrants. They concluded that increased immigration may, indeed, have contributed to the overall drop in violent crime nationwide.

Similarly, Reid, Weis, Adelman, and Jaret (2005) analyzed census data and metropolitan crime reports and found that, not only does immigration not increase crime rates, but that recent immigration actually has a crime-reducing effect on homicides and thefts. They note that one explanation for this association may be that an influx of immigrants often revitalizes blighted urban areas in ways that lead to reductions in crime, and concluded that "municipalities seeking to reduce crime rates may actually benefit by encouraging the development of economically vibrant immigrant communities." (p. 778). Martinez, Stowell, and Lee (2010) also explored this question, finding that the presence of large groups of immigrants reduces homicide rates across the community, lending support to the notion that immigrants reduce segregation and revitalize entire neighborhoods.

Those who support the revitalization argument point to the fact that immigrants are risk-takers by nature, and that entrepreneurship is common in immigrant neighborhoods. A 2012 report from the U.S. Chamber of Commerce and Immigration Policy Center highlights the economic contributions of immigrant entrepreneurs at the local, state, and national levels. They point to a number of studies in cities across the country where immigrants have disproportionately high levels of involvement in the development and growth of small businesses, thus reinvigorating local economies and contributing to overall economic growth.

In addition to the economic revitalization argument, there are other explanations of the link between immigration and reduced crime rates. Davies and Fagan (2012) highlight several reasons, including vibrant immigrant social networks and support systems and intact family and cultural traditions. MacDonald and Saunders (2012) suggest that immigrants may also inculcate in their families a sense of gratitude for the opportunities and improved living conditions relative to their communities of origin, discouraging family members from any involvement in criminal activity.

Similar to the pattern of adults, foreign-born youth commit crimes at lower rates than the general population. MacDonald and Saunders (2012) compared immigrant and native-born youth with multiple risk factors for violent victimization and found that immigrant youth were less vulnerable to commit or experience violent crime. In other words, communities with higher concentrations of immigrants have a particularly strong protective effect against violence, regardless of immigrant status. However, incarceration rates increase with the length of stay in the country, particularly among second- and third-generation immigrants (Rumbaut, Gonzales, Komaie, Morgan, & Tafoya-Estrada, 2006). Among almost all immigrant groups, the likelihood of violence among first-generation immigrants is nearly half that of the third-generation immigrants (Sampson et al., 2005). What accounts for this change across generations? Unfortunately, there is a paucity of research on the causal mechanisms that result in increases in crime rates among the children and grandchildren of immigrants. One explanation was suggested by Waters (1999), who studied 100 years of immigration records in California and found that misunderstandings between immigrant parents and their male children can lead to alienation that promotes gang membership. She also found that juvenile crime most often occurs because of structural differences between immigrants and native-born residents rather than influences from abroad. Indeed, both contemporary and historical immigrants are frequently segregated in poor, high-crime neighborhoods and schools—conditions that may foster delinquency (Suarez-Orozco, 2002). Specifically, while immigrants may bring down crime rates in a neighborhood, segmented assimilation suggests that over time, the children and grandchildren of immigrants may be more influenced by negative neighborhood conditions (Portes, Fernández-Kelly, & Haller, 2005).

Other researchers suggest that acculturation to life in the United States promotes risk behaviors that lead to higher rates of crime. Compared to native-born residents, immigrants have a significant health advantage, but that "healthy migrant effect" deteriorates over time and in second and subsequent generations (Fennelly, 2007). The children of immigrants initially have lower rates of tobacco, alcohol, and illicit drug use, but these rates increase over time in the United States. Some authors speculate that "acculturation" may increase exposure to substance abuse among their peers and to mass media promotions of alcohol (Gfroerer & Tan, 2003). The children of recent immigrants may have strong ties to home and be subject to parental controls that weaken over time as they are increasingly influenced by their American peers. These effects vary among different ethnic origin groups; second- and third-generation Asian-Americans are more likely to report substance abuse than their first-generation counterparts, but not violent or property crimes; for Hispanics, however, the odds of all three types of crimes increase with each successive generation (Bui & Ornuma, 2005). It is important to note that these mechanisms are poorly understood, and the research on immigration and crime has focused largely on major metropolitan areas; more research is needed to explore how immigration is impacting new destination centers for immigrants in smaller towns and cities in the Southeast, Midwest, and elsewhere.

⚔ Unintended Consequences of the Enforcement Policies[2]

The proliferation of immigration enforcement measures designed to target criminals and reduce the threat of terrorism has wide-ranging effects on immigrants, their families, and communities. It contributes to a climate of fear in the immigrant community, even among legal immigrants, and raises concerns about the possible impact of these measures on public safety.

Despite lower crime rates, some immigrant neighborhoods are disproportionately targeted by law enforcement. This may reflect police perceptions of immigrants or the proximity of immigrant groups to higher-crime neighborhoods (Davies & Fagan, 2012). Also, enforcement efforts targeting immigrants vary substantially in different states and counties (see studies by Adams & Newton 2008; Filindra, 2008; Filindra & Tichenor, 2008; Laglagaron, Rodriguez, Silver, & Thanasombat, 2008; National Conference of State Legislatures, 2007, 2008; Ramakrishnan & Wong, 2007; Spiro, 2002; Su, 2009). For example, some communities were subjected to more work site raids than others. However, even in local communities that have not been the sites of ICE actions, undocumented immigrants often complain that they need to curtail routine activities because of a pervasive fear of arrest.

The combination of ICE and local police actions created a general climate of fear that has a negative impact on immigrants' engagement in the public sphere, measured at its most basic level by their willingness to leave their homes to engage in everyday activities. Fennelly and Jones-Correa (2009) conducted surveys and focus groups with predominantly undocumented Latinos in two counties of North Carolina in 2008 and found that the residents were worried, not only about ICE raids, but about the effects of heightened law enforcement. Generally, this enforcement ranged from police stops, to the difficulty in acquiring drivers' licenses, and the risks of deportation if pulled over without one. Such fears changed the patterns of their daily lives and limited residents' abilities to go to the grocery store, to work, to the laundromat, or to provide needed transportation to family members. They found that knowledge of raids and fear of

---

[2] Portions of this section were adapted from a paper by Fennelly and Jones-Correa presented October 2009 at the Conference on Undocumented Hispanic Migration, Connecticut College, New London, CT.

deportation had a direct effect on Latino immigrants' willingness to venture out in public, and this, in turn, is likely to have consequences for their engagement in a wide range of civic activities, from church-going to participation in children's schooling. Well over half (62%) of the Latinos surveyed were worried about deportation. This is similar to findings from the 2008 National Survey of Latinos (Lopez & Minushkin, 2008), in which 57% of foreign-born Latinos said that they worried that they, or a family member or close friend, would be deported.

These depressing effects of immigration enforcement are profoundly felt among the most vulnerable members of the community—families with children and the undocumented. Gonzales (2011) describes the particular impact on undocumented youth as they transition to adulthood. During elementary and high school they are sheltered from the severe barriers that await them as they assume adult roles that require legal status for participation. He notes that the transition has profound implications for their lives as they move from de facto legal to illegal status, and have to "learn to be illegal."

The criminalization of undocumented immigrants increases the likelihood of racial profiling, particularly as local law enforcement becomes more involved in detaining individuals for immigration violations. In 2008, 9% of Latinos nationwide reported being stopped by police or other authorities and asked about their immigration status (Lopez & Minushkin, 2008). In addition to the expanded role for law enforcement in identifying and apprehending undocumented immigrants, laws like Arizona's SB 1070, and some 'copycat' proposals in other states, make the transport of undocumented individuals a criminal offense and allow citizens to bring legal challenges to law enforcement if they believe the police are not sufficiently enforcing the law. This latter provision empowers citizens to become involved in immigration enforcement efforts, which further heightens racial profiling concerns (Bean & Stone, 2011).

Epstein and Goff (2011) suggest that, even with training, it can be difficult for law enforcement officers to avoid making judgments about immigration status without racial cues. Indeed, an analysis of the Secure Communities program found that 93% of those singled out for deportation were from Latin America, raising concerns that Latinos are more likely than other undocumented immigrants to be subject to deportation through the program (Kohli et al., 2011). In spite of these concerns, in 2012 the Supreme Court upheld the "show me your papers" provision of the notorious SB 1070 law in Arizona.

While there have been few empirical studies analyzing the impacts of federal-state collaborations on crime, there are indications that the participation of local police in immigration enforcement affects crime reporting among legal and undocumented immigrants, presenting another potential challenge to public safety. Immigrant families often include a mix of legal permanent residents, U.S. citizens, and undocumented immigrants, a fact that may lead even those who reside legally in the country to avoid contact with law enforcement (Tramonte, 2011). Indeed, in the North Carolina study cited earlier, the authors found that many Hispanics residing legally in the country were unlikely to reach out to police because of the fear of consequences for their extended family, friends, or neighbors (Fennelly & Jones-Correa, 2009). While studies suggest that cooperation with police is higher in neighborhoods with large concentrations of immigrants, strains in police-community relations could reduce this cooperation and lead to increases in crime (Kirk, Papachristos, Fagan, & Tyler, 2012). For example, in Salt Lake City, Utah, Epstein and Goff (2011) analyzed the respective willingness of White and Latino residents to report crimes, with or without cross-deputization (Cross-deputization agreements are agreements that facilitate law personnel to cross borders in criminal cases.) Without cross-deputization, Latinos were significantly more likely to report both violent crime and drug crimes than their White counterparts. However, once cross-deputization was introduced, Latinos were far less likely to report both violent and drug crimes, and the willingness for White residents to report crimes also decreased.

Many law enforcement professionals spoke out against a more prominent role for police in carrying out immigration enforcement efforts. Police rely on information from local residents to prevent and solve crimes. Some law enforcement officials fear that the involvement of police in enforcing immigration violations reduces trust within immigrant communities and may prevent witnesses from coming forward to report crimes. The International Association of Chiefs of Police (IACP) and Major Cities Chiefs Association (MCCA) both issued statements opposing the involvement of local law enforcement in immigration matters due to the potential impacts on cooperation with law enforcement in immigrant communities and the resulting risks to public safety. A survey from the Police Foundation also reflected widespread concern among police chiefs that immigrants will be less likely to come forward to report crimes (Tramonte, 2011). In Houston, after witnesses refused to provide information regarding a homicide, police carried out a public outreach campaign to dispel the notion that officers act on behalf of ICE (Carroll & Pinkerton, 2010).

Many states and municipalities have initiated programs to encourage immigrant reporting of crimes. Over 70 states and cities in the United States have policies preventing law enforcement from asking residents about their immigration status. These so-called "*sanctuary cities*" deliberately extend community policing efforts to immigrant neighborhoods, while continuing to work with DHS when they have apprehended criminals who are subject to immigration detention (Tramonte, 2011).

⊠ How Do We Fix It? Suggestions for Policy Reform

The past decade has seen an unprecedented set of policy measures that transformed the relationship between immigrants and the criminal justice system. While more research is needed to fully understand the complex dynamics, current evidence suggests that efforts to curtail immigration and criminalize immigrants undermine efforts to reduce crime in our communities. At a fundamental level, there is a need to address the false perception of immigrant criminality. As evidence grows about the positive contributions immigrants make to the revitalization and safety of host communities, it is the responsibility of policy makers, media, and other stakeholders to provide an accurate assessment of the varied impacts of immigration on local communities.

As we demonstrated, the myth of the 'criminal alien' is perpetuated by anti-terrorism and law enforcement policies. The recent expansion of immigration enforcement at all levels has important repercussions for law enforcement, the court system, and local communities. In its current form, the immigration enforcement system is a patchwork of state, local, and federal policies that creates confusion for immigrants and law enforcement alike, and reinforces the notion that immigrants increase crime in our neighborhoods and pose a terrorist threat.

There are many aspects of this system that can be improved. The perceived association between immigration and crime led to punitive policies that have little basis in empirical evidence. Increasingly restrictive immigration enforcement measures are costly to implement and have a chilling effect on immigrant communities, impacting legal residents and citizens, as well as the undocumented population. As a result, policies developed in the name of crime reduction may actually undermine public safety by reducing cooperation between all immigrants and law enforcement officials.

In a U.S. Citizenship and Immigration Services (USCIS) statement issued in August of 2012, the agency stated its intention to promote policies that focus on "public safety, border security and the integrity of the immigration system," and accordingly, that the Department of Homeland Security would "exercise prosecutorial discretion as appropriate to ensure that enforcement resources are not expended on low priority cases." As we showed in this chapter, similar statements did not translate into decreases in the detention and deportation of noncriminal aliens in the past; we sincerely hope that these important goals are implemented in the near future.

In the following recommendations, we address ways to ensure that such policies are based on real rather than imagined threats and on proven public safety strategies rather than public opinion.

Expand Community-Based Alternatives to Detention

For most immigration violations, monitoring and detention measures are unnecessary. In circumstances where monitoring is deemed essential, community-based alternatives enjoy a high compliance rate and create fewer disruptions in the lives of immigrants and their families. More of these approaches could be developed and implemented with the active participation of immigrants and their families. Significant human and financial resources could also be spared by adopting a more widespread community-policing model to encourage immigrants to report crime in their communities, and limit detention to those suspected of violent criminal activity.

Scrutinize the Role of the Prison Industry

While public pressure has contributed to the passage of many local immigration-related laws, there is also a growing industry in the private sector that benefits from the expanded use of immigrant surveillance, monitoring, and detention. With a disproportionate number of immigrant detainees being held in private prisons, the role of prison corporations in influencing immigration enforcement legislation and implementation should be subject to greater transparency and accountability.

Pass Comprehensive Immigration Reform

Political pressure should also be brought to bear on the federal government to pass comprehensive immigration reform. Many of the policies being developed at the local level to address concerns over undocumented immigration explicitly mention inaction at the national level. Reform at the national level would provide clarity and consistency in immigration enforcement across states.

KEY TERMS

287(g) federal-state partnership program

Criminal Alien Program

Electronic Monitoring (EM) initiative

Enhanced Supervision Reporting (ESR)

Illegal Immigrant Reform and Immigrant Responsibility Act

Immigration and Nationality Act

Intensive Supervision Appearance Program (ISAP)

National Fugitive Operations Program (NFOP)

Sanctuary cities

Secure Border Initiative (SBI)

USA PATRIOT Act

War on Terror

DISCUSSION QUESTIONS

1. What are the antecedents of the often held belief that immigrants are more likely to commit crimes than nonimmigrants?

2. What data most clearly refute this belief?

3. What strategies could be employed to counteract the myths about immigrants and crime?

WEBSITES FOR ADDITIONAL RESEARCH

Immigration and Customs Enforcement: http://www.ice.gov/

Cornell Law School, Legal Information Institute: http://www.law.cornell.edu/wex/immigration

Immigration Policy Center: http://www.immigrationpolicy.org/ipc-mission

U.S. Citizenship and Immigration Services: http://www.uscis.gov/portal/site/uscis

Ellis Island Museum: http://www.nps.gov/elis/historyculture/index.htm

Amnesty International: http://www.amnesty.org/

National Conference of State Legislators: http://www.ncsl.org/

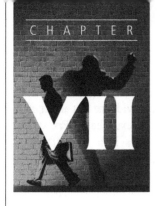

Mandatory Arrest Policies and Intimate Partner Violence

Alesha Durfee

*D*omestic violence (DV) is a pattern of behaviors in which one person attempts to gain power and control over another person. Legal definitions of DV are generally limited to criminal acts, such as battery, sexual assault, kidnapping or unlawful imprisonment, criminal harassment, stalking, and, in some jurisdictions, intimidation. Definitions of DV used by advocates and service providers are less restrictive, and can include threats, isolation, denial, blame, emotional abuse, and economic abuse. While DV spans a number of different forms of violence—including child abuse, parent abuse, and elder abuse—this chapter focuses on *intimate partner violence* (IPV), which is violence that occurs between current or former dating, cohabiting, and married partners.

In the United States, approximately 6.9 million women and 5.3 million men are the victims of IPV each year, and nearly 36% of American women and 29% of American men will be victimized by an intimate partner at some point during their lifetime (Black et al., 2011). For victims, the consequences of IPV are severe—research shows that IPV results in high rates of injury, a significant loss of self-esteem, fear, anxiety, depression, posttraumatic stress disorder, and suicide (Johnson, 2008). IPV also has serious consequences for society; the Centers for Disease Control estimates that the annual cost of IPV in the United States is more than $5.8 billion, including $4.1 billion in direct medical and mental health services to victims (National Center for Injury Prevention and Control, 2003). More recently, Logan, Walker, and Hoyt (2012) estimated that the cost of domestic violence experienced by a woman seeking a civil protection order in Kentucky in the year prior to seeking the order was approximately $35,000.

In an attempt to combat DV, many jurisdictions in the United States have implemented arrest policies for cases of DV reported to law enforcement. The assumption behind mandatory arrest policies is that by increasing the certainty and severity of punishment for acts of DV, potential offenders will be deterred from committing acts of abuse, thereby reducing the prevalence of DV. There are three main types of DV arrest policies: mandatory arrest, pro-arrest, and discretionary arrest. Each type of law requires a certain action of police officers within that jurisdiction, and thus each has different implications for DV victims and perpe-trators. ***Mandatory arrest*** laws require officers to make an arrest if there is evidence that an act of domes-tic violence has taken place or that there is an imminent threat of physical or sexual harm. ***Pro-arrest*** laws do not require that officers make an arrest, but instead explicitly state that arrest is the "preferred" outcome. Finally, ***discretionary arrest*** policies allow officers to make an arrest if there is probable cause that an act of domestic violence has occurred, but do not mandate arrest.

Mandatory arrest policies have been controversial since they were first proposed. There are many arguments as to why mandatory arrest laws are necessary to end DV. Four core arguments summarized by Schneider (2000) include:

1. IPV affects society as a whole. The state has the responsibility of maintaining public order and safety, and arrest is a proper way to do this. Arrest also protects victims and their children.

2. Mandating arrest protects victims. By making arrests mandatory, victims do not have the respon-sibility of deciding whether the abuser should be arrested—thus there is no incentive for the batterer to intimidate the victim.

3. Arresting batterers holds them accountable for their behavior and sends them the message that IPV is criminal and will not be tolerated.

4. Arrests are made in other types of assaults; by treating cases of IPV like other assaults, the state makes it clear that IPV is as serious as other forms of assault.

Yet, others argue that mandatory arrest laws are harmful to victims for several reasons, including:

1. Mandatory arrest laws assume that arrest is always beneficial to victims. Some victims may be harmed by an arrest, including an arrest of the victim for defensive violence, loss of income, child care, and damage to the intimate relationship.

2. Victims will hesitate to contact police because they are afraid their batterer will be arrested.

3. Some evidence suggests that arrest may escalate the violence.

4. By preventing women from making the choice as to whether she wants the abuser arrested, we disempower her and remove her autonomy. In doing so, the state replicates the abusive relation-ship, which is marked by a victim's loss of power and control.

5. By removing the arrest decision from the victim, the state reinforces the idea that battered women are pathological and cannot make rational choices.

Whether they are helpful or harmful, research shows that mandatory arrest policies increase the number of incidents of IPV reported to police and the percentage of cases which result in an arrest. However, mandatory arrest policies also have unintended negative consequences for victims, abusers, and their families. Additionally, mandatory arrest policies have significant impacts on how we as a society view, discuss, and respond to DV and IPV.

This chapter provides an overview of mandatory arrest laws for DV in the United States, including a history of the development of these arrest policies, a description of current arrest policies by state, a sum-mary of the extant research on mandatory arrest policies, and a discussion of some of the unintended consequences of these policies, including how the status characteristics of victims and abusers (such as gender, race, ethnicity, class, sexuality, and immigration status) influence how cases of IPV are treated by law enforcement. Finally, the chapter ends with suggestions for policy reform.

The Back Story: The Creation of Mandatory Arrest Policies in the United States

The criminalization of IPV and the implementation of mandatory arrest policies are a relatively recent phenomenon. The historical reticence of the American legal system to intervene in cases of IPV stems from the legal notion of coverture. Derived from English common law, coverture is the idea that in the eyes of the law, a husband and wife are not two separate individuals, but are instead one entity (Goldfarb, 2011). As they are one entity, a husband cannot be prosecuted for acts of violence against his wife. In fact, prior to the late nineteenth century in the United States, husbands were allowed to physically "chastise" their wives as long as they did not cause any permanent physical damage (Siegel, 1996).

However, the right of husbands to use physical force against their wives was contested in the nineteenth century by both the temperance and women's rights movements. While the temperance movement portrayed IPV as a symptom of the evils of alcohol, the women's rights movement described it as a manifestation of gender inequalities in American society. Although both movements publically called for an end to the sanction of IPV in American law, the solution to the problem of IPV was dramatically different for each movement. For temperance activists, the solution to the problem of violence against women was individualistic—if men could not drink alcohol, they would not engage in physical violence. Thus, making alcohol consumption illegal was an effective prevention strategy. For women's rights activists, the solution to the problem of violence against women was structural—men committed acts of violence against their intimate partners because the oppression of women was legitimated in American society. Thus to end IPV one must effect broader structural and cultural change. This distinction between individualistic and structural solutions to IPV in the nineteenth century was repeated in the 1970s and 1980s when mandatory arrest laws were first proposed as a solution to end IPV.

By 1871, the right of men to engage in physical IPV was no longer formally recognized in American law. In *Commonwealth v. McAfee,* the Massachusetts Supreme Court ruled that "[b]eating or striking a wife violently with the open hand is not one of the rights conferred on a husband by the marriage, even if the wife be drunk or insolent" (Siegel, 1996, p. 2131). States began pushing for the prosecution of abusive husbands, and by 1906 there were 12 states and the District of Columbia, which passed legislation making physical IPV against wives punishable by the whipping post—a punishment designed to physically replicate the wife's victimization. However, prosecution and punishment under these statutes was generally limited to poor men and men of color, limiting the effectiveness of the legislation.

Although by the late nineteenth century it was illegal for men to physically chastise their wives, the courts failed to intervene in many cases of physical IPV because of the notion of the "private" sphere. Because the marital relationship was "private," criminal justice interventions in cases of IPV were considered to be inappropriate and beyond the proper scope of the law. In *State v. Rhodes* (1868), the North Carolina Supreme Court decreed that even though an assault had occurred and that the assault of the defendant's wife was illegal, the defendant should not be punished because the courts should not interfere in domestic relationships. This idea that the courts should not interfere in marital relations led to the decriminalization of IPV, and by the 1920s, most jurisdictions had developed specialized domestic relations courts where parties were encourage to reconcile rather than separate. Police were encouraged to separate the parties and/or mediate the dispute rather than make an arrest, even if there was evidence that a physical assault had occurred. People were encouraged to go to counseling to resolve their conflicts, and victims were expected to take partial responsibility for their own victimization. Battered women were often "regarded as more pathological, more deeply troubled, than the men who batter[ed] them" (Schneider, 2000, p. 23). Just like the solution proposed by temperance activists, the development of specialized family violence courts and the subsequent police response was an individualistic solution to IPV—by addressing pathology, one could end the problem of IPV.

In contrast, the early battered women's movement of the 1970s framed IPV as a manifestation of both systematic oppression against women and the acceptability of violence in American society (Miccio, 2005). The focus of the battered women's movement was on the transformation of American society and the restoration of power and control to women rather than on individual actors. The battered women's movement was "explicitly political"; "domestic violence was linked to women's inferior position within the family, discrimination within the workplace, wage inequity, lack of educational opportunities, the absence of social supports for mothering, and the lack of child care" (Schneider, 2000, p. 23). Thus, the battered women's movement simultaneously advocated for both social and legal change.

One element of this change was shifting the police response to cases of IPV from nonintervention to the arrest of the batterer, primarily through several lawsuits against police departments and the publication of the results of the Spouse Assault Replication Program (SARP). Prior to the passage of domestic violence mandatory arrest laws, relatively few police departments encouraged their officers to make arrests for IPV, even though there were laws explicitly criminalizing IPV (Ferraro, 1989). In fact, most had policies that explicitly discouraged officers from arrests. The 1967 training manual of the International Association of the Chiefs of Police advised officers that "the power of arrest should be exercised as a last resort" in cases of IPV (Sherman, 1992a), and the 1975 training manual of the Oakland Police Department stated that arrest only worsened an IPV situation (Zorza, 1992). Because officers "were trained to do anything except arrest violent husbands," arrest rates in cases of IPV before the implementation of mandatory arrest policies were relatively low (Fagan, 1996, p. 8). Hirschel and Buzawa (2002) estimate that in the 1970s and 1980s arrest rates for IPV were between 7 to 15%. Even when officers made an arrest, cases of domestic violence were less likely to be prosecuted, and sentences for IPV were less serious than for other types of assaults (Fagan, 1996; Sherman, Schmidt, Rogan, & Smith, 1992). Frustrated with what they felt was the inadequacy of the criminal justice system's response to IPV, advocates, activists, and feminists called for the implementation of mandatory arrest policies so that actors in the criminal justice system would be forced to treat IPV as a serious criminal act rather than a private "family" matter.

However, for the early battered women's movement arrest was a "first step" toward a transformation of American culture rather than a goal in and of itself (Miccio, 2005). As IPV was the result of a number of complex social and economic issues, arrest was seen as one element of an integrated response to IPV, and, for arrest to be an effective deterrent, it needed to be accompanied by other changes, such as no-drop prosecution policies and stiffer sentences for IPV. No-drop prosecution policies mean that victims are unable to drop the criminal charges in cases of violence against an intimate partner once charges are filed. Proponents of no-drop policies argue that no-drop policies allow for cases to proceed through the system in the interest of promoting justice for victims. However, opponents of no-drop policies have suggested that such practices ultimately disempower victims (Ford, 2008). Furthermore, some advocates were concerned that law enforcement had a history of abusing their power and that encouraging officers to make arrests in cases of IPV would lead to differential enforcement based on race and socioeconomic status.

Finally, many advocates "saw the state as maintaining, enforcing, and legitimizing male violence against women, not remedying it" and thus did not believe that the state should be used as a resource to stop violence against women (Schneider, 2000, p. 182).

Despite these misgivings, many advocates fought hard for the passage of mandatory arrest policies, and throughout the 1970s and 1980s there were significant changes in both the legal definition of, and response to, IPV (Hirschel & Buzawa, 2002). In addition, several lawsuits resulted in dramatic changes in how police departments responded to cases of IPV (Schneider, 2000; Siegel, 1996). However, at the time, officers could only make an arrest if they either witnessed the assault or if the assault was a felony; if the assault was a misdemeanor and had occurred outside an officer's presence, they could not make an arrest without a warrant. States began passing legislation to authorize warrantless arrests in 1976, and by 1983, 43 states and the District of Columbia authorized officers to make warrantless arrests in cases of domestic violence (Zorza, 1992).

While officers could now make an arrest if they believed that an assault had occurred, they were not mandated to make an arrest. In 1977, Oregon passed the Abuse Prevention Act, the first mandatory arrest law in the United States. The Abuse Prevention Act required officers to make an arrest if the officer believed that an assault had occurred, or if a victim who had a protection order feared that she was in imminent danger of a serious physical assault. However, legislation alone was insufficient to change the police response to IPV. Even after the passage of the Abuse Prevention Act, many departments in Oregon did not change their arrest policies and police training did not change (Zorza, 1992).

A shift in the police response to domestic violence came after empirical evidence showed the impact that arrest policies had on abuser behavior. The first large-scale field experiment examining DV mandatory arrest policies and recidivism was the SARP (Spouse Assault Replication Program). Funded by the National Institute of Justice, the SARP program consisted of six field experiments, the first of which was the ***Minneapolis Domestic Violence Experiment*** (MDVE). The MDVE compared three different approaches to domestic violence—the "traditional" police approach where the two parties were separated, the "psychological" approach where the officers attempted to mediate the dispute using psychological techniques, and the "criminalization" approach where the offender was arrested—to see which was most effective in preventing future acts of violence (Sherman & Berk, 1984). In 1981 and 1982, 314 misdemeanor cases of domestic violence reported to the Minneapolis Police Department were randomly assigned to one of three different groups and treated in accordance with the three approaches to domestic violence. Researchers then followed the victims for six months to see whether they experienced another act of domestic violence.

Results from the MDVE provided support for the idea that arrests reduced recidivism. Only 19% of those perpetrators who were arrested committed another act of domestic violence in the next six months, compared to 37% of perpetrators who were assigned to the psychological group, and 33% of perpetrators assigned to the traditional group (Sherman & Berk, 1984). The deterrent effect of arrest remained statistically significant even when controlling for the perpetrator's race, employment status, education level, and the length of time they were in jail after their arrest. After the findings from the MDVE were made public, the (NIJ) National Institute of Justice funded five other replications. The results of some of the replications actually contradicted the findings of the MDVE—in some cities, while arrest initially deterred some offenders in the short term, arrest actually made some offenders more violent in the long term. For example, in Milwaukee an arrest acted as a deterrent for White offenders: for White offenders, every 10,000 arrests led to 2,504 fewer incidents of domestic violence (Sherman et al., 1992). However, arrest led to *higher* rates of recidivism for Black offenders: every 10,000 arrests led to 1,803 *additional* incidents of domestic violence. The same patterns held true for employment status, marital status, and education level: arrest had an escalation effect for unemployed offenders, unmarried offenders, and offenders with less than a high school education. This effect was attributed to "social marginality." Those offenders with higher stakes in conformity (as measured by higher levels of education, employment, and marriage) are more invested in conforming to social norms than those offenders with lower stakes in conformity. Thus, those offenders with higher stakes in conformity are deterred by the threat of arrest. Those offenders with lower stakes in conformity are additionally marginalized by an arrest, and thus more likely to commit further acts of violence. Arrest only acts as a deterrent for those who have something to lose.

Despite the mixed results of the MDVE and its subsequent replications, the results of the original MDVE dramatically shifted the way that law enforcement responded to cases of DV. After these results were made public, over one-third of all police departments adopted some form of a ***mandatory arrest policy*** (Maxwell, Garner, & Fagan, 2001). In the 1990s (after many states implemented mandatory arrest laws), the prevalence of IPV decreased, the rate at which IPV victimizations were reported to the police increased, and arrest rates for reported cases of IPV increased (Cho & Wilke, 2005). In 1994, Congress passed the federal ***Violence Against Women Act*** (VAWA), which allocated federal funds to state, local, and Indian tribal governments to "develop and strengthen" criminal justice interventions intended to stop violence against women, including funding for states to implement arrest policies that "encourage or mandate" arrests in cases of domestic violence. VAWA was subsequently expanded and reauthorized in 2000, 2005, and 2013.

The Current State of the Policy

Each state has its own policy about arrests in cases of domestic violence, though all 50 states and the District of Columbia have mandatory arrest, pro-arrest, or discretionary arrest policies. As of 2000, 22 states have mandatory arrest laws, including Alaska, Arizona, Colorado, Connecticut, Iowa, Kansas, Louisiana, Maine, Mississippi, Missouri, Nevada, New Jersey, New York, Ohio, Oregon, Rhode Island, South Carolina, South Dakota, Utah, Virginia, Washington, and Wisconsin (Hirschel, Buzawa, Pattavina, & Faggiani, 2007). The District of Columbia also has a mandatory arrest law. Six states have pro-arrest laws: Arkansas, California, Massachusetts, Montana, North Dakota, and Tennessee. Finally, 22 states have discretionary arrest laws: Alabama, Delaware, Florida, Georgia, Hawaii, Idaho, Illinois, Indiana, Kentucky, Maryland, Michigan, Minnesota, Nebraska, New Hampshire, New Mexico, North Carolina, Oklahoma, Pennsylvania, Texas, Vermont, West Virginia, and Wyoming.

Even among states that have mandatory arrest or pro-arrest policies, there are important differences between states as to which incidents of DV must or should result in an arrest. Some of these differences include the type of assault that is threatened and/or committed in order for officers to make an arrest, the time period after the assault in which the arrest must occur, and the relationship between the victim and the offender. For example, in several states the assault must result in bodily injury or been intended to cause bodily injury; thus, cases of intimidation are not covered under their mandatory arrest law. In states such as Ohio, Oregon, and Rhode Island the assault must be a felony, result in an injury, or cause the victim to reasonably fear "imminent serious injury" for the mandatory arrest law to apply. Furthermore, other states have strict requirements as to the maximum amount of time that can elapse between the incident and the arrest—in South Dakota and Washington the assault must have occurred in the previous four hours, while in Mississippi the assault must have occurred in the previous 24 hours.

One of the most important variations in mandatory arrest policies is the victim-offender relationship. In many states violence between dating partners does not meet the legal requirements for mandatory arrest—the offender and the victim must be married, related by marriage or blood, or have a child in common. As many cases of domestic violence are between dating partners, this can be very problematic. By excluding dating relationships from mandatory arrest laws, states treat dating violence less seriously than other forms of domestic violence. As of 2000, 15 of the 22 states with mandatory arrest laws exclude dating relationships from those laws: Arizona, Colorado, Connecticut, Iowa, Kansas, Louisiana, Mississippi, Missouri, New York, Ohio, South Carolina, South Dakota, Utah, Virginia, and Wisconsin (Hirschel et al., 2007).

Another important variation in mandatory arrest policies is whether the policy applies to domestic violence among same-sex partners. According to the National Coalition Against Domestic Violence (NCADV, 2012), Delaware, Montana, and South Carolina have statutes that explicitly exclude same-sex partners from criminal prosecution for domestic violence. Most states have gender-neutral domestic violence statutes; however, as of 2012, same-sex marriage is not legally recognized in 12 of the 15 states with mandatory arrest laws that exclude dating relationships, effectively making mandatory arrest inapplicable to any act of IPV in a same-sex relationship in those states (NCADV, 2012). In those states with gender-neutral domestic violence statutes, unless same-sex couples are specifically included in those statutes, the application of those statutes is left to the discretion of individuals who may or may not recognize a same-sex partnership as a domestic relationship (Pattavina, Hirschel, Buzawa, Faggiani, & Bentley, 2007). Some states that have pro-arrest or discretionary arrest policies still mandate arrest for violations of a protection order (Hirschel et al., 2007). Protection orders are civil orders that prohibit contact between a victim and her abuser. Thirty-three states mandate arrest when a protection order has been violated, including Alaska, California, Colorado, Delaware, Iowa, Kansas, Kentucky, Louisiana, Maine, Maryland, Massachusetts, Minnesota, Mississippi, Missouri, Nebraska, New Hampshire, New Jersey, New Mexico, New York, North Carolina, North Dakota, Oregon, Pennsylvania, Rhode Island, South Carolina, South Dakota, Tennessee, Texas, Utah, Virginia, Washington, West Virginia, and Wisconsin. One key element of VAWA is the full faith and credit provision for protection orders. If a protection order is awarded in one state, all other states must enforce that order. Mandatory arrest laws for protection orders apply to violations of orders in that jurisdiction. Thus if a protection order is awarded to a victim in Alabama (which does not have a mandatory arrest policy), but is violated in Oregon (which has a mandatory arrest policy), officers must make an arrest for that violation. Conversely, if the protection order is awarded in Oregon, but violated in Alabama, an arrest would not be mandated for that violation.

One potential problem with mandatory and pro-arrest policies is that in some cases victims use violence defensively against their abusers. For example, a victim who fears for her safety may push or scratch her abuser in an attempt to get away from him. Because she has committed an assault, if there is a mandatory arrest policy, she may be arrested for domestic violence or she may be arrested along with her abuser. To avoid this problem, many states have added primary aggressor statutes. Primary aggressor statutes require police to determine which party is the primary aggressor and to arrest only that primary aggressor. The primary aggressor is determined through a consideration of a wide range of factors, including the history of IPV in the relationship, the relative severity of injuries, the likelihood of future injuries, and whether the injuries to either party are offensive or defensive. As of 2008, only sixteen states did not have primary aggressor statutes, including Delaware, Hawaii, Idaho, Illinois, Indiana, Kansas, Kentucky, Maine, Massachusetts, New Mexico, North Carolina, Oklahoma, Pennsylvania, Vermont, West Virginia, and Wyoming (Battered Women's Justice Project, 2008).

What Research Has Taught Us: Extant Research on Mandatory Arrest Policies

There are two goals of mandatory arrest policies—to increase the proportion of cases of IPV that result in an arrest and to deter future acts of abuse. Since the passage of mandatory arrest policies, arrests for IPV have increased dramatically. Evidence from several studies shows that before the passage of mandatory arrest laws, arrest rates were approximately 7 to 15%; in the 1990s (after the passage of mandatory and pro-arrest laws) arrest rates increased from 33 to 57% (Dugan, 2003; Eitle, 2005; Hirschel et al., 2007; Jones & Belknap, 1999; Mignon & Holmes, 1995; Pattavina, Buzawa, Hirschel & Faggiani, 2007). Analyses with data from the National Incident Based Reporting System (NIBRS) indicate that this increase is due to the implementation of mandatory and pro-arrest laws; cases of IPV in jurisdictions with mandatory arrest laws are 90% more likely and jurisdictions with pro-arrest laws are 160% more likely to end in an arrest than cases in jurisdictions with discretionary arrest laws (Pattavina, Buzawa, Hirschel, & Faggiani, 2007). Furthermore, Dugan (2003) found that the probability that a household will experience IPV is significantly less in jurisdictions with mandatory arrest policies. In regards to intimate partner homicides, mandatory arrest laws are associated with lower rates of intimate partner homicide for married women, and discretionary arrest laws are associated with lower rates of intimate partner homicide for unmarried men and White unmarried women (Dugan, Rosenfeld, & Nagin, 2003).

Whether mandatory arrest laws are acting as an effective deterrent is a matter of some debate. One problem with using mandatory arrest as a deterrent is that not all cases of IPV are reported to police. According to the National Violence Against Women Survey (NVAWS), among women only 17% of intimate partner rapes and 27% of intimate partner physical assaults are reported to the police (Tjaden & Thoennes, 2000). Many victims who did not contact police said that they felt that the "police couldn't do anything," or that the "police wouldn't believe them," and that they were afraid of reprisal by their abuser. The likelihood that a victim reports IPV to the police increases with the frequency and severity of their victimizations (Jordan, 2004). Dugan (2003) found that although victims were no more likely to report their victimization in jurisdictions with mandatory arrest policies, third parties were significantly less likely to report cases of IPV to police in jurisdictions with mandatory arrest policies than in other jurisdictions. This finding suggests that mandatory arrest policies may act as a deterrent to contacting police.

Does arrest deter abusers from committing additional acts of IPV? One study shows no effect of arrest on recidivism. McFarlane and colleagues (2000) found that six months after the initial incident, women whose partners had been arrested for IPV were no less likely to experience subsequent threats of assault, an assault, or stalking than women whose partners were not arrested. Other research shows that arrest does have an effect on recidivism. Maxwell et al. (2001) did an analysis of pooled data from all six SARP cities and found that arrest deterred male abusers from committing additional acts of domestic violence against female victims, but that the effect of arrest on recidivism was far less than the effect of other offender characteristics, including the age of the offender and the offender's prior criminal record. Furthermore, the deterrent effect of arrest was stronger for some offenders; those male offenders who were older and non-White were more likely to be deterred by arrest than those male offenders who were younger and White. Unlike Sherman and colleagues (1992), Maxwell et al. (2001) also failed to find any evidence that arrest actually increased aggression among any groups of male offenders. Most importantly, whether they had been arrested or not, the majority of the offenders included in the SARP studies did not abuse their intimate partners again. This has important policy implications; the authors argue that even though arrest slightly reduced recidivism, the fact that most offenders do not reoffend means that "policies requiring arrest for all suspects may unnecessarily take a community's resources away from identifying and responding to the worst offenders and victims most at risk" (Maxwell et al., 2001, p. 13).

Another potential problem with arrest is that most criminal justice interventions require the dissolution of the relationship—in some cases a criminal no-contact order can even be issued, preventing the victim and the abuser from any contact. The interests of women who want to maintain the relationship because they still love their abuser may not be served by mandatory arrest policies. Women who seek criminal justice intervention are often "advised to dissolve their relationships" as their situations are "irreparable" and the violence that they experienced can "only be stopped by public intervention and punitive sanctions" (Bumiller, 2010, p. 176; see also James, 1994; Schneider, 2000). Mandatory arrest policies assume that arrest and subsequent criminal sanctions are the best solution for victims of IPV. Furthermore, according to Mills (2003), with the criminalization of IPV, many women who fail to contact law enforcement to report their abuse and/or remain in their abusive relationships are seen as deviant and pathological rather than as autonomous, agentic individuals actively working toward safety using other resources. However, others have responded to Mills's criticism of mandatory arrest policies by stating that "when a woman, for whatever reason, has decided that enough is enough, a strong criminal justice system response can be effective" and that in these cases mandatory arrest policies may be the best solution to IPV (Raphael, 2004, p. 1361).

 ## Gender, Race, Ethnicity, Class, Sexuality, and Immigration Status Implications

Mandatory and pro-arrest policies have had differential impacts on victims based on gender, race, ethnicity, class, sexuality, and immigration status. First advanced by Kimberlé Crenshaw (1991), intersectionality theory critiques traditional feminist approaches to understanding the impacts of gender and race (and, by extension, other dimensions of identity) as failing to recognize their interdependence, and emphasizes that the marginalization and oppression of many women is "social and systemic" in nature rather than "isolated and individual" (p. 1241). Although this section discusses each of these elements individually, they should be viewed as "interlocking" systems of oppression, experienced simultaneously.

Gender

One unintended consequence of mandatory and pro-arrest policies is the dramatic increase in the number of women arrested for domestic violence. As noted previously, arrest rates for both men and women increased since the passage of mandatory and pro-arrest laws. What is notable is that the increase in the number of women arrested for domestic violence far outpaced the increase in the number of men arrested for domestic violence. For example, in California, between 1987 and 2000, arrests of women for domestic violence increased by 500%, while arrests of men for domestic violence increased by only 136% (DeLeon-Granados, Wells, & Binsbacher, 2006). Similar gendered disproportionalities in increases in arrests were observed in Connecticut, Colorado, New Hampshire, and Minnesota (Crager, Cousin, & Hardy, 2003).

There are several explanations given for the marked increase in the number of women arrested for domestic violence, including that women are becoming more violent in their intimate relationships (DeLeon-Granados et al., 2006). However, evidence from the NCVS indicates that the increase in arrests is not due to an increase in offending. From 1993 to 2010, when IPV arrest rates for women were increasing, the rate of IPV victimizations with male victims decreased from 3.0 to 1.1 per 1,000 persons (Catalano, 2012). Susan Miller (2005) conducted interviews about arrest and female-perpetrated IPV with social service providers—all stated that they believed that the increase in the number of women arrested for IPV was not due to an increased use of violence. Meda Chesney-Lind (2002) argues that women are being arrested more frequently for IPV, not because they are becoming more violent, but because the meaning, motivation, and context for their violence are being ignored by law enforcement. Of those women arrested for domestic violence and sent to treatment programs, Miller found that most were "the very people that the criminal justice system is supposed to help, not hurt by first arresting them, then treating them as perpetrators, and finally mandating them to batterer intervention programs" (2005, p. 125).

A more likely explanation for the increase in the disproportionate number of women arrested is the mandatory arrest policy itself. The fact that officers *must* make an arrest when an incident of domestic violence is reported to law enforcement has led to increases in the number of "victim-defendants" and cases of "dual arrests." ***Victim-defendants*** are victims who are mistakenly identified by police as the abuser and arrested for domestic violence. Crager et al. (2003) found that between 1995 and 1999, there were 500 women served by domestic violence agencies in King County, Washington, who reported that they were previously arrested for domestic violence. In 2000, 187 women were identified as the victim in at least one incident, and as the perpetrator in at least one incident of domestic violence reported to the Seattle Police Department. The problem of arresting a victim as a perpetrator can be especially problematic in jurisdictions with mandatory arrest policies and without primary aggressor statutes. Often officers recognize that the person who used violence is the victim, but they feel compelled to make an arrest because they are in a jurisdiction with a mandatory arrest policy. One officer explained "you don't want to arrest the woman, but you have to because she committed the crime. You know she is just trying to defend herself and she has been beaten for years, but you still got to arrest her" (Miller, 2005, p. 64).

Mandatory arrest policies have also led to the problem of "***dual arrests***." Dual arrests occur when both partners have committed acts of violence against one another, both are identified as perpetrators, and then both are arrested for IPV. Estimates of dual arrests range from 1 to 33%, with more recent studies reporting lower rates of dual arrest (Hirschel et al., 2007; Martin, 1997; Mignon & Holmes, 1995). Officers may rely on dual arrest when officers are "reluctant to fully investigate the context within which an incident of family violence occurs" (Finn & Bettis, 2006, p. 282). Officers may not see dual arrest as a punitive measure; some officers interviewed by Finn and Bettis (2006) said that the arrest was "helpful" to the female partner by encouraging her to participate in the prosecution of her male partner, and by facilitating contact with social service agencies. A shelter worker interviewed by Miller (2005) said that

> if they [police officers] see any mark, any scratch at all, police will charge, regardless if it was due to fighting back, or inflicted because of being the initial aggressor. I think police are far more free or willing to charge both parties these days than they used to be. (p. 78)

Being arrested has significant impacts on women who are victims of domestic violence, including their help-seeking behaviors and access to resources. Women who are mistakenly arrested along with their abuser are less likely to use the police as a resource in the future, and domestic violence agencies may reject their requests for victim services as they are also labeled as an "abuser" (Crager et al., 2003). Additionally, since they have been arrested for a crime, they may also be prosecuted for domestic violence. Many female victim-defendants charged with crimes are "eager to get the case over with," and, even though there may not be enough evidence to convict at trial, plead guilty (Miller, 2005, p. 85; see also Crager et al., 2003). A guilty plea can lead to numerous issues: forced enrollment in batterer's treatment programs, probation, jail time, fees and restitution payments; a loss of employment or employment opportunities in certain occupations; a loss of public housing benefits; deportation; a denial of welfare benefits; ineligibility for federal college financial aid; child custody issues, including having Child Protective Services investigate them for child abuse; and the termination of parental rights, or having custody awarded to the abuser (Miller, 2005; National Clearinghouse for the Defense of Battered Women, 2010). Thus, this issue of "victim-defendants" and "dual arrests" is of significant importance and a real problem for women.

Race and Ethnicity

Research also shows that the race and ethnicity of the victim and the abuser have important implications for how cases of IPV are treated by police. Women of color are disproportionately impacted by mandatory arrest policies, partially due to a higher risk of IPV victimization. While IPV is prevalent among all racial and ethnic groups, some have higher rates of IPV. According to the National Intimate Partner and Sexual Violence Survey, 46% of Native American women and 44% of African American women will be victimized by an intimate partner at some point during their lifetime, as compared to 35% of White women, 37% of Hispanic women, and 20% of Asian and Pacific Islander women (Black et al., 2011).

Historically, state intervention in cases of IPV has differed dramatically by race and ethnicity. Given that most scholarship examining race and mandatory arrest in cases of IPV focuses exclusively on Black victims and offenders (Coker, 2000), this section primarily focuses on the experiences of Black women. After the Civil War, IPV was used as an excuse both by the state and by organizations like the Klu Klux Klan to regulate the behavior of Black men (Siegel, 1996). Cases of IPV with Black offenders were responded to more harshly than cases with White offenders, and corporeal punishment for Black men for the commission of IPV was common, especially in the Southern states.

After the decriminalization of IPV in the early twentieth century, but before the advent of mandatory arrest laws, police officers were often less responsive to IPV against women of color than White women. The failure of the police to "respond at all" in cases of IPV against women of color, argues Coker (2000), is because police believed that violence was "an unremarkable event in the households of poor people of color and that police intervention is therefore likely to be ineffective or unnecessary" (p. 1033). In 1976, five Black women filed a lawsuit against the Oakland Police Department claiming that officers failed to respond to cases of IPV appropriately and that Black victims were not given the same treatment as White victims when they contacted the police (Ptacek, 1999; Zorza, 1992). The case *Scott v. Hart* was settled in 1979, with the Oakland police agreeing to respond to IPV calls more quickly, to make arrests more frequently, to give victims information about local resources designed to help IPV victims, and to enforce civil court orders.

In the 1970s and 1980s, mandatory arrest laws were seen as an important tool in forcing the criminal justice system to take cases of IPV against women of color more seriously. Yet, these efforts to end IPV against women of color through criminalization were "undermined" by "hostile and racially discriminatory police practices" (Ptacek, 1999, p. 38). For many women of color, given the differential treatment of men of color by the criminal justice system, "the state is not a source of comfort, but a cause for mistrust or anger," and "any feelings of relief that an arrest of their batterers might otherwise bring may be trumped by feelings of guilt, fear and concern about the fate of their partners in the criminal justice system" (Fedders, 1997, p. 292). This leads to a quandary for many women of color—with so many resources devoted to the enforcement of mandatory arrest policies, the criminal justice system is one of the few resources available to them to achieve safety. This may be why women of color contact the police at higher rates than White women. Black women are significantly more likely to report IPV to the police than are White women, and the victimization of Black women by Black men is more likely to be reported than the victimization of White women by White men (Bachman & Coker 1995; Rennison & Welchans, 2000). Hispanic women are also significantly more likely to report IPV to the police than are non-Hispanic women (Rennison & Welchans, 2000).

Nevertheless, women of color and their abusive partners are treated poorly in comparison to White victims and offenders. Racial stereotypes may make officers more likely to believe that men of color are more dangerous than White men (Fedders, 1997). Police officers may also be less sympathetic to women of color than White women. Fedders (1997) argues that in order for the police to make an arrest, they must believe that an assault has occurred, and that they may be less likely to believe women of color than White women. Furthermore, stereotypes about IPV emphasize traditional notions of victimhood, which are often "defined by a White norm" and are thus inaccessible to women of color (Goodmark, 2008, p. 85). Women of color may also be more likely to be arrested themselves for IPV under mandatory arrest laws as they may be seen as more physically aggressive than White women and their defensive violence viewed instead as IPV perpetration (Chesney-Lind, 2002). As one Black woman told Ritchie (1996), "the judge took one look at me and said, 'You look pretty mean; I bet you could really hurt a man'" (p. 119). For all of these reasons, several scholars argue that "mandatory arrest laws will inevitably result in increased prosecution and consequently, increased oppression for Black men and women in the criminal justice system" (Ruttenberg, 1994, p. 179). It is perhaps unsurprising then that African American women are far less likely to support mandatory arrest laws than are White women (Smith, 2001).

Class

Mandatory arrest policies have differential impacts on victims and abusers based on socioeconomic status. Women living in poverty are more likely than other women to experience IPV. According to the National Family Violence Survey, women with annual incomes of $10,000 or less are 3.5 times more likely to experience IPV than women with annual incomes of $40,000 or more (Straus & Gelles, 1990). Sixty percent of low-income and homeless women report that they have been physically abused by a male intimate partner during adulthood (Browne & Bassuk, 1997), far more than the 25% lifetime victimization rate for all American women (Tjaden & Thoennes, 2000). Not only is poverty a risk factor for victimization, IPV victimization can often lead to poverty. A study in the early 1990s found that 50% of homeless women and children were fleeing domestic violence (Zorza, 1991). When poor women are victimized, the state is more likely to formally intervene than when other women are victimized—44% of low-income and homeless women stated that the police had been called at least once in response to their partner's violence (Browne & Bassuk, 1997), as compared to only 17 to 27% of all American women (Tjaden & Thoennes, 2000). Thus, understanding the impacts of police intervention and mandatory arrest policies for IPV is critically important for impoverished women.

Mandatory arrest policies have both positive and negative impacts on poor women. Coker (2000) argues that the best way to determine the impacts of a policy on poor women is through a material resources test. Poverty keeps women in abusive relationships because they have no other options. Thus, policies that increase the material resources of battered women are positive and should be implemented; those that decrease their material resources or place them at higher risk of harm are negative and should not be implemented. Coker (2000) cites several studies that show that victims whose abusers are arrested report that they have greater levels of assistance from the police: officers may transport victims to DV shelters and/or give these victims information about housing programs and domestic violence shelters, economic assistance programs, legal assistance programs, and other resources designed to assist victims of IPV. Victims whose abusers are not arrested report that they do not receive these same services from the police. Therefore, the arrest of the batterer is associated with greater material resources for poor women and, according to the material resources test, mandatory arrest policies are beneficial for poor women.

Yet, mandatory arrest policies also have negative impacts on poor women. The arrest of the batterer can also be associated with diminished material resources: the arrest of the batterer can lead to a loss of income, which has drastic consequences for poor women. If a no-contact order is issued, the batterer can no longer care for any children, which may make it impossible for the victim to work, go to job training, attend school, or comply with welfare work requirements. The arrest of the abuser can also lead to a loss of resources from informal support networks, including the abuser's friends and family. An arrest for domestic violence also brings the risk of additional state interventions, including custodial evaluations by Child Protection Services workers and investigations into substance use and criminal activity by the victim. Victims living in poverty may also be arrested themselves for IPV, either as a "victim defendant" or in a dual arrest, and poor women are less likely to be able to afford a lawyer to defend them against criminal charges. Finally, as noted previously, initial analyses with SARP data showed that arrest actually escalated the violence against women whose abusive partners were unemployed (Sherman et al., 1992), although subsequent analyses with the data failed to find evidence of this escalation effect (Maxwell, Garner, & Fagan, 2001). For all of these reasons, mandatory arrest policies have significant negative effects on women living in poverty.

Sexuality

Another factor in assessing the impacts of mandatory arrest policies is sexuality. Although IPV in same-sex couples is studied less frequently than IPV in heterosexual couples, it is estimated that the prevalence of IPV among same-sex couples is about the same as for heterosexual couples (Pattavina, Hirschel, Buzawa, Faggiani, & Bentley, 2007). However, as noted previously, cases of same-sex IPV are excluded from mandatory and pro-arrest laws in many jurisdictions. Thus, in these jurisdictions, mandatory and pro-arrest laws have differential impacts on victims of IPV based on their sexuality.

In addition to the laws themselves, there are other factors that make mandatory arrest policies less effective in combating same-sex IPV compared to heterosexual IPV. In order for a mandatory arrest law to apply, the victimization must be reported to police, and there are several reasons why lesbian and gay victims may be more hesitant than heterosexual victims to contact police. First, inherent in reporting same-sex IPV is a formal acknowledgement that one is in a same-sex relationship. This "outing" is such a significant barrier to seeking help that many abusers use it as a tactic to keep victims in abusive same-sex relationships. Victims may not contact police because they do not want to publically acknowledge their sexuality or that they are in a same-sex relationship. Second, homophobia is prevalent in American society, and victims may not contact law enforcement because they fear that police officers, prosecutors, judges, and other criminal justice officials are homophobic or treat them differently than heterosexual victims of IPV (Lundy, 1993). Given the failure of same-sex IPV to be included in mandatory and pro-arrest laws, this is a rational fear.

Even if the victimization is reported, an officer's decision to make an arrest may be different in cases of same-sex IPV than in cases of heterosexual IPV. According to analysis of law enforcement data by

Pattavina et al. (2007), officers are no less likely to make an arrest in cases of same-sex IPV than in cases of heterosexual IPV—officers made arrests in 50% of all cases of IPV reported to law enforcement. However, the effects of mandatory arrest policies differ by sexuality. Similar to cases of heterosexual IPV, cases of lesbian IPV in jurisdictions with mandatory arrest policies are more likely to result in an arrest than cases of lesbian IPV in jurisdictions with pro-arrest or discretionary arrest policies (Pattavina et al., 2007). Yet, cases of IPV between gay men in jurisdictions with mandatory arrest policies are no more likely to result in an arrest than are cases of gay IPV in other jurisdictions. Thus, mandatory arrest laws appear to have less of an effect on the decision to arrest in cases of gay IPV than for cases of lesbian IPV or heterosexual IPV.

Two things should be noted about the study. First, only cases of physical IPV and intimidation were included in the study—sexual IPV was excluded from the analysis. It is likely that given societal stigmas and stereotypes surrounding sexual activity and same-sex partnerships that arrest patterns for sexual IPV in same-sex couples are different than arrest patterns for sexual IPV in heterosexual couples, and that the impact of mandatory arrest policies on arrests for sexual IPV are different for same-sex couples than for heterosexual couples. Second, only incidents that were classified as physical assaults or intimidations by the responding officers were included in the study. If an officer believed that the incident did not merit a police report, or if he or she did not feel that the victimization was serious enough to classify it as an assault, it was not included in the study. It is possible that there are incidents of reported IPV with responding officers who are homophobic, or who do not consider same-sex IPV as serious as heterosexual IPV, that are never included in official law enforcement data. For example, in a study by Bernstein and Kostelac (2002), fully 25% of police officers stated that they had engaged in at least one form of antilesbian or antigay behavior. If these cases are not in the data analyzed by Pattavina et al. (2007), this selection bias may be masking important differences in the effects of mandatory arrest policies on arrests in cases of same-sex IPV.

Finally, mandatory arrest policies can lead to higher rates of "victim-defendants" and dual arrests for cases of same-sex IPV. According to Lundy (1993), victims in same-sex relationships are more likely to physically defend themselves than are victims in heterosexual relationships. As noted previously, victims who engage in defensive violence may be arrested (either alone or as a dual arrest) for IPV in jurisdictions with mandatory arrest policies. Same-sex victims of IPV may be more likely to be seen as equal aggressors than as victims; the

> myth of mutual battering is particularly invidious for same-sex couples, since a common misconception in both the heterosexual and homosexual communities is that any violence between two men or two women is by its very nature "just fighting" which is actively initiated by both parties. (Lundy 1993, p. 283)

This may be exacerbated by the fact that victims of same-sex IPV may be the same size as their abuser when stereotypes of IPV emphasize the greater physical size and strength of the abuser and the relative smaller size and physical weakness of the victim.

Immigration Status

The decision by policy makers and law enforcement to combat IPV through mandatory arrest policies also has important consequences for immigrant women, especially undocumented immigrants. Immigrant women already face serious obstacles to leaving abusive intimate relationships: Social isolation and cultural alienation, a lack of knowledge about available services, culturally inappropriate services, language barriers, few economic resources, diminished job opportunities, an inability to qualify for many economic assistance programs, and societal discrimination and anti-immigrant attitudes—all of these elements can keep immigrant women in abusive relationships (Dasgupta, 2000; Dutton, Orloff, & Hass, 2000; Menjívar & Salcido, 2002). In addition, many battered immigrant women are undocumented or their citizenship status is dependent on their abuser. Fearing that they or their children and/or their abusive partner may be deported, many immigrant women do not contact the police when they are victimized, especially if they know that officers must arrest their abuser. Thus, efforts to combat IPV through criminalization and mandatory arrest policies are less effective for immigrant women (especially undocumented women) than for nonimmigrant women.

In anticipation of this, the Violence Against Women Act (VAWA) includes a provision for immigrant women where they can self-petition for citizenship status for themselves and their undocumented children if their abusive spouse is a U.S. citizen or lawful permanent resident. A second provision in VAWA allows abused immigrant women in deportation or removal proceedings to have their removal from the United States cancelled. While these provisions have assisted many abused immigrant women, there are some women who have not been able to obtain citizenship status through VAWA. First, VAWA requires that victims must prove that they have been abused. Given the many barriers that prevent abused immigrant women from accessing services, some immigrant victims do not have police reports, medical records, court orders, or other forms of external documentation that can help substantiate their claims of abuse. Second, VAWA requires that victims are of "good moral character." Victims who have committed crimes may not qualify for self-petition status, and if he or she is arrested for IPV, under mandatory arrest laws for engaging in defensive violence, an immigrant victim may no longer meet this requirement. Third, same-sex marriages are not recognized by the federal government under the Defense of Marriage Act, and thus same-sex spouses—even those legally married in a state which recognizes same-sex marriage—are not eligible for the federal self-petition program. Finally, and most importantly, an abused immigrant woman must be aware of these provisions under VAWA for her to take advantage of them. If she is unaware of these provisions or believes she will not be able to access them, and if she is worried that she, her children, or her abuser may be deported, she will not contact police when she is abused. Thus, mandatory arrest laws are a less effective response to IPV for immigrant women, even with the provisions afforded by VAWA.

How Do We Fix It? Suggestions for Policy Reform

The following are policy recommendations to make mandatory arrest policies more effective tools in combating IPV while at the same time reducing their costs to victims:

Implement "Mandatory Action" Policies Instead of Mandatory Arrest Policies

Even with adequate training, mandatory arrest policies require officers to make an arrest—they remove officer discretion and preclude victim decision making. Sherman (1992b) argues that instead of mandatory arrest policies, jurisdictions should adopt "mandatory action" policies. A **mandatory action policy** requires officers to take action in cases of IPV; that action can be an arrest, but it can take a number of forms other than an arrest, including giving victims information about available local, state, and federal resources, transporting a victim to a DV shelter, transporting a victim or an offender to a substance abuse treatment facility, and assistance in mobilizing a victim's informal support networks (Sherman, 1992b). Some police departments already provide IPV victims with these services through civilian volunteer programs. Mandatory action policies allow officers to make arrests when they feel it is warranted, or when victims prefer arrest, but also give officers the flexibility to take other action against the offender and/or facilitate victim access to available resources when they perceive that this is a better response to IPV and more beneficial to the victim than simply arresting the offender.

Make "Mandatory Action" Policies Part of a "Coordinated Community Response" to IPV

Mandatory arrest laws should not be the sole societal response to IPV, but should instead be one facet of a "coordinated community response." A coordinated community response is a comprehensive, holistic approach to serving IPV victims where DV advocates, therapists, police, prosecutors, judges, probation officers, and other service providers coordinate their efforts to provide

> follow-up support and advocacy for victims, aggressive and prompt prosecution, active monitoring of offender compliance with probation conditions, court mandated participation in batterer intervention programs, strengthening of civil remedies, and monitoring of the system-wide response to domestic violence cases. (Shepard, Falk, & Elliot, 2002, p. 552)

Shepard, Falk, and Elliot (2002) found that improving communication between police, battered women's advocates, and probation officers about the danger assessments of offenders was linked to lower rates of recidivism. However, many governmental coordinated community response protocols are limited to coordinated efforts by police, prosecutors, court advocates, and treatment providers for the batterer. Effective coordinated community response programs must include material resources for victims. A comprehensive approach to cases of IPV that includes material resources for IPV victims, including assistance with housing, child care, employment, substance abuse treatment, civil legal assistance, assistance with immigration issues, and transportation, is more effective than simply focusing intervention efforts on the offender.

Incorporate Primary Aggressor Statutes into Mandatory Action Policies

Mandatory arrest laws without primary aggressor statutes are actively harmful to victims; if there is no primary aggressor statute, officers have no discretion and must arrest victims for engaging in defensive violence. Mandatory action policies must include primary aggressor statutes in order to avoid the problem of victim-defendants and dual arrests. Even when there are primary aggressor statutes, officers who do not have a background in IPV and are not adequately trained to make an accurate assessment may mistakenly identify victims as aggressors and arrest them for IPV, either by themselves or as a dual arrest. Consequently, in order for the policy to be effective, jurisdictions with a mandatory action policy that includes a primary aggressor statute must provide officers with sufficient training on IPV. This training should include (a) information about the prevalence of IPV, the cycle of violence, the different types of abusive behaviors that are often used to gain power and control over an intimate partner (including information about the Power and Control Wheel); (b) the four forms of IPV identified by Michael Johnson (2008) and how to differentiate between defensive and aggressive forms of violence; (c) the consequences of IPV on victims and their families; (d) typical help-seeking behaviors of IPV victims; (e) common needs of IPV victims; and (f) local, state, and federal resources available to assist IPV victims. The implementation of primary aggressor stat-utes and training officers to make better assessments may be a more cost-effective approach than the arrest, prosecution, and subsequent state action for victims of defensive violence.

Increase Formal Sanctions for IPV When an Arrest Is Made

In order for an arrest to be an effective deterrent, it must be paired with other criminal justice reforms, such as no-drop prosecution policies, and stiffer sentences for IPV. The assumption behind man-datory arrest policies is that we can effectively prevent IPV if we change individual behavior through what criminologists call "deterrence theory" (Pate & Hamilton, 1992). Deterrence theory assumes that indi-viduals are rational actors and weigh the costs and benefits of any action before engaging in criminal behaviors. By mandating arrest in cases of IPV reported to the police, we increase the formal sanction for committing IPV and increase the certainty that the formal sanction is applied. In addition to these formal sanctions, mandating arrest also increases the informal sanctions of committing an act of IPV—the social stigma of being arrested, attachment costs like the loss of the intimate relationship, and commit-ment costs, such as the loss of a job or other economic opportunities (Pate & Hamilton, 1992).

Yet, arrest in isolation is a relatively weak formal sanction, and in some jurisdictions can be limited to just a few hours in jail. According to the NVAWS, only 1% of those offenders who commit an act of physical IPV and 2% of those offenders who commit an act of sexual IPV are ever convicted of IPV and serve jail or prison time (Tjaden & Thoennes, 2000). Even under mandatory arrest policies, it is far from certain that offenders will face serious formal sanctions for their crime. By arresting the offender for IPV, but failing to prosecute the abuser, "the abuser not only receives the message that his behavior will be ignored by the legal system, but may also come away believing that abusive behavior is justified or within his rights" (Murphy, Musser, & Maton, 1998, p. 265). Murphy, Musser, and Maton (1998) found that receiving a guilty verdict for IPV, receiving probation before judgement, and being ordered to probation and domestic vio-lence counseling were associated with significantly lower rates of recidivism. Interestingly, suspended sentences and an order to drug and alcohol counseling were not effective in deterring a reoffense. If arrest is to act as a deterrent, it must be coupled with no-drop prosecution policies, sentences for IPV that include jail or prison time, effective probation monitoring, and mandatory domestic violence counseling.

Conclusion

Mandatory arrest policies have achieved some of their intended goals. First, since the implementation of mandatory arrest policies, there has been an increase in the number of arrests that police make in cases of reported IPV (Dugan, 2003; Eitle, 2005; Hirschel et al., 2007; Jones & Belknap, 1999; Mignon & Holmes, 1995; Pattavina et al., 2007). Second, arrests for IPV are also associated with slightly lower rates of recidivism, suggesting that in general, victims are safer when their abuser is arrested than when he is not (Maxwell, Garner, & Fagan, 2001; Sherman & Berk, 1984). Third, arrests for IPV convey the message to offenders, victims, their children, and society as a whole that IPV is a crime, is as significant as other forms of assault, and that it will not be tolerated.

At the same time, "legal reform based on a model of treating domestic violence like other crimes has engendered a host of unforeseen problems" (Goldfarb, 2011, p. 61). Mandatory arrest policies have severe unintended consequences for victims. These include increases in the number of victims arrested and prosecuted for IPV; the incarceration of victims for IPV and/or other criminal activity; additional economic burdens for victims, including a loss of child support; a loss of informal support networks; increased state surveillance of victims; a loss of custody of children; the "outing" of gay and lesbian victims; deportations; and, in many cases, the destruction of an intimate relationship which the victim did not want to terminate. Some evidence also suggests that for certain offenders—unemployed offenders, Black offenders, offenders with less than a high school education, and unmarried offenders—arrest may actually escalate the risk of future violence (Sherman et al., 1992). Many of these consequences disproportionally impact the most disadvantaged and marginalized victims of IPV—women of color, poor women, gay and lesbian victims, and immigrant women—the very victims these types of policies were intended to help.

But, changes in current mandatory arrest policies can reduce some of these costs to victims while retaining the beneficial elements of the policies. By replacing mandatory arrest policies with mandatory action policies, making mandatory action policies part of a coordinated community response to IPV, incorporating primary aggressor statutes into mandatory action policies, and increasing formal criminal justice sanctions after an arrest is made, we can more effectively combat IPV in American society. The implementation of mandatory arrest policies was an important and necessary development in the governmental response to IPV, and these policies were a critical catalyst to changing how police departments and society as a whole conceptualized, discussed, and responded to IPV. The information about mandatory arrest policies and the policy suggestions presented here can help jurisdictions make needed adjustments to current policies.

KEY TERMS

Discretionary arrest policy

Domestic violence (DV)

Dual arrests

Intimate Partner Violence (IPV)

Mandatory action policy

Mandatory arrest policy

Minneapolis Domestic Violence Experiment

Pro-arrest policy

Victim-defendants

Violence Against Women Act (VAWA)

DISCUSSION QUESTIONS

1. What is a mandatory arrest policy? How does it differ from pro-arrest and discretionary arrest policies?

2. What factors led to the adoption of mandatory arrest policies in the United States?

3. What types of unintended consequences do mandatory arrest policies have? Who is most likely to experience these unintended consequences? Can you think of other unintended consequences not discussed in this chapter?

4. The domestic violence arrest policies for each state are published online. What type of arrest policy does your state have? What types of incidents are included in that policy? Are police mandated to arrest in cases of same-sex intimate partner violence and/or intimate partner violence in dating relationships in your state?

5. Given the benefits and costs of mandatory arrest policies identified by Durfee, do you think that your state should mandate arrest? Why or why not?

WEBSITES FOR ADDITIONAL RESEARCH

National Online Resource Center on Violence Against Women: http://www.vawnet.org/research/

American Bar Association: http://www.americanbar.org/groups/domestic_violence/resources/statistics.html

U.S. Office on Violence Against Women: http://www.ovw.usdoj.gov/

National Conference of State Legislators: http://www.ncsl.org/

Federal Domestic Violence Laws: http://www.justice.gov/usao/gan/documents/federallaws.pdf

National Violence Against Women Prevention Resource Center: http://www.musc.edu/vawprevention/

Rutgers Center on Violence Against Women and Children: http://socialwork.rutgers.edu/Centersand Programs/VAWC.aspx

International Center for Research on Women: http://www.icrw.org/what-we-do/violence-against-women

CHAPTER

VIII

From "Just Say No!" to "Well, Maybe"—The War on Drugs and Sensible Alternatives

Clayton J. Mosher and Scott Akins

A s compared to other Western countries, the United States places a great deal of emphasis on criminal justice responses to illegal drug use[1]. With the most recent "War on Drugs" that began in the mid-1980s, the criminal justice system emphasis became even more pronounced: arrests for drug offenses increased, the sentences for drug offenses were lengthened significantly, and the number of people incarcerated for the commission of drug crimes similarly increased. These policies were apparently implemented with the goal of preventing drug use and drug-related harm, but after 30 years and billions of dollars in criminal justice system expenditures, it is clear that these policies have failed to achieve these goals.

In this chapter, we critically examine these policies, focusing on their effectiveness (or more appropriately, the lack thereof), their economic and social costs, and several unintended consequences that result from them. We begin with a brief discussion of the history of drug legislation in the United States followed by a description of a variety of potential approaches to drug regulation. We then examine trends in arrests and incarcerations for drug offenses and discuss social class and racial inequality in the application of drug laws. We proceed to a discussion of *mandatory minimum sentencing* policies, which have a disproportionately negative impact on the poor and members of minority groups. We also discuss ancillary policies, such as the denial of welfare and student aid to individuals who are convicted of drug offenses; these policies similarly have a negative impact on the poor and members of minority groups. The next section of the chapter discusses alternative approaches to drug regulation that were implemented in other Western countries. We conclude the chapter with a discussion of recent changes in the response to illegal drugs in the United States at the state and federal levels.

---

[1] In this chapter, we address policies related to drugs that are currently illegal in the United States. It is important to note, however, that considerably more harm, including deaths, is associated with legal drugs, such as alcohol, tobacco, and prescription/pharmaceutical drugs.

The Back Story: The History of Drug Laws in the United States

In the 19th century, consciousness-altering substances were sold openly in the United States. Medicine, which lacked the scientific basis it would eventually develop in the 20th century, relied extensively on painkillers to "treat" patients—many of these products contained various derivatives of opium. In 1910, morphine was the most frequently used medical drug, while alcohol was the fifth most commonly used medical drug. The Bayer chemical company successfully synthesized heroin in 1898 and sold the drug over the counter. Cocaine was aggressively marketed and advertised as a cure for hay fever and sinus problems; it was also used as a food additive and was an ingredient in soft drinks, such as Coca-Cola (Mosher & Akins, 2007).

In the early 20th century in the United States, addiction to drugs was fairly common, facilitated by a mass production of drugs and advertising of the products and by physicians and pharmacists who supplied opiate drugs to addicts. Estimates of the number of drug addicts in 1915 ranged from 200,000 to 275,000, with concentrations in the south and among members of the middle and upper classes (Brecher, 1972). However, consistent with subsequent drug laws in the United States (see Table 8.1), the first state and local government efforts to restrict the non-medical use of drugs was not aimed at middle and upper-class users, but instead at the immigrant Chinese population who were associated with opiate use.

Table 8.1 United States Drug Policy Timeline

United States Drug Policy		
1906	Pure Food & Drug Act	Established the Food & Drug Administration (FDA). Labeling of drugs now required over concerns of unlabeled use of animal products, addictive, or harmful substances. Drug could contain these, so long as labeled. Resulted in appreciable drop in addiction in U.S.
1909	Opium Exclusion Act	Banned imported, non-medicinal opium smoking
1914	Harrison Narcotics Tax Act	Opium and cocaine distributors must register and pay tax. Act is a tax only—opiates and narcotics still available through prescriptions. Addiction viewed as a medical issue, not criminal justice issue.
1919	18th Amendment (Volstead Act)	Established the federal prohibition of alcohol in the U.S. Federal enforcement of alcohol prohibition began in 1920.
1922	Narcotic Drug Import & Export Act	Use of narcotics limited to medical use.
1924	Heroin Act	Heroin manufacture illegal
1926	Rolleston Committee in UK	Established medical, not criminal justice, response to addiction in UK. Prompted court cases in U.S., in which medical authority lost to criminal justice interest on issues of addiction

Table 8.1	(Continued)	
United States Drug Policy		
1933	21st Amendment	Overturned 18th Amendment
1937	Marihuana Tax Act	Control of marijuana similar to narcotics: through tax on grower, distributor, seller, buyer. Superseded by Controlled Substance Act of 1970
1938	Food, Drug, and Cosmetic Act	FDA authority over drug safety established, extended beyond mere labeling. Drugs defined, established drugs administered by prescription vs. non-prescription
1942	Opium Poppy Control Act	Established that growers must have license to grow opium poppies
1951	Durham-Humphrey Amendment	Established guidelines for prescription drugs
1951	Boggs Amendment to Harrison Narcotic Act	Established first mandatory sentences for narcotics violations
1956	Narcotics Control Act	Imposed severe penalties for drug violation
1962	Kafauver-Harris Amendments	Essentially established the FDA as agency responsible for testing and approving drugs. Drugs must be effective and approved before human trials can begin
1963	Methadone Maintenance	Methadone introduced in U.S. as alternative to heroin for heroin addicts
1965	Drug Abuse Control Amendments	Regulation of amphetamines and barbiturates as "dangerous drugs," established ongoing regulation of other drugs in future. First federal prohibition of particular substances
1966	Narcotic Addict Rehabilitation Act	Allowed treatment in lieu of jail for drug offenders
1968	The Drug Abuse Control Amendments (DACA) Amendments	Suspended sentence & expungement for offenders with no repeat drug violation within 1 year
1969–1970	Methadone treatment became standard practice in Washington, DC	Methadone treatment for heroin addicts began in Washington, DC, jails. When Nixon expanded funding throughout Washington, DC, burglaries decreased 41%
1970	Comprehensive Drug Abuse Prevention and Control Act (Controlled Substances Act)	Updated all narcotic laws in U.S. First effort to control all drugs through enforcement (Department of Justice), not just through taxation (Treasury). Established Justice oversight for most controlled substances, separate commission to study marijuana
1971	Nixon declared "War On Drugs"	Nixon declared War on Drugs in June 1971 speech, declaring drugs "public enemy number 1." Despite tough rhetoric, Nixon spent more money on treatment than enforcement

(Continued)

Table 8.1 (Continued)

United States Drug Policy		
1972	Drug Abuse Office and Treatment Act	Established federal funds for drug prevention and treatment
1973	Methadone Control Act	Act established the regulations for methadone dispensation and licensing
1973	Heroin Trafficking Act	Increased penalties for heroin
1973	Alcohol, Drug Abuse and Mental Health Administration (ADAMHA) established	Former Agencies consolidated: National Institute of Mental Health (NIMH), National Institute on Drug Abuse (NIDA), and National Institute on Alcohol Abuse and Alcoholism (NIAAA)
1973	Drug Enforcement Administration (DEA)	Bureau of Narcotics and Dangerous Drugs reorganized into DEA, the "super-agency" to handle all aspects of illegal drug issue in U.S., including enforcement, customs, and school education. U.S. policy criticized internationally for demonization of addiction over harm reduction
1976	Carter moved to decriminalize cannabis	Candidate Jimmy Carter campaigned for presidency on decriminalization of cannabis campaign
1978	Alcohol and Drug Abuse Education Amendments	Responsibility for drug education became part of Department of Education
1980	Drug Abuse, Prevention, Treatment, and Rehabilitation Amendments	Extended prevention, education, and treatment efforts for drug abuse and addiction
1984	Just Say No	First Lady Nancy Reagan introduced "Just Say No" campaign. Birth of Drug Abuse Resistance Education (DARE)
1984	Drug Analogue (Designer Drug) Act	Made designer drugs with similar effects & structure subject to same law as existing drugs
1985	Crack as a social problem	Crack emerged as a social problem during the 1980's
1986	Anti-Drug Abuse Act of 1986	Increased penalties for drug trafficking, established mandatory minimums for drugs 100:1 sentence disparity between powdered/crack cocaine, leading to racial disparities in sentencing
1988	Senator John Kerry, U.S. Senate Committee on Foreign Relations	Senate report alleged CIA involved with cocaine sales, used proceeds to fund arms purchases
1988	Anti-Drug Abuse Act of 1988	Established office of National Drug Control Policy
1988	Omnibus Drug Act (Chemical Diversion and Trafficking Act)	Increased penalties for drug users and traffickers. Addressed money laundering and weapons in drug markets; allowed seizure of vehicles and assets used in drug trade

Table 8.1	(Continued)	
United States Drug Policy		
1990	Bush escalated "War On Drugs"	President Bush administration approved 50% spending increase for War on Drugs. Spending increase earmarked for enforcement, not prevention or treatment
1992	Clinton on cannabis	President Clinton admitted to smoking cannabis, but not inhaling
1992	Alcohol, Drug Abuse and Mental Health Administration (ADAMHA) reorganized	Alcohol, Drug Abuse and Mental Health Administration (ADAMHA) reorganization: National Institute on Drug Abuse (NIDA), National Institute on Mental Health (NIMA) and National Institute on Alcohol Abuse and Alcoholism (NIAAA) moved to National Institute of Health; programs moved to Substance Abuse and Mental Health Services Administration (SAMHSA)
1994	Violent Crime Control and Law Enforcement Act	Largest crime bill in U.S. history. In addition to weapon and violent crime provisions, mandated drug testing for federal parolees
1995	U.S. Sentencing Commission recommended revisions on mandatory minimum sentences	U.S. Sentencing Commission sought to address sentencing disparity in federal sentencing guidelines. Congress rejected recommendations of the very Commission charged with making specific recommendations to Congress
1996	Comprehensive Methamphetamine Control Act	Limited access to equipment and chemicals used in production of methamphetamines
2005	Combat Methamphetamine Act	Pseudophedrine (active ingredient in Sudafed) classified as Schedule V substance; ID required for purchase. Methamphetamine production decreased in U.S.
2010	Fair Sentencing Act	Sentencing disparity between crack and powdered cocaine reduced from 100:1 to 18:1

Source: Adapted from Mallicoat & Ireland (2013).

The first federal law regulating drugs in the United States—the Pure Food and Drug Act—was passed in 1906. This law did not make the use of narcotic and other drugs illegal, but required manufacturers of such products to list the ingredients, including the quantity of alcohol and other drugs. Specific regulation of drugs by the U.S. federal government began in 1914 with the passage of the Harrison Narcotics Act. Racial issues played a major role in the passage of this legislation, particularly with respect to the inclusion of cocaine as one of the regulated drugs. Cocaine was portrayed as a drug that was disproportionately used by Blacks, which gave them superhuman strength and contributed to assaults on Whites, particularly sexual assaults against white women (Mitchell, 2009). The Marihuana Tax Act of 1937, the first federal law banning marijuana, was similarly influenced by racial fears. The drug was portrayed as one that was disproportionately used by Mexican immigrants and black jazz musicians, who were also alleged to be involved in distributing the substance to young people (Mosher, 1999).

⊠ The Current State of Drug Policies in the United States

"*Drug Policy*" refers to the laws and procedures implemented by governments to deal with drug use and problems related to such use. The language used to describe drug policy is often vague and inconsistent, and the "drug policy" for any given country typically involves dozens of individual policies enacted (where relevant) at the federal, state, and local levels that are aimed at the control of psychoactive drug consumption, and harm related to the use of drugs.

The most restrictive form of drug policy is drug *criminalization* (or drug prohibition), under which the production, manufacture, sale, and/or possession/consumption of certain drugs are violations of one or more criminal statutes. In practical terms, this means that drug problems are largely handled through the criminal justice system, although the severity of sanctions related to violations of the laws, and the level of discretion exercised by criminal justice system agents, may vary substantially based on the behavior in question (e.g., possession vs. dealing), the particular substance, the amount of the substance involved, and a host of other factors. As is documented in more detail below, drug criminalization is the approach that dominates (for certain drugs) in the United States. Critics of the criminalization approach point out that it is very expensive, has little or no deterrent effect on drug use, and comes with a number of other often negative consequences, which are described in detail below.

The next most restrictive form of drug policy is *de facto legalization*. This approach to drug offenses might be more appropriately termed "drug procedure" rather than "drug policy," as de facto legalization does not represent any formal policy, but rather the informal yet systematic practice of not enforcing drug laws (typically marijuana possession) by law enforcement.

Decriminalization is the process of removing some form of conduct, previously defined as criminal, from the jurisdiction of criminal justice agencies. Many have noted that while the policy is referred to as decriminalization, it is better termed *depenalization* (MacCoun & Reuter, 1997) as the offense in question, although still illegal, cannot result in incarceration of the offender. Offenders are still processed and punished for violations of the law, but in a limited way (often equivalent to a traffic ticket).

The most permissive form of drug regulation policy is drug *legalization*. The general understanding of drug legalization is that some or all drugs become "legal" in the sense that, under certain circumstances, they can be purchased from government approved vendors and consumed. All criminal and civil penalties associated with use of the substance are removed—thus the substance(s) in question become regulated in much the same way that alcohol is currently regulated in the United States. Importantly, however, even under drug legalization policies, ancillary behaviors associated with drug use (i.e., driving under the influence of drugs) may be criminalized.

An additional set of policies and strategies aimed at reducing the harms caused by drug use and the policies designed to regulate drugs is known as *harm reduction* (also known as harm minimization). These policies do not focus on the attempted elimination of drug use and addiction—advocates of harm reduction strategies typically view the pursuit of a "drug-free world" as a completely unrealistic objective. By necessity, the policy approaches suggested by harm reduction advocates vary with respect to the particular drug and the drug-related behavior in question. The general message is that policy should not make firm distinctions between drug users and those who produce and sell drugs; that "soft" and "hard" drugs should not be treated similarly as they pose substantially different risks to users; and that ideology should never take precedence over practicality in attempts to minimize drug-related harm (Goode, 1997). President Jimmy Carter made a harm reduction-based appeal to Congress in his 1977 testimony, commenting, "Penalties against drug use should not be more damaging to an individual than the use of the drug itself. Nowhere is this clearer than in the laws against possession of marijuana for personal use" (Carter, 1977).

With respect to the approach to dealing with harder drugs (e.g., amphetamines, cocaine, heroin) the message from supporters of harm reduction approaches is somewhat more ambiguous. Proposals for the outright legalization of these substances are not the norm among harm reduction advocates, but strict criminal justice sanctions, such as lengthy prison sentences for possession/use of these substances, are typically seen as misguided, ineffective, and counterproductive. In the context of these harder drugs (which pose completely different addiction risks as compared to marijuana, for example), harm reduction advocates tend to view drug use and addiction as primarily health, and not criminal justice system, issues. They are thus more likely to promote some form of decriminalization and/or policy that uses the law as a tool to mandate treatment for users, instead of imposing the law as a mechanism to incarcerate large numbers of drug users. Needle exchange programs and clean needle distribution are also commonly advocated (and effective) approaches to reduce the harm associated with heroin or other illicit opiate injection—in particular the spread of HIV, hepatitis, and other blood-borne diseases (Ferrini, 2000).

Another common, albeit slightly more controversial, harm reduction strategy for the treatment of heroin (and other opiate) addiction is opiate replacement therapy. Opiate replacement therapy involves the substitution of one type of opiate for another, either temporarily or on a long-term basis, in the belief that the substituted drug is less problematic in some way(s). Several drugs are used in this manner, including buprenorphine and slow-release oral morphine, but the most well-known drug used for opiate replacement therapy is methadone. Methadone is a synthetic opiate that is cross-tolerant with other drugs in the opiate category, meaning that taking methadone provides tolerance for all drugs in the category (e.g., heroin) (O'Brien, 1997).

Methadone maintenance typically involves the addict taking an orally administered and standardized dose of methadone, the effects of which last for 12 to 24 hours, with accompanying reductions in the intense cravings commonly associated with opiate addiction (Gahlinger, 2001). When methadone is taken orally and at stable doses, it does not provide any euphoria or "high," and cognition, alertness, and higher mental functions are not impaired (Nadelmann, 1996; O'Brien, 1997). However, this form of drug treatment is more controversial than some others because, by definition, methadone maintenance involves substance dependency—it is precisely because the individual develops an adequate level of tolerance to methadone that the drug "works" in the prevention of heroin use. Critics of methadone maintenance programs also point out that addicts may horde and/or sell prescribed methadone or combine it with a drug like Xanax to obtain a heroin-like high (Negroponte, 2005). Despite these criticisms, methadone maintenance has been found to be effective in the treatment of chronic heroin and other opiate addiction, reducing heroin use, behaviors associated with high HIV risk, crime related to substance use, and levels of unemployment (Leshner, 1999; Marsch, 1998). It is one of the few harm reduction strategies currently embraced by the U.S. federal government's Office of National Drug Control Policy (ONDCP, 2000).

It is important to note that in the United States, harm reduction is an approach that disproportionately relies on dealing with the problems created by *legal* drug use, especially alcohol, and is much less likely to be employed to address problems stemming from the use of currently illegal substances. For example, alcohol consumption is allowed (even to the point of intoxication), but is regulated in a variety of ways intended to reduce the harms that may result from its use. As such, there are policies designed to control access to alcohol: (a) legal age restrictions; (b) consumption/possession regulations; (c) hours of sale and zoning restrictions on establishments selling the drug; (d) regulations on the advertising of alcohol products; (e) regulations on the purity and potency of alcohol products; and (f) provisions of extensive treatment options for those who become dependent on alcohol. The United States also penalizes the harmful consequences associated with the use of alcohol—for example, laws against drunk driving and public intoxication—but not use of the substance itself. As is addressed in more detail later, harm reduction advocates propose that similar policies should be adopted to reduce the harm associated with some, or all, currently illegal drugs.

As noted, the dominant drug regulation policy in the United States for approximately the last 100 years has been criminalization. The passage of the 1914 Harrison Narcotics Control Act launched a policy of arresting and incarcerating increasingly large numbers of users and traffickers in illicit drugs (Brecher, 1972; Musto, 1999) with a disproportional impact on members of minority groups and the poor. Contemporary policies toward illegal drugs in the United States are consistent with principles established early in the 20th century, with a particular focus on a law enforcement approach to the drug problem and stringent penalties attached to violations of drug laws. In 2009, there were 1,663,582 arrests for drug offenses in the United States comprising approximately 12% of the total arrests in that year, and constituting about the same number of arrests as for murder, rape, robbery, burglary, and theft combined (Bureau of Justice Statistics, 2010). And, despite the rhetoric on the part of government and law enforcement officials that the War on Drugs is focused on those who traffic in these substances, arrests for possession of drugs were about four times greater than those for trafficking. Although the rhetoric states that the War on Drugs is also focused on "hard drugs," in 2009, 51.6% of all drug arrests involved marijuana (Bureau of Justice Statistics, 2010), and of the 858,408 arrests for marijuana in that year, 88.4% were for simple possession of the substance.

Given the tremendous number of arrests for drug offenses and the severe penalties that result from convictions for such offenses, the drug war also contributed to unprecedented levels of imprisonment in the United States (Austin & Irwin, 2012). At the end of 2010, there were 2,266,800 adults incarcerated in the United States (Bureau of Justice Statistics, 2011), translating to an incarceration rate of more than 700 per 100,000/population. On December 31, 2011, there were 197,050 prisoners under federal jurisdiction, and of these, 94,600, or 48%, were serving time for drug offenses. At the state level, 237,000 prisoners were serving time for drug offenses, representing 17% of the total number of adults incarcerated in state prisons. And as of the mid-2000s, the United States had 100,000 more people incarcerated for drug offenses than the European Union had for all offenses combined, despite the fact that the European Union had 100 million more inhabitants (Wood, Tyndal, Zhang, Montaner, & Kerr, 2003).

Specific (and Ancillary) Drug Policies

Mandatory Minimum Sentences

Mandatory minimum sentencing policies have been a component of criminal laws in the United States since 1790 (Schulhofer, 1993) but had their greatest impact in the last three decades. Interestingly, in the 1979 Comprehensive Drug Abuse and Control Act, the U.S. Congress concluded that mandatory minimum sentences had not realized their intended purpose of deterring drug offenders, and most mandatory minimum sentencing policies were repealed at that time. However, prompted at least in part by the "crack cocaine epidemic" of the mid-1980s, the federal government and several state governments enacted mandatory minimum penalties for drug offenses in the 1980s (some states, such as New York, enacted such statutes in the 1970s). As of 2012, there were 171 mandatory minimum sentencing statutes in the United States, and approximately 80% were for drug law violations (Tabichnick, 2012).

Most relevant in the context of issues addressed in this chapter, at the federal level, the 1988 Anti-Drug Abuse[2] Act created a host of mandatory minimum penalties for drug offenses, with the most important being a distinction between crack and powder cocaine. Under this legislation, a first-time offender convicted of possession of 5.01 grams of crack cocaine was subject to a mandatory minimum penalty of five years imprisonment. If the individual possessed only 5.0 grams of cocaine or less, they were subject to a maximum sentence of one year imprisonment (Wilkins, Newton, & Steer, 1993). In contrast, for powder cocaine, the five-year mandatory minimum sentence did not apply until the individual possessed more than 500 grams of the substance. In passing this legislation, apparently in response to an alleged crack cocaine "epidemic" in the United States (Reinarman & Levine, 1997), Congress ignored the fact that crack and powder cocaine are essentially the same drugs pharmacologically and have the same effects and consequences (Hatsukami & Fischman, 1996). Congress also failed to offer any rationale for the selection of the 100 to 1 ratio in amounts of powder versus crack cocaine that triggered the mandatory minimum penalties (Sklansky, 1995).

Related to the points regarding racial disparities in the application of drug laws, it is important to note that African Americans (and, to a lesser extent, Hispanics) were far more likely to be arrested and prosecuted under federal crack cocaine statutes than were Whites. A United States Sentencing Commission study in 1992 found that in 16 states, including states with large populations, such as Connecticut, New Jersey, and Illinois, not a single white person had been prosecuted under federal crack laws (Gelacak, 1997). Another study by the Sentencing Commission found that in 1994, Blacks accounted for over 90% of federal prosecutions for crack offenses (Gelacak, 1997).

These racial differences in prosecutions and sentencing under the federal crack laws must be considered in light of data on racial differences in the use of drugs in general and crack cocaine in particular. Although it is true that hardcore drug use and the negative consequences associated with such use are more common in inner-city areas where minorities tend to be concentrated, overall drug use figures for 1990 reported by the National Institute on Drug Abuse (NIDA) indicated that Whites comprised 77% of the estimated 1.3 million users of illegal drugs in the United States, while Blacks comprised 15%. The United States Sentencing Commission acknowledged the racial disparities in sentencing that resulted from the crack/powder cocaine distinction, and while not willing to admit that the law was racially discriminatory in its intent, the Commission commented; "If the impact of the law is discriminatory, the problem is no less regardless of the intent. The problem is particularly acute because the disparate impact arises from a penalty structure for two different forms of the same substance" (Gelacak, 1997, p. 2).

The federal Anti-Drug Abuse Act of 1998 also provided enhanced mandatory minimum penalties for individuals convicted of selling drugs within 1,000 feet of playgrounds, youth centers, swimming pools, video arcades, and other locations where young people are believed to congregate (Gray, 2001)—a number of individual states enacted similar laws. Although many of these laws have since been repealed, it is worth considering how they were applied in particular states. In Massachusetts, legislation provided a two-year mandatory minimum penalty for selling drugs within 1,000 feet of a primary, secondary, or vocational school. A study on the application of these laws in the city of New Bedford found that 84% of all drug trafficking cases within the city limits occurred within school zones. However, a review of the case files revealed that only one of the 443 transactions that occurred involved the actual sale of drugs to children,

---

[2] Earlier, the 1986 Anti-Drug Abuse Act also created the same distinction between crack and powder cocaine trafficking.

and more than 70% of the cases occurred when school was not in session. The authors of this study concluded that the outcome of the legislation did not result in better protection of children from exposure to drugs, but instead, resulted in an escalation of the severity of penalties for violations of drug laws (Brownsberger & Aromaa, 2003).

A similar study focusing on the application of school zone laws in the state of New Jersey found that African Americans and Hispanics, who comprised 27% of the state's population, constituted 96% of all prison inmates in the state whose most serious offense was a school zone violation (New Jersey Commission to Review Criminal Sentencing, 2005). Of 90 reported school zone cases studied in detail by the Commission, not one involved the selling of drugs to minors, and only two of the cases actually occurred on school property. The Commission concluded that the school zone policies were racially discriminatory and recommended significant changes in the laws; however, it was not until 2010 that mandatory minimum penalties for individuals convicted of selling drugs in school zones were eliminated in the state of New Jersey.

Medical Marijuana Laws

A significant development in the drug policy arena is related to the passage of medical marijuana laws in several states. Marijuana has been used for medicinal purposes for at least 300 years, and more than 100 articles on the therapeutic uses of the substance were published in scientific journals between 1840 and 1900. Cannabis was listed in the *United States Pharmacopeia* as a recognized medicine from 1850 until 1942 and could be purchased in local pharmacies in some states until the mid-1920s (Davenport-Hines, 2001). While there is certainly not a consensus on the medical utility of marijuana, a number of prominent organizations and individuals support use of the drug for medicinal purposes. Reports by the National Institutes of Health and the Institute of Medicine noted that cannabis and its constituents may have some medical utility (National Institutes of Health, 1997), and in a publication from the National Academy Press it was noted that "accumulated data indicate a therapeutic potential for cannabinoid drugs, particularly for symptoms, such as pain relief, control of nausea and vomiting, and appetite stimulation" (Joy, Watson, & Benson, 1999, p. 3). This report also pointed out that, with the exception of the harms associated with administering marijuana through smoking, the adverse effects of the drug "are within the range of effects tolerated for other medications" (1999, p. 4). Other organizations in favor of allowing the use of medical marijuana include the American Public Health Association, the Federation of American Scientists, the Physicians' Association for AIDS Care, the Lymphoma Association of America, and the National Association of Prosecutors and Criminal Defense Attorneys (Zimmer & Morgan, 1997). The *New England Journal of Medicine* and the *Journal of the American Medical Association* have also taken editorial stances in favor of medical marijuana.

In 1988, Francis L. Young, the Chief Administrative Law Judge of the Drug Enforcement Administration, recommended that marijuana be removed from Schedule I of the Controlled Substances Act so that it could be used for medical purposes. Young noted that cannabis fulfilled the legal requirement of currently accepted medical use in treatment and noted that it was "one of the safest therapeutically active substances known to man" (as quoted in Grinspoon & Bakalar, 1995, p. 1875). However, the federal government's Drug Enforcement Administration (DEA) ignored this recommendation, and since then, DEA agents and other federal government officials have actively engaged in a campaign of pursuing medical marijuana users and providers in states where medical marijuana legislation has been enacted.

As of April 2013, 19 states and the District of Columbia passed legislation allowing marijuana use for medicinal purposes. Although it would appear on the surface that these state laws allow marijuana to be used for medical purposes, they are in conflict with federal legislation, which continues to list marijuana as a Schedule I drug, and also with Article IV of the Constitution, which holds that federal law shall be the "law of the land" and hence prevail over state laws.

In response to medical marijuana initiatives passed in Arizona and California in the 1990s, President Clinton's drug czar Barry McCaffrey, threatened to arrest any doctor who merely *mentioned* to a patient that marijuana might help them (Boyd & Hitt, 2002) and at one point referred to medical marijuana as "Cheech and Chong medicine" (as quoted in Forbes, 2000). President George W. Bush's drug czar John Walters was even more strident in his opposition to medical marijuana laws, at one point referring to medical marijuana as "medicinal crack" (as quoted in Drug Policy Alliance, 2003). In what some have argued was a violation of the 1939 Hatch Act (which prevents federal government officials from using their authority to affect the outcome of an election), Walters actively campaigned against a marijuana decriminalization ballot initiative in the state of Nevada in 2000, arguing, among other things, that passage of the law would make Nevada a "vacation spot for drug traffickers" (as quoted in Janofsky, 2002). Walters also campaigned against a proposed medical marijuana law in Maryland in 2002, but Maryland Governor Robert Ehrlich eventually approved the legislation, marking the first time a Republican governor had done so (Drug Policy Alliance, 2003).

Proposed medical marijuana legislation was also blocked by federal authorities in Washington, DC, where in September of 2002, a federal appeals court overturned (without providing any rationale), a previous court ruling that had cleared the way for a medical marijuana ballot initiative to be considered by voters in the District of Columbia (Santana, 2002). This was the second time the measure had been blocked in the District of Columbia—in 1998, voters approved a medical marijuana initiative by a vote of 69% to 31%, but Congress prevented the law from going into effect.

As a presidential candidate as well as after taking office, President Obama indicated that his administration would take a "hands-off" approach to medical marijuana (Egelko, 2011). This stance was reflected in a 2009 statement by federal Justice Department officials which indicated that, as a general rule, prosecutors should not focus their resources on "individuals whose actions are in clear and unambiguous compliance with existing state laws providing for the medical use of marijuana" (as cited in Baker, 2011). However, a 2011 Justice Department memo seemed to partially contradict the previous statement, in stating "we maintain the authority to enforce [federal law] vigorously against individuals and organizations that participate in unlawful manufacturing and distribution activity involving marijuana, even if such activities are permitted under state law" (as cited in Baker, 2011). In addition, the 2011 National Drug Control Strategy claimed that marijuana was "addictive and unsafe," and devoted a full five pages to attacking marijuana legalization and medical marijuana.

Under the Obama administration, there have been at least 200 raids and 70 indictments against medical marijuana providers in six states (Martin, 2012). Although some of these raids focused on medical marijuana dispensaries that were located close to schools, one legislator from Washington state (which had recently allowed for the sale of liquor in grocery stores) questioned why marijuana dispensaries were seemingly more dangerous to young people than were grocers (Martin, 2012).

As Ethan Nadlemann, Director of the Drug Policy Alliance pointed out in a *New York Times* editorial (Nadelmann, 2011) in addition to the hundreds of raids of medical marijuana dispensaries that have been conducted by the Drug Enforcement Administration, pressures are also being exerted on medical marijuana businesses by other federal government agencies. Nadelmann notes, for example, that the Treasury Department has forced banks to close the accounts of medical marijuana businesses that are operating legally under state laws; that the Internal Revenue Service has required dispensary owners to pay punitive taxes that are not imposed on any other businesses; and that the Bureau of Alcohol, Tobacco, and Firearms ruled that medical marijuana patients cannot legally purchase firearms. Importantly, Nadelmann notes that these federal efforts will not be successful in stopping the trade in marijuana, but instead serve only to push it back underground, resulting in potentially higher levels of violence and other social harms.

Marijuana Legalization Measures

Despite the federal government's stance on marijuana, in recent years, some states have included marijuana legalization measures on voters' ballots. Rivas (2010) argues that three factors are driving the momentum behind these measures: (a) demographic factors—baby boomers who consumed marijuana in their youth, and do not share previous generations' fear of the drug; (b) economic factors that have reduced criminal justice system budgets (and, more generally, the budgets of state governments), forcing states to seek alternative revenue sources; and (c) the level of drug-related violence in Mexico.

In the fall of 2010, a marijuana legalization measure, Proposition 19 (the "Regulate, Control, and Tax Cannabis Act") was included on the ballot in the state of California (McKinley, 2010). Some political opinion polls indicated that this measure had a fairly good chance of being approved by voters, and in an interesting preemptive move, Governor Arnold Schwarzenegger signed a law just prior to the vote that made the penalty for marijuana possession in the state of California equivalent to a traffic ticket—a $100 fine and no provision for jail time. Schwarzenegger's strategy was important, because one of the primary arguments of supporters of Proposition 19 was that the state's marijuana laws were too costly to enforce and prosecute (Lagos, 2010). In opposition to this law, there were pronouncements by law enforcement officials, such as the police chief in Pleasant Hill, California, who argued "if the price drops [as was predicted if the legislation passed] more people are going to buy it. Low income people are going to buy marijuana instead of buying food, which happens with substance abusers" (as quoted in Wohlsen, 2010). Interestingly, one of the largest financial contributors to the campaign against marijuana legalization in California was the state's beer and beverage distributors, who likely believed their profits would suffer if marijuana was legalized and Californians chose marijuana (instead of alcohol) as their recreational drug. Although Proposition 19 was ultimately defeated by a margin of 56.5% opposed versus 43.5% in favor, younger voters were much more likely to support the measure, and 65% of voters in San Francisco approved it (Proposition 19, 2010).

More recently, in the fall 2012 elections, the states of Colorado, Oregon, and Washington included marijuana legalization measures on their ballots. Colorado's measure, known as Amendment 64, permitted retail stores to sell marijuana, and taxed and regulated the substance in a fashion similar to alcohol. Among the supporters of the Colorado legislation was Bruce Madison, former associate medical director at the University of Colorado School of Medicine who noted that Colorado's marijuana laws "waste millions of dollars by ruining thousands of lives by unnecessary arrest and incarceration, and [cause] the deaths of hundreds of people killed in black market criminal activities" (as quoted in Horwitz, 2012).

In the state of Washington, prior to the inclusion of the marijuana legalization measure on the 2012 ballot, Governor Christine Gregoire (as well as Rhode Island Governor Lincoln Chafee) petitioned the Drug Enforcement Administration to reclassify marijuana as a Schedule II drug, thereby recognizing its medicinal value (Martin, 2011). Washington's measure made it legal for individuals 21 years of age and older to possess up to one ounce of marijuana, and it was estimated that the state would receive approximately $500 million in taxes and licensing fees per year (Carson, 2012).

Among the supporters of the Washington legislation were several prominent politicians in the state, former federal prosecutor John McKay, Seattle's City Attorney, and its mayor and city council

(Garber & Miletich, 2011). King County Sheriff Steve Strachan, himself a former Drug Abuse Resistance Education Officer, also supported the legalization campaign, commenting, "with alcohol being highly regulated, we're able to have a more reasonable conversation about it" (as quoted in Westneat, 2012). The legalization campaign also had considerable financial backing from the Drug Policy Alliance, international travel guide Rick Steves, and Progressive Insurance founder Peter Lewis.

Although the marijuana legalization measure in the state of Oregon did not pass, voters in Colorado and Washington approved the measures (with approximately 55% in favor in both states). While President Obama, in an interview with Barbara Walters of ABC News suggested that his administration had "bigger fish to fry," and that it "would not make sense for us to see a top priority as going after recreational [marijuana] users in states that have determined that it's legal" (as quoted in Weiner, 2012), it remains to be seen how marijuana legalization is handled in the two states. There is also considerable ambiguity regarding how the laws are interpreted by state and local law enforcement and criminal justice system officials; there are also questions surrounding laws related to driving under the influence of marijuana, and drug-testing of employees, among others.

Drug Courts

An alternative to mass incarceration of drug offenders which has become increasingly popular over the last three decades, and which might be construed as consistent with harm reduction policies, is drug courts. The first ***drug court*** was established in Miami, Florida, in 1989, and as of 2011, over 2,600 drug courts exist in the United States (National Drug Court Resource Center, 2012).

Although there is considerable variation across drug court programs with respect to who is eligible and how programs are administered, compared to the traditional legal model of dealing with drug offenders, these courts are based on a "restorative justice" or "therapeutic jurisprudence" paradigm. This means that the process is less about assigning blame and punishment and more about achieving positive change in the life of the offender (Jensen & Mosher, 2006). Offenders enrolled in these courts are expected to participate in drug treatment as a condition of avoiding prison, with the understanding that sanctions (including the possibility of incarceration) may result if they do not comply with the requirements of the treatment program. Drug courts use the threat of sanctions in combination with rewards for compliance in order to keep offenders motivated to participate in treatment.

Generally, offenders in drug court programs appear more frequently in front of judges and are required to enter into an intensive treatment program; undergo frequent, random urinalysis; receive sanctions for failure to comply with program requirements; encouraged to become drug-free; and urged to develop vocational and other skills to promote reentry into the community. Most studies assessing the effectiveness of drug courts found them to be reasonably effective in reducing drug use and recidivism among those who complete the program, at least in the short term (Bahr, Harris, Strobel, & Taylor, 2012; Belenko, 2001; Shaffer, 2011). Perhaps more importantly, many studies lauded drug courts for producing substantial cost savings when compared to incarceration (Downey & Roman, 2010; Washington State Institute for Public Policy, 2002).

Despite ongoing support from many criminal justice system officials and researchers, drug courts are under increased criticism in recent years. While few doubt that drug courts represent significant improvement over strictly punitive responses to drug law violations, among other things, critics asserted that the reported high success rates of these courts is inflated and also that drug courts may serve to perpetuate existing racial and ethnic inequalities in the criminal justice system. With respect to the first issue and relying only on methodologically sound studies, two separate meta-analyses of drug court outcomes found reductions in recidivism of drug court completers, but the reductions were only 9% (Shaffer, 2011) and 12% (Mitchell, Wilson, Eggers, & Mackenzie, 2012) respectively. Clearly, this is much less than the 75% reduction in recidivism claimed by the National Association of Drug Court Professionals (www.NADCP.org).

In addition, there is mounting evidence of class, gender, and racial/ethnic biases becoming further institutionalized as a result of inequities found in drug courts. Research suggests that these programs may reproduce class stratification, as individuals who are unemployed or undereducated are less likely to complete drug court programs (Brown, 2010), and individuals with already limited financial resources and employment opportunities are further burdened by the intensive reporting and transportation requirements (Drug Policy Alliance, 2011). Racial and ethnic disparities have also been reported. African Americans are less likely to complete drug court programs (Brown, Zuelsdorff, & Gassman, 2009; McKean & Warren-Gordon, 2011), and non-White graduates of juvenile drug courts do not experience the same recidivism benefits as Whites (Carter & Barker, 2011). A shortage of culturally sensitive programming for people of color has also been noted (Justice Policy Institute, 2011a), as well as a reduced likelihood of being admitted to drug courts and evidence of more severe sanctioning of minorities for rule violations (McKean & Warren-Gordon, 2011).

Critics of drug courts also examined their larger impacts in terms of "net-widening" and "mesh-tightening." *Net-widening* refers to the broadening of criminal justice system influence as an increasing number of individuals are brought into the system. According to some researchers, the benevolent intentions attached to the belief that all drug users need treatment has contributed to a growth in drug arrests and drug prosecutions (Gardiner, 2008; Hoffman, 1999). A *mesh-tightening* effect may also be created by the increased formality and intensive monitoring of drug court clients, making it more difficult for them to exit the criminal justice system once they are enrolled in a drug court program. Drug court clients are more closely scrutinized than traditional probationers (particularly with respect to frequent drug testing), leading officials to discover and sanction minor offenses that may have previously gone unnoticed, or were ignored. In short, while it is once again important to emphasize that drug courts generally represent a less costly and more humane approach to dealing with drug offenders than incarceration, they do not appear to be the panacea that some credited.

Race, Gender, and Class Implications of Drug Policies in the United States

The consequences of U.S. drug policies extend beyond the incarceration of hundreds of thousands of individuals—these policies also contribute to, and often exacerbate, existing racial/ethnic and social inequalities. For example, members of racial/ethnic minority groups constitute more than 75% of federal drug inmates (Bureau of Prisons Quick Facts, 2010) and more than 80% at the state level (Mauer, 2009). African Americans are the most disproportionately incarcerated group, representing 49% of those incarcerated for drug offenses in 2010, but only 13% of the total population (Guerino, Harrison, & Sabol, 2011). African Americans are disproportionately incarcerated for drug offenses in 97% of the largest counties (Beatty, Petteruti, & Ziedenberg, 2007) and compared to Whites are at least twice as likely to receive a sentence of incarceration for drug convictions in every state.

Although the disproportions are not as great, Hispanic Americans comprise 16% of the U.S. population, but 21.6% of those incarcerated for drug offenses (Guerino et al., 2011). Although limited data exist to make such comparisons, Native Americans are imprisoned for drug offenses at rates higher than Whites in states where they comprise a significant proportion of the population, such as Washington state (Lee & Vukich, 2001) and Montana (Ross, 1998), and this is also true of the native Hawaiians in Hawaii (Thompson, 2010).

Data on class biases in incarceration for drug offenses are more difficult to obtain, but it is notable that as drug incarceration rates peaked in the mid-1990s, more than half of state and federal prisoners had annual incomes of less than $10,000 and one-fifth made less than $3,000 (Reiman, 1998). States with higher poverty rates tend to have higher incarceration rates (Beckett & Western, 2001), and counties with higher rates of unemployment and poverty were found to imprison drug offenders at higher rates (Beatty et al., 2007).

While the majority of imprisoned drug offenders are male, the growth in incarceration for drug offenses is also unevenly felt by women. During the most recent war on drugs, the relative growth in the number of women in prison for drug offenses was even greater than for males (Mauer & King, 2007)— as of 2005, 29% of incarcerated women had committed drug offenses, compared with 19% of men (Harrison & Beck, 2005). Additionally, two-thirds of women imprisoned for drug crimes have children under the age of 18 (Mumola, 2000).

Particularly affected have been women of color, who have much higher rates of incarceration for drug offenses than White women (Lapidus et al., 2005). In the state of New York, for example, women of minority backgrounds comprise 91% of those incarcerated for drug offenses, but only 32% of the population (Lapidus et al., 2005). Similarly, in California, women of color represent 54% of drug prisoners and 38% of the population. There are also intersections of class and race—37% of women in prison for drug offenses in the late 1990s earned less than $600 per month, and 30% received public assistance (Greenfield & Snell, 2000).

Although Mauer (2009) noted that as of the mid-2000s, racial disparities in incarceration for drug law violations were declining and he concluded, "While these trends are welcome as a possible indication of a change in policy and practice, they need to be tempered by an assessment of the overall scale of imprisonment and punishment" (p. 19). He also speculated that because so many African Americans have already been incarcerated, there are fewer Blacks on the streets to arrest (Fears, 2009). Race, class, and gender implications are further explored below as unintended consequences of our drug criminalization policies.

Unintended Consequences of U.S. Drug Criminalization Policies

A number of additional federal and state policies containing drug-offense penalties and restrictions were enacted over the past 20 years that extend the impacts of the drug war into other social realms. Such policies have not only led to unintended consequences for society in general, but these effects further exacerbated racial and social class disparities. In 1996, welfare reform legislation (the Personal Responsibility and Work Opportunities Reconciliation Act), denied, for life, federal welfare benefits to any individual convicted of a felony drug offense, including access to food stamps and temporary aid to needy families (Schwartz, 2002). It is important to note that this provision does not apply to individuals who commit murder, rape, and other serious crimes. The law also allowed states to require drug and alcohol testing of anyone seeking welfare. As of 2002, more than 92,000 women were denied access to welfare as a result of felony drug convictions (Kirkorian, 2002) and the legislation resulted in even more deleterious effects on women of color (Allard, 2002). While it is encouraging to note that a number of states recognize the problems associated with this policy and use the option to not enforce these Welfare Reform Act provisions, the fact that these laws are in place at the federal level and that close to half the states continue to enforce them is cause for concern. Additionally, as of 2011, 31 states and Congress were considering legislation to require ongoing drug testing of welfare and food stamp recipients, despite evidence that testing does not deter drug use (Office of the Assistant Secretary for Planning and Evaluation, 2011).

Public housing eligibility is also impacted by drug war legislation. Under the 1988 Anti-Drug Abuse Act, public housing agencies were required to evict tenants if the tenant, a member of their own family, or guests were involved in "drug-related crimes"—these laws potentially affect the more than three million residents of federally funded housing in the United States. Similarly, under the "One-Strike" initiative within the 1996 federal welfare reform legislation, local public housing authorities were given access to background checks on applicants, and were able to deny housing or evict tenants for any involvement in illegal drug use or sales. Clearly, these public housing policies target poor (and often minority) urban individuals and contribute to the discriminatory impacts of the drug war.

Under provisions of the 1998 Higher Education Act, individuals applying for federal financial aid are required to answer a question regarding their prior drug convictions. If applicants indicate they have a conviction for a drug offense, or if they refuse to answer the question, they are sent a follow-up questionnaire that asks them to provide information on the type and number of drug convictions they have, as well as the date the convictions occurred (Students for Sensible Drug Policy, 2006). Individuals who indicate they have a conviction for a drug offense, including possession of marijuana, or who refuse to answer the question can be denied federal student aid.

Students for Sensible Drug Policy (2006) estimated that since the drug conviction question was added to federal student aid applications in the 2001–2002 school year, 189,065 applicants (approximately one in every 400) had their requests for financial aid denied because of their answers to this question. Davenport-Hines (2001) notes that this law, similar to other drug legislation in the United States, has a disproportionately negative impact on the poor and members of minority groups. Similarly, a *New York Times* editorial commented, "By narrowing access to affordable education, the federal government further diminishes the prospects of young people who are already at risk of becoming lifetime burdens to society. . . . It doesn't take a genius to see that barring young offenders from college leads to more crime, not less" (Cutting College Aid, 2005).

Collectively, the drug-related welfare, public housing, and education laws (among others) provide for lifelong penalties that amplify the impacts of drug convictions. Both the welfare and student aid laws ultimately serve to further reduce employment opportunities (that are already severely limited) for ex-offenders, increasing the likelihood that they will be forced into the secondary labor market or illicit employment. As a result of these laws, ex-offenders (and particularly people of color) experience difficulties in finding affordable housing. By indirectly penalizing family members of those convicted of nonviolent drug offenses, future generations are also negatively impacted due to the connection between stable family environments and children's future educational attainment (Allard, 2002).

As of 2010, 12 states also had disenfranchisement statutes that disqualify individuals convicted of (drug and other) felony offenses from voting, even after such individuals served their sentences (Sentencing Project, 2010). With a significant proportion of felony convictions in recent decades stemming from the drug war, the concentration of drug convictions in poor and minority communities further exacerbates existing disadvantages by reducing the opportunity to effect political change. Estimates suggest that 1.4 million African American males (13%) are currently disenfranchised, and it is projected that 30% of African American males will lose voting rights at some point in their life, and 40% will lose these rights permanently in certain states (Sentencing Project, 2010).

The discussion of specific drug and ancillary legislation above leaves little doubt that in the United States, the criminalization approach to drugs and the attendant drug war has a significant impact for both the criminal justice system as well as society as a whole. There is also virtually no scientific evidence to suggest that these laws have been effective in their apparent goals of reducing drug use in American society. What we do know is that these laws have disproportionately impacted the poor and members of minority groups in ways that were never intended.

What Research Has Taught Us: Outcomes Associated With Less Punitive Drug Policies

Several other countries (and a handful of states in the United States) adopted drug control policies that diverge from a strict criminalization model. Although care must be taken when making cross-national comparisons, research on these "policy experiments" can inform us about what works and what does not work in drug policy. In general, in countries following a shift to less punitive forms of drug policy (the "sky did not fall" approach), the rates of drug use did not substantially increase, and in some cases drug use even declined (see, for example, EMCDDA, European Monitoring Centre for Drugs and Drug Addiction, 2011). Next, we provide a short summary of some of the most notable "drug policy experiments" and the research related to these policies.

Among the most well-known examples of a country with more permissive drug policies is the Netherlands. Since 1976, the Dutch have employed a policy of de facto legalization for marijuana (there is a misconception that marijuana is legalized in the Netherlands, but this is not the case). The Dutch legislation is based on the principle of the separation of markets for soft (cannabis) and hard (heroin, cocaine, amphetamines, etc.) drugs in order to prevent users from entering the criminal underworld (EMCDDA, 2009). As of the early 2000s, estimates suggested that there were between 1,200 and 1,500 "coffee shops" (about one per 1,200 inhabitants) in the Netherlands that sold cannabis products. Most of these establishments offer a variety of marijuana and hashish with varying potency levels, and the typical coffee shop menu lists from five to 20 different varieties of cannabis, as well as coffee, teas, and baked goods that contain the substance (Reid, 2002). Thus, marijuana consumption is tolerated, provided that coffee shop proprietors abide by a number of regulations. These include that sales must be limited to five grams of marijuana per person, per visit; that no hard drugs are sold in the establishments; that the coffee shops do not advertise drugs; that there is no community nuisance created by their presence; that the shops sell marijuana only to adults; and that the coffee shops do not stock more than 500 grams of cannabis (Netherlands Ministry of Health, 2003). Growing or importing marijuana remains illegal in the Netherlands, so coffee shop proprietors risk legal sanctions when obtaining the drugs (this is the so-called "front door, back door problem"—that is, what happens at the front door is legal, what happens at the back door is not).

It is notable that rates of current marijuana use in the Netherlands remain below marijuana use rates in the United States, and below use rates of many other European countries, including those with more punitive cannabis policies. Rates of marijuana consumption in the Netherlands are comparable to those of adjacent countries, such as Belgium and Germany, and are considerably lower than in Britain, France, and Spain (Blickman & Jelsma, 2009). It is important to note, however, that despite perceptions that they are ubiquitous in the Netherlands, the number of coffee shops selling cannabis has steadily declined from a peak of approximately 1,500 in the mid-1990s to 702 in 2008 (Blickman & Jelsma, 2009). And, in December of 2008 (and despite the fact that 80% of Dutch citizens were opposed (Treble, 2008), Dutch officials announced that at least one-fifth of the remaining marijuana cafes in the country would be forced to close. The legislation forced the coffee shops to become members-only clubs and to close those that were located near schools (Pignal, 2010).

Perhaps more importantly, given allegations that marijuana is a "*gateway drug,*" by definition a drug that opens the door to the use of other, harder drugs, the Netherlands has comparatively lower rates of cocaine, heroin, and amphetamine use (MacCoun, 2011). Dutch officials claim that this is at least partially attributable to their practice of allowing quasi-legal access to marijuana (by far, the most commonly used illegal drug) and thus creating a social barrier between the cannabis and hard drug markets (Zimmer & Morgan, 1997).

While certainly known for their liberal policies on marijuana, the Dutch have also adopted harm reduction approaches for other substances. They offer support and assistance to heroin users in the country, with the result that the average age of heroin users increased from approximately 25 in the late 1970s to 36 in the late 1990s (Gray, 1999). Over the same period, the average age of heroin users in the United States declined from 25 to 19. The Dutch have also taken steps to reduce the harm associated with ecstasy (MDMA) use. Although MDMA is still illegal and classified as a hard drug in the Netherlands, ecstasy users can take their pills to drug treatment centers to have the chemical contents analyzed (Richburg, 2001). This program provides ecstasy users with information regarding the effects they can expect from consuming the substance and has the additional advantage of providing public health officials with current information regarding what types of ecstasy are on the market and a profile of users (Cumming, 2004).

Over the past decade, several other European countries loosened penalties on illegal drugs and several decriminalized a wide range of substances. The most sweeping reforms were made in Portugal, which in 2001 decriminalized not just marijuana possession, but possession of *all* drugs for personal use. In 1999, Portugal had the highest rate of drug-related deaths in the European Union, and approximately 100,000 people (nearly one percent of the population) were heroin addicts (Specter, 2011). Under the 2001 legislation, the use and possession of drugs do not constitute criminal offenses, but instead are treated as "administrative offenses" (van het Loo, van Beusekom, & Kahan, 2002). In Portugal, individuals found possessing small quantities of drugs and who the police believe are not involved in more serious offenses like drug trafficking appear before a panel consisting of a doctor, social worker, and lawyer. While these commissions can impose sanctions on users, the main objective is to "explore the need for treatment and to promote healthy recovery" (EMCDDA, 2004).

Treatment and prevention methods became the primary focus of drug policy in Portugal, expanding and incorporating evidence-based practices. In addition, safe injection facilities and needle exchanges were established in many areas where drug problems were concentrated; methadone substitution therapy became the norm for those with opiate addiction; doctors and pharmacies began providing safe access to methadone and heroin maintenance doses; and healthcare professionals were employed to make regular visits to problem areas.

Evaluations of the Portuguese approach to drug regulation have generally been positive, indicating that the country is experiencing reductions in drug use (problematic and otherwise), crime, and drug-related deaths. The most comprehensive analysis of the Portuguese experiment is provided by a report written in 2009 by Glenn Greenwald for the CATO Institute, a Washington-based think tank. Greenwald notes, "judged by virtually every metric, the Portuguese decriminalization framework has been a resounding success" (p. 1). In 2001, Portugal experienced close to 400 drug-related deaths, the majority of these from opiate overdoses (Hughes & Stevens, 2012). However, in 2009, there were only 54 drug-related deaths in the country (EMCDDA, 2011). In addition, the rate of Hepatitis-C among intravenous drug users was 29% in 2009, among the lowest rates in all of Europe (United Nations Office on Drugs and Crime (UNODC), 2011); the number of new HIV cases dropped from nearly 1,400 in 2000 to fewer than 400 in 2006 (Greenwald, 2009), and the number of people seeking drug treatment more than doubled (Szalavitz, 2009).

Perhaps most importantly in the context of evaluating the Portuguese approach, several studies have found that, despite predictions to the contrary, there is little evidence to suggest that drug use in Portugal has increased (Greenwald 2009; Hughes & Stevens, 2012). Although data on past-year drug use indicate that the percentage of Portuguese citizens using drugs increased slightly (from 3.4% in 2001 to 3.7% in 2007 (Hughes & Stevens, 2010), only 16% of Portuguese students reported lifetime use of marijuana in a 2007 survey (European School Survey Project on Alcohol and Other Drugs (ESPAD), 2011). Also, lifetime use of heroin declined from 2.6% to 1.8% between 2001 and 2006 (Hughes & Stevens, 2012).

An additional example of successful harm reduction drug control strategies comes from Canada. Although, similar to the United States, Canada has a long history of stringent drug policies with a criminal justice focus (in fact, Canada's first drug legislation, the Opium and Narcotic Drug Act, was passed in 1908, predating the U.S. Harrison Narcotics Act by six years (Mosher, 1999)), although in the early 2000s, there were indications that Canada was moving toward policies based on harm reduction principles. For example, regulations that came into effect in Canada in 2001 allowed certain individuals access to medical marijuana; a special committee of the Canadian Senate recommended the legalization of cannabis possession and use in 2002 (Canada, 2002); and there were also indications in the early 2000s that in some jurisdictions, at least, marijuana had been de facto decriminalized (i.e., law enforcement officials tolerated and did not arrest users of the substance) (Mosher & Akins 2007).

In addition to the developments surrounding marijuana, some Canadian jurisdictions adopted harm reduction policies in order to address problems related to intravenous drug use. In the early 2000s, the city of Vancouver, British Columbia, had an estimated 12,000 intravenous drug users in a population of 1.3 million, and more than 4,500 of these users lived in a 12-block section of the city known as the downtown eastside. This area had a drug overdose rate that was five times higher than any other Canadian city, and the highest HIV infection rate of any jurisdiction in the Western world. More than 1,000 drug users died in this area over the course of a decade, with 416 overdose deaths in 1998 alone (Glionna, 2003). In response to this situation, Vancouver implemented a "four pillars" approach to drug issues—focusing on treatment, prevention, enforcement, and harm reduction—and established a safe drug injection facility (known as "Insite") for intravenous drug users (Mulgrew, 2007).

An evaluation of the first year of operation of this facility revealed that there were approximately 600 visits a day, and although there were more than 1,000 overdose cases, none were fatal. This study also found that the site led to reductions in the number of people injecting drugs in public in the downtown eastside of Vancouver, as well as fewer discarded syringes and less injection-related litter in the area (British Columbia Center for Excellence in HIV/AIDS, 2004; see also Wood et al., 2007). Participation in the safe injection facility was also associated with a 30% increase of entry into drug detoxification programs (Strathdee & Pollini, 2007), and a study published in the *Canadian Medical Journal* (Bayoumi & Zaric, 2008) estimated that Insite would save the province of British Columbia $14 million and prevent 1,000 HIV infections over a 10-year period. Several other more recent evaluations of this safe injection facility reported similarly positive results (Beyrer, 2011; Marshall, Milloy, Wood, Montaner, & Kerr, 2011; Pinkerton, 2010).

In addition to the Vancouver safe injection site, a special Canadian House of Commons committee on drug issues supported the creation of federally approved safe injection sites for hardcore users of heroin or cocaine, the expansion of methadone maintenance programs, and needle exchange programs (MacCharles, 2002). In response to the recommendations of this House of Commons report, Canada initiated a heroin maintenance study in 2003, the first of its kind implemented in North America. Under this program, which was initiated in the major metropolitan cities of Vancouver, Toronto, and Montreal, 80 heroin addicts in each city received free heroin and were able to inject the drug up to three times per day at a drug treatment center. Addicts also received counseling at the end of the first year and were to be weaned off heroin, or offered methadone withdrawal and counseling for an additional year (Carey, 2003). Evaluations of this program found that participating addicts experienced improved physical and mental health, and committed fewer crimes (Smith, 2009)[3].

Although space restrictions do not permit a complete accounting of these developments, drug policy discussions in several other European countries, including Britain, Germany, Spain, and in Australia and New Zealand emphasized harm reduction approaches, and several of these countries adopted certain aspects of the larger harm reduction philosophies. The harm reduction dialogue is also becoming increasingly prominent in Central and South American countries. For example, in 2009, the Latin American Commission on Drugs and Democracy, led by former Brazilian president Fernando Henrique Cardoso (and including former presidents Ernesto Zedillo of Mexico and Cesar Gaviria of Colombia) published a report which referred to the drug war led by the United States as a "failed war" and recommended that governments consider alternatives, including the decriminalization of marijuana (de Cordoba, 2009). Cardoso, Gaviria, and Zedillo also published an editorial in the *Wall Street Journal* in which they argued:

> In order to drastically reduce the harm caused by narcotics, the long-term solution is to reduce the demand for drugs in the main consumer countries ... We must start by changing the status of addicts from drug buyers in the illegal market to patients cared for by the public health system. ... By treating consumption as a matter of public health, we will enable police to focus their efforts on the critical issue: the fight against organized crime. (February 23, 2009)

More recently, the 2011 Global Commission on Drugs, whose members included the former presidents of Mexico, Brazil, and Columbia, the Prime Minister of Greece, former United Nations Secretary Kofi Annan, former U.S. Secretary of State George Schultz, and British billionaire Richard Branson, among others, called for radical changes in drug policy. The commission noted that its starting point was a recognition that the global drug problem is "a set of interlinked health and social problems to be managed rather than a war to be won" (2011, p. 4). The Commission report argued that drug policies should be guided by the following principles: (a) drug policies should be based on solid empirical and scientific evidence, and (b) drug policies must be based on human rights and public health principles.

Data from the drug policy experiments and developments discussed above (and those in other nations) suggest that less punitive drug control policy is a viable alternative to a strict criminalization model. Patterns of drug use do not appear to increase significantly following a shift to a less punitive approach, and may even decrease, particularly for hard drugs. There are also a number of ancillary benefits to users' health status, treatment participation, and reduced law enforcement and criminal justice system expenditures.

---

[3] While the developments described above indicate a move toward harm reduction drug policies in Canada, it is important to note that there is by no means consensus that drug policies in Canada should be softened. In particular, the current Canadian conservative federal government has attempted to shut down (unsuccessfully) the Insite safe injection facility and has proposed more severe penalties for some drug and drug-related crimes (MacQueen, 2010).

How Do We Fix It: Recent Developments in United States Drug Policies

A study by the National Center on Addiction and Substance Abuse (2009) estimated that in 2005, federal, state, and local governments spent at least $467.7 billion (combined) responding to substance abuse and addiction, which represents close to 11% of their (combined) $4.4 trillion budgets. The study also estimated that of every dollar spent by federal and state governments in 2005, only 1.9 cents was spent on prevention and treatment, 1.4 cents on taxation and regulation, 0.7 cents on interdiction of drugs, and 0.4 cents on drug-related research. The remaining funds were devoted to "shoveling up the wreckage", with health care costs totaling $207.2 billion and $47 billion on criminal justice system expenditures. The report noted that "the federal government spends more than 30 times as much to cope with the health consequences of addiction as it spends on prevention, treatment, and research" (p. 3). The key question is, how can we move beyond our costly, ineffective, and harmful policies toward drugs?

Bruce Alexander (1990) noted that one of the primary reasons drug policies are ineffective, and in many cases counterproductive, is that they are typically determined by national/federal law. He argued that one possible avenue to more rational and progressive drug regulations is for such laws to be "as local as possible" (p. 293). The policies allowing for medical use of marijuana in 19 states and the District of Columbia and recent developments in several states toward the legalization of marijuana suggest that many states are rethinking their severe policies toward drugs. While part of the impetus for these changes is related to a growing recognition that drug treatment can be effective, a number of states moved to relax their policies as a result of the costs associated with incarcerating large numbers of drug offenders.

Treatment in Lieu of Incarceration Laws

The state of California, which passed Proposition 215 (The Compassionate Use Act) allowing for the use of medical marijuana in 1996, also passed Proposition 36 (The Substance Use and Crime Prevention Act) in 2000. This legislation allowed individuals convicted of their first and second nonviolent drug possession offenses the option of participating in drug treatment instead of being incarcerated. The law also allowed offenders on probation or parole for certain offenses and after violations of drug-related provisions of their probation or parole to receive treatment in lieu of incarceration (Uelmen, Abrahamson, Appel, Cox, & Taylor, 2002). Individuals convicted of drug trafficking or other felony offenses were not eligible for this program. Although there have been some negative consequences associated with this legislation, in its first year of operation, Proposition 36 was estimated to have saved the state of California $275 million (Haake, 2003).

Sentencing Reductions

In recent years, there has been progress in reducing or eliminating some of the "tough on crime" sentencing practices that dominated the criminal justice system and resulted in significant changes to sentencing practices. In 2002, the state of Washington passed legislation that reduced by six months the 21- to 27-month mandatory minimum sentence for first-time convictions for trafficking in heroin and cocaine, and also eliminated the "triple-scoring" sentences for nonviolent drug offenders. This law was projected to save Washington state $45 million per year, with the money saved as a result of reductions in the length of sentences being devoted to funding drug courts in the state.

Also in Seattle, Washington, a 2003 ballot initiative required police to make marijuana possession their lowest law enforcement priority. Although (then) federal drug czar John Walters expressed opposition to this law, (then) Seattle Police Chief (and current drug czar in the Obama administration) Gil Kerlikowske, commented:

> The one thing that is pretty clear here is that there's strong recognition that the drug issues and the drug problem are not just a law enforcement or criminal justice problem . . . Just arresting the same people, putting handcuffs on the same people, makes no sense. (as quoted in Pope, 2003)

In 1973, the state of New York enacted legislation (known as the Rockefeller drug laws) that created mandatory minimum sentences of 15 years to life for possession of four ounces of drugs (this penalty was equivalent to the penalty for second degree murder in the state of New York). Similar to the federal drug legislation discussed above, these laws disproportionately affected African Americans (and to a lesser extent, Hispanics) and led to high levels of incarceration in the state of New York. After considerable opposition to these laws in the late 1990s and 2000s, New York Governor David Paterson in 2009 admitted that the laws were counterproductive and revised them. Under the revisions, mandatory minimum sentences for drug laws were removed, and judges were allowed to sentence drug offenders to shorter terms of incarceration, and also to order substance abusers to enter drug treatment programs in lieu of prison (Davis, 2012). Importantly, the changes in the New York legislation were retroactive, allowing more than 1,000 prisoners to apply to be resentenced (Canfield, 2009). It was estimated that the repeal of the Rockefeller drug laws would save the state of New York approximately $250 million per year, primarily in reduced incarceration costs (Hastings, 2009).

In 1995, the Sentencing Commission unanimously recommended to Congress that the 100 to 1 ratio between powder and crack cocaine for the purposes of sentencing be reduced to one to one. However, these recommendations were rejected by Congress and President Clinton. It wasn't until 2010 under the Obama administration that the ***Fair Sentencing Act*** was passed. Under this legislation, the gap between crack and powder cocaine sentencing ratios were narrowed from 100 to 1 to 18 to 1 (Douglas, 2010). Prior to the passage of this legislation, former Republican Congressman J. C. Watts and former Congressman and former head of the Drug Enforcement Administration Asa Hutchinson wrote an editorial in the *Washington Post* calling for the attorney general to change the law; earlier, Hutchinson implied that changing the federal crack cocaine law would flood the streets of the United States with violent felons. Watts and Hutchinson argued, "The truth is that for years our legal system has enforced an unfair approach to sentencing federal crack offenders. . . . it makes no sense that somebody arrested for a crack cocaine offense should receive a substantially longer prison term than somebody who is convicted of a powder cocaine offense" (Watts & Hutchinson, 2008). In defending the eventual change in this legislation, and acknowledging the harm done by the crack/powder cocaine distinction, Attorney General Eric Holder concurred with Watts and Hutchinson and commented, "There is simply no logical reason why their [crack cocaine users/traffickers] sentences should be more severe than those of other cocaine offenders" (as quoted in Serrano, Savage, & Williams, 2011). Under the change in this legislation, an estimated 12,000 federal prisoners, the vast majority of whom were from racial minority groups, were eligible for sentence reductions, with an average reduction of approximately three years (Schwartz, 2011). While this change should be viewed as a positive development in the larger context of drug policy, a federal appeals court judge in Chicago, noting that the disparity between crack and powder cocaine had not been completely eliminated, commented that the Act was misnamed, suggesting that instead it should have been called "the not quite as fair as it could be sentencing act" (as quoted in Liptak, 2011).

And, as Michelle Alexander (2010) comments, "merely reducing sentence length, by itself, does not disturb the basic architecture of the new Jim Crow" (p.14).

 ## Conclusion

While, as noted above, many Western nations address drug use as primarily public health issues and have implemented harm reduction policies to address substance use and abuse, the United States has a long history of dealing with drug problems through the criminal justice system. There is little evidence to suggest that criminal justice system responses to drug use are effective in reducing such use, and these policies simultaneously create a number of social and economic problems. The most problematic consequences of these policies are that they contribute significantly to unprecedented levels of incarceration in the United States and disproportionately impact members of minority groups and the lower social classes.

A 1997 publication from the Office of National Drug Control Policy asserted "the foremost objective of the Office of National Drug Control Policy is to create a national drug control strategy based on science rather than ideology" (p. 1). Similar sentiment was echoed in the 2012 National Drug Control Policy statement, which noted that the federal government's strategy to reduce drug use and its consequences would be based on a "collaborative, balanced, and science-based approach" (ONDCP, 2012, p. 1). In light of the policies and activities of the federal government with respect to drugs as reviewed above, this assertion needs to be questioned.

For many countries, the shift to a set of drug policies based on harm reduction principles transpired in recognition of the substantial challenges and costs, both social and financial, that accompany drug criminalization and their stringent enforcement. Throughout this chapter, we emphasized the challenges facing countries that adopted such policies. Conversely, harm reduction advocates emphasize policies that consider and attempt to balance the damage done by the *response* to drug use against the harms of drug use *per se*. As an analogy, Hunt (2005) urges us to consider the regulation of automobile use. He notes that although there are many hazards associated with driving—including considerable environmental damage, injuries, and deaths—elimination of driving is clearly not a realistic strategy. Instead, countries have enacted laws on speed limits, the control of vehicle emissions, and seat belt and other safety devices as harm reduction strategies to reduce the risks associated with the use of automobiles. Harm reduction policies involve similar goals for drug use.

Finally, while the passage of laws allowing for the medical use of marijuana, marijuana legalization measures, and the more general softening of drug policies in individual states may portend larger changes in drug policies in the United States, it appears as though the federal government feels as though such policies represent a threat to federal hegemony in the drug policy arena.

KEY TERMS

Criminalization	Drug policy	Mandatory minimum sentencing
Decriminalization	Fair Sentencing Act	
De facto legalization	Gateway drug	Mesh-tightening
Depenalization	Harm reduction	Net-widening
Drug court	Legalization	

DISCUSSION QUESTIONS

1. Discuss the key distinctions between forms of drug policy (criminalization, de facto legalization, decriminalization, legalization, harm reduction). What is the dominant form of drug policy in the United States?

2. Discuss racial disparities in the application/enforcement of drug laws in the United States. Why do these disparities exist (and persist)?

3. There are indications that U.S. drug policies may be "softening." Discuss the reasons for this, and examine recent developments in drug policies in your state.

WEBSITES FOR ADDITIONAL RESEARCH

Office of National Drug Policy: http://www.whitehouse.gov/ondcp

National Institute on Drug Abuse: http://www.drugabuse.gov/related-topics/criminal-justice-drug-abuse

UCLA Integrated Substance Abuse Programs: http://www.uclaisap.org/

Drug Policy Alliance: http://www.drugpolicy.org/

Substance Abuse and Mental Health Services Administration: http://www.samhsa.gov/

RAND Drug Policy Research Center: http://www.rand.org/multi/dprc.html

Bureau of Alcohol, Tobacco, Firearms and Explosives: http://www.atf.gov/

National Drug Research Institute (Australia): http://ndri.curtin.edu.au/

UK Drug Policy Commission (UK): http://www.ukdpc.org.uk/

Alcohol and Drug Findings (UK): http://findings.org.uk/aboutDAF.htm

CHAPTER

IX

Controlling the Sexual Offender

Chrysanthi Leon and Ashley Kilmer

While drug crimes now account for the largest share of offenses registered in the prison system, the proportion of sex offenders has also increased, partly due to the public and political fascination with these so-called "monstrous offenders" (Leon, 2011a). Since the 1980s, lawmakers at every level (municipal, state, and federal) have passed new laws and policies that focus on convicted sex offenders (Simon & Leon, 2007). These include mandatory reporting of suspected child abuse, community notification of registered sex offenders, and civil commitment (hospitalization) for some sex offenders (Meloy, Miller, & Curtis, 2008). This chapter follows the development of laws designed to control the sexual offender and highlights some of the challenges in the enforcement of these policies.

The Back Story on Sexual Offenders

In recent history, sex offenses, particularly those committed against children, often generate an intense reaction, which is observable in media coverage (Leon, 2011a). Few people would disagree that serious and repeated sex offending behavior is a severe social problem requiring attention (Wright, 2009). This attention and response on the part of society is typically in the form of passing legislation that outlines sanctions and community-based policy practices aimed at keeping sex offenders either incapacitated or closely supervised so that they can no longer victimize another child or adult. In theory, these laws are intended to prevent known sex offenders from committing further crimes (known as "*recidivism*") as well as provide safety and support to victims of sex offenses (Center for Sex Offender Management, 2008; Cohen & Jeglic, 2007; Ohio Department of Rehabilitation and Correction, 2007; Wright, 2009). However, the realities of these laws often deviate from the intended aims because of legislation and policies enacted irrationally without consideration of the potential unintended consequences of such overly restrictive, punitive actions (Farkas & Stichman, 2002; Mercado, Alverez, & Levenson, 2008).

Historians and criminologists argue about the relationship between ideas about sex crimes and their impact on policy and practice, but archival data show that since at least the 1920s, popular beliefs regarding specific problems of sex offenders and appropriate solutions have remained largely the same (Leon, 2011a). In particular, the public has long believed that sex offenders exhibit both moral degeneracy and compulsive sickness, and that such a confounding pathology requires preventative detention (like civil commitment) to stop any escalation into more serious crimes. While brief spurts of interest in treatment for sex offenders appeared in the 1960s, the general public believes that sex offender treatment is pointless.

One area of change involves the recognition of victims. Social movements have drawn attention to the general tendency to discredit victims and to dismiss women and children who protest their sexual abuse (Rose, 1977; Whittier, 2009). In what we might think of as the "bad old days" (although in some jurisdictions and among some practitioners these dismissive attitudes still prevail), the law and its agents sent the message that sexual violence and sexual offending were really "not so bad" (Frohmann, 1997). Professional discretion was used to divert some sexual offending entirely from the system, or to provide nuisance-worthy slaps on the wrist, while other offending was diverted into treatment, and a fraction of offenders received "deserved" punishment equivalent to other serious criminal offending. This shameful legacy is part of what creates the particular salience of contemporary efforts to prosecute sex crimes and to provide adequate punishment and protection for victims. As the experiments with treatment and diversion for sex offenders have failed in often dramatic ways (Leon 2011a), crime victim advocates use these examples to call for crackdowns on offenders. This is evident in the frequent passage of laws named in honor of child victims (Simon, 2007).

The criminal justice system and the larger political system continue to function against this historical backdrop. Part of addressing this legacy of leaving victims unprotected has meant efforts to increase capacities within criminal justice, such as improved training for police and prosecutors who respond to sex crime victims (Horney & Spohn, 1991), and the collection and attempts to process DNA evidence in the face of staggering backlogs in rape kits (Telsavaara & Arrigo, 2006). While these improvements are real and significant, far less has been achieved in terms of increased accountability for offenders (Beichner & Spohn, 2005). Specifically, despite public awareness and political pontificating on behalf of sex crime victims, convictions for forcible rape have remained relatively constant (Bachman & Paternoster, 1993), while "other sex offenses" (the category that counts all nonrape sex offenses) have increased (Leon, 2011a). Prosecutions for offenders who know their victims are less likely than for the stereotypical offense by a stranger (Tjaden & Thoennes, 2006); it is also true that sentences for non-stranger assailants remain shorter than sentences for stranger perpetrators (McCormick, Maric, Seto, & Barbaree, 1998), which reflects the persistent impacts of rape and sexual assault myths (e.g., widely accepted false beliefs that excuse sexual assault; see Burt, 1998).

Although most sex offenders are still not held accountable (see Figure 9.1, later in this chapter), the fraction who are charged, arrested, and convicted face much more stringent restrictions than in the past. While fears about sex criminals have long held purchase in the public's imagination (Freedman, 1987), today the kind of sexual offending that qualifies a person for inclusion in the category of dangerous sexual offender has spread to include offenders who in previous generations would have been handled informally or through therapeutic intervention (Leon, 2011a, pp. 43–44). For example, in the 1960s, prosecutors who were willing to plead down to misdemeanors did so knowing that the offenders could be civilly committed (i.e., using another form of social control to compensate for a lesser criminal charge). This type of discretion at the front end is now severely curtailed. In addition, more cases make it into the criminal justice system. Mandated reporting laws now trigger law enforcement proceedings in cases which, in previous eras, would have remained unreported. Although most of these new laws that reduce discretion and widen the net for sexual offenders originated in the states, eventually federal laws mandated compliance if states wished to continue receiving federal money for criminal justice. Altogether, this leaves little room for attorneys and judges to challenge predominant biases or to support alternative sanctions unless there is robust evidence against future dangerousness or deviance.

⊠ The Current State of the Policy

The current state of sex offender legislation differs from the past in that it shifted from a diverse set of tools that were used to divert and to punish sex offenders in varying ways, to a more or less one-size-fits-all policy of strict supervision of convicted offenders (both adult and juvenile) following their release back into the community. The intensive supervision of sex offenders is justified through high profile cases involving convicted (or alleged) sex offenders committing new sexual offenses against children, which include kidnapping, violence, and even homicide. The public's horror and outcry from these tragedies is often cited in the today's federally mandated sex offender notification and registration legislation as well as in many of the current local ordinances, including Megan's law and Jessica's law, to name a few.

Washington was the first state to enact legislation that regulated the management and supervision of sex offenders (Wright, 2009). These laws were passed in response to two cases of sexual assault and homicide against children. The first involved a sex offender named Wesley Dodd who molested, tortured, and ultimately killed three young boys. The second case involved an offender named Earl Shriner who kidnapped a 7-year-old boy, molested him, cut off his penis, and left him for dead. Both offenders had already served sentences for prior sex offenses, and both admitted that they planned to commit these offenses on their release from prison. In response, Washington's Community Protection Act of 1990 detailed new policies for the monitoring of sex offenders once they reenter the community following incarceration (Wright, 2009). While several states adopted similar legislation following the Washington cases, the first federal law of this kind was not enacted until 1994.

The *Jacob Wetterling Crimes Against Children and Sexually Violent Offender Registration Act of 1994* (Office of Justice Programs, n.d.) was the first federal law to require a statewide sex offender registration system. Jacob Wetterling was an 11-year-old boy who was abducted near his home in St. Joseph, Minnesota, by a masked stranger in 1989. While his body has never been found, his abduction closely mirrored the case of another boy who was abducted and sexually assaulted earlier that year, leading law enforcement to believe they were in search of a repeat sex offender. Jacob's mother, Patty Wetterling, actively fought for improved sex offender registration requirements in Minnesota and was appointed to a governor's task force to more formally fight for this legislation. In 1994, the United States Congress passed the Jacob Wetterling Crimes Against Children and Sexually Violent Offender Registration Act in honor of Jacob and his family. This Act amended the Violent Crime Control and Law Enforcement Act in order to mandate states to use 10% of their budget for law enforcement to establish a statewide sex offender registration system (Ohio Department of Rehabilitation and Correction, 2007; Sample & Bray, 2006). Sex offenders were required to provide their residential addresses to law enforcement, which then entered and maintained this information in a database (Ohio Department of Rehabilitation and Correction, 2007). This Act applied to all sex offenders equally, regardless of the type of offense they had committed, or their risk to reoffend.

In 1994, twice-convicted pedophile Jesse Timmendequas lured 7-year-old Megan Kanka to his home with the story that he had acquired a new puppy and that she was invited to see it. Timmendequas then sexually assaulted and murdered Megan (Sample & Bray, 2006). Although most known sex offenders will not commit a new sex crime, and only a tiny fraction commit homicide (Langevin, 2003; Zimring & Leon, 2008;), these crimes against children were given widespread media attention and prompted citizens to demand harsher monitoring of all sex offenders released from prison. Kanka's mother fought to change the existing law, arguing that the registration requirements outlined in the Jacob Wetterling Act were not sufficient to ensure community safety (Wright, 2009). In 1996, *Megan's Law* (named after Megan Kanka) required that registration information (originally required to be collected from offenders under the Jacob Wetterling Act) now be available to the public. This is known as *community notification*. As of the year 2000, all fifty states had developed a sex offender registry accessible to the public (Sample & Bray, 2006). Megan's Law also required that states have procedures in place for disseminating information to citizens regarding certain sex offenders who live or work in their communities (Ohio Department of Rehabilitation and Correction, 2007). Active community notification (when police distribute information about particular offenders) is usually reserved for offenders designated the highest risk to reoffend. However, public access to sex offender registration information is available for all sex offenders, regardless of their risk level (Cohen & Jeglic, 2007), including information on juveniles (Leon, Burton, & Alvare, 2011).

In 1996, the *Pam Lychner Sexual Offender Tracking and Identification Act* was also enacted at the federal level as a subsection of the Jacob Wetterling Act. This new act established a national database maintained by the FBI to track all sex offenders convicted of an offense against a minor or of a violent sexual offense (Logan, 2009). In 1996, Pam Lychner was a real estate agent preparing to show a vacant home to a potential buyer when the man who arrived at the house, a repeat sex offender, violently assaulted her (Office of Justice Programs, n.d.). As a direct result of her experience, Pam Lychner later founded "Justice for All," a victims' rights advocacy group that fought for harsher sentencing laws for violent offenders. She then assisted in drafting the bill that later became the Pam Lychner Sexual Offender Tracking and Identification Act to honor her, following her death in July of 1996 on TWA Flight 800 that crashed off the coast of Long Island (Office of Justice Programs, n.d.).

More legislation followed. In 2000, the United States Congress passed the *Campus Sex Crimes Prevention Act* (Logan, 2009) to further amend the *Violent Crime Control and Law Enforcement Act of 1994*. Under this new section of the Act, registered sex offenders are now required to report their attendance or employment at any higher education institutions. This information is entered into the state registries, and colleges and universities can request information from law enforcement agencies on sex offenders attending their school (Wright, 2009).

In addition to registration and notification laws, sex offenders are often subjected to restrictions on their residential, recreational, and employment choices. Communities can enact local ordinances that prohibit offenders from living a certain distance (usually 1,000 feet) from schools, parks, daycare centers, or other locations where children gather, regardless of whether the offender previously had a child or adult victim (Duwe, Donnay, & Tewksbury, 2008; Ohio Department of Rehabilitation and Correction, 2007;). In some instances, if the coverage of local ordinances is particularly dense, sex offenders may not be able to live in certain towns at all because they would always be within 1000 feet of a prohibited area (Ohio Department of Rehabilitation and Correction, 2007). In fact, in a study on residency restrictions in San Diego, results indicated that sex offenders could permissibly live in only 27% of the total amount of living space available in the city (Wartell, 2007, in Wright, 2009).

Finally, the Adam Walsh Child Protection and Safety Act of 2006 (H.R. 4472) was designed to fill in the gaps and close any loopholes discovered in the previous Acts that were passed in the 1990s. Title I of the *Adam Walsh Act* is the Sex Offender Registration and Notification Act (SORNA), which requires that sex offenders provide additional registration information, such as vehicle information and Internet identi-fiers, as well as requiring offenders to check in with law enforcement in person to update and verify their registration information on a regular basis (Ohio Department of Rehabilitation and Correction, 2007). Additionally, SORNA requires that DNA samples be taken and kept on file for all registered sex offenders.

Perhaps one of the most controversial and debated legislative responses to sex offending is the use of ***civil commitment*** to continue to incapacitate sex offenders. Civil commitment laws were originally cre-ated to treat and incapacitate mentally ill sex offenders (often coined "sexual psychopaths") who psy-chologists believed to be unable to control their sexual and violent impulses (Cohen & Jeglic, 2007); this treatment was offered instead of incarceration (Leon, 2011a). This kind of civil commitment as an alterna-tive to prison was aligned with the popular belief at the time that sexual offending was a psychological disorder, and that with enough time, could be "cured" (Leon, 2011a). During the 1950s, this legislation, which was originally designed to incapacitate dangerous sex offenders like serial killer Albert Fish, was also applied to homosexuals, and to individuals who engaged in non-contact sexual behaviors like exhibi-tionism (Leon, 2011a, pp. 80–81, 94–96; Wright, 2009). Although states' definitions of "sexual psychopath" varied widely, all states required that in order to be committed, a sex offender must have an existing men-tal illness and present a danger to themselves or others. Once a committed offender was deemed as no longer a threat to themselves or others, they were then able to be released. However, it is extremely difficult to assess whether someone is truly suffering from a mental illness, whether their illness is cured or in remission, or more importantly, whether they present a danger to themselves or others (Wright, 2009).

While this earlier generation of civil commitment laws fell out of favor, the wave of attention brought to child sexual abuse in the 1990s led to a new approach: Incarcerated sex offenders nearing the end of their sentence could be transferred to a hospital for indefinite civil commitment. The Adam Walsh Act also contained Section 301 (called the "Jimmy Ryce State Civil Commitment Program for Sexually Dangerous Persons") that provided grants to states to once again develop civil commitment programs for eligible offenders, illustrating the continued popularity of indefinite incapacitation of sexual offenders. By 2007, twenty states plus the federal government had enacted new civil commitment provisions for sex offenders—all following the model of Washington state's law. These civil commitment laws provided a way to keep sex offenders incapacitated and locked up, even after they had served their entire sentences. While the stated goal of civil commitment is to provide treatment to sex offenders, research has indicated that most civilly committed sex offenders actually do not receive any sex-offender specific treatment dur-ing their commitment. In California, one study found that only 20% of civilly committed sex offenders received any type of sex-offender oriented treatment, even though the stated primary reason for the com-mitment was to receive treatment (Cohen & Jeglic, 2007). Since the commitment is based on treatment without a definite length of sentence, sex offenders could be (and have been) locked up indefinitely. Civil commitment also carries with it an extreme cost—more than the cost of incarceration and outpatient treatment. As of 2000, it costs states on average $350 dollars per day for each sex offender who was civilly committed, which is far more than the daily costs per inmate of most prisons (Cohen & Jeglic, 2007).

It is clear from the current trend in sex offender legislation that citizens are fearful of sex offenders committing future offenses, particularly against children. As a result, society is supportive of harsh, restrictive legislation that keeps all sex offenders, regardless of their offense, under very strict supervision and provides offender information to the public so that individuals are aware of sex offenders living in their area (Craun & Theriot, 2009). However, current legislation and policy are not grounded in empirical evidence regarding sex offender behavior; recent scholarship disputes that these policies actually result in less sexual offending, reduced sexual recidivism, or greater community safety (Leon, 2011b).

Policy makers' and legislators' perceptions of sexual offending behavior influence the policies that they draft and support (Sample & Kadleck, 2008). A study done in Illinois found that legislators who were involved in drafting sex offender legislation or actively supported sex offender legislation frequently reported believing that sex offender recidivism was higher than recidivism rates for other types of crimes, and that sex offenders were mentally ill and dangerous. The legislators surveyed also reported that they used media to gain information about the scope of the "sex offender problem" in the United States (Sample & Kadleck, 2008). This study lends support to the belief that much sex offender legislation is fueled by misperceptions about sex offending behavior (often developed as a result of high profile cases portrayed in the media). Legislators feel that if they create legislation that requires the close supervision of sex offenders that the "sex offender problem" is lessened. The assumptions behind such legislation are (a) all sex offenders recidivate at high levels, (b) if sex offenders are closely monitored by law enforcement agencies and their presence is well known in the community, they have less opportunity to commit a new sex offense, and (c) these laws prevent non-sex offenders from committing a first offense. If these assumptions are true, then empirical research should validate the assumptions listed above. This is not the case.

What Research Has Taught Us

As evidenced by the fact that most national sex offender legislation is named after the victims of particularly tragic cases, these policies tend to be fueled by emotional responses to such tragedies. It turns out that the empirical evidence often contradicts the emotional impulse.

Sex Offenders and Repeat Crimes (Recidivism)

Commonly held beliefs among the public and policy makers view all sex offenders as a similar group of deviant offenders who prefer to target strangers and have high rates of repeat offending. Research on sex offender characteristics and behavior found that these beliefs are not true. In reality, sex offenders are neither specially deviant, nor specialists in terms of sticking to sex offenses. Before addressing these facts, it is important to recognize that those sex offenders who are available for study typically include only those who have been caught by criminal justice officials or who have sought treatment. As depicted in Figure 9.1, this limits our knowledge of the larger group of sexual offenders. All sex offenders who fall in the dark section of the largest circle, outside the smaller circles, have not been detected by authorities: they are lost in the "dark field." As a result, available research is limited to those offenders detected by criminal justice authorities or who are engaged in treatment, either voluntarily or under order by the justice system) (e.g., see Becker, Stinson, Tromp, & Messer, 2003). As Figure 9.1 indicates, most sex offenders are unknown and unstudied.

Notwithstanding the dark field, we do know that convicted sex offenders are actually a highly diverse group of offenders with a multitude of different characteristics, victim preferences, and motivations for offending (Robertiello & Terry, 2007); very few have a psychiatric disorder. Studies of sex offenders in correctional and clinical samples provided a number of different models for explaining sexually deviant conduct. For most offenders, these explanations involve a combination of factors, as opposed to the fictional account of a compulsive offender who cannot resist a pathological urge. While mental illness plays a role in some offending, for the majority of offenders, it does not (See, generally, Strassberg, Eastvold, Kenney, & Suchy, 2012; Marshall, 2007).

Most sex offenders are like other criminal offenders: People convicted of sex crimes are typically generalists with other criminal involvements. A large representative sample in 1994 of 38,000 offenders

Figure 9.1	Limitations to Sex Offender Studies

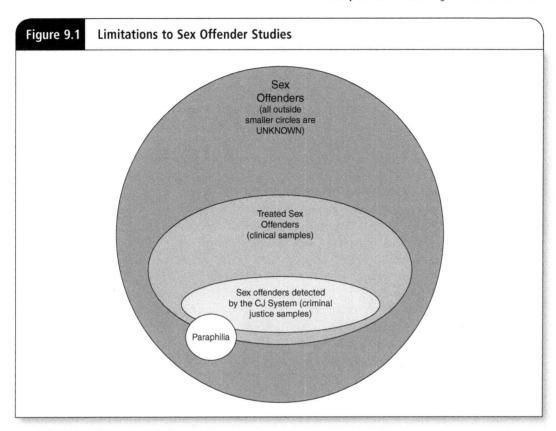

released from prison in 15 states demonstrates what many other studies also ascertained (Miethe, Olson, & Mitchell, 2006). Miethe and colleagues found that the "sex offenders" in their sample (released prisoners who were most recently incarcerated for a sex offense) had criminal records showing far *less **specialization*** than other offender types. Rather than "sex offenders," they were criminals who had a recent sex offense in their history along with other kinds of offending: The longer the criminal record of the sex offender, the less likely they were to be specialists. This contrasted with prisoners incarcerated for property and public order offenses, who were more likely to specialize in these types of offenses, the longer their criminal career.

Another piece of the misunderstanding surrounding sex offenders includes their relationship to victims. Most sexual offense victims are assaulted or abused by someone they know, not attacked or abducted by a stranger. In fact, almost 50% of all sexual abuse against children under the age of six, and approximately 42% of sexual abuse offenses against children between the ages of six and eleven, are committed by a relative of the child (Craun & Theriot, 2009). In terms of sexual offenses involving adult victims, one survey found that nearly 98% of female victims reported knowing the perpetrator (Craun & Theriot, 2009). This particular misperception results in public support for legislation that requires sex offender registration information to be available to the general public, community notification policies, and residency restrictions, all of which may be misleading the public. While a community resident worries about the sex offender who lives two blocks away, they are unaware or ignore the fact that acquaintances and relatives are much more likely to pose the real threat.

Finally, recidivism rates for sex offenders are not as high as the public perceives. Research on sex offender recidivism found that not only do recidivism rates vary by offender characteristics (e.g., type of offense, relationship to victim, etc.), but are relatively low (Sample & Bray, 2006). Despite our gut feeling that sex offenders must be repeat offenders, many decades of empirical research demonstrates that most convicted sex offenders do not commit new crimes (Zimring & Leon, 2008).

A large representative sample of released prisoners were followed for three years, and the results reveal that *sex offenders are less likely to re-offend* (Langan & Levin, 2002, pp. 6–8). See Figure 9.2, which shows that the majority of those prisoners were arrested at least once within 3 years of release (67.5%, shown by the large white circle). Figure 9.2 also includes two smaller circles which show who committed new sex offenses: The shaded circle shows that 22% of those prisoners who were not called sex offenders (i.e., they were in prison for something else, and thus were not on the registry) subsequently committed a new offense that was a sex offense. This is in striking contrast to the small circle that represents repeat sex crimes: Just 5.3% of those prisoners were called sex offenders (i.e., they were incarcerated for a prior sex offense) and then went on to commit new sex crimes.

Another way to appreciate the low recidivism rate for sex offenders is to compare them with other kinds of offenders. In the same study, offenders with the highest rearrest rates were those who stole motor vehicles (78.8%), those who possessed or sold stolen property (77.4%), and burglars (74.0%) (Langan & Levin, 2002). Those with the lowest rearrest rates for any kind of crime were rapists (46.0%), those who committed sexual assault (41.4%), and those convicted of homicide (40.7%).

This finding of low recidivism is confirmed by studies with longer follow-up periods. A meta-analysis (a study which combines numerous studies and controls for variation in the study design) with an average follow-up of 4 to 5 years found an average sex offense recidivism rate of 13.4% ($N = 23,393$; 18.9% for 1,839 rapists and 12.7% for 9,603 child molesters) (Hanson & Bussiere, 1998; see also Hanson & Morton-Bourgon, 2004). These results are also evident in state-specific studies. For example, in a report to the Ohio

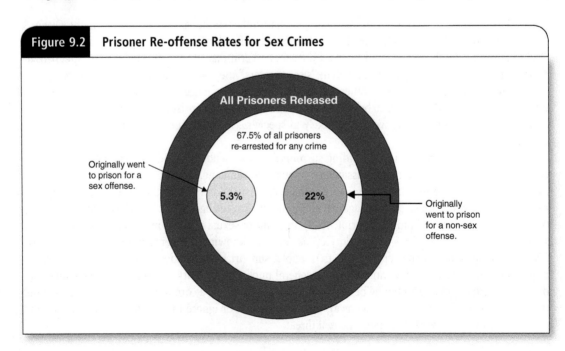

Figure 9.2   Prisoner Re-offense Rates for Sex Crimes

All Prisoners Released

67.5% of all prisoners re-arrested for any crime

Originally went to prison for a sex offense.

5.3%

22%

Originally went to prison for a non-sex offense.

Sentencing Commission in 2005, it was reported that Ohio sex offenders had a recidivism rate of only 8% for a sex-related offense and 14% for a non-sex offense during a 10-year follow-up period (Office of Criminal Justice Services, 2006).

The Impact of Laws on Known and Unknown Offenders

Research conducted in the years following the enactment of current sex offender policies evaluates the impact on reducing sex offender recidivism. Early studies found mixed results for the effectiveness of registration and notification legislation, as well as for residency restrictions (Center for Sex Offender Management, 2008). Some states have reported that offender registration and notification laws have deterred offenders from recidivating and have found significantly lower rates of recidivism in groups that are required to register compared to offender recidivism rates prior to the implementation of registration laws. However, these studies lack methodological rigor, and are also offset by studies from other states that found no such impacts; some studies even indicated that these laws may actually be contributing to *increases* in offenders' risk to recidivate (Center for Sex Offender Management, 2008). Research also indicated that sex offender legislation is associated with a false sense of security in citizens (since most offenders victimize someone who is known to them, not strangers in their neighborhood), increased hostility and vigilantism against sex offenders by community members, and obstacles for offenders seeking housing and employment (Center for Sex Offender Management, 2008).

It is evident from this research that commonly held beliefs regarding sex offenders and their behavior are not accurate. However, sex offender legislation and policies continue to use these misperceptions and justifications for laws that impact nearly every sex offender, regardless of their risk to reoffend, creating overly restrictive and punitive conditions of supervision that may result in an array of negative consequences. A report to the Ohio Criminal Sentencing Commission in 2006 listed several unintended consequences of the state's registration and notification laws. These included misleading the public, negatively impacting family members of offenders and victims, hindering offender reentry, increasing displacement, increasing vandalism and retribution, and a reluctance to report offenses (Office of Criminal Justice Services, 2006). Furthermore, the report suggested that some of these issues increase an offender's stress level and sense of isolation, two factors that play a significant role in an offender's risk to reoffend (Office of Criminal Justice Services, 2006). Research on sex offender legislation and policies primarily focused on offender registration and community notification practices and whether these strategies at supervising sex offenders resulted in lower rates of recidivism among convicted sex offenders. An early study in 1995 was one of the first outcome studies examining the effectiveness of community notification laws (Schram & Milloy, 1995). This study was conducted in Washington and examined the rearrest rates of 90 sex offenders who operated under the highest level of notification and 90 matched offenders who were released prior to the enactment of the notification law. At the end of a 54-month follow-up period for both offense groups, the authors report that there were no significant differences in rearrest rates for the two groups. However, the authors state that the findings, while not statistically significant, tend to suggest that the sex offenders in the community notification group were rearrested at a quicker rate than the group that were released prior to the enactment of the law. Despite the limitations of this early study (particularly, the small sample of sex offenders used in analyses), the findings do not support the effectiveness of community notification practices in reducing recidivism.

A more recent study by Sandler, Freeman, and Socia on the effectiveness of New York's registration and notification laws was published in 2008. This study used time-series analyses to examine arrest rates for sexual offenses before and after the implementation of New York's Sex Offender Registration Act (executed in 1996) in order to see whether the laws reduced recidivism rates or deterred first-time offenders. The authors used data from the New York State offender criminal history files provided by the New York State Division of Criminal Justice Services. Twenty-one years of New York State monthly arrest counts were collected beginning in January 1986 (ten years prior to the enactment of the registration and notification law) to December of 2006, eleven years following the enactment of the law (Sandler, Freeman, & Socia, 2008). Results indicated that the enactment of the registration and notification laws had no significant impact on rates of sexual offending (total sex offenses, rapes, and child molestations). More importantly, the study also revealed that approximately 95% of arrests for sexual offenses (both before and after the enactment of the registration and notification law) were first-time sex offenders, not new offenses by previously convicted sex offenders (recall Figure 9.2). Therefore, the vast majority of sex offenses were committed by individuals who were not listed and would never have been on a sex offender registry (following the enactment of the law). The authors concluded that the legislation, which was originally designed to limit convicted sex offenders' opportunities to recidivate, targets only a very small percentage of those committing sexual offenses and is ineffective at deterring first-time offenders who are committing the vast majority of offenses (Sandler et al., 2008).

Studies that examined the impact of residency restriction ordinances focused on whether these policies reduced the risk of sex offenders coming into contact with potential victims, particularly children. A 2008 study found that only a handful of the offenders in their sample made direct contact with a child victim that was located within one mile of their residence. In addition, of those offenders who did make direct contact with a victim, none of them did so near a school, park, daycare center, or any other location that is typically included in the residency restriction statutes. These findings fail to support the effectiveness of these types of policies at reducing victimization of children (Duwe, Donnay, & Tewksbury, 2008).

Some critics of current sex offender legislation posit that these overly punitive laws may actually lead to an increase in recidivism and sexual violence, citing the tenets of criminological theories (Wakefield, 2006). Wakefield described the harmful effects of registration and notification laws and residency restrictions, in the context of labeling theory and secondary deviance. The author states that these laws lead offenders to feel stigmatized, isolated, and rejected by their community, obstacles that they may feel they can never overcome. The negative feelings associated with these obstacles may lead offenders to engage in a self-fulfilling prophecy and ultimately commit a new offense (Wakefield, 2006).

According to social control theory, social bonds keep individuals from initially engaging in deviant behavior, and may possibly be what prevents offenders from engaging in future criminal acts (Kilmer, 2012). Close ties with family members, engagement in conventional activities like employment, and connectedness to one's community through involvement in community activities (all of which are considered important social bonds) are extremely difficult to secure for sex offenders once they reenter society following incarceration. As a result, offenders may feel isolated, alienated, and frustrated all of which are shown to be linked to an increased risk for recidivism (Ohio Department of Rehabilitation and Correction, 2007; Tewksbury & Zgoba, 2010). Therefore, overly harsh sex offender legislation and policies, particularly residency restrictions, may be preventing sex offenders from developing strong social bonds and ultimately be responsible for increasing the offender's risk to recidivate (Levenson, 2006; Levenson & Cotter, 2005; Levenson & Hern, 2007).

When all sex offenders are grouped together as a homogeneous, high-risk population, legislation is applied to every offender, which potentially reduces the benefits of these laws and could possibly contribute to recidivism. The current sex offender legislation requires law enforcement to monitor and supervise all sex offenders, regardless of their offense type. In addition, offense type, not individualized risk assessment, typically determines the duration and conditions for the offender's registration and contact with law enforcement (Leon et al., 2011).

Therefore, agencies are overburdened with the number of offenders they have to supervise, and officers may not be able to provide the level of supervision that is required, which can result in high-risk offenders slipping through the cracks. Some argue that resources are better used if they are focused only on those offenders at highest risk to recidivate rather than every offender equally (Leon et al., 2011). That way, high-risk offenders are placed under careful supervision, and low-risk offenders can more easily reintegrate back into society, thus lowering their sense of isolation and stress, and ultimately reducing their risk to reoffend (Robbers, 2009). It is therefore important for legislators to realize that sex offenders are a very heterogeneous group with varying motivations for their behavior as well as other unique characteristics that influence their risk to recidivate.

Race, Gender, and Class Implications of the Policy

Feminists and advocates are troubled by the lack of progress in holding sex offenders accountable, and this may be partly attributed to the misleading sense of accomplishment which popular sex offender laws perpetuate (Janus, 2006; Leon, 2011a; Schultz, 2005). By focusing on the subgroup of sex offenders who have been caught and convicted (recall Figure 9.1, which illustrates how many offenders remain unknown), we assuage our fears and concerns, but do little to impact future sex crimes or the structural conditions, including views of women and other rape myths that allow sexual violence to continue (Burt, 1998; Frohmann, 1997). Research also shows that sex offender legislation may perpetuate racial and economic inequality. In a study with the general conclusion that the unintended consequences of residency restrictions dramatically overshadow their purported benefit, Socia (2011) demonstrates how offenders are pushed into overpopulated areas, which has particular implications for economically disadvantaged offenders and for impoverished neighborhoods. In an examination of counties in upstate New York that are representative of the typical parcel density found throughout the United States, Socia measured effects on housing availability, affordability, and social disorganization. He found that sex offenders who must move into the least restricted neighborhoods under the most severe residence restrictions have few housing or rental options. If these few sparsely populated neighborhoods do not contain enough housing for all sex offenders who might have to move there, then homelessness likely increases, which further inhibits the ability to manage and support the offender in the community. Several other recent articles further examined the collateral consequences of these laws on particular communities (Hughes & Burchfield, 2008; Hughes & Kadleck, 2008; Mustaine, Tewksbury, & Stengel, 2006; Zevitz, 2004).

Sex Offenses Committed by Youths

When youth under age 18 are caught engaged in sexual contact, including sexual acts involving force, or with much older youth sexually touching younger children, but also including mutually agreed-on sexual contact, those youth can be taken to court and *adjudicated delinquent* on sex charges (the juvenile court system does not use the word "convicted" in order to avoid stigmatizing youth and to distinguish them from adult proceedings). Prosecutors can also waive these youth to adult court if they feel the charges are serious enough. Approximately 15 to 17% of reported sex offenses are committed by youth (Andrade, Vincent, & Saleh, 2006; Miner, 2002). While some juveniles may offend as a result of motivations similar to their adult counterparts, juveniles may also have unique motivators that are typically not found in adult offender populations and therefore may have different risk factors and treatment needs (Andrade et al., 2006; Miner, 2002).

Importantly, research also shows that young people who commit sex crimes rarely grow up to be adult sex offenders. Most recently, Zimring and his colleagues examined a Philadelphia birth cohort, which included 13,160 boys and 14,000 girls born in 1958 and followed them through age twenty-six (Zimring, Jennings, Piquero, & Hays, 2009). Even though they used a more inclusive measure than is typically used (police contact as opposed to arrest, adjudication, or conviction), the data did not show a connection between juvenile sexual offending and adult sexual offending.

However, many of the legal and clinical responses to juvenile sexual offending mirror responses seen in the adult population. Stemming from the misconceptions of adult sex offending, legislators fear that juvenile sex offending is becoming increasingly widespread and that juveniles have a high risk of recidivism, similar to their adult counterparts (Letourneau & Miner, 2005). Despite the research, youth adjudicated as sex offenders are subjected to more severe and longer sentences than other juvenile offenders and in some states, they are also subjected to registration, community notification, and civil commitment (Chaffin, 2008; Letourneau & Miner, 2005); under the Adam Walsh Act, just like adult offenders, juveniles are included in public registries, although a few states refused to comply (Freeman & Sandler 2010).

How Do We Fix It? Suggestions for Policy Reform

Advocates and policy makers face public pressures to "do something" about sexual offending, and this overshadows the use of empirical evidence to reform public policies: Symbolic responses often take precedence over implementation concerns and related unintended consequences. Attempts to reform the laws have to be framed in terms of real advances in addressing sexual violence. This requires an emphasis on the harms done by sweeping all sexual offending into the same category and the related dilution of law enforcement and other resources.

Reform efforts must differentiate. For example, fixes to the current broad laws should be framed as reallocating resources to focus on the truly dangerous. The Jaycee Lee Duggard/Phillip Garrido case is an illustrative one: Had the California probation officers assigned to visit Garrido been able to focus on a small caseload of high-risk offenders, then there is the likelihood that they would have provided more than cursory oversight of his house and would have identified the kidnap and rape victim Jaycee Lee Duggard rather than allowing him to terrorize her for eighteen years (Strobel, 2009).

Reformers who challenge sex offender policies must be wary of supporting any recommended changes that appear to go "soft" on sex offenders. This can be done by emphasizing that most needed reforms come *after punishment*. Amendments to registration and residency restriction policies do not change the available sentence structure for sex offenses (Leon et al., 2011). Reforms instead address the separate issue of more sensibly managing sex offenders *after their punishment* to bring policies in line with facts, not emotions.

KEY TERMS

Adam Walsh Act

Campus Sex Crimes Prevention Act

Civil commitment

Community notification

Jacob Wetterling Crimes Against Children and Sexually

Violent Offender Registration Act of 1994

Megan's Law

Pam Lychner Sexual Offender Tracking and Identification Act

Recidivism

Specialization

Violent Crime Control and Law Enforcement Act of 1994

DISCUSSION QUESTIONS

1. There is a great deal of controversy surrounding civil commitment laws. Explain the controversy.

2. How do sex offender recidivism rates and patterns compare to criminals convicted of nonsexual offenses?

3. Describe the similarities and differences between the Jacob Wetterling Act, Megan's Law, and the Pam Lychner Act.

WEBSITES FOR ADDITIONAL RESEARCH

Association for the Treatment of Sexual Abusers: http://www.atsa.com/

National Conference of State Legislators: http://www.ncsl.org/issues-research/justice/sex-offender-enactments-database.aspx

Center for Sex Offender Management: http://www.csom.org/

National Institute of Justice: http://www.nij.gov/

Vera Institute: http://www.vera.org/

Urban Institute: http://www.urban.org/

CHAPTER

X

Public Policy and White-Collar and Corporate Crime

Henry N. Pontell and Gilbert Geis

White-collar and corporate crime constitute one of the more intransigent problems confronting law enforcement in the United States and, indeed, throughout the world. The core difficulty is that by definition these offenses are committed by persons who have power in the worlds of business, politics, or the professions. The status of white-collar criminals is reflected in the biases in criminal codes that favor them. In addition, efforts to discover and penalize white-collar and corporate crimes are largely in the hands of persons with the same background and beliefs as those who are perpetrating the offenses. Take one glaring example: the lobbying of legislators. This is an obvious form of bribery. But, the definition of bribery is established by the same legislators who are bribed by the lobbyists, who most assuredly expect some quid pro quo in the nature of favorable legislative treatment. Typically, the lobbyists get what they have paid for, and often a great deal more. In 1707, the English satirist Jonathan Swift repeated a telling comment that had been made by a prominent church official some six centuries earlier: "Laws are like cobwebs which may catch small flies, but let wasps and hornets break through" (Swift, 1707, p. 19).

Illustrative of lobbying tactics was the 2012 conviction of Zehy Jesus and Sandy Annabi in a New York federal district court in one of the rare instances of a successful bribery prosecution. In a city just north of Manhattan, Mr. Jesus gave Ms. Annabi, the majority leader of the city council in Yonkers, $195,000. She then changed her pivotal vote in regard to approval of a controversial luxury mall and housing complex that Mr. Jesus wanted to construct. The defense claimed that the money was really an expression of Mr. Jesus's intense love of the recipient, stressing that he had lost 150 pounds over four years in order to impress her, and that he had showered her with gifts. "It was not her vote, but her body he sought," Jesus's lawyer maintained in his rather brazen opening statement (Weiser, 2012). Perhaps the defense attorney concluded during the jury selection process that a formidable number of members of the panel hearing the case were streetwise and cynical New Yorkers.

There are many reasons why a campaign against the massive problem of white-collar and corporate crime is exceedingly difficult to accomplish, and we subsequently detail some of these considerations in this chapter, along with establishing the background and current context in which white-collar crimes and corporate offenses take place.

The Back Story

Throughout recorded time, naysaying prophets have preached against the perils of unbridled power, which is employed only for self-interest in order to enrich those who exercise it, at the expense of those in inferior positions. Middlemen who profited from the productive labor of farmers were treated scornfully in the Bible as were usurers, or persons who lent money and expected more in return than they had advanced. It was only in the Middle Ages that prominent theologians began to locate divine justification for the accumulation of wealth at the expense of the polity.

In the United States, the prime motivation for the revolution that resulted in the separation of the colonies from the British Empire appears to have been an attempt to create a republic, as contrasted to a monarchy, in which leadership was placed in the hands of persons (only men at the time, and not Black men) who would duplicate the idyllic times during the Augustan epoch in the Roman empire (Galinsky, 1998; Reinhold & Alessi, 1978). The leaders served without pay and equitably advanced the interests of the entire population. Exemplifying this ideal was Samuel Adams of Massachusetts, one of the United States' Founding Fathers. As one of his biographers observes, Adams was educated at Harvard College and was, "a character out of the classical [that is, Roman] past" (Maier, 1980, p. 37). Another writer indicates that Adams had "neither personal ambition nor the desire for wealth. He ... gloried in his poverty" (Wood, 2011, p. 140).

The utopian dream of disinterested and nonpartisan leadership disappeared in short order. As the Pulitzer Prize–winning historian Gordon Wood pointed out:

> Far from sacrificing their private good for the good of the whole, Americans of the early Republic came to see that the individual's pursuit of wealth or happiness (the two were now interchangeable) were not only inevitable, but justifiable in a free state. (Wood, 2011, p. 75)

Over more than two centuries of existence, it is this view that prevails in America.

The unsavory history of behavior that now would be regarded as white-collar crime permeates the chronicles of bygone U.S. history. The most glaring financial skullduggery took place in connection with the construction of the railroads. The so-called Robber Barons (Josephson, 1934) bribed members of Congress to grant them funds to build railroad tracks across the continent, and then developed schemes that allowed them to personally pocket a goodly portion of the public funds that they were awarded. "The Southern Pacific Railroad," it has been pointed out, "under the rapacious and unscrupulous leadership of Collis Huntington was widely believed to dictate policy to the legislature and to dispose of California state matters generally as best suited its own interests" (Turner, 1985, p. 140). It was an accurate belief (Lewis, 1938). Another commentator summed up the nefarious activities of the railroad moguls, describing the perpetrators as "cold-hearted, sordid, selfish men" (Boardman, 1977, p. 62).

Investigative writers, who came to be known as muckrakers, also exposed a series of notorious scandals. They focused on matters such as corruption in the politics of the country's major cities (Steffens, 1904), abominable conditions in the Chicago meat-packing plants (Sinclair, 1906), and monopoly practices in the oil industry (Tarbell, 1904). As the years went by, there was no letup in the big-time law breaking by a roster of persons with the power to do so, culminating in the Great American Meltdown that began in 2008. There typically are half-hearted policy reactions to glaring misdeeds when they are brought to the attention of the public and the politicians. Generally, the actions by legislators went only so far as they believed necessary to placate their middling-class constituents, and not so far as to alienate the rich who financed their campaigns. For instance, the Sherman Antitrust Act was passed in 1890 to try to eliminate monopolistic practices that undercut the ideal of an open competitive marketplace, but the Act was enforced in a languid manner, initially singling out labor unions for prosecution. The Department of Justice filed only nine cases during the five years following passage of the Act, and merely 22 cases during the Act's first 22 years of existence (Dewey, 1990). Typical of this early period was an unsuccessful 1895 government antitrust lawsuit *United States v. E. C. Knight.* The Supreme Court declared that the E.C. Knight Company, which controlled 98% of the country's sugar-refining capacity, was a monopoly of "manufacture" and not of "commerce," and was therefore exempt from the reach of the **Sherman Act**, although the company obviously entered into commerce when selling the sugar that it refined (*United States v. E. C. Knight,* 1895).

Subsequently, the Sherman Act was sustained by the Clayton Act, the Robinson-Patman Act, and other measures. This strengthened law was employed by the **Federal Trade Commission (FTC)** to force motion picture producers and distributors to divest themselves of the theaters that they owned and that they favored over competitors when releasing films (*United States v. Paramount Pictures,* 1948, 1949). Over time, studios were also ordered to end illegal tying relationships where outlets were allowed to screen top-rated films only if they agreed to simultaneously rent "oaters," low-budget westerns that filled out the double-feature, newsreel, and serial (e.g., *Perils of Pauline*) productions that constituted the movie showings of the time (Conant, 1960).

Antitrust enforcement subsequently was eviscerated by economists, mainly academics, who pretended to predict the future of amalgamations and pricing tactics of powerhouse companies. It is not unreasonable to suspect that the economists' ideological preferences played a considerable part in their speculative ventures as well as those of the courts that came to rely on these murky crystal-ball readings. Wal-Mart, for instance, prevailed in a leading antitrust case in American courts (*Wal-Mart Drug Stores v. American Drugs* (1995; Kelley, 1997), but was considered by the German Supreme Court to illegally stifle competition, among a myriad of other specifications of wrongdoing. Wal-Mart ceased operations in Germany and publicly proclaimed that it had learned a lesson.

This is not to say that regulatory oversight does not accomplish some worthwhile ends. Just as we will never know how many persons are inhibited from committing murder, not because of their conscience, but because they fear the legal consequences, we will never know how many possible white-collar criminals are deterred from violating the law because of the law itself.

The FDA, Thalidomide, and RUR-426

There also are exemplary illustrations of regulatory vigilance in the United States that prevented what otherwise could have become tragic disasters. Probably the best known involved the **Food and Drug Administration (FDA)** and the marketing of the medication Thalidomide. The original 1907 law that established the FDA was strengthened in 1938 after more than one hundred people, mostly children, died from taking a sulphanilamide preparation mixed with a toxic chemical that was added to sweeten its taste (Carpenter, 2010; Hilts, 2003). The resulting legislation was characteristic of remedial actions that so often are taken only after severe damage aroused the public.

Thalidomide was developed in the early 1950s in West Germany by Chemie Grünthal, a German pharmaceutical company, and was marketed vigorously as an antidote to a range of human health problems, most particularly morning sickness during the early stage of pregnancy. By 1907, an estimated one million Germans were taking the drug on a daily basis. The producing company advertised what proved to be an ill-fated claim:

> In pregnancy and during the lactation period, the female organism is under great stress. Sleeplessness, unrest, and tension are constant complaints. The administration of a sedative that will hurt neither the mother nor the child is now possible. (Teff & Munro, 1976, p. 1)

Thalidomide proved to have teratogenic effects. In West Germany, about 4,000 children suffered birth defects known as phocomelia, deformities, such as abnormally formed limb growth, stunted arms and legs, misshapen hands and feet, as well as damaged internal organs. By the time the drug was withdrawn in 1960, some 10,000 children in 46 countries were born deformed from their mother's use of thalidomide during the first trimester of their pregnancy.

Frances Kelsey was a medical officer in the federal Food and Drug Administration in Washington when she determined that thalidomide was unfit for sale in the United States, despite intense pressure from the pharmaceutical company that acquired the right to market it in America. Kelsey had a degree in pharmacology from McGill University in Canada and had coauthored a text on the subject. She also possessed a PhD and a medical degree. Of particular importance was the fact that she previously worked as an editor of *Journal of the American Medical Association (JAMA)*. When she took the job at the FDA, she remembered that many of the scientifically poor articles submitted to *JAMA* extolling the virtues of a new drug were written by the same physicians who purported to have conducted research about the value and safety of pharmacological products that were now seeking FDA approval.

More than 500 samples of Thalidomide were distributed by its American outlet to doctors, but fortunately almost all were given to patients who were past the first pregnancy trimester. Because of Kelsey's wariness and integrity, only 17 American children were born with thalidomide-produced deformities. Most of their mothers acquired the drug when their husbands were stationed at an overseas military base. Later, President John Kennedy would present Kelsey with the Distinguished Federal Civilian Service Award (Daemmrich, 2002).

The FDA, its moment of glory well behind it, would show an unscientific, political face when it ingloriously caved in to political pressure in 2004 and disapproved the perfectly safe RU486—the morning-after birth control medicine. This rejection occurred after it had reviewed 40 studies and more than 15,000 pages of data regarding the drug and despite the 23 to 4 vote of its panel of expert medical scholars and the favorable recommendation of the FDA staff. After so strong an endorsement, agency veterans could not recall any other time when the organization failed to approve a drug. In several overseas jurisdictions, the morning-after pills were then being sold over-the-counter. A stated reason for the FDA rejection was that availability of the pills would encourage more and "unsafe" sexual promiscuity. A critic sarcastically noted that the FDA would hardly turn down a drug that treated undesirable levels of cholesterol because it encouraged the eating of cheeseburgers.

In 2009, the FDA was induced to acknowledge the conclusions of a barrage of scientific evidence and approved the sale of morning-after medications. The approval was on a non-prescription "behind-the-counter" basis, meaning that they would have to request the drug and was only approved for women 18 years of age and over. Women under 17 were required to present a prescription, a stipulation that a federal district court judge ruled unconstitutional (*Tummino v. Torti*, 2009). On April 5, 2013, a Federal District Court ruled that Plan B (the morning after pill) be made available over-the-counter to girls of all ages (*Tummino v. Hamburg*, 2013).

The Current State of the Policy

Perhaps the most appropriate word to describe the current state of policy in the United States regarding individual and corporate white-collar crime is "erratic." Notoriously, the government failed to file charges against highly placed individuals and corporations. As far as can be determined, it was decided in high government circles during the last part of the Bush administration and during the Obama presidency that bringing criminal charges against prominent businessmen who had done woefully aberrant things, acts that might reasonably be charged as criminal, was a matter best overlooked since to prosecute them would undermine already-skeptical views about the powers-that-are and the marketplace. In a powerful piece of investigative journalism, Gretchen Morgenson and Louise Story reported that because of the seeming fragility of America's financial system, it was Timothy Geithner, the Secretary of the Treasury and once a player in the world of high finance, who persuaded prosecutors to ignore Wall Street crimes. The aim, the reporters wrote, was "a desire to calm markets, a goal that could be compromised by a hard-charging attorney general" (Morgenson & Story, 2011, p. A1). Bank robbers could only wish they had it so good.

The most visible aspect of this approach was the use of civil suits launched by the **Securities and Exchange Commission (SEC)** against some of the more prominent malefactors and the companies they piloted. The Bank of America, for instance, agreed to a fine of $155 million for its failure to notify stockholders that its acquisition of Merrill Lynch also involved the assumption of millions of dollars awarded to more than one hundred employees of the near-defunct company. No person involved in the composition or approval of the incomplete and misleading statement that went out to shareholders was held either civilly or criminally responsible. Typically, the Bank of America, when agreeing to pay the fine, insisted that the court acknowledge that the payment did not indicate guilt, a traditional dodge aimed at helping a company prevail against later lawsuits. The judge in a related case involving Citigroup asked rhetorically why a company would pay a $285 million fine, and at the same time insist that it was not guilty of having done anything that was against the law. The SEC, which launched the civil cases and approved the settlement terms, appealed the ruling that the losing party must admit guilt. An appellate court in a unanimous decision endorsed the SEC argument that if companies were forced to admit guilt when settling cases, court actions would grind to a halt. A spokesperson for the SEC implicitly acknowledged the power of the corporate world that made his agency support so illogical a concession:

> As we have said consistently, we agree to settlements when the terms reflect what we reasonably believe we could obtain if we prevailed at trial, without the risk of delay and uncertainty that comes with litigation. Equally important, the approach preserves resources that we can use to stop other frauds and protect other victims. (Wyatt, 2012, p. B7)

The idea that the corporate world has superior resources that keep the government from taking a sensible position is unsettling (see generally Pontell, 1984). Besides, of course, the alleged protection of victims is a "closing the barn door after the horses are gone" fiction. Most importantly, the public never gets to hear from those on the witness stand the sordid details of the acts that cost the company, that is its shareholders and ultimately its customers, these hundreds of millions of dollars.

Broken Windows and White-Collar Crime

The failure to bring to justice the malefactors, and the default in the criminological scholarly community to attend assiduously to this major national economic crisis, is exemplified by the work of James Q. Wilson, who likely was the most prominent public commentator on criminal behavior. When Wilson died early in 2012, the myriad of media obituaries focused on the "broken windows" theory that he advanced in collaboration with George Kelling. Kelling and Wilson suggested that minor neighborhood irritants needed to be remedied in order to create an atmosphere that would discourage more serious street crimes. They argued that indifference to incidents such as petty acts of vandalism and graffiti created an atmosphere that encouraged robberies, burglaries, and other major crimes (Kelling & Wilson, 1982).

There was a curious element in Wilson's work. He employed the term "crime" to refer exclusively to traditional street offenses perpetrated by low-status offenders. In his influential work, *Thinking About Crime,* Wilson defended this emphasis: "This book [does not deal] with white-collar crime," Wilson wrote.

> Partly this reflects the limits of my own knowledge, but it also reflects my conviction, which I believe is the conviction of most citizens, that predatory street crime is a far more serious matter than consumer fraud [or] antitrust violations.... because predatory street crime makes difficult or impossible maintenance of meaningful human communities. (Wilson, 1975, p. 407)

One could observe that the **Great Economic Meltdown** made it exceedingly difficult or impossible to maintain meaningful human communities in areas where a barrage of foreclosures was fueled by sales tactics that resulted in the subprime crisis, and homeowners found that skullduggery by scavenger lenders forced them to lose their homes. The lenders, who themselves profited handsomely, readily unloaded the high-risk obligations on investment firms which bundled them together and sold them to unwary investors (Posner, 2011). Here, we had a striking example—not of broken windows—but of catastrophically abandoned residences initiated and fostered by white-collar crime.

Predatory street crimes, the object of Wilson's attention, net their perpetrators far less loot than the bonuses, sometimes illegally obtained (e.g., the hundred or more Merrill Lynch awards) by corporate executives whose businesses have virtually or actually gone bust. It could be argued also that Wilson's observation about the "conviction of most citizens" about crime seriousness is at least in part a function of the information and opinions promulgated by writers like Wilson. He added the following cynical comment to his initial observations about "broken windows": "I am rather tolerant of some forms of civic corruption," he wrote, noting in parentheses that "if a good mayor can stay in office and govern effectively only by making a few deals with highway contractors and insurance agents, I do not get overly alarmed" (Wilson, 1975, pp. 407–408). It is the homeless vagrants who irritate motorists by making a few passes at their car windows and then asking for a handout that Wilson finds so in need of a law enforcement crackdown.

The tolerance of broken windows in the financial world can be linked to the indifference about vigorous oversight, which is characterized by numerous current developments. A priority of the U.S. Chamber of Commerce is to weaken the restraints on business imposed by the **Sarbanes-Oxley Act,** formally known as the Public Company Reform and Investor Protection Act. The Act got through Congress in 2002 only because the Enron-Arthur Andersen debacle hit the headlines and aroused public ire. Sarbanes-Oxley requires chief executive and chief financial officers to attest to the fact that their financial reports are accurate. If their certification proves to be wrong, they can be made to reimburse the company for any equity-based compensation they received and any profit they obtained from sales of the company's stock.

The law also demands that auditors cease doing consulting work with their clients unless the client's board of directors approves of the arrangement (Fletcher & Prett, 2003; Welytok, 2008).

What Research Has Taught Us

The Savings and Loan Debacle

Easily the most instructive policy element in the collapse of the Savings and Loan industry in the1980s is that it is foolhardy to remove oversight (at the urging of lobbyists) from the persons who stand to profit handsomely from the unregulated enterprises that they control or will come to control—particularly once these same persons comprehend that these entities can become the equivalent of the prototypical streets paved with gold that at one time attracted a wave of immigrants from Europe to the United States. After the collapse of so many savings and loan institutions, it is easy to believe in the pithy conclusion that "The easiest way to rob a bank is to own one" (Black, 2005).

The devastation of the savings and loan (S&L or "thrift") industry in the 1980s cost American taxpayers well over a hundred billion dollars, and there is persuasive evidence that white-collar crime was a key element in this economic disaster. The General Accounting Office reported that 70 to 80% of the thrift failures was tied to criminal behavior, and in every one of the 26 cases it investigated in detail, it determined that there was significant criminal behavior that led to the insolvency (General Accounting Office, 1989). When S&Ls found themselves locked into loans that carried low interest rates while they were obligated to pay depositors much higher rates, the thrift industry lobbied the sympathetic Reagan administration to discard the regulatory infrastructure that held the industry together for almost half a century. Reagan's position on white-collar crime was made clear when he was huckstering on the radio for General Electric (GE) decades earlier. He proclaimed that punishing the flagrant antitrust conspiracy of the GE executives was not called for because they were not criminals at heart, and that he doubted that any of them would ever intentionally double park (Braithwaite & Geis, 1982, pp. 292–293).

S&L *deregulation* was like giving the fattest kid on the block the key to a nearby candy store. It was justified on the grounds that the capitalist system possesses built-in mechanisms that make certain that miscreants eventually police themselves. More persuasive is the observation made by Alexander Hamilton, one of the country's founders on laissez-faire and self-regulation notions: "This is one of those wild speculative paradoxes that has gotten into credit with us. It must be rejected by anybody acquainted with commercial history" (Syrett & Cooke, 1961, p. 96). As Hamilton indicated centuries ago, this self-serving claim of self-regulation should be thrown on the ideological junk pile where it belongs.

The deregulation (some called it "unregulation") dropped the requirement that an S&L have at least 400 stockholders, none of whom could own more than a 25% interest in the institution. In the new free atmosphere, money was lent to dummy corporations, and bank assets were hidden by being transferred to the manager's wife under her maiden name. Crooked deals were cut with lawyers, accountants, and appraisers—the latter wildly inflated the value of land holdings so that it appeared that a financially woebegone S&L was flourishing. Huge sums of money were funneled to influential legislators in order to keep the maleficent S&Ls out of harm's way (Calavita, Pontell, & Tillman, 1997; Pizzo, Fricker, & Muolo, 1989).

A senior enforcement officer noted the difficulty of dealing with the horrendous mess created by the S&L crimes: "I feel like it's the Alaska oil spill. I feel like I'm out there with a roll of paper towels. The task is so huge, and what I'm worrying about is where can I get some more paper towels? I stand out there with my roll and I look at the sea of oil coming at me" (Pontell, Calavita, & Tillman, 1994, p. 400).

More than 1,000 criminal cases were filed against S&L manipulators, a vivid contrast to the hands-off policy adopted in the later economic meltdown offenses.

Enron, Arthur Andersen, and Others

An autopsy of the corpse of the Arthur Andersen auditing giant is instructive to reveal the complex dynamics of white-collar crime prosecutions (Tofler & Reingold, 2003). Founded in 1913; by the beginning of the current century Arthur Andersen was known as one of the "Big Six," the kingpins of the auditing world. It had 340 offices in 34 countries, 85,000 employees, and $3.5 billion in annual revenue. Government enforcement agencies finally got fed up with Andersen's irresponsible—and often illegal—behavior. In 1997, the company paid out more than $90 million to settle with investors in Colonial Reality of West Hartford, Connecticut, one of Andersen's clients. The year before its troubles with Enron, Andersen paid $10 million to settle a class action lawsuit filed by shareholders in Sunbeam, another firm that Andersen audited. In addition, Andersen's accountants failed to detect a Ponzi scheme run by the Baptist Foundation of America. Settling claims in that instance cost Andersen $21 million. Then there was a $229 million payment in a 2001 suit involving a Waste Management's earnings report that Andersen was said to have inflated by $1.4 billion through deliberate recourse to unacceptable accounting methods. As part of the settlement of that case, Andersen was enjoined by the court against again engaging in such behavior (Geis, 2013). When the case involving Enron went to court, a deputy attorney general declared that in deciding to prosecute Andersen criminally, his office had taken into account "the firm's history of wrongdoing" (Laufer, 2006, p. 45).

The prosecution focused on the shredding of documents relevant to the Enron auditing after the Andersen managers learned that they were being investigated. More than a ton of documents were destroyed in all-night endeavors as well as 30,000 emails. When Andersen was convicted, its clients fled to other firms and it collapsed. The U.S. Supreme Court, on the grounds that the prosecution had not proved beyond a reasonable doubt that the shredding was no more than a routine house-cleaning, reversed the conviction (*Arthur Andersen LLP v. United States*, 2005). But, it was too late; the Big Six was now the Big Five.

Prior to that conviction, businesses and investors in the United States were profiting so magnificently that they had no interest in questioning the tactics that were causing this bumper economy. Then the dominos began to fall: World Com, Global Crossing, Adelphia, General Re, the American International Group (AIG), ImClone, and Tyco International were all companies that found themselves in serious trouble (Rosoff, Pontell, & Tillman, 2004).

Consequences of White-Collar and Corporate Crimes: The Monstrous Meltdown

As the first decade of the new century neared its end, for those delighted Americans who were routinely "making hay while the sun shines" in business, and also achieving marvelous profits with their stock market investments, the ever-expanding bubble came to a crashing halt. Huge investment firms found themselves deeply in debt as the bottom fell out of the housing loans they packaged as credit derivatives. Unemployment rose, further compounding the impossibility of homeowners, who had been gulled into absurd mortgage arrangements, to meet their payments. House values went "underwater," that is, a house often was not worth what the purchaser owed on it. This fueled a barrage of foreclosures. Banks became wary of making loans, so in turn, businesses that depended on such financing to meet payrolls also gave up the ghost.

It would be much too dreary a recital to go through the roster of unsavory acts, often white-collar crimes, which were part of what actually was a depression, but was camouflaged as a recession, or more dramatically called the ***Great Economic Meltdown***.

We highlight a few of the markers along the way that demonstrate the nature of the activities fundamental to the depressing depression.

Bear Stearns

In March 2008, Bear Stearns, the fifth largest investment company in the United States, became the first of the giants to topple. Its risk management department had accumulated a debt of $1.5 billion. The firm sold itself to J. P. Morgan Chase at $10 a share; it had earlier sold on the New York Stock Exchange for $172 a share. Its situation was best summed up by the son of a former manager who was describing the company's executives: "Few come dishonest; none leave honest" (Cohan, 2009, p. 188).

Ralph Cioffi and Matthew Tummin, managers of the company's hedge fund arm, became the first from any of the juggernauts implicated in the meltdown to be tried criminally, and so far they are the only prominent persons. They were charged with securities fraud, wire fraud, and conspiracy. Among other things, they sold $2 million of their own investment in a hedge fund that they were pushing without informing their customers about their actions, although internal emails indicated that they regarded the fund as a bad investment.

Both men were found not guilty in 2000 by a jury after eight hours of deliberation. The decision largely rested on the panel members' assumption that the defendants were doing what people in their position always did. But, there was lifestyle fallout from the defendants' lost jobs and the fees they incurred. Cioffi, for instance, sold his house in New Jersey and began renting. He also unloaded a Long Island home and gave up a luxurious Fifth Avenue dwelling in New York City, although he managed to retain a retreat in Vermont.

The SEC, undoubtedly embarrassed by its criminal court defeat, refused to abandon the case, and in 2012 reached a civil settlement with the defendants: Cioffi had to cough up $700,000 of his profits and pay a $100,000 civil penalty; Tummin was assessed $200,000 of profit money and fined $50,000. The federal district judge who approved the agreement, scornfully called the assessed sums "chump change," a phrase that dictionaries equate to "chickenfeed" and define as an inconsequential amount. Coiffi was planning to relocate in Florida where he expected to open an investment firm.

The American International Group (AIG)

AIG was the largest insurance company in the United States and the 18th largest public company in the world. It was ruled over for 37 years by Maurice Raymond Greenberg, nicknamed Hank Greenberg after a home run slugger who played for the Detroit Tigers. Greenberg's holdings in AIG were worth more than $3 billion dollars. One of his favorite work maxims was: "All I want from life is an unfair advantage" (Shelp & Ehbar, 2000, p. 146). He and his underlings saw to it that they did get an unfair advantage, although it sometimes involved playing fast and loose on the edge of legal codes. In 2003, the company admitted that it had intentionally misrepresented its earnings to regulators. Greenberg's announcement that he would plead his Fifth Amendment right against self-incrimination and not respond at a Congressional hearing led the AIG Board of Directors to fire him. In 2009, Greenberg and the company's former chief financial officer paid $1 million to the SEC to settle the allegation of ersatz corporate reports. Interestingly, Greenberg maintained that rather than settle, he would have mightily fought any criminal charges.

AIG was deeply involved in the arcane credit derivative market, a market that Warren Buffett, the second richest American (behind Bill Gates), called "weeds priced as flowers" and branded as "financial weapons of mass destruction" (McDonald & Robinson, 2009, p. 161). However, because of the high risk, they were hot Wall Street items since a seller could make exorbitant profits. In the fall of 2008, the government bailed AIG out of its dire liquidity crisis to the tune of $173 billion.

Lehman Brothers Holdings

The government's corporate rescue operations rather quixotically took a brief halt when it came to Lehman Brothers, the country's fourth largest investment bank. The company had been fudging its balance sheet and was short $600 billion. The casino capitalism of Lehman was aided and abetted by the top scores awarded to the company's toxic holdings by a prominent credit rating agency. The downfall of Lehman Brothers came when it could not finalize its purchase by Barclay's in England (the British government objected) or the Bank of America. Lehman's filing for bankruptcy in September 2008 was the largest such default in American history. Richard Fuld, the Lehman CEO, summarized the situation in a short sentence: "We were overwhelmed," he announced. He did not mention that his own cash bonuses had totaled $250 million between 2004 and 2007, and that his company had distributed more than $16 billion in bonuses to its executives during the same time period. In 2008, as Lehman was approaching financial disaster it depleted its limited resources by more than $10 billion through year-end bonuses, stock buybacks, and dividend payments (Dillian, 2011; Ward, 2010).

Dodd-Frank Remedial Legislation

It is not without a considerable element of irony that the Congressional action to plug loopholes that had permitted the meltdown to occur bears the name of Christopher Dodd, the chair of the Senate Banking Committee. Dodd was one of the "Friends of Angelo." Angelo was Angelo Mozilo, the chief executive of the Countrywide Financial Corporation, which at its height financed one out of every five American home mortgages. At its nadir, Countrywide was rescued through a $4 billion purchase by the Bank of America that was aided by government bailout funds (Bruck, 2009; Michaelson, 2009).

Among other complications, Countryside offered sweetheart terms to persons the company believed supported its legislative agenda. Dodd's mortgages with Countrywide involved his Washington, DC, residence and his home in Connecticut and were estimated to save him $75,000. The Senate Ethics Committee concluded only that Dodd should have been more careful about involvement in what some might interpret as corruption. The lenient verdict likely had something to do with Dodd's decision not to run for reelection. Compounding the irony was the fact that Dodd's father, Thomas, also at one time a Connecticut senator, was one of the few members of the Senate to be censured by it. In his case, the charge was the expenditure of campaign funds for personal use, but it also was said that Dodd had double-billed on at least one out-of-town trip, charging both the government and the travel sponsor for his expenses.

The Dodd-Frank measure claimed to be the most drastic overhaul of the country's financial arrangements since legislative reforms that followed the Great Depression in the 1930s. It was an extraordinarily far-ranging and complex measure whose highlights we only note here in a general way: It called for (a) the consolidation of regulatory agencies; (b) increased transparency in regard to credit derivatives; (c) the creation of a new consumer protection agency and tightened rules that sought to increase investor protection; (d) new procedures that would make it unlikely that the government (e.g., taxpayers) again would have to bail out defaulting enterprises; and (e) upgraded standards for auditors and credit rating agencies.

Among the 264 rules in the ***Dodd-Frank Act*** was one that specified that companies of a certain size must report the ratio between the compensation of their CEOs and median earnings of their employees. A provision that personally helped many Americans was one that put a cap on the escalating fees that banks were getting for the use of debit cards. Not surprisingly, many banks raised the costs they were imposing for the "management" of depositors' money in order to compensate for the lesser amounts they could garner from debit card transactions.

Liberals found the constraints on business introduced by Dodd-Frank insufficient while conservatives thought them too demanding and likely to damage the country's economic health. Cynics suspected that astute attorneys and clever MBAs will find a way to get around the more intrusive elements of the Dodd-Frank Act, which was renamed in Congress from the "Wall Street Reform and Consumer Protection Act" to the "Restoring Financial Stability Act" in order not to tarnish Wall Street.

What Took Place Thereafter

The presidential campaign of 2012 did little to buttress faith in the likelihood that the average citizen was getting a square deal from the government. George (Mitt) Romney, the Republican candidate, was reported to have paid 13.9% in taxes on his multi-million dollar income, a situation possible only because of code provisions favoring a person, like himself, who lives off the capital gains of his vast fortune. Warren Buffett, the second richest man in the United States, went public with the information that his secretary paid taxes at a higher rate than he did.

The CREW Report

It was discovered that Ron Paul, a member of the U.S. House of Representatives from Texas, one of Mitt Romney's opponents for the presidential nomination, paid salaries or fees totaling more than $300,000 from money contributed to his electoral campaign. The money went to his daughter, brother, grandson, daughter's mother-in-law, granddaughter, and granddaughter-in-law. The information appeared in a 2012 report by the Citizens for Responsibility and Ethics in Washington (CREW), a nonprofit group founded in 2003 that, in its words, aims to explore, deter, and litigate legal and ethical wrongdoing by members of Congress. Its report noted that "a shocking 248 House members used their positions to financially benefit themselves or family members" (Citizens for Responsibility and Ethics in Washington, 2012, p. F13). Specific findings included the following:

- 82 members (40 Democrats and 42 Republicans) paid family members through their congressional offices, campaign committees, and political actions committees.
- 38 members (24 Democrats and 14 Republicans) earmarked in appropriation bills funds to a family business, employer, or associated nonprofit organizations.

The report and some of its commentators were careful to point out that notwithstanding the blatant nepotism of these dealings, they were not necessarily illegal, but some might well have crossed that line, such as payments to a baby sitter, and rental of a seaplane in the Caribbean.

Fraud in the World of Medicine

The ravages visited on federal and state medical benefit programs by doctors and other health service persons are staggering (Jesilow, Pontell, & Geis, 1993). In 2012, for instance, the Wycoff Medical Center in Brooklyn, New York, was going hat in hand to city and state authorities bewailing the cuts in the assistance given to the facility, which is located in one of the city's poorest neighborhoods. Meanwhile, the hospital's chief executive officer was driving to work in a Bentley Continental GTE, an automobile worth $160,000. The hospital paid thousands of dollars to insure the car and, when the executive lost his driver's license because of an accident, hospital security guards chauffeured him and his wife around the clock in a Cadillac Escalade and a Lincoln Town Car. Additionally, some members of the hospital Board of Directors were involved in enterprises that posed conflicts of interest with their hospital obligations (Hartocollis, 2012).

Race, Class, and Gender Implications of the Policy

By definition, white-collar and corporate crimes are related to matters of class. Neither women, African Americans, nor members of any other minority racial or ethnic groups have figured prominently in the annals of such crimes. A major reason for this situation is that White males have dominated the power structure of the United States. This situation is currently undergoing change in regard to women and Asian Americans, and somewhat less so in regard to Blacks. Women now comprise a majority of the undergraduate college and university enrollments, and they outnumber men in most graduate programs. Law, medical, and business schools also report rapidly escalating rosters of females; presumably, this translates at some ratio—probably not an equivalent one—to their assumption of leading positions in the legal, medical, and business areas.

It is uncertain what, if any, impact this development will have on white-collar and corporate crime. It could reasonably be argued that the character traits necessary for ascension to power suggest that those women who reach those peaks will be as dishonest as the men they replace. Indeed, women likely have to outshine men in terms of aggressiveness, toughness, and winner-take-all qualities in order to reach the pinnacle of worldly success. On the other hand, women as a gender, more than men, tend to be nurturing and cooperative rather than confrontational and highly competitive. A study of female doctors, for instance, found them willing to spend more (unpaid) time with patients discussing their ailment, less mercenary, and comparatively uninvolved in status-enhancing professional activities. Part of the explanation for this may lie in the fact that women physicians tend to be married to male doctors and enjoy excellent family incomes; male doctors choose their mates more randomly (Geis, Geis, & Jesilow, 1991).

How Do We Fix It?

The laws regarding white-collar and corporate crime are both inadequate and, as noted, overly favorable to business. In criminal law, the issue of intent (*mens rea*) is one of the higher barriers that must be surmounted to obtain a criminal conviction; it is particularly difficult to reach in cases involving white-collar offenses. The highly publicized prosecution of Martha Stewart, the well-known guru of all things chic, is illustrative. Stewart seemingly violated the law against insider trading, specifically, buying or selling a stock when you have information about developments that are not yet public knowledge. But, it is very difficult to prove intent regarding acts committed on the basis of insider information. The accused can always claim that it was no more than coincidence that his or her action and the steep rise or decline of the stock they traded merely happened to coincide; they always planned to sell or buy the stock when it reached a certain level. In Stewart's case, she lied before a grand jury, which means she violated a principle holy to career street criminals: Never tell them anything, and let the state prove its case without your verbal contribution. Perjury was a much easier charge to prove and therefore to succeed in obtaining the conviction and imprisonment of Martha Stewart (Toobin, 2003).

White-collar and corporate crimes typically involve arcane matters that juries (and/or judges) may find difficult to understand. Pollution, product and occupational safety prosecutions often need to use complex scientific evidence of causation that meets the "beyond a reasonable" standard for a conviction.

Corporations and Criminal Law

Under law, corporations are regarded as individuals, and except without the Fifth Amendment guarantee against self-incrimination, they have all the rights of individual defendants. The first step in granting these privileges to corporations came in the case of the *New York Central and Hudson River Railroad v. United States* (1908) and was reinforced by the prestigious American Law Institute (Geis & DiMento, 2002). A much overdue reform would jettison the corporation-as-person approach and see the formulation of a special innovative body of law that deals specifically and only with corporate criminal actions. We endorse the suggestion of Maria Boss and Barbara Crutchfield George (1992): "Legislators should consider taking corporate crime completely out of the current context. . . . and should focus their efforts on creating new laws specific to white-collar crime that utilize nontraditional penalties and standards imposing accountability and 'front-end' compliance requirements" (pp. 57–58).

Attorneys and White-Collar and Corporate Crime

Individual white-collar offenders also enjoy pretrial and courtroom advantages, and many business executives have contracts that guarantee that their corporate employer pays the fees of private attorneys, if the executive is charged with criminal behavior. It is arguable whether state and federal prosecutors as a group are superior or inferior to members of the private bar who defend persons accused of white-collar crime. It is common for lawyers to gain experience as government prosecutors and then sign up with private firms that offer much more lucrative salaries. They then turn their talents toward defending the kinds of persons they prosecuted, often opposing lawyers who were their subordinates when they worked for the government. John E. Hueston and Sean M. Berkowitz, the pair of prosecutors who successfully convicted Kenneth Lay and Jeffrey Skilling, the majordomos of Enron, gave up their government jobs soon after that trial. Heuston became a litigator for the 200-person firm of Irell & Manelle in Newport Beach, California, while Berkowitz accepted a partnership in Latham & Watkins, a global firm with more than 2,000 employees.

In interviews with leading members of the white-collar criminal defense bar who are headquartered in New York City, Kenneth Mann, now a judge in Israel, found that they almost invariably assumed that their client was guilty. The lawyers studied by Mann saw their task as delaying the case as long as possible so that concern and memories would fade. They knew that it was unethical to encourage clients to fabricate, but they were adept at formulating strategic scenarios and indicating their likely consequences: "If you say this, it will leave you open to an attack by the prosecutor because. . . ." "If you say the same thing this way, the prosecutor will be stymied." The defense counsel often has a particularly difficult task preparing an accused white-collar criminal for what could be a harrowing discovery examination. Their clients generally were not accustomed to being interrogated, but rather to giving orders that are not questioned. At trial, upper-class offenders are often treated more gingerly by the prosecution, since they present an appearance of great respectability to jurors. Ultimately, the shrewd and talented (and expensive) defense attorney will negotiate the most favorable plea bargain possible. Avoiding trial is a top priority (Mann, 1985).

Virtue as a National Need

The initial step toward formulating a curative context aimed at controlling white-collar and corporate crime is to discard the common belief that selfishness and greed are inherent, genetically determined human traits. There are compelling illustrations of human beings and societal arrangements where the personal accumulation of wealth is deplored. Among various Native American and Native Canadian tribes, for instance, prestige has been attached to those who divest themselves as thoroughly as possible of things that are superfluous to a decent style of living (Jonaitis, 1991). And there assuredly are innumerable examples of persons in past and present times who in defiance of seeming imperatives regarding the accumulation of money (i.e., yachts, Jaguars, and jewels), decided to live the simplest of lives. India's Mahatma Gandhi (Fischer, 1997; Lelyveld, 2011) and America's Henry David Thoreau (Harding, 1982) are prototypes for such a lifestyle choice. Unfortunately, few Americans take seriously the Biblical warning that those who accumulate great wealth will have difficulty ascending to a heavenly berth.

It undoubtedly is naive and disingenuous to expect that such a commendable ethos is able to take hold in contemporary capitalistic nations like the United States, or, for that matter, in authoritarian nations like China. In what he regarded as his major scholarly contribution, political scientist James Q. Wilson argued that human beings are born with a strong moral sense of decency, and remain so unless corrupted by their surrounding environment. Among his attempts to document this position, Wilson argued (rather feebly) that people leave tips in a restaurant where they never anticipate they will return (Wilson, 1993).

Be that as it may, a public policy directed at inhibiting white-collar and corporate crime will be most effective if the ethos of a society is so restructured that the idea of goodness is transmitted efficiently and thoroughly through the indoctrinating institutions, which mold the character of individuals and groups. It is expected that this is a hopeless task in universal terms, but it is a tenet that in certain places (e.g., business schools) ought to be strenuously attempted.

It seems that white-collar and corporate crime should be much easier to repress than traditional street offenses. For corporations, their structure is more susceptible to court-ordered alterations than is the personality or the psyche of the typical street offender. A company can be forced to unload that part of its operation that has been the source of law violations. Participation of a government agency in the dismemberment helps to ensure that any sale is to a business with an exemplary record of compliance.

It also can be reasonably argued that compared to street offenders, white-collar and corporate criminals are more responsive to legal threats—they will presumably avoid legal infractions for fear of public disgrace, and will be more inhibited by principles of deterrence, incapacitation, and rehabilitation. Street criminals may learn new law-breaking tricks in prison; a process not likely for, say, antitrust violators.

In addition, upper-class violators are not persons on the outer rims of society who commit burglaries and robberies in order to purchase a further dose of an illegal drug, or to secure funds to keep the party going (Wright & Decker, 1994, 1997). They are individuals and executives of entities who characteristically live in a style that is the envy of most of us less favored. They are usually well-educated, which presumes that they are capable of making reasonably accurate linkages between causes and effects—that is, that they are aware that *if* they break the law, and are caught, that serious consequences for their lifestyle, reputations, and the well-being of their families possibly result.

However, given the number of possible scenarios in the previous paragraph, no simple-minded conclusions can be drawn from it. For one thing, business executives, physicians, auditors, and members of the federal administrative apparatus never have sufficient information to be able to calculate with certainty the odds that they are breaking the law, and further what their fate will be if they get caught. Very often their employer will take the hit to protect them. They also are aware that sentences for white-collar crimes tend to be indulgent—forget about Bernie Madoff, who was not a mainstream player. The cliché is that any offender will emerge from a jail or prison sentence with a fine suntan, and an improved backhand.

In the end, we come back to where we began with the discussion of remedial actions. In order to tamp down major forms of white-collar and corporate crime, there are many recommendations: tighter regulations, tougher and more certain penalties, new legislation (especially in regard to lobbying) tighter congressional earmarks, and restricted campaign contributions are all necessitated.

The most dramatic incident in the wake of the meltdown demonstrated the need to create a climate of honesty and virtue that is instilled into the very essence of persons with power. Greg Smith, a middle manager at Goldman Sachs, one of the investment giants, went public with his resignation from the company after almost twelve years of employment. Smith lamented that the tone in his workplace had deteriorated into selfishness and callousness, and had become "toxic" and "destructive." Customers often were referred to as "muppets," a British term for idiots. The interests of clients were constantly being overruled by the prospect of making money on a deal. Stocks were being pushed that the seller knew were poor buys. "The integrity problem was too big to ignore," insisted Smith (2012, p. A22).

As long as financiers at Goldman Sachs and other persons with status and power do not demonstrate a sense of moral rectitude, and instead feel justified in gulling other human beings, laws and regulatory oversight will do little more than nibble at the edges of white-collar and corporate evils. An effort to change the commercial culture of a nation represents a gigantic and perhaps unachievable challenge. Frighteningly, such an achievement, or some significant part of it, may be essential for the continued eminence of the United States as an admirable nation—if not for the country's eventual survival.

KEY TERMS

Deregulation	Food and Drug Administration (FDA)	Securities and Exchange Commission (SEC)
Dodd-Frank Act		
Federal Trade Commission (FTC)	Great Economic Meltdown	Sherman Act
	Sarbanes-Oxley Act	

DISCUSSION QUESTIONS

1. How are the statuses of white-collar criminals reflected in statutes that favor them? Give two specific examples from cases in the chapter.

2. Do you believe that the traditional half-hearted policy responses to white-collar and corporate crime have changed? Explain your response with examples.

3. Do you agree with the authors' conclusions regarding how to fix policy responses to white-collar and corporate crime so that they can be more effective? Explain why or why not.

WEBSITES FOR ADDITIONAL RESEARCH

U.S. Securities and Exchange Commission: http://www.sec.gov/

Federal Bureau of Investigation, White Collar Crime Division: http://www.fbi.gov/about-us/investigate/white_collar/whitecollarcrime

National White Collar Crime Center: http://www.nw3c.org/Home

U.S. Treasury Dept., Financial Crimes Enforcement Network: http://www.fincen.gov/

National Health care Anti-Fraud Association: http://www.nhcaa.org/

National Institute of Justice—http://www.ojp.usdoj.gov/nij

Sarbanes-Oxley Law: http://www.sec.gov/about/laws/soa2002.pdf

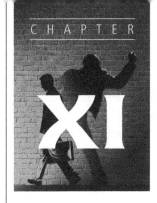

CHAPTER

XI

America's "War on Gangs": Response to a Real Threat or a Moral Panic?

John Hagedorn and Meda Chesney-Lind

his chapter provides an overview of the gang problem in the United States as well as an assessment of policies generated to prevent, intervene, and suppress gang membership. We open with a brief history of the relationship of gangs to the fields of social work and sociology. Following that, we critically assess the role of the media, particularly modern corporate media, in the construction of the modern gang problem—tracing the shift from a sympathetic, poverty, and subcultural narrative (when the gangs were White), to a more menacing narrative as people of color started forming gangs. We also consider the role of gender in gangs, since that is an often missing piece, although, as our chapter indicates the media are increasingly willing to demonize girls involved in gangs as well as boys.

As a modern gang city, and one that continues to have its share of gang and crime problems, we elect Chicago as an instructive case study in what is going right (and mostly wrong) with our national response to the gang problem. We consider the media coverage and the facts in what is seen as Chicago's gang-driven homicide rate. We also review evidence on the effectiveness of specific gang programs like the use of street outreach workers (which actually increased gang cohesion), to current school-based prevention programs like G.R.E.A.T. (Gang Resistance Education and Training), and intervention efforts like the media favorite CeaseFire. All these programs are shown to be ineffective, at best, or counterproductive. Other misguided crime control strategies (like the war on drugs), police brutality and corruption, and mass incarceration have impacted the gang problem, largely by fueling the development of prison gangs that tend to increase gang cohesion, violence, and crime involvement.

There are six factors to keep in mind as we discuss our current policy toward gangs:

1. **Gangs serve as a proxy for "the other" and as targets of punitive criminal justice policies.** A century ago immigrants from southern Europe were seen as threats to American culture and values just as Mexicans are today (Huntington, 2004). Because of the legacy of slavery and the racism that enabled it, African Americans have consistently occupied a special niche in the ranks of the demonized, and a century and a half after emancipation, they remain the most impoverished and oppressed group in the United States; in the same way, non-European gangs were always seen as representing a "dangerous class."

2. **As the racial composition of gangs changed, the conventional perspective on gangs changed from seeing them as mainly delinquents to now defining them as hardened criminals.** Rather than an emphasis on the 1950s approach of outreach and diversion, gang members are now typically treated as beyond the reach of rehabilitation, are often targeted by special police units (and laws), and are viewed as fit only for incapacitation by long prison sentences. The involvement of gangs in nationalist and social movements in the sixties has been either forgotten or dismissed as trickery.

3. **Despite sharply falling rates of crime and violence, *mass incarceration* emerged as the main "solution" to the "gang problem."** The "race to incarcerate" in the United States has taken place at the same time as crime, and specifically violent crime in the United States has dropped to the lowest level since the 1960s. This inconvenient fact has not stopped flamboyant rhetoric by politicians warning of "out of control" violence and framing gangs as "urban terrorists." Mass incarceration is also related to the increase of prison gangs and expansion of their influence, both inside and outside of prisons.

4. **For both male and female gang members, the media play a crucial role in their demonization, pushing rationality into the background of both court proceedings and criminal justice policy.** While gang violence is a very real problem in some communities across the country, sharply declining rates of crime and violence have not caused a drop in media sensationalism toward offenders.

5. **Despite some countertrends, gang-involved juveniles are being routinely prosecuted as adults.** The rationale for a juvenile justice system, the progressive era notion that children must be treated differently than adults, is still not an accepted principle of policy (Feld, 1991). This is particularly the case when gang youth are arrested and charged.

6. **Finally, gang violence provided the backdrop for the development of a variety of "magic bullets" purporting to be "the" cure to the gang problem.** Police departments adopted Compstat[1] and implemented a host of "zero-tolerance" gang policies in some cities, even as violence dropped in nearly all cities nationwide. University-based programs like CeaseFire (now called Cure Violence is an antiviolence program and initiative of the Chicago Project for Violence Prevention aimed at reducing street violence by using outreach workers to interrupt potentially violent situations) received massive media attention through the popular documentary *The Interrupters* while also claiming credit for declining rates of violence. Scientific evaluations, however, do not support their claims. School-based gang prevention programs like G.R.E.A.T., while increasing positive attitudes toward police, show no long-term reduction in gang membership (Howell, 2012).

---

[1] A widely used data-driven police accountability program. Retrieved from http://www.policefoundation.org/pdf/compstatinpractice.pdf

Considering the history of U.S. criminal justice policy toward gangs, combined with today's historic low rates of violence, we conclude that both the current definition of the gang problem as well as the often well-funded criminal justice programs are driven by a "moral panic" rather than an accurate assessment of the phenomenon.

The Back Story

Gangs, in many ways, are inextricably tied to the origins of the fields of criminology and social work (Addams, 1920; Deegan, 1988; Thrasher, 1927). Gangs have also long been a staple of sensationalistic media crime coverage, which in turn means that the media themselves are key players in the development of crime policy around this social problem, and ultimately around the "crime problem" in general (see Barak, 1995; Barlow, 1998; Surette, 1992). Finally, controlling gangs was also a major justification for the growth of urban police forces as these institutions of social control emerged in the immigrant-rich, industrial cities of the late 1800s and early 20th century (Lane, 1971; Monkkonen, 1981).

In fact, gang policy and the treatment of juvenile offenders became a key subject for the core debates about the direction of social reform, poverty, and the "crime problem"—a pattern we contend continues to this day. Consider that at the turn of the last century and the progressive era, sociologists like Jane Addams were working in immigrant communities establishing settlement houses, focusing on literacy, and job training while other elements of the progressive establishment were laying the foundation for the first juvenile courts. The emerging field of social work was crafting a gang and crime policy that was essentially community-based youth work aimed at long-term integration of youth into adult life. It was assumed that most white male youth in gangs would "mature out" of adolescent gangs. The theoretical rationales behind these assumptions were clearly the core founding principles of criminology, including social disorganization theory (Shaw & McKay, 1969), which posited that boys were attracted to gangs because conventional institutions had broken down. Cultural deviance theories looked at the attraction of gang subcultures to lower class youth (Cohen, 1955; Miller, 1958). Policies toward gangs in the 1950, like the New York City Youth Board (1960), reflected a belief in a temporary, age-limited nature of delinquency. In the first part of the 20th century, the emerging field of social work competed with harder attitudes of the police, as seen in the lyrics of the now iconic song, "Gee Officer Krupke" from West Side Story. Here, members of the Jets, after being threatened by a surly and brutal police officer, somewhat cynically act out a future encounter where they will plead that their backgrounds explain their behavior, noting that "Our mothers all are junkies, / Our fathers all are drunks. / Golly Moses, natcherly we're punks!" and concluding with "We ain't no delinquents, / We're misunderstood."[2]

The 1960s marked changes on many fronts. New minority gangs became politicized and attracted to nationalist and civil rights movements. Groups with a nationalist identity, such as the Black Panther Party, Young Lords, and Brown Berets, competed with the gangster identity for the attention and interest of ghetto and barrio youth (Perkins, 1987). However, at the same time gangs like the Vice Lords and Crips began the takeover of vice markets in major cities. Also, the Italian mafia retreated to more profitable and less risky ventures, such as gambling, managing the Teamsters Pension Fund, and controlling Las Vegas

---

[2] "Gee, Officer Krupke" from "West Side Story" by Leonard Bernstein and Stephen Sondheim. © Copyright 1956, 1957, 1958, 1959 by Amberson Holdings LLC and Stephen Sondheim. Copyright renewed. Leonard Bernstein Music Publishing Company LLC, publisher. Boosey & Hawkes, agent for rental. International copyright secured. Reprinted by permission of Boosey & Hawkes, Inc.

casinos (Russo, 2001). People in gangs began to be treated as adults involved with "organized crime," and the social work programs of the past were overshadowed by new gang squad enforcement units. Gradually, the origins of the current policy, known as the ***war on gangs***, evolved as an obvious outgrowth of the Republican emphasis on "law and order" and the "war on drugs." This policy, in fact, masked an increasingly racialized strategy of policing, control, and imprisonment (Garland, 2001; Sherman, 1971).

This political and nationalist turn of the gangs ended in mass incarceration in the 1980s, which resulted in elevating the position of those members within the gangs who wanted to control illicit vice markets over the gang members who identified with the more politicized, prosocial elements (Hagedorn, 2008). Prison became increasingly important in gang culture and affairs, as the gangs took over and replaced the "lifers" in the hierarchy of the prison inmate subculture; witness the infamous Stateville Penitentiary in Illinois (Jacobs, 1977).

Media and the Framing of Crime and Gangs

However, the back story is not just about the gangs. It is also about how the corporate media during this period began to play a more central role in the construction and comprehension of the gang and crime problem, which resulted in very significant consequences for the country. There are many complex reasons for this evolution, some of which relate to media consolidation practices during this period, but also the rise of increasingly conservative media barons like Rupert Murdock (Bagdikian, 2000). For a variety of reasons, whether discussing print or television, conservative media tends to turn to sensationalistic crime stories along with celebrity gossip and scandals as reliable front page staples. For newspapers and television with shrinking newsrooms and little appetite to engage in serious investigative journalism, this mix provides a compelling and profitable filler (Hamilton, 1998; McManus, 1994).

Criminologists have been somewhat slow to analyze this trend, having reserved analytical interest in journalism to efforts to explore whether the "if it bleeds, it leads" form of journalism increases the public's fear of crime. In fact, we now know that media exposure to crime stories do have an impact. Heavier viewers of local television news are more likely to fear crime and criminal victimization (Romer, Jamison, & Aday, 2003). This is attributed to "pervasive coverage of violent crime stories," which also tends to increase the fear of African American and other minorities who are disproportionately featured in crime stories (Romer, Jamison, & DeCoteau, 1998). A broader question, though, is the degree to which crime journalism influences punitive crime policies specific to gang policy, such as "the war on drugs," and "mass incarcerations."

The Current State of the Policy

After years of decline, officials now claim the number of gangs is increasing. The most recent police estimates put the number of gangs in the United States at 27,000 and the number of gang members at approximately 788,000. Supposedly, this represents a 25% increase in the number of jurisdictions reporting gang problems since the nation recorded a twelve-year low in 2001 (National Gang Center, 2009). In 2007, nearly all large cities (86%) reported gang problems, which represents an increase of approximately 50% since 1983, when the gang problem in our country was just beginning to grow (Curry, Fox, Ball, & Stone, 1992; National Gang Center, 2009). However, official estimates of gangs must be used with extreme caution since political factors may enter into police reports (see Miller, 1975), and gangs do not typically keep membership rosters, and never provide them to officials. That said, gangs have long been a feature of the urban landscape in the United States and they show no signs of going away.

Modern day estimates of gang membership sometimes fail to include female participants. Researchers who asked youths if they had ever been in a gang (self-report) found that 3% of boys (aged 12–16) and 1% of girls reported that they were in a gang (Greene & Pranis, 2007, p. 36); this statistic means that girls comprise roughly one quarter of all the youth in gangs. A study conducted in England and Wales, with a slightly broader definition of gang, found that girls comprised roughly half of those classified as belonging to a "delinquent youth group" (Sharp, Aldridge, & Medina, 2006, p. 3). By contrast, police estimates of the number of girls in gangs are frequently very low (often considerably below 10%) (Curry, Ball & Fox, 1994; National Gang Center, 2009). Studies of gang problems done by researchers in the field tend to line up with the self-report data and find that girls are roughly 20% to 46% of those involved in gangs (Miller, 2002, pp. 68–105). All this research points to the importance of paying attention to girls when seeking to prevent gang membership.

One explanation for the different estimates of the number of girls in gangs is a function of the age of the sample surveyed, since girls tend to join gangs at a younger age, and leave gangs earlier than boys (Peterson, Miller, & Esbensen, 2001; Williams, Curry, & Cohen, 2002). A study done of youth ages 11 to 15 found that nearly half the gang members were girls, but one surveying an older group (13–19) found only a fifth were girls (Esbensen & Huizinga, 1993). In the population of young people selected to evaluate the anti-gang program G.R.E.A.T., girls comprised 38% of those reporting gang membership in the eighth-grade sample (Esbensen, Deschanes, & Winfree, 1999). One researcher noted that this is about the same age that girls are attracted to scouting (Quicker, 1983).

The predominant policy response to gangs has focused almost exclusively on harsh, criminal justice responses, which could safely be described as a "war on gangs." As a result, virtually every policy is designed to make it easier to incarcerate gang members for long periods of time. Specifically, U.S. gang policy has been dominated by sentencing enhancements, vertical prosecution programs, and gang injunctions, all of which fuel mass incarceration.[3] ***Sentencing enhancements*** add a given amount of time to a person's sentence for being a gang member, and for committing a crime in furtherance of the gang. ***Vertical prosecution programs*** assign a single prosecutor to a gang member for all of the crimes they are charged with (now or in the future). This single prosecutor (or group of prosecutors in large jurisdictions) often works closely with local police agencies. The purpose is to have a prosecutor familiar with the gang member's history so that he or she is less likely to plea bargain the case, thus the court is more likely to charge the suspect with every possible crime and enhancement so that they receive the longest possible sentence. Finally, ***gang injunctions*** are civil orders that prohibit named gang members from associating with one another, congregating in specific areas, or doing other things stipulated in the injunction. They are highly controversial because they are applied without due process protections and can prohibit named persons from engaging in normally legal activities. Gang injunctions only need to meet the preponderance of evidence threshold rather than the more stringent "beyond a reasonable doubt" standard, and cited individuals are not entitled to an attorney (unless they are currently on probation). Finally, and significantly, gang injunctions are most often used in disadvantaged minority neighborhoods and in gang areas that are adjacent to affluent communities.

---

[3] Some may argue that policy responses also include prevention and intervention programs. We contend that resources spent on prevention and intervention are minimal at best, and do not work. Therefore, we do not include them here.

⊠ Race, Class, and Gender Implications of the Policy

Today, much of the discussion about gangs is centered on issues of race and ethnicity. In criminological theory during the first half of the 20th century, race and gender were disregarded in favor of class (Irwin & Chesney-Lind, 2008). African Americans were considered just another ethnic group, and women in gangs received scant attention by researchers. In terms of policy, girls were identified as either "tomboys" or "seductresses," and policies advocating charm schools and teaching women to conform to gender norms was the chief program for girls—if there was one at all (Chesney-Lind & Hagedorn, 1999). For males, the expectation that "boys would be boys" produced the conclusion that they would eventually mature out of an ethnically neutral gang; therefore, generic delinquency programs were recommended to deal with immature juveniles. The essential role played by various forms of masculinities in gang membership was ignored, even as the gang member was dubbed a "rogue male" by early influential criminologists (Cohen, 1955).

The one major exception to the absence of any discussion about ethnicity was the institutionalization of the Mafia in the 1930s in large cities, and the focus on Italians. Existing literature on gangs has almost completely excluded the Mafia, with the partial exception of Ianni's (1975) study of ethnic succession. Italian gangs were ultimately labeled and treated as "organized crime," and their history (e.g., corruption of police, and integration with urban machines) is seen as irrelevant when reviewing the majority of gang literature. Two things are clear: ethnic and racial stereotypes are prevalent in American society (Chiricos & Eschholz, 2002; Gilliam & Iyengar, 2000) and courts (Hagedorn & Maclean, 2012), and the media play a prominent role in the maintenance of these stereotypes (Welch, Fenwick, & Roberts, 1998). This is evident because the key frames or narratives used by the general public to understand the "crime problem" are provided by the media coverage of crime (Goffman, 1974). Coverage of gangs provides the perfect setting for the corporate media to racialize the crime problem, without seeming overtly racist.

Gang members are reliable and dramatic staples in these media crime scripts, with their unique tattoos, their distinctive clothing styles, their propensity to "hang out" in open street settings, and their reliance on urban graffiti as a communication device (White, 1996). Social science studies over the past decades have pointed out that media coverage is not correlated with actual gang activity, but with sensational events, and often conflates and falsely equates gangs and violence (Miller, 1975; Sullivan, 2005).

Importantly, media-driven stereotypes of crime and offenders are often accompanied with narratives that tend to stress either culpability or innocence leaving the reading public with fairly clear ideas about who should be forgiven and who deserves the punishment. Consistent with that premise, Chiricos and Eschholz (2002) noted that the dominant perception of crime as a minority phenomenon likely influenced "the dramatic escalation of punitiveness toward criminals in the past 20 years, with incarceration rates tripling despite stagnant . . . crime rates" (p. 401). They further stated that the ways in which minorities are portrayed in the media reinforce the notion that these groups "constitute a 'social threat' that warrants a punitive response by the criminal justice system" (2002, p. 416).

Girls are also demonized by the media for their gang identities—consider the Chicago trial of Jacqueline Montañez. In 1992, Montañez and two female gang members killed two rival gang members. Prosecutors spared no rhetoric at her trial:

> Jacqueline Montañez is a cold, calculating, vicious murderer full of hate beyond her years. She showed no remorse at the trial and I believe today shows no remorse about what happened. She planned and perpetrated a crime by luring them with a promise of a good time. She and her fellow

gang members got together and went on that mission. And then executed Hector Reyes and Jimmie Cruz in a manner that Al Capone would be proud of .... Jacqueline Montañez, Judge, has become the teen queen of criminals.... She stands 15 years old, but by her actions, she's a seasoned veteran, a cold-blooded assassin. (Krejci, 1993)

The judge lamented that the youthful age of Montañez made her ineligible for the death penalty, and she was sentenced to life without parole. But no one, neither the prosecutor, mass media, or her own defense attorneys, ever asked why a young girl would commit such a violent act? Presumably, any reading of the literature of women and violence (Chesney-Lind & Pasko, 2004) would mandate a search for child-hood sexual or physical abuse in her background. In Montañez's case, she was raped and beaten by her stepfather beginning at the age of seven. She ran away repeatedly, but was returned by police to her step-father who continued the abuse until her teenage years. When she finally ran away for good, she joined the rival gang of her stepfather; consequently, the killings were obviously much more complex than simple gang revenge.[4]

The punitive propensity in the U.S. gang policies all too often ignores the context of offending and appeals to fear and racial animosity for support of policies of mass incarceration (Alexander, 2010). As Jacqueline Montañez says poignantly, "I did what they said I did, but I'm not who they say I am" (Amnesty International, 2011, p. 9). Our moral panic over gangs gets in the way of an investigation of all the facts and replaces humane and sound justice policy with fear.

⊠ Unintended Consequences of the Policy: The Fallacy of Increasing Gang Violence

This chapter argues that punitive policies of mass incarceration are related to factors other than gangs as an alleged "real threat" and in large part are explained by media demonization and popular stereo-types of criminals and crime. At the end of the 1980s and early 1990s, along with law enforcement interests (e.g., the L.A. Sheriff's office, which conducted large scale gang trainings around the country), the corporate media actively participated in generating a "moral panic" around the gang problem—think of movies like "Colors" and "Boys in the Hood". Following arguments by Loic Wacquant (2009), Michelle Alexander's thesis in 2010 agreed that punitive policies, like those directed at ethnic youth gangs, were related to racial domination; these positions are convincing to us. The intent of this section is to illustrate that framing gangs as a "real threat" (regardless of why we believe that is occurring) ignores the actual trends of violence in the United States. We believe the explanations for this violence are found elsewhere.

We begin by looking at changes in the U.S. homicide rate over the past century.

The homicide rate in the United States in 2010 at 4.8 per 100,000 people is about the same as it was in 1950, which is often pictured as being a period of law and order. The 2010 rate is lower than it was in 1920 and exactly the same as it was in 1908.[5]

---

[4] See affidavits and other supporting materials plus links to Amnesty International articles at http://jacquelinemontanez.com. The "juvenile life without parole" sentence for Montañez was seemingly overturned by the U.S. Supreme Court in *Miller vs Alabama*, but the State of Illinois refuses to apply this decision to any prior cases. Refer to http://www.supremecourt.gov/oral_arguments/argument_transcripts/10-9646.pdf.

[5] Refer to http://polyticks.com/polyticks/beararms/liars/usa.htm

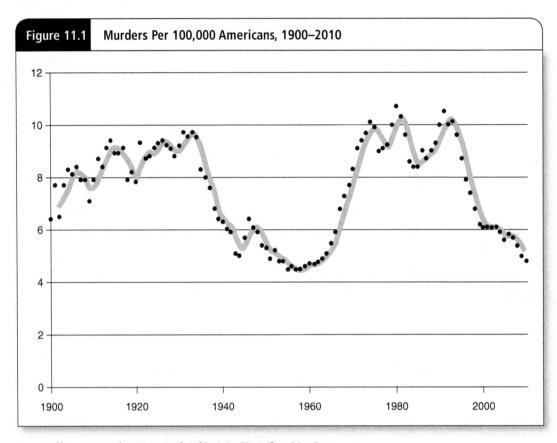

| Figure 11.1 | Murders Per 100,000 Americans, 1900–2010 |

Sources: Eckberg, *Demography,* 1995; National Vital Statistics; FBI Uniform Crime Reports.

The absolute number of homicides in the United States in 2010 was 14,748, which is actually *12 fewer* than the 14,760 people murdered in 1969, despite a U.S. population increase of over 100 million people in the past 40 years (Fox & Zawitz, 2007). *In other words, there is no gang homicide epidemic in the United States today.* We are experiencing record low rates of violence not seen for over a century. So, how has this good news about serious crime translated into correctional policy?

Some observers say that homicides were reduced because more offenders were locked up, but Blumstein and Wallman (2000) pointed out that the drops in homicide preceded punitive policing policies, and the expansion of incarceration practices in the 1990s. While academic debates generally found little impact of incarceration on homicide rates (see Black & Orsagh, 1978; Rosenfeld, 2000), the recently published United Nations Global Study on Homicide helps us better understand how gangs influence the variation in rates of violence (Me, Bisogno, & Malby, 2011).

To summarize this important report, homicide rates vary across regions based on their level of development. In other words, where there are vast areas of social exclusion, such as sub-Saharan Africa, homicide is at a high level. In addition, in some countries and cities, such as Medillín, Colombia, or Juarez, Mexico, homicide reaches terrifying heights. These elevated levels of homicide are the result of wars by gangs, cartels, or militias, often over control of drug markets. Any sudden jumps and declines in levels of violence are typically related to gangs making war, or as in the case of El Salvador recently, making peace (Hayden, 2012).

The history of homicide in the United States finds major increases in the 1920s were clearly related to gang wars over beer and alcohol, and in the 1990s the wars were over crack cocaine markets. The increases in the 1970s, the United Nations report suggests, are better understood as a desperate response to the devastating impact of deindustrialization (Wilson, 1987) or to increases in the hopelessness of the urban Black population after the winding down of the civil rights movement (Me et al., 2011). This period also included the expansion of and conflict between newly formed Black gangs in major U.S. cities.

By the end of the 1990s, the gang/crack wars had ended and in most cities there were significantly lower rates of violence. We contend that this signifies that the Justice Department reports of an upsurge in gang activity is unrelated to the actual recorded rates of violence. We argue that this claim of an upsurge in gang activity is more related to media demonization of violence by "dark others" (see Kingsbury, 2008). This "moral panic" exploits real fears of personal safety, and also manipulates deeply embedded racism in the U.S. public, which has led to the creation of a vast network of expensive and repressive *gulags* or penal camps. This policy has two major unintended consequences.

First, the vast increases in incarceration and enhanced penalties for gang members led to the takeover of the inmate subculture by street gangs, who are now the most powerful force inside prison walls (Camp & Camp, 1985; Fleisher & Decker, 2001). Almost all of the criminological literature makes sharp distinctions between prison and street gangs, That has never been the case in Chicago (Jacobs, 1977), and today gangs from prisons are dominating, or attempting to control, street drug markets everywhere (Hayden, 2004; Moore & Williams, 2010). In a period of mass incarceration, with so many young Black males being released and then quickly returning to prison for violating conditions of parole, the prison has become continuous with the community, and gangs can no longer be understood separate from their typically incarcerated leadership. The large numbers of gang members going in and out of the prison system means persisting ties of varying strength exist between gangs both inside and outside the prison walls.

Secondly, the war on gangs has led to the application of RICO (Racketeer Influenced and Corrupt Organizations Act), or organized crime conspiracy statutes against gang members. The recent passage in the state of Illinois of a "street gang RICO statute" means that the state has joined more than two dozen other states in using RICO statutes to target street gangs and not the mafia (Garcia, 2012). Aside from widening the net by increasing the incarceration of gang members, the impact or ramifications on family and friends of these RICO and conspiracy charges has been relatively uninvestigated. Susan Phillips's 2012 book, *Operation Fly Trap,* is the first book to look carefully at the human impact of conspiracy charges, chronicling the broken families and how the war on gangs encourages street violence. It is a chilling and important piece of research. We also need to reiterate with Michelle Alexander (2010) that prison disenfranchises felons, which, she argues, makes incarceration a key element in a criminal system that functions as the "new Jim Crow."

What Research Has Taught Us About Gangs

Since 2001, there has been a tendency to conflate the wars on gangs and drugs with the war on terror. Gangs are now frequently being reframed by media and law enforcement as "urban terrorists" (Killebrew,

2008), which often justifies police brutality and denial of civil liberties. For example, MS-13 (a transnational criminal gang) has been called a "mutating virus and international menace."[6] Anti-gang legislation, such as in Illinois and California, typically contain "urban or street gang terrorist" in the title.[7]

Punitive policies continue to be popular with prosecutors and the public. The recent 5 to 4 Supreme Court decision in **Miller v. Alabama** (2012) declared a sentence of life without parole for juveniles was unconstitutional, following the earlier ruling that declared that the death penalty was unconstitutional for youth under 18 (**Roper v. Simmons**, 2005).[8] At the same time, the trend continues toward waiving juveniles (particularly gang-involved youth) to criminal court to be tried as adults.[9] The use of the waiver, particularly with those persons labeled as gang members, has shown no overall decline over 25 years, despite declining rates of crime and violence. About one in every one hundred youth adjudicated delinquent is waived to adult court. These data demonstrate that we have not decisively broken from the fears of John Dilulio's predictions that the nineties would see a generation of young, hyperviolent "super-predators." (Adams & Addie, 2010).

Most criminological reviews of gang programming (e.g., Howell's *Gangs in America's Communities)* omit any mention of the impact of mass incarceration, and avoid discussing the everyday problems of minority youth when dealing with law enforcement, such as overly aggressive policing, brutality, and corruption. Federally funded gang programs tend to have a very one-sided view of the police in poor minority communities; they see them as agents of social control and not as problems themselves. Also, including the police as part of the problem is virtually unknown in the federally funded universe of gang research.

For example, the highly touted G.R.E.A.T. program purports to be a gang and violence prevention program, but formal evaluations (see a review in Howell, 2012) have not found any long-term effects on gang membership (Esbensen, 2004). The main impact of the program appears to be a short-term change in attitudes of youth toward law enforcement. The G.R.E.A.T. program is more ceremonial than substantive and appears to be little more than a 21st century version of "Officer Friendly."

A second example is the Department of Justice "comprehensive model" (Howell, 2012)[10] of gang programming that was based on Irving Spergel's Little Village Gang Violence Reduction Project in Chicago. What Howell and the Department of Justice (DOJ) fail to disclose is that Spergel's project was sabotaged by the Chicago police and ultimately denied funding (Spergel et al., 2003).[11] In the final Report to the project, the late Dr. Spergel laments: "The Mayor and the Superintendent of the Chicago Police Department still had not learned that the gang problem was a complex human, organizational, and community problem that could not be resolved by hard-line police policy alone" (Spergel et al., 2003, p. 18).

---

[6] Ling, L. (Writer). (2000). *The world's most dangerous gang* [DVD]. Washington, DC: National Geographic.
[7] For example (740 ILCS 147/1), referred to as the "Illinois Streetgang Terrorism Omnibus Prevention Act."
[8] Note that many states, like Illinois, simply refuse to apply the ban on juvenile life without parole sentences to past cases, including Jacqueline Montañez.
[9] For example, see Institute for Law and Justice, specifically sections on Prosecutor and Judicial Decision making in Juvenile Waiver Cases. Retrieved from http://www.ilj.org/focus_areas/gangs_and_juvenile_justice.html
[10] http://www.nationalgangcenter.gov/Comprehensive-Gang-Model/About
[11] Spergel also expanded on this issue in a personal conversation to the first author, and in a formal talk to one of his classes.

In fact, Chicago provides a good example of what public policy has not learned from research on gangs and violence; hence, Chicago is an excellent setting for an exploration of whether gang wars are a response to a real threat or may more closely resemble a moral panic.

Gangs, Chicago, and Homicide

Gangs in Chicago date back to the 19th century and are synonymous with Chicago from the time of Al Capone until the present day. The sharp rise in 2012 in the number of Chicago's homicides has been attributed to a gang problem, and also described as "worse than any city" (Belkin, 2012; Davey, 2012; Reynolds, 2012). While Chicago's violent crime rates, particularly homicide rates, have varied over the years, they have always been much higher than the rates of the United States as a whole. Chicago's highest murder levels coincided with the beer wars of the 1920s, gang violence associated with the deindustrialization of the 1970s, and the crack wars of the 1990s. This pattern, it should be recalled, is consistent with conclusions from the United Nations Global Study on Homicide (Me et. al, 2011).

As noted earlier, Chicago's modest declines in homicide rates beginning in the mid-1990s are similar to those in other cities and in the United States nationally. Prior to 2012, both the Chicago Police and CeaseFire, a university-based program that purports to "interrupt" gang retaliations, were loudly claiming credit for these reductions in gang violence, which occurred throughout the United States and in nearly every Chicago neighborhood. The program CeaseFire was the subject of a Hollywood documentary, *The Interrupters,* that popularized its violence interruption approach and disseminated it worldwide. For their part, the Chicago Police adopted the New York City approach to crime reduction, Compstat, a law enforcement strategy to map crimes, identify "hotspots" and problems, and ultimately devise solutions and which demands accountability from police for reducing "the numbers." This program is effectively belittled in the HBO show, *The Wire.* The Chicago police also adapted David Kennedy's original CeaseFire program, renamed Violence Reduction Strategy, aiming to replicate the sharp drops in murder rates that occurred in Boston. Kennedy claimed reducing violence in central cities is "easy"[12] and argued that police tactics can intimidate gang members to bring "an end to violence in inner-city America" (Kennedy, 2011).

But, 2012 saw a quick, if temporary, halt to this reckless rhetoric. Chicago became the "Wild, Wild, Midwest" (Daly, 2012) and the nationwide center of attention after experiencing a 40% increase in homicides during the first six months of the year. The magic bullets of the Chicago police force and the CeaseFire program didn't seem so magic anymore.[13] Although the current police superintendent McCarthy

Table 11.1	Homicide Rates in Chicago and in the U.S. 1900–2010	
	Chicago	United States
1900	6.0	1.2
1910	9.2	**4.6**
1920	10.5	6.8
1930	**14.6**	8.8
1940	7.1	6.3
1950	7.9	**4.6**
1960	10.3	5.1
1970	24.0	7.9
1980	28.7	10.2
1990	32.9	9.4
2000	22.1	5.5
2010	**15.4**	**4.8**

Source: U.S. Rates 1910–1940 from http://www.druglibrary.org/schaffer/Library/homrate1.htm; 1950–2000 and http://www.disastercenter.com/crime/uscrime.htm. Chicago rates from Chicago Homicide Data Base and Chicago Police Department statistics.

[12] http://gangsandthemedia.blogspot.com/2011/10/interruptors-why-i-dont-like-this-movie.html
[13] In fact, earlier evaluations of CeaseFire had pointed out the program had little or no effect in a city where violence was already decreasing in all neighborhoods. See particularly Block's and Papachristos' formal evaluations. http://www.chicagojustice.org/foi/relevant-documents-of-interest/ceasefire/Northwestern-CeaseFire-Evaluation-Appendices.pdf

and Mayor Emanuel continued to blame gangs for the increase, why gang violence would rise now after more than a decade of declines was unintelligible and embarrassingly contradicted their previous claims of police and CeaseFire "success."

Frantic policy proposals of all sorts were floated, the most highly touted a state RICO statute directly aimed at street gangs (Moore, 2012), with mandatory sentences for gun possession applying only to gang members, and multiple "get tough on gangs" tactics (Byrne, 2009). Superintendent McCarthy also angrily called for the "elimination" of the Maniac Latin Disciples, a 60-year-old gang that will certainly far outlast the superintendent's term in office (Main, 2011).[14]

The increase in violence in 2012 wrenched up official rhetoric to induce the media into a classic moral panic. But a calm, scientific examination of what is really going on paints a different picture. First, the increases in the first part of 2012 were real, but Chicago's homicide rate is still about the same as it was in 1930. Homicides today in Chicago, even if the increases of the first six months of 2012 continued, are half the rates of the mid-1990s, and less than in 2008. Taking into account both before and after the 2012 increases, Chicago's murder rate still holds steady at less than half of Detroit's (43.3/100,000 in 2010) and about four times higher than New York City's (4.5/100,000).[15] Nothing has really changed in Chicago's rank as a city of high/moderate homicide levels.

Second, levels of homicide, as we've seen from the United Nations report, are related to "social isolation and alienation" which remains at a high level in Chicago particularly in the Black community (Me et al., 2011). Chicago's Black community has still not recovered from the Jon Burge era, labeled such because a former police commander tortured more than 100 Black male gang members with nary a complaint from fellow officers or politicians aware of the human rights violations (Conroy, 2000). A series of corruption and human rights scandals involving police units robbing gangs of drugs and selling them has also contributed to intense alienation on the streets.[16] Chicago's 19% Black unemployment rate is the third highest in the nation, nearly three times higher than for whites (Boodhoo, 2012). Press reports find a correlation between the poorest and most segregated neighborhoods and high homicide rates (Bogira, 2012).

What did not occur in 2012 is a major gang war. Researchers found that the current spate in violence is largely spontaneous and related to desperation more than organization. Since the crack wars of the 1990s, Chicago gangs have fractured, with gang leadership no longer in control of street soldiers (Hagedorn, 2008; Moore & Williams, 2010).

This means that any policies are misplaced that target Chicago gang leaders as responsible for the increase in homicides. Since gang leaders no longer control the streets and the violence, attempts to intimidate gang leaders or to negotiate with them to reduce violence are largely ineffective. Chicago is neither Mexico nor El Salvador. Gangs are not waging an all-out war over drug markets, as in Mexico, and they no longer have the legitimate authority to call a truce, as in El Salvador. While it is likely that the decreases of the last half of 2012 are examples of "regression to the mean," that has not stopped police and others from claiming credit for reductions in violence.[17]

---

[14] See also http://gangsandthemedia.blogspot.com/2011/07/obliterating-gangs-in-chicago.html

[15] New York City rates: http://www.disastercenter.com/crime/nycrime.htm. For Detroit http://www.detroitmi.gov/DepartmentsandAgencies/PoliceDepartment/CrimeStatistics.aspx

[16] For example, watch this *60 Minutes* segment on Chicago's SOS unit where the leader of a corrupt unit seeks to hire a gang hitman to kill a fellow officer threatening to testify against him. Retrieved from http://www.cbsnews.com/2100-18560_162-4139413.html

[17] E.g., "Police Supt. Garry McCarthy said his strategies are beginning to drive down shootings and slayings." http://www.suntimes.com/news/crime/14164166-418/citys-rising-murder-rate-beginning-to-drop-top-cop-says.html

In the policy world, when magic bullets are fired, the best response is to duck. Of course, evaluations of specific tactics in Chicago this year are not yet possible. But, the real lesson of the current events in Chicago is that a "moral panic" over gang violence obscures a rational analysis of the factual situation—which is what social science and this article require. But, if magic bullets are blanks, does that mean we are helpless? No.

How Do We Fix It? Suggestions for Policy Reform

We end our chapter by asking for *attention to detail* when conducting any discussion or evaluation on gangs: first, to understand that in order to know what to do about gangs, requires understanding them, their alienation, and why young boys and girls join a gang; and then demands that we base our policies on their actual patterns of behavior, not what the mass media say about them. Chicago is a clear, if sad, example of what happens when media hype trumps reality in the construction of the crime problem.

Attention to detail means understanding the extensiveness of violence in boys and girls lives. And to shape our response to youth violence with a clear understanding of the day-to-day traumas that many youth in extremely violent homes, neighborhoods, and schools experience. To examine patterns and create sensible policy does not excuse violence, but rather means that any successful policy must understand the pain of victims. Most often the victims of violence are other youth, and they need interventions that seek to reduce violence and the impact of violence. We call special attention to violence against women in and around gangs and the need for shelters and gender-specific programming (Firmin, 2011).

Given our analysis, no policy can be implemented without a cultural struggle against demonization. In other words, if gang members are dehumanized, then any policy solutions devised will also be inhumane. Demonization has enabled extremely brutal and corrupt police practices, as was dramatically clear in the Rampart scandal involving the Los Angeles Police Department's anti-gang unit (see Markovitz, 2011) or the two-decade-long torture spree in Chicago by Jon Burge. *Attention to detail* means considering the lives of gang members, police, neighbors, victims, and all citizens as *human beings,* not as devils or monsters. Special attention is recommended to combat demonization in court, where prosecutors find it useful to paint gang offenders in the worst possible light (Jackson, 2004). This does not advance the cause of justice.

We call for *attention to detail* in better investigative journalism of police practices as well as exposés of the conditions of social exclusion and racism in minority and poor communities. We encourage the development of a new cadre of citizen journalists, in both the web and print media, and encourage more public support for genuine investigative journalism, which has all but disappeared.

Major media are now increasingly under the control of corporate barons who employ racist media frames of crime stories to justify often draconian and racist policing practices while also stoking the imprisonment binge. Along with salacious celebrity gossip, these moguls use these methods of selling papers to distract readers from the war mongering, corporate greed, and income inequality that actually jeopardize the future of our country. University researchers must do their part to document and challenge these media distortions and to get the word out about how a balanced and public health approach to drug addiction and gang violence can cost less and be far more effective in preventing youth 𝑓

The discipline of cultural criminology promises just this outcome, because it
assessments of corporate media images while also challenging the d
like graffiti (see Ferrell, 1996).

Attention to detail means that we must not forget the pressing need for structural changes, including more jobs in "truly disadvantaged" communities in our cities where gangs flourish. We need to create a meaningful alternative to the endless supply of jobs generated by the illegal drug trade (Hagedorn, 2001). We do not believe that the expansion of the military and our perpetual involvement in foreign wars is an acceptable alternative to jobs creation. The most likely result of violence, as Hannah Arendt (1969) famously said, is "more violence." We believe Arendt's words apply to our militaristic foreign policy.

In tandem with more jobs, there should be fewer prisons. There is no excuse for the United States to have 5% of the world's population, but imprison 25% of the world's prisoners. Senator Jim Webb, who is leading a national commission to look into the problem, notes sensibly and prophetically

> America imprisons 756 inmates for every 100,000 residents, a rate nearly five times the world's average. About one in every 31 adults in this country is in jail, or on supervised release. Either we are the most evil people in the world, or we are doing something terribly wrong. (Webb, 2009)

We agree.

If we pay *attention to detail* in our correctional populations, we see that it is minority nonviolent drug-related offenders, not a declining number of violent gang members, who make up most of the correctional population. Many studies have found that one way to begin to wind down the war on drugs is to decriminalize marijuana, which would immediately eliminate over half of all drug arrests (FBI, 2011). This action also undermines the hyperviolent drug cartels in Mexico, which rely on marijuana criminalization for much of their profits (Beittel, 2012). Additionally, it creates fewer recruits for prison-based gangs. Clearly, a public health, harm reduction, approach to the use and sale of drugs removes much of the current "market" for illegal drugs.

If we take a serious look at repairing the nation's tattered infrastructure, there might well be entry-level jobs for motivated, but marginalized young people. Likewise, if we prioritized women and children, we would support education and training programs (with childcare) so that young women of color could imagine positions for themselves in health care or the service industry with benefits and a future. Investing the dollars we now have committed to incarceration in the rebuilding of communities would make the often sordid and violent drug trade far less attractive to desperate young people.

Attention to detail means studying history, and we not forgetting the influence that the social movements of the 1960s had on gangs. The Black liberation and civil rights movements in those times won over many of the very poor, and politics competed with criminality for the allegiance of gang members and other street youth. Such movements may still be the most effective means to reduce violence and promote prosocial actions.

We need to be more cautious in accepting at face value "magic bullet" programs like police and school "zero tolerance" programs, or university-based programs like CeaseFire. To solve the chronic problem of violence in certain communities, we should place more attention on supporting and empowering communities, particularly African American and Latino neighborhoods, so that they can work with their own youth. If youth feel that they are a part of a vital community and they have a sense of their own future, they are less drawn to sources of identity built on masculine display, conspicuous consumption, and hyperviolence (what might be called "gangsta mentality"). Likewise, if girls can reconnect with their families and schools so that they do not have to turn to gangs as surrogate family, we can imagine communities where gangs do not rule the streets. We believe the involvement of gang youth with their peers and neighbors in social movements toward justice and equality is an essential component of solving America's gang problem.

Finally, *attention to detail* means we need to make certain that those charged with controlling crime do not mimic the same masculine norms of hyperviolence and corruption popularly associated with gangs. Police cannot combat gangs if they have a gangster mentality. Added to that, meaningful civilian oversight of the police and penal institutions is vital so that organizations do not perpetuate the gang problem, as has been the case with prison gangs.

We conclude that the gang problem in the United States is better understood by social scientists as "moral panic" rather than a "real threat." This does not mean violence is not a serious problem, particularly for many poor Black and Latino communities. We think policy responses need to be based on empathy for victims and offenders alike. It also needs to be based on a real understanding of the many reasons why youth engage in criminal behavior and join gangs. At the very top of our agenda is the rejection of mass incarceration that is largely based on the demonization of racial and ethnic communities as "gang ridden" and beyond redemption.

KEY TERMS

Gang injunctions	Sentencing enhancements	War on gangs
Mass incarceration	Vertical prosecution programs	

DISCUSSION QUESTIONS

1. What are "magic bullets" and how does this concept explain limitations of programs dealing with gangs?

2. What role has the media played in inflating the "gang problem"?

3. What did Jacqueline Montañez mean by her statement: "I did what you said I did, but I'm not who you say I am?" Why does it matter? In what ways can stereotypes of gangs actually cause harm?

WEBSITES FOR ADDITIONAL RESEARCH

National Criminal Justice Reference Service: https://www.ncjrs.gov/

National Gang Center: http://www.nationalgangcenter.gov/

National Gang Crime Research Center: http://www.ngcrc.com/

Street Gangs in Los Angeles: http://www.streetgangs.com/

Los Angeles Police Department: http://www.lapdonline.org

XII

Juvenile Waiver Policies

Aaron Kupchik and Megan Gosse

The first juvenile court was created in 1899 in Chicago. Its founders promoted it as a way to help youth in need by responding to youth crime in developmentally appropriate ways. The creation of this type of court was a very popular legal reform, and states across the United States quickly copied Chicago's idea and began their own juvenile courts.

More than 100 years later, the system of juvenile courts is still in place. But, often children under age 18 are prosecuted in adult criminal courts instead of juvenile courts, due to a policy called juvenile waiver. Waived juveniles are identified as better suited for the adult court, and their cases are transferred, or waived, there. In this chapter, we describe how the numbers and use of juvenile waiver policies has expanded in recent years and the effects of these policies.

✄ The Back Story

The development of the juvenile justice system in Cook County (Chicago) in 1899 was preceded by massive social change, including transformations like urbanization and immigration (Platt, 2009; Rothman, 2002). Rapid immigration and urbanization in the late 19th century meant that large numbers of youth, many of them poor and from immigrant families, were forced to fend for themselves on urban streets. Their parents often worked long hours in factories, leaving these youth with little supervision as they traveled within high-crime impoverished areas.

At the same time, ideas about childhood were changing in the United States. Historians described the late 19th century as a time when broadly held ideas about childhood, including perceptions of the abilities and vulnerabilities of children as well as of the "value" of children, were changing (see Feld, 1999; Zelizer, 1985). Children were increasingly seen as different from adults because they were: (a) vulnerable and in need of protection from cruel city streets, (b) innocent, in that they were not fully responsible for their mistakes due to their immaturity, and (c) emotionally priceless, as adults began to cherish children more for sentimental reasons than for their ability to contribute financially to the family.

These two trends—increasing numbers of poor, unsupervised, often immigrant youth, and the growing recognition of children's needs and their differences from adults—led to broad changes in how society dealt with juvenile delinquents and to the creation of the first juvenile court. Rhetorically, at least, the new juvenile justice system followed the ideas that juveniles, due to their age and lack of maturity, were more in need of rehabilitation than punishment. Children were also viewed as having a lower level of culpability (blameworthiness) than adults, since they lacked adult-like maturity (Bortner, 1986; Fritsch, Caeti, & Hemmens, 1996). The court system was designed to be a "confidential, informal, and non-adversarial forum to deal with crime related and other problems of children" (Houghtalin & Mays, 1991, p. 394). Juveniles were viewed as relatively blameless, since the court's founders believed that improper parenting and negative community influences were the root causes of their delinquency (Applegate, Davis, & Cullen, 2009). As a result, children were seen as more innocent, less able to form criminal intent, and more amenable to treatment and rehabilitation than adults (Fritsch et al., 1996; Kurlychek & Johnson, 2004).

Yet, the founders of the first court realized that not all youth fit this description, as some juvenile offenders were so dangerous or stubborn in their offending that they were beyond the juvenile court's ability to help. These youth were sent to the adult courts, or waived to the adult court for prosecution and punishment (see Kupchik, 2006; Tanenhaus, 2004). This practice was relatively rare since the founders of the juvenile court were optimistic that they could reasonably respond to most delinquent youth.

In the 1970s and 1980s, the juvenile court came under attack. Juvenile crime was rising, and critics argued that the rehabilitative nature of the juvenile justice system was too soft on crime, too coddling of offenders. These critics insisted on a more retributive approach, where punishment was the central goal instead of rehabilitation; such an approach follows the maxim "an eye for an eye" in prescribing punishment rather than trying to fix the problems that led to the delinquency (Applegate et al., 2009; Fritsch et al., 1996; Steiner & Wright, 2006; Steiner, Hemmens, & Bell, 2006). Though juvenile courts were able to waive the most difficult youth to adult court, critics argued that this happened too infrequently. As a result, 49 states amended their statutes during the 1990s to "get tough" on crime, increasing the number of juvenile offenders prosecuted as adults. The purpose of these new laws was to make it easier for judges or prosecutors to waive youth to adult court so that they could be treated as hardened offenders rather than as errant youth. Punishment rather than rehabilitation was now the central concern guiding the sentencing of these juveniles. Those accused of serious crimes were to be held fully accountable and have to take full responsibility for their acts, two ideas that were previously foreign to the juvenile justice system (Fritsch et al., 1996; Urbina, 2005). Slogans like "If you are old enough to do the crime, you are old enough to do the time" started appearing in the media, and political campaigns championed a "get tough" on crime position (Kurlychek & Johnson, 2004).

These laws worked in different ways. One type of waiver law that became more common during this time is usually referred to as "*statutory exclusion.*" These laws apply to specific age/crime combinations and dictate that youth of certain ages arrested for certain offenses are automatically waived to the adult system. In Maryland, for example, juveniles 14 and older are automatically waived for capital offenses, and those 16 and older are waived for a host of personal and weapon offenses (Kurlychek & Johnson, 2010). In addition, certain states have "*once waived, always waived*" legislation, which states that after a juvenile is waived once to criminal court, all subsequent charges against the juvenile, regardless of the severity of the offense, have to be charged in criminal court. Other laws expanded the original type of waiver practice, known as "*judicial waiver,*" where judges decide which juveniles should be waived. These new laws made it easier for judges to waive youth based on their *discretion*, by removing barriers like minimum age requirements for waiver. In these cases, a judge has to determine if the juvenile is amenable to the treatment options available in the juvenile court. If the judge feels the juvenile will not benefit from the treatment offered by the juvenile court, the judge transfers the juvenile to adult court. Also, these decisions usually take into account the age of the offender and the offense committed (Griffin, 2003).

But, perhaps the most substantial shift was that states across the United States gave greater power to prosecutors to decide which youth should be waived. Many states adopted "***direct file***" laws that allow prosecutors to file juvenile cases directly to the adult court, prior to any appearance before a judge (also known as ***prosecutorial waiver***) (Applegate et al., 2009). Fifteen states allow the use of direct file, and while some have restrictive criteria about who can be waived, other states give the prosecutor a great deal of freedom and discretion to make this decision. For example, in Florida prosecutors have few restrictions on directly filing juvenile cases in adult court, thus the waiver of juveniles to the adult court is very easily accomplished. One consequence of this broad prosecutorial authority in Florida is that racial and ethnic minority youth are disproportionately transferred to the adult system, with studies finding Black youth over twice as likely to be transferred (Bishop, Frazier, & Henretta, 1989).

The Current State of the Policy

It is very difficult to estimate exactly how many youth under the age of 18 are prosecuted in adult court, for two reasons. One reason is that there are many different ways for a youth to be waived to adult court.[1] Most states allow for judicial waiver, where a judge can decide which youth should be sent to the adult system. In some states, judges must follow presumptive judicial waiver laws, where a judge has little ability to deviate from the presumption that a case will be waived, based on specific criteria. In other states, judges *must* waive certain cases, if certain criteria are met. But, other cases can be directly filed in the adult court by a prosecutor, and yet others are automatically excluded from the juvenile court. In most states, the age of the offender and type of crime determine which of these many waiver mechanisms can and will be applied to a particular case.

Just to make things even more confusing, more than half of all the states also use a "once waived, always waived" rule; this rule states that if a youth is waived to the adult court at any time, that juvenile is automatically considered an adult for any further criminal offense, regardless of their age and how trivial the offense. Conversely, about half of the states allow for a "reverse waiver," which means that after a juvenile's case gets waived to the adult court, it can still be waived back down to the juvenile court. In other words, waiver laws are very complicated, with most states using multiple—sometimes even competing—waiver mechanisms.

The second reason why it is difficult to estimate how many youth are prosecuted as adults is simply that we don't bother to count them. The number of youth who are waived by judges is counted each year—however, this is the least common method of waiver (Griffin et al., 2011). There is no national count of youth whose cases are directly filed in the adult court, or who are excluded by law from the juvenile court, because many jurisdictions don't define them as juveniles. Once a juvenile gets treated as an adult, their legal status within the criminal justice system is that they are, officially, an adult. Thus, a thirteen-year-old in middle school, who enjoys absolutely none of the rights or privileges of an adult (e.g., voting, purchasing alcohol or cigarettes, driving) and who is classified as a dependent and a minor by all other government agencies, no longer counts as a juvenile for criminal justice statistics once she or he is waived to the adult court.

---

[1] For an excellent recent summary of states' waiver laws, see Griffin, Addie, Adams, and Firestine (2011); this summary informs the following discussion of contemporary waiver laws and rates of waiver.

Nationwide, we know that about 8,500 youth were judicially waived in 2007 (Griffin et al., 2011). Based on a 1998 report from the Department of Justice, we can use this number to estimate the number of youth waived by other means (Rainville & Smith, 2003). This report was based on research in 40 large counties in the United States where the researchers tracked cases of all the juvenile defendants who were waived to adult courts. It found that in these counties, judicially waived youth represented about one-fourth of all waived youth (Rainville & Smith, 2003), suggesting that approximately another 25,500 youth were waived in 2007 from direct file and statutory exclusion laws, nationwide.

Yet, neither of these estimates includes youth who are beyond their state's age of majority. This is important because 13 states define being an adult (for criminal justice purposes only) at either 16 or 17. In New York, for example, *all* 16- and 17-year-olds who are arrested for *any* offense are automatically defined as adults, with no opportunity whatsoever for prosecution in the juvenile court (thus, when a prosecutor on *Law and Order* wrestles with the decision to prosecute a 17-year-old as an adult, the television show offers an incorrect view of New York's laws). Based on their states' ages of majority, Griffin et al. (2011) attempted to estimate the number of youth younger than 18 who were prosecuted as adults; they estimated that up to 175,000 youth reach adult court this way! These youth aren't normally considered under other counts of waived youth, even though they are younger than 18 and prosecuted in adult courts.

Though these estimates may be helpful, they are estimates, not counts, and should be interpreted with caution. Moreover, extrapolations are severely complicated by the fact that states waive youth at very different rates. For example, among the 13 states that collect and report data on waiver fairly well, the rate of waiver varies from 7.1 per 100,000 youth in North Carolina to 164.7 per 100,000 in Florida (Griffin et al., 2011)—this variation among the states would likely be larger if all the states were included in the comparison.

Another way to view the contemporary use of waiver policies is to look at a high profile case. Consider, for example, the case of Jordan Brown, who killed his father's pregnant fiancée in 2009 in Pennsylvania, when Jordan was 11 years old (Balingit, 2012). Jordan's case was initially heard in the adult court, but eventually he was sent down to the juvenile court where in April of 2012, he was adjudicated delinquent (the euphemism for "convicted" used in the juvenile court) for the murder of his father's fiancée and her unborn baby. Jordan's crime was horrific and clearly deserves some form of serious punishment that can both protect the public from a severely troubled youth and respond to public outrage over the crime. But, given the severe immaturity of the average 11-year-old, the prospect (and initial action) of prosecuting Jordan as an adult raises interesting questions. Does it make sense to prosecute a preadolescent as an adult if he lacks anywhere near an adult capacity of maturity and reasoning, including the ability to understand the consequences of his actions, think about the future, or empathize with others? Is the answer to this question influenced by the fact that conviction for this offense in the criminal court would have resulted in a mandatory sentence of life in prison without possibility of parole?

Jordan's case also underscores the complexity of waiver law. Because of Pennsylvania waiver laws, his case began in the adult court, which states that the judge conducts what is known as a "decertification hearing"; here, the judge decides if the case should be "decertified," or waived down to the juvenile court. The judge denied the defense's request for decertification, arguing that because he refused to admit guilt and take responsibility for the crime, Jordan failed to show he was amenable to rehabilitative treatment (amenability to treatment is one component of the decertification decision). Jordan's attorneys successfully argued to the Pennsylvania Superior Court that it was unconstitutional to force him to admit guilt (thus foregoing his right to a trial) in order to be prosecuted as a juvenile (Juvenile Law Center, 2012). This disagreement shows the complexity of Pennsylvania's waiver laws and lack of clarity—even among judges—about how waiver decisions should be made.

As we discuss below, a growing body of evidence suggests that waiver laws may produce more harm than good. Perhaps in recognition of this, a number of states are beginning to undo some of their waiver mechanisms. In Connecticut, the criminal age of majority was raised to 18 from 16. Other states have enacted smaller changes, such as limiting the offenses for which a juvenile can be waived (see Arya, 2011). For example, in 2010 Colorado raised its minimum age of direct file eligibility from 14 to 16 for most offenses, meaning that prosecutors cannot directly file juveniles younger than 16 (other than those charged with murder or a sex offense) to adult court. Though waiver is still a common and popular practice, these modest legal reforms suggest that we may see a substantial reduction of the use of waiver at some point in the near future.

What Research Has Taught Us: Outcomes of Waiver Laws

There are a few key goals of waiver laws: to sentence serious offenders more severely than could be done in the juvenile court; to judge serious juvenile offenders based on what they have done, not on who they are; and to protect the public from serious juvenile offenders. The research evidence suggests that waiver laws may have met the first goal, but have failed at the other goals.

Early research examining whether waived youth are punished more severely than youth in the juvenile court shows mixed results; some studies find that juveniles who get waived are more likely to be convicted and incarcerated than youth in the juvenile court, while other studies find that they are less likely to be convicted and incarcerated (see Howell, 1996). If the latter is true, it is probably because adult court judges who are accustomed to sentencing hardened adult offenders may look sympathetically at waived youth and attempt to rehabilitate rather than punish them severely. However, more recent research has done a better job of comparing similar cases and controlling for factors like juveniles' prior records. This literature tends to report that youth prosecuted in criminal court do indeed receive harsher punishments than those tried in juvenile court (Jordan & Myers, 2011; Kupchik, Fagan, & Liberman, 2003). Moreover, recent research suggests that youth who are waived often receive even harsher punishment than young adults who are charged with the same crimes (e.g., Kurlychek & Johnson, 2004, 2010; Steiner, 2009). Thus, overall the research finds that waiver to adult court is successful at providing harsh punishment for juveniles.

When we look at how these waived youth are judged, however, we find that waiver laws are less successful. In theory, waiver to adult court means that the defendant's immaturity should no longer matter, only their offense (see Kupchik, 2006). As slogans, such as "you do the crime, you do the time" suggest, waiver laws are meant to select some youth who no longer deserve the individualized decision making of the juvenile court and now must be judged only for the harms they committed. Waiver laws are intended in part as a message that at least for these youth, it doesn't matter if they have dysfunctional homes or learning disabilities—only their crimes matter. Yet, research that examines how youth in criminal court are judged finds that these waived youth are still judged with their immaturity in mind. Though this research is sparse and based on case studies that may not be generalizable to all jurisdictions, it finds that judges, prosecutors, and defense attorneys do still consider the immaturity of waived youth and try to allow them room for rehabilitation (Barrett, 2012; Kupchik, 2006). For example, this research finds that adult court judges often delay sentencing on juveniles' cases while the juvenile is sent to drug treatment, counseling, or other therapeutic programs. If the juveniles do well in these programs, and prove their ability to reform their behavior, judges often suspend their prison sentence. Thus, when they believe the circumstances of a particular case warrant it, court actors actually bypass some aspects of waiver laws in an effort to act like a juvenile court, not an adult court; in these cases they allow children the opportunity to learn from their mistakes rather than assuming they are fully responsible for their crimes.

Nevertheless, perhaps the most important outcome to consider is public safety. Waiver laws are intended both to protect the public by teaching young criminals a lesson and to prevent crime among youth who may be frightened by the harsh sentences given to young offenders. This was certainly a central promise of politicians who wrote new waiver laws in the 1990s, suggesting that only by creating harsh waiver laws could we tackle increasing rates of serious juvenile crime. By this important measure, waiver laws are a colossal failure. Several studies in different parts of the country and using very different methodologies were conducted looking at both general deterrence (whether waiver laws prevent crime among the whole population of youth) and specific deterrence (whether the experience of waiver prevents a return to crime, or recidivism, among the specific youth who are waived) (see Bishop, Frazier, Lanza-Kaduce, & Winner, 1996; Fagan, 1996; Fagan, Kupchik, & Liberman, 2003; Jensen & Metsger, 1994; Lanza-Kaduce, Frazier, Lane, & Bishop, 2002; Myers, 2001; Singer & MacDowall, 1988; Steiner & Wright, 2006; Winner, Lanza-Kaduce, Bishop, & Frazier, 1997). Recent reviews of this research conducted both for the U.S. Department of Justice (Redding, 2010) and the Centers for Disease Control (Hahn et al., 2007; see also McGowan et al., 2007) find that these studies converge on two general conclusions: waiver laws have no general deterrent effect (they have no impact on juvenile crime rates, generally), and among youth who are waived, the waiver laws may *increase* rates of crime, particularly *violent* crime.

It is not fully clear why waiver laws might increase crime. It's possible that the mark of an adult conviction makes it more difficult for waived youth to find employment and even a place to live (e.g., many housing projects evict residents if a family member has been convicted of certain crimes[2]), which makes them more likely to return to crime rather than moving forward with productive lives. It's also likely that because they are sent to the adult system, these juveniles miss out on potentially helpful treatment they could have received in the juvenile court system. Although the research still has not fully explained why we see this result, it is now clear that the increased use of waiver that began in the 1970s puts the public at greater risk of criminal victimization, particularly violent victimization.

◈ Race, Class, and Gender Implications

Another serious problem with the broad use of waiver is that waiver policies increase racial inequality in the juvenile justice system. Several studies find that youth of color are considerably more likely than White youth charged with the same crimes to be waived to the criminal court (e.g., Bortner, Zatz, & Hawkins, 2000). While self-report studies show White adolescents use drugs just as often as African American adolescents, 75% of juvenile drug offense defendants are Black, and 95% of youth sent to adult prison for drug charges are youth of color (Young & Gainsborough, 2000).

---

[2] The federal government's "One Strike" policy encourages public housing authorities to evict families if their children are convicted of any offenses, leading to homelessness among youth whose families face the choice of kicking out their children, or eviction for the whole family (Kaplan & Rossman, 2011).

Once in the criminal court, youth of color also face more severe punishments than similarly situated White youth. For example, Jordan & Freiburger (2010), found that compared to Whites, a Black youth's chances of receiving probation rather than jail time were decreased and both Blacks and Hispanics were significantly more likely to receive prison rather than a jail sentence compared to Whites. Finally, having previous encounters with the juvenile justice system increased the probability of receiving prison rather than jail for Black youth, but not for Whites. Because youth are much more likely to face severe punishment in the adult system than in the juvenile system, and their incarceration in adult facilities often leads to severe problems like physical attack (Forst, Fagan, & Vivona, 1989) and PTSD (Fagan & Kupchik, 2011), this racial discrepancy in the use of waiver means that minority youth are subjected to hurtful outcomes at greater rates than White youth.

Furthermore, the racial discrepancies caused by waiver do not cease once the juveniles are released, since the stigma of criminal court conviction continues to harm youths for years to come. In contrast, juvenile court convictions are often sealed and confidential, which means that the youth are less likely to be punished when seeking jobs, housing, or public benefits. Yet, this stigma that results from waiver has different consequences according to a juvenile's race. For example, in an extensive study of the long-term harm of a criminal conviction to one's future prospects, Devah Pager (2007) conducted an experiment where Black and White young men claiming to have criminal convictions searched for employment. She found that contact with the criminal justice system substantially decreased employment opportunities for youths, indicating the stigma of prison as the factor preventing them from employment. For instance, 34% of Whites without a criminal record received callbacks compared to only 17% of Whites with a criminal record; indicating a criminal record reduces their chance of callback by 50% (Pager, 2007). Unfortunately, this statistic was much worse for African Americans. Despite similar resumés, the results indicated that among Blacks who did not have a criminal record, only 14% received callbacks, compared to 34% of Whites without criminal records and 17% of Whites with a criminal record. Therefore, the effect of a criminal record is much more pronounced for Blacks than it is Whites. This is again evident from the report that employers asked several Black applicants before submitting their application if they had a criminal history. None of the White applicants were asked the same question (Pager, 2007).

Overall, evidence on waiver strongly reveals that it increases racial inequality; youth of color are at greater risk than White youth of being waived, which has a long-lasting effect on their ability to eventually become productive citizens. There is less evidence on whether waiver has implications for gender and class dynamics. With regard to gender, this is likely because most waived cases are of males, though additional research is needed to clarify this issue. With regard to class, this is probably because juvenile and criminal justice systems rarely collect data on socioeconomic status, thus it is difficult to measure the class backgrounds of juveniles.

⬛ Unintended Consequences of Juvenile Waiver Policies

Above, contrary to the goals of waiver policies, we discussed how waiver leads to increased crime rates and less overall public safety. Yet, there are other downfalls to the widespread use of juvenile waiver as well. One important consequence is that waived juveniles who are incarcerated often do their time in adult correctional facilities rather than juvenile facilities. Research shows distinct differences for youth between the adult and the juvenile correctional experience. Simon Singer (1996) describes how youth and adult systems differ physically and structurally.

Masten Park, like other [Division for Youth] facilities, differs from adult prisons in several important ways. First, they are physically different. Secure facilities for juveniles are much smaller than most maximum security adult prisons. Like other juvenile facilities, there are no prison cells with iron bars in place of doors. Juvenile institutions contain a much lower staff-to-inmate ratio. Masten Park's daily average of 100 juvenile offenders contrasts sharply with another correctional facility in western New York, Attica, which houses over 2,000 adult inmates. (p. 167)

With such a large number of inmates and the low staff-to-inmate ratio, juveniles in adult prisons are much less likely to receive educational or counseling services. Once waived to the adult system, the child also loses protective and rehabilitative services (Redding, 2003). According to one study, juveniles facing time in adult prisons are almost eight times more likely to commit suicide, five times more likely to be sexually assaulted, two times more likely to be beaten by a staff member, and 50% more likely to be attacked with a weapon (see Forst et al., 1989; Young & Gainsborough, 2000). Other research indicates that compared to juveniles in adult facilities, those in juvenile facilities develop more supportive, mentoring relationships with staff that can be helpful for their successful reintegration to society after their release (Kupchik, 2007). Moreover, juveniles in adult facilities report significantly higher levels of posttraumatic stress disorder (PTSD) and other symptoms of mental illness compared to similar offenders serving time in juvenile facilities (Fagan & Kupchik, 2011). In other words, because they are waived to the adult system and often incarcerated in adult facilities, these youth are more likely to be victimized, receive less treatment, and leave the facilities in worse shape than youth who are retained in the juvenile system.

Unfortunately, the problems with youth being transferred to the adult system do not stop once they are released. As we mentioned above, several long-term consequences are associated with transfer of youth, including a public record, being charged as an adult on subsequent offenses, having to report conviction on employment applications, as well as losing the right to vote and serve in the military. Gainful employment and an education are both activities that have been shown to reduce recidivism. A felony record can automatically disqualify employment in certain licensed or professional occupations, jobs in health care or skilled trades, as well as public sector employment (Western, Kling, & Weiman, 2001). This has a tremendous impact for a juvenile who may still spend the majority of his or her life outside of prison. He or she has very limited opportunities to find employment that affords a decent living, which consequently could provoke the return to illegal and more profitable activities (Needels, 1996). While research has shown there is no causal link between having a criminal record and posing a risk to campus safety, more and more college campuses are including criminal records on applications. Taking away the chance to attend college greatly impacts these juveniles, because studies show that education greatly reduces recidivism by increasing employment opportunities (Center for Community Alternatives, 2011).

Suggestions for Policy Reform

At this point, the evidence is clear that the current waiver policies should be changed. Pretending that children who make mistakes are equally responsible for their crimes as adults runs contrary to all science on adolescent development (e.g., Steinberg, 2009). Punishing juveniles as adults exposes them to harsh treatment and fails to help them refrain from crime in the future. But, perhaps most importantly, the evidence now strongly suggests that waiving large numbers of juveniles to the adult court only increases crime and puts the public at greater risk of victimization.

None of this signifies that juveniles should *never* be tried as adults, but that the waiver practice should be used sparingly, only for the most severe cases, and where it is necessary for public safety or where juvenile justice penalties proved ineffective. Policies need to be revised, such as in the state of New York where all 14- and 15-year-olds arrested for any of seventeen felony offenses are automatically waived to the adult system, and where *all* 16- and 17-year-olds arrested for *any* offense are considered adults. These policies allow little room for informed professionals to evaluate individual youth to determine whether they are in fact beyond the capacity of the juvenile court.

It is also important to limit the use of direct file, the type of waiver that allows prosecutors authority over who is waived and who stays in the juvenile court. Though they may be well-intentioned, prosecutors typically have only a portion of the relevant information available to them. They usually know only about the offense committed, and nothing about the juvenile and his or her home life, history of victimization, efforts to succeed in school, or other factors that should be taken into account in deciding whether the youth deserves to be prosecuted as a juvenile or an adult.

The solution is fairly straightforward: return to a system of judicial discretion and limited use of waiver. This was the practice of most juvenile courts before the wave of legislation from the 1970s through the 1990s, which led to so many youth being waived to the adult court. A system of judicial waiver allows judges to make balanced decisions after hearing from both prosecutors and defense attorneys, and after weighing all the information, not just the facts relating to the offense itself. Only cases in which serious violence takes place, or cases where the juvenile has exhausted options available through juvenile court and continues to offend, should be waived to the adult court. This system protects youth from the hazards of waiver, protects the public from the higher crime rates that result from the frequent use of waiver, and allows the juvenile court to make sensible decisions and treat youth.

Another important policy reform is to begin counting the number of people younger than age 18 who are prosecuted and punished as adults. It seems ridiculous that in this information age, we simply don't know how many youth are waived to the adult system. Without better information, it is difficult to track who is waived, how many are waived, and what outcomes result.

Finally, additional research is necessary to study gender and class implications of waiver. We discussed the racial implications found in several prior studies; yet, we know very little about the extent to which female youth are particularly affected by waiver to criminal court or whether social class shapes waiver experiences. The issue of gender implications is particularly important since arrest rates of female juveniles relative to those of males increased considerably in recent years (see Chesney-Lind & Irwin, 2007). We hope that researchers can remedy these gaps in our knowledge as additional data on waiver are collected.

KEY TERMS

Direct file	Judicial waiver	Prosecutorial waiver
Discretion	Once waived, always waived	Statutory exclusion

DISCUSSION QUESTIONS

1. How have states in the United States changed the way they respond to youth crime in recent decades?

2. How do current juvenile waiver policies reflect change in the treatment of delinquent youth?

3. What are the advantages and disadvantages of prosecuting juveniles in adult courts?

WEBSITES FOR ADDITIONAL RESEARCH

Center on Juvenile and Criminal Justice: http://www.cjcj.org/

National Center for Juvenile Justice: http://www.ncjj.org/Default.aspx

Office of Juvenile Justice and Delinquency Prevention: http://www.ojjdp.gov/

The Justice Research Center: http://www.thejrc.com/

The Urban Institute: http://www.urban.org/justice/juvjustice.cfm

MacArthur Foundation: http://www.macfound.org/networks/research-network-on-adolescent-development-juvenil/

Annie E. Casey Foundation: http://www.aecf.org/

Center for Court Innovation: http://www.courtinnovation.org/

American Bar Association: http://www.americanbar.org/groups/criminal_justice.html

Campaign for Youth Justice: http://www.campaignforyouthjustice.org/about-us.html

Juvenile Law Center: http://www.jlc.org/

National Center for Juvenile Justice: http://www.ncjj.org/

National Council on Crime and Delinquency: http://www.nccdglobal.org/

CHAPTER

XIII

Criminal Justice Responses to the Mentally Ill

Henry F. Fradella and Rebecca Smith-Casey

Mentally ill criminal offenders often attract substantial attention from a broad cross section of society, particularly in the media. One of the most famous cases in history involving a mentally ill offender is the 1981 assassination attempt on President Ronald Reagan by John Hinckley Jr. Hinckley, who was diagnosed with schizophrenia, was found not guilty by reason of insanity in 1982 and since that time remains under institutional care at St. Elizabeth's Hospital in Washington, DC. It does not take an assassination attempt on a U.S. President, however, for the media to devote significant attention to the crimes committed by mentally ill offenders, or those presumed to be. Consider the following recent cases:

- Just before Christmas of 2012, 20-year-old Adam Lanza committed the most deadly school shooting spree in U.S. history. Armed with three of his mother's guns, he killed 20 children and 6 adults inside an elementary school in Newtown, Connecticut, before turning a gun on himself. Details about his mental status remain fuzzy, but news reports suggested that Lanza committed these acts after learning his mother was preparing to commit him to a psychiatric facility. But, much of what was reported in the news was either hearsay or conjecture. As of this writing, the fact is that it is not yet known whether Lanza had a history of psychiatric illness or if he had been exhibiting signs of a psychotic breakdown. Yet, reports of Lanza's purported mental status filled speculative media accounts of his heinous crime.

- In the summer of 2012, James Holmes killed 12 people and wounded 58 others inside an Aurora, Colorado, movie theater during a screening of *The Dark Knight Rises*. As of this writing, his case is pending, but his defense attorneys represented to the court that Holmes was mentally ill at the time of the shooting massacre and, therefore, they intend to litigate an insanity defense. In fact, before Holmes dropped out of a PhD program in neuroscience at the University of Colorado's Anschutz campus, he sought mental health assistance from professionals associated with the university's mental health services. Details of Holmes's mental status have not yet been made public, but any mental illnesses revealed are likely to play a central role in his defense. Moreover, there will surely be significant questions about the civil liability of the university employed mental health professionals for their actions (or inactions) after meeting with Holmes and assessing his potential *dangerousness*.

- In 2011, Jared Loughner opened fire on a crowd of people in a Tucson, Arizona, shopping center parking lot. The shooting killed six people, including a federal judge, and injured 13 others, including U.S. Representative Gabrielle Giffords, whose treatment was followed intently by the media up until her resignation from her congressional seat in 2012. Loughner had been diagnosed with schizophrenia. He spent more than a year and a half in a secure *mental hospital* where mental health professionals worked to restore his competency to stand trial. In August 2012, a federal judge found that his competency was restored through treatment and then accepted Loughner's guilty plea. He was subsequently sentenced to life in prison without the possibility of parole.
- In April 2007, Seung Hoi Cho, who had been treated over a period of time for a variety of psychiatric symptoms, embarked on a shooting spree at Virginia Tech University, killing 32 people and injuring dozens more. At various times in his life, Cho had been diagnosed with major depression, social anxiety disorder, selective mutism, and an otherwise unspecified mood disorder.
- In 2001, Andrea Yates killed her five children by drowning them in the bathtub. Although diagnosed with postpartum depression and postpartum psychosis, Yates was initially convicted of five counts of murder. Her convictions were set aside by an appellate court when it was revealed that a mental health expert falsified evidence in the case. On retrial, she was found guilty by reason of insanity and committed to the North Texas State Hospital, where she remained until 2007, before being transferred to a minimum security hospital.

The interplay between the media and criminal justice may be greater today than ever before—between the 24-hour news cycle's unquenchable thirst for reporting sensational crimes and Hollywood's seemingly endless depiction of crime stories in television and film (Surette, 2011). But, other factors beyond the media contribute to the pervasive narratives of offenders with mental illnesses, such as the prevalence of mentally ill offenders committing crimes, the lack of access to mental health services that might prevent mentally ill people from committing crimes, and the poor outcomes that result from the way that those offenders are treated.

The Back Story: Historical Foundations

Since the founding of the United States, people with *serious mental illnesses (SMIs)* were often confined in jails rather than hospitals. That slowly began to change in the 1820s and 1830s with early reform efforts in Massachusetts. Between 1840 and 1880, the first wave of major treatment reforms for the mentally ill had taken firm root. Advances in the behavioral sciences in the early twentieth century spurred a second wave of reforms that produced little fruit. Advances in psychiatry in the 1950s and 1960s ushered in a third wave of reform efforts that produced profound effects, most notably the advent of psychotropic medication that allowed the mentally ill to lead lives outside the walls of institutions. But, the unintended consequences of those reforms led to the current situation, namely with hundreds of thousands of incarcerated inmates who have SMIs that not only affect their behavior, but also impact the lives of correctional officials, the other inmates, and the courts (see Fradella, 2003).

First-Wave Reform Efforts: From Jails and Prisons to Asylums

In the early part of the 1800s, a Massachusetts minister, Rev. Louis Dwight, began a crusade to improve the shockingly inhumane living conditions of mentally ill offenders when he delivered Bibles to prisoners. His efforts led the state legislature first to appoint a commission to investigate his claims, and then to enact a law making it illegal to confine the mentally ill in jails rather than in hospitals (Grob, 1966, as cited in Torrey, Kennard, Eslinger, Lamb, & Pavle, 2010). A few years later, Massachusetts constructed the State Lunatic Asylum at Worcester to house up to 120 patients.

In the early 1840s, Dorothea Dix began to build on Reverend Dwight's early efforts. As a nurse, she witnessed the atrocious living conditions of inmates with SMIs, such as the caging and whipping of people experiencing psychotic symptoms in futile efforts to control their behavior (Viney & Zorich, 1982). Dix eventually visited in excess of 300 jails and 18 state prisons, documenting the cruel treatment of the incarcerated mentally ill (Dix, 1975, as cited in Torrey et al., 2010). As a function of her era predating the dawn of modern psychology and psychiatry, her views were radical for the time, although through her presentation of detailed case studies, Dix successfully convinced policy makers that more humane conditions for the mentally ill could lead to their improved functioning. By the time she died in 1887, she had visited every state east of the Mississippi River and 13 European countries (Viney & Zorich, 1982). Dix's efforts on both sides of the Atlantic are credited with facilitating the construction of 32 psychiatric hospitals and 15 schools for the "feeble minded" across the eastern United States, and her work had great impact on reform efforts in Europe (Viney & Zorich, 1982). According to Torrey and colleagues (2010), her reform efforts were so successful that by 1880, the U.S. Census "identified 40,942 'insane persons' in 'hospitals and *asylums* for the insane'[,]" but only "397 'insane persons' in jails and prisons, constituting less than 1% (0.7%) of the jail and prison population" at that time (p. 14). Largely as a result of her accomplishments, the *Encyclopedia of Human Behavior* describes Dorothea Dix as "the most effective advocate of humanitarian reform in American mental institutions during the nineteenth century" (Goldenson, 1970, p. 341).

The first wave of reforms was based primarily on moral arguments about the ethical treatment of people with SMIs. These reform efforts brought long-lasting changes. The movement's emphasis on caring for the mentally ill fostered acceptance of a medical-psychological model of mental illness rather than theories of demonic possession that had prevailed until that time (Grob, 1966; Morrissey & Goldman, 1986). This, in turn, led to the establishment of asylums that were supposed to offer compassionate treatment of the mentally ill.

The spread of asylums was effective in moving those with SMIs out of jails and prisons and into treatment facilities. Indeed, until the 1960s, most studies found similar prevalence rates (i.e., less than 2%) of the mentally ill in jails and prisons as reported in the 1880 Census (e.g., Bromberg & Thompson, 1937). Rather, those with SMIs "were treated as patients, not as criminals, and were sent to mental hospitals [even though] the hospitals had little treatment to offer them at that time" (Torrey et al., 2010, p. 14). But, the goal of providing compassionate treatment to people with SMIs was never fully realized.

Asylums actually predate the first-wave reform movement. The first public asylum, Eastern State Hospital, was created in 1773 in Williamsburg, Virginia (*New York Times*, 1900). But most early asylums established in the United States were created by Protestants whose religious convictions led them to believe that it was their religious duty to care for "the less fortunate members of society" (Morrissey & Goldman, 1986, p. 14). Many of these asylums established a patient-care model based on the principles espoused by the Quakers at the time, who believed that people with SMIs should be treated "in a comfortable, clean, family atmosphere, in the tranquil surroundings of a country house" (Parry-Jones, 1988, p. 408). Indeed, the term "asylum" stems from the notion of a place of refuge—"a quiet haven in which the shattered bark might find a means of reparation or of safety (p. 408). This philosophy guided most of the private asylums throughout the 1800s. Public asylums were generally created with this same patient-care model in mind. But, lack of public funding and sufficient staffing led public asylums to become sprawling, overcrowded places where people with SMIs lived in "bleak, impoverished wards" that served merely as custodial institutions rather than treatment facilities (Parry-Jones, 1988, p. 408; see also Morrissey & Goldman, 1986). Moreover, as the U.S. population increased, so did the demand for custody arrangements for those with SMIs. As a result, the wealthy largely turned to private, pastoral facilities while the poor filled public asylums that became human warehouses, which served as "a general-purpose solution to the welfare burdens of a society undergoing rapid industrialization and stratification along social class and ethnic lines" (Morrissey & Goldman, 1986, p. 17). In other words, treatment became a concern secondary to low-cost custody and community protection (Rothman, 1970).

Second-Wave Reform Efforts: The Rise of Psychiatry and Psychology

Around the turn of the 20th century, a scientific approach to mental illness began to take a firm hold. Scientific advances in neurology, psychiatry, psychology, and social work were spawned as a result of the work of researchers such as Adolf Meyer and William James. Their work focused on therapeutic treatments of mental disorders, "especially by early intervention in acute cases" (Morrissey & Goldman, 1986, p. 18; see also Deutsch, 1944).

The second-wave reform efforts led to the creation of "psychopathic hospitals" for the acute treatment of people with SMIs, most of which were affiliated with research universities (Morrissey & Goldman, 1986). Other mental health facilities, mostly clinics, were also created as a result of the increasing medicalization of mental illness care. But, these facilities, just as the psychopathic hospitals, were designed to provide acute care; patients with SMIs who needed long-term care were eventually sent to state asylums where they received little, if any, real care.

Some scholars argued that the various forms of mental institutions that operated between the late 1800s and the mid-1900s were driven primarily by humanitarian concerns to care for those with mental illness (e.g., Grob, 1994; Ziff, 2004). Others, however, argued that asylums and mental hospitals primarily served a social control function to reinforce individual conformity with prevailing societal expectations—especially in poor, immigrant populations (e.g., Foucault, 1965; Rothman, 1970; Scull, 1991). Whatever the motivations, it is clear that public mental hospitals proliferated in the first half of the twentieth century and their patient population ballooned from 150,000 in 1903 to 512,000 in 1950—"a rate of growth nearly twice as large as the rate of increase in the U.S. population as a whole" (Morrissey & Goldman, 1986, p. 19). Moreover, in spite of scientific advances in the behavioral sciences, most state facilities remained primarily custodial in nature, providing long-term custody not only to those with SMIs, but also to the poor and disabled who could not care for themselves.

Third-Wave Reform Efforts: The Community Mental Health Movement

The third wave of reform is referred to as the Community Mental Health (CMH) movement. CMH efforts emerged in the aftermath of the Second World War as a function of several significant factors. First, new psychosocial techniques developed during the war to provide acute care for those in military service proved to be successful on the front lines (Morrissey & Goldman, 1986; Spiegel & Grinker, 1945). Psychiatrists who returned to practice after serving in the military brought these techniques back with them and taught others in state mental hospitals how to use them. Second, increased understanding of the importance of aftercare led mental hospitals to open outpatient clinics to serve those who were discharged after inpatient treatment while, at the same time, regular hospitals opened acute psychiatric care units (Morrissey & Goldman, 1986; Linn, 1961). Third, the federal government enacted a series of laws that not only established the National Institute of Mental Health, but also created far-reaching policies to foster mental health in the United States (Morrissey & Goldman, 1986; Foley & Sharfstein, 1983). Fourth, charges of neglect, abuse, and dehumanizing conditions in many state-run mental hospitals—such as those described in landmark sociological studies like Ervin Goffman's *Asylums* (1961), and those depicted in the movie *One Flew Over the Cuckoo's Nest* (Douglas, Zaentz, & Forman, 1975)—led civil libertarians and other activists to advocate for sweeping treatment reforms for those with SMIs. And perhaps most importantly, new psychotropic medications were introduced in the 1950s and 1960s (Talbott, 1982). These antipsychotic drugs—including Haldol, Mellaril, Moban, Navane, Perphenazine, Prolixin, Stelazine, and Thorazine—altered brain chemistry by regulating neurotransmitters. In doing so, these drugs enhance clarity of thought in those affected by psychosis, control for emotions, and prevent interference with rational thought processes. These developments led to the widespread release of the mentally ill through **deinstitutionalization** policies, which sought to reintroduce these patients to the community for supportive services.

The CMH movement spurred civil liberties activists to seek tightening of the methods which were used to involuntarily civilly commit the mentally ill. Prior to the 1950s, most states had only loose protections to prevent a person from being involuntarily hospitalized for psychiatric treatment. "Some jurisdictions statutorily authorized civil commitment for those persons defined as being a 'social menace' or 'a fit and proper candidate for institutionalization'" (Fradella, 2008, p. 1972). But the advent of antipsychotic medicines, combined with the social movements of the 1960s—the CMH movement included—generated action by both legislatures and the courts to recognize that people with mental illnesses possessed a range of liberty interests protected by the U.S. Constitution, including "community-situated treatment, due process procedural protections, the right to treatment, medical and constitutional minimal standards in treatment, and the right to refuse treatment" (Arrigio, 1992/1993, pp. 139–140).

The landmark decision in **Lessard v. Schmidt** (1972) was decided at a time before many of the modern due process protections associated with civil commitment were enacted. Indeed, *Lessard* was largely responsible for transforming the legal landscape concerning due process in civil commitments (Mossman, Schwartz, & Elam, 2012). The case centered on a woman who was involuntarily hospitalized following an *ex parte* hearing about which she never received notice. She won her class action suit enjoining the state of Wisconsin from enforcing its involuntary commitment statute. One of the provisions the court ordered as part of its remedy in *Lessard* was to require evidence of risk as demonstrated by an actual threat or an *overt act*—some observable behavior from which dangerousness could be inferred. Several states subsequently adopted the overt act requirement as part of their own due process reforms, while other states did not (Mossman et al., 2012).

In the wake of *Lessard,* most states tightened their civil commitment laws so that mental illness alone, even if serious, did not suffice as the singular reason for commitment. Significantly, someone could only be involuntarily committed for treatment if a court found, by clear and convincing evidence, that the person represented a danger to themselves or to others (see *Addington v. Texas,* 1979). Although this *dangerousness* standard is universally concerned with imminent physical harm to oneself or to others, in about 30 states, it also includes dangerousness to oneself because of grave disability. This is described as a condition where someone is unable to provide for their basic needs, such as food, clothing, shelter, health, or safety, but often only with the caveat that a failure to assist the person would result in a substantial deterioration of their previous ability to function on their own (Fradella, 2008).

The federal government also played an important role in facilitating deinstitutionalization. The CMH movement was successful in getting Congress to include incentives for moving patients out of psychiatric hospitals and into ***community-based treatment*** programs. Most notably, Medicaid and Medicare legislation passed in 1965 "purposefully excluded payments to 'institutions for the treatment of mental diseases' because the programs were not designed to supplant state control and financing of psychiatric facilities" (Harcourt, 2011, p. 67). This gave states an incentive to move psychiatric patients out of their hospitals and into communities where they became eligible for "Supplemental Security Income . . . Medicaid, food stamps, and other federal benefits" (p. 67).

Deinstitutionalization caused the resident population of state mental hospitals to decline by more than 75% between 1955 and 1980, while during this time frame more than 700 CMH centers were created (Morrissey & Goldman, 1986; Morrissey, 1982). As a result, state mental hospitals were closed across the country. But, on their release from mental hospitals, those people with SMIs rather than receiving community-based care were largely ignored because adequate funding was not provided to communities to support the needs of these patients (Bassuk & Gerson, 1978).

> Deinstitutionalized patients encountered the hostility and rejection of the general public and the reluctance of community mental health and welfare agencies to assume responsibility for their care. Tens of thousands ended up in rooming houses, foster homes, nursing homes, run-down hotels, and on the streets. (Morrissey & Goldman, 1986, pp. 21–22)

The population in state mental hospitals peaked at more than 558,200 patients in 1955; that number stands in sharp contrast to the fewer than 70,000 patients with SMIs who were housed in public psychiatric hospitals in the mid-1990s (The Sentencing Project, 2002). By 2006, there were only 228 state psychiatric hospitals operating 49,000 beds, nearly a third of which were occupied by forensic patients—those "committed by the criminal courts because their competency to stand trial has been questioned, they have been found incompetent and have not regained competency, or they were adjudicated as not guilty by reason of insanity" (Fisher, Geller, & Pandiani, 2009, p. 679).

The overly optimistic CMH movement left tens of thousands of former patients "homeless or living in substandard housing, often without treatment, supervision, or social support" (Goldman & Morrissey, 1985, p. 729). Sadly, this state of affairs largely continues today; many communities currently have no services in place to assist those with SMIs. Largely as a function of these deficiencies, the mentally ill are often arrested for so-called "nuisance crimes," which leads to prolonged contacts with the criminal justice system among people who are often unable to conform their behaviors to the rules of society due to their severe and chronic psychiatric issues.

On the other end of the spectrum, lack of access to quality mental health services has dire consequences, as it appears to have had for the Aurora movie theater victims in the James Holmes case. In the wake of Adam Lanza's school massacre in Newtown, Connecticut, President Obama stated, "We are going to need to work on making access to mental health care at least as easy as access to getting a gun." This is a tall order since between 2009 and 2012, states cut more than $4.35 billion in public mental health spending, or about 12% of the total budget; as a result, more than 3,200 psychiatric hospital beds, or 6 of the total, have disappeared and another 1,249 beds are in danger of being lost (Glober, Miller, & Sadowski, 2012).

The Current State of the Policy

In contrast to the height of mental hospitalizations in 1955 when there was one public psychiatric bed for every 300 people in the United States, only one such bed currently exists in both public and private facilities for every 3,000 people. In other words, without including private facilities or beds in psychiatric units of general hospitals, people with SMIs were 10 times more likely to find space available in public psychiatric hospitals in 1955 than could be found at the start of the 21st century at general hospitals, public psychiatric hospitals, and private psychiatric facilities *combined* (Torrey et al., 2010). Conversely, there are more than three times as many people with SMIs incarcerated in correctional institutions today than there are in psychiatric hospitals; thus, "America's jails and prisons have become our new mental hospitals" (Torrey et al., 2010, p. 3).

Estimates of Mentally Ill Inmates

Currently available data indicate that approximately 7.1 million adults were under the supervision of state or federal correctional authorities in the United States at the end of 2010 (Glaze, 2011)—the most recent year providing official statistics. Of these people, roughly 2.26 million were incarcerated in prisons and jails (Glaze, 2011, p. 2). A sizable portion of this population suffer from SMIs.

One study concluded that up to 17.5% of inmates in state prisons had schizophrenia, bipolar disorder, or major depression (Veysey & Bichler-Robertson, 2002). Another study found that 16.6% of inmates in five jails met the diagnostic criteria for SMIs that included schizophrenia, schizophrenia spectrum disorder, schizoaffective disorder, bipolar disorder, brief psychotic disorder, delusional disorder, and psychotic disorder not otherwise specified (Steadman, Osher, Robbins, Case, & Samuels, 2009). And a 2006 survey conducted by the U.S. Department of Justice concluded upwards of 24% of inmates in certain metropolitan jails evidenced symptomology of a psychotic disorder (James & Glaze, 2006).

> Studies show that the number of persons with SMIs in the prison system has risen from 7% in 1982 to 10–19% of jail populations, 18–27% of state prison populations, and 16–21% of federal prison populations. To put these prevalence estimates into perspective, the current rate of SMIs in jails and prisons is two to four times higher than rates of SMIs found among the general public. (Litschge & Vaughn, 2009, p. 542 [internal citations omitted]; see also Skeem, Manchak, & Peterson, 2010)

Based on these studies and official reports from many states, Torrey and colleagues (2010) concluded that we "have thus effectively returned to conditions that last existed in the United States in the 1840s" when Dorothea Dix first began her campaign against imprisoning the mentally ill in jails (see Figure 13.1). This conclusion is supported by the fact that the largest psychiatric facility in the United States is New York City's Rikers Island, which is estimated to hold 3,000 mentally ill offenders at any given time (Stephey, 2007).

In addition to the high rates of those with SMIs placed in correctional institutions designed to punish offenders rather than provide treatment, it is important to note that substance abuse is high among those with SMIs. It is estimated that between 50 and 75% of all mentally ill offenders in jails have co-occurring substance abuse problems (Skeem et al., 2010). In part, this may be due

| Figure 13.1 | Percentage of Jail and Prison Inmates With Serious Mental Illness |

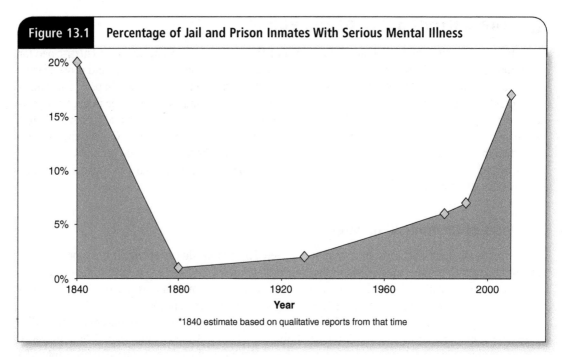

*1840 estimate based on qualitative reports from that time

Source: Torrey et al. (2010)

to those with SMIs self-medicating with alcohol and/or illicit drugs to help relieve the unpleasant or painful symptoms of their disorders (e.g., Dixon, 1999; Khantzian, 1997; Modestin, Nussbaumer, Angst, Scheidegger, & Hell, 1997; Robinson, Sareen, Cox, & Bolton, 2009; Strakowski & DelBello, 2000).

Explanations for the High Prevalence of Inmates with SMIs

There are several possible explanations as to why there are so many people with SMIs in correctional facilities. First, much research demonstrates that police frequently arrest the mentally ill with whom they come into contact (Borum, Swanson, Swartz, & Hiday, 1997; Steadman, Cocozza, & Melick, 1978; Torrey et al., 1992). To some, the most obvious explanation for this is that the police do not understand the behaviors exhibited by people with SMIs and, therefore, make arrests based on misconceptions (e.g., Hylton, 1995). In landmark studies conducted in the 1980s, Teplin (1984, 1990) found that police were more likely to arrest people displaying psychiatric symptoms than those engaging in similar nuisance behaviors, but who do not outwardly show any signs of mental illness. But, other research questioned these findings. For example, after controlling for variables linked to police decision making, such as non-compliance and the relationship between the victim and offender, Engel and Silver (2001) found that police were actually less likely to arrest offenders with mental illnesses. The differences in results may be a function of methodology. Teplin used clinical definitions while Engel and Silver relied on officer's perceptions of mental illness.

Second, in many U.S. jurisdictions—especially those where police departments subscribe to Broken Windows policing, formal criminal justice enforcement emerged as a significant—if not the preferred—response to disorderly people (Kelling & Coles, 1996). People with SMIs, especially those who are homeless, loud, or otherwise disorderly, often face formal arrests in these locales.

Third, it is clear that police often arrest the mentally ill to help them obtain services. Teplin and Pruett (1992) reported that police often make so-called "***mercy bookings***" to ensure that arrestees had a place to sleep, especially in extreme weather conditions, and were fed two or three meals each day. Torrey and colleagues (1992) similarly found that police arrested people with SMIs to keep them in a relatively safe environment until treatment space became available at mental health facilities.

Fourth, research suggests that many people with SMIs are arrested and criminally incarcerated due to a lack of availability of any mental health alternatives—even though such an alternative would have been preferable (Dupont & Cochran, 2000; Lurigio, Snowden, & Watson, 2006). Indeed, well-trained officers often recognize when people they encounter need mental health services, but nonetheless make arrests either because community resources are completely unavailable, or are so inadequate that frustration leads officers to doubt the feasibility of any public health options (Engel & Silver, 2001; Hails & Borum, 2003; Thompson, Reuland, & Souweine, 2003).

Finally, the high prevalence rates of inmates with SMIs call into question the fairness of the criminal justice system's treatment of mentally ill. Mentally ill offenders who commit minor crimes are the "frequent flyers" of local and county jail systems (Torrey et al., 2010). Largely due to frequency of arrests and the lack of coordination between the criminal justice and mental health systems, these offenders typically receive little or no aftercare treatment after their release from jail, which, in turn, can lead them to decompensation and rearrest (see Solomon, Osborne, LoBuglio, Mellow, & Mukamal, 2008).

People with SMIs who commit serious offenses often fare no better in light of hostility to criminal defenses of excuse, such as diminished capacity or insanity. Traditionally, the doctrine of competency to stand trial and the insanity defense were both designed to prevent those with SMIs from being subjected to criminal prosecution and punishment (Schug & Fradella, 2014). But, the standard for adjudicative competency is quite low, and detainees often languish for months awaiting trial while issues related to determining competency are hashed out by mental health experts, attorneys, and the courts (Schug & Fradella, 2014). And in the wake of John Hinckley's insanity acquittal for the attempted assignation of President Ronald Reagan, the federal government and more than two-thirds of U.S. states either significantly restricted the insanity defense or outright abolished it (Fradella, 2007). Similarly, legislatures, judges, and jurors have all proven to be hostile toward insanity and diminished capacity defenses, collectively contributing to the "sharp increase in the number of mentally ill people in prisons" since the mid-1980s (p. 120). Fradella argued that the U.S. Supreme Court's decision in *Clark v. Arizona* (2006) illustrated this hostility to defenses of excuse based on mental illness, and signaled a continued narrowing of the law in a manner that leads to the incarceration of those with SMIs. These prisoners cost more to incarcerate (Torrey et al., 2010), cause significant management problems for correctional officials and the courts (Fradella, 2003), and frequently decompensate to the point that roughly half of them attempt to commit suicide (Goss, Peterson, Smith, Kalb, & Brodey, 2002).

Case Study: *Clark v. Arizona*

In Flagstaff, Arizona in the early morning hours of June 21, 2000, 17-year-old Eric Clark was driving his pickup truck around a residential neighborhood with the radio blaring loud music. Police Officer Jeffrey Moritz pulled over Clark's truck in response to complaints. Less than a minute after approaching Clark and telling him to "stay where he was," Clark shot the officer and ran away. Before he died, the officer contacted the police dispatcher for help. Clark was apprehended later that day with gunpowder residue on his hands. The gun used to kill the officer was subsequently found close to where Clark had been arrested.

At Clark's trial, friends, family, classmates, and school officials all testified about his "increasingly bizarre behavior over the year before the shooting."

For example, witnesses testified that paranoid delusions led Clark to rig a fishing line with beads and wind chimes at home to alert him to intrusion by invaders, and to keep a bird in his automobile to warn of airborne poison. There was lay and expert testimony that Clark thought Flagstaff was populated with "aliens" (some impersonating government agents), the "aliens" were trying to kill him, and bullets were the only way to stop them. A psychiatrist testified that Clark was suffering from paranoid schizophrenia with delusions about "aliens" when he killed Officer Moritz, and he concluded that Clark was incapable of luring the officer or understanding right from wrong, and that he was thus insane at the time of the killing. In rebuttal, a psychiatrist for the State gave his opinion that Clark's paranoid schizophrenia did not keep him from appreciating the wrongfulness of his conduct, as shown by his actions before and after the shooting (e.g., circling the residential block with music blaring as if to lure the police to intervene, evading the police after the shooting, and hiding the gun) (p. 745).

At trial, Clark admitted that he shot and killed Moritz, but contended that he should be excused from criminal responsibility because he suffered from paranoid schizophrenia. Specifically, Clark sought to offer psychiatric evidence both to support an insanity-based defense and to prove that he failed to act with the *mens rea* required for a murder conviction because he delusionally thought he was shooting an alien. Relying on Arizona state precedent that prohibited diminished capacity evidence, the trial court refused to allow Clark to present evidence of mental illness to rebut *mens rea*, limiting such evidence strictly to consideration of his insanity claim.

Although the trial court determined that Clark "was indisputably afflicted with paranoid schizophrenia at the time of the shooting," it found him guilty nonetheless, concluding that his mental illness "did not . . . distort his perception of reality so severely that he did not know his actions were wrong" (p. 746). The court thus determined Clark had failed to prove he was insane by clear and convincing evidence as required under Arizona's narrow formulation of the "guilty except insane" defense. Moreover, given the state of Arizona's bar on diminished capacity evidence, Clark was convicted and sentenced to life in prison with the possibility of parole only after serving 25 years.

Clark challenged his conviction on due process grounds, arguing that Arizona's bar on relevant psychiatric evidence interferes with a criminal defendant's "meaningful opportunity to present a complete defense" (p. 789). Over a strong dissent, a majority of the U.S. Supreme Court rejected this argument and affirmed Clark's conviction. The Court reasoned the nature of mental-disease and capacity evidence gives rise to several risks that can be diminished "by channeling the consideration of such evidence to the insanity"—namely the "controversial character of some categories of mental

(Continued)

disease," "the potential of mental-disease evidence to mislead," and "the danger of according greater certainty to capacity evidence than experts claim for it" (p. 774).

Source: Schug & Fradella (2014).

In summary, a wide range of factors contributes to the high incarceration rates of the mentally ill: the failure of many CMH initiatives in the wake of mass deinstitutionalization; decreased funding for public psychiatric services; tight restrictions on the involuntary civil commitment of the mentally ill; and get-tough on crime and disorder policies, ranging from Broken Windows policing to the narrowing of criminal defenses of excuse. Collectively, these factors led many to conclude that people with SMIs are "criminalized"—a phenomenon often referred to as *the criminalization of the mentally ill* or *the criminalization of mental illness* (see Abramson, 1972; Fisher, Silver, & Wolff, 2006; PrisonPolicy.org., 2011; Slate & Johnson, 2008; Torrey et al., 2010). In essence, behaviors caused by mental illness that were once managed in the mental health system have now become behaviors that are referred to the criminal justice system.

It should be noted that some scholars have questioned the criminalization hypothesis, arguing that the criminal behavior exhibited by only a small, albeit important, minority of offenders (estimated as just under 10%) is a direct result of either psychosis or survival crimes related to poverty (Junginger, Claypoole, Laygo, & Crisanti, 2006; Peterson, Skeem, Hart, Vidal, & Keith, 2010). But these studies suffer from some methodological limitations insofar as they focus primarily on those convicted of only serious offenses and on those with SMIs. The researchers readily acknowledge that less serious offenses are often driven by hostility, disinhibition, and emotional reactivity that might be exacerbated by mental illnesses that do not rise to the level of being labeled "serious" (i.e., those that do not involve psychosis). For example, Junginger and colleagues (2006) concluded that co-occurring substance abuse disorders led to a sizable minority of offenses in the population they studied. Thus, although there are limited data to suggest that SMIs are not "criminalized" per se, there is little doubt that mentally ill offenders are in need of treatment that not only can reduce recidivism but also promote successful community reentry for this population of offenders. Consider the following data.

Upon release from prison, mentally ill offenders recidivate at high rates (e.g., Messina, Burdon, Hagopian, & Prendergast, 2004). In fact, parolees with mental illness are nearly twice as likely as their non-mentally ill counterparts to return to prison within one year of release (Eno-Louden & Skeem, 2011), and between 39% and 70% reoffended within 27 to 55 months, depending on the type of crime for which they were originally convicted (Case, Steadman, Dupuis, & Morris, 2009; Lovell, Gagliardi, & Peterson, 2002; Theurer & Lovell, 2008). Since one of the primary goals of the criminal justice system is to reduce recidivism rates, a number of initiatives attempted to reduce recidivism in this population of offenders; many of these initiatives were funded by a federal grant program established under the Mentally Ill Offender Treatment and Crime Reduction Act (MIOTCRA) of 2004.

The Mentally Ill Offender Treatment and Crime Reduction Act of 2004

The *Mentally Ill Offender Treatment and Crime Reduction Act (MIOTCRA)* was signed into law in 2004 by President George W. Bush. The law created the ***Justice and Mental Health***

Collaboration Program (JMHCP) to assist state and local governments create collaboratives between criminal justice and mental health systems. Congress reauthorized the Act in 2008 for an additional period of five years and expanded opportunities for training aimed at assisting law enforcement in the identification of persons and response to persons with mental illness and assessment of those in custody for mental health and/or substance abuse treatment needs.

Under the Act's grant program, $50 million was available for state and local government use. The grant application process requires collaborative efforts between law enforcement or criminal justice agencies and mental health services in an effort to most effectively deal with the intersection of the two systems when dealing with deviant behaviors that occur as a result of mental illness. According to the Criminal Justice/Mental Health Consensus Project of the Council of State Governments (2012), this grant money was used to develop and implement training programs for law enforcement, ***mental health courts***, and a variety of corrections-based treatment initiatives. Evaluation research on a number of these programs suggests that some are more effective than others. Before exploring such research, it should be noted that MIOTCRA was criticized for limiting grant money to diversion programs that serve only *nonviolent* criminal offenders; money to assist people with SMIs who committed violent offenses was limited to correctional-based treatments in jails or prisons or reentry programs after release (e.g., Danjczek, 2007).

What Research Has Taught Us

Skeem, Manchak, and Peterson (2010) conducted a meta-analysis of the effectiveness of a number of programs aimed at reducing recidivism rates of mentally ill offenders. They focused on six types of programs, including four employing criminal justice models (jail diversion, mental health courts, specialty mental health probation/parole programs, and aftercare/re-entry programs) and two utilizing mental health models (Forensic Assertive Community Treatment [F-ACT] programs and Forensic Intensive Case Management [FICM] programs). Overall, they found mixed evidence that these programs reduce recidivism, with the evidence for both mental health-based programs and jail-diversion programs showing little to no effectiveness in reducing recidivism. They speculated that this may be due, in part, to these programs' heavy reliance on case management services. In contrast, three of the criminal justice-based programs demonstrated varying levels of success and, therefore, deserve some explanation.

Mental Health Courts

Perhaps because evaluation research generally indicated significant levels of success in reducing recidivism through mental health courts compared to most of the other policies targeted at reducing the recidivism by mentally ill offenders, these specialty courts have grown in use and popularity since the first one was established in 1997. By 2012, roughly 250 mental health courts were established and that number is consistently growing. These courts are staffed by specially trained personnel experienced in working with mentally ill offenders and are based on a therapeutic jurisprudence model rather than an adversarial justice style (Council of State Governments, 2012; Mann, 2011). The mental health courts typically include judges, social workers, probation officers, and attorneys who have received special training regarding mental illness, psychotropic medication, and substance abuse, in direct contrast to the "mixed bag" of training and education normally found in non-mental health court adjudication.

Mental health courts are remarkably diverse. The clinical diagnoses that qualify arrestees for participation in mental health court vary significantly across the country, as do court procedures and completion requirements (Mann, 2011; Redlich, Hoover, Summers, & Steadman, 2010). The types of cases mental health courts adjudicate also vary: 85% accept misdemeanor cases; 75% handle felony cases; however, only 20% accept violent felony cases; and only 1% handle seriously violent felony cases (Mann, 2011).

Technically, participation in mental health court programs is supposed to be voluntary. Upon agreeing to participate, new participants are required to sign contracts that typically include commitments to take prescribed medications, attend and engage in treatment appointments, return to the court for status review hearings, come to court on time, meet with case managers or probation officers, and to follow any other individual requirements deemed necessary (Mann, 2011; Redlich et al., 2010). The use of sanctions to enforce these provisions varies significantly across mental health courts. However, Redlich and colleagues (2010) found that although between 65 and 76% of mental health court participants reported that they chose to enroll in the programs, most indicated that they did not know the court was voluntary, had not been informed of the program requirements prior to enrolling, and were unaware that they could stop participation if they so desired.

Community-based treatment is the defining characteristic of these courts (Almquist & Dodd, 2009). Yet, "despite being common, outpatient care appears not to have been intensive" (Luskin, 2012, p. 9). Nonetheless, the increased number and kinds of treatments mental health court participants receive decrease both inpatient and emergency room treatments (Luskin, 2012).

Empirical evaluations of mental health courts generally found them to be effective at reducing recidivism (Herinckx, Swart, Ama, Dolezal, & King, 2005; Moore & Hiday, 2006; Trupin & Richards, 2003). McNiel and Binder (2007) reported that mental health court participants experienced longer periods before any new charges for both violent and nonviolent offenses were filed against them than a comparison group processed through criminal courts—a pattern that persisted after completion of the mental health court program. Dirks-Linhorst and Linhorst (2012) found that the rearrest rate of 351 defendants who successfully completed a mental health court program was 14.5%, as compared to 38% among defendants who were negatively terminated from the program and 25.8% of defendants who chose not to participate. These results are similar to the decrease in rearrest rates that Herinckx and his colleagues (2005) found where the average number of arrests prior to mental health court participation was 1.99, but one year after entry into a mental health court program, the mean number of arrests dropped to 0.48. In part, determining the person who reoffends may be a function of program completion. Moore and Hiday (2006) found that 26.9% of participants who completed mental health court were rearrested within one year, compared to the rearrest rate of 70.0% for those who did not complete the program. Moore and Hiday also examined the factors associated with recidivism. They found that demographic factors and most criminal history factors were not significant related to reoffending; however, one criminal history factor proved salient: More severe prior offenses significantly increased the odds of rearrest.

In contrast, at least two studies concluded that there is little difference in reoffending levels between mental health court graduates and those who do not complete such programs. Although Christy, Poythress, Boothroyd, Petrila, and Mehra (2005) reported that 47% of mental health court participants were rearrested within a year of the initial court appearance compared to 56% in the comparison group, this difference was not statistically significant. Cosden, Ellens, Schnell, and Yamini-Diouf (2005) similarly reported small, nonsignificant differences in rearrests, convictions leading to imprisonment, and number of days spent in jail over a four-year period (two years before and after initial admission to a mental health court program). The intense variations in mental health court policies and programs may be responsible for these divergent findings.

Specialty Mental Health Probation

More than 100 U.S. jurisdictions created programs where probation officers manage specialized, reduced size caseloads of mentally ill probationers working directly with treatment providers (Eno-Louden, Skeem, Camp, Vidal, & Peterson, 2012). Because these specialty probation officers "more frequently discussed probationers' general mental health than any individual criminogenic need"; "chiefly questioned, directed, affirmed, and supported (rather than confronted) probationers"; and "relied more heavily on neutral strategies and positive pressures (e.g., inducements) rather than negative pressures (e.g., threats of incarceration) to monitor and enforce compliance" (p. 109), specialty probationers were modestly less likely to be rearrested or have their probation revoked over a one-year period than offenders assigned to traditional probation. But, given the modest levels of success associated with most of the specialty probation programs that have been empirically evaluated, the third option of reentry and an aftercare program might be a better approach as this alternative was found to have support by which Skeem and colleagues (2010).

Prisoner Reentry and Aftercare Programs

The first year after release from jail or prison is a particularly salient time for monitoring offenders with SMIs since 77% of reoffending occurs within this time (Lovell et al., 2002). High rates of reoffending can be tied to a number of factors, including medication non-compliance, lack of treatment services, a return to disorganized community settings, and poor support services. Accordingly, a number of jurisdictions formed collaborative programs between correctional and mental health services to provide some continuity of care, many of which have been effective at reducing recidivism rates, even for those with co-occurring substance abuse disorders (Kesten et al., 2012; Sacks, Chaple, Sacks, McKendrick, & Cleland, 2012). For example, a study by Sacks, Sacks, McKendrick, Banks, and Stommel (2004), which randomly assigned male inmates with co-occurring serious mental illness and chemical abuse (MICA) disorders to either modified therapeutic community (MTC) or mental health (MH) treatment programs, found that mentally-ill offenders receiving aftercare and reentry services were three times less likely to be reincarcerated within a year than those who received no such treatment interventions (5% vs. 16%). Similarly, a comprehensive jail aftercare and reentry program in Harris County, Texas, was found by Held, Brown, Frost, Hickey, and Buck (2012) to reduce the total number of rearrests significantly for both felonies and misdemeanors (see Figure 13.2).

The most promising reentry and aftercare programs are those that combine "interagency collaboration, housing support, and intensive, integrated clinical attention to mental health and substance abuse problems" (Theurer & Lovell, 2008, p. 400). As the Council of State Governments (2002) stated, "[w]ithout housing that is integrated with mental health, substance abuse, employment, and other services, many people with mental illness end up being homeless, disconnected from community supports, and thus more likely to . . . become involved with the criminal justice system" (p. 8). It should come as no surprise that such comprehensive programs can be quite expensive, reaching an annual cost of approximately $20,000 per person in some jurisdictions (Frisman, Swanson, Marín, & Leavitt-Smith, 2010). However, given that the average cost of incarcerating an inmate ranges between $18,000 to $50,000 per year with an average cost per inmate of $36,000 (*The Economist*, 2010), such reentry programs represent a solid investment from a cost-benefit standpoint (Torrey, 2011). Moreover, even in jurisdictions where the cost of reentry programs exceeds incarceration costs, such an investment protects the public from future crime associated with untreated mental illness while simultaneously providing "a better set of mental health and justice outcomes for people with mental health problems and their communities" (Wolff, Bjerklie, & Maschi, 2005, p. 38).

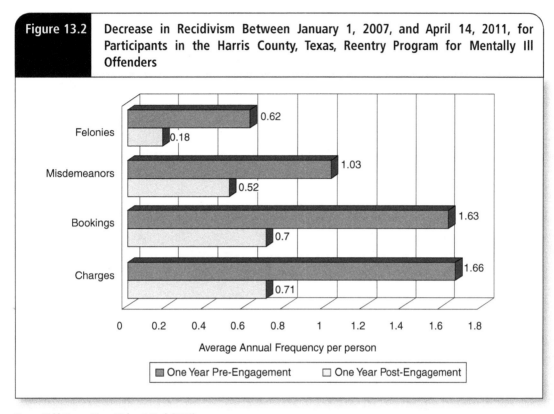

Figure 13.2 Decrease in Recidivism Between January 1, 2007, and April 14, 2011, for Participants in the Harris County, Texas, Reentry Program for Mentally Ill Offenders

Source: Held, Brown, Frost, Hickey, & Buck (2012).

 Differences Involving Race, Ethnicity, Gender, and Class

As explored in several other chapters of this book, there are significant race, gender, and class disparities in U.S. incarceration rates that are separate from any issues surrounding mental illness. But these disparities may be amplified in mentally ill arrestees since many factors that are generally correlated with arrest decisions are also correlated with the presence of mental illness.

Race and Ethnicity

"Cultural factors affect how individuals define, evaluate, seek help for, and present their health problems to family members, friends, and service providers" (U.S. Department of Health and Human Services, 2001, p. 18). This can not only lead members of different racial and ethnic groups to express symptoms differently, but also can lead clinicians to misinterpret these differences (Peters, Bartoi, & Sherman, 2008).

There is remarkably little research on racial/ethnic differences in the way police interact with the mentally ill. In one of the few such studies, Cooper, McLearen, and Zapf (2004) found no racial differences in the decision to arrest people who presented with psychiatric symptoms. However, police were more likely to seek involuntary psychiatric commitment of Whites than Blacks. The implications of this research are troubling insofar as it suggests that Whites "will be diverted to the mental health system, whereas African Americans will find themselves in jail for the same actions" (p. 306). Moreover, another research finding suggests that once taken to jail, minority suspects may not be properly screened for mental illness. Certain screening instruments used on arrestees, such as Brief Jail Mental Health Screen, are more likely to miss symptoms in Blacks and Latinos than Whites, resulting in underreferrals for these racial and ethnic minorities for psychiatric services (Prins, Osher, Steadman, Robbins, & Case, 2012). Thus, not only does there appear to be a racial disparity in terms of who is initially treated as a psychiatric case (rather than a criminal justice one), but also it appears that racial and ethnic minorities are less likely to receive treatment for mental illness after arrest, which, in turn, can lead to higher rates of reoffending and rearrest. At least one study provides evidence for this outcome in areas with high minority populations. Grekin, Jemelka, and Trupin (1994) found that

> counties with a high proportion of a particular minority send more mentally ill members of that minority to prison and fewer to state hospitals than expected. This trend was strongest for Hispanics, but was also strong for Blacks and Native Americans. (p. 417)

Gender

Both men and women with SMIs present with similar risks of aggression, psychosocial characteristics, mental health histories, mental health problems, and criminogenic needs (Nicholls, Brink, Greaves, Lussier, & Verdun-Jones, 2009). Yet, incarcerated women with SMIs outnumber incarcerated men with SMIs by a ratio of more than two to one (Steadman et al., 2009). Although this is somewhat surprising in light of the fact that females are more likely to be diverted into treatment than their male counterparts (see Albonetti & Hepburn, 1996), it may be explained as a function of interaction between gender and age. Luskin (2001) found that younger women were the beneficiaries of diversion in mental health treatment programs in comparison to younger men, but older women were disadvantaged. She explained this finding by speculating for females, "youth indicates someone who is not yet committed to a criminal identity" whereas a youthful male who commits crimes "signals danger" (p. 231). As women age, however, whatever benefits they experience as a function of discretionary decision-making concerning diversion disappear.

Age differences among women notwithstanding, there are significant gender differences between male and female offenders with mental illnesses. Females tend to be

> more likely to have a history of engagement with social services, and report more trauma. Although more than half of both male and female mentally ill offenders (61% of the men and 56% of the women) did not complete high school, 20% of the mentally ill female offenders report some college education in comparison to 4% of the men. . . . [N]early three-fourths of the female mentally ill offenders (72%) report substance abuse problems in comparison to only half (48%) of the men. From a correctional standpoint, this is not counterintuitive considering the majority of female offenders are serving time for drug-related offenses and also have substance abuse problems. (Hartwell, 2001, p. 4)

As a result of these differences, gender-specific treatment programs for female offenders with SMIs are warranted. "Monitoring women who return home to families and children post release is prudent given their abuse histories" (Hartwell, 2001, p. 7). And females' higher incidence of co-occurring substance abuse disorders should result in their working with clinicians who possess "expertise in integrated or dual diagnosis treatment in prison, during their transition, and while living in the community" (p. 7). Finally, Hartwell found that men with SMIs who commit serious crimes, such as rape and murder, tend to be "transitioned immediately to inpatient hospitalization" after their release from prison and subsequently receive more "intensive and collaborative treatment and monitoring across several agencies (mental health and criminal justice) to assure public safety" (p. 7). The same is not true for women, who tend to be released into the community. As Hartwell pointed out, this raises "the question as to whether or not the mental health system responds similarly across gender and if the risk potential to others by males is perceived more seriously" (p. 8).

Socioeconomic Status

Poverty and declining economic status have long been important themes in research on the social consequences of mental disorders. Studies consistently found that those people from lower socioeconomic backgrounds are more likely to be diagnosed with SMIs than those of more economically privileged backgrounds (e.g., Lurigio, 2011). But SMIs can actually cause (or at least contribute significantly to) poverty. Consider that in 1939, Faris and Dunham (as cited in Fisher et al., 2006) described a "downward drift" of schizophrenic patients, leading them to increasingly worsening socioeconomic positions; a situation that persists today. People with untreated SMIs experience symptoms that can interfere significantly with daily functioning, making it difficult, if not impossible, to hold down a job, maintain housing, and obtain medical and mental health care. These factors often coalesce in ways that result in homelessness and the commission of "survival crimes," such as theft, trespassing, and panhandling (Fisher et al., 2006).

Even when subsidized housing or group-home living is made available to those with SMIs, such facilities tend to be located in low-income areas because people in middle class or affluent neighborhoods often block efforts to locate this type of housing near their homes (Fisher et al., 2006). Thus, those with SMIs tend to live in low-income areas where illicit drugs are prevalent. Given the high co-occurrence of SMIs and substance abuse disorders, this combination can lead to the commission of other illegal activities, "including larceny, drug trafficking, and prostitution" in an effort to support drug use (Fisher et al., 2006, p. 552). Moreover, high crime rates in low-income neighborhoods can lead to additional violence. For example, Silver, Mulvey, and Monahan (1999) found that patients who resided in high-poverty neighborhoods following discharge were more likely to engage in violence than patients discharged into neighborhoods with less poverty.

Unintended Consequences of the Policy

Given the comparative effectiveness of several of the criminal justice interventions discussed previously which leverage access to much needed community services, these programs can inadvertently increase police willingness to make "mercy bookings." In other words, the structured treatment that mental health courts and reentry/aftercare programs offer can create incentives for police to arrest those with SMIs in order to get them the services they need (Bazelon Center for Mental Health Law, 2012). At first blush, one might be tempted to conclude that since the humanitarian motivations underlying such mercy arrests result in people with SMIs obtaining the services they need, justice system involvement is not necessarily a bad thing. But there are numerous, serious unintended consequences to using the criminal justice system to address the public health need of people with SMIs.

First, there are several negative consequences stemming directly from arrest and incarceration. These traumas can aggravate the symptoms of many SMIs, causing not only an unnecessary increase in suffering for the affected person, but also manifesting in behaviors that lead to violence that can injure those with SMIs, police officers, innocent bystanders, correctional officers, and other inmates in jails and prisons (see Gur, 2010). And arrests have collateral social consequences as well, which range from "stigmatization based on a criminal record" to the "resulting denial of housing or employment or treatment services—even if charges are dropped" (Bazelon Center for Mental Health, 2003, p. 2).

Second, because police often serve as the first responders to situations involving people with SMIs, significant resources must be devoted to training police to interact with this population to avoid unnecessary victimization. Today, many police departments have established a ***Crisis Intervention Team*** (CIT) to avoid situations where officers mistake the symptoms of SMIs and respond using unnecessary levels of force, sometimes resulting in preventable deaths (Gur, 2010; Stephey, 2007). But CIT programs are not cure-alls. Certainly it costs a significant amount of money to establish these programs and then train officers. But, perhaps more importantly, we do not know if CITs actually reduce violence and victimization experiences by both police and people with SMIs during encounters between the two, nor has it been established that CIT programs are actually effective in reducing the arrests of persons with SMIs (see Watson et al., 2010).

Third, using the criminal justice system as the "front door to access mental health care" (Seltzer, 2005, p. 583) places enormous financial burdens on state and local governments forced to increase budgets to accommodate the expenditures required to deal with these complex problems. According to Johnson (2011), states with large populations of prisoners must commit large portions of their state budgets to operating criminal justice services. The implications of these increasing criminal justice budgets are cuts to other programs in the state, when ironically these same cuts to public health or housing programs may help prevent some offenses from occurring that lead to incarceration.

State and city-wide expenditures continue to rise as more and more offenders requiring psychiatric treatment are relegated to the care and custody of jails and prisons. For instance, the Los Angeles County Jail spent $10 million on psychiatric medication in 2001, and the State of Ohio in 2005 was treating 8,371 mentally ill offenders at a cost of $67 million a year. In Florida the number of mentally ill inmates in jails and prisons is believed to outnumber those in state run psychiatric facilities by 5 to 1; yet, the minimum cost to care for a mentally ill person in a Florida jail costs in excess of $40,000 and $60,000 in a Florida prison. Compare those figures to the roughly $20,000 cost of providing intensive CMH treatment for those with SMIs (www.PrisonPolicy.org). Overall, it is calculated that imprisoning mentally ill offenders costs the United States roughly $9 billion per year (Slate & Johnson, 2008).

Fourth, mentally ill inmates create enormous problems for the corrections system. The three largest providers of psychiatric care in the United States are New York's Rikers Island Jail, Illinois' Cook County Jail, and California's Los Angeles Jail (Slate & Johnson, 2008). The fact that so many mentally ill offenders are being held in our jails and prisons means that many of these prisoners are in daily contact with corrections officers who have not received proper training in effectively and safely dealing with psychiatric populations (Gur, 2010). This lack of training and understanding can lead to increases in conflicts, physical altercations, and injuries of both corrections officers and inmates (Steadman et al., 2009). Indeed, people with SMIs are often victimized while incarcerated (Gur, 2010; Human Rights Watch, 2009). Failing to provide incarcerated inmates with constitutionally minimum levels of medical care, as well as failing to protect these inmates from foreseeable victimization while incarcerated, further adds to the budgetary strain local and state governments experience as a result of the criminalization of mental illness. "Perhaps the best example of this is Sheriff Joe Arpaio who, claiming to be the toughest sheriff in the country, has cost taxpayers of Phoenix millions of dollars in lawsuit settlements for violating the civil rights of inmates with mental and medical needs" (Johnson, 2011, p. 19).

At great cost, some larger correctional facilities have special units devoted to housing "special needs" populations and staff receive at least some training in working with the mentally ill. But, even in such units, those with SMIs face a number of risks, not the least of which is decompensation, where the severity of the mental illness or the associated symptoms increases. The incarceration environment is one where inmates with SMIs "are more likely to violate rules or be injured in fights (Gur, 2010, p. 228; James & Glaze, 2006).

Finally, the funding consequences linked with the criminalization of mental illness offenders produces an untenable situation because in some U.S. jurisdictions, funds are no longer available to support public mental health outside of the correctional setting. As a result, some states, like Iowa, have turned to re-committing offenders with SMIs after serving their sentences back into the same prison system that released them because the state has no other facility for referral (Fuller, 2011). The beginning of 2011 saw 75 mentally ill offenders committed to prisons under this arrangement, some of whom had been civilly committed to the prison for a period of several years (Fuller, 2011). In essence, this means that citizens who have served their sentences are still being remanded to prison as the result of their mental illness, because there are no adequate mental health treatment facilities left where they can be civilly committed for treatment. This is the purest example of our jails and prisons becoming de facto psychiatric facilities, and it raises the question that the due process rights of these mentally ill offenders are being violated by virtue of the fact they have "served their time" and yet are not being released from prison.

⊠ How Do We Fix It? Suggestions for Policy Reform

There is no shortage of calls for changes in policy to address the many problems with the revolving-door cycle of incarcerating those with SMIs in jails and prisons and then releasing them only to have them return to the criminal justice system (e.g., Torrey et al., 2010; Vitiello, 2010). In the final section of this chapter, we explore some of the most common recommendations.

Legislative Changes to Address Financial Problems

Two legislative changes could go a long way toward improving policies to assist mentally ill offenders. First, as noted earlier, MIOTCRA limited its diversion programs to serve only non-violent criminal offenders. If MIOTCRA were amended to fund diversion programs that reached violent offenders as well, that many more people with SMIs could benefit from mental health court supervision.

Second, the statutory restriction for using Medicaid funds to support mentally ill individuals in "institutions for mental diseases" should be lifted. This ban encourages states "to empty hospitals, even if the patients end up in jails or homeless" (Torrey et al., 2010, p. 12). Moreover, "there are no fiscal incentives to follow up and make sure the patients receive care once they leave the hospitals (p. 12). Accordingly, this restriction on Medicaid use should be repealed.

Increased Diversion Efforts by Expanding the Number and Scope of Mental Health Courts

As previously summarized, most of the studies evaluating the effectiveness of mental health courts finds them to be effective at reducing recidivism (Dirks-Linhorst & Linhorst, 2012; Herinckx et al. (2005);

McNiel & Binder, 2007; Moore & Hiday, 2006; Trupin & Richards, 2003) and improving mental health functioning (Boothroyd, Poythress, McGaha, & Petrila, 2003). But there are many communities without this option available. Therefore, it presumes good public policy to advocate for the increase of the number of mental health courts. But care must be taken to ensure that these courts are properly staffed and funded, lest the courts become so backlogged and unable to provide services that their effectiveness is compromised. But adequate court resources are not sufficient since the success or failure of any mental health court program depends "on the ability of the mental health system to treat effectively those diverted from the criminal justice system (Litschge & Vaughn, 2009, p. 550). Thus, as discussed more fully below, inadequacies in the mental health system must also be addressed.

Regardless of the availability of mental health courts, there is a question of whether any criminal justice system involvement is necessary at all, especially in many misdemeanor cases. Consider that Fisher and colleagues (2006) noted that a review of records of mentally ill offenders arrested for nuisance crimes and referred to the forensic evaluation unit of a state hospital in Massachusetts found that many of these offenders would have met criteria for an involuntary hospitalization if the police had not arrested them and instead taken them for psychiatric emergency services. If that's the case, does the criminal justice system need to be involved at all? As Skeem and colleagues (2010) suggested, providing psychiatric treatment to those with SMIs before they violate the criminal law could prevent the criminal justice system from even being involved with people who should be treated as patients rather than offenders. Thus, the best public policy options may lie outside the criminal justice system.

Reform Civil Commitment Laws

Torrey and colleagues (2010) called for significant changes in civil commitment laws. Specifically, they seek the statutory authority to commit those who need treatment without regard to their ***dangerousness***. "Many times, it is this very dangerousness standard that necessitates law enforcement involvement. Mentally ill individuals should be able to access treatment before they become dangerous or commit a crime, not after" (p. 12). At first blush, this proposal seems logical and warranted. But, two concerns threaten its viability.

First, lax due process protections in the civil commitment arena were one of the reasons that civil liberties activists championed the tightening of these laws in the 1960s and 1970s. Legislators need to vote to loosen these laws over the objections of both civil libertarians and advocates for the mentally ill who oppose involuntary hospitalization. Moreover, when such laws are challenged in the courts, judges not only have to decide if the autonomy and privacy rights of the individual are outweighed by societal interests in caring for the mentally ill against their wishes, but also have to ensure that statutes provide sufficient safeguards are in place to guarantee due process. This is not, however, a difficult task; New York appears to have done so quite successfully (see Litschge & Vaughn, 2009; New York State Office of Mental Health, 2005).

Second, even if better laws could be enacted that eased the dangerousness criteria for commitment while still honoring due process rights, increasing the number of civil commitments is not possible if there are insufficient beds in psychiatric facilities to care for the civilly committed patients . Given how few beds are available, and in light of the incredible budgetary pressures on most states since the Great Recession of 2008, it is highly unlikely that most states can afford to expand the number of psychiatric beds available to accommodate need. Moreover, although there is an argument to be made that the funds currently used to pay for the incarceration of mentally ill offenders in jails in prisons could be shifted out of the criminal justice system and into the public health system to pay for these beds, the politics of doing so is likely a significant obstacle. Consider that many other social services, most notably education, have been cut as public budgets have diminished. Reasonable arguments can certainly be made that education and other services need to be funded before expanded access to psychiatric hospital beds.

However, there may be a middle ground. In the past few years, many states have modified their civil commitment laws to allow for outpatient civil commitments of mentally ill people in crisis (Slate, 2009, p. 21). Outpatient civil commitment is more commonly referred to as assisted outpatient treatment (AOT). AOT "requires selected seriously mentally ill persons to take medication under court order as a condition for living in the community" (Torrey et al., 2010, p. 12). According to the Treatment Advocacy Center (2012), 44 states have laws that authorize AOT. Empirical studies of AOT lend significant support to this policy recommendation, as AOT has been demonstrated not only to reduce dramatically the arrest rate of the mentally ill (New York State Office of Mental Health, 2005; Swanson et al., 2000), but also to significantly decrease their use of alcohol and drugs, psychiatric rehospitalizations, homelessness, suicides, and violent behaviors (Fernandez & Nygard, 1990; Munetz, Grande, Kleist, & Peterson, 1996; Phelan et al., 2010; Rohland, 1998; Swartz et al., 2010; Zanni & deVeau, 1986). Moreover, there is evidence that several of these positive outcomes continue even after court supervision ends (Van Dorn et al., 2010).

Improve Services for the Mentally Ill Within and Beyond the Criminal Justice System

Offenders with SMIs generally fall into three categories: those who were arrested for "simply displaying the signs and symptoms of mental illness in public"; those who committed petty, nuisance, or survival crimes; and those who commit serious crimes, including those that are violent (Lurigio, 2011, p. 12). Those who fall within the first group do not belong in the criminal justice system at all. They need psychiatric services that need to be offered through an improved public health system. When police encounter such individuals, they should be able to take them for treatment without ever making a formal arrest. The aforementioned improvements in outpatient civil commitment laws vis-à-vis AOT gives police the authority to do so and improves the public health outcomes for the mentally ill without ever involving them in the criminal justice system.

The second group of offenders should be diverted to mental health courts. But, we need to conceptualize the primary purpose of these specialized courts as serving a public health function, not a criminal justice role. Measures of success need to go beyond mere recidivism statistics. Indeed, the myth that treating psychiatric systems can improve recidivism rates must be dispelled. There are no studies which empirically demonstrate that alleviating psychiatric symptoms—in and of itself—affects recidivism among offenders with SMIs (Lurigio, 2011). Thus, improvements which address only the treatment of psychiatric systems are not likely to reduce recidivism. To accomplish the goal of reducing recidivism, psychiatric treatments need to be paired with other interventions aimed at criminogenic factors (Skeem et al., 2010), such as substance abuse, lack of education, lack of employment, and community disorganization. Toward that end, mental health courts need to pair offenders with a variety of social service agencies in much the same way that prison parolees are paired in the comprehensive reentry and aftercare programs that demonstrated so much success at rehabilitating the whole person. This would not only help these people "get back on their feet," but also help them avoid subsequent involvement in the criminal justice system (Council of State Governments, 2002; Kesten et al., 2012; Sacks et al., 2004, 2012; Skeem et al., 2010; Theurer & Lovell, 2008; Wolff et al., 2005).

The third group of offenders—those who commit serious crimes—pose the most significant policy challenges. To be sure, those who are imprisoned need treatment while incarcerated and, after release, they must be placed into comprehensive reentry and aftercare programs that help them comply with rules governing their release, thereby avoiding probation and parole violations and reducing the incidence of new offenses. But those correctionally based treatment, reentry, and aftercare programs do not address the true problem of incarcerating offenders with SMIs in jails or prisons in the first place. Three changes to law and policy could make a significant difference in reducing the number of people with SMIs in correctional institutions, and the final proposal might even serve to reduce the commission of crime by this population.

Initially, the narrowing of the criminal defenses of excuse that began in the 1970s and accelerated dramatically in the wake of John Hinckley Jr.'s case must be revisited. In *Clark v. Arizona* (2006), the U.S. Supreme Court upheld the authority of states to severely limit a mentally ill criminal defendant from offering some of the most probative evidence concerning his or her guilt. To prove that Eric Clark committed murder, the prosecution in the *Clark* case introduced evidence that the defendant spoke of wanting to kill police and then argued that to carry out this plan, the defendant lured police to the scene by blaring music from his truck while circling a block in a residential neighborhood. The defendant, however, was barred from introducing largely undisputed evidence about the nature of paranoid schizophrenia and how the disease caused, or could have caused, his actions. Specifically, the trial court was barred from considering expert testimony that people with schizophrenia often play music loudly to drown out the voices in their heads, which would have directly undercut the assertion that Clark did so to lure police officers to his car. The unworkable evidentiary framework upheld in *Clark* prevent the defense from arguing what should have been straightforward defense, namely that the defendant "did not commit the crime with which he was charged" because he lacked the requisite *mens rea* (*Clark v. Arizona*, 2006, p. 801, Kennedy, J., dissenting). The Supreme Court must revisit this misguided result and hold that barring the admissibility of such evidence violates due process (Fradella, 2007). Of course, dangerous people with SMIs like Eric Clark do not belong on the streets where they are free to maim or kill. But they do not belong in prisons either where they burden the correctional system and receive little or no treatment for their SMIs. Rather, such defendants should be remanded for treatment to secure psychiatric hospitals.

Next, the jurisdiction of mental health courts should be expanded to include the authority to adjudicate violent felony offenses. As Mann (2011) pointed out, 80% of mental health court systems do not accept any violent felony cases and only 1% handle those involving serious crimes of violence. If defendants who commit crimes like robbery and aggravated assault as a function of their SMIs had their cases handled through a system that subscribed to a therapeutic jurisprudence model, these offenders could get the comprehensive help they need while being monitored for compliance in ways that help to increase public safety.

Finally, and most importantly, we must make improvements to the mental health system and related social services so that people with SMIs do not commit serious crimes in the first place. Significantly expanded use of AOT can help to effectuate this desirable outcome. Those with SMIs need both psychiatric care (including access to psychotropic medications, when appropriate) and interventions aimed at criminogenic factors, such as job training, substance abuse treatment, and housing assistance (Skeem et al., 2010). Such multimodal services are likely to bring significant secondary benefits largely unrelated to the narrow metric of recidivism. Providing better treatment for the mentally ill likely reduces psychiatric symptoms in ways that allow the mentally ill to "become sober and employed, find and retain stable housing, develop better self-control, return to school, [and] mend relationships with family" (Lurigio, 2011, p. 15). These benefits, in turn, reduce calls to police and correspondingly reduce the number of inmates with SMIs, because mentally ill people receiving mentally appropriate treatment and adequate social services are better able to follow societal rules so that they do not run afoul of the law to begin with.

KEY TERMS

Asylum	Deinstitutionalization	Mental hospital
Community-based treatment	Justice and Mental Health Collaboration Program (JMHCP)	Mentally Ill Offender Treatment and Crime Reduction Act (MIOTCRA)
Community Mental Health (CMH)		
Crisis Intervention Team (CIT)	*Lessard v. Schmidt*	"Mercy booking"
Dangerousness	Mental health courts	Serious mental illness (SMI)

DISCUSSION QUESTIONS

1. Compare and contrast the first- and second-wave efforts to reform the criminal justice system's treatment of offenders with mental illness with the efforts of the community mental health movement. How were these efforts alike? How did they differ? Which, in your opinion, was the most successful? Why?

2. What are the primary reasons offered to explain why there are so many people with serious mental illness in U.S. correctional facilities?

3. Explain the criminalization hypothesis. What evidence supports it? What evidence calls it into question?

4. In your opinion, which two of the four criminal justice-based programs aimed at reducing recidivism rates of mentally ill offenders are the most promising? Evaluate the effectiveness of these programs using empirical evidence. How might these programs be expanded to further reduce recidivism rates of mentally ill offenders?

5. What do you think is the most effective noncriminal justice policy that, if implemented, would most improve services for people with serious mentally illnesses? Explain your reasoning.

WEBSITES FOR ADDITIONAL RESEARCH

Substance Abuse and Mental Health Services Administration: http://www.samhsa.gov/

U.S. Substance Abuse & Mental Health Services Administration National Registry of Evidence-Based Programs and Practices: http://www.nrepp.samhsa.gov/

California Courts: http://www.courts.ca.gov/5982.htm

Bureau of Justice Assistance, https://www.bja.gov/

National Center for State Courts: http://www.ncsc.org/Topics/Problem-Solving-Courts/Mental-Health-Courts/Resource-Guide.aspx

Center for Court Innovation: http://www.courtinnovation.org/

Council of State Governments Consensus Project: http://consensusproject.org/

National Council for Community Behavioral Healthcare: http://www.thenationalcouncil.org/cs/home

Mentally Ill Offender Treatment and Crime Reduction Act (MIOTCRA): http://www.gpo.gov/fdsys/pkg/PLAW-108pub1414/html/PLAW-108pub1414.htm

Treatment Advocacy Center: http://www.treatmentadvocacycenter.org/

National Institute of Mental Health: http://www.nimh.nih.gov/index.shtml

CHAPTER

XIV

Gender Responsive Practices

Barbara Koons-Witt and Courtney Crittenden

Gender-responsive practices are policies and programs based on the recognized needs of women offenders. These practices acknowledge that there are gendered pathways to crime, meaning there are various biological, psychological, and social factors that are unique to the female offender (Salisbury & Van Voorhis, 2009). Moreover, these practices recognize that programs and policies need to be geared toward women's differences and unique needs in order for the female offender to succeed after exiting the correctional system and negotiating reentry to society. In the current chapter, we examine gender-responsive practices in the criminal justice system. We begin by reviewing the background and the need for gender-responsive practices for women offenders. Next, we focus on current gender-responsive practices used in prisons for women, and finally, we discuss the future of these policies for women and their involvement in the criminal justice system.

The Back Story: The Need for Gender-Responsive Practices

Historically, women suffered from neglect in the criminal justice system and in criminal justice research (Belknap, 2007; Grana, 2010; Koons, Burrow, Morash, & Bynum, 1997). One of the major reasons that women experience this oversight is the fact that women are a minority in the offender population and the corrections system (Belknap, 2007; Butler, 1997; Glaze & Maruschak, 2008; Koons et al., 1997; Mumola, 2000; Owen, 2001); in fact, they are often referred to as an *invisible population* (Belknap, 2007). Moreover, Salisbury and Van Voorhis (2009) note that, "because crime is predominately a 'man's game,' it comes as no surprise that most criminological knowledge focuses on how and why men engage in criminal activity" (p. 541). Yet, women are coming into the criminal justice system at a greater rate than ever before, and from 1980 to 1998, the number of incarcerated women increased over 500% (Morash & Schram, 2002). What is more, the number of women coming into the correctional system since 1970 is more than twice the rate of men (Belknap, 2010). These dramatic trends have resulted in more attention and research on women offenders.

Brief Profile of Women Offenders

Female offenders share many commonalities and are often quite different from their male counterparts. When women commit crimes, they are typically supervised in the community rather than being incarcerated (Glaze, 2010). This is because women compared to men are usually much less violent, have less extensive criminal histories (Belknap, 2007), and are more likely to be arrested (and incarcerated) for drug or property offenses than for violent offenses (Brown & Bloom, 2009; Glaze & Maruschak, 2008; Mumola, 2000; Owen, 2001). Even when women are incarcerated for a violent offense, these offenses are typically less serious crimes than those committed by violent men (Belknap, 2007; Chesney-Lind, 2004; Sokoloff, 2005). Once in prison, women are regarded as less serious than their male counterparts because they are not as likely to riot or cause other major disturbances within the prison facility (Belknap, 2007; Rafter, 1990).

Women are likely to have extensive histories of victimization (Browne, Miller, & Maguin, 1999; Chesney-Lind, 2004; DeHart, 2008; Gilfus, 1992), drug use and abuse (Chesney-Lind, 2004; Glaze & Maruschak, 2008; Mumola, 2000), and mental health issues—especially in comparison to the general population (James & Glaze, 2006; Lord, 2008). Many women in prison are also likely to come from situations of poverty and broken homes (Chesney-Lind, 2004; Simon & Ahn-Redding, 2005) and have a striking lack of education (Belknap, 2010; Bloom, Owen, & Covington, 2005; Schram, 2003). These women are also highly likely to be mothers (Bloom et al., 2005; Chesney-Lind, 2004; Glaze & Maruschak, 2008; Leverentz, 2006; Morash & Schram, 2002; Simon & Ahn-Redding, 2005). Finally, minority women are overrepresented in the offender and prisoner populations (Glaze & Maruschak, 2008; Simon & Ahn-Redding, 2005; Sokoloff, 2005). Oftentimes, an accumulation of these multiple factors affect women's criminality. All of these factors separate women from their male counterparts and warrant differential treatment from men. However, the treatment of women by the correctional system was not always the most appropriate for them.

Historical Perspective of Treatment and Programming

Throughout its history, the correctional system used various methods to control and treat women and generally, the treatment has been inferior to the treatment received by that of their male counterparts (Rafter, 1990). Historically, they received stereotypical programming due to the dominant societal ideal of a *"good woman"* which reflected the attitudes of mainstream society in regards to what it meant to be a proper woman in society (Grana, 2010). Many of the women who came into contact with the criminal justice system were viewed as *"fallen women"*; therefore, their time in prison was used to retrain them in the image of a "good woman." They received programs that focused on traditional gender roles, such as sewing, cleaning, cooking, and other domestic duties (Fox, 1984; Rafter, 1990). Very few programs trained women to be self-sufficient and/or earn a living on their own.

Beginning in the late 1960s and early 1970s, critics pushed for the equal treatment of men and women in prisons (Fox, 1984); yet, this too was later condemned since the standard used to define equal was based on males (Belknap, 2003; Chesney-Lind, 2004; Morash & Schram, 2002; van Wormer, 2010). Under equal treatment, women basically received programs that were designed for men and simply added to women's prisons in an effort to ensure "equality" (Rafter, 1990). In the late 1980s and early 1990s, feminist scholars argued that women in the criminal justice system were different enough from their male counterparts to warrant their own study (Covington, 2000). This focus on women resulted in the development of a theoretical point of view known as the (gendered) pathways perspective. The pathways perspective acknowledges that men and women take different paths to delinquency and criminality. Additionally, it notes that the most common paths for women consist of surviving trauma and abuse, poverty, and substance use/abuse (Belknap, 2003; Bloom et al., 2005).

The push for equitable and gender-responsive treatment also began in the early 1990s. Equitable treatment does not mean sameness, but instead refers to equal funding and programming options that are developed respectively for the needs of men and women prisoners (Bloom, 2012). Indeed, women are not identical to men, but "look" rather different from them in regards to the offenses they commit, their personal histories, their pathways to crime, and their risk factors and needs (Bloom et al., 2004; Wright, Van Voorhis, Salisbury, & Bauman, 2012). There were two major justifications for the gender-specific push: (a) the dramatic increase of incarcerated women and (b) differential needs and risk factors posed by women (Bloom, 1999; Morash, Bynum, & Koons, 1998).

One of the first major studies of **gender-specific practices** was conducted by Morash and colleagues in their examination of prison administrators' opinions of management, treatment, and offender needs for women inmates. In this study, prison administrators noted the need for gender-specific classifications because **gender-neutral classifications** were less effective in their ability to correctly classify the needs and security risks of women (Morash et al., 1998). Additionally, administrators recognized that women need their own management style (Koons et al., 1997; Morash et al., 1998), and they identified successful elements of women's programs that appeared to be promising in meeting their specific needs (Morash et al., 1998). Morash and colleagues (1998) concluded that the development and expansion of gender-specific practices was needed.

Bloom and her colleagues contributed to the gender-specific literature with the development of six gender-responsive guidelines (Bloom, 1999; Bloom et al., 2004, 2005). These principles have since been used to develop programs for women offenders. The gender-responsive principles, as outlined by Bloom and her colleagues (2004), include the following:

1. *Gender:* Acknowledge that gender makes a difference.

2. *Environment:* Create an environment based on safety, respect, and dignity.

3. *Relationships:* Develop policies, practices, and programs that are relational and promote healthy connections to children, family, significant others, and the community.

4. *Services and Supervision:* Address substance abuse, trauma, and mental health issues through comprehensive, integrated, and culturally relevant services and appropriate supervision.

5. *Socio-economic Status:* Provide women with opportunities to improve their socioeconomic conditions.

6. *Community:* Establish a system of community supervision and reentry with comprehensive, collaborative services (p. 43).

Taken as a whole, the principles outlined above recognize the unique criminal pathways of women offenders. First, the principles acknowledge the many difficulties that women experience in their childhood (e.g., childhood abuse and neglect, family instability). Second, the principles identify the significance of relationships for women. These include relationships between women and their parents, their intimate partners, their children, and their friends. Third, the principles detail the importance of prior abuse and victimization for women. They address this issue in terms of needed program environments, programming, and supervision approaches. Finally, the principles demonstrate the interconnectedness of issues that women offenders face and the importance of addressing them in a holistic manner and throughout all parts of the correctional system. Again, these principles developed by Bloom and her colleagues guide much of the gender-responsive research and program development, which when taken altogether can work toward rehabilitating women by addressing their specific experiences, circumstances, and needs.

The Current State of Gender-Responsive Practices and Research

Researchers and practitioners alike have made progress in making the case for gender-responsive policies and practices. Due to their smaller numbers and less serious forms of offending, women have endured decades of being overlooked and neglected in research and in the formulation of criminal justice policies and practices (Bloom et al., 2004). As a result of our increased attention toward female offenders beginning in the 1960s and 1970s, and a growing body of research since then on women's involvement in the criminal justice system, it is safe to say that gender does matter.

We know that there are vital differences between males and females and their involvement in the criminal justice system. These differences include pathways to delinquency and crime, and ultimately to the legal system. Recent research highlights gender differences in offenses, criminal backgrounds, and risk factors (Bloom et al., 2004; Wright et al., 2012). All of these are is important to consider because in addition to them providing us with a better understanding of women offenders, they also present us with a framework for how women offenders should be dealt with by the criminal justice system. While it is necessary to consider how gender-responsive practices can inform criminal justice policies across the entire system (Bloom et al., 2004), in the sections below we focus on the significance of gender-responsive practices in the correctional system in terms of classification and assessment, programming, and management/supervision areas for women prisoners and review what we know from current research.

Assessment of Risk and Needs

Once sentenced to prison, entering offenders typically spend several weeks being evaluated and assessed for security and programming reasons in a reception and orientation center or wing (Clear, Cole, Reisig, & Petrosino, 2012). Prisoners are most frequently classified into minimum, medium, or maximum security levels that reflect an increasing degree of risk for harming themselves or other prisoners, escaping, or recidivating (Farr, 2000; Wright, Salisbury, & Van Voorhis, 2007). Since the female inmate population is comparatively smaller than the male inmate population, female housing options are often more limited so this security classification is not always possible (e.g., there may be only one female corrections institution in a particular state). An inmate's designated security level has other consequences for them. Custody level can also dictate prisoner's access to resources, certain programming, and services within the institution (Farr, 2000; Wright et. al., 2007).

Prisons have historically classified incarcerated women using instruments that were developed for and validated on incarcerated men (Burke & Adams, 1991; Farr, 2000; Morash et al., 1998; Hardyman & Van Voorhis, 2004). Many practitioners and researchers believed that the assessments did not work for women (Burke & Adams, 1991; Reisig, Holtfreter, & Morash, 2006; Taylor & Blanchette, 2009; Van Voorhis,

Wright, Salisbury, & Bauman, 2010) and that they did a poor job in matching women to proper custody levels or needed programming and services (Hardyman & Van Voorhis, 2004). One national survey conducted during the mid-1990s found that about three in four states used the same classification instrument for both male and female prisoners, and only a few states (three, or 6%) used classification tools that were different from those used by men and were specifically designed for female inmates (Morash et al., 1998).

The general goal of classification systems is to maintain order inside prisons, prevent escapes, and ensure community safety. Most women are not violent, do not commit serious infractions while incarcerated, and rarely riot or try to escape prison (Belknap, 2007; Rafter, 1990). Essentially, women commit less serious forms of crimes and serve their prison time differently than men (Kruttschnitt, Gartner, & Miller, 2000; Owen, 1998). Classification systems fail to recognize these differences. Correctional administrators generally feel that women prisoners are over-classified into higher security levels than either needed or appropriate (Morash et al., 1998). Over-classification can happen due to a number of reasons. First, instruments can inaccurately predict that a sizable number of women will harm themselves or other inmates in the prison. Second, because of their small numbers, females who are assessed as low risk may be confined in one institution meant to manage varying security levels; therefore, their setting is more restrictive than required (Morash & Schram, 2002). Additionally, gender-neutral assessment tools are believed to over-classify many women involved in violent crimes because they ignore the context or circumstance associated with women's use of violence. For example, women may use violence in response to their abuse, or when they are with male partners (Farr, 2000). In other words, women's use of violence in these incidents means something substantively different given the context; thus, they do not necessarily represent the same threat or risk for violence and disturbances behind bars as their male counterparts. Some states use overrides to address this issue. One classification study on women found that 1 in 5 state agencies utilized classification overrides between 18% and 70% of the time with women (Van Voorhis & Presser, 2001). Risk assessments ought to reflect women's experiences and behaviors and should identify and connect women to proper custody levels and necessary programs.

In addition to determining the level of risk for women, many prisons assess women for mental health and medical problems and for other programming areas, including substance abuse, family issues, relationships, education level, and job skills (Morash & Schram, 2002). Morash and colleagues found that a considerable number of states assessed all incoming women offenders for substance abuse (86%), mental health (86%), medical problems (76%), and education level (86%). The study also found that states frequently assessed all incoming women prisoners for vocational choice (60%), spousal abuse (52%), childhood sexual abuse (50%), and the presence of children (48%). Overall, they found that the assessments produced difficulties matching women to needed programs, and that this was further complicated by overcrowding, a restricted number of available housing options, and the lack of needed bed space in certain facilities and programs (Morash et. al., 1998; Morash & Schram, 2002). In conclusion, several studies from the 1990s suggest that correctional administrators and those working with women offenders questioned the utility of assessment and classification systems for women offenders in terms of both placing women at appropriate custody levels and identifying and connecting women to needed programming and services within prisons.

Beginning in the late 1990s and continuing through to the current decade, several initiatives were undertaken to develop and validate gender-specific classification and assessment systems, building on early efforts that identified concerns with existing assessment tools. Van Voorhis along with colleagues and in cooperation with the National Institute of Corrections (NIC) embarked on a project to determine if "gender-responsive factors are risk factors for institutional misconduct and community recidivism, as well as whether these factors improve the classification of women when they are considered in classification assessment tools" (Wright et al., 2012). This work on the part of Van Voorhis and others resulted in the development of two types of assessments, referred to as Women's Risk and Needs Assessments, or WRNA (Buell, 2010). The one assessment, referred to as "the trailer," is used to supplement an existing risk/needs assessment instrument like the LSI-R (The Level of Service Inventory-Revised), while the second assessment is utilized as an independent or "stand-alone" risk/need assessment instrument (Van Voorhis et al., 2008). In addition to incorporating "strength-based" items, the new assessments highlighted issues involving mental health, healthy relationships, stress related to parenting roles, prior abuse, and self-efficacy (Buell, 2010).

Current Research. Researchers involved in the NIC project report that early indications at least suggest that "risk assessments incorporating factors shared by men and women (gender-neutral) and those noted in the gender-responsive literature were found to be predictive/valid for women offenders" (Van Voorhis et al., 2010, p. 263). In fact, several programming needs for women appear to be risk factors for their adjustment to prison. Van Voorhis found that needs associated with a history of abuse and victimization, mental health and substance abuse problems, and difficult or unhealthy intimate relationships were linked to the occurrence of serious behavior misconducts within the first year of incarceration for women (Wright et al., 2012).

Taylor and Blanchette (2009) contend in their research that women's pathways to crime must inform risk assessments for women. They note, "immense value is gained by recognizing women offender's unique life experiences, offending context, and social location. The complex question is how to account fairly and justly for gendered pathways to crime" (p. 224). This area requires additional research since there is a continuing debate over whether gender-neutral or gender-specific risk factors *best* predict misconducts by women prisoners. There is some evidence that a gender-neutral assessment like the LSI-R is useful in assessing women offenders; however, Morash (2009) raises the question as to whether it is the *best* predictor for them. Some researchers continue to argue that gender-specific risk assessments are the best way to account for women's needs, especially when added to gender-neutral assessments (Taylor & Blanchette, 2009; Van Voorhis et al., 2010; Wright, Van Voorhis, Salisbury, & Bauman, 2009), meaning that both gender-neutral and gender-specific assessments are needed to understand risk factors and predict misconducts for women.

Correctional Programming

Women in prison have many needs that can and should be met by the correctional system. These needs include medical and mental health issues, substance abuse treatment, parenting and family relationship issues, and education and job skills training. Given the array of programs needs and the fact that many of these issues are interconnected, it is important that prisons use holistic approaches that can be individually tailored to women (Adams, Leukefeld, & Peden, 2008; Browne et al., 1999; Koons et al., 1997). Programs and services should also emphasize building strengths, skills, and empowerment for women offenders (Koons et al., 1997; Morash et al., 1998; Morash & Schram, 2002) and should include wraparound services for them in the community as well (Adams et al., 2008).

Physical Health

Women prisoners have considerable health problems that must be addressed while they are incarcerated. They are likely to have more health issues than both men and women in the general population, and also more than incarcerated men (Anderson, 2003). Many women come to prison with very little prior preventive medical care and a history of limited access to proper health care in the community (Daane, 2003; van Wormer, 2010). Some of these health care needs are unique to women and are related to their reproductive systems (e.g., pregnancy and prenatal care, gynecological needs). Their needs in prison may range from prenatal care to treatment of sexually transmitted diseases, or even treatment for major illnesses, such as cancer (Anderson, 2003; Daane, 2003). They may also have chronic health problems due to prior abuse (DeHart, 2008). Prisons have difficulty providing adequate health care services to women offenders. Despite the fact that more health care services are provided in today's correctional system than in the past, there continues to be concerns, including (1) limited access to treatment compared to their male counterparts; (2) poor quality care; and (3) the use of unqualified medical professionals that show little concern for women and their health care needs (Anderson, 2003, p. 55).

Abuse and Victimization

The Pathways Perspective (research on women's pathways into crime) highlights the prominence that prior abuse and victimization play in women's involvement in crime and the criminal justice system. Research consistently demonstrates that incarcerated women have extensive histories of abuse and violence (Browne et al., 1999; DeHart, 2008; Gilfus, 1992) and report higher levels of prior abuse than do male inmates, 57% versus 16%, respectively (Harlow, 1999; see also, Belknap, 2003). Their abuse includes physical, sexual, and emotional incidents (Browne et al., 1999; Gilfus, 1992; Glaze & Maruschak, 2008). What is more, they tend to experience abuse and violence throughout their lifetime (i.e., childhood, adolescence, and adulthood) at the hands of multiple victimizers (DeHart, 2008). Many of these women offenders turn to drugs so that they can handle the pain and trauma; researchers refer to this as "self medication" (Chesney-Lind, 2000; McClellan, Farabee, & Crouch, 1997; Morash & Schram, 2002). For some women, prisons represent a "safe haven" for them away from their abuser and the chaos that is their life on the outside (Henriques & Manatu-Rupert, 2001). Access to programming to address trauma and abuse is essential since it represents an opportunity to counsel women about healthy relationships, empowerment, and responses other than turning to alcohol and other drugs.

Mental Health

Mental health issues are substantial among the correctional population and the problem has steadily worsened over the last several decades (Lord, 2008; Morash & Schram, 2002). National statistics from 2005 suggest that over half of all prison and jail inmates have some form of mental health problems (James & Glaze, 2006). The problem appears to be more exacerbated among female inmates, with 73% of female prison inmates (vs. 55% of males) and 75% of female jail inmates (vs. 63% of males) identified as having a mental health problem (James & Glaze, 2006). In sum, female inmates are considerably more likely than their male counterparts to suffer from mental illness, with a vast majority of women suffering from some mental health deficiency (Glaze & Maruschak, 2008).

Mentally ill women have difficulty understanding the prison environment, following rules, and participating in available programming. Referred to as "prison's untouchables" by a former prison superintendent, mentally ill women are frequently misunderstood, stigmatized, and find themselves at the lowest end of the prison hierarchy (Lord, 2008). Because of their erratic behavior and propensity to harm themselves and others without warning, they are often isolated within the prison setting. Prisons are not equipped to handle the large number of incarcerated women with mental illnesses (Lord, 2008), and lack the necessary programming, services, staff, and bed space necessary to effectively address this population. Essentially, mentally ill women in prison remain stigmatized and misunderstood with few resources to remedy their circumstances (Lord, 2008).

Substance Abuse

Female offenders have serious drug histories with many reporting use of drugs in the month leading up to their current imprisonment (Mumola, 2000). In fact, illegal drug use is higher among women than men prisoners (Greenfeld & Snell, 1999; McClellan et al., 1997). Correctional systems do not have enough programs and services to address the level of need of the large number of women in prisons or entering prisons with drug-related problems. Providing drug treatment for women while they are in prison and then in the community setting is critically important (Johnston, 1995; Owen, 2001), but treatment must recognize the differences in patterns of substance abuse between men and women.

Correctional addictions programs do not necessarily assess the multiple problems of women offenders. Women are frequently placed in programs that were designed for males (e.g., use confrontational approaches), and which do not typically work well for them (Shearer, 2003). Experiences with abuse and violence are pervasive among women prisoners, and they frequently deal with feelings of worthlessness, depression, and the need to please others around them (Shearer, 2003). Programs for women prisoners need to address the mental health problems (i.e., anxiety, depression) and traumatic experiences (i.e., victimization, abuse) that are often associated with drug use. Women's drug use is also connected to other high-risk behaviors, such as the sharing of needles, exchanging sex for drugs, contracting sexually transmitted diseases, and engaging in unprotected sex with multiple partners (Shearer, 2003). Nevertheless, studies show that women can succeed in drug abuse programs (Dowden & Blanchette, 2002; Johnston, 1995).

Children and Family Relationships

Almost 66% of women prisoners report leaving at least one dependent child behind when they entered the prison system (Glaze & Maruschak, 2008). Incarcerated mothers feel a great deal of shame and regret for how their own decisions have negatively impacted their children's lives. They worry about who will care for their children during their incarceration and fear the possibility of losing their parental rights (Morash & Schram, 2002). To avoid losing custody of their children, incarcerated women may resort to placing the children in tenuous environments that are themselves rife with chaos, danger, drug use, abuse, and violence (Sharp, 2003). Children of incarcerated women may react to the separation by getting angry, depressed, doing poorly in school, and acting out in other ways (Morash & Schram, 2002). It is important to provide opportunities and programming that encourage continued communication and contact between incarcerated women and their kids with many prisons offering some form of parenting programs or visitation programs to help maintain and strengthen this relationship (Sharp, 2003). These programs are important since children can serve as a motivating factor for women offenders (Brown & Bloom, 2009); therefore, facilitating a positive and healthy relationship between both should be an important objective for the correctional system.

Education and Job Skills

Providing educational programs and job training programs to incarcerated women is needed since many of their crimes are economic in nature (e.g., shoplifting, embezzlement, credit card fraud, etc.), and many prisoners need to be self-sufficient and provide for themselves and their families once they reenter society (Schram, Koons-Witt, Williams, & McShane, 2006). Women prisoners have poor educational backgrounds; many do not have a high school diploma (Brown & Bloom, 2009; Mumola, 2000). Most correctional systems provide some level of educational programming to prisoners. These programs typically involve GED (General Educational Development) programs, and to a lesser extent access to college-level courses (Pollock, 2004).

Many incarcerated women have very limited job skills, lack experience in the formal labor market, and are more likely to be unemployed when they are arrested than are incarcerated men (Greenfeld & Snell, 1999). Offering vocational programs to women is one way to provide them with marketable skills and training; however, job programs should reflect a wide array of employment opportunities and not simply reinforce cultural stereotypes of women. Vocational programs that are considered stereotypical for women include cosmetology, clerical or office work, food services, and domestic work. Alternative vocational programs (i.e., nontraditional vocational programming for women) include auto repair, welding, carpentry, electrical work, and plumbing (Schram, 2003). Research by Schram (2003) suggests that participation in these types of programs can depend on how women prisoners view these specific jobs. Despite this concern, it is still necessary to offer women vocational programs that provide them with new and marketable job skills. Furthermore, programming should provide them with job skills that pay decent wages and help them to become self-sufficient in the community.

As previously stated, it is important to provide women offenders with gender-responsive programming while they are in prison, and in the community, if they are released on parole. Researchers make a strong case describing the differences between men and women offenders, recognizing their distinct pathways, and identifying the unique programs and services women offenders need; yet, program evaluations and evidence-based research studies remain limited (Morash et al., 1998). A review of evaluation literature in the 1990s located reports for 68 corrections programs for women, with just 12 of these programs specifically measuring outcomes, and only six of those looking at recidivism as an outcome measure (Morash et al., 1998).

In order to understand what might work in programming for women offenders, Morash studied promising approaches for women offenders and asked respondents from correctional systems across the country to identify programs in their respective jurisdictions which were particularly effective or promising in meeting the needs of women in their system. While a total of 242 innovative programs were identified as a result of this process, there were 17 states where respondents could not identify a promising program for women offenders (Morash et al., 1998). For those respondents who named a promising program, they were asked to indicate what program elements were linked to the success of the program. Among the characteristics mentioned were (a) program staff that were dedicated, caring, and who were role models; (b) programs that were comprehensive; (c) programs with peer influence and support; (d) programs with many types of resources; (e) programs that provided women offenders with skills; (f) programs that established safe and comforting environments; and (g) programs that used nonaggressive management approaches and had support from custody staff (adapted from Exhibit 4 in Morash et al., 1998, p. 7).

These are important factors to consider when designing and implementing gender-responsive programs for women offenders. Additional program evaluations have completed since the study by Morash and her colleagues, and some have found success in reducing recidivism among other program outcomes (Dowden & Blanchette, 2002; Gehring, Van Voorhis, & Bell, 2010; Kennon, Mackintosh, & Myers, 2009; Robbins, Martin, & Surratt, 2009). However, it is evident that more evaluation research of women's programming is needed (Kendall, 1998; Ritchie, 2001).

Funding agencies and decision makers are increasingly requiring the documentation of program effects through process and outcome evaluations (Bloom, 2012). Program evaluations are necessary because they highlight factors that are linked to program success and failure as measured by both short- and long-term impact on participants. In addition to the usual measures of recidivism, Bloom (2012) suggests that outcome evaluations use indicators of program participation, completion, recovery from drugs and trauma, receiving a GED or other degree/trade, obtaining employment, safe housing, assuming custody of children, and maintaining one's physical and mental health as possible measures of a program's impact (p. 26).

Equally clear is the need for more program evaluations to make certain that programs are meeting women's needs and reducing recidivism (Robbins et al., 2009). Again, women want to participate in correctional programs, they want to better themselves (Glaze & Maruschak, 2008; Lord, 2008); however, if they are participating in programs that do not work and are not effective, then essentially they have not improved or changed their circumstances. Yes, they will eventually leave prison and reenter the community, but nothing will have changed. They will undoubtedly face the same problems that brought them to prison in the first place. Evaluations of correctional programming for women prisoners are a necessary requirement if we want evidence-based research and findings to inform policies and decision making in the corrections field.

Correctional Management and Supervision

For correctional agencies, the management and supervision of offenders generally includes, among other things, staffing, operations, and security. Unlike assessment and programming, far less attention is paid to gender-responsive practices in the management and supervision of women prisoners (e.g., day-to-day operations of institutions and related policies). Despite this observation, we argue that management and supervision practices are critically important for women prisoners. The policies that govern women's prisons, and the perspectives of those who manage facilities for women offenders and who come into contact with them through their work in security and programming, can impact how women serve their time and experience the prison setting.

Due to their small numbers, women prisoners are clearly a marginal group in correctional systems. They typically comprise between 5% and 7% of those housed in state prisons (Greenfeld & Snell, 1999; Simon & Ahn-Redding, 2005). Their marginal status influences them in very direct and fundamental ways. Case in point, while there are some correctional systems around the country that are responding to the needs of women offenders, many prison systems still subscribe to the view that "an inmate is an inmate" and use the same policies to address both male and female inmate populations (Pollock, 2004; Schram et al., 2004; Wright et al., 2012). The reality that correctional policies that are gender-neutral are being used to train correctional staff, secure prison facilities, transport inmates (including pregnant inmates), house, clothe, and feed inmates is problematic. Standard policies and procedures that govern searches, use of restraints, and isolation can re-traumatize women who have experiences with prior abuse, victimization and violence, and mental health problems (Covington & Bloom, 2003).

Prior research indicates that there is a different feeling or atmosphere to women's prisons (Pollock, 2004), yet, policy is generally developed to manage the behavior of the larger male inmate population and neglects these key distinctions (Bloom et al., 2004; Camp, Hardyman, May, & Camp, 2008). Of the state agencies which participated in a study of staffing policies for women's prisons, 83% indicated that they "do not use female-specific methods to determine the number of security staff required to support women's institutions," and 80% reported that they "do not use female-specific criteria for establishing, adding, and/ or deleting posts in women's institutions ..." (Camp et al., 2008, p. 110).

Correctional officers and staff with experience working in male and female institutions acknowledge differences in the type of supervision needed when working with female inmates (Camp et al., 2008; Morash et al., 1998). Training should reflect similarities and differences between male and female prisoners, should acknowledge the need for gender-responsive policies, and evidence-based practices. For example, custody staff should be trained by mental health professionals to become familiar with women prisoners' histories of trauma, depression, and other illnesses so that they can appropriately identify and respond to these women (Camp et al., 2008). This includes learning how to respond to requests for more time, attention, and interactions with women prisoners in an informed and professional way (Camp et al., 2008). Staff should be made aware of distinct differences between men and women in terms of their pathways to prison, their risk factors, and programming needs. Training also needs to prepare staff with information on how women offenders adapt to and experience prison differently than male offenders, and should train staff on how to avoid responses to female inmates that are stereotypical (i.e., treating them like children), and disempowering them (Schram et al., 2004).

Some of these concerns may be alleviated in part by identifying employees who want to work in women's institutions (Wright et al., 2012). This is vital since staff members may feel hesitant to work with women prisoners because it is "not real corrections" (Buell, 2010), or they view the work as being more difficult and challenging (Pollock, 1984, 1995; Schram et al., 2004). Corrections officers often find that it is easier to work with male inmates than female inmates. For instance, officers believe that male inmates are much more likely to follow orders, whereas female prisoners tend to question orders more, and frequently are more emotional (Pollock, 1986; Schram et al., 2004). Pollock's (1986) interviews with corrections officers illustrate perceived differences between male and female inmates:

> Women tend to show their problems more. Things bother them more so they have to act out more than men. So that part there makes it a little harder, because you have more problems to deal with. [male corrections officer] (p. 98)

> They had to know, why? How come? They would be more apt to question what I said. Whether they knew I was right or wrong. They would have to question it just for the sake of questioning it. [female corrections officer] (p. 98)

Current correctional policies and training fail to prepare officers for assignments to women's institutions, and what they should expect when supervising and interacting with women prisoners. Buell (2010) states that "applying a practice to a female offender in the exact same way it is applied to a male may have different results" (p. 1).

> At the same time, Pollock (1986) found corrections officers who preferred working with women prisoners because they were more interesting to be around, they learned a great deal from the experiences, and they liked the challenge and believed they could be more effective in helping women offenders.

> Several officers in the study made the following observations as to why they liked working with women prisoners:

> Men are less stressful to work with, but you get bored with them. . . . You keep active with the women so I enjoy that more. They have more problems you had to deal with. [female corrections officer] (p. 99)

I find it a lot more challenging because they are so demanding and because they appear to care a lot more about what's happening to them while they're incarcerated. I found the men boring to work with. Minimal problems and minimal hassles and they just wanted to do time and most of them were able to do that, and it was very dull. There was no challenge to that, although it was easier, less stressful. [female corrections officer] (p. 99)

Interestingly, some of the same issues identified as negative reasons for not wanting to work with women were identified as positive reasons for working in women's prisons. Thus, it is important that correctional agencies identify those employees who value working with women offenders and see their work in women's prisons in a positive light (Wright et al., 2012). Having dedicated and caring staff members that are qualified and can serve as credible role models are important for women offenders (Koons et al., 1997).

Research involving the effectiveness of gender-responsive practices for the supervision and management of women offenders is more limited in scope than in the assessment and programming areas. However, there are several efforts underway to expand our understanding of gender-responsive principles and their application in both institutional and community corrections. The National Institute of Corrections (NIC) and the Center for Effective Public Policy (CEPP) have been working together to develop a *Gender-Informed Practices Assessment (GIPA)* tool that determines the degree to which women's prisons and correctional systems adhere to gender-responsive principles and evidence-based practices for women offenders (National Institute of Corrections, n.d.). The Gender-Informed Practices Assessment examines each of the following areas: (a) facility; (b) management and operations; (c) staffing and training; (d) facility culture; (e) offender management; (f) assessment and classification; (g) case and transitional planning; (h) research-based program areas; (i) services; and (j) quality assurance and evaluation (National Institute of Corrections, n.d., pp. 1–9). This project seems promising and should continue to provide prisons and agencies with useful feedback concerning what they are doing well and what areas need improving in order to bring them in line with gender-informed policies and practices.

A second initiative includes the use of the *Women Offender Case Management Model (WOCMM)* in the probation field. This model emphasizes an "enriched case management approach to address the risk, need, and responsivity issues that are critical for success with women" (Orbis Partners, 2009, p. 1). WOCMM is a dynamic initiative and is delivered employing a multidisciplinary team. It uses an individualized service plan, provides women with an array of services and opportunities, focuses on women's existing strengths, and uses a process that monitors the progress of women probationers (Orbis Partners, 2009). An outcome evaluation of the WOCMM program in Connecticut found limited success. While some success was found with the model program, the differences failed to reach statistical significance. It is important to note however, that the follow-up period and the measurement of recidivism was limited to the first six months (Orbis Partners, 2009).

The Gender-Informed Practices Assessment (GIPA) and the Women Offender Case Management Model (WOCMM) are two examples of gender-responsive approaches to addressing female offenders within the corrections field. Each line of research is important because they both emphasize the need to address women in a comprehensive and holistic manner. Gender-responsive practices for women in corrections not only entails providing needed programming and services for women, but also includes the establishment of gender-informed philosophy and leadership, structure or environment and culture, and an acknowledgement as to how gender influences behavior in prison and under community supervision.

Considerations of Race/Ethnicity and Class in Gender-Responsive Practices

In addition to gender, other statuses like race, ethnicity, and class are important in shaping women's experiences. According to Bloom, "race and class can also determine views of gender-appropriate roles and behavior. Differences exist among women based on race and socioeconomic status or class" (Bloom et al., 2004, p. 32). These differences are reflected by the variations of those who enter into the criminal justice system. For instance, the imprisonment rates for women differ by race, with Black females having the highest incarceration rate (149 per 100,000), followed by the incarceration rate for Hispanic females (75 per 100,000) and the rate for White females (50 per 100,000) (Sabol, West, & Cooper, 2009).

The war on drugs policies of the last several decades had a tremendous impact on Black females with some researchers equating the era to a war on poor women and women of color (Bush-Baskette, 1999; van Wormer & Kaplan, 2006). Many of these women were once punished in the community setting, but instead more recently have been incarcerated for their involvement in drug-related crimes (Bush-Baskette, 1999; Bloom et al., 2004). The war on drugs campaign had a disproportionate impact on women offenders. From the mid-1980s to the mid-1990s, approximately one-third (32%) of the increase in male incarceration rates were attributed to drug offenses, whereas about half (49%) of the increase in female incarceration rates during this time were attributed to drug offenses (Mauer, Potler, & Wolf, 1999). Furthermore, the number of women sentenced to state prisons for drug-related crimes grew by 888% compared to 116% for violent offenses and property crimes respectively (Mauer et al., 1999, p. 5). The result of these drug and sentencing policies was that more women, especially ones with limited economic resources and women of color, were incarcerated in higher numbers than previously (Bloom et al., 2004) and represented a disproportionate share of those sentenced to prisons around the country (Mauer et al., 1999).

Black women face complex social conditions and extreme powerlessness outside of prison. According to Henriques and Manatu-Rupert (2001), "it appears that the gendered roles African American women learn, aspire to, and seek so desperately to maintain work to imprison them. It appears, too, that these women have been imprisoned at various points in their lives in other, more symbolic ways as a result of their social exclusion, witness to the economic frustration felt by African American men, and their abuse and victimization that is an outgrowth of this inequality at both the social and economic levels in the Unites States" (Henriques & Manatu-Rupert, 2001, p. 224). Morash and Schram (2002) state that, "at the heart of a gender-responsive program is the recognition that women exist in a social context and structure that affords access to choices and opportunities according to class, race, ethnicity, and gender. Gender-responsive programs change women and their circumstances so that they get out of destructive relationships, get access to good jobs, and can negotiate effectively for resources from welfare and health care providers" (p. 167). In sum, gender-responsive practices must not only address the unique needs of women overall, but they also must recognize that there are key differences among women offenders; differences that take into account experiences influenced by social location and oppression that are linked to race, ethnicity, and class identities.

How Do We Fix It? The Future and Gender-Responsive Practices

Gender-responsive practices are relevant to both male and female offenders; consequently, our approaches to both populations should reflect the unique needs of *all* who come into contact with the criminal justice system. Understanding the pathways offenders take into the criminal justice system helps us respond appropriately to their risks and needs. Because males are the dominant offender population, much of our understanding of offenders to date, and the policies and practices used to process and punish them, are based on our knowledge of men. Both researchers and practitioners argue that women offenders require a different approach, one that is responsive to their unique needs and experiences and informed by research. Put simply, gender along with race and socioeconomic status shape women's lives in critical ways. Scholars believe that gender-informed practices are necessary so that women offenders can succeed in negotiating the prison system and in reentering society as more prepared, productive, and empowered citizens (Bloom et al., 2004).

In the first section of the current chapter, we discussed the background and importance of gender-responsive practices for women offenders. We found that women offenders have endured a history of neglect, oversight, and approaches steeped in traditional gender stereotypes (Fox, 1984; Grana, 2010; Rafter, 1990). At certain points in history, incarcerated women were treated the "same" or equal to their male counterparts and at other times they were treated differently from males (Rafter, 1990). After decades of research involving women offenders and considerable debate as to whether our response should be informed by equality or equity, a substantial amount of research now supports the belief that gender matters and that there is a serious need for policies and practices that acknowledge these distinct differences. In other words, the approaches we use with women offenders should reflect parity and equitable treatment. Equitable treatment rejects the notion of sameness and instead promotes equal funding and programming options that are appropriate and correspond to the needs of incarcerated men *and* the needs of incarcerated women (Bloom, 2012).

In the second section of this chapter, we detailed the current state of gender-responsive practices in the correctional system, focusing specifically on assessment and classification, programming, and managing or supervision of women prisoners. We found that progress has been made on several fronts. For instance, Van Voorhis and the National Institute of Corrections collaborated together to develop and validate gender-informed assessment tools that correctional systems can use as either a supplement (i.e., referred to as a "trailer") to an existing instrument, or as a "stand-alone" tool. Preliminary research suggests that there are gender-responsive factors that can improve on gender-neutral instruments (Wright et al., 2007; Wright et al., 2009). This is an area where research should continue to examine the usefulness of gender-informed assessment tools and continue to determine what is best to use with incarcerated women.

In this section, we also discussed what gender-responsive programming might look like and what management or supervision approaches for working with women offenders might entail. Needed programming areas include mental health and abuse, substance abuse, parenting, and job skills training (Koons et al., 1997). Again, a sizable amount of research details women's programmatic needs and required services; however, we know very little about the actual impact of programs and their overall effectiveness. In terms of management and the supervision of incarcerated women, research suggests that women are less violent, pose less of a risk while in prison (Belknap, 2007; Rafter, 1990), and do their time in different ways than incarcerated men (e.g., they are more emotional, talkative, seek out connections to others, worry about their kids) (Schram et al., 2004). Interest and attention in this area of corrections is growing. Researchers believe that gender-responsive practices have relevance here as well, in terms of management and supervision styles that are appropriate to use when working with women who have histories of abuse, tend to value relationships, and experience their time in prison differently than do men. This is an important area of research, and further work on initiatives such as GIPA and the WOMCC are warranted.

One of the most important lessons learned from the current chapter is that gender-responsive practices are informative for *all parts* of the criminal justice system. Bloom, Owen, and Covington (2004) maintain that it is necessary to examine the gendered effects of public policy. They state

> although their numbers have grown, . . . public policy has ignored the context of women's lives and that women offenders have disproportionately suffered from the impact of ill-informed public policy. The policies—both within the criminal justice system and other social arenas— ignore the realities of gender. (p. 31)

Future research should focus on how policies in the sentencing area (i.e., mandatory minimums and truth-in-sentencing initiatives) influence women's sanctioning and increasingly incarcerate women for non-violent offenses. Many women who are currently incarcerated for their offenses could be effectively sanctioned under community supervision.

The criminal justice system may not know where to begin when determining the relevance of gender-responsive practices for their agencies and overall system. Bloom and her colleagues (2004) suggest that those who are interested in developing gender-informed policies and approaches should ask themselves the following questions so that gender-informed knowledge can guide their decisions:

- How can correctional policy address the differences in the behavior and needs of female and male offenders?
- What challenges do these gender differences create in community and institutional corrections?
- How do these differences affect correctional practice, operations, and supervision in terms of system outcomes and offender-level measures of needs?
- How can policy and practice be optimized to best meet criminal justice system goals for women offenders? (p. 44)

In conclusion, it is important that the criminal justice system recognize that gender matters and that key differences between men and women offenders are reflected in the policies and practices that are used. The criminal justice system and researchers need to continuously review and assess in the creation and implementation of policies and programs for offenders and inmates. As we have discussed, too often policies are used in the criminal justice system that have the sanctioning and management of males as their goal. Yes, women make up a small minority of the offender population in all aspects of the criminal justice system; however, failing to recognize how they are different from the majority population places them at a considerable disadvantage in their treatment and response from the system. If we continue to neglect women offenders and the factors that bring them to our attention in the criminal justice system, then the women are doomed to return. More importantly, not only will they return, but it is highly likely that their children will enter the criminal justice system as well. For these reasons, we encourage those who are involved in research on women offenders and those who directly work with them to continue their work. Until the criminal justice system is fully prepared to address the unique issues of women offenders, we remain less than effective in our ability to treat and rehabilitate this offender population.

KEY TERMS

"Fallen woman"

Gender-Informed Practices Assessment (GIPA)

Gender-neutral classification

Gender-responsive practices

Gender-specific practices

"Good woman"

Invisible population

Women Offender Case Management Model (WOCMM)

DISCUSSION QUESTIONS

1. Gender-responsive practices take into account the recognized needs of women in the correctional system. Why is it important to account for these needs? How are their needs similar to and different from those of their male counterparts?

2. Barbara Bloom and her colleagues outline six (6) gender-responsive principles. What is the purpose of these principles? How do they work to inform programming and treatment options for women?

3. Working in a female prison is arguably different for correctional officers than working in a male prison. What are the differences and how might correctional officers be better prepared to work with women prisoners? What are some promising practices currently being undertaken in the correctional system regarding the management of women prisoners?

4. Why is it necessary to consider race/ethnicity and class in the use of gender-responsive practices?

WEBSITES FOR ADDITIONAL RESEARCH

National Institute of Corrections, Women Offenders Project: http://nicic.gov/WomenOffenders

National Reentry Resource Center (Council of State Governments Justice Center): http://www.national-reentryresourcecenter.org/

National Resource Center on Justice Involved Women: http://cjinvolvedwomen.org/

Center for Effective Public Policy: http://cepp.com/

Directory of Programs for Women with Criminal Justice Involvement Web Site: http://nicic.gov/WODP/

National Council on Crime and Delinquency: http://www.nccdglobal.org/what-we-do/center-for-girls-young-women

University of Cincinnati, Women's Risk Needs Assessment Project: http://www.uc.edu/womenoffenders.html

Women's Prison Association: http://www.wpaonline.org/

Restorative Justice

Donna Decker Morris

Restorative justice represents a paradigmatic shift in society's response to crime. The established criminal justice system involves only two parties—the government and the defendant. The victim and/or members of the community impacted by the crime are generally considered irrelevant, except as witnesses. When a crime occurs, the issues are determining what law was violated and finding, prosecuting, and punishing the perpetrator. In contrast, restorative justice recognizes and includes victims and the community as integral participants in the process. Moreover, restorative justice considers the much broader questions: who was harmed by the crime, what is the nature of the harm, and how can the harm be repaired (Braithwaite, 2003, p. 1; Perry, 2002; Roche, 2006; Umbreit & Greenwood, 1999; Umbreit, Vos, Coates, & Lightfoot, 2007; Van Ness & Strong, 1997; Zehr, 1995, 2002)?

Restorative justice takes many forms, but for the justice to be considered restorative, there are several necessary elements. There must be a focus on reparation of harm, assisting the victim(s), offender accountability, and protection of the victim and all involved in the crime and its aftermath. Involvement of all stakeholders—victim, offender, families/community, and government—and usually the inclusion of some sort of dialogue process is also critical. With this inclusive approach, there is a restructuring of community and government roles in promoting reparations and restoration of persons and the community, with an increased role for the community impacted by the crime. Finally, as much as possible, restorative justice promotes the reintegration of victims and offenders into their community(ies). Common restorative program forms include victim-offender dialogue, group conferencing, circles, and/or community boards; however, these dialogue processes are only a portion of what makes a program restorative.

The Back Story: Historical Perspectives on Restorative Justice

The theory and practice of *restorative justice* have evolved during the past forty years from multiple sources, including community and social justice efforts, recognition and adoption of some indigenous people's response to crime, the victim's rights movement, peacemaking/faith-based initiatives, and alternative conflict resolution scholarship and practice. Detailed histories of the development of restorative justice have been presented by scholars like Paul McCold, Daniel Van Ness and Karen Heetderks Strong, and Mark Umbreit and colleagues (McCold, 2008; Van Ness & Strong, 2010; Umbreit et al., 2007). For a brief chronology of restorative justice practices, refer to Box 15.1.

BOX 15.1: Timeline of Restorative Justice Practices

1971—V/O (Victim-Offender) Mediation—Minnesota Restitution Center diversion & restitution program in Minnesota for adult male property offenders & Night Prosecutor Program—diversion in Columbus, Ohio

1974/5—VORP programs (Victim-Offender Reconciliation Programs)—"Kitchener experiment" in Canada, followed by VORP program

1976—Circle process first used in criminal case in Canada

1977—Brooklyn Dispute Center funded by Victim/Witness Assistance Project—V/O Mediation

1978—Three experimental neighborhood justice (V/O Mediation) centers funded by DOJ—still operating in Atlanta, Los Angeles, & Kansas City

1978—VORP in U.S. in Elkhart, Indiana

1980s—Expansion of community mediation centers and VOM (Victim-Offender Mediation) programs with funding from federal & private foundation sources

1982—Circle process in Navajo Peacemaker Courts

1989—New Zealand juvenile justice reform—conferencing model implemented nationally

1991—Family Group Conferencing (FGC) started by police (community policing context) in Wagga Wagga, Australia

1991—Sentencing circle process began by judge in Yukon, Canada

1993—Balanced and Restorative Justice (BARJ) Project—national initiative of the Office of Juvenile Justice and Delinquency Prevention (OJJDP)

1994—Group conferencing model introduced in United States

1995—Reparative board programs established in Vermont

1998—Restorative justice circles in Minnesota implemented off reservations

1990s—International development of RJ (restorative justice) programs

1999—Nova Scotia Restorative Justice Program initiated in four communities; expanded provincewide by 2001

2000—10th UN Congress on Prevention of Crime adopted resolution promoting RJ in criminal justice process

2002—UN Economic and Social Council adopted Resolution on Restorative Justice: "Basic Principles on the Use of Restorative Justice Programmes in Criminal Matters" [E/CN.15/2002/5/Add.1]

Currently—Hundreds of individual programs in U.S. and hundreds of international programs, many of which are systemwide

Community Justice

Community justice has been defined as referring "to all variants of crime prevention and justice activities that explicitly include the community in their processes and set the enhancement of community quality of life as a goal" (Karp & Clear, 2000, p. 1). Key elements in community justice include viewing the community as an "***active agent***" in partnership with traditional justice entities, taking a problem solving approach to enhance public safety, building capacity within the community, evaluations based on community outcomes—not just crime control or recidivism, and restorative justice as the orientation (Roman, Moore, Jenkins, & Small, 2002, p.7; Bazemore & Schiff, 2001; Karp & Clear, 2000). Thus, the focus in community justice efforts is the community itself and the quality of life for persons living in a particular location, not merely responses to crime, especially particular instances of crime (Crawford & Clear, 2001). Formal community justice programs began in the 1980s with community policing and drug courts, and since then have expanded with initiation of community courts, community prosecutor programs, and similar efforts. (e.g., see Clear, Hamilton, & Cadora, 2011; Nicholl, 1999; Bazemore & Schiff, 2001). Community justice programs seek to focus resources in high crime areas and engage citizens in ways that not only attack specific crime problems using formal social controls of the criminal justice system, but also improve quality of life and promote social justice in neighborhoods; this is achieved through increased resources and collaboration in ways that strengthen informal social controls. For it is recognized that strong informal social controls provide the most significant deterrence of crime. Thus, community justice efforts combine programs, such as community policing, citizen patrols and neighborhood watches, community courts with focused social services and community service requirements, halfway houses, and similar programs, and services to promote citizen and community involvement. These programs seek to reduce crime through increased detection and arrests of offenders, but also to assist offenders in rebuilding their lives, to avoid future crime involvement, and to assist citizens in the community with development (Clear et al., 2011; Gilbert & Settles, 2007; Bazemore & Schiff, 2001). An example of concerted efforts to restore a community is demonstrated by the Red Hook Community Justice Center, which was created in 2000 in New York (Center for Court Innovation, 2012).

In addition to formal community justice programs, grassroots social justice efforts not only inform community justice, but also more directly contribute to development of restorative justice. Out of the 1960s and 1970s movements for civil rights, women's rights, economic rights, and the human rights of indigenous people emerged greater consciousness of the negative impacts of the criminal justice system on disadvantaged communities and the need to empower people within communities. This was in contrast to the increased professionalization of criminal justice and social service programs during that time. As a result, the need to improve social justice as a predicate for stronger communities is recognized by proponents of community justice initiatives (Clear et al., 2011).

Out of this recognition of the need to empower communities and the emerging development of conflict resolution thinking, community mediation centers were developed in many locations, providing mediation of disputes, many of which might otherwise result in criminal processing. In some instances these were separate from the criminal justice system, and in other cases community mediation organizations collaborated with the criminal justice system through the mediation of disputes referred by the police or the courts. In what appears to be the earliest such program, the Institute for Mediation and Conflict Resolution was established in 1969 in New York City to mediate community conflicts and personal disputes. The first recognized examples of direct collaboration by community mediation organizations with the criminal justice system in the United States occurred in 1971 with establishment of the mediation diversion project through the Minnesota Restitution Center and the Night Prosecutor Program in

Columbus, Ohio. In the subsequent twenty years, many community mediation organizations emerged across the United States, with similar entities developing in Australia, the United Kingdom, and Europe. By 1990, approximately 400 community mediation organizations existed in the United States, with a few locations like the State of New York providing formal, legislated public support for a network of mediation centers, although in most states there was limited governmental support and collaboration (McCold, 2008; National Association For Community Mediation (NAFCM), 2012). Community mediation inclined toward a focus on interpersonal and community disputes where offenders and victims, or mutual offenders, knew each other and resolution of the underlying conflict was necessary to prevent further problems. In part as a result of this, the community mediation approach had a tendency to approach the conflict from a neutral stance and to see both sides as equal parties in the "dispute." At times, this approach was in conflict with the emerging *victims' rights movement* and what developed as fundamental principles of restorative justice of focusing on the nature of the harm and repairing the harm—not merely reaching an agreement to settle the immediate "dispute." However, as community mediation matured, it frequently became a provider of victim-protective as well as community-focused restorative justice programs, often in collaboration with the formal justice system diversion efforts.

Victims' Rights Movement

The victims' rights movement was another major influence in the development of restorative justice. In modern Western criminal justice systems, victims were relegated to witnesses for the prosecution at best, and often disregarded entirely in the process of government prosecution against criminal defendants. This was not always the case. In ancient times, most crimes were viewed as offenses against the individual victims and there were systems of restitution for victims for the harms caused by the particular crimes, with enforcement assisted by whatever governmental authority. This was true even in early colonial America, although this no longer applied in continental Europe because increasingly powerful monarchies developed in the Middle Ages, and crimes were transformed into offenses against the king's peace rather than offenses against individual victims. Through fines or confiscation of property, punishment, both physical and financial, was meted out by governmental authorities with any money collected going into the monarch's treasury. The only remedy left for victims was to attempt to recover through the developing civil court systems (Tobolowsky, Gaboury, Jackson, & Blackburn, 2010). Thus, in practical terms restitution for victims became virtually impossible (Roberts, 1990).

The development of the academic study of what became known as victimology started in the mid-twentieth century, evolved into the modern-day victim's movement in the 1960s and 1970s, and was then followed by formal, governmental recognition and national and state legislation in the 1980s (Roberts, 1990; Tobolowsky et al., 2010). Significant reforms achieved were: the recognition of crime victims' rights to information from the prosecution about the cases against the person who had harmed them; consideration of the impact of the crime on them during sentencing, achieved through victim impact statements; the opportunity to be heard during proceedings involving the offender; the opportunity to receive reparations; the provision of direct services to address victims' needs; and the prevention for further harm (i.e., evidence shield laws in rape cases) during prosecutions (Tobolowsky et al., 2010; Van Ness & Strong, 2010).

In some of the early Victim Offender Reconciliation Programs (VORPs) and other restorative justice programs, too much emphasis may have been placed on reconciliation and efforts to help offenders and endeavors to reduce recidivism. In these instances, victims felt pressured to participate and were expected to forgive the offenders and accept reconciliation, which further imposed duress and harm on the victims, contrary to the intended philosophy. As a result, there was a time that victims' advocates were inclined to oppose restorative justice programs. Their concerns, however, were recognized and adaptations were made by restorative justice proponents to refocus and help to ensure victim protections, which resulted in greater collaboration and increased sensitivity to victims' needs by proponents of restorative justice (Umbreit et al., 2007). Also, in the mid-1990s in the United States, the Balanced and Restorative Justice (BARJ) approach was developed and researched with support by the U.S. Department of Justice to provide best practice models for implementation which addressed the needs of victims as well as juvenile offenders (Pranis & Bazemore, 1999). In 1994, the American Bar Association (ABA) approved *Criminal Justice Policy on Victim Offender Mediation/Dialogue* recommending adoption of restorative dialogue in courts throughout the country, but including recommended protections for both victims and offenders, such as voluntary participation (American Bar Association, 1994). In 1995, a leader of the victims' rights movement endorsed broad implementation of restorative justice programs in a monograph published by the National Organization for Victim Assistance (NOVA), *Restorative Community Justice: A Call to Action* (Young, 1995). While most no longer see restorative justice as contrary to victims' rights and needs, collaborative efforts are continuing for groups and agencies, and for restorative justice programs to truly protect the needs of victims (see Achilles, 2004; Achilles & Stutzman-Amstutz, 2008; Amstutz, 2004; Herman, 2004; Strang, 2004).

First Nation Peoples and Village-Based Cultural Philosophies

In contrast to the individualistic philosophies of modern European-based cultures, including the United States, communitarian philosophies of first nation peoples and village-based cultures emphasize community harmony and community harm when crime occurs were also influential in the development of restorative justice. For example, after a crime, the process used for addressing the crime and its consequences, the goals of the process, and the decision-making sources of authority generate justice models that contrast with European-based justice systems (see, Schweigert, 2002a and 2002b). Traditions from the Maori of New Zealand and the Native Americans of North America have been particularly influential beyond their own cultures, while practices from many other cultures have also contributed.

Many indigenous cultures use relatively informal processes to deal with crime. In contrast to a formal police/prosecution/judicial system, community leaders are called on or initiate the response when a crime occurs. The process is often dialogue-based and usually involves not only the victim and offender, but often family members and others in the community who know the immediate parties or were in some way impacted by the crime. For example, the Navajo way of peacemaking is directed by appropriate *naat'aanii* (respected members of the community who are the natural leaders) who engage others in a talking-out process; a process where people discuss what happened—including varying perceptions of what happened, why the events happened, feelings about what happened and the impact on them and their relationships with others, and then what to do to repair the harm and prevent future problems (Zion & Yazzie, 2008). This process of finding consensus through dialogue is also evident in the methods used by other indigenous cultures for resolving conflict arising from crimes or other harms (e.g., application of *ubuntu* (African concept of one's humanity as expressed in relationship to others/community) approach, see Louw, 2006).

Specific practices of conference and circles have emerged from these consensus-based processes. The Navajo Nation on its reservation in the southwestern United States in 1982 formally established Peacemaker Courts employing restorative circles for criminal cases (McCold, 2008). The first incorporation of a Native American circle process into a Western criminal justice system is generally considered the sentencing circle applied to a case in the Yukon Territory of Canada in 1992. Circles have been adapted to non-aboriginal settings and are starting to be used in programs throughout North America and in other parts of the world (Van Ness & Strong, 2010). The application of this circles process ranges from the use of original **sentencing circles**, to corrections settings involving conflict reduction or reentry programs, to school-based programs dealing with youth (Pranis, 2005).

Sources of authority for determining whether a crime has occurred and what should be done about it are based on the unwritten cultural norms, or customs, of the community rather than written laws adopted by a formal government entity (see Zion & Yazzie, 2008). What drives the processes, however, are the philosophical roots and resulting goals. Following the disruption by a crime, the community seeks to restore harmony or peace in the relationships among community members for the good of the entire community. For example, Navajo peacemaking seeks to find and follow the appropriate "life way" based on talking out the problems involved with, and created by, the crime, its impact, the participants' understandings and feelings, and then by application of the "problem-solving concept of *nahat'a*." This problem-solving component is much more than simply resolving the "dispute" in Western terms. Rather, Navajo peacemaking explores how to repair the harm in its broadest sense, how to prevent it from happening again, and thus to restore the right relations among the people (Zion and Yazzie, 2008, p. 152). Similarly, the southern African concept of *ubuntu* also emphasizes relationships among people and the healing of breaches in relationships, including the community, when crimes occur (Louw, 2008). This concept was incorporated into the South African government's statement of principles for "development of social welfare policies and programmes" (South African Department of Welfare, 1997, p. 10).

Ubuntu is defined as

> The principle of caring for each other's well-being . . . and a spirit of mutual support . . . Each individual's humanity is ideally expressed through his or her relationship with others and theirs in turn through a recognition of the individual's humanity. Ubuntu means that people are people through other people. It also acknowledges both the rights and the responsibilities of every citizen in promoting individual and society well-being. (p. 12)

At the same time, being truly human under *ubuntu* means respecting each person and implicitly recognizing and protecting differences among people, which protects individuals and limits forced consensus through dialogue (Louw, 2008, 167). Thus, under the principle of *ubuntu* the goal of criminal justice is the healing and restoration for all concerned, not prosecution and punishment of the offender (Louw, 2008).

Central to rebuilding relationships within the community in such traditional processes is reparation for the victims. Providing reparations or some form of compensation for the victims serves to make amends for the wrong and relieve the perpetrators' shame from offending community norms, thus providing the basis for rebuilding relationships within the community (e.g., Howley, 2002).

In the 1980s in New Zealand, the Maoris became increasingly concerned about the impact of the western-style criminal justice system that was at odds with their traditional, communitarian culture. Too many of their children were being removed from their families and communities by the government's criminal justice system. The authorities were likewise concerned with the high levels of incarceration of children and with their recidivism. Following proposals, dialogue, and pilot programs, the result was the passage of the groundbreaking *Children, Young Persons and Their Families Act of 1989* that established a restorative justice system, with conferencing as a central component, for all juvenile cases, except homicides, throughout New Zealand. It is also significant that the process rested on a family welfare model with major involvement by the Department of Social Welfare (McCold, 2008; MacRae & Zehr, 2004). Thus, New Zealand was the first country to implement nationwide a restorative justice process for juveniles rooted in first nation traditions.

Faith-Based Influences

Faith-based organizations and individuals also played a significant role in developing restorative justice practice and philosophy. The Mennonite Central Committee was instrumental in the Kitchener experiment and in the subsequent establishment of the Community Justice Initiatives Association's *victim offender reconciliation program (VORP)* in Ontario, Canada, as well as the establishment of the first VORP program in the United States in Elkhardt, Indiana (McCold, 2008; Peachy, 1989; Umbreit, Coates, Kalanj, Lipkin, & Petros, 1995). The Center for Justice and Peacebuilding of Eastern Mennonite University supports scholarship and restorative justice programs and is the home of Howard Zehr, often referred to as the grandfather of restorative justice (Van Ness & Strong, 2010). Prison Fellowship International supports many programs working with victims and with prisoners (both within prisons and for reentry), and also provides an online clearinghouse for restorative justice news and information. The major faith traditions promote respect for all persons, compassion, and healing, which can be described as a positive peace among people, exemplified in the concept of *shalom* (Hadley, 2008; Van Ness & Strong, 2010).

Common Themes in Restorative Justice Programming

Common threads found in all these cited sources is the recognition of the failures of formal, government controlled, punitive criminal justice systems; a desire for a more humane system that strengthens communities and provides healing for victims; and opportunities for offenders to rejoin those communities. The restorative justice vision is a transformative one; it does not merely involve a different response approach to instances of crime by the criminal justice system, but instead reflects "a holistic change in the way we do justice in the world" (Braithwaite, 2003, p. 1). Thus, restorative justice is considered the means for creating a positive peace in our communities and society instead of an ineffective, negative peace based on a strong police presence (the occupying force model), incarceration, and further disintegration of communities (Zehr, 1995; Van Ness & Strong, 2010).

The Current State of the Policy

The principles and practices which developed and coalesced into what is generally known as restorative justice emerged approximately 40 years ago as a result of deep discontent with, and recognition of, the failures of established criminal justice systems. However, to date in the United States, despite multiple, isolated and often diversionary or net-widening programs, restorative justice has limited systemic impact. In reality, in many respects the criminal justice system in the United States has become even worse. Disadvantaged populations are alienated from the justice system and tend to perceive it as not legitimate. While some progress has been made in reducing re-victimization by the system and state practices vary considerably, many victims are still generally ignored, with only victims of serious, violent crimes generally receiving advocacy assistance, opportunities to be heard in sentencing decisions, and notices of results and offenders' status. Lengths of prison sentences and incarceration rates have increased dramatically, to the point that this country leads the world in the imprisonment of its citizens—not an enviable first-place position (e.g., Bonta, Jesseman, Rugge, & Cormier, 2008). Recidivism rates for persons released from prisons range from approximately 35% for first time juvenile offenders to an average of about 43%, measured as reincarceration for adults incarcerated in state prisons and released in 2004 (Pew Center on the States, 2011). Combining state and federal expenditures, the United States spends approximately 57 billion dollars annually to incarcerate its citizens, which does not even include the cost of "supervision" of over 5 million persons on probation or parole (Guerino, Harrison, & Sabol, 2011; Glaze, 2010; Pew Center on the States, 2011). Yet, finally there are signs that policy makers and the public may be recognizing the problems with the criminal justice system, in part due to the enormous costs as well as the high levels of recidivism. Consequently, policy makers and the public may be receptive to recognizing that restorative justice provides a better approach.

From the first programs in the United States in the early 1970's in New York, Minnesota, and Ohio, restorative justice programs in some form spread throughout the United States, with over 400 programs in existence today. Restorative justice programs also expanded worldwide. In 2002, the United Nations Economic and Social Council adopted a Resolution on Restorative Justice, titled *Basic Principles on the Use of Restorative Justice Programmes in Criminal Matters*. This was followed by the adoption of a call to implement restorative justice programs by the 11th United Nations Congress on Crime in the Bangkok Declaration:

> To promote the interests of victims and the rehabilitation of offenders, we recognize the importance of further developing restorative justice policies, procedures and programmes that include alternatives to prosecution, thereby avoiding possible adverse effects of imprisonment, helping to decrease the caseload of criminal courts and promoting the incorporation of restorative justice approaches into criminal justice systems, as appropriate. (Article 32)

In 2006, the United Nations Office on Drugs and Crimes published a *Handbook on Restorative Justice Programs,* which included "Basic Principles on the Use of Restorative Justice Programmes in Criminal Matters" as an appendix. Currently, well over 80 countries implement at least some restorative justice programs (Van Ness, 2005), including several countries which have adopted broadly based national or state/province level programs (e.g., Archibald & Llewellyn, 2006).

Basic principles of restorative justice include (a) focusing on the harm caused by the crime—especially to the victim, but also to the community and offender rather than merely on the rule violation; (b) seeking to repair the harm; (c) accountability for repairing harm, primarily the offenders, but in some cases others may have obligations to repair harms; (d) involving all stakeholders—victim and community as well as offender and government—in decision making through a collaborative process; and (e) reintegration/restoration of victim, offender, and community (Raye & Roberts, 2004; Umbreit, 2001; Van Ness & Strong, 2010; Zehr, 2002). As Howard Zehr explained, restorative justice is based on a "commonsense understanding of wrongdoing" that views crime as "a violation of people and of personal relationships" that "create obligations ... to put right the wrongs" (Zehr, 2002, p. 19). This is in contrast to typical criminal justice systems that focus on the rule violations and punishment for offenders of the violations (Zehr, 2002; Van Ness & Strong, 2010).

Restorative justice tends to be misperceived as a "get out of jail free" approach that is soft on crime, or as an ill-conceived reversion to disparate, personal justice which reinforces unequal bargaining and deprivation of constitutional protections, without any consistency on application of the law (Delgado, 2000). Neither view is accurate. In a restorative justice process, offenders must take responsibility for their actions, which is in contrast to the legal due process model where offenders deny responsibility. Offenders must repair the harm they caused as much as possible, in contrast to the traditional criminal justice approach of punishment without reparation to the victims. While there are increasingly criminal dispositions that include some attempt to order restitution or community service, these changes actually reflect the impact of the victim's rights and restorative justice movements, although as currently practiced the attempts are only limited and not truly restorative. Moreover, in cases of serious offenses as well as in cases in which offenders are considered a threat to the community or refuse to accept responsibility, offenders are likely incarcerated, at least for some period of time.

Even with some of the problems that may arise with the improper application of restorative justice, the problems pale in comparison to the failures of the current system. Even Delgado in his criticism of restorative justice admits that the current criminal justice system almost completely fails to live up to the supposed positive ideals of consistency in application of law and punishment, protection of due process, and use of punishment to satisfy "society's need for retribution or vengeance" (Delgado, 2000, p. 761). The retributive model assumes that justice is achieved by carrying out society's need for vengeance by inflicting pain on the offender in supposed equal measure to the pain inflicted on a victim. Of course, such "justice" conceives of fairness as an equality of suffering, which only results in an overall increase in pain in the world (Walgrave, 2004). This idea of justice as fairness in equality of pain totally breaks down and fails to account for victimless and status crimes. Retributive justice then becomes blatantly the application of coercive power to cause pain to those persons who have arguably not harmed anyone else—except perhaps themselves in a paternalistic sense. In these situations, also, retributive justice only serves to double the pain imposed on the so-called offender.

Four major restorative justice models emerged in the criminal justice context: ***victim-offender mediation***/dialogue, ***family group conferencing***, ***community reparative boards***, and ***peacemaking circles*** or sentencing circles (Bazemore & Umbreit, 2002). These programs are applied in various stages across the entire spectrum of the criminal justice process—from diversion, particularly with juveniles; pre-conviction, as an adjunct to plea bargaining; post-conviction and pre-sentence, which may or may not impact sentencing; post-sentence as part of the sentencing process or requirements; separately, at the request of those impacted by the crime; and increasingly in reentry. In addition, victim impact panels are increasingly used in corrections settings, as well as the importation of mediation, conferencing, and circles into correctional settings (Gaboury & Ruth-Heffelbower, 2010). Other restorative justice programs may include community courts, drug courts, or community service and restitution options to the extent that these programs implement restorative justice principles and practices.

Victim-offender mediation and family group conferencing involve direct dialogue between the victim and offender. In general, participants in the victim-offender mediation model are limited to the victim, offender, and mediator, although in juvenile matters the parents are also usually present. Even in adult dialogues, supporters or others impacted by the crime may be present. However, the number of participants is generally quite small. Moreover, in the mediation model supporters generally have somewhat limited roles (Bazemore & Umbreit, 2002). In contrast, family group conferencing includes the victim, the victim's family and supporters, the offender, the offender's family and supporters, and other community members who may have been harmed or affected by the crime (Bazemore & Umbreit, 2002; Bradshaw & Roseborough, 2005; MacRae & Zehr, 2004). These two models are the most frequently used and studied, particularly the victim-offender mediation model (Bazemore & Umbreit, 2002; Latimer, Dowden, & Muise, 2005; Umbreit, Coates, & Vos, 2001; Pelikan & Trenczek, 2008).

It should be noted that the term "mediation" is a contested concept, although there seems to be little dispute about the general nature of the process—a dialogue between the victim and offender facilitated by a mediator. Early programs in the United States used the term "victim offender reconciliation pro-grams" (VORP). Because of concerns with the connotations of the term "reconciliation" by victims and the emerging victims' rights movement, the term "victim offender mediation" (VOM) is now more commonly used. However, even the term "mediation" generated concern, because of the implications that it was similar to the settlement-driven process often used in civil matters. Also, because of continuing concerns from victims and prosecutors/criminal justice personnel that mediation implied a "neutral" mediator facilitating a "dispute" between equal parties, in contrast to a criminal matter with an identified victim who needs to be protected and/or at a minimum, an identified offender who has committed a crime. In part because of these concerns that the term "mediation" implies mediator's neutrality and a settlement-driven process, as often the case in court-affiliated civil mediation, VOM became frequently labeled restor-ative dialogue or restorative conferencing (Umbreit, Coates, & Vos, 2008). Of course, these terms do not clearly distinguish a dialogue between two or a few people from a dialogue involving several or many people, which can be the case in group conferencing or circles, nor do the terms distinguish the process differences.

A foundation of restorative justice theory is that the process is transformational for the individuals involved. For the victims, the intended effect of a restorative justice process is to provide healing, repara-tion for the harm caused by the crime, and a restored sense of safety and integration in the community. The offender is expected to take responsibility for his or her actions, experience remorse, make repara-tions, and through this process be reintegrated into the community in a positive way. Accordingly, it is expected that the offender is then less likely to reoffend (Bazemore & Umbreit, 2002; Moore & McDonald, 2002; McGarrell & Hipple, 2007; Schweigert, 2002b). In part, it is this promise of stopping the cycle of criminal behavior, especially with juveniles, that has made restorative justice increasingly appealing for criminal justice professionals and policy makers, even without sharing the more philosophical concepts of restorative justice proponents.

In addition to diversionary, pre-conviction, or immediate post-conviction sentencing applications of restorative justice, increasingly restorative justice is being applied in correctional settings. Within prisons, circles and restorative dialogue are being used to reduce violence, especially among inmates with lengthy prison sentences. In some cases, victim-offender dialogues are taking place between victims (or family member survivors) and the perpetrator of violent offenses, such as rape or murder. These take place at the request of victims who have questions only the offender can answer or who want to confront the person who caused so much harm. The results often go far beyond what offenders thought possible and provide a basis for healing, for the victim, and also even for the offender (Gaboury & Ruth-Heffelbower, 2010).

Another frequent correctional approach is the use of victim impact panels in preparation for reentry. In these cases, victims from the community engage in facilitated dialogues with an offender or offenders through victim impact panels. In these panels, the victims are representative in that they do not meet directly with those who personally offended against them; instead, victims speak to strangers about their experiences. The victims who participated in these panels report high levels of satisfaction. Victim impact panels are employed in nearly every state in the United States. The primary purpose of these victim impact panels is to promote acceptance of responsibility and to reduce recidivism on completion of the offender's lengthy sentence. Some reported results from such programs are highly promising, with reduced recidi-vism rates following reentry. Another reentry model is conferencing or a narrower restorative dialogue among the offenders and their families. Reentry is highly stressful for both the offender and the offender's family, especially after lengthy incarcerations. Restorative dialogue assists both the offender and family members (Gaboury & Ruth-Heffelbower, 2010).

⊠ What Research Has Taught Us

Restorative justice practices have been extensively studied in North America, Australia, New Zealand, the United Kingdom, and Europe. Reflecting the dominant models used in the various countries, in Europe and North America the great majority of research was on victim offender dialogue (mediation) programs, with group conferencing mainly studied in New Zealand and Australia. Existing research analyzed recidivism and various qualitative measures of satisfaction, procedural justice (fairness, opportunity to be heard), and emotional benefits for victims (e.g., reduced fear, healing). Overall, the results of this research are highly favorable for restorative justice programs, especially victim-offender dialogue. This research is summarized and then followed by a discussion of program-generated difficulties, and further research needs.

In North America, most of the research on victim-offender mediation (VOM) programs for juveniles reports decreased recidivism, although some results varied (Umbreit et al., 2001). Some of this research was questioned due to design flaws, such as absence of control groups, non-equivalent control groups, and self-selection bias (Bradshaw & Roseborough, 2005; Umbreit et al., 2001). It should be noted, however, that these methodological problems are largely an artifact of program and funding limitations, since with few exceptions there was insufficient funding and institutional support for strong experimental designs, particularly random assignments with control groups. Also, definitions of recidivism ranged from reconviction within one year to any re-involvement with the juvenile justice system, making generalization across studies more difficult (Bradshaw & Roseborough, 2005). However, in a large cross-site analysis of victim-offender mediation programs using matched control groups from programs in the midwestern and western United States, Umbreit (2001) reported significant reduction in recidivism of juveniles in the mediation programs compared to similar offenders in court-administered restitution programs. A reanalysis of four previous studies also reported a significant reduction in recidivism by juveniles who participated in victim-offender mediation (Nugent, Umbreit, Winamaki, & Paddock, 2001). And in a recent meta-analysis of previous studies, the effectiveness of victim-offender mediation in reducing recidivism was confirmed (Bradshaw, Roseborough, & Umbreit, 2006).

Another meta-analysis of restorative justice programs, including both published and unpublished research, also reported a significant reduction in recidivism (Latimer et al., 2005). In this study, programs meeting the operational definition of "restorative justice" as "a voluntary, community-based response to criminal behavior that attempts to bring together the victim, the offender, and the community, in an effort to address the harm caused by the criminal behavior" were included in the analysis so that programs implementing various models at varying stages of the criminal justice process were included (Latimer et al., 2005, p.131). This analysis also included adults as well as juveniles. A more recent meta-analysis which up-dated these previous studies found not only overall reduced recidivism from restorative conferencing, but also greater effects in more recent program studies, possibly reflecting better program designs and training of facilitators (Bonta, Jesseman et al., 2008).

A study of long-term effects of a restorative justice juvenile diversion program in a largely rural and small city midwestern population found that referral to the restorative justice program, reduced juvenile recidivism both quantitatively and qualitatively (severity of re-offense) relative to a matched sample comparison group. Although originally designed as a victim-offender dialogue program, in practice this program served as a hybrid program, which included victim-offender dialogue when appropriate or possible and, when a dialogue was not appropriate or possible, then the program used informal community panels, or even simply dialogue with the program facilitator. At intervals over four years, the study evaluated both long-term effects and survival rates and controlled for various factors, such as age, race, gender, urban (small city) versus rural residence, seriousness of offense, and prior offenses (Bergseth & Bouffard, 2007). Restorative dialogue programs, in particular victim-offender mediation, yielded high levels of satisfaction and perceptions of fairness by victims and offenders, which was in marked contrast with levels of satisfaction and perceptions of fairness by victims and offenders in the traditional criminal justice system. Participants in victim-offender mediation perceived both the process and resulting agreements to be fair to both victims and offenders. Significantly, these high levels of satisfaction and perceptions of fairness also produced satisfaction and perceptions of fairness of the criminal justice system itself by participants in VOM (Umbreit et al., 2008).

In Europe, VOM is also the predominant restorative justice model applied, with similar success. Victims and offenders report high levels of satisfaction with the process and outcomes. Also, victims participating in restorative justice programs had significantly higher levels of satisfaction than victims in the regular criminal justice system. In addition, offenders participating in restorative processes had lower rates of recidivism (Pelikan & Trenczek, 2008).

Less empirical research is available on family group conferencing (FGC). In a recent meta-analysis of restorative justice dialogue programs, the available research on family group conferencing using control groups reflected mixed results. Although restorative justice dialogue programs, including both VOM and FGC, produced significant reductions in juvenile recidivism, the effect for VOM programs was significantly greater than for FGC programs. One study found that the impact of FGC programs differed little or not at all from the impact of traditional juvenile justice approaches (Bradshaw & Roseborough, 2005). However, among young first-time offenders who participated in family group conferencing, a recently reported study in Indianapolis using an experimental design found significantly reduced recidivism, both in terms of frequency and survival of effect (McGarrell & Hipple, 2007). Research in Australia and New Zealand also showed some mixed results, but particularly in New Zealand, conferencing produced reductions in re-offending (Maxwell, Morris, & Hayes, 2008). A major factor reflected in these different results may be in the program designs and the role of the facilitator. For example, some of the programs with less favorable results used police facilitators, while more successful ones used social service or community facilitators who are not directly part of the prosecuting agencies. In addition, the nature of the offense involved may also be a factor, since there may be little difference in results between traditional process and restorative justice referrals for young, first-time offenders who committed minor offenses.

In addition to measures of recidivism, research on conferencing in New Zealand and Australia measured perceptions of procedural and substantive justice. Participants in conferences showed much greater satisfaction with conferencing than with the courts, indicating they felt the conferences were fair procedurally and produced fair results. Both victims and offenders also believed they had a greater opportunity to be heard and allowed input into the outcome, especially in New Zealand where non-police facilitators were used.

A recent study of a community-based restorative justice program in a major metropolitan area in the southwest with a diverse juvenile population also found reduced recidivism for juveniles in the restorative justice program compared to juveniles in the traditionally processed comparison group whose terms of diversion were defined by probation officers. The restorative justice diversion program studied consisted of community justice committees which combined elements of group conferencing and community reparative boards. In their analyses, the researchers not only controlled for factors, such as race, gender, age, offense, and number of prior offenses between groups, but also considered the mediating effect of these factors on program impact. For example, the restorative justice program produced an even greater reduction in recidivism for girls than for boys (Rodriguez, 2007).

Various research concerns in the extant restorative justice literature have been identified, both by the researchers and by critics, including the nature or lack of comparison groups, potential self-selection bias, non-response bias, definition of recidivism, and effect of other potential meditating factors (e.g., gender, age, etc.) (Bergseth & Bouffard, 2007; Bradshaw & Roseborough, 2005; Bradshaw et al., 2006; Latimer et al., 2005; Lemmon et al., 2012; McGarrell & Hipple, 2007; Rodriguez, 2007). For example, until recently, gender had been largely ignored in the reported literature; the studies involved predominantly male populations (see summary in Latimer et al., 2005). However, Rodriguez (2007) found that gender had a significant mediating effect; the impact of the restorative justice diversion program studied on reducing juvenile recidivism was even more pronounced for girls than for the boys. Further research is also needed on the impact of program design, particularly the degree to which programs follow best practices in both design and in training/selection of dialogue facilitators, referral criteria, and the degree to which the programs are restorative (e.g., Zehr, 2002). Often a problem in conducting research in this area is that the researchers have little control over design features and referral criteria. Both cooperation from agencies and criminal justice professionals in designing programs that can more thoroughly test these issues, as well as finding sources of funding to develop and evaluate such programs, are needed to refine our understanding of restorative justice programs and define best practices for replication.

Race, Gender, and Class Implications

Gender implications in restorative justice vary based on whether the perspective is offender or victim based. With respect to offenders, much of the research focused on male offenders (Latimer et al., 2005). More recent research that assessed programs with substantial numbers of female juvenile offenders found a greater reduction in recidivism for girls referred to the restorative justice program compared to a matched sample. Thus, while the restorative justice intervention decreased recidivism for both boys and girls, the effect was even stronger for girls (Rodriguez, 2007). Additional research is needed to consider whether there are differences in gender impact, under what circumstances, and why.

Whether victims' experience with restorative justice is mediated by gender is an important question, but one which has not been considered empirically. Conceptually, restorative justice is seen as holding great promise for improving victims' lives (Achilles, 2004; Strang, 2004). For victims of domestic violence and sexual assault, who are predominantly female, practitioners were often reluctant to apply restorative dialogue processes because of concern of the power imbalances or the emotional trauma from the violence/assaults. On the other hand, restorative justice in these situations may provide increased benefits due to the victim-focus and empowerment of restorative justice.

Established criminal justice systems disproportionately impact persons from lower socioeconomic classes, minorities, and women both in terms of the rate and levels of punishment and lack of recognition and voice in deciding what is prohibited and how the punishment is enacted (e.g., Jenkins, 2004; Hakiaha, 2004). Incarceration rates are a prime example. In the United States, the incarceration of Black males is six to seven times the rate of incarceration of White males (Mauer & King, 2007; Glaze, 2010) resulting in a drastically skewed overall incarceration of African Americans. Of the 2.2 million people incarcerated in the United States in 2005, 900,000 are African American even though African Americans represent only 12.8% of the population (Mauer & King, 2007; U.S. Census Bureau, 2013). Moreover, there is substantial variation of Black-to-White incarceration rates among the states, from 13.6% (Oklahoma) to 1.9% (Hawaii), with seven states maintaining a Black-to-White incarceration rate of more than ten to one. Even worse, incarceration of young Black men is even more concentrated, with one in nine or 11.7% of all African American men ages 25 to 29 in the United States in prison (Mauer & King, 2007).

The resulting impact on African American communities is enormous in terms of employment prospects, family relations, family and community stability, and voting participation. Michelle Alexander labeled the practices of the criminal justice system as "the new Jim Crow." Through the criminal justice system, African Americans, especially men, are not only denied the ability to vote in massive numbers, but also "subject to legalized discrimination in employment, housing, education, public benefits, and jury service," similar to their ancestors. She notes, "we use our criminal justice system to label people of color 'criminals' and then engage in all the practices [of discrimination] we supposedly left behind" (Alexander, 2012, pp. 1–2).

Although the rate is much less than for AfricanAmericans, incarceration rates for Hispanics nationally is about twice the rate of non-Hispanic Whites. This varies considerably by state, however, as does the ratio of Hispanic-to-White incarceration which varies from a high of 6.6% in Connecticut to less than one-to-one (under-representation of Hispanics) in several other states. Moreover, the rate of Hispanic incarceration is increasing (Mauer & King, 2007).

Conceptually, restorative justice could reduce these disparities by empowering the primary stakeholders—victims, offenders, and community—to address crimes. Jenkins (2004) noted that restorative principles are consistent with an Afrocentric approach to crime, but that a more explicitly Afrocentric theoretical approach that emphasized community and reduced governmental dominance would enhance restorative justice practices. However, there is scant analysis or research evaluating the impact of restorative justice practices on communities of color. To the extent that racial impacts were considered in existing research on restorative justice programs, no racial differences in the positive effects of restorative justice was found; specifically, restorative justice programs lead to similar reductions in recidivism for African American and Hispanics as for Whites (e.g., Rodriguez, 2007). Yet, reducing recidivism in general does not change the definitions of "crime" or selective enforcement, which can often disproportionately target persons of color, such as the disparate treatment of crack cocaine offenders.

As a corollary to disproportionate impact, aspects of the criminal justice system are viewed as illegitimate by racial minorities and the poor (e.g., Gau & Brunson, 2010; Jenkins, 2004). Similarly, women who contest sexual or domestic violence can experience the criminal justice system as illegitimate when not only do the laws not protect them, but the system further victimizes them if they seek enforcement (e.g., Estrich, 1987; Gaarder & Presser, 2008).

In political and legal philosophy, legitimacy is founded on having an equal voice in the development of laws and on perceptions of fairness of the laws (Rawls, 1971/1999). Furthermore, people tend to obey the law when they perceive it as legitimate, whereas perceptions that the law or system is illegitimate undermine compliance with the law (Tyler, 2006). Therefore, for those on whom the laws and punishments are disproportionately imposed—racial minorities and the poor—and those who are not provided adequate protection by the law, or are further victimized by legal systems (e.g., women who suffer from victimization of sexual and domestic violence), legitimacy and compliance are undermined. In addition, in the criminal justice system juveniles with no power or say in the process also share these concerns, which can be further compounded by considerations of race, class, and gender.

As discussed in the next section on reform suggestions, restorative justice holds great promise for changing these dynamics, or at least lessening the harmful impacts. With citizens working in partnership with the criminal justice and judicial systems, communities can be rebuilt. An example is the Redhook Community Justice Center in New York City, which opened in 2000 (Center for Court Innovation, 2012).

Through accepting responsibility and working to repair harm, individual lives can be rebuilt so that formerly despairing and offending people can become productive members of their communities. In New Zealand prior to implementation of a restorative justice approach for all juveniles with the enactment and implementation of the Children, Young Persons, and Their Families Act of 1989, Maori youth were disproportionately incarcerated (MacRae & Zehr, 2004). Victims can find healing through acknowledgment of the pain they suffered, acceptance, and support by members of their communities as well as reparations from offenders. Thus, restorative justice mechanisms can empower people within their own communities to discuss the impacts of crime and develop plans to respond and repair the harms. Significantly, in disadvantaged communities repair of harms often involves providing services for offenders to enable them to be reintegrated into a safer community. This local empowerment can then provide the springboard for reduced marginalization and extension of their voices into the political arena.

How Do We Fix It? Suggestions for Reform

"Never doubt that a small group of thoughtful, committed, citizens can
change the world. Indeed, it is the only thing that ever has."

Margaret Mead

Suggestions for reform involve micro and macro elements. Several leaders in the restorative justice movement have noted concerns with actual or potential problems in implementation of restorative practices. These suggestions address design, evaluation, and essentially quality control elements for restorative justice programs in order to achieve proper implementation. A macro discussion is an attempt to discuss an overall redesign of the criminal justice system that melds the existing legal system with restorative justice, while still preserving rule of law, due process, and public safety principles. Collaboratively thinking through what such a system would actually look like and how it might function in a legal context is necessary if we are going to move toward a more just and effective system.

Areas of concern with implementation of restorative justice involve ensuring best practices, maximizing the extent programs or practices are truly restorative, and preventing "net-widening" while maximizing use. Best practices include such characteristics as voluntary participation, sensitivity to victims' needs, proper training of dialogue facilitators, and adopting a respectful dialogue/encounter process rather than an agreement-driven process (Umbreit, 2001). Howard Zehr proposed six questions for analyzing the extent to which particular applications are effective and restorative: Do they address harm/needs/causes, are they victim-oriented, do they encourage offenders to take responsibility, is there stakeholder involvement, is there dialogue and stakeholder decision making, and do they respect all stakeholders (Zehr, 2002, p. 55). Van Ness and Strong posited three key principles for implementing restorative justice: (a) working to heal victims, offenders, and communities; (b) opportunity for all stakeholders for active involvement in justice processes; and (c) rethinking and reordering the roles of government and communities in achieving both order and peace. As an alternative to focusing on a best practices approach, Van Ness and Strong further recommended focusing on restorative values as guideposts for design, evaluation, and training: assuming responsibility for making amends, assistance for affected persons, collaboration and consensual decision making, empowerment of affected persons, opportunity for encounter, inclusion of affected parties, moral education through reinforcement of community standards, protection of physical and emotional safety as a primary concern, reintegration, and finally, resolution of the issues surrounding the offense and its aftermath (Van Ness & Strong, 2010).

As noted above, advocates for restorative justice argue for systemic change, essentially a transformation of thinking as well as practice, recognizing that the two are intertwined. Van Ness and Strong applied the principles and values they identified to redefine various models of a minimally restorative system to a fully restorative system (Van Ness & Strong, 2010). Similarly, others also argue that policy makers and practitioners need to carefully implement and monitor programs to ensure that such programs include necessary elements of a truly restorative system, follow best practices, and avoid undermining the restorative process through co-optation by system professionals or net-widening (Van Ness & Strong, 2010; Bazemore & Schiff, 2001; Zehr, 2002).

Nevertheless, too little attention has been given to overall design in practical terms, although Van Ness and Strong do identify five models for implementing restorative justice. The "*augmentation model*" is essentially what currently exists in the United States and in most other jurisdictions, where some parties may be referred to and choose alternative restorative justice programs at various stages in the contemporary criminal justice proceedings. The reverse of this augmentation model, is when the "*safety net model*" of restorative justice becomes the primary system for responding to crime with relatively few cases processed in the traditional system. Alternatively, a dual track model envisions parallel systems with the decision about whether to proceed through restorative justice or traditional criminal proceedings made by the stakeholders. A hybrid model processes cases first through one system and then the other in a linear fashion, while a unitary model handles all cases through a restorative justice process, which the authors note presents the most challenges to consider (Van Ness & Strong, 2010). However, none of the authors adequately consider the law in their discussions.

When we are talking about a response to crime, it would seem that a threshold question must be how to best achieve justice in our responses to crime, with justice defined as achieving fairness and what is morally right (e.g., Rawls, 1999). Note that fairness and what is morally right includes justice for victims and the community as well as for offenders. Moreover, this definition of justice does not include vengeance nor arbitrary and discretionary punishments.

On a macro level, it is difficult to see how anyone can argue that the retributive criminal justice system in the United States dispenses "justice." When an African American disabled youth is sentenced to 162 years in prison without possibility of parole as a first-time offender, is this justice? Add to that information, the crime was for a brief series of robberies of commercial establishments, with his convictions based mainly on the testimony of five accomplices who cut plea deals with sentences of nine to 22 years in prison. Based on this example alone, can it be argued that our criminal justice system even dispenses proportional or equal punishment, let alone justice (Brown, 2012)? Our prison system has also been called the "new Jim Crow" for its massive incarceration of African Americans, largely resulting from the so-called "war on drugs" (Alexander, 2012). A very large portion of persons incarcerated or on probation suffer from mental illness, but receive punishment instead of treatment. Victims continue to be sidelined and often ignored. Too many people are incarcerated, and sometimes even executed, when they are actually innocent. Debtors' prisons have been on the rise, where people are incarcerated when they are simply unable to pay fines, only to have continued fines added to their debts by for-profit collection and jail companies (Bronner, 2012). The list of examples could go on—this is the reality of the criminal justice system experienced by massive numbers of our citizens. Thus, it is small wonder that many people who experience these injustices perceive the criminal justice system, including the laws, as illegitimate. Rather than generating respect for law and acceptance of the laws as a reflection of appropriate social norms, the current system tends to generate perceptions of illegitimacy and rejection of the law itself.

On the other hand, legal principles and protections enshrined in our judicial institutions set a gold standard for human rights—rule of law, due process, equal protection, and justice. Occasionally, for those with sufficient resources or whose cause may be taken on as test cases, the criminal justice system lives up to those ideals. Certainly, legal constraints limit injustice to some degree. It is generally recognized, for example, that the local warlord, "bigman," or the U.S. equivalent in the form of county sheriff or judge, should not be able to arbitrarily make up the law. Instead, rule of law principles require established rules governing future conduct by all parties and define rewards and punishments for complying with and breaching the rules. In the criminal justice context, among other rights, accused are legally entitled to a speedy trial, to be informed of the charges against them, to have legal counsel represent them, to be free from coercion so as not to incriminate themselves, to obtain a trial by jury of their peers, and to challenge the legality of the charges against them, or the conduct of those prosecuting them. These rights have been established and given meaning through judicial proceedings. Recently, for example, the U.S. Supreme Court ruled that the imposition of a life sentence without possibility of parole for juveniles violates the Eighth Amendment's ban on cruel and unusual punishment (*Graham v. Florida,* 2010). Equal protection and due process protections that have meaning through case decisions also constrain arbitrary abuse of power. Thus, concerns about maintaining legal proceedings and judicial decisions to advance as well as reinforce concepts of justice and their application are appropriate (see Fiss, 1984). Without test cases, development of the law stagnates.

In the movement to make criminal justice more fair and humane as well as provide real remedies for persons harmed by crime (i.e., be restorative), the importance of rule of law is not adequately recognized and discussed. Additionally, we cannot lose sight of the important advances in human rights that rule of law principles and practices have achieved. On a global scale, international efforts to promote rule of law are seen as critical to ensuring stability, economic and political development, and human rights.

Nevertheless, in the current implementation of the criminal justice system, justice tends to be lost along with respect for the fundamental legal system, while human lives are often further harmed by the system itself. While the law seeks a shared understanding of normative behavior and social order necessarily relies to a large extent on voluntary compliance with the law, when the legal system is viewed as illegitimate by substantial segments of the population, shared understanding and voluntary compliance are decreased. On the other hand, wholesale adoption of community-based justice without following legal limits may create similar injustices rather than the healing and more humane society it seeks (see, Wojkowska, 2006). We cannot forget that communities may be oppressive, both in terms of seeking vengeance against persons who have committed crimes, and in punishing people, even victims, who challenge cultural stereotypes or are seen as threatening the harmony of the community by trying to assert their own human rights, such as freedom from domestic abuse. Examples abound in many developing countries of the oppression of such community based "justice." At the same time, advances in the law would also be curtailed by largely replacing the legal system with restorative processes. The challenge, it seems, for restorative justice should not be to supplant the legal system or to promote a parallel and competing system as has been suggested by some or understood by others. The challenge is to develop a system that integrates the best aspects of each.

What I propose is melding the two models, an idea that was generated while observing the Village Courts in Papua New Guinea. The Village Courts attempt to integrate indigenous traditions and restorative processes with the formal justice system. Although in Papua New Guinea the system is fraught with enormous political and economic problems, the basic model is sound.

Rather than being a parallel system, the Village Courts function to provide community-based justice which can then be enforced in the traditional system when the process does not result in compliance. Established by the Village Courts Act in 1973 and modified and expanded by the Village Courts Act of 1989, the Village Courts seek to apply restorative justice based on the Melanesian tradition of mediation and local custom (normative practices) to promote harmony in the communities. The Village Courts consider civil and customary law cases and minor criminal matters and may order reparations, fines, and community service, but not imprisonment. With judicial system reforms in 2000, restorative justice was established as one of the "pillars" of the Papua New Guinean justice system with efforts to expand and improve the Village Courts (Papua New Guinea Law & Justice Sector, 2000; Kimisopa, 2007). Recently, there were more than 1,100 village courts in Papua New Guinea, a country with a land mass equivalent to California and a population of approximately seven million.

As a British Commonwealth country, the formal judicial system is very similar to that of the United States, with an independent judiciary that functions as a separate branch of government and a tiered court system, in order of descending jurisdiction, consisting of a supreme court, national courts, district courts, and village courts. The supreme, national, and district courts are part of the formal court system with judges or magistrates appointed and applying constitutional, legislative, and common law (with incremental incorporation of local customary law into British/Australian common law). On election or nomination by each local area council, village court officers, who are respected members of their communities, are appointed by the government; the officers in each village court, who receive training in procedures, legal limits, and mediation skills, are several magistrates, with one of the magistrates serving as chair or chief magistrate, a clerk who maintains written records of the court's proceedings, and one or more peace officers.

The village courts apply local custom law in a three-tiered process. Significantly, the village courts are limited both in cases they can consider and results by constitutional law and legislation. Initially, when a dispute arises, one or more magistrates may try to conciliate the matter informally. If this fails to resolve the dispute or when an offense has been committed, a formal mediation is held in which all affected parties and members of the community have the opportunity to discuss the matter. The mediation process is essentially the same as practiced in community mediation centers in the United States, with opportunity for all concerned to express what happened and the impact, discuss what is needed to resolve the dispute (in civil cases), or repair the harm (in a criminal cases), and jointly decide what will happen, which is then recorded as the mediated agreement (personal observation, 2008). A distinction, however, is that the mediation agreement is recorded for two purposes: for reference in the event a party does not comply, and for review by the government for compliance with constitutional and legislative requirements. Subsequently, if the agreement is breached, the case proceeds to a hearing (similar to an informal, but binding, arbitration hearing) before the magistrates, who after hearing from the parties involved, decide the matter by consensus of the magistrates and issue an order. If the order is then breached, the aggrieved party can take the order to the district court for consideration and formal action.

This general model could work very well in Western legal systems. Although precise details require discussion, a proposed framework for our system is as follows. Community justice centers are established, coordinating with existing community mediation organizations and civil society community organizations, operated mainly by members of the community who receive specialized training and with some administrative support, and collaborating with local governmental organizations. Once established, citizens could access the community-based process on their own initiative, or on referral from community agencies, including civil society as well as government agencies. Law enforcement entities would initially refer matters to the community justice centers within specified jurisdictional ranges (misdemeanors and nonviolent, low-level felonies) and/or refer based on voluntary choice by victims and offenders. The community justice centers would function within the communities, using existing space in such locations as schools, community centers, churches, and so forth. If victims objected to a restorative process or offenders either objected or were not willing to accept responsibility, then those cases would move forward to be processed through the traditional system. Also, seriously violent crimes and severe white-collar crimes would initially route through the traditional system, although restorative justice processes should be integrated into those proceedings. For example, as much as possible, victims should have a voice in the process involving repair of harms, as a mandatory consideration in sentencing orders, and with opportunities for restorative dialogue provided at appropriate stages. In tandem, there should be opportunities for offenders to engage in various restorative options, including during any incarceration and prerelease. The restorative processes and partnerships provided and developed in the community justice centers should also serve as resources for providing restorative dialogue and other restorative options to more serious offender cases handled in the traditional court system, as well as for reentry programs.

Adapting the village courts system to the existing system in the United States provides several advantages. First, this can provide the mechanism to implement restorative justice universally as the primary entry point through community courts, staffed by trained members of the community, and as the provider and/or coordinator of restorative processes in serious offender cases. Second, savings in traditional system costs, including savings from reduced use of incarceration for non-serious cases, can be used to fund the community court system, which includes citizen mediators/magistrates as well as some full-time staff, similar to community mediation organizations. Third, these citizen justice centers can provide significantly greater access to justice for many citizens without adequate access, including not only the poor and marginalized groups, but also the middle class and other victims (See Wojkowska, 2006). Fourth, particularly in marginalized communities, this system of citizen courts can be expected to increase perceptions of legitimacy of the legal system, since it would not be justice administered through an occupying force but rather by the community itself, resulting in increased public safety through greater compliance with the law. Fifth, with oversight by the traditional legal system and jurisdictional and, to some extent, outcome limitations, concerns about potential for excess or evasion of responsibility of offenders is obviated. Sixth, with a tiered system where orders from the citizen courts can be enforced through the traditional system in the event of noncompliance, participants are ensured enforcement without duplication of effort and resources. Seventh, with an integrated system, significant legal issues can still be processed through the traditional system in order to advance the law.

It is hoped that this proposal meets the challenge of blending the best of both restorative and traditional justice systems. At the least, perhaps it can start a practical conversation about how to blend the two systems.

KEY TERMS

Active agent

Augmentation model

Community justice

Community reparative boards

Family group conferencing

Peacemaking circles

Restorative justice

Safety net model

Sentencing circles

Victim-offender mediation

Victim Offender Reconciliation Program (VORP)

Victims' Rights Movement

DISCUSSION QUESTIONS

1. What were the major influences or sources in the development of restorative justice?

2. Identify the principles of restorative justice and define restorative justice incorporating those principles.

3. What does the research on restorative justice demonstrate and what additional research is needed?

4. How can restorative justice be implemented to improve the justice system as well as promote public safety?

WEBSITES FOR ADDITIONAL RESEARCH

Restorative Justice Online (Prison Fellowship International): http://www.restorativejustice.org/

National Institute of Justice: http://www.nij.gov/

Restorative Justice Research Network: http://www.iars.org.uk/content/RJRN

Restorative Justice Council (UK): http://www.restorativejustice.org.uk/resources/research/

UK Justice: http://www.justice.gov.uk/youth-justice/working-with-victims/restorative-justice

International Institute of Restorative Practices: http://www.realjustice.org/

Australian Institute of Criminology: http://www.aic.gov.au/index.html

Jerry Lee Center of Criminology at Penn State: http://crim.sas.upenn.edu/jerry-lee-center-criminology/research

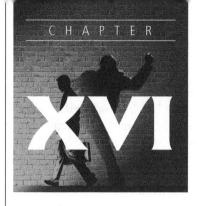

Three Strikes: Passage, Implementation, Evaluation, and Reform

Elsa Chen

The first Three Strikes policy was adopted by ballot initiative in Washington state in 1993. Since then, about half of the states and the federal court system have adopted Three Strikes laws. *Three Strikes laws* are based on the following premises: Repeat offenders are responsible for a substantial share of violent crime; increases in sentencing severity can serve to reduce *recidivism* through both *incapacitation* and *deterrence*; and the most incorrigible criminals deserve particularly punitive sentences. In the early to mid-1990s, as the United States' crime rate was reaching a peak and states were serving as laboratories for innovations in crime reduction strategies, these rationales served as the basis for numerous "tough-on-crime" policy efforts throughout the nation.

While Three Strikes laws share a common name, the details of the laws vary widely from one state to another. Variation exists in the number and types of offenses that are defined as strikes, the number and nature of convictions required to trigger an enhanced sentence, and the mandatory sentence that must be served by a repeat offender (Clark, Austin, & Henry, 1997; National Conference of State Legislatures, 1996). By August 1998, California had sentenced 4,468 third-strikers and 36,043 second-strikers under the law (Dickey, 1998). In comparison, Washington, which enacted its Three Strikes statute a year earlier, had sentenced approximately 120 third-strike offenders and three second-strikers under its more restrictive law (Dickey, 1998). By the end of 2006, every state with a Three Strikes law, other than California, reported fewer than 400 second- or third-strike convictions (Chen, 2008a). In contrast, by the end of 2003, a total of 80,087 second strikers and 7,332 third-strikers had been imprisoned in California (California District Attorneys Association, 2004).

California's law differed from those in other states in two respects: it included a *"second strike" provision*, and it was not limited to violent and serious offenders. The *"second strike" provision*, which is still in place, requires that any individual convicted of a felony automatically receives a doubled sentence if he or she has a proven prior serious or violent offense (a "strike") on his or her record. Until November 2012, an individual who had two proven "strikes" and was convicted of any subsequent felony could receive the "third strike" sentence of 25 years to life in prison. While the list of serious and violent offenses that count as "strikes" comprises about 26 crimes and enhancements as defined in California Penal Code sections 667.5(c) and 1192.7(c), over 500 felonies could trigger the third strike sentence, including numerous property and drug crimes, and a long list of *"wobbler"* offenses that could be charged as either felonies or misdemeanors. This distinctive aspect of the law changed when *Proposition 36* was passed by ballot referendum in November 2012. As of November 7, 2012, the second-strike provision remains in place, but the current offense must be serious or violent in order to trigger the third-strike sentence of 25 years to life in prison. This change brought California's law more in line with the policies in place in the rest of the nation.

This chapter focuses on California's Three Strikes policy, which for its first eighteen years of existence was the nation's broadest and most frequently used policy of this type. I begin with an explanation of the law and why and how it was originally passed. I continue with a discussion of the law's implementation and an assessment of its effects on crime. Next, efforts to modify the law, including Proposition 66, which failed in 2004, and Proposition 36, which passed in November 2012, are reviewed. The chapter concludes with some thoughts about the future of Three Strikes in California, as well as suggestions for further research on the topic.

▧ The Back Story: How the Idea Became Reality

According to political scientist John Kingdon, the success of policy ideas depends on the confluence of favorable circumstances with regard to problem recognition, the generation of policy proposals, and the political environment as well as the presence of "policy entrepreneurs" ready to devote energy and resources to their preferred proposals when the right "window of opportunity" arises (Kingdon, 1984). The passage of the Three Strikes law in 1994 fits Kingdon's theoretical framework well.

Violent crime was a well-recognized problem in the early 1990s. While the crime rate was rising across the United States, California faced a particularly severe situation. The state had the second highest violent crime rate in the nation in 1993 (U.S. Department of Justice—Federal Bureau of Investigation, 1993). Violent crime, as measured by both the Uniform Crime Reports and the National Crime Victimization Survey, had been rising steadily for about a decade (U.S. Department of Justice, Office of Justice Programs, 1985–1996), and criminal justice experts predicted that the situation would only worsen in the foreseeable future (Ruth & Reitz, 2003). Frequent media reports of rampant and random violence heightened the public's awareness and fear of violent crime (Ruth & Reitz, 2003). Meanwhile, frustrations ran high over the apparent ineffectiveness of the existing state of sentencing and incarceration. A report by former U.S. Attorney General William Barr cited an alarming statistic: Violent offenders nationwide were serving an average of only 37% of their sentences before being released (Barr, 1992).

Support for increased toughness on crime was high among both the general public and political leaders. The Gallup poll found that the proportion of people who identified crime as "the most important issue facing the country today" rose from nearly zero in 1991 to a peak of over 50% in 1994 (Turner, Fain,

Greenwood, Chen, & Chiesa, 2001). Other opinion polls indicated that the public had low confidence in the criminal justice system, felt that courts were not dealing harshly enough with criminals, and were increasingly willing to prioritize punishment over rehabilitation and to spend money to control the crime rate (Turner et al., 2001). Mentions of "crime" in the presidential papers and "violent crime" in the congressional record also peaked in 1994 (Turner et al., 2001).

States and local jurisdictions hastened to adopt policy efforts to control and reverse these trends. Congress passed a comprehensive Violent Crime Control and Law Enforcement Act in 1994, which provided grants to the states to fund crime-fighting initiatives, including building prisons, lengthening time served for inmates convicted of violent crimes, expanding "boot camps" for delinquent youth, monitoring sex offenders, and hiring police officers (U.S. Congress, 1994). Other ideas proliferated, including "zero-tolerance" policing in New York (Kelling & Bratton, 1998), efforts to abolish or curtail the use of parole in Texas (Petersilia, 1999), the use of prison chain gangs in Alabama and Arizona (Burley, 1997), the adoption of gang injunctions in Los Angeles (Gibeaut, 1998), and active use of the death penalty in Texas (Sorensen, Wrinkle, Brewer, & Marquart, 1999). Three Strikes was just one of a myriad of "tough on crime" proposals attracting the attention of the public and policy makers throughout the United States.

The California Three Strikes law was not initially written by a policy expert, but rather by a professional photographer from Fresno, Mike Reynolds, whose 18-year-old daughter, Kimber, had been shot and killed in a robbery attempt in June 1992 (Skelton, 1993). In his grief and anger, Mike Reynolds drafted a proposal loosely modeled on the measure that had passed by ballot initiative in the state of Washington, but with changes that made it far broader in scope. With support from his Assemblyman, Bill Jones, Reynolds originally attempted to get the Three Strikes law passed through the California legislature. Despite the best efforts of Reynolds and Jones, the proposal's most persistent advocates, "Three Strikes" initially received only lukewarm support in the legislature and among the public. The measure was defeated in the Assembly Public Safety Committee when it was first introduced (Moore, 1999). However, a compelling "focusing event," the heinous kidnap and murder of a young girl by a repeat offender, provided the window of opportunity for Three Strikes' advocates to attract the public and political attention and approval they needed for the bill to succeed.

In October 1993, twelve-year-old Polly Klaas was abducted at knifepoint from her suburban Petaluma, California, home during a slumber party. Her strangled body was eventually found at an abandoned lumber mill (Anderson, 1994). She had been murdered by Richard Allen Davis, a repeat offender with an 11-page-long rap sheet, listing 17 prior arrests, including three for kidnapping and sexual abuse (Franklin, 1994). Davis was remorseless and repulsive in his attitude and behavior (Vitiello, 1997a). At the time that he murdered Polly Klaas, he had recently been freed from prison after being released for good behavior halfway through a 16-year sentence for kidnapping. The events of this case and Davis's name and photograph were highly publicized by the media in California and beyond. Polly Klaas's victimization and Davis's arrest and trial drew the public's attention to the issues of repeat offenders and early prison releases. The petition in support of the Three Strikes ballot initiative, which had until then collected only 20,000 signatures, rapidly accumulated well over the 385,000 signatures required to put it on the November 1994 ballot. The initiative also attracted the support of powerful interest groups and political candidates during that election year (Vitiello, 1997b). The National Rifle Association offered political and financial support for Three Strikes, as did the 24,000-member California Correctional Peace Officers Association, another politically powerful group. Three Strikes also had the support of the California Gun Owners Association, the Republican Party, and the campaign committees of Governor Pete Wilson and United States Senate candidate Michael Huffington (Vitiello, 1997a).

Realizing that this policy proposal had attracted a groundswell of public support, the California legislature passed the Three Strikes bill, and the governor signed it, in March 1994. Eight months later, the Three Strikes ballot initiative, Proposition 184, was approved with 71.9% of the popular vote in the 1994 California election. While the ballot initiative reiterated the language already approved by the legislature, it strengthened Three Strikes; changes to laws passed by ballot initiative in California require a majority vote in a subsequent ballot initiative or a two-thirds vote in both the Senate and Assembly rather than a simple majority vote in the state legislature (League of Women Voters California Education Fund, 2010).[1] This was a primary reason that the law remained unchanged for eighteen years.

The Current State of the Implementation of Three Strikes

While Three Strikes is a statewide law, its implementation is carried out at the county level. Research has found that substantial variation exists in the law's application from county to county, and even from case to case within counties. A major source of discretion is the ability to dismiss or ignore prior serious or violent offenses, which must be "***pled and proved***," to avoid triggering a second- or third-strike sentence. Prosecutors have always been granted this discretion, and the California Supreme Court's decision in *People v. Superior Court (Romero)* extended similar decision-making authority to judges (California Legislative Analyst's Office, 1997). A second source of discretion is the prosecutor's authority to determine whether to charge what is known as a "***wobbler***" offense as a misdemeanor, which carries a maximum sentence of one year in jail, or as a felony, which could carry a 25 years to life prison sentence if it were charged as a third strike under the original form of the law (Chen, 2008b).

The penal code allows prior strike convictions to be dismissed or ignored by prosecutors or judges "in the furtherance of justice." This discretion is used very frequently. A study using data from 2006 found that among California prison inmates admitted to prison between 2002 and 2006 with two prior serious or violent convictions before the current felony conviction, only 14% were actually serving sentences of 25 to life, even though they were all technically eligible for the third-strike sentence (Chen, 2013). Frequent use of prosecutorial and judicial discretion has served as a "***safety valve***," helping to prevent California's already overcrowded prisons from becoming even more overwhelmed with nonserious and nonviolent inmates, and keeping the costs of implementation below some of the highest initial estimates (California Legislative Analyst's Office, 2005; Greenwood, Rydell, Abrahamse, Caulkins, Chiesa, Model, & Klein, 1994). Strong evidence indicates that much of the variation in implementation results from prosecutors' and/or judges' exercise of this discretion in an effort to restore some proportionality to sentencing under Three Strikes. A clear positive correlation was found between the severity of an offender's current offense and the likelihood of having received a 25-to-life sentence (Chen, 2013). Furthermore, all else equal, eligible offenders with a higher number of serious and violent priors were also more likely to be serving third-strike sentences (Chen, 2013).

What Research Has Taught Us: The Effects of Three Strikes

Three Strikes was passed in California with the stated intention of enhancing public safety through the incapacitation and deterrence of repeat offenders. As evidence of the law's effectiveness at crime reduction,

---

[1] An exception to this occurs if the text of the initiative expressly permits legislative amendments.

proponents of the law point to the fact that crime rates have declined dramatically in California since the law's passage. For example, in opposition to Proposition 36, the "Save Three Strikes" web page stated: "What's to fix? Shortly after 3 Strikes passed in 1994, California crime dropped in half. Half the crime also has meant half the criminals" (www.savethreestrikes.com). Statements like this imply that Three Strikes was responsible for the dramatic decline in crime rates, but fail to acknowledge other facts: crime rates began dropping before Three Strikes was enacted; crime rates fell as much and even more in many states that did not adopt Three Strikes; and declines in crime were no larger in California counties with high rates of Three Strikes usage than in counties that applied the third-strike penalty sparingly (Chen, 2008a; Zimring, Hawkins, & Kamin, 2001).

Several methodologically rigorous analyses have investigated whether the Three Strikes' crime reduction objective has been accomplished. Prominent criminologist Michael Tonry provided a summary of fifteen major published empirical analyses of the deterrent effects of Three Strikes in California, and found that only one concluded that the policy had led to a statistically significant reduction in crime (Tonry, 2009). The other 14 studies concurred that California's Three Strikes law did not significantly reduce crime, despite the fact that the researchers relied on a variety of different units of analysis (including cities, counties, and states) and statistical methods (including econometric time-series designs, noneconometric time-series comparisons between California and other states, time-series comparisons of counties in California with varying rates of Three Strikes usage, and comparisons of different demographic populations within California) (Tonry, 2009). In fact, three of the studies found an association between Three Strikes and higher homicide rates, which the authors attributed to an increased motivation among those facing third strikes to eliminate victims, witnesses, and/or law enforcement officers (Kovandzic, Sloan, & Vieraitis, 2002; Marvell & Moody, 2001; Moody, Marvell, & Kaminski, 2002).

According to a cross-sectional, time-series analysis of state-level data from all 50 states over 20 years, California's Three Strikes law, despite its breadth, had little impact on crime trends above and beyond the effects of the narrower Three Strikes laws in other states (Chen, 2008a). This conclusion seems counterintuitive, given that 100,000 felons have been sent to prison for second and third strikes in California, and so many fewer have been sentenced under the law in other states. How, one might ask, could the incapacitation of so many criminals have had no clear effect on crime rates? One possible explanation is capacity constraints. Because California's prisons have been full beyond capacity since before Three Strikes was adopted, keeping Three Strikes inmates incarcerated longer has prevented non-strikers from serving as much time in prison. The most violent and serious offenders with third-strike sentences probably would have received long sentences, even in the absence of Three Strikes. However, if nonviolent, nonserious, aging third-strike inmates serving long mandatory prison sentences are less dangerous than the other criminals who were prevented from remaining in prison because of limited capacity, then declines in violent and serious crimes could very well not occur (Chen, 2012).

Although Three Strikes had negligible effects on crime in California, it had substantial effects on the correctional population and the state's budget. A study conducted by the nonprofit Justice Policy Institute attributed about $10.5 billion in additional prison and jail expenditures from March 1994 to September 2003 to the law, with $6.3 billion the result of longer prison terms (Ehlers, Schiraldi, & Ziedenberg, 2004). More than half of the cost was for the incarceration of individuals whose third strike was nonviolent (Cost of 'three strikes' law, 2004). A May 2010 report on California's prisons by the California State Auditor concluded, about 25 percent of the inmate population was incarcerated under the three strikes law . . . On average, we estimate that these individuals' sentences are nine years longer because of the requirements of the three strikes law and that these additional years of incarceration represent a cost to the State of $19.2 billion. (California State Auditor, 2010)

These costs, combined with severe budget constraints in California and questions about the law's fairness, were among the driving forces behind efforts to reform the law and eventually the approval of Proposition 36 in 2012.

⊠ Race, Class, and Gender Implications of the Policy

Considerable variation also exists between counties in the exercise of prosecutorial and judicial discretion to dismiss or ignore prior strikes (Greenwood, Everingham, Chen, Abrahamse, Merritt, & Chiesa, 1998). For all or part of the law's existence, the chief District Attorneys in three of California's 58 counties (Los Angeles, San Francisco, and recently, Santa Clara) have already been directing deputy DAs to charge third strikes in a manner consistent with the post-Proposition 36 law (email interview with Debbie Mesloh, Public Information Officer, Office of San Francisco District Attorney Kamala D. Harris, October 17, 2006; Van Derbeken, 2004; Whitaker, 2000). As a matter of policy, several other district attorneys have filed third-strike sentences against all or most eligible offenders (Bowers, 2001). In other jurisdictions, third strikes have been charged on a case-by-case basis with no overarching policy. This resulted in considerable geographic disparity in offenders' chances of receiving a 25-to-life sentence (Bowers, 2001; Zimring et al., 2001).

The odds of a third-strike sentence are influenced not only by characteristics of the defendant and his crime, but also by characteristics of the jurisdiction where an offender is sentenced. For example, as the proportion of Republicans in the county population increases, so does the likelihood that an offender receives a third-strike sentence, even when offense, prior record, and other variables are controlled (Chen, 2013). This is not surprising, since California District Attorneys and judges are elected political officials and are therefore motivated to demonstrate accountability and responsiveness to the views of their constituents. In addition, as the proportion of Latinos in the local population increases, so does the probability of receiving a third-strike sentence (Chen, 2013). The odds of a third-strike sentence are also higher where the unemployment rate is higher (Chen, 2013).

In addition to geographic disparities, racial disparities emerged in the application of Three Strikes in California. Although African Americans make up only 6% of California's population, they comprise 34% of second-strikers in prison, and about 44% of third-strikers (Chen, 2008b). Even when legally relevant characteristics, such as current offense, prior record, and parole status are held constant, African Americans face 40% higher odds of a third-strike sentence than Whites (Chen, 2013). Prior studies found similar evidence of discrimination against African Americans in the application of habitual-offender laws in Florida (Crawford, 2000; Crawford, Chiricos, & Kleck, 1998; Crow & Johnson, 2008). Although prior research conducted in other states found disparities between Latinos and Whites in the application of mandatory minimum and habitual offender sentencing policies (Crow & Johnson, 2008; Ulmer, Kurlychek, & Kramer, 2007), evidence of similar disparities has not been found in California.

Racial disparity between Blacks and Whites is more severe when it comes to lesser offenses. The gap between Blacks and Whites in the odds of receiving a third-strike sentence is greater for property and drug offenses than for violent offenses. The difference between Blacks and Whites in their odds of a third-strike sentence is 76% for property crimes, 52% for drug crimes, and 35% for violent crimes (Chen, 2008b). Blacks also have 56% higher odds than Whites of receiving a third-strike sentence for a wobbler offense, whereas the difference between Blacks and Whites is 44% percent for non-wobbler offenses (Chen, 2008b). This statistic is consistent with the "liberation hypothesis," which suggests that there is likely to be some consensus regarding appropriate punishments for the most egregious offenses, but less agreement regarding punishments for less serious crimes; therefore decisions regarding the latter may be more susceptible to the influence of personal opinions and biases of criminal justice decision makers (Kalven & Zeisel, 1966; Spohn & Cederblom, 1991).

It would be as unwise as it is impractical to advocate for the elimination of prosecutorial discretion in sentencing decisions. Discretion is a necessity when decisions are being made about humans whose characteristics and circumstances are not easily distilled into a few data points entered into a formula. Discretion also allows for more efficient allocation of scarce courtroom and correctional resources. However, the findings described above indicate that discretion has been exercised widely, but not uniformly, in the implementation of Three Strikes, and the variation is sometimes associated with factors that should not influence the administration of justice. The implementation of California's Proposition 36, which removed the option to charge a third strike for a nonserious, nonviolent offense, is expected to reduce unwarranted disparities by removing much of the room for variation in the application of the Three Strikes law.

How Do We Fix It? Efforts to Reform Three Strikes

From the start, opponents to Three Strikes challenged components of the law in court. In 1996, the California Supreme Court ruled in *People v. Superior Court (Romero)* that judges (rather than only prosecutors) had the discretion to dismiss prior felony convictions in the implementation of the law (California Legislative Analyst's Office, 2005). In *People v. Fuhrman* (1997), the state Supreme Court upheld a lower court's decision to permit multiple strike convictions to be charged from a single criminal incident (California Legislative Analyst's Office, 2005). The constitutionality of Three Strikes under the Eighth Amendment was upheld by the United States Supreme Court in *Ewing v. California* (2003). The plaintiff, who had received a 25-to-life sentence for stealing a set of golf clubs, argued that Three Strikes constituted cruel and unusual punishment because the sentence was grossly disproportionate to the offense (California Legislative Analyst's Office, 2005; Vitiello, 2003). Likewise, the U.S. Supreme Court ruled in *Lockyer v. Andrade* (2003) that a sentence of 50 years to life for two third-strike counts of petty theft (for stealing about $155 worth of videotapes from two different Kmart stores) did not violate the Eighth Amendment (Horn, 2004).

In addition to challenges in court, efforts to modify the law have been made through two ballot initiatives subsequent to the original Three Strikes initiative. The first, Proposition 66, appeared on the ballot in November 2004. Proposition 66 sought to require that all three offenses needed to be serious or violent in order to trigger the 25-to-life sentence. It also tried to remove burglary of an unoccupied residence, attempted burglary, and six other crimes from the list of "serious and violent" felonies that could count as strikes. The measure also required all strikes to be tried and convicted separately so that multiple strikes could not result from one criminal act. Inmates whose cases did not meet the terms of the modified law were eligible for resentencing. Finally, in an effort to allay the fears of those whose memories of Polly Klaas had not faded, Proposition 66 required 25-to-life prison terms for second-time child molesters (California Legislative Analyst's Office, 2004).

The "Yes on Proposition 66" campaign was funded by over $5 million in donations from a handful of wealthy individuals, while the "No on Prop. 66" side received only about $71,000 from the California Organization of Police and Sheriffs (National Institute on Money in State Politics, 2004; Teji, 2011). The measure led by a margin of 62% to 21% among registered voters responding to a *Los Angeles Times* poll conducted just two weeks before the election, and by an even greater margin according a Field Poll taken earlier in October 2004 (Mathews, 2004). However, election results reflected an enormous shift in public opinion just before the election. Ultimately, the measure lost. Analysts attributed the measure's sudden loss of voter support to several factors. Confident in his own reelection bid, Governor Arnold Schwarzenegger refocused his energies during the two weeks leading up to election day on a media campaign to defeat Proposition 66 that was financed by last minute donations, including $3.5 million from Henry T. Nicholas III, a billionaire whose daughter had been a murder victim, and over $138,000 from the California Correctional Peace Officers Association, which represents the state's prison guards (Kravets, 2004; Teji, 2011). Television ads, including one starring Schwarzenegger, "shifted debate on the proposition from images of drug addicts and petty thieves serving unfairly harsh prison sentences to hardened criminals receiving get-out-of-jail-free passes" (Martin, 2004). The wording of Proposition 66 also contained ambiguities that raised fears regarding the potential early release thousands of prison inmates, and its efforts to redefine "serious and violent crime" seemed too extensive to many critics (Kravets, 2004; Martin, 2004). Finally, Schwarzenegger portrayed wealthy businessman Jerry Keenan's $2 million contribution to the "Yes on 66" campaign as an effort to buy freedom for his son, who was serving prison time for two vehicular manslaughter convictions (Kravets, 2004). Concerns raised by these issues were serious enough to convince 53.2% of California voters to vote against this effort to reform Three Strikes (Mathews, 2004).

Eight years later, in the context of a very different economic and political climate, California's voters approved Proposition 36 by a margin of 69.3% to 30.7% (Bowen, 2012), with majority support in every one of the state's 58 counties (Leonard & Dolan, 2012b). This ballot measure, passed on November 6, 2012, and effective the next day, made two major changes to the "Three Strikes and You're Out" sentencing policy:

- Nonserious or nonviolent new felonies no longer trigger third-strike sentences of 25 to life. All three offenses must now be serious or violent.
- Proposition 36 also applies retroactively to certain inmates sentenced to 25-to-life for nonviolent, nonserious third strikes. Based on data from the California Department of Corrections and Rehabilitation (CDCR), approximately 2,900 current prison inmates may be eligible for resentencing as "second strikers." Successful petitioners will receive shortened sentences, and some will be released on the basis of time served (California Secretary of State, 2012).

At the same time, the existing law's "second strike" provision remains intact. The revised law still requires a doubled sentence for any offender with two prior serious or violent felonies who is convicted of a new nonserious, nonviolent felony. In addition, Proposition 36 is written so that offenders whose priors include particularly egregious crimes like murder, rape, or child molestation do not benefit; they remain eligible for 25-to-life third-strike sentences and are excluded from resentencing consideration, even if their most recent crimes are nonserious and nonviolent (Bowen, 2012).

Proposition 36 succeeded in 2012 where Proposition 66 failed in 2004 for many reasons. One was a decline in the importance of criminal justice as a salient political issue and the heightened prominence of a state budget crisis in the minds of the public. With crime rates declining or constant over the past decade, the public no longer perceived tough crime policies as urgently needed. Facing a state budget shortfall, cuts in social welfare benefits and services, poorly performing schools, and higher taxes, California voters were no longer in the mood to prioritize expensive crime-fighting approaches above other budgetary priorities. A well-publicized report by an organization called California Common Sense reported that in 2011, after three decades of growth in spending on prisons and declines in spending on higher education, the former surpassed the latter (Anand, 2012). A public opinion poll conducted by the Public Policy Institute of California in 2012 found that 64% of Californians were willing to pay higher taxes for K-12 schools, and 54% willing to pay for health and human services, but only 17% wanted to pay for prisons, and 81% opposed any such efforts (Skelton, 2013). Another poll found that 62% agreed that the governor and legislature should cut prison spending to prevent additional cuts to education, health and social services (Californians for Safety and Justice, 2012). The nonpartisan California Legislative Analyst's office estimated that Proposition 36 would save taxpayers $70 million to $90 million a year (California Legislative Analyst's Office, 2012), and the measure's advocates effectively emphasized these cost savings in their messages to voters.

Polls conducted during and after the election indicated that proponents of Proposition 36 succeeded in convincing the majority of voters, including conservatives, that Three Strikes in its original form was not only too expensive, but also unfair (Turner, 2012). Although critics of Three Strikes had complained about sentencing disproportionalities associated with Three Strikes since before the original law's passage in 1994, it took many years before moral and legal arguments, and numerous well-publicized real-life examples, such as individuals sentenced to 25-to-life for offenses like stealing a loaf of bread, a pair of gloves, or a slice of pizza (Furillo, 2012), raised the public's concerns about the law's fairness beyond the level necessary to create policy change. There were also doubts about the law's effectiveness. Advocates for reform pointed to the substantial body of expert research conducted over many years that reached the consensus that the California Three Strikes law had not effectively reduced crime as its proponents had contended (Tonry, 2009).

While crafting the language of the 2012 initiative, the authors of Proposition 36 avoided some of the pitfalls that had damaged prospects for success for Proposition 66 in 2004. Proposition 36 did not narrow Three Strikes as much as Proposition 66 would have, the language was less ambiguous, and it included specific provisions exempting the worst violent offenders from reduced sentences and leaving ample room for prosecutorial and judicial discretion in the resentencing process.

The political environment was far more conducive to Three Strikes reform in 2012 than in 2004. While Proposition 66 was defeated in large part through the efforts of Republican governor Arnold Schwarzenegger, Proposition 36 appeared on the ballot with the support of the state's popular Democratic governor, Jerry Brown, who was a persistent and outspoken advocate of exercising fiscal responsibility, balancing the state's budget through difficult decisions, and regaining control over the growth in California's prison populations (Skelton, 2013).

Bipartisan support also contributed to Proposition 36's success (Leonard & Dolan, 2012a). Although the measure was opposed by the California District Attorneys Association, three prominent DAs, Steve Cooley of Los Angeles, Jeff Rosen of Santa Clara County (which includes San Jose, California's third-largest city), and George Gascón of San Francisco strongly supported Proposition 36 in advertisements, media interviews, and public appearances (Austin, 2012). These three counties are home to 40% of California's voters (Kaplan, 2012b). The law also had public support from other prominent Republicans, including Los Angeles Police Chief Charlie Beck (Austin, 2012); a Texas-based conservative criminal justice reform group called Right on Crime, whose signatories included Jeb Bush and Newt Gingrich (Kaplan, 2012b) and prominent fiscal conservatives, such as anti-tax crusader Grover Norquist, who stated, "the Three

Strikes Reform Act is tough on crime without being tough on taxpayers. It will put a stop to wasting hundreds of millions in taxpayers' hard-earned money, while protecting people from violent crime" (Turner, 2012). The ballot measure earned the support of 51% of Republican voters along with 81% of Democrats and 74% of independent voters (Californians for Safety and Justice, 2012).[2]

Finally, Proposition 36 was well-funded, receiving $1 million in support from George Soros, nearly $1 million from Stanford Law School professor and business investor David Mills, and several other substantial donations (KCET, 2012). The opponents were considerably less well-financed, and the California Correctional Peace Officers' Association, whose generous donations had contributed to the success of Three Strikes and the defeat of Proposition 66, did not make a contribution to the "No on 36" campaign (Furillo, 2012).

Like the original Three Strikes proposal, Proposition 36 met many of John Kingdon's (1984) criteria for effective transformation of an idea into policy. This effort at reform succeeded in 2012 because of the public's belief that it would address important problems, because of the merits of the policy proposal as well as the well-documented shortcomings of the law it was designed to modify, and because of favorable political conditions.

Future Directions: What Lies Ahead for Three Strikes in California?

Now that Three Strikes reform has been passed, the next steps are implementation, evaluation, and continued change, if appropriate. Like the original Three Strikes law, the revised policy is being implemented at the county level. While Proposition 36 is expected to reduce geographic disparity, there remain opportunities to exercise discretion in the revised law, and perhaps even more so in Proposition 36 resentencing.

Based on data from the California Department of Corrections and Rehabilitation (CDCR), approximately 2,900 current prison inmates may be eligible for resentencing as "second strikers." Geographically from ten California counties, 92% of the inmates who are eligible for resentencing were convicted, and would therefore be considered for resentencing.[3] The resentencing provision of Three Strikes is expected to proceed quickly in some counties and more slowly in others (Kaplan, 2012a). Discussions with public defenders and alternate defenders from several counties reveal that variation already exists between counties in many aspects of Proposition 36 implementation, including efforts to communicate with inmates who are eligible for resentencing, procedures for resentencing application, personnel and other resources allocated to resentencing, and challenges from DAs.[4]

Proposition 36 added the following language to the Penal Code (emphasis mine):

> If a defendant has two or more prior serious and/or violent felony convictions as defined in subdivision (c) of Section 667.5 or subdivision (c) of Section 1192.7 *that have been pled and*

---

[2] At the same time, most Republicans opposed another ballot measure up for a vote, Proposition 34 to abolish the death penalty, which did not pass.

[3] They are Los Angeles (976 inmates), San Bernardino (317), San Diego (258), Kern (226), Santa Clara (209), Riverside (207), Sacramento (207), Orange (152), Fresno (67), and Kings (67). Source: Stanford Three Strikes Project.

[4] These discussions took place at a Proposition 36 Implementation Summit at Stanford University on November 19, 2012, and during a subsequent conference call on December 17, 2012.

proved, and the current offense is not a serious or violent felony . . . the defendant shall be sentenced pursuant to paragraph (1) of subdivision (e) [i.e., doubled sentence] unless the prosecution *pleads and proves* [one of several exceptions].[5]

The italicized "pled and proved" clauses remain subject to discretionary treatment. Prosecutors can continue to opt not to prove some or all prior strikes or exceptions. Furthermore, one exception, listed in section 667(e)(2)(C)(iii), is that "the defendant used a firearm, was armed with a firearm, or intended to cause great bodily injury to another person." "Intention" may be subject to interpretation by prosecutors, juries, and/or judges.

Regarding resentencing, the Penal Code was amended to read (emphasis mine):

An inmate is eligible for resentencing if: (1) The inmate is serving an indeterminate term of life imprisonment imposed pursuant to [the Three Strikes law] . . . *unless the court, in its discretion, determines that resentencing the petitioner would pose an unreasonable risk of danger to public safety* . . . In exercising its discretion . . . the court may consider: (1) the petitioner's criminal conviction history, including the type of crimes committed, the extent of injury to victims, the length of prior prison commitments, and the remoteness of the crimes; (2) the petitioner's disciplinary record and record of rehabilitation while incarcerated; and (3) any other evidence the court, within its discretion, determines to be relevant in deciding whether a new sentence would result in an unreasonable risk of danger to public safety.[6]

Substantial room for discretion has clearly and intentionally been written into the law. Prosecutors and resentencing judges retain the authority to assess an offender's dangerousness, and they are afforded considerable latitude with regard to the factors that they may consider in this assessment. DAs have the opportunity to provide arguments against sentence reduction or release during resentencing hearings. Public Defenders in some counties do not anticipate much opposition from their prosecutorial counterparts, but a few DAs have already filed challenges in response to early petitions for resentencing, and still others are expected to challenge most or all petitions that come before them (Lee, 2013).

Variation in administrative processes may also lead to differences in outcomes between and within counties. In many jurisdictions, the Public Defender's office has taken responsibility for initiating contact with most or all offenders who may be eligible for resentencing, reviewing files to confirm eligibility, filing petitions, and representing clients in hearings. However, many Public Defenders have limited staff and funds to allocate to this process. Moreover, some counties do not have Public Defenders, instead providing indigent defense on a contract basis. It is not yet clear how resentencing will be handled in these counties. There will also be variation in legal counsel among resentencing applicants, with most represented by public or alternate defenders, others represented by private attorneys, and yet others representing themselves. Research is needed to determine the extent to which the factors described here influence the outcomes of offenders seeking resentencing.

---

[5] California Penal Code Section 667(e)(2)(C). The exceptions include conviction for certain felony sex offenses, child molestation, homicide, "solicitation to commit murder," "assault with a machine gun on a peace officer or firefighter," "possession of a weapon of mass destruction," and "any serious and/or violent felony offense punishable in California by life imprisonment or death."
[6] California Penal Code section 1170.126(e).

Another area of concern in the implementation of Three Strikes after Proposition 36 is what will happen to the inmates who earn early release through the resentencing process. Some will be resentenced to time served and released unconditionally, which means that they will no longer be under any form of correctional supervision, so they will lack access to the range of services normally offered to parolees (Kaplan, 2013). For these inmates, release from prison will be welcome, but challenging, particularly if they had not anticipated or prepared for their freedom well in advance and do not receive adequate resources, such as transitional housing, job training, employment assistance, or mental health care, to facilitate successful reintegration into society (Kaplan, 2013). According to criminologist Joan Petersilia, 38% of third-strikers receive mental health treatment in prison, compared to 22% of inmates in the general population (Kaplan, 2013). The average age of inmates eligible for resentencing is over 50, while for other inmates it has historically been around the age of 30.[7] This age difference makes resentenced third-strikers statistically less likely to reoffend compared to the average person released from prison, but it may also be associated with greater challenges with regard to health and employment.

In addition to current inmates eligible for resentencing, future offenders may be influenced by the revisions to Three Strikes. Many nonviolent, nonserious offenders will be spared the lengthy sentences that they might have received if Proposition 36 had not passed. Therefore, the biggest question regarding Three Strikes in the future may be whether the recent modifications to the law will change the behavior of potential criminals. Opponents to Proposition 36, like Three Strikes author Mike Reynolds, predict that watering down Three Strikes will embolden criminals and endanger the public by reducing the law's deterrent effect (Leonard, 2012). Supporters of Proposition 36 argue that crime is unlikely to rise, pointing to the fact that crime rates are actually lower in counties where Three Strikes was used sparingly than in counties where DAs adhered more strictly to the law (Leonard, 2012), and they cite scholarly studies discussed earlier in this chapter that question whether the original law had a deterrent effect at all. Rigorous research is needed to determine which predictions are more accurate.

It will be a methodological challenge to separate the effects of Proposition 36 from the potentially larger effects of other changes that occurred in California's criminal justice system around the same time, most notably the implementation of Assembly Bill 109, a major criminal justice "realignment" effort enacted in October 2011 after the United States Supreme Court's *Plata v. Brown* decision, which upheld a District Court's order to reduce overcrowding in the state's prisons (Schlanger, 2013). As a result of AB 109, offenders whose crimes are nonviolent, nonserious, and not sex offenses, who have no serious or violent prior convictions, are now sentenced to terms in county jail, community supervision in the counties, or split sentences combining jail and community supervision instead of state prison (California Department of Corrections and Rehabilitation, 2012). Furthermore, some inmates will be eligible for post-release community supervision administered by the counties rather than parole, which is administered by the state (Silbert, 2012). In the first year of realignment, California's prison population shrank by about 26,000 inmates, to its lowest level since May 1995 (Mintz, 2013). Citing anecdotal evidence, some local law enforcement officials have blamed the influx of former prison inmates into local communities for recent increases in crime rates, while others have expressed skepticism about these assertions (Bulwa & Berton, 2013). Claims regarding realignment's effects on crime rates have yet to be confirmed or disproven by research, but if any effects exist, they may confound the observed relationship between the modified Three Strikes law and crime.

---

[7] Source: personal correspondence with data analyst Jerome McGuire, California Senate Public Safety Committee, September 18, 2012.

The Legislative Analyst's Office (LAO) estimated that Proposition 36 would reduce prison and parole costs by $70 million to $90 million per year, with one-time resentencing costs of "a few million dollars statewide over a couple of years" (California Legislative Analyst's Office, 2012). However, the LAO's report added that the true savings would depend on many factors, such as the level of government services required by released offenders, potential revenue from released inmates who enter the workforce, and costs associated with any changes in the crime rate resulting from changes in the law (California Legislative Analyst's Office, 2012). More data will have to be collected over time to determine the costs of the revised Three Strikes law and the savings associated with Proposition 36.

⊠ Conclusion

Three Strikes and other habitual offender laws were among many "tough on crime" policy efforts adopted throughout the nation in the early to mid-1990s in response to rapidly rising crime rates and frustration over the perceived failure of rehabilitative approaches to criminal justice (Ruth & Reitz, 2003). Although crime rates have declined nationwide over the last two decades, these laws remain in place in about half the states and the federal court system. Until November 2012, one state, California, had a Three Strikes law in place that was unusually draconian. The law's passage in 1994 resulted from the confluence of many factors, including California's system of direct democracy, which allows members of the public to bypass the legislature to enact laws, an atmosphere of public alarm over high and rising crime rates, and a critical focusing event, the abduction and murder of Polly Klaas and the subsequent arrest and trial of Richard Allen Davis, who epitomized the problem of lenient treatment of repeat violent offenders.

As Three Strikes was implemented by county court systems, substantial geographic disparities emerged in the law's implementation, with some District Attorneys charging all eligible offenders with third strikes, and others reserving third-strike charges for only the most serious and violent criminals. Racial disparities have also been found in the law's application, with African American defendants far more likely than Whites to be sentenced to 25-to-life under the law.

Questions over the law's fairness led to efforts to modify or repeal the law in the courts and at the ballot box. In 2012, a successful ballot initiative, Proposition 36, considerably narrowed the range of offenses that can trigger a third-strike sentence. Research is needed to assess the effects of this change. If future analyses find that recent modifications to Three Strikes decrease unwarranted disparities in the law's application without increasing crime, we might conclude that the first eighteen years of the law's existence in California constituted a wide-ranging experiment in sentencing policy with immense monetary and social costs with limited benefits.

The public's willingness to reform Three Strikes came at a time of dramatic change in California's approaches to correctional policy. While severe budget constraints and an ongoing recession have forced policy makers throughout the United States to make difficult choices, these dire fiscal circumstances also opened a window of opportunity for innovative reform in criminal justice policy. Recognition of the high cost of incarceration increased political officials' willingness to consider less-expensive intermediate sanctions for certain offenders. Concerns about persistently high recidivism rates and the easing of prison overcrowding as a result of realignment provided correctional authorities with incentives and opportunities to again think more seriously about rehabilitation. The influx of ex-inmates into local communities as a result of both realignment and the end of long prison terms imposed during the 1990s has directed the attention of policy makers and the public to the importance of reentry and reintegration. California voters' acceptance of recent changes to Three Strikes may reflect the beginning of a shift from the "get-tough" attitudes and policies of the 1990s toward more balanced, affordable, and effective approaches to criminal sentencing.

KEY TERMS

Deterrence

Incapacitation

"Pled and proved" clauses

Proposition 36

Recidivism

Safety valve

Second strike provision

Three Strikes law

Wobbler

DISCUSSION QUESTIONS

1. The Three Strikes ballot initiative passed with overwhelming voter support in 1994. What factors led to this success at the ballot box?

2. The implementation of the law varied widely between counties. Why? Aside from geographic disparities, what other disparities emerged in the law's implementation and outcomes? How could those disparities be reduced?

3. Three Strikes was passed in California with the intention of reducing crime, particularly serious and violent crime. What did researchers find when they analyzed the law's effects on crime? How can these findings be explained?

4. Why did Proposition 66 to reform Three Strikes fail in 2004, while Proposition 36 passed in 2012?

WEBSITES FOR ADDITIONAL RESEARCH

UC Irvine's Center for Evidence-Based Corrections: http://ucicorrections.seweb.uci.edu/

Justice Policy Institute: http://www.justicepolicy.org/index.html

RAND: http://www.rand.org/topics/law-and-business.html

Urban Institute: http://www.urban.org/

Vera Institute: http://www.vera.org/

CHAPTER

XVII

The Supermax: Issues and Challenges

Brett Garland, H. Daniel Butler, and Benjamin Steiner

Prisons confine individuals who, by virtue of their behavior, are considered a threat to public safety, but correctional administrators also bear the responsibility of protecting the confined. Inmate assaults and rule violations threaten the safety of inmates and staff. Super-maximum security facilities (hereafter referred to as supermax) offer a solution to inmates that habitually violate prison rules of conduct. Supermax confinement has been defined as

> a highly restrictive, high-custody, housing unit within a secure facility or an entire secure facility that isolates inmates from the general prison population and from each other due to grievous crimes, repetitive assaultive or violent institutional behavior, the threat of escape or actual escape from high-custody facility(s), or inciting or threatening to incite disturbances in a correctional institution. (Riveland, 1999, p. 6)

Inmates housed in supermax confinement are typically locked down in single cells for 23-hours a day and provided limited opportunities to shower and exercise (Haney, 2003; Richards, 2008). A National Institute of Corrections report published in 1997 noted differences in supermax units across state, federal, and Canadian prison systems. The report indicated that 22 of 34 Departments of Corrections (DOCs) that operated a supermax facility permitted inmates to be released directly to the community following supermax confinement. Twenty-three DOCs had a transitional process where prisoners could earn transfer from the supermax to less secure facilities. Sixteen permitted inmate-to-inmate contact in a supermax, and 13 offered supermax prisoners program opportunities outside their cells. Supermax inmates were provided library services in 25 DOCs, education programs in 21, anger management training in 12, and substances abuse training in 9 DOCs.

Supermax prisons have ignited controversy in academic and correctional discourse due to the nature of supermax confinement, but isolating inmates who pose safety and security risks from the general prison population to minimize institutional disturbances is not a new idea. Institutional segregation has existed for decades in most high-security prisons in the United States. At its roots, the modern supermax is a **segregation unit**. What makes supermax confinement different from other institutional segregation units is that it typically involves long-term placement and supermax prisons may exist as stand-alone institutions rather than one part of an existing prison (Riveland, 1999; Stickrath & Bucholtz, 2003).

The supermax continues an impressive trend of U.S. contributions to correctional history. Similar to other American penal innovations, such as probation and the reformatory prison, the supermax has its champions and critics. This chapter describes the rise of the supermax from its early beginnings at **Alcatraz** and **Marion federal prisons**. We critically examine justifications for supermax confinement and explore its financial and legal implications. The chapter concludes with recommendations for improving supermax policy and guiding research on this controversial practice.

The Back Story: The Rise of Supermax Confinement

Although the widespread use of supermax confinement is a relatively recent phenomenon, early American prison administrators frequently used solitary confinement, a technique that supermax prisons employ today. In the 1700s and early 1800s, prison administrators often housed inmates in single cells in order to isolate them from the ills of society and all forms of human contact (Pizarro, Stenius, & Pratt, 2006; Stickrath & Bucholtz, 2003; Toch, 2001). In the mid to late 1800s, prison administrators limited the use of solitary confinement due to the harsh effects isolation had on inmates (e.g., development of mental illnesses) (Pizarro & Stenius, 2013; Toch, 2003). Scholars remain divided about which prison constitutes the first true supermax facility. Chase Riveland (1999) and Ward and Werlich (2003) suggested that the Alcatraz penitentiary, located outside San Francisco, California, was the first supermax prison, while Stephen Richards (2008) and R. D. King (1999) argued that the federal penitentiary at Marion, Illinois, was the first long-term lockdown facility.

Alcatraz was opened by the Federal Bureau of Prisons in 1934, and it operated for 29 years (Riveland, 1999). During its operation, Alcatraz housed some of the most notorious offenders (e.g., Al Capone) in the United States (Ward & Werlich, 2003). However, there are several key differences between Alcatraz and modern supermax facilities (King, 1999; Ward & Werlich, 2003). For instance, Alcatraz did not house problematic inmates who violated institutional rules, but instead imprisoned hardened criminals and escape risk inmates (Ward & Werlich, 2003). The rules at Alcatraz also allowed inmates to work outside their cells and spend time in the exercise yard with other inmates. Many modern supermax facilities do not permit inmates outside of their cells for work or allow them to interact with other inmates (King, 1999). However, the rules at Alcatraz were strict and vigorously enforced (Ward & Werlich, 2003). Primarily due to the cost of operating Alcatraz, the facility was closed in 1963.

The federal penitentiary at Marion, Illinois, opened in 1963 and was designed to replace Alcatraz. Similar to Alcatraz, inmates housed in Marion were designated as unfit or too dangerous to be housed in general population prisons. Initially, inmates housed in Marion spent most of their time in solitary confinement, but they also participated in some rehabilitative programming. In the 1970s, administrators at Marion began using blocks of control unit cells, where inmates would spend 23 hours locked down in single cells (Ward & Werlich, 2003). In 1983, however, two correctional officers at Marion were murdered, which resulted in a significant increase in security. Marion became the first prolonged lockdown prison in the United States (King, 1999; Richards, 2008). The strict long-term lockdown status lasted 24 years, and effectively transformed Marion into a control unit, or what is currently referred to as a supermax prison (Richards, 2008). A description of life inside Marion following the elevation to supermax status can be described as follows:

> Even under these restraints, no inmate was to be moved from his cell for any reason without a supervisor and several officers to escort him. Basic law libraries were installed in each unit to reduce the opportunity for inmates to pass messages and contraband from unit to unit, hidden in legal papers and law books. Weightlifting and bodybuilding equipment was removed and exercise was limited to walking or jogging in a very small area, calisthenics, and the use of a chin-up bar. (Ward & Werlich, 2003, p. 58)

Marion was downgraded to a medium security prison in 2007, but it still serves as a model supermax facility for the states (Richards, 2008).

Drawing from the ideas applied in the federal system at Alcatraz and Marion, many states constructed supermax prisons during the 1980s and 1990s in an effort to separate, isolate, and control problematic inmates (Mears & Castro, 2006). In many respects, the rise of supermax prisons reflect an outgrowth of what Feeley and Simon (1992) termed the "new penology" (see also Pizarro et al., 2006; Ward & Werlich, 2003; Wells, Johnson, & Henningsen, 2002). According to Feeley and Simon (1992), the primary goal of imprisonment evolved during the 1980s from a focus on individual considerations (e.g., rehabilitation) into the management or control of large offender populations with a heavier focus on risk assessment and custodial classification. Supermax prisons embody the new penology in that their primary purpose is to physically separate the highest-risk inmates, or so called "worst of the worst," from the general inmate population. These high-risk inmates are then managed by restricting their opportunities for deviance through separation and isolation.

In 1984, only one prison in the United States fit the description of a supermax prison (National Institute of Correction, 1997). By 1999, however, approximately two-thirds of the states had supermax prisons and approximately 20,000 inmates were housed in supermax confinement (King, 1999). By 2005, the number of states operating a supermax prison had increased to 44 and roughly 25,000 inmates were confined in supermax housing (Mears, 2006). With the expansion of supermax prisons in the United States, these facilities largely remain an American solution for handling high risk offenders (King, 1999).

The Current State of the Policy: Is the Supermax a "Good" Correctional Practice?

Supermax prisons are tasked with achieving multiple goals (Mears & Watson, 2006). Mears and Castro's (2006) national survey of prison wardens revealed that over 95% of wardens agree that supermax prisons should strive to increase safety, order, and control throughout the prison system as well as segregate violent and disruptive inmates. Wardens overwhelmingly advocated using supermax confinement to improve inmate conduct (84%), decrease prison riots (82%), reduce prison gang influence (79%), and prevent inmate escapes (72%). The main arguments for supermax confinement attaining these goals are grounded in incapacitation and deterrence theories. This section of our chapter breaks down these arguments, provides an overview of supermax research, and discusses relevant financial and legal issues.

Incapacitation

Incapacitation refers to isolating harmful people to increase the safety of others by reducing opportunities for victimization. The existence of prison systems, not just supermax units, is justified in part because of this premise. In fact, the astronomical growth in U.S. prisons since the mid-1970s was fueled largely by a belief in the potential of incapacitation (Garland, 2001; Zimring & Hawkins, 1995). Supermax prisons are used to incapacitate within prison systems by segregating the highest risk inmates, making them physically incapable of committing offenses directly within the general prisoner population. Supermax units also pursue broader incapacitative goals for society by enhancing physical security over problematic and escape-prone inmates (Mears, 2006). Very few escapes from supermax facilities have been documented, although these observations must be tempered by the fact that there have been very few escapes from prisons of any security level.

The incapacitation justification for reducing system-wide violence and disorder is also tied to the notion that people sent to supermax units are not just perpetrators of prison disruption, but that they have a facilitation effect on institutional violence and disorder (Mears & Reisig, 2006). The facilitation argument maintains that certain inmates influence the actions of others. For example, a number of correctional departments experience gang-related problems in their prison systems. Some gangs, such as the Aryan Brotherhood and Mexican Mafia, demonstrate a vertical organizational structure, which implies that the actions of ground-level "soldiers" are inspired and directed by gang leaders (Seiter, 2005). If the leadership is disbanded through supermax segregation, one potential outcome is that the lower-ranking members become less active without orders from the gang leaders (Mears & Reisig, 2006).

Another argument is that removing troublesome inmates from the general population creates a better environment throughout the general population facilities. Even though prisons house people regarded as hostile, unruly, dangerous, and difficult, our correctional institutions are not erupting in riots on a daily basis. Rather, American prisons typically appear quite orderly, which has been attributed in part to an embedded and self-imposed inmate code of conduct (Bottoms, 1999; Crouch & Marquart, 1990; Engel & Rothman, 1983). A key aspect of this conduct code that generates order is the recognition that extreme rule violations by one or a few people, such as stabbings and massive destruction of property, can result in uncomfortable living arrangements for all inmates, including complete lockdowns in housing units (Johnson, 2002; Useem & Kimball, 1989). If a few "bad apples" are acting out and multiple inmates are feeding into the behavior, then the removal of those nonconforming inmates could normalize the prison environment and lead to more orderly behavior in observance of the inmate code (Kurki & Morris, 2001; Mears & Reisig, 2006; Ward & Werlich, 2003). With fewer problem inmates within the general inmate population, inmate programs, such as education classes, vocational training, and cognitive therapy, should function more efficiently (Mears & Reisig, 2006). This latter result is a critical benefit as the integration of inmate programs in prisons is related to greater order and less violence (Byrne & Hummer, 2008a).

There are several counterarguments that question the utility of the incapacitation strategy. One key assumption of the incapacitation argument is that the inmates who are the most likely to habitually commit extreme acts of violence and disruption can be identified (Mears & Reisig, 2006). In other words, the incapacitation position hinges on being able to predict the future behavior of troublesome inmates (Walker, 2011). It is one thing to place a disruptive inmate in lockdown; it is another to be certain that the isolated inmate would continue his or her disruptive path if given alternative sanctions and left in the general population. Although past behavior is one of the best predictors of future behavior offender risk assessment instruments have been shown to over or under classify a notable percentage of the inmate population (Wright, Clear, & Dickson, 1984). While segregating problem inmates from the rest of the prison population keeps them from personally injuring staff and inmates in the general population, we simply do not know how much direct harm is prevented.

Supermax prisons could increase violence and disruptive behavior by placing staff and inmates in environments (i.e., supermax units) with higher concentrations of serious and violent offenders in relatively small locations. In effect, the supermax itself might create a "hot spot" of institutional violence and disorder. The number of prison assaults are greater in higher security facilities than in lower security institutions (Byrne & Hummer, 2008b), but no studies have made comparisons specifically with supermax facilities. Supermax prisons may create "self-fulfilling" prophecies among inmates, where inmates accept the violent, "worst of the worst" label and proceed to act accordingly (King, Steiner, & Breach, 2008).

Questions also exist regarding how effectively supermax placements can reduce the influence of supermax-confined inmates, especially inmates affiliated with prison gangs and security threat groups. Incarcerated gang leaders have ordered acts of violence and controlled street gang activities outside the prison. Supermax inmates can also send messages through other inmates and staff to direct violence and other illegal activities like drug distribution in the general population. Well-developed coding schemes have been constructed by prison gangs to issue commands and avoid detection from institutional authorities (Mears & Reisig, 2006). Unfortunately, the success of message communication from supermax prisoners to general population inmates has not been empirically examined.

Removing gang leaders from the general population also has the potential to create power vacuums that encourage violent encounters. Layered organizational structures can sometimes serve to constrain the aggressive and unruly tendencies of members (McAdam, 1986; McCauley & Segal, 1987; Piven & Cloward, 1977; Smith, 1994). Those in charge have an interest in reigning in disorderly behavior so that the group's plans are not exposed and administrative surveillance is not increased. When the leadership unravels, the organizational constraints loosen and members begin questioning who is in charge. This outcome can set the stage for physical confrontations to fill vacant leadership roles. Additionally, those engaging in prohibited activities, such as extortion and drug distribution, whether individually or in small groups may become emboldened and consequently more active in their misconduct due to the absence of a control-oriented leadership structure (Decker, Bynum, & Weisel, 1998; Jankowski, 1991; Shelden, Tracy, & Brown, 2004)

Another possibility that may decrease the impact of the supermax incapacitation strategy relates to the realities of prison gang organizational structure. The counterarguments above assume that gangs are well organized in prisons. While hierarchical structures can exist in street and prison gangs, many gangs are not highly organized (Decker et al., 1998). In less organized gangs, leadership is transitory and members are less inclined to act on the instructions of a leader (Shelden et al., 2004; Jankowski, 1991). For these types of gangs in prisons, placing the current leader in isolation may have limited influence on gang member behavior.

Inmates not affiliated with gangs are also capable of creating problems within prisons. One example is an inmate resistant to institutional control who takes every opportunity to destroy property and harass staff, such as tearing out sinks and toilets from walls and throwing fecal matter from cells at officers. The typical correctional response to this destructive behavior is placement in a segregation unit. However, if inmates engaging in such behavior are released from segregation only to continue the misconduct, the general prisoner population might interpret this as indicating that prison authorities and staff are unable to adequately handle such problems. Therefore, other inmates could be encouraged to defy prison authority merely from the example set by the unruly prisoner, and not from any specific orders or directions. These types of situations involving inmates who appear undeterred by prison authority are cited when analyzing the initial stages of prison riots (Useem & Kimball, 1989). Unfortunately, it is difficult to assess inmate perceptions and responses to high profile displays of defiance. This lack of knowledge makes it difficult to assess the incapacitative value of supermax placements for undeterred inmates similar to the one described. In all, if extremely troublesome inmates are removed from the general population and there is no appreciable influence on levels of inmate misconduct, the argument regarding the normalization of the prison environment through the segregation of the "worst of the worst" is difficult to justify (Mears & Reisig, 2006).

Deterrence

Deterrence can be divided into two types: general and specific. Regarding supermax prisons, ***general deterrence*** refers to discouraging general population inmates from engaging in seriously disruptive behavior due to the threat of placement in supermax confinement. ***Specific deterrence*** refers to the actual experience of supermax confinement discouraging future deviance among inmates who are placed there. For deterrence to work, it was theorized long ago that the punishment associated with a criminal act or prison violation must be swift, certain, and proportionate to the offense committed (Beccaria, 1986).

The criminal justice system is often portrayed as incapable of achieving or sustaining deterrent outcomes for a variety of reasons, such as an overburdened court system that delays punishment and extensive plea bargaining which dilutes the punitiveness of criminal sanctions. However, the prison disciplinary system is quite different from the criminal justice system. One fundamental difference is that punishment for prison rule violations is more swiftly imposed than in the criminal justice system. Prisoners are afforded limited due process protections when misconduct is reported. In addition, conduct adjustment boards are not as backlogged as the criminal courts. Accordingly, it is likely that judgments regarding misconduct that might result in supermax housing are quickly determined.

Research suggests that the certainty of punishment is the most critical component for achieving effective deterrence (Wright, 2010). It is here that the deterrent power of supermax prisons must be questioned. King's (2005) interviews with supermax prisoners in Minnesota and Colorado revealed that supermax placements were perceived by inmates to be arbitrary and the duration of confinement far too discretionary. This is not a surprising discovery as it fits with Samuel Walker's (2011) law of criminal justice thermodynamics. That is, increasing the severity of a penalty leads to less frequent application, and, when applied less often, its use becomes more arbitrary.

From a general deterrence perspective, if prisoners perceive a weak probability of going to the supermax for committing a serious rule violation, the certainty aspect is not fulfilled. An equally important consideration is that getting caught committing a violation that can incur supermax placement might seem unlikely to inmates. For example, a predatory inmate rapist may be confident that fellow offenders will uphold the code against snitching and not report sexual assaults (Fleisher & Krienert, 2009). Kingpins in the underground drug economy of prisons may see little chance of authorities identifying them as major drug distributors. Research suggests general deterrence may not be effective because so few inmates are sent to supermax prisons, approximately 2% of the inmate population (Mears & Reisig, 2006; Riveland, 1999).

The impact of the *potential* consequences of supermax in the general population is one aspect to consider, but actually *experiencing* supermax confinement (i.e. specific deterrence) brings its own unique considerations. Serving time in the isolated confines of a supermax unit is typically portrayed as a severely unpleasant experience. The supermax represents the pinnacle of incarceration deprivations, which have long been associated with the term "pains of imprisonment" (Johnson, 2002; Sykes, 1958). Supermax confinement encapsulates deprivation by restricting physical movement and removing social contact, such as phone and visitation privileges. Psychological effects from extreme and prolonged isolation are regarded as the most challenging part of supermax confinement (King et al., 2008; Mears & Watson, 2006; Pizarro & Stenius, 2013). Scientifically based studies on the specific impact of isolation in a supermax on a prisoner's mental state have not yet materialized. Nonetheless, scholars are quick to point out that solitary confinement in any form produces psychological consequences, such as cognitive disruption, memory decay, heightened anxiety, depression, and suicidal ideation (Grassian, 1983; Haney, 2003, 2008; Kupers, 1996; Rhodes, 2005). A study of Washington state inmates assigned to a supermax unit indicated that one out of every four to five residents experienced mental health issues during their confinement; however, the findings do not identify if these symptoms were attributable to supermax conditions or prior psychological impairments (Cloyes, Lovell, Allen, & Rhodes, 2006; Lovell, Cloyes, Allen, & Rhodes, 2000).

Due to the harsh environment of supermax confinement, it may be expected that inmates will abstain from institutional misconduct to prevent returning to segregation. However, the unpleasant aspects of supermax confinement that are designed to deter misbehavior could also serve to increase misbehavior. If inmates do not believe that supermax classification decisions were just, they might react with defiance (Ward & Werlich, 2003). This emotional discontent could elevate hostility against the prison system, resulting in increased violence and disruption (King, 2005). Supermax confinement may also increase mental deterioration among inmates, which can result in loss of self-control and higher levels of impulsivity (Haney, 2003).

What Research Has Taught Us: The Impact of Supermax Prisons

A few studies assessed whether supermax facilities contribute to decreases in violence and disorder. Ward and Werlich (2003) examined records of inmates who were either confined in Alcatraz or Marion to evaluate the effects of supermax confinement. Ward and Werlich found that 3% of Alcatraz inmates who were recirculated into the federal prison system returned to Alcatraz for disciplinary problems. Approximately 50% of Alcatraz inmates avoided returning to prison after their release, compared to 37% of maximum-security inmates confined in Leavenworth Federal Penitentiary. Roughly 16% of prisoners housed in Marion returned to Marion following their transfer to a different facility. The re-imprisonment rate for Marion inmates was 49%, nearly the same as the rate among Alcatraz inmates.

Ward and Werlich (2003) arrived at the following conclusion:

> The post-release measures for the Alcatraz prisoners, the decline in misconduct, which allowed more than 80% of the Marion prisoners to remain in lower custody institutions to which they were transferred, and the ability of half of the Marion cohort to stay out of prison to date provide evidence, *albeit tentative,* that the predictions of destructive behavioral consequences, namely violence, resulting from long-term incarceration in supermax prisons do not appear to hold true for most of the men in these populations of federal prisoners. (p. 64)

Although the prisoners at Leavenworth returned to prison at lower rates than Alcatraz inmates, Ward and Werlich emphasized that the expectation would be that there were much higher return rates for supermax inmates, if significant psychological damage was inflicted in the supermax units.

Briggs, Sundt, and Castellano (2003) examined the impact of the implementation of supermax facilities on inmate-on-inmate and inmate-on-staff violence in three state prison systems: Arizona, Illinois, and Minnesota. Specifically, these researchers examined whether system-wide violence decreased after the supermax units were opened. Briggs and colleagues found no statistically significant decreases in inmate-on-inmate violence that could be attributed to the implementation of a supermax unit in any state. Mixed results emerged from the analysis of inmate-on-staff violence. In the periods following the implementation of supermax units, assaults against staff decreased in Illinois, increased temporarily in Arizona, and stayed the same in Minnesota.

Lovell, Johnson, and Cain (2007) examined the effects on recidivism of exposure to supermax confinement in Washington state, while Mears and Bales (2009) conducted a similar study with data collected from inmates confined in Florida. In general, both studies revealed that the odds of recidivism were the same between offenders exposed to supermax confinement and offenders not exposed to supermax confinement. However, Lovell et al. (2007) observed that offenders released directly from a supermax prison were more likely to reoffend than offenders directly released from another prison. Mears and Bales (2009) found that offenders exposed to supermax confinement were more likely to recidivate via violent offenses than offenders who were not confined in a supermax prison.

These four studies have broken fresh ground in the supermax literature, but additional research is needed. Researchers Ward and Werlich and Briggs and colleagues examined whether supermax prisons achieve their top goal, which is reducing inmate violence and disorder. Unfortunately, both studies have methodological limitations which limit strong conclusions. For example, Ward and Werlich's approach to examine inmate returns to supermax prisons after recirculation into the general population does not measure system-wide impact, and studying Alcatraz as a supermax prison is highly questionable. Briggs and colleagues examined how levels of violence fluctuated before and after implementation of a supermax prison, but did not consider other variables which might simultaneously affect prison violence. For example, changes in staff-inmate ratios, prison policy, management style, officer training, access to rehabilitation programs, physical security and inmate monitoring technology all could influence prison violence. In addition, Briggs et al. acknowledge potential problems with incorporating the Minnesota supermax into their study, because of its description as a podular-design unit providing extensive opportunities for educational and rehabilitative programming. The Lovell, Johnson, and Cain research in 2007 and the Mears and Bales studies in 2009 focused on recidivism effects from supermax confinement, notwithstanding the statistic that only 24% of prison wardens feel that lowering crime levels should be a supermax goal (Mears & Castro, 2006). The ultimate conclusion from the research thus far is that the question of whether supermax incarceration is a good correctional policy is far from answerable, necessitating more sophisticated studies.

⧅ Race, Class, and Gender Implications

Mass incarceration, which began in the 1980s, has contributed to the disproportionate imprisonment of racial and ethnic minorities (Alexander, 2012; Travis, 2005), as well as notable increases in the rate of imprisonment among women relative to men (Beck & Harrison, 2001; Guerino et al., 2011). Estimates suggest that approximately one in three Black males and one in six Hispanic males will be incarcerated during their lifetime, compared to only one in 17 White males (e.g., Bonczar & Beck, 2003). Similarly, although the odds of imprisonment are still much higher for men relative to women, the gender gap has closed considerably over the past 30 years (Guerino et al., 2011). The overall growth in prison populations has provided new challenges to correctional administrators, including managing increasingly heterogeneous populations of inmates. Correctional administrators have used supermax facilities to manage some of the problems resulting from the increases in the prison population, such as reducing gang influence, increasing public safety, and punishing violent inmates (Mears & Watson, 2006). Yet, little is known about the race, class, and gender composition of inmates in supermax confinement.

The limited knowledge concerning female inmates and supermax confinement is probably attributable to the fact that women are rarely (if ever) placed in supermax confinement. For instance, Mears and Bales (2009) reported that only nine women released from prison between 1996 and 2001 in the state of Florida had served time in supermax confinement. Lovell et al. (2007) observed that Washington state's supermax program was only used for men. Women respond differently to incarceration than men, and female inmates are less likely than men to engage in the type of violent behaviors that result in supermax placement (Lord, 2008). Thus, supermax confinement for female inmates may simply not be needed in most states.

Social class is a difficult concept to study among prison inmates because nearly all inmates are drawn from lower socioeconomic strata. Prison inmates are also drawn disproportionately from disadvantaged neighborhoods (Rose & Clear, 1998; Sampson & Loeffler, 2010). Perhaps for this reason, no studies have examined the link between social class and supermax placement. Closely tied to class, however, is race and ethnicity. Black individuals, for example, are much more likely than White individuals to reside in disadvantaged areas, and this has been the case for a number of generations (Sharkey, 2008; Wilson, 2010). Further, compared to residents of disadvantaged White neighborhoods, residents of disadvantaged Black neighborhoods experience greater levels of social isolation and disadvantage (Krivo & Peterson 1996; Sampson & Bean, 2006). Evidence also suggests that other ethnic minority groups (e.g., Hispanics) might also experience greater disadvantage compared to Whites (Sampson & Bean, 2006).

Regarding race and ethnicity, some researchers observed that minority inmates are more likely to experience supermax confinement than Whites (Lowen & Isaacs, 2012; Mears & Bales, 2009; O'Keefe, 2008; Reiter, 2012). For instance, researchers found that Hispanic inmates were more likely to experience supermax confinement than White inmates or Black inmates in California, Colorado, and Arizona (see Lowen & Isaacs, 2012; O'Keefe, 2008; Reiter, 2012). In California, approximately 56% of all inmates released from supermax confinement in 2007 were Hispanic, compared to 42% who were Black or White (Reiter, 2012). Similar trends were found between 1997 and 2007, and Hispanic inmates also served longer periods of time in supermax units, compared to other racial/ethnic groups (Reiter, 2012). O'Keefe (2008) also found that Hispanic inmates were overrepresented in Colorado's administrative segregation units and in supermax admissions, compared to Whites or Blacks. Mears and Bales (2009) reported that 75% of their sample of inmates released from prison between 1996 and 2001 who were housed in supermax confinement were Black, while 5% were Hispanic, and 20% were White. By contrast, Lovell et al. (2007) reported that only 35% of their sample of supermax inmates in Washington state were nonwhite.

It is important to note that none of the studies discussed above focused specifically on understanding whether race or ethnicity influenced supermax placement. Since inmates are typically placed in supermax confinement for disruptive behavior, researchers inferred that the overrepresentation of minority offenders in supermax confinement is attributable to potential affiliations with gangs, such as the dominance of Latino affiliated gangs in California and Arizona (Lowen & Isaacs, 2012; Reiter, 2012), or that minority inmates are more likely to commit rule infractions, which could lead to supermax placement. An inmate's race or ethnicity is often used as one identifying characteristic of membership in a gang or security threat group because prison gangs are often racially divided (Gaes, Wallace, Gilman, Klein-Saffran, & Suppa, 2002; Goodman, 2008). Evidence concerning the link between race and ethnicity and prison misconduct is mixed (Bottoms, 1999; Camp, Gaes, Langan, & Saylor, 2003; Griffin & Hepburn, 2006; Morris, Longmire, Buffington-Vollum, & Vollum, 2010; Sorensen, Cunningham, Vigen, & Woods, 2011; Steiner & Wooldredge, 2009a; 2009b; Wooldredge, 1991), although a meta-analysis did find an overall positive effect of minority status on rule violations (Gendreau, Goggin, & Law, 1997). Some researchers observed that Black or Hispanic inmates are more likely than other inmates to commit violent misconduct (e.g., assaults on inmates) (see, e.g., Berg & DeLisi, 2006; Gaes et al., 2002; Harer & Steffensmeier, 1996; Huebner, 2003; Sorensen, Wrinkle, & Gutierrez, 1998; Steiner & Wooldredge, 2009a; 2009b; Wooldredge, 1994), although the evidence is certainly not conclusive (Camp et al., 2003; Griffin & Hepburn, 2006; Wright & Goodstein, 1989). If minority inmates are more likely to be involved in prison gangs or commit violent rule infractions, then it stands to reason that they would also be more likely to "earn" a placement in supermax confinement.

Given the evidence presented above, the disparate confinement of minority groups in supermax custody does present an important avenue for future study. More research is clearly needed to assess the extent to which supermax length of stay, treatment, and programming amenities differentiate between minority and White inmates.

Implications of the Policy

Financial Costs

While the intent of this chapter is not to pit benefits against costs, it is important to recognize the substantial financial investments required to build and sustain a supermax. Supermax prisons are expensive due to the retrofitting of cells or construction of new facilities that are designed to house violent, disruptive, and problematic inmates in prolonged solitary confinement (Riveland, 1999). These institutions require architectural designs and numerous technological devices that add to operational expenses. Steel-frame doors, single-cells with electronically controlled doors, and recording monitors represent a few of the technological advances used to enhance security within these facilities. The Tamms penitentiary in Illinois cost taxpayers roughly 75 million dollars to construct (Kurki & Morris, 2001), while construction of the Pelican Bay State prison in California cost over 250 million dollars (King et al., 2008).

In addition to the costs associated with constructing and maintaining supermax facilities, staffing and training costs are considerably higher for supermax facilities (Riveland, 1999). It is not uncommon for policies pertaining to supermax confinement to dictate that all inmates housed in supermax housing need to be escorted in shackles by more than one officer each time they exit their cell (see, e.g., King et al., 2008). Policies like these, along with the extra security required in facilities that house a state's highest risk inmates, demand a higher number of allocated staff for these facilities compared to lower security facilities. For example, the Ohio Department of Rehabilitation and Correction allocates approximately one security staff member for every two inmates housed in its supermax facility compared to a ratio of nearly three to one at Ohio's maximum security facility, and ratios of six or seven to one at close security facilities in that state. All of this translates into higher costs associated with operating supermax facilities compared to lower security facilities. Each prisoner housed in the Tamms Penitentiary costs the state of Illinois $36,000 annually, which is nearly double the cost associated with housing an inmate in a maximum security facility in that state (Kurki & Morris, 2001). The cost of housing a supermax inmate in Colorado is

$32,000 per year or close to $90 per day, compared to $18,500 per year and just over $50 a day at a maximum security institution in that state (Pizarro & Stenius, 2013). The daily cost of housing an inmate in Ohio's supermax facility is 50% higher than the comparable cost at Ohio's maximum security facility and roughly 100% higher than the comparable cost at Ohio's close security facilities.

Legal Issues

Determining the wisdom of a criminal justice policy is not simply a question of whether it provides desired results, but also whether the policy can withstand constitutional scrutiny. The isolated conditions of supermax confinement along with due process considerations related to supermax placement and review hearings have generated considerable legal debate (Goode, 2012; Haney, 2003; Matthews, 2010). Most suits filed on behalf of inmates have challenged the conditions of supermax confinement (King et al., 2008; *Madrid v. Gomez*, 1995). These suits allege that supermax confinement or aspects of supermax confinement violate inmates' right to protection from cruel and unusual punishment guaranteed under the Eighth Amendment to the U.S. Constitution. Although some suits filed on inmates' behalf have been successful, the use of solitary confinement has typically been found constitutional (e.g., *Ford v. Bd. of Managers of N.J. State Prison*, 1969; *Madrid v. Gomez*, 1995). However, courts have not provided unconditional support for the use of supermax facilities, but instead tried to balance needs pertaining to institutional security alongside protecting inmates rights, specifically the mentally ill (Haney, 2003).

With regard to objective conditions of confinement (e.g., exercise, clothing), the courts have often evaluated the constitutionality of supermax confinement by applying the "evolving standards of decency" test, which states a community's "broad and idealistic concepts of dignity, civilized standards, humanity, and decency are useful and useable" (*Jackson v. Bishop*, 1968, p. 404). Under the evolving standard of decency test, the legality of supermax confinement rests, in part, with the public's standard of what constitutes acceptable punishment (Toch, 2001). Courts have also wrestled with the degree of psychological deterioration that constitutes a violation of the Eighth Amendment because harms associated with psychological punishment are more difficult to define and quantify than injuries suffered from corporal punishment. The standard by which courts have evaluated psychological punishment and corresponding medical care is the deliberate indifference test, or whether the conditions harm the inmate or present a serious risk of substantial harm, and whether the officials are intentionally or purposefully indifferent to that risk (*Wilson v. Seiter*, 1991).

Inmate lawsuits have argued conditions of confinement worsen an individual's mental state (Goode, 2012; *Madrid v. Gomez*, 1995, *Ruiz v. Johnson*, 1999). Specifically, these suits have alleged that prolonged exposure to supermax confinement results in sensory deprivation that contributes to psychological deterioration that inhibits inmates' ability to function during and after incarceration (Grassian & Friedman, 1986; Haney, 2003). Some suits challenging the constitutionality of supermax confinement have argued that sensory deprivation in conjunction with preexisting mental disorders worsens the mental state of inmates in supermax confinement (see *Madrid v. Gomez*, 1995; *Ruiz v. Johnson*, 1999). In *Ruiz v. Johnson* (1999), the Supreme Court held that prison administrators acted in deliberate indifference in handling supermax inmates with mental illnesses. Other cases pertaining to the conditions associated with supermax confinement that were decided on behalf of inmates include *Madrid v. Gomez* (1995), *Taifa v. Bayh* (1994), and *Jones 'El v. Berge* (2001). Taken together, these decisions state that although the use of supermax confinement may not directly violate the constitution, its practice and implementation require prison administrators to closely monitor inmates suitable for placement.

The process by which inmates are placed in supermax confinement has also been subject to litigation. For example, an inmate entering prison may sometimes move directly to supermax confinement simply due to the nature of their committing offense or gang membership. A study of Mississippi State Penitentiary's supermax unit (Unit 32) revealed approximately 800 inmates were indiscriminately classified, such as admitting non-violent inmates, confining inmates for their criminal offense, and placing protective custody inmates in Unit 32 (Kupers et al., 2009). In response to a suit alleging cruel and unusual punishment and violations of due process rights, the Mississippi Department of Corrections agreed to reevaluate their inmate classification process, which ultimately led to the transfer of 800 inmates from supermax confinement. Specifically, revisions to the classification process required that inmates engage in unambiguous behaviors that constitute a threat to the institution before they could be housed in supermax confinement (Kupers et al., 2009).

In 2005, the U.S. Supreme Court's unanimous decision in *Wilkinson v. Austin* further clarified the admission requirements for supermax confinement. Current and former inmates of the Ohio State Penitentiary filed suit against the Ohio Department of Rehabilitation and Corrections in reference to the Department's policy governing inmate admissions to supermax confinement. The suit alleged that the policy violated inmates' due process rights as applied by the Fourteenth Amendment.

After the suit was filed, the Department implemented a new policy governing the admission process for supermax confinement. Under the new policy, inmates were provided a presentation of the facts leading to placement in supermax confinement and an opportunity to contest allegations or placement decisions. If a classification reviewer overturned a placement decision or a reviewer disagreed with a placement decision, then the placement process was to be terminated. The policy also stated that inmates housed in supermax confinement would be reviewed within the first 30 days of confinement and annually thereafter. In addition to the procedures regarding admission to supermax confinement outlined in the new policy, in 2004, the Sixth Circuit Court went one step further when they ruled that the Department must document specific behaviors to be considered during the decision. However, the Supreme Court reversed the Sixth Circuit Court's decision stating that Ohio's new policy was compliant with the Fourteenth Amendment's procedural due process requirement. Among other things, the Court stated that the provision of "notice of the factual basis for a decision and a fair opportunity for rebuttal are among the most important procedural mechanisms for purposes of avoiding erroneous deprivations" (p. 183).

In the *Wilkinson v. Austin* decision, the Court acknowledged that Ohio has a vested interest in the use and implementation of supermax units to prevent gang violence and disorderly inmates from harming others. However, the Court did confirm the Sixth Circuit Court's ruling that placement in supermax units triggers a "liberty" interest, which means inmates should not be indiscriminately admitted to supermax units without adequate due process. This is because the restrictive and "atypical" conditions of confinement in supermax units should be used in circumstances where an inmate poses a consistent or serious problem to correctional administrators. More recently, the U.S. District Court for the Northern District of California also held that due process applies during inmate transfer proceedings. Specifically, the court held inmates are guaranteed minimal procedural protections, such as the ability to defend oneself prior to supermax confinement, a hearing within a reasonable time following admission to segregation, a notice of charges that led to supermax placement, and an opportunity to represent oneself during classification reviews (*Lira v. California Director of Corrections*, 2008).

Classification reviews decide whether continual placement in supermax confinement is necessary. In most states, internal administrative review committees oversee the length of stay, appeals, and progress inmates make within supermax confinement. Critics of these processes argue that determining inmate progress may be problematic because inmates have few opportunities to show behavioral change within supermax cells due to lack of available programming and inability to engage in social interactions with others (Haney, 2003).

In a national study of supermax prisons, Riveland (1999) concluded that the review process for inmates in administrative segregation is largely indeterminate, and an inmate's chance of classification review is predicated by his or her threat to the institution. Determination of the threat an inmate poses to the institution is a subjective process, but most states define a list of inmate behaviors perceived as threats to the safety and security of the institution. For instance, Kurki and Morris (2001) found inmates in Tamms Penitentiary, Illinois undergo a placement review before the transfer committee every ninety days. Transfer can be denied if the inmate is affiliated with a gang or is believed to pose a considerable threat (e.g., behavior that endangers inmates or staff) to institutional safety. Inmates only go before the transfer committee themselves on an annual basis, and this meeting can occur at the inmate's cell door. Based on the court's decision in *Lira v. California Director of Corrections* (2008), however, it appears that courts require that some basic due process protections are afforded to inmates at review hearings, such as an opportunity to represent themselves during classification reviews.

How Do We Fix It? The Future of the Supermax

Although the literature is inconclusive regarding the importance of supermax prisons, the tone in the scholarly literature is decidedly negative. Supermax confinement is described as creating monsters (King et al., 2008) and the correctional equivalent of "waste management" (Pizzaro & Narag, 2008). Suspicion regarding supermax prisons seems related to the negative connotations attached to solitary confinement. It is important to reiterate here that supermax prisons are simply an extension of institutional segregation, which is a staple of American corrections (Pizarro et al., 2006). What makes supermax confinement different is the extended amount of confinement in isolated settings. With so little concrete research on supermax facilities, it is hard to understand why people would strongly support or strongly oppose this practice. It may be that deeper philosophical orientations are at work in shaping perspectives on the supermax. The supermax could be viewed as a microcosm of the broader "get tough" incarceration movement of the past few decades. Consequently, a lack of faith in the supermax could be tied to dissatisfaction with this larger movement, whereas support could be linked to acceptance of tougher imprisonment policies. One thing is unquestionable: Supermax units are now embedded across the U.S. correctional landscape. Recognizing that an empirically based judgment of the supermax is not yet possible, this final section offers some tentative suggestions for operating and researching supermax facilities.

Recommendation #1: Require a careful evaluation by state and federal policy makers and practitioners in correctional fields to determine the need for supermax units

As an extension of institutional segregation practices, there seems little need for separate supermax units or entire supermax prisons if existing prison segregation units are able to effectively meet the demand (Mears, 2006). Adding a supermax prison unnecessarily to the existing bureaucracy increases strain on correctional administrators for operating an efficient and cost effective prison system.

Evaluating the need for supermax prisons must take into account alternative strategies for responding to highly dangerous and disruptive inmates. Riveland (1999) notes that the supermax is essentially a concentration approach to dealing with severe prisoner misconduct. The supermax provides one centralized location where the most problematic prisoners can be monitored in a setting designed to house high-risk offenders. Prior to the implementation of supermax facilities, a dispersion strategy was popular in state prison systems and this strategy continues to be the norm in many other Western countries (King, 1999). The dispersion strategy relocates the most troublesome inmates to other prison units which, in theory, prevents difficult offenders from bonding and offers staff directly supervising them some relief. The real question is whether modern American prison systems, many of which are overcrowded and receiving more gang members, have the capacity to effectively disperse problem offenders.

The need for supermax prisons may be offset by decreasing the number of eligible candidates for supermax confinement through readjusting the correctional environment. Some initiatives have been launched to improve correctional staff culture in the hope that positive effects will follow for inmates. A correctional staff culture that is less tolerant of staff-inmate harassment and achieves a greater "buy in" to programmatic efforts might engender a safer prison environment (Byrne, Hummer, & Taxman, 2008; Crawley & Crawley, 2008). Despite these efforts, it is reasonable to assume that acts of extreme violence and disorder will nonetheless remain part of prison life. The question becomes whether changes in the institutional environment can have sufficient impact so that existing institutional segregation units and non-isolation disciplinary measures can control disorderly inmates without the necessity of supermax classification.

Assessing the need of supermax facilities also requires careful consideration of net-widening effects. Net widening, within this context, refers to the process of admitting inmates to supermax custody because of available unit space, not necessarily due to misconduct (King, 2005). Many inmates engage in assaults and disruptive behaviors during their commitment periods, but supermax confinement is meant for the highest risk inmates. If "nuisance" inmates are sent to a supermax prison, supermax prisons are not serving their intended goals and net widening occurs. This phenomenon also has negative cost implications because less restrictive environments are cheaper than supermax confinement.

Recommendation #2: Identify clear goals for the supermax and closely monitor progress toward achievement of these goals

Mears and Watson (2006) list a number of goals pursuable by supermax prisons, including increasing institutional safety, increasing order and control throughout prison systems, reducing gang influence, punishing dangerous and disruptive inmates, enhancing public safety, and improving operational efficiency (2006, p. 242). The authors specify concrete performance measures which correspond to a specific goal. For example, the number of murders and assaults of staff and prisoners can measure the goal of increasing prison safety, the number of attempted and successful escapes can measure the goal of increasing public safety, and the proportion of inmates identified as gang members and the number of intimidation incidents by gang members can measure the goal of reducing prison gang influence.

Correctional officials and administrators should be cautious in developing goals for supermax prisons because heralding the supermax as a panacea for all correctional ills is a recipe for failure. A supermax unit typically contains a very small proportion of the overall prisoner population, sometimes less than 2% (King, 1999). It is hard to imagine how interventions affecting such small numbers can achieve multiple goals and produce substantial systemwide impacts. The supermax facility might best be conceived as a unit strictly for (a) containing inmates who engaged in or established plans to enact the most extreme acts of violence, such as conspiring to lead a prison takeover, or brutally assaulting a correctional officer or inmate, and (b) preventing inmates from escaping who have attempted or succeeded at escape in the past. Before creating goals pertaining to controlling gang influence and presence, each prison system should carefully analyze the extent and organizational structure and activities of prison gangs. As noted earlier in the chapter, supermax confinement may be ineffective at preventing or disrupting gang ties and behavior.

It is important to also recognize the limitations of performance measures for a single intervention like a supermax prison. Performance measures can be affected by a wide variety of institutional, managerial, and social forces, and separating the individual contributions of these factors is a complex task. The difficulty in evaluating a supermax from an academic standpoint is that it is virtually impossible, if not highly unethical, to place equivalent offender groups randomly into a supermax unit or another maximum-security, but less restrictive setting. Evaluations of how effectively a supermax pursues its goals are likely to compare inmate conduct among offenders who pose different levels of risk to the public and prison system.

Recommendation #3: Develop clear policies and procedures for determining supermax placement, length of confinement, and custody review

All policies and procedures should naturally be in line with the goals pursued by an agency. In this case, clear policies and procedures help to limit discretion in classifying inmates to supermax units. It is probable that procedures for supermax placement and length of confinement vary across jurisdictions. For instance, one state's guidelines for assigning prisoners to a supermax uses language like "professional judgment of the classifying official," "conduct or continued presence at [his] current institution poses a serious or chronic threat," "conspired to introduce contraband that may pose a serious threat to the security of the prison," and "demonstrated the ability to compromise the integrity of staff" (Stickrath & Bucholtz, 2003, p. 4). The problem is that these phrases are susceptible to considerable interpretation. What exactly is a serious threat beyond any other? Is an inmate threatening to strike another a nonserious threat whereas a threat of violence made with a clenched fist is labeled serious? What examples represent contraband that poses a serious threat? Violence and institutional disruption can arise from conflict grounded in various aspects of the underground prison economy, and technically this underground economy consists primarily, if not entirely, of contraband. What signifies compromising the integrity of staff? Is an inmate compromising staff integrity if he is successful at playing mind games with officers and gets them to consider slacking off on their security responsibilities?

Our intention here is not to simply highlight weaknesses in supermax admission policies, but to suggest areas of improvement. That being said, correctional policy makers should aim for constructing unambiguous policies given that versatile applications of supermax classification have potential to undermine prison authority and increase the probability of danger and disruption. For example, distinctions in policy made between physical violence that might "injure" versus "likely cause the deaths" of inmate or staff victims. Restricting contraband distribution that warrants supermax placement to those forms that can directly result in violence. In another instance, a policy could specify that prisoners caught smuggling dangerous weapons like knives and guns into the prison, are sent to a supermax unit. On the other hand, deal with the smuggling of cigarettes and drugs through alternative means, such as extensive loss of privileges and loss of earned credit time.

Riveland (1999) also recommended that high-level correctional administrators possess the final authority for approving placement and release from a supermax. Outside opinions from a correctional official not directly associated with the prison where an incident occurred could increase the objectivity of placement decisions. This practice might also be viewed favorably by prisoners skeptical of motivations behind placement decisions and thereby increase the perceived legitimacy of supermax classification.

According to Riveland (1999), most prison agencies use an indeterminate placement method for determining the length of stay in a supermax facility. Riveland notes that release may be influenced by "perceived risk the inmate presents, behavior changes, the amount of time left in the inmate's sentence, changes in the inmate's willingness to renounce gang ties, or other factors" (p. 10). At the same time, the duration of supermax confinement should be carefully evaluated to ensure that an inmate does not spend any more time than needed in such conditions. In addition, drafting guidelines for length of stay should incorporate an understanding that certain forms of inmate misconduct in the supermax unit do not necessarily justify longer stays. Inmates under strict supervision are likely to challenge staff due to the amplification of captor and captive roles in isolated confinement settings. For instance, greater incidents of inmate-staff disrespect are expected. At the very least, supermax inmates should have an expected release date (which most prisons hopefully already identify during admission to a solitary confinement unit), and the types of behaviors which delay or accelerate release communicated clearly to them.

Finally, states should bring their supermax admission and transfer policies in line with the *Wilkinson* and *Lira* decisions discussed above. The courts were clear regarding inmates liberty interests, as they pertain to supermax confinement, and states seeking to avoid expensive litigation and ensure due process is provided to inmates should revise their policies in a manner that is consistent with these decisions. Most importantly, inmates who are subjected to potential placement in supermax confinement should be given notice of the factual basis for the decision and an opportunity to challenge the decision.

Recommendation # 4: Require qualified, well-trained staff for supermax units

The heightened security required for 23-hour confinement creates intense interactions between staff and inmates. The officers working these units need to be trained to recognize behavioral cues signaling increased agitation and volatility, and also to deescalate these situations before they become explosive (King, 2005). By definition, a supermax unit does create a hot spot of potential violence toward both staff and inmates. In this environment, it can be rather easy for staff to objectify and dehumanize the inmates. Haney (2008) implied that isolated confinement creates an "ecology of cruelty" in the correctional workplace. However, this phenomenon has yet to be substantiated empirically in supermax prisons. Nonetheless, supermax staff must be carefully selected and closely supervised by high-ranking managers. Because working in a supermax prison may adversely affect morale and burnout (Mears & Watson, 2006), it is in the best interest of management, staff, and inmates that the employees assigned to supermax units are knowledgeable, skilled, focused, and driven to professionally perform their jobs. If supermax units hold the "worst of the worst," it is reasonable that the facility should be staffed by the "best of the best."

Recommendation #5: Integrate into all supermax policy and training the close monitoring for mental health problems, and the provision for appropriate aftercare

Although advocates of the deterrent impact of a supermax expect some level of physical and mental discomfort to occur from this type of confinement, prison officials have to be cautious that the discomfort does not rise to the level of mental health impairment. Fortunately, recent research explored the use of measures to assess psychosocial states during supermax placement. Cloyes et al. (2006) examined measures tapping into withdrawal retardation, anxious depression, agitation excitement, and hostile suspiciousness. Inmates need to be evaluated routinely by clinical professionals at various stages of their isolation on several dimensions of mental health so that exposure to supermax confinement does not result in more harm than good. This is important considering a high percentage of supermax inmates are released back to society at some point.

Fortunately, most supermax prisoners are released back into the general prisoner population; relatively few return straight to society (National Institute of Corrections, 1997). Although researchers have yet to adequately document the post-isolation experience, adjustment difficulties are probable. Careful attention should be given to step-down programs which gradually reacquaint former supermax inmates to the daily aspects of inmate life. Mental health counselors need to continue monitoring prisoners following supermax confinement, especially their level of hostility toward staff and inmates. For supermax inmates returning directly from isolation to society, prerelease counselors should make this group a high priority and take extra precautions to ensure the smoothest post-release transition possible.

Conclusion

Supermax prisons emerged on the correctional landscape as a solution to reducing inmate violence systemwide. Due to potential psychological damage, financial implications, legal concerns, and a lack of empirical support, supermax confinement has received substantial criticism. Still, at least 44 states currently operate a supermax unit. Although the practice of using supermax confinement is relatively new and its future uncertain, there are indications that it will become a permanent fixture within the U.S. corrections system. Supermax prisons fit with the modern emphasis on risk management, and the concentration strategy of isolating problem inmates generates commonsense appeal. Although a number of academics and practitioners questioned the utility of supermax confinement, few studies of the effectiveness of these facilities exist. Until additional research is carried out, the contribution of supermax prisons to prison management remains in question.

KEY TERMS

Alcatraz	Marion federal prison	Supermax prison
General deterrence	Segregation unit	
Incapacitation	Specific deterrence	

DISCUSSION QUESTIONS

1. Which arguments do you find most and least compelling regarding the concept of the supermax? Can you identify an argument for or against supermax prisons that was not identified in this chapter?

2. What is the ideal mission statement and architectural design for a supermax in your state prison system? What specific suggestions can you give to correctional policy makers who are considering building a supermax in a state where one does not yet exist?

3. Do you feel there is a need for supermax prisons for female inmates? Why or why not?

WEBSITES FOR ADDITIONAL RESEARCH

National Institute of Corrections: http://nicic.gov/

National Institute of Justice: http://www.nij.gov/

Urban Institute: http://www.urban.org/

Vera Institute: http://www.vera.org/

Supermaxed.com: http://www.supermaxed.com/

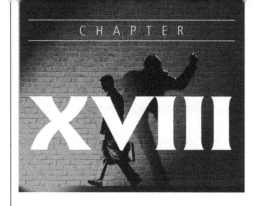

CHAPTER

XVIII

Capital Punishment

Robert M. Bohm

ew criminal justice policy issues are as controversial as capital punishment, or the death penalty. Yet, most people know little about the history of the ultimate sanction or its administration. This chapter attempts to rectify that situation by presenting the modern history of capital punishment in the United States. The chapter begins with a description of the successful challenge to capital punishment's constitutionality that occurred in the 1960s and culminated with its temporary abolition in 1972. It continues with an examination of the penalty's reinstatement four short years later and the new procedures that now govern its administration. Whether these new procedures have eliminated or significantly reduced the problems with the administration of capital punishment under the old, unconstitutional procedures is discussed next. Especially emphasized are race, gender, and class matters. The chapter ends with policy suggestions about what can be done to fix the problems that remain.

The Back Story

Despite its ban by several states, a successful challenge to capital punishment's constitutionality did not occur until the 1960s. Led by the American Civil Liberties Union (ACLU) and, especially, the NAACP Legal Defense and Educational Fund (LDF), neither of which was a death penalty abolitionist organization, the challenge to capital punishment has been referred to as the "final act of the [black] Civil Rights movement" (Bedau, 2009, p. 617; Haines, 1996, p. 43). LDF lawyers turned their attention to the death penalty in the 1960s primarily because of the racially discriminatory way it was being administered. A series of cases (and defeats for the LDF lawyers) set the stage for what would turn out to be the landmark case of *Furman v. Georgia*, decided by the U.S. Supreme Court (the "Court") on January 29, 1972.

Furman's lawyers argued to the Supreme Court that unfettered jury discretion in imposing death for murder resulted in arbitrary or capricious sentencing in violation of their client's Fourteenth Amendment right to due process and his Eighth Amendment right not to be subjected to cruel and unusual punishment. In a 5 to 4 decision, the Court ruled in favor of Furman and set aside death sentences for the first

293

time in its history. It is important to note that the Court did not declare the death penalty itself unconstitutional; it held as unconstitutional only the statutes under which the death penalty was then being administered.

The backlash against the *Furman* decision was immediate and widespread. Many people, including those who had never given the death penalty issue much thought, were incensed at what they perceived as the Supreme Court's arrogance in ignoring the will of the majority and its elected representatives. They clamored to have the penalty restored. Obliging their constituents, the elected representatives of 35 states proceeded to adopt new death penalty statutes designed to meet the Court's objections (Lain, 2007). The new death penalty laws took two forms. Twenty-two states removed all discretion from the process by mandating capital punishment on conviction for certain crimes (**"mandatory" death penalty statutes**). Other states provided specific guidelines that judges and juries were to use in deciding if death was the appropriate sentence in a particular case, known as **"guided discretion" death penalty statutes** (Bowers & Steiner, 1999).

The constitutionality of the new death penalty statutes was quickly challenged, and on July 2, 1976, the Supreme Court announced its rulings in five test cases. In *Woodson v. North Carolina* and *Roberts v. Louisiana* the Court rejected, by a vote of 5 to 4, mandatory statutes that automatically imposed death sentences for defined capital crimes. Justice Potter Stewart explained why the Court rejected the mandatory statutes. According to Stewart, to impose the same penalty on all convicted murderers, even though all defendants are different, is just as capricious as imposing a penalty randomly (Woodward & Armstrong, 1979). To alleviate this problem, some sentencing guidelines were necessary. Thus, in **Gregg v. Georgia,** *Jurek v. Texas,* and *Proffitt v. Florida* (hereafter referred to as the *Gregg* decision), the Court, by a vote of 7 to 2, approved guided discretion statutes that set standards for juries and judges to use when deciding whether to impose the death penalty. With the *Gregg* decision, executions in the United States resumed the following year with the execution of Gary Gilmore by firing squad in Utah. Gilmore's execution was the first execution in the United States in a decade. In those jurisdictions that administer it, guided discretion statutes govern the death penalty today.

The Current State of the Policy

In *Gregg,* the Court's majority concluded that the guided discretion statutes struck a reasonable balance between giving the jury some direction and allowing it to consider the defendant's background and character and the circumstances of the crime. In doing so, they respected the defendant's basic human dignity, as required by the Eighth Amendment, and, as an added bonus, prevented jury nullification (Acker, 1996). **Jury nullification** refers to a jury's knowing and deliberate refusal to apply the law, because in this case, a mandatory death sentence was considered contrary to the jury's sense of justice, morality, or fairness (Garner, 2000). In most death penalty states, guided discretion statutes list aggravating factors and, at least in some of those states, mitigating factors. **Aggravating factors** are facts or situations that increase the blameworthiness for a criminal act (for example, creating a great risk of death to many persons, or committing a capital felony that is especially heinous, atrocious, or cruel). **Mitigating factors** are facts or situations that do not justify or excuse a criminal act, but reduce the degree of blameworthiness and thus may reduce the punishment (for example, having no significant history of prior criminal activity, or being under a certain age at the time of the crime). Whether listed in the statute or not, the Court has ruled that judges and juries must consider any mitigating factors proffered by the defense, as long as they are supported by evidence. Generally, aggravating factors are weighed against mitigating factors. If aggravating factors outweigh mitigating factors, then the appropriate sentence is death. On the other hand, if mitigating factors outweigh aggravating factors, then the appropriate sentence in most death penalty states is life imprisonment without opportunity of parole (LWOP).

The Court also approved three other major procedural reforms in *Gregg* decision: bifurcated trials; ***automatic appellate review*** of convictions and sentences, usually by a state's highest appellate court; and proportionality review. A ***bifurcated trial*** is a two-stage trial—unlike the one-stage trial in other felony cases—consisting of a guilt phase and a separate penalty phase (the presentation of aggravating and mitigating factors occurs during the penalty phase). ***Proportionality review*** is a process whereby state appellate courts compare the sentence in the case before it with sentences imposed in similar cases in the state. Its purpose is to identify sentencing disparities and aid in their elimination. Although the Court considers them desirable, neither automatic appellate review nor proportionality review is constitutionally required. In addition to automatic appellate review, defendants sentenced to death also have a dual system of ***collateral review***, that is, they may challenge their convictions and/or sentences through both state postconviction proceedings and federal habeas corpus petitions. The procedures that govern capital punishment today are referred to as "***super due process***" (Radin, 1980).

What Research Has Taught Us

The Court's majority believed that the new procedural safeguards approved in *Gregg* would rid the death penalty of the problems cited in *Furman*. This leap of faith on the Court's part was not based on any evidence, because there was none. No jurisdiction in the United States had ever used all of the elements of super due process. However, now, more than 35 years later, it is possible to determine whether the Court's faith in the new death penalty process was justified. The evidence shows that super due process has not met the Court's expectations, especially at the trialcourt level. As a result of the review process, a large number of convictions and/or sentences in death penalty cases have been reversed—a reversal rate many times higher than in noncapital cases. The errors discovered, moreover, are not insignificant legal technicalities, but are the result of violations of fundamental constitutional protections (e.g., ineffective assistance of counsel, prosecutor misconduct, unconstitutional jury instructions, and judge/jury bias). From 1976 through May 2012, 140 inmates in 26 states have been released from death row because of evidence of their innocence (Death Penalty Information Center, 2012a). Not known is the number of death row inmates still awaiting their executions despite their innocence or the number of innocent inmates who already were executed.

Regardless, innocence was not the reason the Court invalidated death penalty statutes in *Furman*. Nor, for that matter, were the issues of cost or ***general deterrence***. The reason for the Court's landmark decision was that unfettered jury discretion resulted in an arbitrary and discriminatory application of the penalty. In *Gregg*, as noted, the Court was optimistic that super due process would significantly reduce or eliminate the problem. Below, evidence of arbitrary application of the death penalty under super due process is examined, followed by recent evidence on cost and general deterrence. Although the latter two issues were not the focus of the *Furman* Court, they currently are important to both sides of the death penalty debate. The issue of discriminatory application of the death penalty is examined in the next major section on race, gender, and class implications of the policy.

▧ Arbitrary Application

To apply the death penalty arbitrarily or capriciously is to administer it randomly. Capital punishment in the United States today is a lottery where an unlucky few death-eligible offenders are executed, while the vast majority of death-eligible offenders are not. Only about 1% of all death–eligible offenders were executed under super due process, and there is no meaningful way to distinguish between the eligible offenders who have been executed and those who have not (see Dieter, 2011). One might assume that the few death-eligible offenders who have been executed represent the "worst of the worst," but the "worst of the worst" sometimes escape execution, while murderers who clearly are not among the "worst of the worst" do not. An example of the first category is serial killer Gary Ridgway, the so-called "Green River Killer," who, in 2003, admitted to killing 48 women during a span of two decades. Ridgeway was not sentenced to death, but to consecutive LWOP sentences for each murder.

Arbitrariness is also evident in the way the death penalty is applied across jurisdictions and over time. Thirty-five separate jurisdictions in the United States have capital punishment statutes (33 states, the federal government, and the U.S. military), while 18 jurisdictions do not (17 states and the District of Columbia). So, whether a killer (only murderers have been executed post-*Gregg*) receives the death penalty depends on the jurisdiction where the death-eligible murder was committed. A murderer who kills his victim in Missouri may be sentenced to death, while a murderer who kills his victim in Illinois—perhaps less than a mile away from the Missouri killing—could not be sentenced to death today, but could have been sentenced to death before 2011—the year Illinois abolished its death penalty. Some people may argue that the preceding example is not evidence of arbitrary application, but, instead, is a function of the United States' federal system of government. Perhaps. But, the federal system of government cannot explain county-level variation within death penalty states.

A recent study found that only 15 of 3,148 counties in the United States (less than 1%) accounted for 30% of all executions since 1976; nine of those 15 counties were in Texas (Baumgartner, 2012). Another recent study discovered that only 10% of U.S. counties accounted for all death sentences imposed between 2004 and 2009, and only 5% of U.S. counties accounted for all death sentences imposed between 2007 and 2009 (Smith, 2010). The researchers reported that the concentration of death sentences in those counties was not a function of the heinousness of the murders committed, or the incorrigibility of the offenders. Rather, in some counties prosecutors sought the death penalty, and in other counties in the same state they did not, even for the same or more aggravated death-eligible murders.

Data of county-level variation within states indicate that greater numbers of death-eligible homicides do not increase the overall probability of a death sentence, as one might expect. Rather, the data show that the odds of being sentenced to death are either greater in counties with fewer death-eligible homicides, or not related to the number of death-eligible homicides at all. It may be that where capital murders are few, those that are committed receive harsher punishment. Another explanation has to do with the costs of capital punishment. Counties that can afford it may seek the death penalty in all cases that warrant it, while poor counties may have to pick and choose among death-eligible cases, pursuing the death penalty in only some cases, or not at all. Poor counties simply may not be able to afford the death penalty (Dieter, 2005). Regardless of the reason, the result is arbitrary application.

Cost

Under super due process, although the actual procedures used to cause death may be relatively inexpensive, the process of getting to that point is quite costly. Capital punishment is so expensive that some states have decided to abolish the death penalty altogether (e.g., New Jersey in 2007 and New Mexico in 2009), while some counties, as noted above, elected not to pursue the death penalty in death-eligible cases.

In 2000, the average cost per execution in the United States (i.e., the entire process) was estimated to range from about $2.5 million to $5 million (see Cook & Slawson, 1993; Dieter, 1992; Liebman, Fagan, & West, 2000; NJADP, 2005; Roman, Chalfin, & Knight, 2009; Spangenberg & Walsh, 1989). Extraordinary cases can cost more. For example, the state of Florida reportedly spent $10 million to execute serial murderer Ted Bundy in 1989 (Muwakkil, 1989), and the federal government spent more than $100 million to execute mass murderer Timothy McVeigh in 2001 (Michel & Herbeck, 2001).

The average cost of a LWOP sentence is much less. For example, California spends approximately $137 million a year on the death penalty, whereas a comparable system that sentences the same inmates to LWOP costs only about $11.5 million per year (Dieter, 2009). The death penalty cost New Jersey taxpayers approximately $11 million a year between 1983 and the end of 2005, even though New Jersey did not execute anyone during that period. That is $253 million "over and above the costs that would have been incurred had the state utilized a sentence of life without parole instead of death" (NJADP, 2005). As noted previously, New Jersey abolished its death penalty in 2007.

The costs of a death sentence will probably always be more expensive than the costs of an LWOP sentence because super due process is required only in capital cases (see *Harmelin v. Michigan*, 1991). Another consideration is that

> death penalty costs are accrued upfront, especially at trial and for the early appeals, while life-in-prison costs are spread out over many decades. A million dollars spent today is a lot more costly to the state than a million dollars that can be paid gradually over 40 years. (Dieter, 2005)

It should also be remembered that whenever a capital trial does not result in a death sentence and execution, the added costs associated with the death penalty process were incurred without any "return" on the state's investment of resources. In other words, the enormous costs of capital punishment are not a product of the number of executions, but rather the number of people that death penalty jurisdictions attempted to execute (Haines, 1996). Consequently, since 1977, California has executed only 13 people, making the cost of each execution more than $250 million (Dieter, 2009). Between 1978 and 1999, Maryland executed only 5 people at a cost of about $37 million per execution (Dieter, 2009). And, as noted above, between 1983 and the end of 2005, New Jersey spent $253 million on its death penalty, even though it executed no one during that period (NJADP, 2005).

As the evidence shows, capital punishment in the United States is much more expensive than alternative noncapital punishments, including LWOP. Perhaps this added expense could be justified if it could be shown that a capital punishment sentence saves more lives than a noncapital punishment sentence, that is, if capital punishment has a marginal deterrent effect. That possibility is examined next.

General Deterrence

In the context of capital punishment, the broad deterrence question is whether or not executions prevent people other than the person executed from committing capital crimes. Despite decades of research, there is no evidence that capital punishment has a marginal deterrent effect, or that it deters more effectively than an alternative noncapital punishment, such as LWOP.

Until 1975, there were no scientific data showing that capital punishment had a significant (or greater than a chance) effect on homicide or murder rates. Despite more than 40 years of research and dozens of studies, this finding was sustained. In 1975, economics professor Isaac Ehrlich published the first scientific study to report a deterrent effect for capital punishment (Ehrlich, 1975). Ehrlich examined the simultaneous effect of several variables on homicide rates during the years 1933 to 1969. He found that "an additional execution per year over the period in question may have resulted, on average, in seven or eight fewer murders" (Ehrlich, 1975, p. 414).

Ehrlich's findings drew considerable attention. Most of the attention was critical, and numerous methodological flaws with his research were cited. Dozens of studies were subsequently conducted, and most of them failed to find a deterrent effect for the death penalty. In fact, some of them discovered a counterdeterrent or brutalization effect (that is, executions may cause murders rather than deter them). Recently, a new wave of deterrence studies, many of them conducted by economists like Ehrlich, found a deterrent effect for capital punishment.

In response to these studies, Yang and Lester (2008) conducted a meta-analysis of 104 studies of the deterrent effect of capital punishment published in peer-reviewed journals after 1975. A meta-analysis is the statistical analysis of a large collection of analysis results for the purpose of integrating the findings. Of the 104 deterrence studies, only 95 had adequate data that allowed the researchers to report an effect size. Yang and Lester reported that 60 of the studies found a deterrent effect, while 35 of the studies discovered a counterdeterrent or brutalization effect.

Critical analyses of the newer econometric studies faulted them for some of the same problems that invalidated Ehrlich's earlier research, plus some new ones. Among the long list of criticisms is that none of the studies determines the marginal effect of executions. Furthermore, the dramatic recent decrease in homicide rates in New York, Texas, and California seems to demonstrate the deterrent superiority of LWOP over executions because in capital cases LWOP sentences are more frequently given than death sentences (Fagan, 2005; also see Berk, 2005).

In 1989, following a comprehensive review of death penalty research by a panel of distinguished scholars, the American Society of Criminology—the largest association of criminologists in the nation—passed a resolution condemning capital punishment and calling for its abolition. Among the reasons for the Society's position was the absence of "consistent evidence of crime deterrence through execution" (Petersilia, 1990). Also, a 1996 survey of 67 current and past presidents of the top three criminology professional organizations—the American Society of Criminology, the Academy of Criminal Justice Sciences, and the Law and Society Association—found that about "80% of them believe that the death penalty is no greater a deterrent to homicide than long imprisonment" (Radelet & Akers, 1996).

✄ Race, Gender, and Class Implications of the Policy

As noted previously, the *Gregg* Court believed that super due process would eliminate (or at least dramatically reduce) discriminatory application of the death penalty. It has not. Capital punishment in the United States continues to be plagued by discrimination based on race, gender, and class.

Class

Justice William O. Douglas wrote in his *Furman* decision, "One searches our chronicles in vain for the execution of any member of the affluent strata of this society" (*Furman v. Georgia*, 1972, pp. 251–252), and attorney Bryan Stevenson observed that capital punishment really means "them without the capital gets the punishment" (Stevenson, 2004, p. 95). A major reason wealth matters is that the wealthy are able to hire the best attorneys. In many capital cases, the outcome depends more on an attorney's skill than what actually happened (Dow, 2005).

That the wealthy are practically immune to the death penalty is supported by a recent study of 504 adult defendants indicted for capital murder in Harris County (Houston), Texas, from 1992 to 1999 (Phillips, 2009). Harris County, Texas, is notorious for being the capital punishment capital of the United States. If Harris County were a state, it would rank second only to Texas as the state with the most post-*Gregg* executions. Harris County also is noteworthy because it does not have a public defender system. All criminal defendants are represented by privately retained lawyers or appointed counsel. The study found that all but one of the 504 defendants were poor (based on the median household income of the defendant's neighborhood, i.e., census block group). The one exception was multimillionaire Robert Angelton, who was accused of hiring his brother to kill his wife. Not surprisingly, Angelton was acquitted of the capital murder at trial.

In another study using the same Harris County data, the victim's social class or social status was discovered to frequently determine whether the prosecutor sought, and the jury imposed, the death penalty (Phillips, 2010). Prosecutors were more likely to seek the death penalty and juries were more likely to impose the death penalty in cases of high-status victims than in cases of low-status victims. High-status victims were defined as wealthy (based on median household income in victim's residential neighborhood), integrated (married or widowed), sophisticated (college degree), conventional (White or Hispanic), and respectable (clean criminal record). Low-status victims, on the other hand, were poor, marginal (separated, divorced, or single), unsophisticated (no college degree), unconventional (Black or Asian), and disrespectable (prior criminal record). Thus, not only does the offender's social status determine death eligibility, but also so does the victim's social status.

Gender

The death penalty is rarely inflicted on women, even though women commit roughly one in ten criminal homicides where the gender of the offender is known (Federal Bureau of Investigation, 2010b). (The percentage of women who commit death-eligible homicides is unknown.) Approximately 20,000 people have been legally executed in the United States since 1608, and about 3% (approximately 569) of those have been women; most of them (nearly 90%) were executed prior to 1866 (Schneider & Smykla, 1991).

It is estimated that under current death penalty laws, if women and men were treated equally and no factor other than offense was considered, then women would receive between 4% and 6% of all death sentences (Rapaport, 1993). Under post–*Furman* statutes, however, women have received about 2% of all death sentences—2 to 8 death sentences a year—167 total between January 1, 1973, and late 2010 (Streib, 2010). Only 12 women have been executed under super due process as of this writing (Death Penalty Information Center, 2012b). The reason is that from arrest through execution, women are filtered from the process.

Streib (1993) identified two principal sources of this gender discrimination: (a) the conscious or subconscious attitudes of key actors in the criminal justice process and (b) death penalty laws, themselves. Streib contends that the aggravating and mitigating circumstances enumerated in death penalty laws bias the application of the death penalty in favor of women. For example, among aggravating factors that generally advantage women over men charged with capital crimes are those that pertain to (a) previous criminal record (women are less likely than men to have one), (b) premeditation (homicides by women tend to be unplanned and sudden acts), and (c) felony–murders (women are rarely involved in them) (Streib, 1993). Mitigating factors that tend to advantage women involve: (a) committing a capital crime while under extreme mental or emotional disturbance (female murderers are perceived to be more emotionally disturbed than male murderers) and (b) acting under the substantial domination of another person (when both women and men are involved in a capital crime, the man is generally considered the principal actor) (Streib, 1993).

As for the key actors in the criminal justice process, judges (who are predominately male) admit that, in general, they tend to be more lenient toward female offenders. They also tend to believe that women are better candidates for rehabilitation than are men. Jurors also tend to be more lenient toward female offenders, particularly in cases of serious crimes (Streib 1993).

Race

Super due process also fails to end racial discrimination in the imposition of the death penalty. According to an "evaluation synthesis" of 28 post–*Furman* studies prepared by the U.S. General Accounting Office (GAO) and published in 1990,

> more than half of the studies found that race of defendant influenced the likelihood of being charged with a capital crime or receiving the death penalty ... [and in] more than three-fourths of the studies that identified a race-of-defendant effect ... black defendants were more likely to receive the death penalty. (U.S. General Accounting Office, 1990, p. 6)

An update of the GAO study prepared for the American Bar Association (ABA) showed that in nearly half of the death penalty states, race of defendant was a significant predictor of who would receive a death sentence. In all but two of those states (Florida and Tennessee), Black defendants were more likely to receive a death sentence (Baldus & Woodworth, 1997). Likewise, a 1994 study by the *Houston Post* found that in Harris County, Texas (Houston), Blacks were sentenced to death twice as often as Whites (Bright, 1997a, p. 4). A more recent study of Harris County, Texas, published in 2008 found that death sentences were still more likely to be imposed on Black defendants than on White defendants (Phillips, 2008). Another study examined a sample of death-eligible murderers in Philadelphia, Pennsylvania, between 1983 and 1993 (Baldus, Woodworth, Zuckerman, Weiner, & Broffitt, 1998). African Americans were found to have a nearly four times greater chance of receiving a death sentence than similarly situated defendants, even after controlling for a variety of factors, including severity of offense and background of defendant. Also discovered was that race made the most difference in the "mid–range" of severity or aggravation cases in which prosecutors and jurors exercise the most discretion in seeking and imposing the death penalty.

Available evidence indicates that super due process has not eliminated a second, less obvious form of racial discrimination: victim-based racial discrimination. Whether the death penalty is imposed continues to depend on the race of the victim. Research shows that the killers of Whites, regardless of their race, are much more likely to be sentenced to death than are the killers of non-Whites.

The ABA study discussed previously found evidence of race-of-victim disparities in 93% of death penalty states, and in all but one of those states (Delaware) White–victim cases were more likely to receive death sentences (Baldus & Woodworth, 1997). The GAO evaluation synthesis further revealed that in 82 percent of the studies, race of victim was found to influence the likelihood of being charged with capital murder or receiving the death penalty. . . . This finding was remarkably consistent across data sets, states, data collection methods, and analytic techniques. (U.S. General Accounting Office, 1990, p. 5)

The report also noted that "the race of victim influence was stronger for the earlier stages of the judicial process (e.g., prosecutorial decision to charge defendant with a capital offense, decision to proceed to trial rather than plea bargain) than in later stages" (U.S. General Accounting Office, 1990, p. 5).

More recent data do not indicate any change in the situation. As of January 1, 2010, about 80% of the victims of those persons executed under post–*Furman* statutes have been White, and only about 13% have been Black. Yet, 56% of defendants executed have been White, while 35% have been black (Criminal Justice Project, 2010). Discrimination seems apparent because, historically, capital crimes were generally intraracial (see Zahn, 1989). For example, in 2009, White offenders murdered 84% of white victims, and Black offenders murdered 91% of Black victims (when race of victim and offender were known) (Federal Bureau of Investigation, 2010a). Still, uncertainty remains about whether the data show discrimination because only about 20% of murders and nonnegligent manslaughters are capital crimes. It seems likely that the percentage of interracial murders may be somewhat greater for capital murders than it is for noncapital murders.

Studies found that the source of racial disparity/discrimination under super due process is located predominately in the discretionary actions of prosecutors and, to a lesser extent, juries. (Evidence suggests that prosecutors and juries are also sources of arbitrariness in the death penalty's application.) Baldus and his colleagues declare that "the exercise of prosecutorial discretion [in seeking a death sentence] is the principal source of the race-of-victim disparities observed in the system" (Baldus, Woodworth, & Pulaski, 1990, p. 403). In Georgia (and in other states) a capital sentencing hearing is a preliminary stage in the process that leads to a capital trial. Under Georgia's post–*Furman* statute, Black defendants whose victims were White were advanced to a capital sentencing hearing by prosecutors at a rate nearly five times that of Black defendants whose victims were Black, and more than three times the rate of White defendants whose victims were Black (Baldus, Pulaski, & Woodworth, 1983). Other research found that prosecutors sought the death penalty in 70% of cases involving Black defendants and White victims and in only 35% of the cases involving other racial combinations (Bright, 1997b). A study of Maryland's death penalty found that, after controlling for relevant case characteristics, the killers of White victims, especially if they were Black, were substantially more likely than the killers of non-whites to be charged by prosecutors with a capital crime and for the charge to "stick," that is, not be withdrawn by the prosecutor once the death notification was filed (Paternoster & Brame, 2003).

In Florida, prosecutors have "upgraded" and "downgraded" potential capital cases under super due process by alleging aggravating circumstances, charging defendants with an accompanying felony, ignoring evidence in police reports, and withholding an accompanying charge depending on the race of the offender and of the victim (Bowers, 1984; Radelet, 1981; Radelet & Pierce, 1985). Radelet and Pierce (1985) report that "cases in which blacks were accused of killing whites were the most likely to be upgraded and least likely to be downgraded" (p. 6). Prosecutors also have reduced death-eligible cases with White defendant or Black victim to noncapital ones through plea bargaining, or they have foregone a penalty trial and thus waived the death penalty, even when a defendant was convicted by a jury of a capital offense (Baldus et al., 1990). Prosecutors engaged in similar actions in other states (Baldus et al., 1990; Gross & Mauro, 1989; Sorensen & Wallace, 1999).

How Do We Fix It? Suggestions for Reform

After more than 35 years of the Court's "tinkering with the machinery of death," to use former Justice Harry Blackmun's evocative phrase (*Callins v. Collins*, 1994), it may be impossible to fix capital punishment in the United States, if "fixing" it means substantially reducing the problems of arbitrary and discriminatory application, and especially the problems of wrongful convictions and executions. Thus, the only way to fix the problems with capital punishment is to abolish it. However, short of total abolition there are numerous reforms that proponents of the penalty hope will make the capital punishment process less egregious. The problem with reform is that capital punishment, like any other sanction, invariably is imposed arbitrarily and too often in a discriminatory way. In addition, errors and mistakes are made by all of its participants and continue to plague the entire capital punishment process. To err is human. The problems are individual and structural, intentional and accidental. After 35 years of trying, further reform efforts are probably a fool's errand.

Good Defense Attorneys Can Make a Difference[1]

The quality of legal representation is arguably the most critical problem with the current capital punishment process. Unfortunately, most capital defendants are indigent and are not represented by privately retained defense counsel skilled in the complexities of capital jurisprudence, but instead are represented by court-appointed lawyers or public defenders who are inexperienced, overworked, understaffed, unprepared, less resourceful, less independent, poorly compensated, and, in some cases, have been reprimanded, disciplined, or subsequently disbarred (Bedau, 1982; Bowers, 1984; Coyle, Strasser, & Lavelle, 1990; Dow, 2002, 2005; Mello & Perkins, 1998).

In 2003, the American Bar Association's House of Delegates approved a revised edition of its 1989 guidelines for the appointment and performance of defense counsel in death penalty cases. The revised edition was created because of deficiencies in the older guidelines. However, as of May 2012, only three death penalty states—Kansas, Kentucky, and Oregon—explicitly follow the ABA guidelines (National Center for State Courts, 2012). The reason is twofold. First, according to critics of the guidelines, they are too expensive to implement (Post, 2004). Second, the Supreme Court has not required them. In fact, in *Strickland v. Washington* (1984), the case that provided a test for determining when counsel is ineffective, the Court adamantly refused to adopt performance guidelines for evaluating counsel in capital cases (Williams, 2005). It gave three reasons for its position. First, the Court pointed out the purpose of the effective assistance guarantee was "not to improve the quality of legal representation" (*Strickland v. Washington*, 1984, p. 699). Second, the Court opined that "no particular set of detailed rules for counsel's conduct can satisfactorily take account of the variety of circumstances faced by defense counsel or the range of legitimate decisions regarding how best to represent a criminal defendant" (pp. 708–709). Third, the Court was concerned that the adoption of specific standards would encourage ineffectiveness claims, which would discourage many attorneys from representing defendants in capital cases.

As of May 23, 2012, only three death penalty states adopted the 2003 ABA guidelines; however, 28 of the 33 death penalty states adopted their own minimum guidelines or standards for the appointment of counsel

---

[1] Space limitations preclude a detailed discussion of possible reforms; the interested reader should consult the following sources: Scheck, Neufeld, and Dwyer, 2001; State of Illinois, 2002; and The Constitution Project, 2005. Unless indicated otherwise, the information presented below is from these sources.

at either the trial or appellate level, or both in capital cases (National Center for State Courts, 2012). The only death penalty states that have not yet adopted any minimum guidelines or standards are Delaware, Mississippi, New Hampshire, Ohio, South Dakota, and Wyoming. Clearly, these standards are better than no standards at all, but none of them can be considered particularly rigorous; they are truly minimum standards.

In addition, defense counsel in capital cases (including those in states with guidelines or standards) rarely has the resources necessary to mount an effective defense. It is not unusual for attorneys in capital cases to be compensated at less than minimum wage, and states have been known to appoint attorneys in capital cases who submitted the lowest bids (Bright, 1997b).

Punish the Misconduct of Defense Attorneys

Most acts of misconduct by defense attorneys in capital cases should result in the attorney being disciplined by the state bar association. Where applicable, such disciplined attorneys should be removed from the roster of attorneys eligible to handle death penalty cases. For egregious cases of misconduct, defense attorneys should be disbarred.

Improve Police Investigations, Interrogations, and the Handling of Evidence

Police should keep an open and objective mind during investigations. They should investigate crimes rather than trying to build a case against a likely suspect. Once a suspect has been identified, the police should continue to pursue all reasonable leads, whether they point toward or away from the suspect.

To reduce the number of false confessions, defense counsel should be provided to indigent suspects during police interrogation in potential death penalty cases. When there is doubt about whether the suspect is indigent, defense counsel should be provided. Police should also make a reasonable attempt to determine if a suspect is mentally retarded. If the suspect is deemed mentally retarded, the police should not ask leading questions (mentally retarded suspects are inclined to agree with the police version of events) and/or suggest that they believe the suspect is guilty.

In potential death penalty cases, the entire police custodial interrogation should be videorecorded to help validate the interrogation and confessions. Where videorecording is not feasible, audiorecording should be substituted. Interviews with significant witnesses in homicide cases should also be electronically recorded.

To make certain that the police provide all the evidence in their possession to the prosecution (a) all relevant evidence, including exculpatory evidence and its location, should be listed on schedules by the police, (b) specific police officers or employees should be assigned recordkeeping responsibility, and (c) prosecutors should be given certified written copies of the evidence schedules by the police.

Improve Eyewitness Identification Techniques and Procedures

Experts agree that the accuracy of eyewitness identifications could be greatly improved if several policy reforms were adopted in all jurisdictions, including the videotaping of all lineups, photo spreads, and other identification processes so that later any biases, suggestions, or hints that infected the process could be exposed and evaluated. In addition, convictions for murder based on the testimony of a single eyewitness or accomplice, without any other corroboration, should never be eligible for the death penalty.

Punish Police Misconduct

Depending on the seriousness of the misconduct, offending police officers should be reprimanded, suspended without pay, decertified (if applicable), or terminated. Particularly serious misconduct by police officers should be prosecuted in the federal courts.

Improve the Work and Credibility of Crime Lab Technicians

To promote greater credibility in the work of crime lab technicians, such labs and their budgets should be independent and not under the supervision of a police department or prosecutor's office, as is typically the case. Crime labs should also be accredited by professional organizations and subject to regulatory oversight and external blind proficiency testing (in which samples are sent in as ordinary evidence to corroborate the validity of results). Agent technicians who make mistakes should be disciplined.

Require DNA Testing

DNA testing should be required in cases in which DNA evidence is available and there is a reasonable probability that the DNA results could exonerate the defendant

Set Rigorous Standards for Jailhouse Snitches/Informants

Before allowing a jailhouse snitch/informant to testify, a committee of prosecutors should be able to provide satisfactory answers to the following questions: (a) Is there corroborating evidence to support their statement, other than the testimony of another snitch? (b) Does the statement provide details of the crime, or lead to evidence that could only be known by the perpetrator? (c) Could the incriminating evidence have been obtained from a source other than the accused, such as press accounts or legal proceedings? (d) Does the snitch/informant have a reputation for being dishonest? And (e) Does the snitch/informant regularly provide incriminating evidence? There should be a presumption that the testimony of a jailhouse snitch/informant is unreliable, and the prosecutor should be required to overcome that presumption before a jury is allowed to hear the evidence. Any deal that police officers or prosecutors make with a snitch/informant should be recorded, preferably videotaped. Finally, the uncorroborated testimony of a jailhouse snitch/informant witness about the confession or admission of the defendant should never be the sole basis for imposition of a death penalty.

Guide Prosecutors' Decisions to Seek the Death Penalty

Statewide written protocols should be developed to guide county prosecutors in making death penalty determinations. The guidelines should include the requirement that each county prosecutor establish within his or her office a committee to review homicide cases where the death penalty may be sought in order to assist the prosecutor in making the decision. Prior to trial, the governor should appoint a statewide committee to review death eligibility decisions made by prosecutors. When the committee decides that death is not the appropriate sentence in the case, the prosecutor should not be authorized to overrule and to seek the death penalty. Committee authorization of the death penalty should become mandatory and required by statute.

Improve Disclosure Requirements

The prosecutor should be required to file a certificate with the court at least 14 days before the date set for the trial guaranteeing that all material that is required to be disclosed to the defense has been disclosed. Following conviction, the prosecutor should have a continuing obligation to make timely disclosure to the defendant's counsel, or the defendant if not represented by counsel, of the existence of evidence known to the prosecutor that tends to negate the guilt of the defendant or mitigate the defendant's capital sentence.

Punish Prosecutor Misconduct

For extreme misconduct, prosecutors should be criminally prosecuted. At the least, statutes should be narrowed that grant prosecutors broad immunity from civil suits in cases of intentional misconduct. For egregious cases of misconduct, prosecutors should be disbarred.

Better Training and Certification of Trial Judges in Capital Cases

Capital case training should be provided for all trial judges who preside over capital cases. The training should be required before a judge hears a capital case. A statewide bench manual covering capital cases should also be developed and used. Trial judges should be certified to hear capital cases by the state supreme court or the chief judges of judicial circuits. Certification should be based on experience and training. Only certified judges should hear capital cases.

Give Trial Judges Veto Power

The trial judge should have to indicate on the record whether he or she agrees with the jury's sentence of death. When the judge does not agree with the jury's death sentence, the defendant must not be sentenced to death.

Eliminate Time Limits and Other Constraints on Claims of Actual Innocence

Claims of actual innocence in capital cases based on newly discovered evidence should be heard by a court of record any time after conviction, without regard for other post–conviction matters or timing. Also, state "closed discovery" laws should be repealed. Those laws prevent defense attorneys or journalists from reviewing evidence following a conviction, thus making the detection of miscarriages of justice even more difficult.

Improve the Clemency Process

To make officials more accountable in their decision making, clemency boards should hold public hearings to determine their recommendations to the governor. Governors should meet personally with attorneys and should be required to provide the public with an explanation of their clemency decisions. Better yet, to depoliticize the process, clemency decisions should not be made by governors, but, instead by respected three-judge panels.

Moratorium

Short of total abolition, some observers, including some respected individuals who support the death penalty in principle, have called for a moratorium on executions until some of the more egregious problems with its administration are fixed.

 # Conclusion

Currently, the United States is one of only 57 countries in the world to retain the death penalty; more than 70% of the world's nations have abolished it in law or in practice (Amnesty International, 2012). As noted previously, 35 jurisdictions in the United States have capital punishment statutes; 18 jurisdictions do not. In 19 of those 35 jurisdictions, fewer than 10 inmates have been executed since 1976. Three of those 19 jurisdictions—Kansas, New Hampshire, and the U.S. military—have not executed anyone since at least 1976. On the other hand, five death penalty jurisdictions have executed nearly two-thirds of the inmates executed since 1976: Texas, Virginia, Oklahoma, Florida, and Missouri. Texas, alone, accounts for 37% of all executions in the United States since 1976. Thus, except for fewer than 30% of the world's countries, a handful of states in the United States, and a few counties in those states, the death penalty is a dying practice. Clearly, those countries and states without a death penalty (or without imposing the death penalty) are able to administer justice and avoid calamities without capital punishment.

KEY TERMS

Aggravating factor	*Furman v. Georgia*	Mandatory death penalty statutes
Arbitrariness	General deterrence	
Automatic appellate review	*Gregg v. Georgia*	Mitigating factor
	Guided discretion death penalty statutes	Proportionality review
Bifurcated trial		Super due process
Collateral review	Jury nullification	

DISCUSSION QUESTIONS

1. Discuss the three procedural reforms to the death penalty made by the Court in the case *Gregg v. Georgia.*

2. In *Furman,* the Court overturned the death penalty, arguing that it was arbitrary and discriminatory. Has the practice of capital punisment today resolved the concerns of the *Furman* court? Why or why not?

3. Discuss the feasibility of the suggested reforms to capital punishment. What is needed from the criminal justice system in order to satisfy these concerns?

WEBSITES FOR ADDITIONAL RESEARCH

Death Penalty Information Center: http://www.deathpenaltyinfo.org/

Death Penalty Focus: http://www.deathpenalty.org/

Amnesty International: http://www.amnestyusa.org/

PEW Forum: http://www.pewforum.org/topics/issues/Death-Penalty/

Sentencing Project: http://www.sentencingproject.org/template/index.cfm

National Registry of Exonerations: http://www.law.umich.edu/special/exoneration/Pages/about.aspx

Innocence Project: http://www.innocenceproject.org/

CHAPTER

XIX

Reentry and Rehabilitation

Generating Successful Outcomes During Challenging Times

Faith E. Lutze and Roger L. Schaefer

eentry to the community from prison is a process that poses many challenges both to the ex-offender experiencing the transition and the professionals tasked with managing the process. For the ex-offender it means reengaging with family, friends, work, and treatment while navigating the pitfalls of encountering criminal peers, living in high-risk neighborhoods, and managing impulsive behaviors. For the ***community corrections officer*** it means working with the offender to monitor compliance with court-ordered conditions; guiding ex-offenders through legal, economic, emotional, and social challenges; and managing the multiple criminal justice, social services, and public health partnerships necessary to effectively transition ex-offenders into the community. Therefore, ***community corrections*** is one of the most important components of the criminal justice system because it has the power to intervene on multiple levels over time to influence positive outcomes for the individual, the community, and the system. Although community corrections is extremely important to the overall success of the criminal justice system, it has not generally garnered the respect that it deserves.

Since the demise of the rehabilitative ideal beginning in the 1970s, community corrections was often criticized for being "soft on crime" and ineffective in keeping the community safe from dangerous offenders released from prison. In recent decades, community corrections experienced somewhat of an identity crisis: trying to adhere to its rehabilitative origins (designed to engage the ex-offender in the reentry process), while attempting to achieve contemporary legitimacy within a crime control era focused on strict monitoring, rule enforcement, and sanctioning noncompliance. This has caused an ideological debate within the profession about whether community corrections should provide rehabilitation or punishment, support or accountability, guidance or coercion, social work or law enforcement. Ironically, this conflict often leaves community corrections vulnerable to being ineffective at both meeting the individual needs of the ex-offender and the safety needs of the community.

In this chapter, we argue that it is time for community corrections to move beyond oversimplistic ideologically defined approaches to supervision, and resolve the rehabilitation or punishment debate by implementing balanced, evidence-based interventions designed to reduce recidivism and improve long-term reintegration. First, we place community corrections and prisoner reentry into a political, economic, and social context as it relates to contemporary circumstances that pose serious challenges to community corrections and successful reentry. Second, we present what is known about effective strategies to reduce recidivism and achieve reintegration at both the individual level of intervention and at the agency level of operation. Finally, we recommend strategies that can be implemented by policy makers as they take responsibility for supporting and intelligently guiding the future of community corrections.

As a brief review of the current political, economic, and social context of community corrections shows, there are serious challenges confronting community corrections due to an ongoing political emphasis on narrowly defined punitive policies, the contemporary fiscal crises, and the existence of distressed communities attempting to absorb ex-offenders. It is within this reality that community corrections exists and must be managed to achieve success.

The Back Story: The Political, Economic, and Social Context of Community Corrections

Until recently, the corrections system of the United States was driven by a philosophy of offender reform and rehabilitation. Community supervision became institutionalized during the Progressive Era (1900–1920) with the establishment of the indeterminate sentence to accommodate individual differences in reform and the early release of "cured" inmates from prisons by parole boards. Ex-prisoners, once reformed in the prison, needed the assistance of parole officers to achieve full reintegration into the community (Pisciotta, 1994). Rehabilitation continued to dominate corrections until the 1970s when major social and political upheaval caused both liberals and conservatives alike to question the integrity and effectiveness of the rehabilitative model as the core philosophy guiding corrections (Cullen & Jonson, 2012).

The political unrest of the 1960s, including several prison riots and increasing crime rates, attracted scrutiny to many criminal justice practices (see Cullen & Jonson, 2012; Garland, 2001). Liberals questioned the power of the state concluding that rehabilitation was never truly implemented and indeterminate sentences allowed for discriminatory practices resulting in longer and harsher punishments for the poor and racial minorities. Conservatives argued that the social unrest and rising crime rates were due to a weakened police force, lenient judges, and permissive parole boards. Many contended, however, that the total demise of rehabilitation was completed with the publication of the Martinson Report (Martinson, 1974).

Martinson (1974) reviewed 231 studies of correctional interventions and reported that one could not reliably conclude what works in correctional rehabilitation because of the broad array of programs and the poor quality of many of the studies. The timing of his report leant strong support for the critics of rehabilitation, and the results were rapidly translated into "***nothing works***" in correctional rehabilitation. Although the Martinson study was almost immediately rebutted by Palmer (1975) and by Martinson (1979) himself. After reassessing his own data, Martinson determined that programs that were theoretically informed and targeted appropriate populations did indeed work; however, the damage had been done and the momentum opposing rehabilitation was too strong to be altered.

The agreement between liberals and conservatives also ended with the belief that rehabilitation should be abandoned, and their disagreement began with a fury about what should be the guiding philosophy of the criminal justice system, and specifically corrections, into the future (see Cullen & Jonson, 2012). Liberals argued for restricting discretion in order to limit state power and to implement due process protections to rid the system of abuse and discrimination against poor and minority offenders. Conservatives argued to limit the discretion of lenient judges and to get tough on crime through more punitive crime control measures to ensure the rights of victims and to provide for safer communities. In the end, the conservative crime control model, steeped in deterrence and retribution, directed the criminal justice system and each of its institutions. The initiation of the "war on crime," followed by the "war on drugs," had a dramatic impact, not only on the criminal justice system and corrections, but also on our communities. The full impact of these philosophical changes from rehabilitation to crime control, retribution, and deterrence and the practical impact of the resulting policies on corrections, offenders, and communities would not become fully understood until much later (Clear, 2007; Cullen & Jonson, 2012; Garland, 2001; Mele & Miller, 2005; Petersilia, 2003; Travis, 2005).

Beginning in the 1970s, the punitive shift in the political environment of the United States led to increases in prison admissions, longer sentences, mandatory minimum sentences, reductions in prison programs, and laws restricting publicly funded social support for convicted felons (Garland, 2001; Mele & Miller, 2005; Petersilia, 2003). Cumulatively, these policies led to a dramatic increase in our prison and jail populations with approximately 2.5 million people incarcerated and as a result, approximately 740,000 inmates released from prison each year. Combined with those persons who are already under supervision, approximately 5 million people are under some form of state control while living in the community (The Pew Center on the States, 2009). This increase in the corrections population created a significant burden for state and county governments, the prison system, community corrections, and the communities affected by the return of the offenders.

The economic burden caused by the institutional expansion of corrections caused severe limits on state and local governments' ability to invest in cost effective and successful prevention programs, public health, education, and other social services that are related to easing the pains of poverty and other conditions highly correlated with crime. For instance, many states during the 1980s and 1990s responded to increasing prison populations by attempting to build their way out of the crisis by spending an estimated $47 billion on prison construction nationally, then followed by billions spent annually to operate existing prisons (SCJS, Sourcebook of Criminal Justice Statistics, 2006; The Pew Center on the States, 2009). Interestingly, the recent recession has forced many states to cut education, public health, and social service budgets in order to sustain corrections expenditures (Grattet, Petersilia, Lin, & Beckman, 2009; Hughes, 2006; Petersilia, 2003).[1]

In spite of the fact that most of the corrections population resides within community corrections, in many jurisdictions there are competing needs and political pressure to favor prisons over community corrections (Lehman & Labecki, 1998). Therefore, since the late 1970s community corrections spending stagnated (Petersilia, 2002). The disproportionate spending on prisons is evident with only 32% of the correctional population incarcerated, yet that same population consumes 88% of correctional

---

[1] For instance, spending on corrections increased 1,173% from 1997 to 2003 compared to 505% for education, 572% for hospitals and health care, 577% for interest on debt, and 766% for public welfare (Hughes, 2006, p. 4).

costs (The Pew Center on the States, 2009). Within prison spending, most of the resources are directed toward labor costs, maintaining the physical plant, and goods and services with many state and federal corrections systems cutting education and vocational programs, substance abuse and mental health counseling, and life skills courses designed to engage inmates in pro-social activities and reduce recidivism (Petersilia, 2003). Even though prisons have become more expensive, inmates today are much less likely than those in the past to participate in programs to alleviate the personal and situational conditions that originally brought them to prison.

✖ The Current State of Prison Reentry

Many of the life situations of those released from prison are stark, and the individual challenges they confront in order to become successfully reintegrated are many. The average parolee is male (93%), under the age of 34 (50%), undereducated and oftentimes functionally illiterate (33% < high school diploma), and a racial or ethnic minority (38% Black, 20% Hispanic) (Clear, 2007; Petersilia, 2003; Sabol, West, & Cooper, 2009, pp. 2, 36; Government Accounting Office, 2000). Parolees are also more likely than the general population to suffer from poor mental health, physical health, substance abuse, co-occurring disorders, infectious diseases, learning disabilities, homelessness, and violent victimization (Deadman & MacDonald, 2004; Falshaw, 2005; Petersilia, 2003; Roman & Travis, 2006).

The quality of the prison experiences also affects reentry. Recent research shows that victimization in prison is common with 22% of maximum security federal inmates, 35% of male state inmates, and 24% of female state inmates reporting physical victimization by either staff or other inmates (Listwan, Colvin, Hanley, & Flannery, 2010). Research shows that the harsher the prison environment the more difficult it is to cope with the transition to the community and living in unsafe neighborhoods often results in a persistent and heightened awareness to avoid victimization and a sense of isolation, fear, distrust, learned helplessness, and the perception that one is alone to deal with psychological distress (see Lutze & Kigerl, 2013).

The communities that offenders are most often released to are stressed neighborhoods. Poor communities often have fewer resources available from private sector businesses resulting in few if any places to purchase basic goods, such as food, clothing, or other life staples (Clear, 2007; Rank, 2004). Public institutions, although present, are also limited and represented by failing public schools, overcrowded medical clinics with little to offer in preventative care, and social service agencies that are often perceived by residents as controlling versus empowering (Jones, 2010; Raphael, 2000). The cumulative effect of limited private services and underresourced and overburdened public sector services results in greater distances to travel for jobs, fewer businesses to purchase goods and services, less education, poorer health, and higher odds of early death (Rank, 2004).

Yet, it is within this political, economic, and social context that ex-offenders and community corrections professionals are expected to succeed. Community corrections is given the responsibility of successfully managing ex-offenders at the end of a cross-systems journey (i.e., public education, public health, social services, and criminal justice) made by offenders that has not prepared them, either before or during prison, for reentry into a community context that is diminished in its capacity to support successful reentry. We argue, however, that even within these very challenging circumstances, we know how to bring about effective change that will enhance successful reintegration, reduce recidivism, and bring the role of community corrections within reasonable expectations for achieving success. Understanding the conditions and experiences of those involved in reentry leads to a clearer understanding of why some correctional programs work to reduce recidivism and why so many fail.

Race, Gender, and Class Implications of the Policy

It is also clear that poor and minority Americans, especially African Americans and *Latinos*, painfully experience more than others the effects of punitive crime control policies (Unnever & Cullen, 2010; Lutze, 2006; Reiman, 2004). This is evident in that 1 in 45 Whites, 1 in 27 Hispanics, and 1 in 11 Blacks are under some form of state control (The Pew Center on the States, 2009). When race, sex, and social economic class are combined, the statistics are alarming, with young, poor, Black males being incarcerated far more than any other group (The Pew Center on the States, 2009; Travis, Solomon, & Waul, 2001). In poor, urban neighborhoods it is not unusual for 1 in 3 young Black men to be under some form of state control. Black men in general have a 29% lifetime chance of serving at least one year in prison, compared to 16% of Hispanic males (any race), and 5% of White males (Travis, Solomon, & Waul, 2001, p. 12). Poor and minority women have not escaped harsh crime control policies either. As a result of harsh drug laws and mandatory minimums, the number of women in prison has dramatically increased since 1990, especially for young Black women (Sabol, West, & Cooper, 2009; SCJS, 2008). The effects are dire when recognition is given to the fact that these women are also much more likely to have custody of their minor children than are males.

It can also be argued that the economic burden caused by prison expansion has a disproportionate effect on poor communities that the rest of society does not directly experience (Clear, 2007). Due to the fact that poverty is not randomly distributed in the United States, but is often concentrated in urban minority communities, the cost of incarceration does not affect everyone equally (Clear, 2007; Petersilia, 2003; Rank, 2004). Given that most offenders processed by the criminal justice system are poor, and public money has shifted away from education, health, and social services to support our prison system instead, poor communities experience both the disproportionate loss of citizens (primarily young males) due to incarceration and the loss of valuable public services due to the costs of prisons. These sentencing and monetary policies remove productive young males from the general population and away from supporting their families, through both legal and illegal means, while at the same time diminishing public support networks that would traditionally help to fill in the gap. Due to the effects of incarceration, these young men often remain out of productive labor long after release from prison.

The removal of so many young men and increasing numbers of women from communities where incarceration is concentrated creates conditions that are not easily addressed by community corrections, even when possible. There is also a strongly held myth by many politicians and their constituents that the majority of offenders, especially those living in poor communities, can easily or successfully overcome the challenges confronting them on reentry, if only they worked harder (conservative perspective) or greater opportunities were provided to them (liberal perspective) (Rank, 2004). There is a failure by both political camps to understand how the structural inequality that leads to concentrated poverty and incarceration also sabotages an individual's ability to work harder or to take advantage of opportunities, if they should exist. Ongoing structural inequality during both good and bad times creates a climate where state institutions, including social services, police, and corrections, are perceived as intrusive, controlling, and not to be trusted (Clear, 2007; Jones, 2010; Mele & Miller, 2005; Petersilia, 2003; Rank, 2004; Raphael, 2000).

Therefore, a willingness for citizens to work with the very agencies and professionals designated to support reentry efforts, whether community corrections or social services, is diminished.

⊠ What Research Has Taught Us: Evidence-Based Practices and Reentry

The multiple problems confronted by those individuals who are released from prison clearly demonstrate that punitive measures alone will not result in long-term change. Ex-offenders need assistance in dealing with educational and skill deficits, mental health problems, substance abuse, housing, employment, and reintegration with family. They also must change their antisocial attitudes and behaviors that increase their risk to recidivate and threaten community safety. Many new approaches to reentry have emerged based on a greater understanding of the conditions that contribute to reentry failure and an onslaught of methodologically strong research showing that correctional programs work to reduce recidivism. Recent reentry initiatives focus on coordinating services across systems, utilizing evidence-based programs, increasing contact with offenders, providing structure, and holding offenders accountable for their behavior.

What Works to Enhance Success in Community Corrections

Research clearly shows that correctional programs are effective in decreasing recidivism when they are theoretically informed, targeted toward high-risk and high-need offenders, and implemented with structural integrity according to the model's intended design (Andrews & Bonta, 2010; Cullen & Jonson, 2012; MacKenzie, 2006). Evidence-based practice refers to the implementation of programs proven to increase intended outcomes as a result of rigorous scientific evaluation. The most relevant findings related to evidence-based practices in correctional interventions are (a) the development of reliable and valid *risk assessment tools*, (b) the *risk, need, and responsivity (RNR)* model of correctional interventions, (c) *cognitive-behavioral treatment* programs (CBT), (d) singular interventions that focus on offender needs, (e) the integration of *cultural competency* into interventions, and (f) planned and coordinated responses to reentry.

Risk Assessment Tools

An important development related to correctional treatment in the last 30 years is the improvement of risk and need assessments (Andrews & Bonta, 2010). Risk assessments are important because they allow for the classification of offenders into low, moderate, and high-risk groups that guide correction's personnel to determine what level of control and treatment are necessary to have the greatest effect on outcomes. Risk assessment tools allow corrections to move beyond anecdotal and clinical perceptions about what appears to work toward the ability to more accurately specify who is at greatest risk of failure and to target those in the greatest need of services (Andrews & Bonta, 2010).

Risk, Need, and Responsivity

Programs that target offender risks, needs, and responsivity (RNR) have repeatedly been shown to reduce recidivism among high-risk offenders. Risks, as articulated by Andrews and Bonta (2010, p. 20), are "characteristics of people and their circumstances that are associated with an increased chance of criminal activity." They identify criminogenic needs as those risk factors that are "dynamic," meaning they are risk factors that can be changed through interventions (Andrews & Bonta, 2010, p. 21). In general, responsivity is an approach that considers the "ability and learning style of the offender" in an effort to empower him or her in the rehabilitation process (Andrews & Bonta, 2010, p. 49).

Andrews and Bonta (2010) developed the RNR model based on evaluations of the factors statistically related to increased criminal conduct. They determined that there are four key attributes common to the majority of offenders: antisocial attitudes, antisocial peers, antisocial personality, and having a criminal history. They also propose that familial or marital circumstances, educational or vocational attainment or involvement, gratification in leisure or recreational activities, and substance abuse problems are scientifically relevant to criminal conduct. They argue that programs that do not target these risk and criminogenic needs fail to change behavior and impact recidivism. Several large studies showed that interventions that are implemented based on the RNR model are effective in reducing recidivism up to 30%, while those that fail to include the principles of RNR resulted in no effect or may even have an iatrogenic effect by increasing recidivism (see Andrews & Bonta, 2010; Cullen & Jonson, 2012; Lowenkamp, Latessa, & Holsinger, 2006; Lowenkamp, Latessa, & Smith, 2006).

Cognitive-Behavioral Treatment

Another type of intervention proven to be effective founded on rigorous scientific evaluations is cognitive-behavioral treatments (CBT). CBT is a learning-oriented approach that demands that the client engage in the here-and-now in an effort to address problematic thinking and behavioral patterns. Although CBT is sometimes thought of as a single approach, it actually represents a wide range of therapeutic methods (Gideon & Sung, 2011). Therefore, CBT interventions can be adapted to the targeted cognitive processes and behaviors that need to be changed, such as antisocial attitudes, substance abuse, anger, and other behaviors highly correlated with criminal behavior.

Several meta-analyses show that CBT interventions effectively reduce recidivism when used with offender populations (Andrews & Bonta, 2010; Landenberger & Lipsey, 2005; Lowenkamp, Hubbard, Makarios, & Latessa, 2012; MacKenzie, 2000; Wilson, Bouffard, & MacKenzie, 2005). For example, Wilson et al., (2005) found moral recognition therapy resulted in a 33% reduction in recidivism while cognitive restructuring or reasoning approaches resulted in a 16% reduction. Landenberger and Lipsey (2005) found that increased dosages of CBT, as measured by the total number of sessions/hours per week, reduced recidivism by 25% and that CBT programs that utilize a higher standard for quality implementation had a greater impact on reducing recidivism. Similarly, Lipsey, Chapman, and Landenberger (2001) found that while overall those offenders who participated in CBT recidivated at approximately one-third the rate of those who did not participate, programs that were classified as "demonstration" programs were more effective in reducing recidivism. As is discussed later, these findings are important because they provide evidence that implementers of proven intervention models must not alter the core principles of the program, or the strength of the outcomes are diminished.

Singular Interventions Focused on Offender Needs

Individual interventions directed toward education, housing, mental health, substance abuse treatment, and employment also are effective strategies to reduce recidivism and aid in the successful reintegration of ex-offenders into the community. Many offenders who are under community supervision live in the same economically depressed and socially disorganized communities that they did before prison (Clear, 2007; Kirk, 2009, 2012; Kubrin & Stewart, 2006). Thus, many need help with basic human necessities, such as a place to live, personal safety, nourishment, and companionship. While these specific needs are not in and of themselves criminogenic, the pressure put on an offender for these essentials can negatively impact their ability to engage in programs necessary to bring about change (see Lutze & Kigerl, 2013). Therefore, the most successful strategies to reentry often focus on changing attitudes and behaviors (RNR and CBT) while at the same time addressing the basic human needs necessary to clear the path toward program engagement and change.

Educational performance and functionality are identified as important to ex-offenders' ability to be successful. Many offenders have low levels of education and many are functionally illiterate (Petersilia, 2003). This often prevents individuals from fully engaging in treatment or employment. There is sufficient scientific evidence that educational and vocational programs delivered in prison and in the community reduce recidivism and increase employment opportunities. For instance, in a meta-analysis, including educational and vocational programs, Wilson, Gallagher, and MacKenzie (2000) found that basic education programs were associated with lower recidivism rates (41% vs. 50%) compared to those programs that did not offer any educational opportunities. The differences in recidivism were even greater for college-level programs (37% vs. 50%) and vocational training (39% vs. 50%) (Lawrence, Mears, Dubin, & Travis, 2002; Wilson et al., 2000). Similarly, work release and vocational training programs are effective in reducing recidivism and improving work-related skills for ex-offenders (see Seiter & Kadela, 2003).

Substance abuse and drug addiction have also long been connected to poor performance for those being supervised in the community. Drug use violates the conditions of supervision and makes it more difficult to sustain a viable place to live, find employment, and refrain from committing new crimes (Petersilia, 2003). Addiction also diminishes one's cognitive abilities to make proper decisions or to consume new information relevant to supervision and treatment success (Lutze & van Wormer, 2007). Overall, drug treatment programs significantly reduce recidivism and increase other prosocial behaviors (Taxman & Bouffard, 2000; Butzin, O'Connell, Martin, & Incairdi, 2006). For instance, a meta-analysis conducted by Prendergast, Podus, Chang, and Urada (2002) found that substance abuse treatment significantly reduced both substance use and criminal activity and was most effective for younger offenders (also see MacKenzie, 2006). In addition, Butzin and his colleagues (2006) found that drug treatment within the context of therapeutic communities significantly reduced an offender's propensity for rearrest and increased their time in the community. Therapeutic communities are also effective in addressing various aspects of community reentry, particularly helping ex-offenders with co-occurring disorders (MacKenzie, 2006; Deitch, Carleton, Koutsenok, & Marsolais, 2002), and creating a group atmosphere for ex-offenders that provides support and accountability (Kennard & Roberts, 1983; Prendergast & Burdon, 2002).

There is strong evidence that housing instability often leads to incarceration and experiences of incarceration often lead to housing instability (Geller & Curtis, 2011; Metraux & Culhane, 2004, 2006). Without a stable and safe place to live, individuals must constantly worry about where to sleep and how to protect themselves. They also have no place from which to search for work, receive benefits, prepare for treatment, keep their belongings, or take care of their basic human needs (Roman & Travis, 2006). Fortunately, a growing body of research shows that providing housing support significantly reduces recidivism for high-risk/need offenders, substance abusing offenders, and those with serious mental illness (Culhane, Metraux, & Hadley, 2002; Lutze, Hamilton, & Rosky, 2012; Miller & Ngugi, 2009; Worcel, Burrus, Finigan, Sanders, & Allen, 2009).

Cultural Competency

Within all of these successful interventions, increasing evidence strongly suggests that programs need to be culturally competent to enhance outcomes across different groups (see Lutze, 2006; Lutze et al., 2012; Lutze & van Wormer, 2007). Many interventions were historically designed to serve adult male populations and then are extrapolated to other groups with the expectation that they will work just as well. It is well known, however, that interventions are often perceived and experienced differently based on race/ethnicity, gender, class, education, age, and other social demographic characteristics.

Yet, the demographic differences in outcomes within successful programs are oftentimes ignored in favor of reporting the overall success of the program. Although it is important to know what programs are most effective in reducing recidivism overall, it is also relevant to know who they do not work for and why so that positive outcomes can be shared by all participants. Based on a review of cultural competency in drug courts, Lutze and van Wormer (2007, p. 234) conclude "Although we must focus on equality in access to services, giving everyone treatment that is based on a male model of addiction is not equality and may lead to disparity in outcomes." Therefore, cultural competency goes beyond merely building awareness about group differences by requiring an understanding about how life experiences may differ based on demographic characteristics and how these differences may influence perceptions of and engagement in interventions. Poor outcomes may not be because the ex-offender failed to engage in the treatment, but that the treatment failed to engage the ex-offender.

Coordinated Responses to Reentry and a Continuum of Care

The discovery of so many evidence-based practices that are successful in reducing recidivism and increasing community safety led to concerns about how best to deliver what works in a coordinated manner that enhances overall outcomes. Research consistently shows that most ex-offenders fail within the first 90 days of reentry due primarily to technical violations, and an estimated 67% will fail within 3 years (see Hamilton & Campbell, 2013; Petersilia, 2003). Attempting to address the multiple needs of offenders through different service providers and across large bureaucratic systems (criminal justice, social services, public health, education, labor) often results in a fractured response to managing ex-offender's risks and needs. Not surprisingly, offenders are oftentimes overwhelmed trying to navigate multiple systems to access services and to abide by competing sets of expectations. In addition, actions taken within one system oftentimes inadvertently sabotage the work being provided by those in another system serving the same client (Henderson & Hanley, 2006; Lutze & van Wormer, 2007; Taxman & Bouffard, 2000).

During the 1990s, researchers, practitioners, and policy makers developed reentry initiatives that relied on evidence-based practices coordinated across providers and embedded within a continuum of care (Duwe, 2011; Lattimore, Visher, & Lindquist, 2005; Taxman, Shepardson, & Byrne, 2004; Winterfield, Lattimore, Seffey, Brumbaugh, & Lindquist, 2006). These initiatives were designed to address the high-risk period immediately following release, to bridge the gap between prison and community corrections services, and to coordinate across institutions (criminal justice, social services, and public health) in order to provide wraparound services to address both risk and need. As Taxman and Bouffard (2000, p. 42) state, "By each organization focusing on the overall process and not simply on its own goals and responsibilities, services can be implemented in a manner that maximizes their overall efficiency and effectiveness." They propose that integrated service models must become "boundaryless organizations" that share goals and develop mutually beneficial practices at key decision points that are common for both criminal justice and treatment agencies (Taxman & Bouffard, 2000, p. 39).

In addition, within corrections, it became clear that in order to impact the time immediately following release into the community, community corrections interventions actually need to begin by preparing inmates for reentry prior to release from prison. Prerelease preparations within the institution need to include meeting with the community corrections officer, arranging treatment with a community provider, extending drug prescriptions for physical and mental health, obtaining state identification and a social security card, arranging for safe housing, and beginning the search for employment or the continuation of benefits (Petersilia, 2003).[2] After release, services need to be coordinated within and between agencies in order to immediately stabilize high-risk ex-offenders and address their criminogenic and basic life needs.

Research shows that coordinated responses to reentry are effective in reducing recidivism. For example, process evaluations of the *Serious and Violent Offender Reentry Initiatives (SVORI)* show that programs that provide a continuum of care between the prison and the community and provide wraparound services significantly increase the number of services utilized by ex-offenders compared to traditionally supervised parolees (Bouffard & Bergerson, 2006; Lattimore et al., 2005; Winterfield et al., 2006). Outcome evaluations of coordinated approaches to reentry also show promise in that they significantly reduce recidivism and increase many prosocial behaviors, such as gaining employment, reducing drug use, increasing medication compliance, and acquiring stable housing (Bouffard & Bergerson, 2006; Braga, Piehl, & Hureau, 2009; Culhane et al., 2002; Duwe, 2011; Lutze, Hamilton, & Rosky, 2012; Worcel et al., 2009).

Therefore, research provides extensive evidence that correctional rehabilitation programs work to decrease recidivism and increase prosocial behaviors when targeting high-risk/need offenders and when implemented within programs that adhere to the principles of effective treatment. In addition, the process utilized to manage the complex web of services across systems is important to assure that ex-offenders are given the support they need to be successful. In short, evidence-based programs and practices work to reduce recidivism and increase community safety. With this knowledge, it is important that community corrections agencies work to strategically implement what works.

◤ Challenges of Reentry: The Importance of Implementation

When corrections was guided by a rehabilitative ideal, it retained a sense of responsibility for influencing long-term offender change (see Cullen & Jonson, 2012). The shift to the crime control model, however, relieved the corrections system from responsibility for offender change and shifted it solely on the offender and their immediate behavior (Lutze, Johnson, Clear, Latessa, & Slate, 2012). Recent research began to refocus attention on a shared responsibility between the offender and the agencies responsible for managing the process of reintegration. Over time, it became apparent that it is the failure of effective implementation that has seriously handicapped the success of many promising innovations (see Henderson & Hanley, 2006; Pisciotta, 1994; Rothman, 1980). Agencies play an important role in achieving successful offender outcomes if they are structured and administered to incorporate best practices into their daily operations and are held accountable for achieving the agency's mission and goals. In order to be successful, organizations need to (a) prepare for innovation and its implementation within systems, (b) administer

---

[2] Traditionally, many departments of corrections released inmates with a small amount of cash ($50-$100) and a bus ticket to their jurisdiction of conviction and an order to report to their community corrections officer within 24 hours of release (Richards & Jones, 2004).

programs to manage success instead of failure, and (c) structure community supervision strategies to achieve individual and system-level goals through dynamic practices inclusive of both support and accountability.

Preparing for Innovation

Innovations in corrections often sweep into vogue promising to change offender behavior and make a significant impact on recidivism through cost effective simple solutions (see Finckenauer, 1982). Generally, broad claims of success are made by the original program designers, which in turn inspires the quick implementation of similar programs in other jurisdictions with little, if any evidence showing that the program truly works (see Henderson & Hanley, 2006). Innovative programs that are quickly adopted in new jurisdictions are often altered to meet localized conditions that are generally not prepared to implement the program, yet are expected to produce positive results. In the rush to begin the program, little consideration is given to the many barriers to implementation that need to be resolved prior to beginning the program.

Research shows that challenges to implementation are many and can be detrimental if policy makers do not prepare the various stakeholders to receive the innovation. Implementation barriers often include insufficient staff, inadequate funding, poor intra-agency communication, turf battles, staff turnover, agency regulations or policies, inadequate community services, resistance from line staff or supervisors, and inadequate training regarding the core goals and program design (see Lattimore et al., 2005). Oftentimes, implementation is also hampered by barriers to participant enrollment, such as overly stringent eligibility criteria, transfer policies that disrupt participation, inadequate screening, and cumbersome data management systems (see Lattimore et al., 2005). It is not uncommon for a new program to be funded and implemented and only then to discover that it is practically inoperable because of structural barriers or a lack of eligible participants. Therefore, in order for implementation to be effective and result in positive outcomes, policy makers and project leaders need to analyze and prepare the systems and the execution of new reentry initiatives (Henderson & Hanley, 2006).

Managing Organizational Success

Too often overall failure is accepted without consequence in correctional agencies that have become accustomed to the status quo of high rates of recidivism and technical violations (see Latessa, Cullen, & Gendreau, 2002). However, recent research shows that agencies that hire qualified staff as administrators, implement theoretically informed and evidence-based programs, and that build in quality assurance measures to guarantee program integrity over time can reduce recidivism by up to 30% compared to agencies that lack structural integrity (Lowenkamp, Latessa, & Smith, 2006; also see Andrews & Bonta, 2010; Cullen & Jonson, 2012; Lowenkamp, Latessa, & Holsinger, 2006; Taxman et al., 2004). Nevertheless, it appears that community corrections agencies, and many of the programs they rely on to provide services, struggle to operationalize the structural integrity necessary to promote change. For instance, Lowenkamp, Latessa, and Smith (2006) discovered that a majority of the agencies assessed in their study were categorized as operationally "unsatisfactory" (68%) or were rated as "satisfactory, but needs improvement" (35%). Therefore, there is still room to improve the structural quality of community corrections agencies and their ability to support community corrections officers (CCOs) in their work with ex-offenders.

Community Supervision Practices

Research on community corrections officers (CCOs), also known as probation and parole officers, clearly shows that supervision is a dynamic process, whether applied through a social work or law enforcement perspective, or a fluid combination of both. CCOs and their work are often dichotomized as either social work or law enforcement oriented. A social work orientation emphasizes offender's needs related to treatment, life skills, and social support resulting in greater collaboration with social services and health care agencies in addition to criminal justice agencies. A law enforcement orientation emphasizes offender risks to recidivate and an emphasis on surveillance, monitoring, and rule enforcement resulting in greater collaboration with police, code enforcement, and jail rather than treatment and social services. This dichotomy unfortunately led to a narrow conceptualization of the important work community corrections officers provide to the criminal justice system as well as the community.

Narrow and static definitions of community supervision stymie or hinder innovation and minimize the importance of the complex role community corrections officers serve in managing offender change (Lutze et al., 2012; Taxman, 2002). In short, ex-offenders possess both risk and need, and depending on the situation, require a multifaceted approach to impact their behavior. Unlike any other actors in the criminal justice or social service systems, CCOs possess the power and substantial knowledge about where offenders are in the process of change to leverage both support and coercion to influence outcomes (Lutze et al., 2012).Working with offenders over time in the community is a powerful and important position.

Singular approaches to supervision, whether purely rehabilitative or punitive, tend to be less effective than those that are fluid and responsive to an offender's demonstrated risk and need over time. The implementation of ***intensive supervision programs (ISP)*** to control high-risk offenders living in the community is most revealing in this regard. The initial research on ISP revealed that increased control of offenders through surveillance, monitoring compliance, and sanctioning does not reduce recidivism and does increase the detection of technical violations resulting in revocations to prison (Latessa, Travis, Fulton, & Stichman, 1998; Petersilia & Turner, 1993; Taxman, 2002). Yet, several studies of ISPs also show that their failure may be due to a lack of balance between treatment and surveillance and not the intensity of the program per se. For instance, Paparozzi and Gendreau (2005, p. 445) discovered an ISP in New Jersey that reduced recidivism from 10% to 30% by providing a supportive organizational environment conducive to treatment and employed parole officers with balanced "law enforcement/social casework orientations" (also see Jalbert, Rhodes, Flygare, & Kane, 2010). Similarly, Wodahl, Garland, Culhane, and McCarty (2011), in a study of an ISP that implemented both rewards for positive behavior and sanctions for negative behavior, discovered that a ratio of four rewards to every one sanction (4:1) increased the probability of ISP completion to 71%. Paparozzi and Gendereau (2005) contend that many ISP programs tend to overemphasize the risk of failure and ignore offender's strengths that may lead to success. Conversely, they also suggest that programs that overemphasize treatment needs may be too permissive and do not provide adequate boundaries to keep participants in compliance with supervision. Balanced approaches are more likely to be firm, fair, and consistent resulting in greater levels of compliance and program completion.

Studies are also beginning to reveal that the content of interactions between CCOs and ex-offenders are also important to outcomes (Bonta, Rugge et al., 2008; Dowden & Andrews, 2004; Taxman, 2002; Trotter, 2000). Additional time spent on offender's problems, such as antisocial attitudes, relationships, work, and other issues relevant to the offender's ability to cope and problem solve, decreased recidivism compared to time spent on compliance requirements, which tends to result in increased recidivism

(Bonta, Rugge et al., 2008). To make the most out of CCO contacts with offenders, many corrections programs are implementing programs, such as motivational interviewing, to teach CCOs to respond positively to offenders and encourage their motivation to change (Walters, Vader, Nguyen, Harris, & Eells, 2011). Unfortunately, research shows that most CCOs are prevented from spending much time helping individuals because of large caseloads and truncated meeting times. For instance, the majority of CCOs have two to four contacts with offenders each month that range in length from 10 to 20 minutes each and include record-keeping tasks as well as therapeutic discussions (Bonta, Rugge et al., 2008; DeMichele, 2007; Grattet et al., 2009). With caseloads on average greater than 100, supervision has become an exercise in documentation (i.e., urinalyses results, recording contacts, etc.) versus essential interactions with ex-offenders related to their life and reintegration. Therefore, jurisdictions need to provide the structure and time for CCOs to practice in a manner that provides integrity to the process and produces an honest attempt at achieving success.

Expectations for justice systems, agencies, and community corrections officers must change to reflect the potential to achieve successful outcomes versus accepting failure without consequence. Research shows that success can be managed through preparing justice systems and stakeholders for the implementation of innovation, managing success through organizational design focused on the implementation of evidence-based practices, and utilizing dynamic supervision practices that balance support and control.

How Do We Fix It? Policy Recommendations for Reentry and Rehabilitation

We have entered an era of corrections where ignorance is no longer an excuse for sustaining institutional and offender failure. Decades worth of research now presents policy makers, administrators, and community corrections officers with a way forward to attend to offender's needs while simultaneously controlling for risk and improving community safety (see Andrews & Bonta, 2010; Cullen & Jonson, 2012; Petersilia, 2003). It is time for community corrections to be led by policy makers who are informed and willing to invest in correctional interventions that are most likely to produce successful outcomes.

First, it is important to strive for excellence even in very difficult times. While corrections alone cannot solve the macro-level political, economic, and social problems of poverty and the suffering caused in communities by concentrated incarceration, it can work directly with offenders, their families, and the community to interrupt and reduce the persistent hardship caused by a cycle of crime, prison, and recidivism. Policy makers and corrections professionals must stop placing the sole responsibility for failure on individual offenders while ignoring the influence of structural inequality and system-level failure to invest in what works. This is a disservice to both corrections professionals and the communities they serve and makes the goal of achieving safe communities an empty promise. It is time for corrections professionals to hold politicians and their constituents accountable for funding and implementing policies that support community corrections and the associated institutions that serve the vast majority of the correctional population. It is unacceptable for offenders and victims to be the only ones who suffer the consequences of failure when policy makers and corrections agencies have it within their power to significantly increase success.

Second, policy makers must support interagency collaborations that are coordinated and responsive to both offender risks and needs. The problems confronting inmates on release from prison to the community are greater than any one agency can solve. To manage community safety and achieve long-term reintegration, policy makers must provide the leadership and support necessary to allow corrections professionals to span beyond the criminal justice system and effect change by harnessing the expertise and resources of other public and private institutions, such as health and social services, education, victim advocacy, and community groups. It is unreasonable to place the total burden of reform on corrections when so much of what happens to offenders is beyond their scope of practice and their power to change.

Third, innovation must be introduced to systems that are adequately prepared to implement change. Policy makers must be proactive in discerning what correctional programs are worthy of implementation and act to reduce failure due to structural barriers that undermine the success of programs. Although we know that coordinated responses to reentry enhance success of existing evidence-based programs, if these programs are hastily implemented they are likely to be inefficient, costly, and have diminished impact on intended goals.

Fourth, policy makers must insist on the implementation of evidence-based practices. The scientific evidence is strong that interventions that incorporate the principles of risk, need, and responsivity, utilize cognitive behavioral approaches, and target high-risk/need offenders are effective in reducing recidivism. Supervision approaches that rely on evidence-based programs and incorporate balanced styles work to increase compliance and reduce recidivism. Innovators who wish to move beyond tested, evidence-based practices must create programs that are theoretically informed and adhere to the principles of effective treatment before policy makers or professionals consider the program for implementation. Ignorance or indifference is no longer acceptable given the quality of the evidence that supports rehabilitation and balanced approaches to supervision to produce positive outcomes.

Fifth, cultural competency matters and cannot be ignored by policy makers or corrections professionals. The overrepresentation of poor, minority, and urban men and women in our corrections system can no longer be politely ignored. The debate about whether this overrepresentation is due to disparity or discrimination has paralyzed us from moving forward to bring about change. It is time to move beyond acknowledgement of differences and the passiveness of building awareness to an active understanding about how different group's life experiences influence their willingness to engage in the process of supervision and treatment. Without an informed understanding, we will continue to blame offenders for not working harder or taking advantage of opportunities when in reality they just do not trust the systems that have failed them in the past to now meet their needs. Simply extrapolating what works for one group to that of another is no longer acceptable. Therefore, policy makers who fund research must insist that evaluators of correctional programs not just determine whether programs work, but who they work for and why so that success can truly be shared equally by all who participate.

Finally, it is time for policy makers to move community corrections out of the shadow of prisons and achieve parity through acknowledging the interdependent relationship that the success or failure within one directly has on the other. Prisons need to be renovated to create positive outcomes that can be enhanced by community corrections to achieve successful reintegration. Community corrections needs to be empowered to allow CCOs to utilize their expertise and actively engage offenders in the process of change. We can no longer afford, in human or financial costs, to allow either institutional or community corrections to be a passive witness to the carnage caused by high-risk offenders when we fail to actively organize our resources and empower corrections experts to implement evidence-based practices. Failing to invest in, structure, and empower corrections for success is negligence that results in direct harm to our communities. Obviously offenders need to take responsibility for the harm they inflict on others, but this alone is not enough. The mounting evidence on the success of rehabilitation programs, coordinated responses to reentry, and balanced approaches to supervision now makes it obvious that policy makers, corrections leaders, CCOs, and community stakeholders must take responsibility as well.

Community corrections is positioned at the end of the criminal justice system prepared to effectively manage offender risk through providing support, treatment, and accountability within supervision. Corrections professionals are accustomed to working with difficult populations in very difficult circumstances. In spite of the many challenges confronting the system and individual professionals, many innovative programs have been implemented and proven to work over the last 30 years. Community corrections is poised to bring about a revolution in corrections that is rife with innovation and prospects for achieving successful outcomes. Policy makers and corrections professionals must possess the determination to make it happen.

KEY TERMS

Cognitive-behavioral treatment (CBT)

Community corrections

Community Corrections Officer (CCO)

Cultural competency

Intensive supervision program (ISP)

Nothing works

Risk assessment tools

Risk, Need Responsivity (RNR)

Serious and Violent Offender Reentry Initiatives (SVORI)

DISCUSSION QUESTIONS

1. Historically, changes in correctional practices are caused by changes in social or political ideology. However, the authors argue that the unique economic climate contributed to changes in correctional practices. What does this tell us about the nature of criminal justice policy in general and correctional practices in particular?

2. The authors discuss how substance abuse hinders an ex-offender's ability to maintain employment, secure suitable and sustainable housing, and adhere to his or her conditions of community supervision. Strict enforcement of substance-free supervision conditions can lead to high levels of revocation and inflate recidivism rates. What policy changes should be implemented to ensure adherence with supervision conditions and limit supervision revocations while being aware of the realities of addiction?

3. What role, if any, should policy play in reconciling the polarity between the social work and the law enforcement approaches to community-based corrections?

4. Which aspects of current correctional policies impede the development of therapeutic relationships between the community corrections officers and ex-offenders under their supervision? What policies should be enhanced or eliminated to endure the development of therapeutic relationships within the correctional context?

WEBSITES FOR ADDITIONAL RESEARCH

National Reentry Resource Center (Council of State Governments Justice Center): http://www.national-reentryresourcecenter.org/library

National Institute of Justice: http://www.nij.gov/topics/corrections/reentry/

Urban Institute: http://www.urban.org/projects/reentry-portfolio/

UC Irvine's Center for Evidence-Based Corrections: http://ucicorrections.seweb.uci.edu/

CHAPTER

XX

Emerging Issues in Criminal Justice Policy

Christine L. Gardiner and Stacy L. Mallicoat

There are many important criminal justice policy issues on the horizon. We chose to highlight four areas for discussion in this chapter: criminal justice realignment as a policy response to violations of inmates' constitutional rights, juvenile justice policy modifications in response to the U.S. Supreme Court's changing view of juveniles, a renewed debate about gun control policies in response to high profile incidents, and recent 2nd Amendment decisions and 4th Amendment protections in the new digital age. We chose these topics because they represent interesting and complex constitutional issues and they exemplify unique policy responses to specific constitutional concerns.

Incarceration and Realignment: The Case of California

Over the past three decades, tough on crime sentencing practices resulted in dramatic increases in prison populations nationwide. This trend is exemplified by events in California. In 1980, California's prisons held a mere 24,569 individuals: 98% of the incarcerated were men, 38.6% were White, 24% were Hispanic/Latino, and 35.4% were African American (Good & Rouse, 1980). Fast-forward to the end of 2010, and the state's prison population grew to 162,821: 82% of the incarcerated were men and 25.2% were White, 39.8% were Hispanic/Latino, and 28.9% were African American (California Department of Corrections and Rehabilitation (CDCR), 2011a). In an effort to accommodate the rising incarcerated population, the state opened 21 new prison facilities. Today, the 33 state prisons are designed to hold 84,597 inmates (CDCR, n.d.). However, with a current population that almost doubles this capacity, it is fair to say that California is faced with a serious prison overcrowding problem.

Prison overcrowding leads to a number of issues, including many which run the risk of violating the constitutional rights of inmates. Despite their status as an incarcerated individual, inmates retain a number of basic rights under the constitution. However, this was not always the case. Prior to the 1960s, the courts adopted a "hands-off" doctrine when it came to convicted offenders. The U.S. Supreme Court decision in *Cooper v. Pate* (1964) led to significant changes in the role of the courts for the incarcerated population. The *Cooper* decision held that state prisoners have the right to sue in Federal court to address grievances under the Civil Rights Act of 1871. As a result, the gates to the judiciary were thrown open to prisoner claims of constitutional violations under the 1st, 4th, 6th, 8th, and 14th amendments. Since then, several notable cases were decided that relate to the issues of prison conditions. These include *Estelle v. Gamble* (1976), which held that the deliberate indifference to the medical needs of prisoners is a violation of the cruel and unusual doctrine of the 8th amendment, and *Coleman v. Wilson* (1990), which held that prisoners must be provided with basic mental health care.

In response to the poor conditions in California's prisons, inmates filed a class action lawsuit alleging that the state engaged in deliberate indifference in providing quality medical treatment. In 2011, the U.S. Supreme Court decided in favor of the inmates, citing overcrowding as a key factor in the state's inability to provide basic quality physical and mental health care. In response to the decision by the Court, a three judge panel mandated a significant reduction in the state prison population such that the "in-state prison capacity is brought to within 137.5% of institutional design capacity" (*Brown v. Plata*, 2011).

In order to reduce the prison population, the state began to shift lower-level offenders to local custodial and community supervision programs. This process, otherwise known as **realignment**, posits that "officials at the local level are better situated to identify the needs of their communities and create specialized programs for implementation" (Smude, 2012, p.153). There are three major benefits in realignment for California's correctional system. First, the financial costs of incarcerating the largest prison population nationwide have taken its toll. It costs over $47,000 a year to incarcerate an individual, due to rising security and health care costs (Legislative Analyst Office (LAO), 2008–2009). The current state budget crisis led to significant cuts to many areas in the state, including social services, education, government services, and public works. Second, the crisis forced the reduction because of overcrowding in the state prisons as ordered by the courts under *Brown v. Plata* (2011).

Finally, California's correctional system failed to effectively rehabilitate offenders. A review of recidivism rates for those offenders released during the 2007 to 2008 fiscal year demonstrates that 47.4% were returned to prison within one year of release, and 59.2% were returned to prison within two years of release (CDCR, 2011b). In addition, California's rates are generally 15 to 20% higher than national recidivism rates. The majority of these offenders do not return to prison for new offenses. Rather, they violate the technical rules of their release (such as curfew violations, failure to obtain a job, etc.).

California's realignment plan involves a complete overhaul of the state's correctional system in a number of ways. First, California Assembly Bill AB 109 allows for nonviolent, nonserious, and nonsexual offenders to serve their sentence in county jails instead of state prison facilities. While convicted jail inmates are generally convicted of misdemeanors and incarcerated for less than one year, the Public Safety Realignment Act of 2011 revised the definition of felony to permit certain offenders to serve sentences greater than one year in jail facilities. This shifts not only the management of these offenders to local jurisdictions, but the costs of supervising these offenders as well. However, counties are allowed to contract with the state to send these offenders to state facilities (CDCR, 2010). Second, each county created a post-release community supervision (PRCS) program administered by the county probation department as an alternative to parole. The shift of post-incarceration supervision to the county level is limited to three groups: (a) non-violent offenders, (b) non-serious offenders, and (c) low-risk sexual offenders. PRCS applies to these individuals who are released after October 1, 2011. Third, on their release from prison, CDCR no longer has jurisdiction over the individual. This is particularly important in cases of parole revocation. Instead of returning these cases to state prisons, revocations of PRCS will be sent to local jails and sentences will last no longer than 180 days. For those low-level offenders who were sentenced to parole prior to realignment, the state parole agency has the authority to terminate an individual's parole, if they have been violation free for six months. Finally, each county created an executive committee charged with making recommendations for implementing realignment at the local level. The executive committee is composed of the chief probation officer, chief of police/sheriff, district attorney, public defender, presiding judge of the Superior Court, and a representative from the Division of Health and Human Services (CDCR, 2011b).

Even though counties received funds from the state to ensure that they do not bear the financial burden of the realignment process, there was little direction at the state level as to how counties should spend the money and what types of programs to implement (Lofstrom, Petersilia, & Raphael, 2012). As communities consider the types of programming to implement, scholars argue that a successful realignment plan should include wraparound services that focus on collaborative relationships between multiple agencies both at the public and private level. Inmates face a variety of challenges related to the reentry process, including finding a job, a place to live, and dealing with substance abuse issues. Prior to realignment, many offenders did not have access to realignment services. A study by Vera Institute of Justice indicates that only 13% of inmates serving time at the Los Angeles County Jail received any sort of reentry programming while in jail (Sandwick, Tamis, Parsons, & Arauz-Cuadra, 2013). In addition, counties should look to evidence-based research when developing and implementing policies and programs (Krisberg & Taylor-Nicholson, 2011).

To date, we have seen several positive examples of realignment in action. In Santa Clara County, representatives from a variety of public agencies and community partners have come together to streamline services for offenders. Their plan focuses on education, employment, housing, health and well-being, and family reunification as the cornerstones toward successful rehabilitation and reentry (Wilson, 2013). In Merced and San Bernardino counties, professionals from law enforcement, probation, human services, and mental health are housed together at day reporting centers in an effort to work together as a team to serve the needs of AB 109 clients (Giwargis, 2013; San Bernadino County, 2012). These types of collaborative efforts in the community place fewer fiscal demands as the costs of housing an inmate in jail is $156 per day, compared to the $17 per day cost of AB 109 monitoring (Giwargis, 2013).

> To increase public safety in this austere budget environment, we must support cost-effective efforts by states that are grounded in the "best practices" and draw on the latest innovations from public corrections and the faith-based community . . . For many years, reducing recidivism seemed nearly impossible. Now, many states are starting to turn a corner through commonsense and cost-effective reforms. (Pew Center on the States, 2011, p. 6)

While realignment creates significant opportunities for California to transform their correctional system, there are significant risks as well. The legislature created pathways to fund realignment, but many question whether these allocations are sufficient to manage the caseload placed on local jurisdictions. Some officials also expressed concerns about whether local communities could be at risk for due process and equal protection legal challenges by inmates—challenges based on the counties' ability to effectively deliver services due to costs as well as variations between the types of programming that each county offers (Krisberg & Taylor-Nicholson, 2011). While the intent of AB 109 was to create community alternatives to incarceration, many counties focused on expanding jail facilities to house offenders (Reentry Court Solutions, 2013).

Counties that choose to expand their jail capacity will encounter large capital budget outlays, extended periods for design and construction of new facilities, and little public support for more local spending on corrections as opposed to education, sustainable new job creation, health care, and other vital community needs. (Krisberg & Taylor-Nicholson, 2011, p. 5)

If successful, California's realignment plan could represent a model for states nationwide. While critics question whether public safety will be compromised with the expansion of community supervision programs and jails in lieu of prison, only low-risk and low-level offenders will be shifted to these types of programs. In addition, the state may benefit from substantial cost savings by utilizing local criminal justice agencies instead of prisons for low-level offenders (Vuong, Hartney, Krisberg, & Marchionna, 2010). In addition, research indicates that the use of short periods of incarceration or intensive community supervision options are more effective in preventing recidivism (Kleiman, 2009). Finally, the ability to use discretion when determining punishments is key. Unlike state parole, which imposes a mandatory three-year intensive supervision to all offenders released from state prison, the ability to utilize flexible options and customize both individual programs and the system as a whole ultimately benefits the unique needs of individual offenders (Krisberg & Taylor-Nicholson, 2011).

Zero Tolerance and Tough on Crime: Rolling Back on Juvenile Offending

In 1899, the first juvenile court was formed in Chicago, Illinois, under the doctrine of ***parens patriae***. Under this philosophy, the state assumed responsibility for wayward children, removed them from their parents' care, and placed them in institutions under the guise of acting in the best interests of the child. States began to distinguish between the criminal actions of adults and the delinquent actions of youth. By separating juveniles from adult offenders, the juvenile court developed its own set of procedures and practices for dealing with cases of delinquency. This shift represented a new philosophy: "children had to be treated, not punished and the judge should act as a wise and kind parent" (Regoli, Hewitt, & DeLisi, 2009, p. 19). By 1945, all states had juvenile courts (Ferdinand, 1991).

By the end of the 20th century, many of the practices in the juvenile court reflected the retributive philosophy that governed the adult criminal court system. As you learned in Chapter 12 of this text, the use of juvenile waiver policies dominated this practice, as states began to send a message of "do the adult crime, do the adult time" to juveniles by transferring youth who had committed serious infractions to the adult court. Much of these get tough on juvenile crime policies rose to power as a result of growing concerns about significant increases in the number of violent offenses committed by juveniles. Projections by researchers like Wilson (1995) and Dilulio (1996) added fuel to the fire that juvenile superpredators would fuel a crime wave with significant increases to the violent crime rate. Despite the fact that the superpredators never materialized and that violent crimes actually decreased nationwide (Federal Bureau of Investigation (FBI), 2012), these fears led to an increase in tougher laws designed to combat juvenile crime. In addition to increasing the option of transferring juveniles to adult court, states expanded their sentencing options for juvenile offenders, modified confidentiality clauses which created greater open access to juvenile court proceedings and juvenile records, developed additional correctional programs for juvenile institutions, and increased victims' rights within juvenile proceedings (Lawrence & Hesse, 2010).

The expansion of juvenile sentencing practices meant that youth were treated more like adults. While in 1989 the option of the death penalty was prohibited for youth under the age of 16 (see *Stanford v. Kentucky*), nineteen states had laws on the books permitting the use of capital punishment for youths aged 16 and 17. Between 1990 and 2003, 19 people who committed crimes as juveniles were executed in Louisiana, Texas, Georgia, Missouri, Oklahoma, and Virginia (Death Penalty Information Center (DPIC), 2003). The juvenile death penalty was abolished nationwide in 2005 with the U.S. Supreme Court decision in *Roper v. Simmons.* As a result of the "evolving standards of decency that mark the progress of a maturing society," the Court held that the practice of executing juveniles violated the 8th and 14th amendments of the Constitution. As a result, 71 inmates on death rows across twelve states saw their sentences commuted to life without the possibility of parole.

Even in states that either opposed the practice of death entirely, or limited the application to adult offenders, life without parole was available in 39 states for juveniles over the age of 14 (Malcolm & Slattery, 2012). Perhaps one of the most controversial uses of this practice occurred in the case of Lionel Tate. Tate was a 14-year-old boy who was sentenced to life without the possibility of parole in Florida in 1999 for the death of his 6-year-old neighbor. Tate became the youngest offender in the United States to receive a life without parole (LWOP) sentence. Following national attention in opposition to the punishment, his sentence was overturned in January 2004 and he was released on probation. However, he was arrested in 2005 for armed burglary with battery and armed robbery. As a result, he was sentenced to thirty years in prison for violating his probation (Aguayo, 2006).

Tate's case was one where the nature of the charge led to the imposition of a mandatory sentence under the law. In the case of *Miller v. Alabama* (2012), the court held that use of mandatory life without the possibility of parole for juveniles is unconstitutional. Writing for the majority, Justice Kagan cited that 85% of all juvenile LWOP sentences come from states where the sentence is mandatory, which takes away the sentencing discretion in these cases. While the court did not prohibit the use of LWOP sentences for juveniles in general, many states began to implement alternative practices. For example, the Nebraska senate is currently considering a bill to replace juvenile LWOP with a 20-year minimum sentence (Swift, 2013). In 2012, the California legislature passed Senate Bill 9, which involves juveniles sentenced to life without the possibility of parole and permits judges to revisit sentences in these cases after fifteen years and to make adjustments to their sentences, a practice that would "allow judges to go back and review past sentences and look at who this individual has grown up and become" (Burke & Cavanaugh, 2012). Despite a positive record as a juvenile, not all youth successfully transition to their adult lives outside of prison. Like Lionel Tate, John Engel was 14 years old when he was charged with murder in Colorado in 1999. Engel was convicted of murdering his adoptive mother and grandmother. Initially sentenced to thirty-two years, his sentence was converted to a community corrections sentence after serving eight years in a juvenile facility (Shields, 2008). Within three months of his release, Engel was charged with technical violations related to his release and was returned to prison (Aguilar, 2009). Perhaps one of the most ironic twists in this case was that Engel was only five days past his 14th birthday at the time of his crime—under Colorado law, youths under the age of 14 receive a maximum sentence to age 21 to be served in a juvenile facility (Shields, 2008).

At the same time that we saw increases in punitive policies in the juvenile court, *zero-tolerance policies* began to emerge within school environments. Zero-tolerance policies focus on the reduction of drug abuse and violence in schools and requires punishment for any infraction, regardless of its degree of severity, whether it was an accidental mistake or other extenuating circumstance. Zero-tolerance laws gained popularity beginning in 1994, when Congress passed a law requiring a one-year expulsion for any youth who brought a firearm to school (Gun-Free Schools Act, 1994). Despite the intent to create safe spaces in schools for students, zero-tolerance policies resulted in a range of negative consequences. "Zero tolerance often leads to indiscriminate suspensions and expulsions for both serious and mild infractions and disproportionately impacts students from minority status backgrounds and those with disabilities" (National Association of School Psychologists (NASP), 2001).

The roots of zero-tolerance policies are based in the broken windows model of policing, which suggests that communities can prevent larger acts of violence by enforcing minor law infractions, such as loitering, drinking in public, graffiti, and other public nuisance crimes (Wilson & Kelling, 1982). As high profile events of school violence, such as Columbine and Virginia Tech, began to dominate the news, the popularity of zero-tolerance policies in schools increased significantly. Even cases like Sandy Hook, while not a case of school violence per se, impact how school administrators engage in disciplinary decision making. Yet, research demonstrates that such policies have a negative impact, not only on the consistency of discipline in schools, but also decrease the academic achievements of students (American Psychological Association (APA), 2008). In addition, many schools are now utilizing the juvenile justice system to manage classroom disciplinary issues rather than deal with these minor infractions internally (Casella, 2003; APA, 2008).

Recently, many jurisdictions started to rollback zero-tolerance policies, citing concerns that such practices actually increased crime in their schools and communities. "From kids getting kicked out of school for playing games with fingers pointed like guns on the Eastern Shore to chewing their breakfast pastry into "gun-like" shapes in Baltimore" (Allard, 2013), events like these demonstrate that the broad application of zero-tolerance has exceeded its original intent. In Los Angeles, school police officers agreed to stop writing citations for truancy and other minor infractions, and instead refer students to youth programs that help students with the challenges that they face (Watanabe, 2012). In March 2013, Maryland State Senator Jennings introduced The Reasonable School Discipline Act of 2013 (Senate Bill 1058, 2013). Rather than provide a one-size-fits-all philosophy, this proposed bill allows for greater discretion when handing out disciplinary infractions, such as school suspensions and expulsions. In the Denver Public Schools, school resource officers now only respond to serious criminal actions, while the school district implemented restorative justice practices to deal with disruptive students. As a result, the district saw significant decreases in the number of youth who are suspended or expelled (Hing, 2003).

◪ Gun Control Policy: A Renewed Interest in the Second Amendment

Every time a horrific incident involving a gun-toting shooter occurs, there is a strong call to pass tougher gun legislation. There is also an equally strong call to leave our gun laws alone. Few, if any, criminal justice policies are as contentious as gun control. This is because no policy issue is more emblematic of the necessity to balance our desire to control crime against the protection of our constitutional rights than gun control (except possibly the ability of government to invade our privacy).

Like so many other issues, *gun policy* is greatly impacted by public response to high profile incidents. In fact, it has taken front stage lately with the occurrence of several unfortunate and dreadful events involving shooters killing unsuspecting victims with high-powered, and sometimes illegally obtained, weapons. Mass shootings, in particular those committed by young people, have devastated communities and dominated the news in recent years. You may be familiar with some of the most horrific recent examples.

- Dylan Klebold and Eric Harris (both 17 years old) murdered 12 students and a teacher (and injured 21 others) during a rampage at Columbine High School in Colorado on April 20, 1999.
- Cho Seung-Hui, a 23-year-old student at Virginia Tech, killed 32 students (2 in a dorm and 30 in a classroom) before committing suicide on April 16, 2007.
- A former graduate student at Northern Illinois University, Stephen Kazmierczak, shot and killed 5 students and himself (and injured 17 others) when he opened fire in a classroom on February 14, 2008.
- Jared Loughner, a 22-year-old with suspected mental health problems, shot and killed 6 people (and injured 13 others) at a public rally for Senator Gabrielle Giffords in Tucson, Arizona, on January 8, 2011.
- James Holmes (24 years old) set off tear gas in a crowded movie theater showing the premiere of *The Dark Knight Rises*, then shot and killed 12 moviegoers (and injured 58 others) on July 20, 2012.
- Adam Lanza (20 years old) shot and killed 26 people (20 of them 1st graders) at Sandy Hook Elementary School in Newtown, Connecticut, on December 14, 2012.

In a standard year, approximately 30,000 people die from firearm-related incidents (Center for Disease Control (CDC), 2011). Some of these shootings, such as the ones above, received major national news coverage, while many others received only scant local coverage. These stories not only captured the headlines in recent years, they also caused people to question their stance on gun control policies. The latest tragedy in particular, the one in Newtown, Connecticut, shined a bright spotlight on gun control and spurred the nation to investigate and vigorously debate the role of gun policy in these and similar crimes. Immediately after the Newtown incident there was a loud call for tougher gun control and the percent of Americans who supported stricter gun control was at a 10-year high (57%) (Constantini, 2012). That strong support appears to have been short lived, as three months later the percentage of Americans who support stricter gun control dropped to 47% in March of 2013 (Peralta, 2013).

Immediately after the Newtown shooting, President Obama and others called on Congress to pass meaningful gun legislation. This proposed legislation includes controversial measures, such as expanding the use of background checks, particularly at gun shows. While over 40% of guns are sold at gun shows and are often exempt from requiring background checks, opponents of tightening these legislations suggest that such procedures only limit the rights of those who legally possess these weapons. Yet, Adam Lanza, James Holmes, and Jared Loughner all used weapons that were legally obtained. Another hotly debated component of Obama's plan involves the assault weapons ban. Initially passed by Congress in 1994, the assault weapons ban prohibited the manufacturing of all fully automatic firearms and selected semi-automatic firearms as well as high capacity ammunition magazines, though it did not limit the ownership or sales of any of these weapons manufactured prior to the ban. Some questioned the efficacy of the ban, including Senator Lindsay Graham (R) from South Carolina, who stated that "we had the assault weapons ban from 1994 to 2004 and the conclusion was, it did not change crime.... in an appreciable way" (Jackson & Madhani, 2013, p. 6A). In his proposal, President Obama not only called to reinstate the assault weapons ban, but to limit ammunition magazines to ten rounds,[1] and to ban the possession of armor piercing ammunition. In addition, Obama's plan calls for increased funding to improve policing resources

---

[1] Both the Sandy Hook and Aurora Movie Theater shootings involved the use of high capacity magazines, which some have argued contributed to the high death count of victims.

(hire more officers, increase training, etc.), resume social science research on gun violence, reinforce school safety initiatives, and provide funding toward early identification and intervention in our mental health system (Jackson & Madhani, 2013).

As evidence of the contentious nature of gun control policy discussions, Congress has yet to agree on any gun policy issues. Even though more than 90% of Americans support **universal background checks** for all gun purchasers, Congress cannot agree on several particulars (for example, whether background checks are necessary for gun transfers, private sales, or online sales) (Rucker & O'Keefe, 2013). Another major item being debated is the legality of assault-style weapons. Here, one of the main problems is that there is not an agreed-on definition of what constitutes an "**assault-style weapon**" and the process of defining the term is highly contentious. In general, definitions are cosmetic in nature and defined by several features that are typically associated with military weapons, such as magazines that hold a high number of rounds, having a folding stock, a pistol grip, or able to fire a specific number of rounds per second. Given the strength of the National Rifle Association (NRA), and its stance on this issue, it is unlikely that we will see any compromise on this issue in the near future.

For this reason, we are most likely to see substantive gun policy passed at the state level rather than the federal level. This is because politicians at the state level can more easily pass legislation that fits with the personality of their state, without exposing themselves to the risk of not being reelected. We have already seen several states pass comprehensive gun legislation. For example, Colorado Governor Hickenlooper signed landmark legislation in March 2013 that requires background checks for private and online gun sales, and bans magazines that hold more than 15 rounds of ammunition (Moreno, 2013). California, Delaware, and a dozen other states are in the midst of voting on a number of gun laws to ban or strengthen existing bans or restrictions on particular weapons, high capacity magazines, and/or bulk purchases of ammunition, as well as require registration of guns and gun parts (O'Keefe, 2013).

The debate about gun policy has reached new heights, in part because of a 2008 U.S. Supreme Court decision (**District of Columbia v. Heller**). Heller, a Washington, DC, special policeman, carried a gun for work, but was denied a license to keep the gun at home. The U.S. Supreme Court (USSC) held in *District of Columbia v. Heller* (2008) that the **Second Amendment** protects an *individual's* right to possess a firearm for lawful purposes. The USSC's decision was a dramatic departure from earlier precedent because prior to this point, the Second Amendment was interpreted narrowly, within the framework of gun carrying for the purposes of militia service only.[2]

Although the USSC took a strong stand on the Second Amendment's protections, its decision left open many issues regarding our right to bear arms. In his majority opinion, Justice Scalia firmly stated that the Second Amendment guarantees the "individual right to possess and carry weapons in case of confrontation" (*District of Columbia v. Heller*, 2008). He specifically noted the ability of lawmakers to restrict and control who owns firearms (prohibiting felons and the mentally ill from owning is acceptable), how they are carried (concealed weapon prohibitions are acceptable), and where they can be carried (sensitive area prohibitions are acceptable).

Why Is Gun Policy So Contentious?

At the heart of the issue is our Second Amendment right to bear arms contrasted against our strong desire to protect innocent individuals from gun violence. Herbert Packer's due process and **crime control models** of criminal justice help us understand the issue more clearly. On one side of the issue, the due

---

[2] McDonald v. City of Chicago (2010) solidified this new precedent and incorporated this decision to the states through the 14th Amendment.

process side, are individuals who interpret the U.S. Supreme Court's decision to mean that individuals have a constitutional right to possess any type of firearm and that right is more important than public safety concerns. These folks, mostly Libertarians and Republicans, want no restrictions (or very few) restrictions on gun possession and ownership. They contend that any restriction on gun possession weakens and infringes on our constitutional rights.

On the other side of the issue, the crime control side, are individuals who support legislation that limits and controls Americans' access to guns in order to protect public safety. These folks, mostly Democrats, favor what they call "sensible gun policy" that places some restrictions on who can carry, where people can carry, when people can carry, and what people can carry. Crime control advocates argue that if a gun feature is not necessary to protect one's person or property, it should be outlawed (e.g., assault-style weapons). They want to close loopholes that allow criminals and other restricted individuals from purchasing guns and increase penalties on straw purchasers (i.e., people who purchase guns for people who cannot legally purchase them). A good example of this side's views is New York City Mayor Michael Bloomberg's pro-gun control advertising campaign, which featured a gun rights advocate asserting "with rights come responsibilities."

Interestingly, one of the reasons this is such a thorny issue is because individuals who typically support a ***due process model*** find themselves advocating a crime control view and vice versa. Under most circumstances, certainly when discussing 4th and 5th Amendment issues, Democrats and Libertarians support a model that preferences our due process rights over our crime control efforts, and Republicans typically support a model that favors government's ability to control crime over our due process rights. On this issue, however, both sides are on foreign soil—Republicans and Libertarians are joined in a fight to uphold every ounce of our 2nd Amendment constitutional rights while Democrats are in the unique position of arguing to restrict rights in favor of crime control. Of course, the issue is not completely black and white and there are many, many shades of gray.

Given the vast ideological differences on this issue, it is instructive to consult the available scientific research for evidence on effective gun policies. Unfortunately, there is not enough quality research on gun policy to provide guidance about which gun laws tend to work in which circumstances. One of the reasons for this dearth of research is a lack of government funding on the issue. Since 1996, the Center for Disease Control (CDC) has been prohibited from funding any research that may "advocate or promote gun control" (Plumer, 2013). New York City Mayor Michael Bloomberg's advocacy group estimates that this law single-handedly reduced studies on gun violence by 60% (Mayors Against Illegal Guns, 2013).[3] Their recently published report describes how the Washington gun lobby successfully restricted academic studies on gun violence as well as the ability of law enforcement, military, and medical professionals to share information about guns or gun violence (Mayors Against Illegal Guns, 2013). Although government-sponsored grants are not the only source of funding for academic research, they play a pivotal role in setting research agendas. Fortunately, this situation should change shortly, as President Obama signed an executive order in January 2013 directing the CDC to, once again, study the "causes of gun violence." However, shortly after President Obama signed that order, the NRA (the most powerful gun lobby in the nation), mounted a campaign to keep language in the 2014 budget that limited data collection and research on gun violence (Stachelberg, Gerney, & Parsons, 2013). At the end of the day, this demonstrates how politically charged some criminal justice policy research can be; but, the important question that needs to be asked is: Why is the NRA so afraid of scientific research?

---

[3] The NRA retorted with their own "School Safety Report" that recommended arming school personnel and adding armed security guards (or police officers) to schools as a viable and preferred strategy to prevent school violence (Hutchinson, 2013).

⬚ Search and Seizure in the 21st century

The issue of emerging technology has posed challenges for the courts since wiretapping was introduced in the 1870s. The courts, however, are often slow to respond to constitutional issues pertaining to the use of new technologies because of our lengthy judicial process. In fact, it took 60 years before Congress placed the first restrictions on law enforcement's powers to use wiretapping for investigative purposes and 90 years before the Supreme Court required police to obtain a warrant prior to placing a wiretap (*Katz v. United States*, 1967). The use of thermal scanning, pen registers, and trap and trace devices provide additional examples of the courts' failure to protect our 4th Amendment rights from newer and more invasive technologies.

As police continue to take advantage of emerging technology in the 21st century, our 4th Amendment rights (written in the 18th century) inevitably and necessarily will come under much closer scrutiny by the courts. As forward thinking as the framers of the constitution were, they could not possibly have imagined the technological world we live in today. For this reason, the U.S. Supreme Court, as well as our lower courts of appeal, are called on regularly to interpret the intentions of the framers as they pertain to the expanded capacity of today's technology. As a society, we need to consider the significant opportunities and consequences that come with our latest technological innovations and find a balance between protecting public safety and protecting our due process rights. Some important 4th Amendment issues on the horizon that will very likely have a potent effect on average citizens are: the use of drones for law enforcement purposes, collection and use of DNA, and the circumstances under which police may utilize specific technological devices and applications (such as GPS, cell phones, social media) to establish **probable cause** and/or build a case against a suspect.

The 4th Amendment of the Constitution provides Americans the right "to be secure in their persons, houses, papers, and effects, against unreasonable searches and seizures, shall not be violated, and no Warrants shall issue, but upon probable cause . . ." However, this permanent right is subject to an ever changing interpretation of "**unreasonable search**." In order for a search to be considered "unreasonable," (a) an individual must have an **expressed expectation of privacy**, and (b) that expectation must be reasonable (*Katz v. United States,* 1967). This is the cornerstone of our 4th Amendment rights; however, it is important to appreciate that the court's interpretation of "reasonable" will change as technology advances and societal expectations of privacy change. For example, closed-circuit cameras are now part of our daily lives and we expect that we are on camera when we shop at retailers, put gas in our vehicle at the service station, and drive through certain intersections. As such, if we commit a crime or traffic infraction in one of these places we expect that we might get caught, prosecuted, and punished.

Every generation for at least 150 years was concerned with the capabilities of new and remarkable technological innovations to place behavior under surveillance and see or hear things that we thought to be private. Today, just like past generations, astonishing technologies allow the government to look into our daily lives in new ways that require us to consider the implications of those methodologies under the 4th Amendment.

Drones

Drones, or Unmanned Aerial Vehicles (UAVs), are "aircraft that can fly without an onboard human operator" (Thompson, 2012, summary, Para. 2). They can fly on autonomous programming or can be controlled remotely by a ground operator. Drones, which range in size from the size of an insect to the size of a standard jet, were initially developed to be used by our military overseas; but, with the winding down of the war, surplus drones are beginning to enter the U.S. marketplace. A recent government report estimates that there will be 30,000 drones in our airspace by 2033 (Thompson, 2012). Currently, drones can only be flown under 400 feet by persons or agencies that have an FAA-issued Certificate of Authorization to operate an UAV (Thompson, 2012). Although there are only about 300 drones in use in the United States today, Congress signed a bill in 2012 to make it easier to get drone licenses and plans to integrate significantly more drones into our airspace starting in the fall of 2015 (Wolfgang, 2012; Couts, 2012).

Drones are versatile, easy to operate, and relatively inexpensive, which makes them ideal for surveillance, reconnaissance, and many other law enforcement (and non-law enforcement) purposes. For example, drones equipped with laser radar (LIDAR) and license plate readers could render traditional traffic officers obsolete. Depending on if, when, where, and how Congress or the U.S.S.C. allow them to be used for traffic enforcement, drones have the potential to change the driving habits of prudent motorists across the nation.

Additionally, drones can be equipped with a variety of specialized equipment, such as electromagnetic radar (which can create 3D images of concealed objects) and thermal imaging (which uses heat-sensitive technology to display images of things and people). Drones equipped with these powerful technologies will have the awesome (and frightening) capability to see through solid objects (such as walls and ceilings) (Thompson, 2012). Drones can also be equipped with facial or soft biometric recognition software which would allow them to surveil and track specific individuals (Thompson, 2012). Given the capacity to store vast amounts of highly personal information, this feature has important 4th Amendment considerations. Drones could even be equipped with Tasers, bean bags, and other weapons. Despite the fact that only a few law enforcement agencies currently have access to drones, this technology has the potential to revolutionize policing in the very near future.

In June 2011, Rodney Brossart of North Dakota became the first person arrested with the assistance of a drone (Koebler, 2012). He unsuccessfully argued that his 4th Amendment rights were violated when police deployed a borrowed drone to pinpoint his location on his property during a standoff with police (Wolverton, 2012). For purposes of the 4th Amendment, courts will probably liken drones to helicopters and other manned aerial vehicles. While aerial searches (for suspects or over property) do not violate 4th Amendment protections (as was the case above), drone surveillance may.

When determining whether drone surveillance violates the 4th Amendment, the court will likely look at several considerations. The first consideration, and probably the most important, is the location of the search (Thompson, 2012). Individuals have the strongest protections against unreasonable searches inside (and in this case, directly above) their homes. **Fourth Amendment** protections diminish the farther one goes from the house. Curtilage (the area immediately surrounding one's home—e.g., backyard, patio, possibly the driveway) usually provides some privacy protections while open fields provide virtually no privacy protections over public spaces. Thus, drones probably will not be able to legally look through your ceiling or wall into your house, but they probably will be able to check out what is growing or stashed in your backyard. Protections against unreasonable search at or near international borders are almost nonexistent, so we can expect the courts to continue to provide great leeway to law enforcement in these locations.

The length of tracking will also be an important determinant of whether a search warrant is required (Thompson, 2012). The U.S.S.C. ruled in **United States v. Jones** (2012) that long-term tracking constitutes a search and requires a warrant due to the amount of information that can be collected. Other cases have upheld law enforcement officers' ability to track individuals in public for shorter periods of time without a warrant.

Also, the sophistication of technology attached to the drone will most certainly matter in whether or not a warrant is required (Thompson, 2012). Technologies that are accessible to everyone (binoculars, for example) are generally more permissible than are sophisticated, specialized equipment (infrared, radar, etc.). Thus the government (the courts and/or policy makers) will most certainly need to weigh in on the types of equipment that can be affixed to drones for surveillance purposes (standard zoom lenses or high-powered infrared cameras, still photos or video, facial recognition software, etc.) as well as how long the information can be retained and how it can be used.

As drones and other technologies become widely available, the amount of privacy that individuals insist on will shrink. As our expectations of privacy shrink, so too will our 4th Amendment protections against unreasonable searches. This is because our protection against unreasonable searches is premised on our reasonable expectations of privacy in certain situations, and those expectations change with technological innovations. For example, how many drones there are and how they are used will likely change people's minds about the type of surveillance activity that is considered reasonable and thus not protected by the Fourth Amendment (as an example, consider cameras in public spaces).

Despite some generally accepted law enforcement uses for drones (locating missing persons, capturing fleeing criminals, or surveying damage and locating victims after natural disasters), it is clear that the increased surveillance capacity of drones is frightening to many Americans. In addition to the three bills addressing the use of drones by law enforcement currently being debated in Congress (Thompson, 2013), several cities, counties, and states initiated creating their own laws that dictate when, how, and for what purposes police can (or cannot) use drones (Sengupta, 2013). This type of lawmaking at the local level is unusual (though not unheard of) and demonstrates the high level of anxiety that many officials possess regarding this new technology.

DNA

The ability to collect and analyze individuals' DNA is another technological advance that provides a very powerful crime-solving tool for law enforcement agents; yet also challenges our 18th century constitutional protections. Since *California v. Greenwood* (1988), state courts have consistently equated discarded DNA to trash and allowed law enforcement officials to collect discarded DNA for investigative purposes without a warrant. The reasoning is, if you leave it behind (say on a cup or utensil), it is considered abandoned and you have no expectation of privacy. This ruling allows cops (in the real world and on television) to sift through a suspect's trash, or offer a suspect a drink or meal, in order to collect his or her DNA and solve the crime.

All 50 states and the federal government have laws that allow DNA samples to be collected from persons convicted of a felony (Chemerinsky, 2013). But what about collecting DNA from individuals arrested for, yet not convicted of, a crime? Is that legal? At least 21states[4] have laws that allow (or require) the collection of DNA from persons arrested for certain crimes (usually serious, violent, or all felonies). Traditionally, the courts upheld these laws as legal and allowed for the collection of DNA from felony arrestees by likening DNA to fingerprints (see *State of Maryland v. Raines,* 2004; *Anderson v. Commonwealth of Virginia,* 2007) (www.dnaforensics.com/arrestees).

---

[4] The following states allow this practice: Alabama, Alaska, Arizona, California, Colorado, Florida, Indiana, Kansas, Louisiana, Maryland, Michigan, Minnesota, Missouri, New Mexico, North Dakota, South Carolina, South Dakota, Tennessee, Texas, Vermont, Virginia (www.dnaforensics.com).

In 2012, the U.S. Supreme Court granted certiorari in the case of ***Maryland v. King.*** The central issue before the court in *Maryland v. King* is whether DNA can be collected for the purpose of linking a suspect to *other crimes,* crimes that he is not suspected of committing (Chemerinsky, 2013). In other words, can the police "go fishing" with a criminal's DNA without a warrant and without probable cause because the technology exists to do so? In this case, the defense argued that DNA is qualitatively different than fingerprints and that because the DNA was used to link the individual to other crimes, the government needed probable cause and a warrant (Chemerinsky, 2013). The government, on the other hand, asked the court to apply a balancing test and affirm the law based on the minimal intrusion to the suspect in comparison to the potentially great benefits to law enforcement and society (Chemerinsky, 2013). After hearing oral arguments in the case Justice Alito commented that the case is "perhaps the most important criminal procedures case that this court has heard in decades" (Cassens-Weiss, 2013). In June 2013, the U.S. Supreme Court held that the collection of DNA from detained individuals is a legitimate component of the booking process and does not violate the protection against unreasonable search and seizure of the fourth amendment (*Maryland v. King,* 2013).

Another concern is what happens to an arrestee's DNA if the charges against the individual are dropped or the individual is acquitted? Can the person's DNA stay in a countywide or statewide DNA database if they are never convicted of a crime? Moreover, how do familial DNA matches (DNA matches based on a relative's DNA) figure into this conversation about rights and privacy. The answer at the current time is: It depends on the rules established in each state. Federal courts have not ruled on these issues yet, but it is probably only a matter of time.

Other Emerging Technologies

Beyond drones and DNA, GPS, cell phones, and social media are all recent technological innovations that also pose conundrums for the courts and law enforcement agents. Each of these can be used to track our movements and our social connections. The ability to attach a GPS device to a suspect's car means officers less frequently conduct "stakeouts" in the traditional sense. Attaching a GPS to a suspect's car does, however, constitute a search and may require a warrant (*United States v. Jones,* 2012). Short-term tracking is generally allowed without a warrant, as long as the device is affixed to the car while it is parked in public and in a state whose state constitution does not prohibit it[5] (*United States v. Pineda Moreno,* 2010; *United States v. Jones,* 2012).

Cell phones can also provide law enforcement officers with a wealth of information about a person's life and activities–including evidence of wrongdoing. There are already several cases testing the limits of various aspects of this technology (e.g., accessing email, texts, calls, contacts, pictures, and social media accounts as well as GPS functionality with and without warrants). There are too many cases and situations to summarize here, but in general, cell phones can be searched incident to arrest (Seligman, 2012). Although the U.S. Supreme Court has not addressed the issue of warrantless cell phone searches, the Sixth Circuit recently held that police can track suspects via their cell phones without a warrant (*United States v. Skinner,* 2012). It is unclear whether a password-protected smartphone can be searched without a warrant—on the one

---

[5] State constitutions may be more restrictive of government conduct than our federal constitution. Massachusetts, New York, and Washington prohibit the use of tracking devices by government agents unless they have probable cause and a warrant.

hand password protecting one's phone demonstrates an expressed expectation of privacy, but on the other hand courts ruled that there is no expectation of privacy when data are transmitted over public airwaves.

In determining whether law enforcement officers need a search warrant to access information on a suspect's social media account, justices are considering the suspect's privacy settings along with the size of his or her circle of "friends" to determine the individual's expectation of privacy (the larger the circle of "friends" or "followers," the less expectation of privacy).

There is little doubt that modern technology has eroded our reasonable expectations of privacy. With so many new technologies it can be hard to predict which ones may infringe on our 4th Amendment rights. Yet, we can expect courts throughout the nation to be called on frequently to apply our 18th century constitutional guarantees to our 21st century technology.

⊠ Conclusion

We Americans hold dear to our constitutional freedoms; however, sometimes those rights threaten our ability to effectively prevent crime and protect public safety. In these circumstances, we must carefully consider every goal and potential consequence of a policy or piece of legislation. While policy must always operate within the confines of the Constitution, policy can sometimes be dictated by constitutional challenges. For example, correctional realignment in California was a direct response to that state's violations of prisoner's rights. Similarly, recent U.S. Supreme Court rulings concerning the punishment of juveniles has impacted many state's juvenile justice policies and changed how criminal justice practitioners and society respond to our youngest residents. In some cases, such as the case with gun control policy, the court provides broad constitutional strokes as a framework for policy construction, but leaves the particulars to be debated by state, federal, and sometimes local policy makers. Likewise, new and emerging technologies pose significant constitutional questions for our courts. It remains to be seen how policies like these will be addressed by the courts in the future, and the greater implications of the implementation of these practices for our criminal justice system.

KEY TERMS

Assault-style weapon	Gun policy	Second Amendment
Broken windows	*Katz v. United States*	*Stanford v. Kentucky*
Crime control model	*Maryland v. King*	*United States v. Jones*
District of Columbia v. Heller	*Miller v. Alabama*	Universal background checks
Drones	*Parens patriae*	Unreasonable search
Due process model	Probable cause	Zero-tolerance policies
Expressed expectation of privacy	Realignment	
Fourth Amendment	*Roper v. Simmons*	

DISCUSSION QUESTIONS

1. In reviewing each of the emerging policy issues in this chapter, what challenges does the criminal justice system face in implementing these policies? What resources will be required to facilitate success?

2. What sort of constitutional challenges might the courts face within each of these policy issues?

3. Other than the topics mentioned in this book, what do you see as an emerging policy issue facing the criminal justice system in the 21st century?

WEBSITES FOR ADDITIONAL RESEARCH

International Firearm Injury Prevention and Policy: http://www.gunpolicy.org/

Law Center to Prevent Gun Violence: http://smartgunlaws.org/gun-policy/

NRA Institute for Legislative Action: http://www.nraila.org/second-amendment.aspx

American Civil Liberties Union: http://www.aclu.org/criminal-law-reform/search-and-seizure

References

Abramson, M. F. (1972). The criminalization of mentally disordered behavior: Possible side-effect of a new mental health law. *Hospital and Community Psychiatry, 23,* 101–107.

Achilles, M. (2004). Will restorative justice live up to its promise to victims? In H. Zehr & B. Toews (Eds.), *Critical issues in restorative justice.* Monsey, NY: Criminal Justice Press.

Achilles, M., & Stutzman-Amstutz, L. (2008). Responding to the needs of victims: What was promised, what has been delivered. In D. Sullivan & L. Tifft (Eds.), *Handbook of restorative justice.* New York: Routledge.

Acker, J. R. (1996). The death penalty: A 25-year retrospective and a perspective on the future. *Criminal Justice Review, 21,* 139–160.

Adams, B., & Addie, S. (2010). *Delinquency cases waived to criminal court, 2007.* Washington, DC: Office of Juvenile Justice and Delinquency Prevention, U.S. Department of Justice. Retrieved from https://www.ncjrs.gov/pdffiles1/ojjdp/230167.pdf

Adams, B., & Newton, L. (2008, August 28–31). *State laws related to immigration and immigrants: Symbolism or substance?* Paper presented at the annual meeting of the American Political Science Association, Boston, MA.

Adams, S., Leukefeld, C. G., & Peden, A. R. (2008). Substance abuse treatment for women offenders: A research review. *Journal of Addictions Nursing, 19*(2), 61–75.

Addams, J. (1920/1960). *Twenty years at Hull-House.* New York: Signet.

Addington v. Texas, 441 U.S. 418 (1979).

Agnew, R., & Brezina, A. (2011). *Juvenile delinquency: Causes and control* (4th ed.). New York: Oxford University Press.

Aguayo, T. (2006). Youth who killed at 12 will return to prison, but not for life. *New York Times.* Retrieved from http://www.nytimes.com/2006/03/02/national/02tate.html?_r=0

Aguilar, J. (2009, March 5). Back to prison for Longmont double murder. *Daily Camera.* Retrieved from http://www.denverpost.com/news/ci_11844461

Albonetti, C. A., & Hepburn, J. R. (1996). Prosecutorial discretion to defer criminalization: The effects of defendant's ascribed and achieved status characteristics. *Journal of Quantitative Criminology, 12,* 63–81.

Alexander, B. (1990). *Peaceful measures: Canada's way out of the war on drugs.* Toronto, Canada: University of Toronto Press.

Alexander, M. (2012). *The new Jim Crow: Mass incarceration in the age of color blindness.* (2nd ed.). New York: The New Press.

Allard, J. (2013, March 8). New bill on school discipline introduced to Senate. *Star Democrat.* Retrieved from http://www.stardem.com/news/local_news/article_d0d2f350-8838-11e2-95c9-001a4bcf887a.html

Allard, P. (2002). *Life sentences: Denying welfare benefits to women convicted of drug offenses.* Washington, DC: The Sentencing Project.

Almquist, L., & Dodd, E. (2009). *Mental health courts: A guide to research-informed policy and practice.* Retrieved from http://consensusproject.org/jc_publications/mental-health-courts-a-guide-to-research-informedpolicy-and-practice.pdf

American Bar Association. (1994). *Criminal justice policy on victim offender mediation/dialogue* (101B). Chicago, IL: Author. Retrieved from http://www.americanbar.org/groups/criminal_justice/policy/index_aba_criminal_justice_policies_by_meeting.html

American Bar Association. (2010). *Reforming the immigration system: Proposals to promote independence, fairness, efficiency, and professionalism in the adjudication of removal cases.* Washington, DC: ABA Commission on Immigration. Retrieved from http://www.americanbar.org/content/dam/aba/migrated/Immigration/PublicDocuments/full_report_part1.authcheckdam.pdf

American Civil Liberties Union. (2009). *Prolonged immigration detention of individuals who are challenging removal.* (IRP-Institute for Research on Poverty Issue Brief). Washington, DC: Author. Retrieved from http://www.aclu.uwm.edu

American Psychological Association (APA). (2008). Are zero tolerance policies effective in the schools?: An evidentiary review and recommendations. *American Psychologist, 63*(9), 852–862.

Amnesty International. (2009). *Jailed without justice: Immigrant detention in the United States.* Retrieved from http://www.amnestyusa.org/pdfs/JailedWithoutJustice.pdf

Amnesty International. (2011). "This is where I'm going to die": Children facing imprisonment without the possibility of release in the USA. London, UK: Author.

Amnesty International. (2012). *Abolitionist and retentionist countries.* London, UK: Author. Retrieved from http://www.amnesty.org/en/death-penalty/abolitionist-and-retentionist-countries

Amstutz, L. S. (2004). What is the relationship between victim service organizations and restorative justice? In H. Zehr & B. Toews (Eds.), *Critical issues in restorative justice.* Monsey, NY: Criminal Justice Press.

Anand, P. (2012). *Winners and losers: Corrections and higher education in California*. Los Altos, CA: California Common Sense.

Anderson, D. C. (1994, June 12). The crime funnel. *The New York Times Magazine*. Retrieved from http://www.nytimes.com/1994/06/12/magazine/the-crime-funnel.html

Anderson, T. L. (2003). Issues in the availability of health care for women prisoners. In S. F. Sharp (Ed.), *The incarcerated woman: Rehabilitative programming in women's prisons* (pp. 49–60). Upper Saddle River, NJ: Prentice Hall.

Anderson v. Commonwealth of Virginia, 650 S.E.2d 702, 704 (2007)—Record N. 062051.

Andrade, J. T., Vincent, G. M., & Saleh, F. M. (2006). Juvenile sex offenders: A complex population. *Journal of Forensic Science, 51*(1), 163–167.

Andrews, D., & Bonta, J. (2010). *The psychology of criminal conduct* (5th ed.). Cincinnati, OH: Anderson.

Applegate, B. K., Davis, R. K., & Cullen, F. T. (2009). Reconsidering child saving: The extent and correlates of public support for excluding youths from the juvenile court. *Crime and Delinquency, 55*, 51–77.

Archibald, B., & Llewellyn, J. (2006). The challenges of institutionalizing comprehensive restorative justice: Theory and practice in Nova Scotia. *Dalhousie Law Journal, 29*, 297.

Arendt, H. (1969). *On violence*. San Diego, CA: Harcourt & Brace.

Arizona v. United States, 567 U.S. ___, 2012.

Arrigio, B. A. (1992/1993). Paternalism, civil commitment and illness politics: Assessing the current debate and outlining a future direction. *Journal of Law and Health, 7*(2), 131–168.

Arthur Andersen, LLP v. United States, 544 U.S. 606 (2005).

Arya, N. (2011). *State trends: Legislative changes from 2005 to 2010 removing youth from the adult criminal justice system*. Washington, DC: Campaign for Youth Justice.

Austin, J. (2012, November 28). Crime and punishment. *Los Angeles Times*, p. 2.

Austin, J., & Irwin, J. (2012). *It's about time—America's imprisonment binge*. Independence, KY: Cengage.

Bach, R. (2005). Transforming border security: Prevention first. *Homeland Security Affairs, 1*(1), 1–15.

Bachman, R., & Coker, A. L. (1995). Police involvement in domestic violence: The interactive effects of victim injury, offender's history of violence, and race. *Violence and Victims, 10*, 91–106.

Bachman, R., & Paternoster, R. (1993). A contemporary look at the effects of rape law reform: How far have we really come? *Journal of Criminal Law and Criminology, 84*(3), 554–573.

Bagdikian, B. (2000). *The media monopoly* (6th ed.). Boston, MA: Beacon Press.

Bahr, S., Harris, P. E., Strobel, J. H., & Taylor, B. M. (2012). An evaluation of a short-term drug treatment for jail inmates. *International Journal of Offender Therapy and Comparative Criminology, 54*, 667–669.

Bahrampour, T. (2010). Number of illegal immigrants in U.S. drops, report says. *Washington Post*. Retrieved from http://www.washingtonpost.com/wp-dyn/content/article/2010/09/01/AR2010090106940.html

Baker, A., & Rivera, R. (2010, October 26). Study finds street stops by N.Y. police unjustified. *The New York Times*. Retrieved from http://www.nytimes.com/2010/10/27/nyregion/27frisk.html?emc=eta1

Baker, M. (2011, May 3). States reassess marijuana laws after federal warning. *Associated Press*. Retrieved from http://www.ap.org

Baldus, D. C., Pulaski, C., & Woodworth, G. (1983). Comparative review of death sentences: An empirical study of the Georgia experience. *Journal of Criminal Law and Criminology, 74*, pp. 661–753.

Baldus, D. C., & Woodworth, G. (1997). Race discrimination in America's capital punishment system since *Furman v. Georgia* (1972): The evidence of race disparities and the record of our courts and legislatures in addressing this issue. (Report prepared for the American Bar Association). In R. C. Dieter (1998). *The death penalty in Black & White: Who lives, who dies, who decides*. Washington, DC: DPIC, Death Penalty Information Center. Retrieved from http://www.deathpenaltyinfo.org/death-penalty-black-and-white-who-lives-who-dies-who-decides

Baldus, D. C., Woodworth, G. G., & Pulaski, C. A. (1990). *Equal justice and the death penalty: A legal and empirical analysis*. Boston, MA: Northeastern University Press.

Baldus, D. C., Woodworth, G., Zuckerman, D., Weiner, N. A., & Broffitt, B. (1998). Race discrimination and the death penalty in the post-*Furman* era: An empirical and legal overview, with preliminary findings from Philadelphia. *Cornell Law Review, 83*, 1638–1770.

Balingit, M. (2012, April 14). Jordan Brown held responsible for two slayings. *Pittsburgh Post-Gazette*. Retrieved from http://www.post-gazette.com/stories/local/neighborhoods-north/jordan-brown-held-responsible-for-2-homicides-631320/?p=0

Banks, D., & Kyckelhahn, T. (2011). *Characteristics of suspected human trafficking incidents, 2008–2010*. Washington, DC: Bureau of Justice Statistics.

Barak, G. (Ed.). (1995). *Media, process, and the social construction of crime: Studies in newsmaking criminology*. New York: Routledge, Taylor & Francis.

Barker, T. (2010). Law enforcement assistance administration. In B. S. Fisher & S. P. Lab (Eds.), *Encyclopedia of victimology and crime prevention*. London: Sage.

Barlow M. H. (1998). Race and the problem of crime in *Time* and *Newsweek* cover stories, 1946–1995. *Social Justice, 25*.

Barr, W. P. (1992). *Combating violent crime: 24 recommendations to strengthen criminal justice*. Washington, DC: Office of the United States Attorney General.

Barrett, C. J. (2012). *Courting kids: Inside an experimental youth court*. New York: NYU Press.

Bassuk, E., & Gerson, S. (1978). Deinstitutionalization and mental health services. *Scientific American, 238*, 46–53.

Battered Women's Justice Project. (2008). *Primary aggressor statutes*. Retrieved from http://www.bwjp.org/files/bwjp/articles/Primary_Aggressor_Chart_Final.pdf

Baumgartner, F. (2012). *Executions by county*. Washington, DC: Death Penalty Information Center. Retrieved from http://www.deathpenaltyinfo.org/executions-county

Bayoumi, A., & Zaric, G. (2008). The cost-effectiveness of Vancouver's supervised injection facility. *Canadian Medical Association Journal, 179*, 1143–1151.

Bazelon Center for Mental Health Law. (2003). *Criminalization of people with mental illnesses: The role of mental health courts in system reform.* Washington, DC: Author. Retrieved from http://www.portal.state.pa.us/portal/server.pt/document/1037939/doc115bazelon_2003_pdf

Bazelon Center for Mental Health Law. (2102). *Mental health courts.* Retrieved from http://www.bazelon.org/Where-We-Stand/Access-to-Services/Diversion-from-Incarceration-and-Reentry-/Mental-Health-Courts.aspx

Bazemore, G., & Schiff, M. (2001). *Restorative community justice: Repairing harm and transforming communities.* Cincinnati, OH: Anderson.

Bazemore, G., & Umbreit, M. (2002). A comparison of four restorative conferencing models by the office of juvenile justice and delinquency prevention. In J. Perry (Ed.), *Repairing communities through restorative justice* (pp. 67–105). Lanham, MD: American Correctional Association.

Bean, M. G., & Stone, J. (2011). Another view from the ground: How laws like SB1070 and HB2281 erode the intergroup fabric of our community. *Analyses of Social Issues and Public Policy, 12*(1), 144–150.

Beatty, P., Petteruti, A., & Ziedenberg, J. (2007, December). *The vortex: The concentrated racial impact of drug imprisonment and the characteristics of punitive counties.* Washington, DC: Justice Policy Institute.

Beccaria, C. (1986). *On crimes and punishments* (D. Young, Trans.). Indianapolis, IN: Hackett. (Original work published 1764)

Beck, A. J., & Harrison, P. M. (2001). *Prisoners in 2000.* Washington, DC: Bureau of Justice Statistics, Office of Justice Programs, U.S. Department of Justice.

Beck, C., Bratton, W. J., & Kelling, G. L. (2011, Spring). Who will police the criminologists? The dangers of politicized social science. *City Journal, 21*(2).

Becker, J. V., Stinson, J., Tromp, S., & Messer, G. (2003). Characteristics of individuals petitioned for civil commitment. *International Journal of Offender Therapy and Comparative Criminology, 47*(2), 185.

Beckett, K., & Western, B. (2001). Governing social marginality: Welfare, incarceration, and the transformation of state policy. *Punishment and Society, 3*, 43–59.

Bedau, H. A. (Ed.). (1982). *The death penalty in America* (3rd ed.). New York: Oxford University Press.

Bedau, H. A. (2009). Racism, wrongful convictions, and the death penalty. *Tennessee Law Review, 76*, 615–624.

Beichner, D., & Spohn, C. (2005). Prosecutorial charging decisions in sexual assault cases: Examining the impact of a specialized prosecution unit. *Criminal Justice Policy Review, 16*(4), 461–498.

Beittel, J. (2012). *Mexico's drug trafficking organizations: Source and scope of the rising violence.* Washington, DC: Congressional Research Service.

Belenko, S. (2001). *Research on drug courts: A critical review, 2001* (Update). New York: Columbia University National Center on Addiction and Substance Abuse.

Belkin, D. (2012, July 12). Chicago hunts for answers to gang killings: Police build Facebook-like database to prevent swift cycles of retaliation. *Wall Street Journal.* Retrieved from http://online.wsj.com/article/SB10001424052702303644004577520863051001848.html?goback=%2Egde_1314427_member_135339641

Belknap, J. (2003). Responding to the needs of women prisoners. In S. F. Sharp (Ed.), *The incarcerated woman: Rehabilitative programming in women's prisons* (pp. 93–106). Upper Saddle River, NJ: Prentice Hall.

Belknap, J. (2007). *The invisible woman: Gender, crime and justice* (3rd ed.). Belmont, CA: Wadsworth.

Belknap, J. (2010). "Offending women": A double entendre. *The Journal of Criminal Law & Criminology, 100*(3), 1061–1098.

Bellavita, C. (2008). Changing homeland security: What is homeland security? *Homeland Security Affairs, 4*(2), 1–30.

Bennett, B. (2012, July 6). U.S. citizen sues over imprisonment in fingerprint-sharing program. *Los Angeles Times.*

Benson, E. (2012, July 17). Dukakis's regret: What the onetime Democratic nominee learned from the Willie Horton ad. *New York Magazine.* Retrieved from http://nymag.com/news/frank-rich/michael-dukakis-2012-6/

Berg, M., & DeLisi, M. (2006). The correctional melting pot: Race, ethnicity, citizenship, and prison violence. *Journal of Criminal Justice, 34*, 631–642.

Bergseth, K. J., & Bouffard, J. A. (2007). The long-term impact of restorative justice programming for juvenile offenders. *Journal of Criminal Justice, 35*, 433–451. Retrieved from http://www.co.clay.mn.us/depts/attorney/pdfs/berbou07.pdf

Berk, R. (2005). *New claims about executions and general deterrence: Déjà vu all over again?* Los Angeles, CA: Department of Statistics Papers, Department of Statistics, UCLA. Retrieved from http://escholarship.org/uc/item/0q52b0b1

Bernstein, M., & Kostelac, C. (2002). Lavender and blue: Attitudes about homosexuality and behavior towards lesbians and gay men among police officers. *Journal of Contemporary Criminal Justice, 18*, 302–328.

Beyrer, C. (2011). Safe injection facilities save lives. *The Lancet, 377*, 1385–1386.

Bidinotto, R. J. (1988, July). Getting away with murder. *Readers Digest.*

Bishop, D. M., Frazier, C. E., & Henretta, J. C. (1989). Prosecutorial waiver: Case study of a questionable reform. *Crime and Delinquency, 35*, 179–201.

Bishop, D. M., Frazier, C. E., Lanza-Kaduce, L., & Winner, L. (1996). The transfer of juveniles to criminal court: Does it make a difference? *Crime and Delinquency, 42*, 171–191.

Black, M. C., Basile, K. C., Breiding, M. J., Smith, S. G., Walters, M. L., Merrick, M.T., . . . Stevens, M. R. (2011). *The national intimate partner and sexual violence survey (NISVS): 2010 summary report.* Atlanta, GA: National Center for Injury Prevention and Control, Centers for Disease Control and Prevention.

Black T., & Orsagh, T. (1978). New evidence on the efficacy of sanctions as a deterrent to homicide. *Social Science Quarterly, 58*, 616–631.

Black, W. K. (2005). *The best way to rob a bank is to own one: How corporate executives and politicians looted the S&L industry.* Austin: University of Texas Press.

Blickman, T., & Jelsma, M. (2009). *Drug policy reform in practice.* Amsterdam, Netherlands: Transnational Institute.

Block, R. (2008). *Impact of CeaseFire on geographical crime patterns. Appendix B evaluation of CeaseFire-Chicago.* Chicago, IL: National Institute of Justice, Office of Justice Programs. Retrieved from http://www.chicagojustice.org/foi/relevant-documents-of-interest/ceasefire/Northwestern-CeaseFire-Evaluation-Appendices.pdf

Bloom, B. (1999). Gender-responsive programming for women offenders: Guiding principles and practices. *Forum on Corrections Research, 11*(3), 22–27.

Bloom, B. (2012). *Gender-responsive programming for women offenders: Guiding principles and practices.* Ottawa, Canada: Correctional Service of Canada. Retrieved from http://www.csc-scc.gc.ca/text/pblct/forum/e113/113f_e.pdf

Bloom, B., & Covington, S. S. (1998). *Gender-specific programming for female offenders: What is it and why is it important?* Paper presented at the Annual Meeting of the American Society of Criminology, Washington, DC.

Bloom, B., Owen, B., & Covington, S. (2004). Women offenders and the gendered effects of public policy. *Review of Policy Research, 21*(1), 31–48.

Bloom, B., Owen, B., & Covington, S. (2005). *Gender responsive strategies for women offenders: A summary of research, practice, and guiding principles for women offenders.* Washington, DC: National Institute of Corrections, U.S. Department of Justice.

Blueprints for Healthy Youth development. (n.d.). Retrieved from http://www.blueprintsprograms.com

Blumstein A., & Wallman J. (Eds.). (2000). *The crime drop in America* (Rev. ed.). New York: University of Cambridge Press.

Boardman, Jr., F. W. (1977). *America and the robber barons, 1865 to 1913.* New York: Henry Z. Walck.

Bogira, S. (2012, July 26). Concentrated poverty and homicide in Chicago [web log post]. *Chicago Reader.* Chicago, IL. Retrieved from http://www.chicagoreader.com/Bleader/archives/2012/07/26/concentrated-poverty-and-homicide-in-chicago

Bonczar, T. P., & Beck, A. J. (2003). *Lifetime likelihood of going to state or federal prison.* Washington, DC: U.S. Department of Justice, Bureau of Justice Statistics.

Bonta, J., Jesseman, R., Rugge, T., & Cormier, R. (2008). Restorative justice and recidivism: Promises made, promises kept. In D. Sullivan & L. Tifft (Eds.), *Handbook of restorative justice.* New York: Routledge.

Bonta, J., Rugge, T., Scott, T.-L., Bourgon, G., & Yessine, A. K. (2008). Exploring the black box of community supervision. *Journal of Offender Rehabilitation, 47*(3), 248–270.

Boodhoo, N. (2012, July 3). *Black unemployment in Chicago is third highest in nation.* Discussion with Algernon Austin of the Economic Policy Institute on *Eight Forty-Eight* Tuesday morning (WBEZ 91.5). Chicago, IL: Chicago Public Media. Retrieved from http://www.wbez.org/black-unemployment-chicago-third-highest-nation-report-finds-100638

Boos, E. J. (1997). Moving in the direction of justice: College minds—Criminal mentalities. *Journal of Criminal Justice and Popular Culture, 5*, 1–20.

Boothroyd, R., Poythress, N., McGaha, A., & Petrila, J. (2003). The Broward mental health court: Process, outcomes and service utilization. *International Journal of Law and Psychiatry, 26*, 55–71.

Bortner, M. A. (1986). Traditional rhetoric, organizational realities: Remand of juveniles to adult court. *Crime and Delinquency, 32*, 53–73.

Bortner, M. A., Zatz, M. S., & Hawkins, D. F. (2000). Race and transfer: Empirical research and social context. In J. Fagan & F. E. Zimring (Eds.), *The changing borders of juvenile justice: Transfer of adolescents to the criminal court* (pp. 277–320). Chicago, IL: University of Chicago Press.

Borum, R., Swanson, J., Swartz, M., & Hiday, V. (1997). Substance abuse, violent behavior and police encounters among persons with severe mental disorder. *Journal of Contemporary Criminal Justice, 13*(3), 236–250.

Boss, M. S., & George, B. C. (1992). Challenging conventional views of white-collar crime. *Criminal Law Bulletin, 28*, 32–58.

Bottoms, A. (1999). Interpersonal violence and social order in prison. In M. Tonry & J. Petersilia (Eds.), *Crime and justice: A review of research, 26*, 205–282.

Botvin, G., Baker, E., Dusenbury, L., Botvin, W., & Diaz, T. (1995). Long-term follow-up results of a randomized drug abuse prevention trial in a white middle-class population. *Journal of the American Medical Association, 273*, 1106–1112.

Bouffard, J. A., & Bergerson, L. E. (2006). Reentry works: The implementation and effectiveness of a serious and violent offender reentry initiative. *Journal of Offender Rehabilitation, 44*(2/3), 1–129.

Bowen, D. (2012). *Statement of vote: November 6, 2012, general election.* Sacramento: California Secretary of State.

Bowers, J. E. (2001). The integrity of the game is everything: The problem of geographic disparity in three strikes. *New York University Law Review, 76*(4), 1164–1203.

Bowers, W. J., Pierce, G. L., & McDevitt, J. F. (1984). *Legal homicide: Death as punishment in America, 1864–1982.* Boston, MA: Northeastern University Press.

Bowers, W. J., & Steiner, B. D. (1999). Death by default: An empirical demonstration of false and forced choices in capital sentencing. *Texas Law Review, 77*, 605–717.

Boyd, G., & Hitt, J. (2002). This is your bill of rights. In M. Gray (Ed.), *Busted* (pp. 149–154). New York: Thunder's Mouth Press/Nation Books.

Bradshaw, W., & Roseborough, D. (2005). Restorative justice dialogue: The impact of mediation and conferencing on juvenile recidivism. *Federal Probation, 69*(2), 15–21.

Bradshaw, W., Roseborough, D., & Umbreit, M. S. (2006). The effect of victim offender mediation on juvenile offender recidivism: A meta-analysis. *Conflict Resolution Quarterly, 24*, 87–98.

Braga, A. A. (2008). *Problem-oriented policing and crime prevention* (2nd ed.). Monsey, NY: Criminal Justice Press.

Braga, A. A., & Bond, B. J. (2008). Policing crime and disorder hot spots: A randomized controlled trial. *Criminology, 46*(3), 577–607.

Braga, A. A., Hureau, D. M., & Papachristos, A. V. (2012). An ex-post-facto evaluation framework for place-based police interventions. *Evaluation Review, 35*(6), 592–626.

Braga, A. A., Kennedy, D., Waring, E., & Piehl, A. (2001). Problem-oriented policing, deterrence, and youth violence: An evaluation of Boston's Operation Ceasefire. *Journal of Research in Crime and Delinquency, 38*, 195–225.

Braga, A. A., Papachristos, A., & Hureau, D. (2012). Hot spots policing effects on crime. *Campbell Systematic Reviews, 8*.

Braga, A. A., Piehl, M. A., & Hureau, D. (2009). Controlling violent offenders released to the community: An evaluation of the Boston Reentry Initiative. *Journal of Research in Crime and Delinquency, 46*(4), 411–436.

Braga, A. A., & Weisburd, D. L. (2010). *Policing problem places: Crime hotspots and effective prevention*. Oxford, UK: Oxford University Press.

Braga, A. A., Weisburd, D. L., Waring, E. J., Green-Mazerolle, L., Spelman, W., & Gajewski, F. (1999). Problem-oriented policing in violent crime places: A randomized controlled experiment. *Criminology, 37*(3), 541–580.

Braga, A. A., & Winship, C. (2006). Partnership, accountability, and innovation: Clarifying Boston's experience with pulling levers. In D. L. Weisburd & A. A. Braga (Eds.), *Police innovation: Contrasting perspectives*. New York: Cambridge University Press.

Braithwaite, J. (2003). Principles of restorative justice. In A. Von Hirsch, J. Roberts, A. Bottoms, K. Roach, & M. Schiff (Eds.), *Restorative justice and criminal justice: Competing or reconcilable paradigms?* Oxford, UK: Hart.

Braithwaite, J., & Geis, G. (1982). On theory and action for corporate crime control. *Crime & Delinquency, 28*, 202–314.

Brantingham, P. J., & Brantingham, P. L. (1991). *Environmental criminology*. Prospect Heights, IL: Waveland Press.

Brecher, E. (1972). *Licit and illicit drugs*. Boston, MA: Little, Brown.

Brehm, J., & Gates, S. (1997). *Working, shirking, and sabotage: Bureaucratic response to a democratic public*. Ann Arbor: University of Michigan Press.

Bright, S. B. (1997a). *Capital punishment on the 25th anniversary of Furman v. Georgia*. Atlanta, GA: Southern Center for Human Rights.

Bright, S. B. (1997b). Neither equal nor just: The rationing and denial of legal services to the poor when life and liberty are at stake. *Annual Survey of American Law, 1997*, p. 783–836.

Briggs, C. S., Sundt, J. L., & Castellano, T. C. (2003). The effect of supermaximum security prisons on aggregate levels of institutional violence. *Criminology, 41*, 1341–1376.

British Columbia Center for Excellence in HIV/AIDS. (2004). *Evaluation of the supervised injection site: One-year summary*. Vancouver, BC: Author.

Bromberg, W., & Thompson, C. B. (1937). The relation of psychosis, mental defect, and personality types to crime. *Journal of Criminal Law and Criminology, 28*, 70–88.

Bronner, E. (2012). Poor land in jail as companies add huge fees for probation. *New York Times*. Retrieved from http://www.nytimes.com/2012/07/03/us/probation-fees-multiply-as-companies-profit.html?pagewanted=1&nl=todaysheadlines&emc=edit_th_20120703

Brown, B. (2007). Community policing in post-September 11 America: A comment on the concept of community-oriented counterterrorism. *Police Practice and Research, 8*(3), 239–251.

Brown, M., & Bloom, B. (2009). Reentry and renegotiating motherhood: Maternal identity and success on parole. *Crime & Delinquency, 55*(2), 313–336.

Brown, R. (2010). Associations with substance abuse treatment completion rates among drug court participants. *Substance Use and Misuse, 45*, 1874–1891.

Brown, R., Zuelsdorff, M., & Gassman, M. (2009). Treatment retention among African Americans in the Dane County drug treatment court. *Journal of Offender Rehabilitation, 48*, 336–349.

Brown, T. (2012, July 3). Insight: Florida man sees "cruel" face of U.S. justice. *Reuters*. Retrieved from http://news.yahoo.com/insight-florida-man-sees-cruel-face-u-justice-050157061.html

Brown v. Plata, 131 S Ct. 1910 (2011).

Browne, A., & Bassuk, S. S. (1997). Intimate violence in the lives of homeless and poor housed women: Prevalence and patterns in an ethnically diverse sample. *American Journal of Orthopsychiatry, 67*, 261–278.

Browne, A., Miller, B., & Maguin, E. (1999). Prevalence and severity of lifetime physical and sexual victimization among incarcerated women. *International Journal of Law and Psychiatry, 22*(3/4), 301–322.

Brownsberger, W., & Aromaa, S. (2003). Prohibition of drug dealing in school zones. *FAS (Federation of American Scientists) Drug Policy Analysis Bulletin, 9*.

Bruck, C. (2009, June 29). Angelo's ashes: The man who became the face of the financial crisis. *New Yorker*, pp. 49–55.

Buell, M. (2010). NIC's women offender initiative: New research in action. *Corrections Today-Research Notes*. Washington, DC: American Correctional Association. Retrieved from https://aca.org/research/pdf/ResearchNotes_Dec2010.pdf

Bui, H. N., & Ornuma, T. (2005). Immigration and self-reported delinquency: The interplay of immigrant generations, gender, race and ethnicity. *Journal of Crime and Justice, 28*(2), 71–99.

Bullock, J. A., Haddow, G. D., & Coppola, D. P. (2013). *Introduction to homeland security*. Waltham, MA: Butterworth-Heinemann.

Bulwa, D., & Berton, J. (2013, January 13). Slayings rise in Bay Area in 2012. *San Francisco Chronicle*, p. 1.

Bumiller, K. (2010). The nexus of domestic violence reform and social science: From instrument of social change to institutionalized surveillance. *Annual Review of Law and Social Science, 6*, 173–193.

Bureau of Justice Statistics. (2010). *Crime in the United States*. Washington, DC: U.S. Department of Justice.

Bureau of Justice Statistics. (2011). *Prisoners in 2010*. Washington, DC: U.S. Department of Justice.

Bureau of Prisons. (2010, December 25). *Quick facts, last update*. Washington, DC: U.S. Department of Justice. Retrieved from http://www.bop.gov/news/quick.jsp

Burgess, M. (2003). *A brief history of terrorism.* Washington, DC: CDI, Center for Defense Information. Retrieved from http://www.cdi.org/friendlyversion/printversion.cfm?documentID=1502

Burke, M. (Producer), & Cavanaugh, M. (Host). (2012, August 27). *New hope for juveniles sentenced to life without parole* [Television broadcast]. San Diego, CA: KPBS Midday Edition. Retrieved from http://www.kpbs.org/news/2012/aug/27/new-hope-juveniles-sentenced-lwop/

Burke, P., & Adams, L. (1991). *Classification of women offenders in state correctional facilities: A handbook for practitioners.* Washington, DC: Department of Justice, National Institute of Corrections.

Burley, L. M. (1997). History repeats itself in the resurrection of prisoner chain gangs: Alabama's experience raises eighth amendment concerns. *Law and Inequality, 15*(1), 127–156.

Burt, M. R. (1998). Rape myths. In M. E. Odem & J. Clay-Warner (Eds.), *Confronting rape and sexual assault: Worlds of women, No. 3* (pp. 129–144). Wilmington, DE: SR Books/Scholarly Resources.

Bush-Baskette, S. R. (1999). The war on drugs: A war against women? In S. Cook & S. Davies (Eds.), *Harsh punishment: International experiences of women's imprisonment* (pp. 211–229). Boston, MA: Northeastern University Press.

Butcher, K. F., & Piehl, A. M. (1998). Cross-city evidence on the relationship between immigration and crime. *Journal of Policy Analysis and Management, 17*, 457–493.

Butcher, K. F., & Piehl, A. M. (2008, February). Crime corrections, and California: What does immigration have to do with it? *California Counts, 9*(3). Retrieved from http://www.ppic.org/content/pubs/cacounts/CC_208KBCC.pdf

Butler, A. M. (1997). *Gendered justice in the American west: Women prisoners in men's penitentiaries.* Chicago: University of Illinois Press.

Butzin, C. A., O'Connell, D. J., Martin, S. S., & Incairdi, J. A. (2006). Effect of drug treatment during work release on new arrest and incarcerations. *Journal of Criminal Justice, 34*, 557–565.

Byrne, J. (2009, December 4). Gang gun law: New statute mandates prison for gang members caught with loaded weapons. *Chicago Tribune.* Retrieved from Cable News Network [CNN]. (2000). *Debate history: 1988 presidential debates.* Retrieved from http://www.cnn.com/ELECTION/2000/debates/history.story/1988.html

Byrne, J. M., & Hummer, D. (2008a). Examining the impact of institutional culture on prison violence and disorder: An evidence-based review. In J. M. Byrne, D. Hummer, & F. S. Taxman (Eds.), *The culture of prison violence* (pp. 40–90). Boston, MA: Pearson Education.

Byrne, J. M., & Hummer, D. (2008b). The nature and extent of prison violence. In J. M. Byrne, D. Hummer, & F. S. Taxman (Eds.), *The culture of prison violence* (pp. 12–26). Boston, MA: Pearson Education.

Byrne, J. M., Hummer, D., & Taxman, F. S. (2008c). The National Institute of Corrections' institutional culture change initiative: A multisite evaluation. In J. M. Byrne, D. Hummer, & F. S. Taxman (Eds.), *The culture of prison violence* (pp. 137–163). Boston, MA: Pearson.

Calavita, K. (1993). The contradictions of immigration lawmaking. In W. Chambliss & M. Zatz (Eds.), *Making law: The state, the law, and structural contradictions.* Bloomington, IN: Indiana University Press.

Calavita, K. (1996). The new politics of immigration: Balanced budget conservatism and the symbolism of Prop. 187. *Social Problems, 43*(3), 284–305.

Calavita, K., Pontell, H. N., & Tillman, R. H. (1997). *Big money crime: Fraud and politics in the savings and loan crisis.* Berkeley: University of California Press.

California Department of Corrections. (2010). *The cornerstone of California's solution to reduce overcrowding, costs, and recidivism.* Retrieved from http://www.cdcr.ca.gov/realignment

California Department of Corrections and Rehabilitation (CDCR). (n.d.). *California's Correctional Facilities.* Sacramento, CA: Author. Retrieved from http://www.cdcr.ca.gov/visitors/docs/20081124-webmapbooklet%202.pdf

California Department of Corrections and Rehabilitation (CDCR). (2011a). *California prisoners and parolees.* Sacramento, CA: Author. Retrieved from http://www.cdcr.ca.gov/reports_research/offender_information_services_branch/Annual/CalPris/CALPRISd2010.pdf

California Department of Corrections and Rehabilitation (CDCR). (2011b, July 15). *Fact sheet. 2011 public safety realignment.* Sacramento, CA: Author. Retrieved from http://www.cdcr.ca.gov/about_cdcr/docs/realignment-fact-sheet.pdf

California Department of Corrections and Rehabilitation. (2012). *Fact sheet: 2011 public safety realignment.* Sacramento, CA: Author.

California District Attorney's Association. (2004). *Prosecutors' perspective on California's Three Strikes Law: A 10-year retrospective.* Sacramento, CA: Author.

California Legislative Analyst's Office. (1997). *The "three strikes and you're out" law: An update.* Sacramento, CA: Author.

California Legislative Analyst's Office (2004). *Proposition 66: Limitations on "three strikes" law. Sex crimes. Punishment. Initiative statute.* Retrieved from http://www.lao.ca.gov/ballot/2004/66_11_2004.htm

California Legislative Analyst's Office. (2005). *A primer: Three strikes: The impact after more than a decade.* Sacramento, CA: Author.

California Legislative Analyst's Office. (2012). Proposition 36. Three strikes law. Sentencing for repeat felony offenders (Initiative statute). Retrieved from http://www.lao.ca.gov/ballot/2012/36_11_2012.aspx

California Secretary of State. (2012). Official voter information guide: Prop 36. Retrieved from http://voterguide.sos.ca.gov/propositions/36/

California State Auditor. (2010). *California department of corrections and rehabilitation: Inmates sentenced under the three strikes law and a small number of inmates receiving specialty health care represent significant costs.* Sacramento, CA: Author.

California v. Greenwood, 486 U.S. 35 (1988).

Californians for Safety and Justice. (2012). Why California voters passed Proposition 36 and what criminal justice changes they want next. Oakland, CA: Author. Retrieved from http://www.safe-andjust.org/news-media/Nov2012survey

Callins v. Collins, 510 U.S. 1141, 1994.

Camp, C. G., Hardyman, P. L., May, R., & Camp, G. M. (2008). *Prison staffing analysis: A training manual with staffing considerations for special populations.* Washington, DC: U.S. Department of Justice, National Institute of Corrections.

Camp, G., & Camp, C. G. (1985). Prison gangs: Their extent, nature, and impact on prisons. Washington, DC: U.S. Department of Justice.

Camp, S., Gaes, G. G., Langan, N., & Saylor, W. (2003). The influence of prisons on inmate misconduct: A multilevel investigation. *Justice Quarterly, 20*(3), 501–533.

Campbell Collaboration. (n.d.). Retrieved from http://www.cambell-collaboration.org

Campus Sexual Assault Victims' Bill of Rights, Pub. L. No. 102–325, §486(c)(1992).

Canada. (2002). *Report of the Senate special committee on illegal drugs.* Ottawa, Canada: Author.

Canfield, D. (2009, October 8). Drug law reforms in place. *Huffington Post.* Retrieved from http://www.huffingtonpost.com

Caplan, J. M., & Kennedy, L. W. (2010). *Risk terrain modeling manual.* Newark, NJ: Rutgers Center on Public Security.

Cardoso, F., Gaviria, C., & Zedillo, E. (2009). The war on drugs is a failure. *Wall Street Journal.* Retrieved from http://www.online.wsj.com

Carey, B. (2003). Searching for the next Prozac. *Los Angeles Times.* Retrieved from http://www.latimes.com

Carlson, D. K. (2004). *Terrorism fears not partisan; War's progress is.* Washington, DC: The Gallup Organization.

Carlson, D. P. (2005). *When cultures clash: Strategies for strengthening police-community relations* (2nd ed.). Upper Saddle River, NJ: Pearson-Prentice Hall.

Carpenter, D. P. (2010). *Regulation and power: Organizational image and pharmaceutical regulation at the FDA.* Princeton, NJ: Princeton University Press.

Carroll, S., & Pinkerton, J. (2010, February 22). HPD fights lack of trust among immigrant witnesses. *Houston Chronicle.* Retrieved from http://www.chron.com/news/houston-texas/article/HPD-fights-lack-of-trust-among-immigrant-witnesses-1698719.php

Carson, E. A., & Sabol, W. J. (2012). *Prisoners in 2011.* Washington, DC: Bureau of Justice Statistics, U.S. Department of Justice. Retrieved from http://bjs.gov/content/pub/pdf/p11.pdf

Carson, R. (2012, September 30). Washington's marijuana legalization measure creates strange bedfellows among foes, backers. *Tacoma News Tribune.* Retrieved from http://www.thenewstribune.com

Carter, D. (2004). *Law enforcement intelligence: A guide for state, local, and tribal law enforcement agencies.* Washington, DC: Office of Community Oriented Policing Services.

Carter, J. (1977, August 2). *Drug abuse message to the Congress.* Washington, DC: U.S. Government Printing Office.

Carter, W., & Barker, R. (2011). Does completion of juvenile drug court deter adult criminality? *Journal of Social Work Practice in the Addictions, 11,* 181–193.

Case, B., Steadman, H. J., Dupuis, S. A., & Morris, L. S. (2009). Who succeeds in jail diversion programs for persons with mental illness? A multi-site study. *Behavioral Science and Law, 22,* 661–674.

Casella, R. (2003). Zero tolerance policy in schools: Rationale, consequences, and alternatives. *Teachers College Record, 105,* 872–892.

Cassens-Weiss, D. (2013, February 27). Scalia and Kagan appear most skeptical about DNA collection from arrestees. *ABA Journal.* Retrieved from http://www.abajournal.com/news/article/scalia_and_kagan_appear_most_skeptical_about_dna_collection_from_arrestees/

Catalano, S. (2012). *Intimate partner violence, 1993–2010.* Washington, DC: U.S. Department of Justice. Retrieved from http://www.bjs.gov/content/pub/pdf/ipv9310.pdf

Center for Community Alternatives. (2011). *The use of criminal history records in college admissions.* Retrieved from http://www.communityalternatives.org/pdf/Reconsidered-criminal-hist-recs-in-college-admissions.pdf

Center for Court Innovation. (2012). *Red Hook community justice center.* New York: Author. Retrieved from http://www.courtinnovation.org/project/red-hook-community-justice-center

Center for Disease Control (2011). *FastStats: Injury and homicides.* Atlanta, GA: Author. Retrieved from http://www.cdc.gov/nchs/fastats/

Center for Sex Offender Management. (2008). *Legislative trends in sex offender management.* Washington, DC: U.S. Department of Justice, Office of Justice Programs.

Chaffin, M. (2008). Our minds are made up—don't confuse us with the facts: Commentary on policies concerning children with sexual behavior problems and juvenile sex offenders. *Child Maltreatment, 13*(2), 110–121.

Chaiken, J. M., Lawless, M. W., & Stevenson, K. A. (1974). *The impact of police activity on crime: Robberies on the New York City subway system.* New York: RAND.

Champion, D. J. (1989). Private counsels and public defenders: A look at weak cases, prior records, and leniency in plea bargaining. *Journal of Criminal Justice, 17,* 253–263.

Chemerinsky, E. (2013, February 25). Does the Fourth Amendment still fit the 21st century? *ABA Journal.* Retrieved from http://www.abajournal.com/news/article/chemerinsky_does_the_fourth_amendment_still_fit_the_21st_century/

Chen, E. Y. (2008a). Impacts of 'three strikes and you're out' on crime trends in California and throughout the United States. *Journal of Contemporary Criminal Justice, 24*(4), 345–370.

Chen, E. Y. (2008b). The liberation hypothesis and racial and ethnic disparities in the application of California's three strikes law. *Journal of Ethnicity in Criminal Justice, 6*(2), 83–102.

Chen, E. Y. (2012, November 1). Prop 36 will save money and increase fairness. *San Jose Mercury News.* Retrieved from http://www.mercurynews.com/opinion/ci_21905517/elsa-y-chen-prop-36-will-save-money

Chen, E. Y. (2013). In the furtherance of justice, injustice, or both? A multilevel analysis of courtroom context and the implementation of three strikes. *Justice Quarterly,* 1–30.

Chesney-Lind, M. (2000). Women and the criminal justice system: Gender matters. In *Topics in community corrections: Responding to women offenders in the community* (pp. 7–10). Washington, DC: National Institute of Corrections.

Chesney-Lind, M. (2002). Criminalizing victimization: The unintended consequences of pro-arrest policies for girls and women. *Criminology and Public Policy, 2,* 81–90.

Chesney-Lind, M. (2004). *The female offender: Girls, women, and crime* (2nd ed.). Thousand Oaks, CA: Sage.

Chesney-Lind, M., & Hagedorn, J. M. (Eds). (1999). *Female gangs in America: Essays on girls, gangs, and gender.* Chicago, IL: Lakeview Press.

Chesney-Lind, M., & Irwin, K. (2007). *Beyond bad girls: Gender, violence, and hype.* New York: Routledge.

Chesney-Lind, M., Morash, M., & Stevens, T. (2008). Girls' troubles, girls' delinquency, and gender responsive programming: A review. *Australian & New Zealand Journal of Criminology, 41*(1), 162–189.

Chesney-Lind, M., & Pasko, L. (2004). *The female offender: Girls, women, and crime* (2nd ed.). Thousand Oaks, CA: Sage.

Chettiar, I. (2012, January 11). *Criminal justice reform can help with state fiscal woes.* Washington, DC: Center for American Progress. Retrieved from http://www.americanprogress.org/issues/civil-liberties/news/2012/01/11/10970/criminal-justice-reform-can-help-with-state-fiscal-woes/

Chiricos, T., & Eschholz, S. (2002). The racial and ethnic typification of crime and the criminal typification of race and ethnicity in local television news. *Journal of Research in Crime and Delinquency, 39*(4), 400–420.

Chiricos, T., Padgett, K., & Gertz, M. (2000). Fear, TV news, and the reality of crime. *Criminology, 38,* 755–786.

Cho, H., & Wilke, D. J. (2005). How has the Violence Against Women Act affected the response of the criminal justice system to domestic violence? *Journal of Sociology and Social Welfare, 32,* 125–139.

Christy, A., Poythress, N. G., Boothroyd, R. A., Petrila, J., & Mehra, S. (2005). Evaluating the efficiency and community safety goals of the Broward County mental health court. *Behavioral Sciences and the Law, 22,* 227–243.

Citizens for Responsibility and Ethics in Washington. (2012). *Family affair.* Washington, DC: Author.

Clark, J., Austin, J., & Henry, D. A. (1997). *"Three strikes and you're out": A review of state legislation.* Washington, DC: National Institute of Justice.

Clark, M. (July 15, 2013). "Zimmerman verdict renews focus on 'stand your ground' laws." *USA Today.* Retrieved from http://www.usatoday.com/story/news/nation/2013/07/15/stateline-zimmerman-stand-your-ground/2517507/

Clark v. Arizona, 548 U.S. 735 (2006).

Clarke, R. V. (Ed.). (1996). Preventing mass transit crime. *Crime Prevention Studies, 6.*

Clarke, R. V. (1997). *Situational crime prevention* (2nd ed.). Guilderland, NY: Harrow and Heston.

Clarke, R. V., & Weisburd, D. (1994). Diffusion of crime control benefits: Observations on the reverse of displacement. *Crime Prevention Studies, 2.*

Clear, T. R. (2007). *Imprisoning communities: How mass incarceration makes disadvantaged neighborhoods worse.* New York: Oxford University Press.

Clear, T. R., Cole, G. F., Reisig, M. D., & Petrosino, C. (2012). *American corrections in brief.* Belmont, CA: Wadsworth.

Clear, T. R., Hamilton, J. R., Jr., & Cadora, E. (2011). *Community justice* (2nd ed.). New York: Routledge.

Cloyes, K. G., Lovell, D., Allen, D. G., & Rhodes, L. A. (2006). Assessment of psychosocial impairment in a supermaximum security unit sample. *Criminal Justice and Behavior, 33,* 760–781.

Cochran, C. E., Mayer, L. C., Carr, T. R., Cayer, N. J., & McKenzie, M. (2011). *American public policy: An Introduction.* Boston, MA: Wadsworth.

Cohan, W. D. (2009). *House of cards: A tale of hubris and wretched excess on Wall Street.* New York: Doubleday.

Cohen, A. (1955). *Delinquent boys.* Glencoe, IL: The Free Press.

Cohen, L. E., & Felson, M. (1979). Social change and crime rate trends: A routine activity approach. *American Sociological Review, 44,* 588–608.

Cohen, M., & Jeglic, E. (2007). Sex offender legislation in the United States: What do we know? *International Journal of Offender Therapy and Comparative Criminology, 51*(4), 369–383.

Cohen, T. (2013, February 28). House passes Violence Against Women Act after GOP version defeated. *CNN Politics.* Retrieved from http://www.cnn.com/2013/02/28/politics/violence-against-women/index.html

Coker, D. (2000). Shifting power for battered women: Law, material resources, and poor women of color. *University of California, Davis Law Review, 33,* 1009–1056.

Coleman v. Wilson, 912 F. Supp. 1282, 1324 (E.D.Cal.1995).

Conant, M. (1960). *Antitrust in the American motion picture industry.* Berkeley: University of California Press.

Congressional Research Service. (2012). Analysis of data regarding certain individuals identified through Secure Communities: Updating the previous analysis with citizenship. Washington, DC: Author. Retrieved from http://judiciary.house.gov/news/pdfs/Criminal%20Aliens%20Report.pdf

Conroy, J. (2000). *Unspeakable acts, ordinary people: The dynamics of torture* (1st ed.). New York: Knopf.

Constantini, C. (2012, December 12). Support for gun control at 10-year high. *ABC News.* Retrieved from http://abcnews.go.com/ABC_Univision/News/study-support-gun-control-10-year-high/story?id=18015933#.UVsmaazilWc

Cook, P. J., & Slawson, D. B. (1993). *The costs of processing murder cases in North Carolina* (assistance from L. A. Gries). Raleigh, NC: North Carolina Administrative Office of the Courts.

Cooper, V. G., McLearen, A. M., & Zapf, P. A. (2004). Dispositional decisions with the mentally ill: Police perceptions and characteristics. *Police Quarterly, 7,* 295–310.

Cooper v. Pate, 378 U.S. 546 (1964).

Cops, D., & Pleysier, S. (2011). "Doing gender" in fear of crime: The impact of gender identity on reported levels of fear of crime in adolescents and young adults. *British Journal of Criminology, 51*(1), 58–74.

Cornish, D. B., & Clarke, R. V. (Eds.). (1986). *The reasoning criminal.* New York: Springer-Verlag.

Cornish, D. B., & Clarke, R. V. (2003). Opportunities, precipitators, and criminal decisions: A reply to Wortley's critique of situational crime prevention. *Crime Prevention Studies, 16,* 41–96.

Cosden, M., Ellens, J., Schnell, J., & Yamini-Diouf, Y. (2005). Efficacy of a mental health treatment court with assertive community treatment. *Behavioral Sciences and the Law, 23,* 199–214.

Cost of 'three strikes' law. (2004, March 5). *San Francisco Chronicle*. Retrieved from http://www.sfgate.com/opinion/editorials/article/Cost-of-three-strikes-law-2814048.php

Council of State Governments. (2012). *Criminal justice/mental health consensus project*. Arlington, VA: National Alliance on Mental Illness. Retrieved from http://www.consensusproject.org

Couts, A. (2012, September 12). Drones: 13 things you need to know from Congress's new report. *Digital Trends*. Retrieved from http://www.digitaltrends.com/cool-tech/drones-congressional-research-service-report/

Covington, S. S. (2000). Helping women to recover: Creating gender-specific treatment for substance abusing women and girls in community corrections. In M. McMahon (Ed.), *Assessment to assistance: Programs for women in community corrections* (pp. 171–234). Lanham, MD: ACA, American Counseling Association.

Covington, S., & Bloom, B. (2003). Gendered justice: Women in the criminal justice system. In B. Bloom (Ed.), *Gendered justice: Addressing female offenders* (pp. 3–24). Durham, NC: Carolina Academic Press.

Coyle, M., Strasser, F., & Lavelle, M. (1990, June 11). Fatal defense: Trial and error in the nation's death belt. *The National Law Journal, 12*(40), 30–44.

Crager, M., Cousin, M., & Hardy, T. (2003). Victim-defendants: An emerging challenge in responding to domestic violence in Seattle and the King County region. Retrieved from http://www.mincava.umn.edu/documents/victimdefendant/victimdefendant.pdf

Craun S. W., & Theriot, M. T. (2009). Misperceptions of sex offender perpetration: Considering the impact of sex offender registration. *Journal of Interpersonal Violence, 24*(12), 2057–2072.

Crawford, A., & Clear, T. R. (2001). Community justice: Transforming communities through restorative justice? In G. Bazemore & M. Schiff (Eds.), *Restorative community justice: Repairing harm and transforming communities* (pp. 127–149). Cincinnati, OH: Anderson.

Crawford, C. (2000). Gender, race, and habitual offender sentencing in Florida. *Criminology, 38*(1), 263–280.

Crawford, C., Chiricos, T., & Kleck, G. (1998). Race, racial threat, and sentencing of habitual offenders. *Criminology, 36*(3), 481–511.

Crawley, E., & Crawley, P. (2008). Culture, performance, and disorder: The communicative quality of prison violence. In J. M. Byrne, D. Hummer, & F. S. Taxman (Eds.), *The culture of prison violence* (pp. 123–136). Boston, MA: Pearson.

Crenshaw, K. (1991). Mapping the margins: Intersectionality, identity politics, and violence against women of color. *Stanford Law Review, 43*, 1241–1299.

Criminal Justice/Mental Health Consensus Project. (2012). *Mentally Ill Offender Treatment and Crime Reduction Act: Fact sheet*. New York: The Council of State Governments. Retrieved from http://www.consensusproject.org/jc_publications/mentally-ill-offender-treatment-and-crime-reduction-act-fact-sheet/MIOTCRA_Fact_Sheet_2_21_12.pdf

Criminal Justice Project. (2010, Winter). *Death row, USA*. New York: NAACP Legal Defense and Educational Fund.

Critchley, T. A. (1972). *A history of police in England and Wales*. Montclair, NJ: Patterson Smith.

Crouch, B. M., & Marquart, J. W. (1990). Resolving the paradox of reform: Litigation, prisoner violence, and perceptions of risk. *Justice Quarterly, 7*, 103–123.

Crow, M. S., & Johnson, K. A. (2008). Race, ethnicity, and habitual-offender sentencing: A multilevel analysis of individual and contextual threat. *Criminal Justice Policy Review, 19*(1), 63–83.

Culhane, D. P., Metraux, S., & Hadley, T. (2002). Public service reductions associated with placement of homeless persons with severe mental illness in supportive housing. *Housing Policy Debate, 13*(1), 107–163.

Cullen, F., & Jonson, C. (2012). *Correctional theory: Context and consequences*. Thousand Oaks, CA: Sage.

Cumming, A. (2004, November 7). Ecstasy testing rejected. *Sydney Morning Herald*. Retrieved November 7, 2004, from http://www.smh.com.au

Curran, D. J., & Renzetti, C. M. (1994). *Theories of crime*. Boston, MA: Allyn and Bacon.

Curry, G. D., Ball, R. A., & Fox, R. J. (1994). *Gang crime and law enforcement recordkeeping*. Washington, DC: National Institute of Justice.

Curry, G. D., Fox, R. J., Ball, R. A., & Stone, D. (1992). *National assessment of law enforcement anti-gang information resources: Draft 1992*. (Final report). Washington, DC: U.S. Department of Justice, National Institute of Justice.

Cutting college aid, fostering crime. (2005, July 20). (Editorial). *New York Times*. Retrieved from http://www.nytimes.com

Daane, D. M. (2003). Pregnant prisoners: Health, security, and special needs issues. In S. F. Sharp (Ed.), *The incarcerated woman: Rehabilitative programming in women's prisons* (pp. 61–72). Upper Saddle River, NJ: Prentice Hall.

Daemmrich, A. (2002). A tale of two experts: Thalidomide and political engagement in the United States and West Germany. *Social History of Medicine, 15*, 137–158.

Daly, M. (2012, June 13). Spike in shootings, murders creates "wild, wild Midwest" effect in Chicago. *The Daily Beast*. Retrieved from http://www.thedailybeast.com/articles/2012/06/13/spike-in-shootings-murders-creates-wild-wild-midwest-effect-in-chicago.html

Danjczek, L. J. (2007). The Mentally Ill Offender Treatment and Crime Reduction Act and its inappropriate non-violent offender limitation. *Journal of Contemporary Health Law and Policy, 24*, 69–117.

Dasgupta, S.D. (2000). Charting the course: An overview of domestic violence in the South Asian community in the United States. *Journal of Social Distress and the Homeless, 9*, 173–185.

Davenport-Hines, R. (2001). *The pursuit of oblivion: A global history of narcotics*. London, UK: Weidenfeld & Nicholson.

Davey, M. (2012, June 25). Rate of killings rises 38 percent in Chicago in 2012. *New York Times*. Retrieved from http://www.nytimes.com/2012/06/26/us/rate-of-killings-rises-38-percent-in-chicago-in-12.html?pagewanted=all&_r=0

Davies, G., & Fagan, J. (2012). Crime and enforcement in immigrant neighborhoods: Evidence from New York City. *The ANNALS of the American Academy of Political and Social Science, 641*, 99–124.

Davis, D. (2012, April 27). New York drug laws. *Drug Rehab*. Retrieved from http://www.drugrehab.com

Deadman, D., & MacDonald, Z. (2004). Offenders as victims of crime?: An investigation into the relationship between criminal behavior and victimization. *Journal of Royal Statistical Society, 167*(1), 53–67.

Death Penalty Information Center (DPIC). (2003). *Juveniles and the death penalty*. Washington, DC: Author. Retrieved from http://www.deathpenaltyinfo.org/juveniles-and-death-penalty

Death Penalty Information Center. (2012a). *Innocence and the death penalty*. Washington, DC: Author. Retrieved from http://www.deathpenaltyinfo.org/innocence-and-death-penalty

Death Penalty Information Center. (2012b). *Searchable execution database*. Washington, DC: Author. Retrieved from http://www.deathpenaltyinfo.org/women-and-death-penalty

Decker, S. H., Bynum, T. S., & Weisel, D. L. (1998). Gangs as organized crime groups: A tale of two cities. *Justice Quarterly, 15*, 395–423.

de Cordoba, J. (2009, February 12). Latin American panel calls U.S. drug war a failure. *Wall Street Journal*. Retrieved from online. wsj.com

Deegan, M. J. (1988). *Jane Addams and the men of the Chicago School, 1892–1918*. New Brunswick, NJ: Transaction.

De Groof, S. (2008). And my mama said. . . . The (relative) parental influence on fear of crime among adolescent boys and girls. *Youth & Society, 39*(3), 267–293.

DeHart, D. D. (2008). Pathways to prison: Impact of victimization in the lives of incarcerated women. *Violence Against Women, 14*(12), 1362–1381.

Deitch, D., Carleton, S., Koutsenok, I. B., & Marsolais, K. (2002). Therapeutic community treatment in prison. In C. Leukefeld, F. Tims, & D. Farabee (Eds.), *Treatment of drug offenders: Policies and issues* (pp. 127–148). New York: Springer.

DeLeon-Granados, W., Wells, W., & Binsbacher, R. (2006). Arresting developments: Trends in female arrests for domestic violence and proposed explanations. *Violence Against Women, 12*, 355–371.

Delgado, R. (2000). Goodbye to Hammurabi: Analyzing the atavistic appeal of restorative justice. *Stanford Law Review, 52*, 751–775.

DeMichele, M. T. (2007). *Probation and parole's growing caseloads and workload allocation: Strategies for managerial decision making*. Washington, DC: The American Probation & Parole Association, Bureau of Justice Assistance, Office of Justice Programs.

Department of Homeland Security. (2005). Fact sheet: Secure border initiative. *Backgrounder.* Washington, DC: Author. Retrieved from http://www.dhs.gov/xnews/releases/press_release_0794.shtm

Department of Homeland Security. (2006a). Department of Homeland Security unveils comprehensive immigration enforcement strategy for the nation's interior. *Backgrounder*. Washington, DC: Author. Retrieved from http://www.ice.gov/pi/news/newsreleases/articles/060420washington_2.htm

Department of Homeland Security. (2006b). *National infrastructure protection plan*. Washington, DC: Author.

Department of Homeland Security. (2008a). *Homepage*. Retrieved from http://www.dhs.gov/index.shtm

Department of Homeland Security. (2008b). *National response framework*. Washington, DC: Author.

Department of Homeland Security. (2008c). *National incident management system*. Washington, DC: Author.

Department of Homeland Security. (2010). *Quadrennial homeland security review report*. Washington, DC: Author.

Department of Homeland Security. (2012). *FY 2012: Budget in brief.* Retrieved from http://www.dhs.gov/xlibrary/assets/budget-bib-fy2012.pdf

Deutsch, A. (1944). The history of mental hygiene. In J. K. Hall, G. Zilboorg, & H. A. Bunker (Eds.), *One hundred years of American psychiatry* (pp. 325–365). New York: Columbia University Press.

Dewey, D. (1990). *The antitrust experiment in America*. New York: Columbia University Press.

Dickey, W. J. (1998). *"Three strikes": Five years later*. Washington, DC: Campaign for an Effective Crime Policy.

Dieter, R. C. (1992). *Millions misspent: What politicians don't say about the high costs of the death penalty*. Washington, DC: The Death Penalty Information Center. Retrieved from http://www.deathpenaltyinfo.org/node/599

Dieter, R. C. (2005, January 25). *Costs of the death penalty and related issues*. Testimony before the New York State Assembly: Standing Committees on Codes, Judiciary, and Correction. Albany, New York. Retrieved from http://www.deathpenaltyinfo.org/NY-RCD-Test.pdf

Dieter, R. C. (2009). *Smart on crime: Reconsidering the death penalty in a time of economic crisis*. Washington, DC: The Death Penalty Information Center. Retrieved from http://www.death-penaltyinfo.org/documents/CostsRptFinal.pdf

Dieter, R. C. (2011). *Struck by lightning: The continuing arbitrariness of the death penalty thirty-five years after its re-instatement in 1976*. Washington, DC: Death Penalty Information Center. Retrieved from http://www.deathpenaltyinfo.org/documents/StruckByLightning.pdf

Dillian, J. (2011). *Street freak: Money and madness at Lehman Brothers*. New York: Simon & Schuster.

Dilulio, J. (1996, Spring). They're coming: Florida's youth crime bomb. *Impact*, 25–27.

Dirks-Linhorst, P. A., & Linhorst, D. M. (2012). Recidivism outcomes for suburban mental health court defendants. *American Journal of Criminal Justice, 37*, 76–91.

District of Columbia v. Heller, 554 U.S. __, 128 S. Ct. 2783, 171 L. Ed. 2d 637 (2008).

Ditton, J., Chadee, D., Farrall, S., Gilchrist, E., & Bannister, J. (2004). From imitation to intimidation—A note on the curious and changing relationship between the media, crime and fear of crime. *British Journal of Criminology, 44*(4), 595–610.

Dix, D. L. (1975). *On behalf of the insane poor: Selected reports 1842–1862*. New York: Ayer.

Dixon, L. (1999). Dual diagnosis of substance abuse in schizophrenia: Prevalence and impact on outcomes. *Schizophrenia Research, 35*(Suppl. 1), S93–S100.

Douglas, M. (Producer), Zaentz, S. (Producer), & Forman, M. (Director). (1975). *One flew over the cuckoo's nest* [Motion picture]. United States: Fantasy Films and United Artists.

Douglas, W. (2010, July 28). Congress narrows gap in cocaine sentences. *Washington Post*. Retrieved from http://www.washingtonpost.com

Dow, D. R. (2002). How the death penalty really works. In D. R. Dow & M. Dow (Eds.), *Machinery of death: The reality of America's death penalty regime* (pp. 11–35). New York: Routledge.

Dow, D. R. (2005). *Executed on a technicality: Lethal injustice on America's death row*. Boston, MA: Beacon Press.

Dowden, C., & Andrews, D. A. (2004). The importance of staff practice in delivering effective correctional treatment: A meta-analytic review. *International Journal of Offender Therapy and Comparative Criminology, 48*(2), 203–214.

Dowden, C., & Blanchette, K. (2002). An evaluation of the effectiveness of substance abuse programming for female offenders. *International Journal of Offender Therapy and Comparative Criminology, 46*(2), 220–230.

Dowler, K. (2003). Media consumption and public attitudes toward crime and justice: The relationship between fear of crime, punitive attitudes and perceived police effectiveness. *Journal of Criminal Justice and Popular Culture, 10*, 109–126.

Downey, P., & Roman, J. (2010). *A Bayesian meta-analysis of drug court effectiveness*. Washington, DC: Urban Institute.

Doyle, C. (2002). *The USA PATRIOT Act: A Sketch*. (Congressional Research Service Report, RS21203). Washington, DC: Library of Congress.

Drug Policy Alliance. (2003, October 3). *Chretien waiting to inhale*. Retrieved from http://www.drugpolicy.org

Drug Policy Alliance. (2011). *Drug courts are not the answer*. Washington, DC: Author.

Dugan, L. (2003). Domestic violence legislation: Exploring its impact on the likelihood of domestic violence, police involvement, and arrest. *Criminology & Public Policy, 2*, 283–312.

Dugan, L., Rosenfeld, R., & Nagin, D. S. (2003). Exposure reduction or retaliation: The effects of domestic violence resources on intimate-partner homicide. *Law & Society Review, 1*, 169–198.

Dupont, R., & Cochran, S. (2000). Police response to mental health emergencies—barriers to change. *The Journal of the American Academy of Psychiatry and the Law, 28*(3), 338–344.

Dutton, M. A., Orloff, L. E., & Hass, G. S. (2000). Characteristics of help-seeking behaviors, resources and service needs of battered immigrant Latinas: Legal and policy implications. *Georgetown Journal on Poverty Law and Policy, 7*, 245–306.

Duwe, G. (2011). Evaluating the Minnesota Comprehensive Offender Reentry Plan (MCORP): Results from a randomized experiment. *Justice Quarterly*, 1–37.

Duwe, J., Donnay, W., & Tewksbury, R. (2008). Does residential proximity matter? A geographic analysis of sex offense recidivism. *Criminal Justice and Behavior, 35*(4), 484–504.

Eck, J. (1993). The threat of crime displacement. *Problem Solving Quarterly, 6*(3).

Eck, J. (2006). Science, values, and problem-oriented policing: Why problem-oriented policing? In D. L. Weisburd & A. A. Braga (Eds.), *Police innovation: Contrasting perspectives*. New York: Cambridge University Press.

Eck, J. (2010). Policy is in the details: Using external validity to help policy makers. *Criminology and Public Policy, 9*(4), 859–866.

Egelko, B. (2011, July 5). Is Obama changing his tune on marijuana? *San Francisco Chronicle*. Retrieved from http://www.sfgate.com

Ehlers, S., Schiraldi, V., & Ziedenberg, J. (2004). *Still striking out: Ten years of California's three strikes*. Washington, DC: Justice Policy Institute.

Ehrlich, I. (1975). The deterrent effect of capital punishment: A question of life and death. *American Economic Review, 65*, 397–417.

Eichelberger, E. (2013, January 3). Blocking VAWA, the GOP keeps up the war on women. *The Nation*. Retrieved from http://www.the-nation.com/article/171977/gop-blocks-vawa#

Eitle, D. (2005). The influence of mandatory arrest policies, police organizational characteristics, and situational variables on the probability of arrest in domestic violence cases. *Crime & Delinquency, 51*, 573–597.

Elliott, J. F. (1973). *Interception patrol: An examination of the theory of random patrol as a municipal police tactic*. Springfield, IL: Thomas.

Engel, K., & Rothman, S. (1983). Prison violence and the paradox of reform. *The Public Interest, 73*, 91–105.

Engel, R. S., & Silver, E. (2001). Policing mentally-disordered suspects: A re-examination of the criminalization hypothesis. *Criminology, 39*, 225–252.

Eno-Louden, J., & Skeem, J. L. (2011). Parolees with mental disorder: Toward evidence-based practice. *UC Irvine Center for Evidence-Based Corrections Bulletin, 7*(1), 1–9.

Eno-Louden, J., Skeem, J. L., Camp, J., Vidal, S., & Peterson, J. (2012). Supervision practices in specialty mental health probation: What happens in officer–probationer meetings. *Law and Human Behavior, 36*(2), 109–119.

Epstein, L. M., & Goff, P. A. (2011). Safety or liberty?: The bogus trade-off of cross-deputization policy. *Analyses of Social Issues and Public Policy, 11*, 314–324.

Esbensen, F.-A. (2004). *Evaluating G.R.E.A.T, a school-based gang prevention program*. Washington, DC: National Institute of Justice, U.S. Department of Justice. Retrieved from https://www.ncjrs.gov/pdffiles1/198604.pdf

Esbensen, F.-A., Deschenes, E. P, Winfree, L. T., Jr. (1999). Differences between gang girls and gang boys: Results from a multi-site survey. *Youth and Society, 31*(1), 27–53.

Esbensen, F.-A., & Huizinga, D. (1993). Gangs, drugs, and delinquency in a survey of youth. *Criminology, 31*, 565–589.

Estelle v. Gamble, 429 U.S. 97 (1976).

Estep, R., & MacDonald, P. T. (1984). How prime-time crime evolved on TV, 1976 to 1983. In R. Surette (Ed.), *Justice and the media: Issues and research* (pp. 110–123). Springfield, IL: C.C. Thomas.

Estrich, S. (1987). *Real rape: How the legal system victimizes women who say no*. Cambridge, MA: University Press.

European Monitoring Center for Drugs and Addiction (EMCDDA). (2004, December 12). *Country profiles: European legal database on drugs*. Retrieved from http://eldd.emcdda.europe.eu

European Monitoring Center for Drugs and Addiction (EMCDDA). (2009). A cannabis reader: Global issues and local experiences. *Monographs, 8*. Lisbon, Portugal: Author. Retrieved from http://www.emcdda.europa.eu/publications/monographs/cannabis

European Monitoring Centre for Drugs and Addiction (EMCDDA). (2011). *The state of the drugs problem in Europe: Annual*

Report 2011. Lisbon, Portugal: Author. Retrieved from http://www.emcdda.europa.eu/publications/annual-report/2011

European School Survey Project on Alcohol and Other Drugs (ESPAD). (2011). *The 2011 ESPAD report.* Retrieved from http://www.espad.org

Ewing v. California, 538 U.S. 11 (2003).

Fagan, J. (1996). The comparative advantage of juvenile versus criminal court sanctions on recidivism among adolescent felony offenders. *Law & Policy, 18,* 79–113.

Fagan, J. (2005, January 21). *Deterrence and the death penalty: A critical review of new evidence.* Testimony to the New York State Assembly Standing Committee on Codes, Assembly Standing Committee on Judiciary and Assembly Standing Committee on Correction. Hearings on the Future of Capital Punishment in the State of New York. Albany, New York. Retrieved from http://www.findthatfile.com/search-2337438-hPDF/download-documents-fagantestimony.pdf.htm

Fagan, J., Geller, A., Davies, G., & West, V. (2010). Street stops and broken windows revisited: The demography and logic of proactive policing in a safe and changing city. In S. K. Rice & M. D. White (Eds.), *Race, ethnicity, and policing: New and essential readings.* New York: New York University Press.

Fagan, J., & Kupchik, A. (2011). Juvenile incarceration and the pains of imprisonment. *Duke Forum for Law and Social Change, 3,* 29–61.

Fagan, J., Kupchik, A., & Liberman, A. (2003). The comparative impacts of juvenile versus criminal court sanctions on recidivism among adolescent felony offenders: A replication and extension (Final grant report). Washington, DC: Office of Juvenile Justice and Delinquency Prevention.

Falshaw, L. (2005). The link between a history of maltreatment and subsequent offending behavior. *The Journal of Community and Criminal Justice, 4,* 423–434.

Faris, R. E., & Dunham, H. W. (1939). *Mental disorders in urban areas.* Chicago, IL: University of Chicago Press.

Farkas, M. A., & Stichman, A. (2002). Sex offender laws: Can treatment, punishment, incapacitation, and public safety be reconciled? *Criminal Justice Review, 27*(2), 256–283.

Farr, K. A. (2000). Classification for female inmates: Moving forward. *Crime & Delinquency, 46*(1), 3–17.

Farrell, G. (1995). Preventing repeat victimization. In M. Tonry & D. P. Farrington (Eds.), Building a safer society: Strategic approaches to crime prevention. *Crime and Justice: A Review of Research, 19,* 469–534.

Farrell, G., & Sousa, W. (2001). Repeat victimization and hot spots: The overlap and its implications for problem-oriented policing. *Crime Prevention Studies, 12,* 5–25.

Farrington, D. (2000). Explaining and preventing crime: The globalization of knowledge. The American Society of Criminology 1999 Presidential address. *Criminology, 38*(1), 1–24.

Farrington, D., Barnes, J., & Lambert, S. (1996). The concentration of offending in families. *Legal and Criminological Psychology, 1,* 47–63.

Farrington, D., & Welsh, B. (2007). *Saving children from a life of crime: Early risk factors and effective interventions.* New York: Oxford University Press.

Farwell, J. P., & Rohozinski, R. (2011). Stuxnet and the future of cyber war. *Survival: Global Politics and Strategy, 53,* 23–40.

Fears, D. (2009, April 15). State prisons see drop in blacks held for drugs. *Washington Post.* Retrieved from http://www.washingtonpost.com

Fedders, B. (1997). Lobbying for mandatory-arrest policies: Race, class, and the politics of the battered women's movement. *New York University Review of Law & Social Change, 23,* 281–300.

Federal Bureau of Investigation. (2002, September 30). *Financing of terrorism and terrorist acts and related money laundering.* (Briefing). Washington, DC: Author.

Federal Bureau of Investigation. (2010a). *Expanded homicide data Table 6.* Washington, DC: Author. Retrieved from http://www2.fbi.gov/ucr/cius2009/offenses/expanded_information/data/shrtable_06.html

Federal Bureau of Investigation. (2010b). *Crime in the United States, 2010.* Washington, DC: U.S. Department of Justice, Government Printing Office. Retrieved from http://www.fbi.gov/about-us/cjis/ucr/crime-in-the-u.s/2010/crime-in-the-u.s.-2010/tables/10shrtb103.xls

Federal Bureau of Investigation [FBI]. (2011). *Crime in the United States, 2010.* Washington, DC: United States Department of Justice. Retrieved from http://www.fbi.gov/about-us/cjis/ucr/crime-in-the-u.s/2010/crime-in-the-u.s.-2010/tables/10tb133.xls

Federal Bureau of Investigation (FBI). (2012). *Uniform Crime Reports, 2011.* Washington, DC: Author. Retrieved from http://www.fbi.gov/about-us/cjis/ucr/crime-in-the-u.s/2011/crime-in-the-u.s.-2011/violent-crime/violent-crime

Federal Bureau of Investigation (FBI). (2012). *Crime in the United States. Uniform crime reports.* Washington, DC: U.S. Department of Justice. Retrieved from http://www.fbi.gov/about-us/cjis/ucr/crime-in-the-u.s/2011/crime-in-the-u.s.-2011/tables/table-1

Federal Emergency Management Agency. (2012). *Declared disasters by year or state.* Retrieved from http://www.fema.gov/news/disaster_totals_annual.fema

Federal Reserve Bank of San Francisco. (2004, April). *How much currency is circulating in the economy, and how much of it is counterfeit? Is currency included in the money supply statistics?* San Francisco, CA: Author. Retrieved from http://www.frbsf.org/education/activities/drecon/2004/0404.html

Federal Trade Commission. (2012). *Consumer sentinel network data book for January—December 2011.* Washington, DC: Author. Retrieved from http://www.ftc.gov/sentinel/reports/sentinel-annual-reports/sentinel-cy2011.pdf

Federation for American Immigration Reform (FAIR). (2012). *State of Arizona v. United States of America: The Supreme Court hears arguments on SB 1070.* Washington, DC: Author. Retrieved from http://www.fairus.org/DocServer/SB1070_041912.pdf

Feeley, M. M., & Simon, J. (1992). The new penology: Notes on the emerging strategy of corrections and its implications. *Criminology, 30,* 449–475.

Feld, B. C. (1991). The transformation of the juvenile court. *Minnesota Law Review, 75,* 691–725.

Feld, B. C. (1999). *Bad kids: Race and the transformation of the juvenile court.* New York: Oxford University Press.

Fennelly, K. (2007). The healthy migrant phenomenon. In P. F. Walker & E. Day (Eds.), *Immigrant medicine: A comprehensive reference for the care of refugees and immigrants.* New York: Elsevier Press.

Fennelly, K., & Jones-Correa, M. (2009, October). *Immigration enforcement and its effects on Latino lives in two rural North Carolina communities.* Paper presented at the Conference on Undocumented Hispanic Migration, Connecticut College, New London, CT.

Ferdinand, T. N. (1991). History overtakes the juvenile justice system. *Crime & Delinquency, 37*(2), 204–224.

Fernandez, G. A., & Nygard, S. (1990). Impact of involuntary outpatient commitment on the revolving-door syndrome in North Carolina. *Hospital and Community Psychiatry, 41*, 1001–1004.

Ferraro, K. J. (1989). Policing woman battering. *Social Problems, 36*, 61–74.

Ferrell, J. (1996). *Crimes of style: Urban graffiti and the politics of style.* Boston, MA: Northeastern University Press.

Ferrini, R. (2000). American College of Preventative Medicine public policy on needle-exchange programs to reduce drug-associated morbidity and mortality. *American Journal of Preventative Medicine, 18*(2), 173–175.

Filindra, A. (2008, March). *Bringing the states in to the immigration debate: The role of political institutions and interest groups in state-level immigrant policy formation.* Paper presented at the annual meeting of the Western Political Science Association, San Diego, CA.

Filindra, A., & Tichenor, D. (2008, August 28–31). *Beyond myths of federal exclusivity: Regulating immigration and noncitizens in the states.* Paper presented at the annual meeting of the American Political Science Association, Boston, MA.

Financial Action Task Force. (2008). *Terrorist financing.* Retrieved from http://www.fatf-gafi.org/media/fatf/documents/reports/FATF%20Terrorist%20Financing%20Typologies%20Report.pdf

Finckenauer, J. O. (1982). *Scared straight! And the panacea phenomenon.* Englewood Cliffs, NJ: Prentice Hall.

Finn, M. A., & Bettis, P. (2006). Punitive action or gentle persuasion: Exploring police officers' justification for using dual arrest in domestic violence cases. *Violence Against Women, 12*, 268–287.

Firmin, C. (2011). *Female voice in violence project: Final report.* London, UK: Race on the Agenda, ROTA Funders and Partners.

Fischer, L. (1997). *The life of Mahatma Ghandi.* New York: HarperCollins.

Fisher, B. S., & May, D. (2009). College students' crime-related fears on campus: Are fear-provoking cues gendered? *Journal of Contemporary Criminal Justice, 25*(3), 300–321.

Fisher, W. H., Geller, J. L., & Pandiani, J. A. (2009). The changing role of the state psychiatric hospital. *Health Affairs, 28*(3), 676–684.

Fisher, W. H., Silver, E., & Wolff, N. (2006). Beyond criminalization: Toward a criminologically informed mental health policy and services research. *Administration & Policy in Mental Health & Mental Health Services Research, 33*(5), 544–557.

Fiss, O. M. (1984). Against settlement. (Faculty Scholarship Series, Paper 1215). *Yale Law Journal, 93*, 1073.

Fleisher, M. S., & Decker, S. H. (2001). An overview of the challenge of prison gangs. *Corrections Management Quarterly, 5*, 1–9.

Fleisher, M. S., & Krienert, J. L. (2009). *The myth of prison rape: Sexual culture in American prisons.* Lanham, MD: Rowan and Littlefield.

Fletcher, W. H., & Plett, T. N. (2003). *The Sarbanes-Oxley Act: Implementation, significance, and impact.* New York: Nova Science.

Foley, H. A., & Sharfstein, S. S. (1983). *Madness and government: Who cares for the mentally ill?* Arlington, VA: American Psychiatric Press.

Forbes, D. (2000, July 27). Fighting "Cheech and Chong" medicine. *Salon.* Retrieved from http://www.salon.com

Ford, D. A. (2008). No drop prosecution. In C. M. Renzetti & J. L. Edleson (Eds.), *Encyclopedia of interpersonal violence* (Vol. 1). Thousand Oaks, CA: Sage.

Ford v. Bd. of Managers of N.J. State Prison, 407 F.2d 937, 940 (3d Cir. 1969).

Forst, M., Fagan, J., & Vivona, T. S. (1989). Youth in prison and training schools: Perceptions and consequences of the treatment custody dichotomy. *Juvenile and Family Court Journal, 40*, 1–14.

Foucault, M. (1965). *Madness and civilization: A history of insanity in the age of reason.* New York: Vintage Books.

Fox, J. A., & Zawitz, M. W. (2007). *Homicide trends in the United States.* Washington, DC: Bureau of Justice Statistics. Retrieved from http://bjs.gov/content/pub/pdf/htius.pdf

Fox, J. G. (1984). Women's prison policy, prisoner activism, and the impact of the contemporary feminist movement: A case study. *The Prison Journal, 64*(1), 15–36.

Fradella, H. F. (2003). Faith, delusions, and death: A case study of the death of a psychotic inmate as a call for reform. *Journal of Contemporary Criminal Justice, 19*, 98–113.

Fradella, H. F. (2007). *Mental illness and criminal defenses of excuse in contemporary American law.* Bethesda, MD: Academica Press.

Fradella, H. F. (2008). *Forensic psychology: The use of behavioral science in civil and criminal justice* (2nd ed). Belmont, CA: Wadsworth.

Frank, S. A., & Lewis, G. B. (2004). Government employees: Working hard, or hardly working? *American Review of Public Administration, 34*, 36–51.

Franklin, D. (1994, September). The right three strikes: Three strikes and out law. *Washington Monthly, 26*(9).

Freedman, E. B. (1987). Uncontrolled desires: The response to the sexual psychopath, 1920–1960. *The Journal of American History, 74*(1), 83–106.

Freeman, N. J., & Sandler, J. C. (2010). The Adam Walsh Act. *Criminal Justice Policy Review, 21*(1), 31–49.

Frisman, L. K., Swanson, J., Marín, M. C., & Leavitt-Smith, E. (2010). Estimating costs of reentry programs for prisoners with severe mental illnesses. *Correctional Health Care Report, 11*(6), 81–95.

Fritsch, E. J., Caeti, T. J., & Hemmens, C. (1996). Spare the needle but not the punishment: The incarceration of waived youth in Texas prisons. *Crime and Delinquency, 42*, 593–609.

Frohmann, L. (1997). Convictability and discordant locales: Reproducing race, class, and gender ideologies in prosecutorial decision making. *Law and Society Review, 31*(3), 531–556.

Frost, N. A., & Phillips, N. D. (2011). Talking heads: Crime reporting on cable news. *Justice Quarterly, 28*(1), 87–112.

Fuld, L. F. 1971). *Police administration.* Montclair, NJ: Patterson Smith. (Original work published 1909)

Fuller, D. A. (2011). To fix "broken" jails—Fix treatment laws for mental illness. *Sheriff, 63*(7), 30–31.

Furillo, A. (2012, Aug. 22). "Three-strikes" battle returns to fall ballot in California. *Sacramento Bee.* Retrieved from http://www.sacbee.com/2012/08/22/4746637/three-strikes-battle-returns-to.html#storylink=cpy

Furman v Georgia, 408 U.S. 238 (1972).

Gaarder, E., & Presser, L. (2008). A feminist vision of justice? The problems and possibilities of restorative justice for girls and women. In D. Sullivan & L. Tifft (Eds.), *Handbook of restorative justice.* New York: Routledge.

Gaboury, M., & Ruth-Heffelbower, D. (2010). Innovations in correctional settings. In J. P. J. Dussich & J. Schellenberg (Eds.), *The promise of restorative justice: New approaches for criminal justice and beyond.* Boulder, CO: Lynne Rienner.

Gaes, G. G., Wallace, S., Gilman, E., Klein-Saffran, J., & Suppa, S. (2002). The influence of prison gang affiliation on violence and other prison misconduct. *The Prison Journal, 82*(3), 359–385.

Gahlinger, P. (2001). *Illegal drugs: A complete guide to their history, chemistry, use and abuse.* Salt Lake City, UT: Sagebrush Press.

Gaines, L. K., & Kappeler, V. E. (2012). *Homeland security.* Upper Saddle River, NJ: Prentice Hall.

Galinsky, K. (1998). *Augustan culture: An interpretative introduction.* Princeton, NJ: Princeton University Press.

Garber, A., & Miletich, S. (2011, June 21). Former U.S. Attorney McKay backs efforts to legalize pot in Washington. *Seattle Times.* Retrieved from http://www.seattletimes.com

Garcia, M. (2012, June 11). New Illinois law beefs up street gangs prosecution. *Chicago Tribune.* Retrieved from http://articles.chicagotribune.com/2012-06-11/news/chi-new-illinois-law-beefs-up-street-gangs-prosecution-20120611_1_street-gangs-new-illinois-law-law-today

Gardiner, C. (2008). *From inception to implementation: How SACPA has affected the case processing and sentencing of drug offenders in one California county.* (Doctoral dissertation). University of California, Irvine, California.

Gardiner, C. L. (2012). Policing in California. In C. L. Gardiner & S. L. Mallicoat (Eds.), *California's criminal justice system* (pp. 64–96). Durham, NC: Carolina Academic Press.

Garland, D. (2001). *The culture of control: Crime and social order in contemporary society.* Chicago, IL: University of Chicago Press.

Garner, B. A. (Ed.). (2000). *Black's law dictionary* (7th ed. abridged). St. Paul, MN: West.

Garofalo, J. (1981). Crime and the mass media: A selective review of research. *Journal of Research in Crime and Delinquency, 18*, 319–350.

Gau, J. M., & Brunson, R. K. (2010, April). Procedural justice and order maintenance policing: A study of inner-city young men's perceptions of police legitimacy. *Justice Quarterly, 27*(2), 255–278.

Gavett, G. (Writer). (2011, October 18). Record number of illegal immigrants deported in 2011. *Frontline* (Television series episode). Boston, MA: WGBH. Retrieved from http://www.pbs.org/wgbh/pages/frontline/race-multicultural/lost-in-detention/record-number-of-illegal-immigrants-deported-in-2011/

Gehring, K., Van Voorhis, P., & Bell, V. (2010). "What works" for female probationers?: An evaluation of the Moving On program. *Women, Girls, and Criminal Justice, 11*(1), 1, 6–10.

Geis, G. (2013). Unaccountable external auditors, and their role in the economic meltdown. In S. Will & S. Handeleman (Eds.), *How they got away with it: White-collar crime and the financial meltdown.* New York: Columbia University Press.

Geis, G., & DiMento, J. F. C. (2002). Empirical evidence and the legal doctrine of corporate criminal liability. *American Journal of Criminal Law, 29*, 341–375.

Geis, R., Geis, G., & Jesilow, P. (1991). The Amelia Stern syndrome. *Medicine, Science & Law, 33*, 967–971.

Gelacak, M. (1997). *Cocaine and federal sentencing policy.* Washington, DC: United States Sentencing Commission.

Geller, A., & Curtis, M. A. (2011). A sort of homecoming: Incarceration and the housing security of urban men. *Social Science Research, 40*, 1196–1213.

Gendreau, P., Goggin, C. E., & Law, M. A. (1997). Predicting prison misconducts. *Criminal Justice and Behavior, 24*(4), 414–431.

General Accounting Office. (1989). *Thrift failures: Costly failures resulted from regulatory violations and unsafe practices.* Washington, DC: U.S. Government Printing Office.

Gerber, E. R., Lupia, A., McCubbins, M. D., & Kiewiet, D. R. (2001). *Stealing the initiative: How state government responds to direct democracy.* Upper Saddle River, NJ: Prentice Hall.

Gerbner, G., Gross, L., Morgan, M., & Signorielli, N. (1980). The mainstreaming of America: Violence profile no. 11. *Journal of Communication, 30*(3), 10–29.

Gfroerer, J. C., & Tan, L. L. (2003, November). Substance use among foreign-born youths in the United States: Does the length of residence matter? *American Journal of Public Health, 93*(11), 1892–1895.

Gibeaut, J. (1998). Gang busters. *ABA Journal, 84*(1), 64–69.

Gideon, L., & Sung, H. (2011). *Rethinking corrections: Rehabilitation, reentry and reintegration.* Thousand Oaks, CA: Sage.

Gilbert, L. (2012). Patchwork immigration laws and federal enforcement priorities. Social Science Research Network (SSRN) abstract. Retrieved from http://ssrn.com/abstract=2093486

Gilbert, M. J., & Settles, T. L. (2007). The next step: Indigenous development of neighborhood-restorative community justice. *Criminal Justice Review, 32*(1), 5–25.

Gilfus, M. E. (1992). From victims to survivors to offenders. Women's routes of entry and immersion into street crime. *Women & Criminal Justice, 4*(1), 63–90.

Gilliam, F. D., & Iyengar, S. (2000). Prime suspects: The influence of local television news on the viewing public. *American Journal of Political Science, 44*(3), 560–573.

Giwargis, R. (2013, February 28). Merced sheriff unveils vision for AB 109 locally with new Trident Center. *Merced Sun Star*. Retrieved from http://www.mercedsunstar.com/2013/02/28/2849249/merced-sheriff-unveils-three-pronged.html

Glaze, L. E. (2010). *Correctional populations in the United States, 2009*. Washington, DC: U.S. Department of Justice, Bureau of Justice Statistics.

Glaze, L. E. (2011). *Correctional population in the United States, 2010* (Report NCJ231681). Washington, DC: U.S. Department of Justice, Office of Justice Programs, Bureau of Justice Statistics. Retrieved from http://bjs.ojp.usdoj.gov/content/pub/pdf/cpus10.pdf

Glaze, L. E., & Maruschak, L. M. (2008). *Parents of prison and their minor children*. Washington, DC: U.S. Department of Justice, Bureau of Justice Statistics.

Glionna, J. (2003, June 1). Light and darkness in Canada. *Los Angeles Times*. Retrieved from http://www.latimes.com

Global Commission on Drugs. (2011, June). *War on drugs: Report of the Global Commission on Drug policy*. Rio de Janeiro, Brazil: Global Commission on Drugs. Retrieved from http://www.globalcommissionondrugs.org

Glober, R. W., Miller, J. E., & Sadowski, S. R. (2012). *Proceedings on the state budget crisis and the behavioral health treatment gap: The impact on public substance abuse and mental health treatment systems*. Washington, DC: National Association of State Mental Health Program Directors. Retrieved from http://www.nasmhpd.org/docs/Summary-Congressional%20Briefing_March%2022_Website.pdf

Goffman, E. (1961). *Asylums*. New York: Doubleday.

Goffman, E. (1974). *Frame analysis: An essay on the organization of experience*. Cambridge, MA: Harvard University Press.

Golash-Boza, T. M. (2012). *Immigration nation: Raids, detentions, and deportations in post-9/11 America*. Boulder, CO: Paradigm.

Goldenson, R. M. (1970). *The encyclopedia of human behavior: Psychology, psychiatry, and mental health*. Garden City, NY: Doubleday.

Goldfarb, S. F. (2011). A clash of cultures: Women, domestic violence, and law in the United States. In D. L. Hodgson (Ed.), *Gender and culture at the limit of rights* (pp. 55–77). Philadelphia, PA. University of Pennsylvania Press.

Goldman, H. H., & Morrissey, J. P. (1985). The alchemy of mental health policy: Homelessness and the fourth cycle of reform. *American Journal of Public Health, 75*(7), 727–731.

Goldstein, H. (1979). Improving policing: A problem-oriented approach. *Crime and Delinquency, 25*, 236–258.

Gonzales, R. G. (2011). Learning to be illegal: Undocumented youth and shifting legal contexts in the transition to adulthood. *American Sociological Review, 76*(4), 602–619.

Good, D., & Rouse, J. (1980). *Summary statistics of felon prisoners and parolees*. Sacramento, CA: California Department of Corrections. Retrieved from http://www.cdcr.ca.gov/reports_research/offender_information_services_branch/Annual/CalPris/CALPRISd1980.pdf

Goode, E. (1997). *Between politics and reason: The drug legalization debate*. New York: St. Martin's Press.

Goode, E. (2012). Fighting a drawn-out battle against solitary confinement. *New York Times*. Retrieved from http://www.nytimes.com/2012/03/31/us/battles-to-change-prison-policy-of-solitary-confinement.html?pagewanted=all

Goodman, P. (2008). "It's just Black, White, or Hispanic": An observational study of racializing moves in California's segregated prison reception centers. *Law and Society Review, 42*(4), 735–770.

Goodmark, L. (2008). When is a battered woman not a battered woman? When she fights back. *Yale Journal of Law and Feminism, 20*, 75–129.

Gorman, A. (2012, May 14). L.A. county's 911 system burdened by nonemergency calls. *Los Angeles Times*. Retrieved at http://articles.latimes.com/2012/may/14/local/la-me-911-changes-20120515

Gorman, A., & Riccardi, N. (2010, April 28). Calls to boycott Arizona grow over new immigration law. *Los Angeles Times*. Retrieved from http://articles.latimes.com/2010/apr/28/local/la-me-0428-arizona-boycott-20100428

Goss, J. R., Peterson, K., Smith, L. W., Kalb, K., & Brodey, B. B. (2002). Characteristics of suicide attempts in a large urban jail system with an established suicide prevention program. *Psychiatric Services, 53*, 574–579.

Government Accounting Office. (2000). *State and federal prisoners: Profiles of inmate characteristics in 1991 and 1997*. Washington, DC: Author.

Graber, D. (1980). *Crime news and the public*. New York: Prager.

Graham v. Florida. (2010). ___ U.S. ___, 130 S. Ct. 2011; 176 L. Ed. 2d 82.

Grana, S. J. (2010). *Women and justice* (2nd ed.). Lanham, MD: Rowman & Littlefield.

Grassian, S. (1983). Psychopathological effects of solitary confinement. *American Journal of Psychiatry, 140*, 1450–1454.

Grassian, S., & Friedman, N. (1986). Effects of sensory deprivation in psychiatric seclusion and solitary confinement. *International Journal of Law and Psychiatry, 8*(1), 49–65.

Grattet, R., Petersilia, J., Lin, J., & Beckman, M. (2009). Parole violations and revocations in California: Analysis and suggestions for action. *Federal Probation, 73*(1), 2–11.

Gray, J. (2001). *Why our drug laws have failed and what we can do about it*. Philadelphia, PA: Temple University Press.

Gray, M. (1999, September 20). The perils of prohibition. *The Nation*. Retrieved from http://www.thenation.com

Greene, J., & Pranis, K. (2007). *Gang wars: The failure of enforcement tactics and the need for effective public safety strategies*. Washington, DC: The Justice Policy Institute. Retrieved from http://www.justicestrategies.org/sites/default/files/Gang_Wars_Full_Report_2007.pdf

Greene, J. R. (2007). Make police oversight independent and transparent. *Criminology & Public Policy, 6*(4), 747–754.

Greenfeld, L., & Snell, T. (1999). *Women offenders*. Washington, DC: U.S. Department of Justice.

Greenfield, L., & Snell, T. (2000). *Bureau of justice statistics special report: Women offenders*. Washington, DC: Office of Justice Programs. Retrieved from http://www.ojp.usdoj.gov/bjs/pub/pdf/wo.pdf

Greenwald, G. (2009). *Drug decriminalization in Portugal: Lessons for creating fair and successful drug policies.* Washington, DC: Cato Institute.

Greenwood, P., & Turner, S. (2011). Juvenile crime and juvenile justice. In J. Q. Wilson & J. Petersilia (Eds.), *Crime and public policy.* New York: Oxford University Press.

Greenwood, P. W., Everingham, S., Chen, E. Y., Abrahamse, A. F., Merritt, N., & Chiesa, J. (1998). *Three strikes revisited: An early assessment of implementation and effects.* Santa Monica, CA: RAND.

Greenwood, P. W., Rydell, C. P., Abrahamse, A. F., Caulkins, J. P., Chiesa, J., Model, K. E., & Klein, S. P. (1994). *Three strikes and you're out: Estimated benefits and costs of California's new mandatory-sentencing law.* Santa Monica, CA: RAND.

Gregg v. Georgia, 428 U.S. 153 (1976).

Grekin, P. M., Jemelka, R., & Trupin, E. W. (1994). Racial differences in the criminalization of the mentally ill. *Bulletin of the American Academy of Psychiatry & the Law, 22*(3), 411–420.

Griffin, M., & Hepburn, J. (2006). The effect of gang affiliation on violent misconduct among inmates during the early years of confinement. *Criminal Justice and Behavior, 33*(4), 419–448.

Griffin, P. (2003). *Trying and sentencing juveniles as adults: An analysis of state transfer and blended sentencing laws.* Washington, DC: Office of Juvenile Justice and Delinquency Prevention.

Griffin, P., Addie, S., Adams, B., & Firestine, K. (2011). *Trying juveniles as adults: An analysis of state waiver laws and reporting.* Washington, DC: U.S. Department of Justice, Office of Justice Programs, Office of Juvenile Justice and Delinquency Prevention.

Grimshaw, R., & Jefferson, T. (1987). Interpreting policework: Policy and practice in forms of beat policing. London, UK: Allen & Unwin.

Grinspoon, L., & Bakalar, J. (1995). Marijuana as medicine: A plea for reconsideration. *Journal of the American Medical Association, 273,* 1875–1876.

Grob, G. N. (1966). *The state of the mentally ill.* Chapel Hill, NC: University of North Carolina Press.

Grob, G. N. (1994). *The mad among us: A history of the care of America's mentally ill.* Cambridge, MA: Harvard University Press.

Gross, S. R., & Mauro, R. (1989). *Death and discrimination: Racial disparities in capital sentencing.* Boston, MA: Northeastern University Press.

Guerette, R. T. (2009). *Analyzing crime displacement and diffusion: Problem-oriented guides for police.* (Problem-Solving Tools Series No. 10). Washington, DC: Center for Problem-Oriented Policing, U.S. Department of Justice.

Guerino, P., Harrison, P. M., & Sobol, W. (2011). *Prisoners in 2010.* (Report NCJ2366096). (Rev. ed. 2012). Washington, DC: U.S. Department of Justice, Office of Justice Programs, Bureau of Justice Statistics.

Gun-Free Schools Act, 20 USC § 7151 (1994).

Gur, O. M. (2010). Persons with mental illness in the criminal justice system: Police interventions to prevent violence and criminalization. *Journal of Police Crisis Negotiations, 10,* 220–240.

Haake, J. (2003, July 21). UCLA study: Drug rehab has financial benefits over incarceration. *Daily Bruin.* Retrieved from http://www.dailybruin.ucla.edu

Hadley, M. L. (2008). Spiritual foundations of restorative justice. In D. Sullivan & L. Tifft (Eds.), *Handbook of restorative justice.* New York: Routledge.

Hagedorn, J. M. (2001). Gangs and the informal economy. In R. Huff (Ed.), *Gangs in America* (pp. 101–120). Thousand Oaks, CA: Sage.

Hagedorn, J. M. (2008). *A world of gangs: Armed young men and gangsta culture.* Minneapolis, MN: University of Minnesota Press.

Hagedorn, J. M., & MacLean, B. A. (2012). Breaking the frame: Responding to gang stereotyping in capital cases. *The University of Memphis Law Review, 42,* 1–33.

Hahn, R., McGowan, A., Liberman, A., Crosby, A., Fullilove, M., Johnson, R., . . . Stone, G. (2007). Effects on violence of laws and policies facilitating the waiver of youth from the juvenile to the adult justice system: A report on recommendations of the task force on community preventive services. *Morbidity and Mortality Weekly Report, 56,* 1–11.

Hails, J., & Borum, R. (2003). Police training and specialized approaches to respond to people with mental illnesses. *Crime & Delinquency, 49*(1), 52–61.

Haines, H. H. (1996). *Against capital punishment: The anti-death penalty movement in America, 1972–1994.* New York: Oxford University Press.

Hakiaha, M. (2004). What is the state's role in indigenous justice processes? In H. Zehr & B. Toews (Eds.), *Critical issues in restorative justice.* Monsey, NY: Criminal Justice Press.

Hamilton, J. T. (1998). *Channeling violence: The economic market for violent television programming.* Princeton, NJ: Princeton University Press.

Hamilton, Z., & Campbell, C. (2013). A dark figure in corrections: Failure by way of participation. *Criminal Justice and Behavior, 40*(2), 180–202.

Haney, C. (2003). Mental health issues in long-term solitary and "supermax" confinement. *Crime and Delinquency, 49,* 124–156.

Haney, C. (2008). A culture of harm: Taming the dynamics of cruelty in supermax prisons. *Criminal Justice and Behavior, 35,* 956–984.

Hanson, R. K., & Bussiere, M. T. (1998). Predicting relapse: A meta-analysis of sexual offender recidivism studies. *Journal of Consulting and Clinical Psychology, 66*(2), 348–362.

Hanson, R. K., & Morton-Bourgon, K. (2004). *Predictors of sexual recidivism: An updated meta-analysis.* Ottawa, Canada: Public Works and Government Services, Public Safety and Emergency Preparedness.

Harcourt, B. E. (2011). Reducing mass incarceration: Lessons from the deinstitutionalization of mental hospitals in the 1960s. *Ohio State Journal of Criminal Law, 9,* 53–88.

Harcourt, B. E., & Ludwig, J. (2007). Reefer madness: Broken windows policing and misdemeanor marijuana arrests in New York City, 1989–2000. *Criminology & Public Policy, 6*(1), 165–182.

Harding, W. (1982). *The days of Henry Thoreau.* Princeton, NJ: Princeton University Press.

Hardyman, P. L., & Van Voorhis, P. (2004). *Developing gender-specific classification systems for women offenders.* Washington, DC: U.S. Department of Justice, National Institute of Corrections.

Harer, M., & Steffensmeier, D. (1996). Race and prison violence. *Criminology, 34*(3), 323–355.

Harlow, C. W. (1999). *Prior abuse reported by inmates and probationers.* Washington, DC: U.S. Department of Justice, Bureau of Justice Statistics.

Harlow, C. W. (2000). *Defense council in criminal cases.* (Special report). Washington, DC: U.S. Department of Justice, Bureau of Justice Statistics.

Harmelin v. Michigan, 501 U.S 957 (1991).

Harrison, P., & Beck, A. (2005). *Prison and jail inmates at midyear 2004.* Washington, DC: U.S. Department of Justice.

Hart, B. J. (1993). Battered women and the criminal justice system. *American Behavioral Scientist, 36*(5), 624–638.

Hartney, C., & Glesmann, C. (2012). *Prison bed profiteers: How corporations are reshaping criminal justice in the U.S.* Oakland, CA: National Council on Crime and Delinquency. Retrieved from http://nccdglobal.org/sites/default/files/publication_pdf/prison-bed-profiteers.pdf

Hartocollis, A. (2012, March 26). At ailing Brooklyn hospital, insider deals and lavish perks. *New York Times,* pp. A1, A21.

Hartwell, S. (2001). Female mentally ill offenders and their community reintegration needs: An initial examination. *International Journal of Law and Psychiatry, 24,* 1–11.

Hastings, D. (2009, April 4). States pull back after decades of get tough laws. *Associated Press.* Retrieved from http://www.ap.org

Hatsukami, D., & Fischman, M. (1996). Crack cocaine and cocaine hydrochloride: Are the differences myth or reality? *Journal of the American Medical Association, 276,* 1580–1588.

Hayden, T. (2004). *Street wars: Gangs and the future of violence.* New York: New Press.

Hayden T. (2012, May 14). Peace is breaking out among Salvadoran gang members. *The Nation.* Retrieved from http://www.the-nation.com/article/167875/peace-breaking-out-among-salvadoran-gang-members

Held, M. L., Brown, C. A., Frost, L. E., Hickey, J. S., & Buck, D. S. (2012). Integrated primary and behavioral health care in patient-centered medical homes for jail releasees with mental illness. *Criminal Justice & Behavior, 39*(4), 533–551.

Henderson, M. L., & Hanley, D. (2006). Planning for quality: A strategy for reentry initiatives. *Western Criminology Review, 7*(2), 62–78.

Henriques, Z. W., & Manatu-Rupert, N. (2001). Living on the outside: Women before, during, and after imprisonment. *The Prison Journal, 81*(1), 6–19.

Herinckx, H. A., Swart, S. C., Ama, S. M., Dolezal, C. D., & King, S. (2005). Rearrest and linkage to mental health services among defendants of the Clark County mental health court program. *Psychiatric Services, 56*(7), 853–857.

Herman, S. (2004). Is restorative justice possible without a parallel system for victims? In H. Zehr & B. Toews (Eds.), *Critical issues in restorative justice.* Monsey, NY: Criminal Justice Press.

Hernández, D. M. (2009). Pursuant to deportation: Latinos and immigrant detention. In S. Oboler (Ed.), *Behind bars: Latino/as and prison in the United States.* New York: Palgrave Macmillan.

Hilts, P. J. (2003). *Protecting America's health: The FDA, business, and one hundred years of regulation.* New York: Knopf.

Hing, J. (2013, February 21). Denver plugging up its school-to-prison pipeline. *Colorlines.* Retrieved from http://colorlines.com/archives/2013/02/denver_signs_landmark_agreement_to_roll_back_the_school-to-prison_pipeline.html

Hinkle, J. C., & Weisburd, D. (2008). The irony of broken windows policing: A micro-place study of the relationship between disorder, focused police crackdowns, and fear of crime. *Journal of Criminal Justice, 36,* 503–512.

Hirschel, D., & Buzawa, E. (2002). Understanding the context of dual arrest with directions for future research. *Violence Against Women, 8,* 1449–1473.

Hirschel, D., Buzawa, E., Pattavina, A., & Faggiani, D. (2007). Domestic violence and mandatory arrest laws: To what extent do they influence police arrest decisions? *Journal of Criminal Law & Criminology, 98,* 254–298.

Hoffman, M. (1999–2000). The drug court scandal. *North Carolina Law Review, 78*(5), 1437.

Horn, D. (2004). *Lockyer v. Andrade:* California three strikes law survives challenge based on federal law that is anything but "clearly established." *The Journal of Criminal Law and Criminology, 94*(3), 687–722.

Horney, J., & Spohn, C. (1991). Rape law reform and instrumental change in six urban jurisdictions. *Law & Society Review, 25*(1), 117–154.

Horwitz, S. (2004). Cigarette smuggling linked to terrorism. *The Washington Post.* Retrieved from http://www.washingtonpost.com/wp-dyn/articles/A23384–2004Jun7.html

Horwitz, S. (2012, October 11). Marijuana legalization on ballot in three states, but Justice Department remains silent. *Washington Post.* Retrieved from http://www.washingtonpost.com

Houghtalin, M., & Mays, G. L. (1991). Criminal dispositions of New Mexico juveniles transferred to adult court. *Crime and Delinquency, 37,* 393–407.

Howell, J. C. (1996). Juvenile transfers to the criminal justice system: State of the art. *Law & Policy, 18,* 17–60.

Howell, J. C. (2012). *Gangs in America's communities.* Thousand Oaks, CA: Sage.

Howley, P. (2002). *Breaking spears and mending hearts: Peacemakers and restorative justice in Bougainville.* London, UK: Federation Press.

H.R. 4472—109th Congress: Adam Walsh Child Protection and Safety Act of 2006. (2005). In GovTrack.us (database of federal legislation). Retrieved from http://www.govtrack.us/congress/bills/109/

Huebner, B. (2003). Administrative determinants of inmate violence: A multilevel analysis. *Journal of Criminal Justice, 31*(2), 107–117.

Hughes, C., & Stevens, A. (2010). What can we learn from the Portuguese decriminalization of illicit drugs? *British Journal of Criminology, 50*(6), 999–1022.

Hughes, C., & Stevens, A. (2012). A resounding success or a disastrous failure? Re-examining the interpretation of evidence on the Portuguese decriminalization of illicit drugs. *Drug and Alcohol Review, 31,* 101–113.

Hughes, K. A. (2006). *Justice expenditures and employment in the United States, 2003.* Office of Justice Programs, U.S. Department of Justice. Washington, DC: Bureau of Justice Statistics.

Hughes, L. A., & Burchfield, K. B. (2008). Sex offender residence restrictions in Chicago: An environmental injustice? *Justice Quarterly, 25*(4), 647–673.

Hughes, L. A., & Kadleck, C. (2008). Sex offender community notification and community stratification. *Justice Quarterly, 25*(3), 469–495.

Human Rights Watch. (2009, September 22). *Mental illness, human rights, and U.S. prisons: Human rights watch statement for the record to the senate judiciary committee subcommittee on human rights and the law.* New York: Author. Retrieved from http://www.hrw.org/sites/default/files/related_material/Human%20Rights%20Watch%20Statement%20for%20the%20Record_9_22_09.pdf

Human Rights Watch. (2010). *Costly and unfair: Flaws in U.S. immigration detention policies.* New York: Author. Retrieved from http://www.hrw.org/sites/default/files/reports/usimmigration0510webwcover.pdf

Human Rights Watch. (2011). *A costly move: Far and frequent transfers impede hearings for immigrant detainees in the United States.* New York: Author. Retrieved from http://www.hrw.org/sites/default/files/reports/us0611webwcover_0.pdf

Hunt, N. (2005). *A review of the evidence-base for harm reduction approaches to drug use.* Retrieved from http://www.forward-thinking-on-drugs.org

Huntington, S. (2004, March 1). The Hispanic challenge. *Foreign Policy.* Retrieved from http://www.foreignpolicy.com/articles/2004/03/01/the_hispanic_challenge

Hupe, P., & Hill, M. (2007). Street-level bureaucracy and public accountability. *Public Administration Review, 85*(2), 279–299.

Hutchinson, A. (2001, December 5). *Statement before the house government reform committee, subcommittee on criminal justice, drug policy and human resources.* (CRS Report). Washington, DC: Congressional Research Service, Library of Congress.

Hutchinson, A. (2013, April 2). *Report of the National School Shield Task Force.* Fairfax, VA: National School Shield (NSS) Task Force, National Rifle Association. Retrieved from http://www.scribd.com/doc/133630146/NRA-s-National-School-Shield-Report

Hylton, J. H. (1995). Care or control: Health or criminal justice options for the long-term seriously mentally ill in a Canadian province. *International Journal of Law and Psychiatry, 18,* 45–59.

Ianni, F. (1975). *Black mafia.* New York: Simon & Schuster.

ICE, Immigration and Customs Enforcement. (2005). *Fact sheet: Section 287(g) immigration enforcement.* Washington, DC: Author. Retrieved from http://www.ice.gov/pi/news/factsheets/section287g.htm

ICE, Immigration and Customs Enforcement. (2009). *Fact Sheet: Delegation of immigration authority Section 287(g) Immigration and Nationality Act.* Washington, DC: Author. Retrieved from http://www.ice.gov/pi/news/factsheets/section287_g.htm

ICE, Immigration and Customs Enforcement. (2012a). *Fugitive Operations.* Washington, DC: Author. Retrieved from http://www.ice.gov/fugitive-operations/

ICE, Immigration and Customs Enforcement. (2012b). *Secure communities activated jurisdictions.* Washington, DC: Author. Retrieved from http://www.ice.gov/doclib/secure-communities/pdf/sc-activated1.pdf

International Monetary Fund. (2012). *The IMF and the fight against money laundering and the financing of terrorism.* Washington, DC: Author. Retrieved from http://www.imf.org/external/np/exr/facts/aml.htm

Immigration and Customs Enforcement. (2012a). *ICE total removals.* Retrieved from http://www.ice.gov/doclib/about/offices/ero/pdf/ero-removals1.pdf

Immigration and Customs Enforcement. (2012b). *Human trafficking.* Retrieved from http://www.ice.gov/human-trafficking/

Immigration and Customs Enforcement. (2012b). *Human trafficking.* Retrieved from http://www.ice.gov/human-trafficking/

Irwin, K., & Chesney-Lind. M. (2008). Girl's violence: Beyond dangerous masculinity. *Sociology Compass, 2*(3), 837–855.

Jackall, R. (2005). *Street stories: The world of police detectives.* Cambridge, MA: Harvard University Press.

Jackson, A. (2004). *Prosecuting gang cases: What local prosecutors need to know.* Washington, DC: American Prosecutor's Research Institute.

Jackson, D., & Madhani, A. (2013, January 17). Obama challenges Congress to pass new gun regulations. *USA Today.* Retrieved from http://www.usatoday.com/story/news/politics/2013/01/16/line-drawn-on-guns/1566406/ //nimo

Jackson v. Bishop, 404 F.2d 571, 579 (8th Cir. 1968).

Jacobs, J. (1977). *Stateville: The penitentiary in mass society.* Chicago, IL: University of Chicago.

Jalbert, S. K., Rhodes, W., Flygare, C., & Kane, M. (2010). Testing probation outcomes in an evidence-based practice setting: Reduced caseload size and intensive supervision effectiveness. *Journal of Offender Rehabilitation, 49,* 233–253.

James, D. J., & Glaze, L. E. (2006). *Mental health problems of prison and jail inmates.* Washington, DC: U.S. Department of Justice, Bureau of Justice Statistics.

James, N. (1994). Domestic violence: A history of arrest policies and a survey of modern laws. *Family Law Quarterly, 28,* 509–520.

Jankowski, M. S. (1991). *Islands in the street: Gangs and American urban society.* Berkeley, CA: University of California Press.

Janofsky, M. (2002, August 2). Nevadans weigh proposal to make marijuana legal. *New York Times.* Retrieved from http://www.nytimes.com

Janus, E. S. (2006). *Failure to protect: America's sexual predator laws and the rise of the preventive state.* Ithaca, NY: Cornell University Press.

Jenkins, M. (2004). How do culture, class and gender affect the practice of RJ (Part 1). In H. Zehr & B. Toews (Eds.), *Critical issues in restorative justice.* Monsey, NY: Criminal Justice Press.

Jenness, V., & Grattet, R. (2005). The law-in-between: The effects of organizational perviousness on the policing of hate crime. *Social Problems, 52*(3), 337–359.

Jensen, E. L., & Metsger, L. K. (1994). A test of the deterrent effect of legislative waiver on violent juvenile crime. *Crime & Delinquency, 40*, 96–104.

Jensen, E., & Mosher, C. (2006). Adult drug courts: The judicial origins, evaluations of effectiveness, and expansion of the model. *Idaho Law Review, 42*, 433–470.

Jermier, J. M., & Berkes, L. J. (1979). Leader behavior in a police command bureaucracy: A closer look at the quasi-military model. *Administrative Science Quarterly, 24*(1), 1–23.

Jermier, J. M., Slocum, Jr., J. W., Fry, L. W., & Gaines, J. (1991). Organizational subcultures in a soft bureaucracy: Resistance behind the myth and facade of an official culture organization. *Science, 2*(2), 170–194.

Jesilow, P. D., Pontell, H. N., & Geis, G. (1993). *Prescription for profit: How doctors defraud Medicaid.* Berkeley: University of California Press.

Johnson, G. (2012, December 6). Legalizing marijuana: Washington law goes into effect, allowing recreational use of drug. *Huffington Post.* Retrieved from http://www.huffingtonpost.com/2012/12/06/legalizing-marijuana-washington-state_n_2249238.html

Johnson, M. P. (2008). *A typology of domestic violence: Intimate terrorism, violent resistance, and situational couple violence.* Boston, MA: Northeastern University Press.

Johnson, R. (2002). *Hard time: Understanding and reforming the prison* (3rd ed.). Belmont, CA: Wadsworth.

Johnson, W. W. (2011). Rethinking the interface between mental illness, criminal justice and academia. *Justice Quarterly, 28*(1), 15–22.

Johnston, D. (1995). Child custody issues of women prisoners: A preliminary report from the Chicas Project. *The Prison Journal, 75*(2), 222–239.

Jonaitis, A. (1991). *Chiefly feasts: The enduring Kwakiutl potlatch.* Seattle: University of Washington Press.

Jones, N. (2010). *Between good and ghetto: African American girls and inner-city violence.* New Brunswick, NJ: Rutgers University Press.

Jones-Correa, M. (2012). *Contested ground: Immigration in the United States.* Retrieved from http://www.migrationpolicy.org/pubs/TCM-UScasestudy.pdf

Jones, D. A., & Belknap, J. (1999). Police response to battering in a progressive pro-arrest jurisdiction. *Justice Quarterly, 16,* 249–273.

Jones 'El v. Berge, 172 F. Supp. 2d 1128 (2001).

Jordan, C. E. (2004). Intimate partner violence and the justice system: An examination of the interface. *Journal of Interpersonal Violence, 19,* 1412–1434.

Jordan, K. L., & Freiburger, T. L. (2010). Examining the impact of race and ethnicity on the sentencing of juveniles in the adult court. *Criminal Justice Policy Review, 21,* 185–201.

Jordan, K. L., & Myers, D. L. (2011). Juvenile transfer and deterrence: Reexamining the effectiveness of a "get-tough policy." *Crime and Delinquency, 57,* 247–270.

Josephson, M. (1934). *The robber barons: The great American capitalists, 1861–1901.* New York: Harcourt Brace.

Joy, J., Watson, S., & Benson, J. (Eds.). (1999). *Marijuana and medicine: Assessing the science base.* Washington, DC: National Academy Press.

Junginger, J., Claypoole, K., Laygo, R., & Crisanti, A. (2006). Effects of serious mental illness and substance abuse on criminal offense. *Psychiatric Services, 57,* 879–882.

Jurek v. Texas, 428 U.S. 153 (1976).

Justice Policy Institute. (2011a, March). *Addicted to courts: How a growing dependence on drug courts impacts peoples and communities.* Washington, DC: Author. Retrieved from http://www.justicepolicy.org/uploads/justicepolicy/documents/addicted_to_courts_final.pdf

Justice Policy Institute. (2011b). *Gaming the system: How the political strategies of private prison companies promote ineffective incarceration strategies.* Washington, DC: Author. Retrieved from http://www.justicepolicy.org/uploads/justicepolicy/documents/gaming_the_system.pdf

Juvenile Law Center. (2012). *Commonwealth of Pennsylvania v. Jordan Brown.* Retrieved from http://jlc.org/legal-docket/commonwealth-pennsylvania-v-jordan-brown

Kalven, H., & Zeisel, H. (1966). *The American jury.* Boston, MA: Little, Brown.

Kane, J., & Wall, A. (2005). *Identifying the links between white-collar crime and terrorism.* Washington, DC: U.S. Department of Justice.

Kaplan, T. (2012a, November 8). California Prop. 36: Families of some three-strikers hope for early release or shorter sentences. *San Jose Mercury News.*

Kaplan, T. (2012b, November 6). Proposition 36: Voters overwhelmingly ease three strikes law. *San Jose Mercury News.*

Kaplan, T. (2013, January 21). Newly released California "three-strikers" face new challenges. *San Jose Mercury News.*

Kaplan, W. J., & Rossman, D. (2011). Called "out" at home: The one strike eviction policy and juvenile court. *Duke Forum for Law and Social Change, 3,* 109–138.

Karp, D. R., & Clear, T. R. (2000). Community justice: A conceptual framework. In C. M. Friel (Ed.), *Boundary changes in criminal justice organizations: Criminal justice 2000* (Vol. 2, pp. 323–368). Washington, DC: National Criminal Justice Reference Service. Retrieved from https://www.ncjrs.gov/criminal_justice2000/vol_2/02i2.pdf

Katz v. United States, 389 U.S. 347 (1967).

KCET. (2012). *Who's funding Prop 36, the three strikes law revision?* Retrieved from http://www.kcet.org/news/ballotbrief/elections2012/propositions/database-whos-funding-prop-36-three-strikes-law-revision.html

Kelley, R. B. (1997). *Wal-Mart Stores, Inc. v. American Drugs, Inc.*: Drawing the line between predatory and competitive pricing. *Arkansas Law Review, 50,* 103–124.

Kelling, G. L. (1999). *Broken windows and police discretion.* (Research report NCJ17859). Washington, DC: National Institute of Justice.

Kelling, G. L., & Bratton, W. J. (1998). Declining crime rates: Insiders' views of the New York City story. *The Journal of Criminal Law and Criminology, 88*(4), 1217–1232.

Kelling, G. L., & Coles, C. M. (1996). *Fixing broken windows: Restoring order and reducing crime in our communities.* New York: Touchstone.

Kelling, G. L., & Moore, M. H. (1988). The evolving strategy of policing. National Institute of Justice and Harvard University: *Perspectives on Policing, 4,* 1–15.

Kelling, G. L., Pate, A. M., Dieckman, D., & Brown, C. (1974). *The Kansas City patrol experiment: Summary version.* Washington, DC: Police Foundation.

Kelling, G. L., Pate, A., Ferrara, A., Utne, M., & Brown, C. (1981). *The Newark foot patrol experiment.* Washington, DC: Police Foundation.

Kelling, G. L., & Sousa, W. H. (2001). *Do police matter? An analysis of the impact of New York City's police reforms.* (Civic report No. 22). New York: The Manhattan Institute for Policy Research.

Kelling, G. L., & Wilson, J. Q. (1982, March). Broken windows: The police and neighborhood safety. *The Atlantic Monthly,* 29–38.

Kendall, K. (1998). Evaluation of programs for female offenders. In R. Zaplin (Ed.), *Female offenders: Critical perspectives and effective interventions* (pp. 361–379). Gathersburg, MD: Aspen.

Kennard, D., & Roberts, J. (1983). *An introduction to therapeutic communities.* Boston, MA: Routledge & Kegan Paul.

Kennedy, D. (1998). Pulling levers: Getting deterrence right. *National Institute of Justice Journal.* Washington, DC: U.S. Department of Justice.

Kennedy, D. (2006). Old wine in new bottles: Policing and the lessons of pulling levers. In D. L. Weisburd & A. A. Braga (Eds.), *Police innovation: Contrasting perspectives.* New York: Cambridge University Press.

Kennedy, D. (2011). Don't shoot: One man, a street fellowship, and the end of violence in inner-city America. London, UK: Bloomsbury.

Kennedy, D. M., Braga, A. A., & Piehl, A. M. (2001). Developing and implementing Operation Ceasefire. In *Reducing gun violence: The Boston gun project's Operation Ceasefire.* Washington, DC: U.S. Department of Justice.

Kennon, S. S., Mackintosh, V. H., & Myers, B. J. (2009). Parenting education for incarcerated mothers. *The Journal of Correctional Education, 60*(1), 10–30.

Kerwin, D., & Yi-Ying Lin, S. (2009). *Immigrant detention: Can ICE meet its legal imperatives and case management responsibilities?* Retrieved from http://www.migrationpolicy.org/pubs/detentionreportSept1009.pdf

Kessler, D. P., & Piehl, A. M. (1998). The role of discretion in the criminal justice system. *Journal of Law, Economics, and Organization, 14*(2), 256–276.

Kesten, K. L., Leavitt-Smith, E., Rau, D. R., Shelton, D., Zhang, W., Wagner, J., & Trestman, R. L. (2012). Recidivism rates among mentally ill inmates: Impact of the Connecticut offender reentry program. *Journal of Correctional Health Care, 18*(1), 20–28.

Khantzian, E. J. (1997). The self-medication hypothesis of substance use disorders: A reconsideration and recent applications. *Harvard Review of Psychiatry, 4,* 231–244.

Killebrew, R. (2008, Fall). A new threat: The crossover of urban gang warfare and terrorism. *National Strategy Forum Review.* Retrieved from http://smallwarsjournal.com/blog/the-crossover-of-urban-gang-warfare-and-terrorism

Kilmer, A. (2012). *Social control theory and sex offender policy: Are we breaking the bonds needed for success?* Unpublished paper presented at 2012 annual meeting of the American Society of Criminology, Chicago, IL.

Kimisopa, B. (2007). *A just, safe, and secure society: A white paper on law and justice in Papua New Guinea.* Presented to Parliament by the Minister for Justice on the authority of the National Executive Council. Retrieved from http://www.lawandjustice.gov.pg/www/html/49-2007-white-paper-on-law-and-justice.asp

King, K., Steiner, B., & Breach, S. R. (2008). Violence in the supermax: A self-fulfilling prophecy. *Prison Journal, 88,* 144–168.

King, R. D. (1999). The rise and rise of supermax: An American solution in search of a problem? *Punishment and Society, 1,* 163–186.

King, R. D. (2005). The effects of supermax custody. In A. Liebling & S. Maruna (Eds.), *The effects of imprisonment* (pp. 118–145). Portland, OR: Willan.

Kingsbury, A. (2008, December 10). Inside the Feds' war on gang violence. *U.S. News and World Report.* Retrieved from http://www.usnews.com/news/national/articles/2008/12/10/inside-the-feds-war-on-gang-violence

Kingdon, J. W. (1984). *Agendas, alternatives, and public policies.* Boston: Little, Brown.

Kirk, D. S. (2009). A natural experiment on residential change and recidivism: Lessons from Hurricane Katrina. *American Sociological Review, 74*(3), 484–505.

Kirk, D. S. (2012). Residential change as a turning point in the life course of crime: Desistance or temporary cessation? *Criminology, 50*(2), 329–358.

Kirk, D. S., Papachristos, A. V., Fagan, J., & Tyler, T. R. (2012). The paradox of law enforcement in immigrant communities: Does tough immigration enforcement undermine public safety? *The Annals of the American Academy of Political and Social Science, 641,* 79–98.

Kirkorian, G. (2002, February 28). Welfare ban for drug felons harms children, study says. *Los Angeles Times.* Retrieved from http://www.latimes.com

Kleiman, M. (2009). *When brute force fails: How to have less crime and less punishment.* Princeton, NJ: Princeton University Press.

Klite, P., Bardwell, R. A., & Salzman, J. (1997). Local TV news: Getting away with murder. *The Harvard International Journal of Press/Politics, 2*(2), 102–112.

Knouss, R. (2001). National disaster medical system. *Public Health Reports, 116,* 49–52.

Koebler, J. (2012, August 2). Court upholds domestic drone use in arrest of American citizen. *US News and World Reports.* Retrieved from http://www.usnews.com/news/articles/2012/08/02/court-upholds-domestic-drone-use-in-arrest-of-american-citizen

Kohli, A., Markowitz, P. L., & Chavez, L. (2011). *Secure Communities by the numbers: An analysis of demographics and due process.* Berkeley, CA: University of California-Berkeley Law School, The Chief Justice Earl Warren Institute on Law and Social Policy. Retrieved from http://www.law.berkeley.edu/files/Secure_Communities_by_the_Numbers.pdf

Koons, B. A., Burrow, J. D., Morash, M., & Bynum, T. (1997). Expert and offender perceptions of program elements linked to successful outcomes for incarcerated women. *Crime & Delinquency, 43*(4), 512–532.

Kort-Butler, L. A., & Sittner Hartshorn, K. J. (2011). Watching the detectives: Crime programming, fear of crime, and attitudes about the criminal justice system. *Sociological Quarterly, 52*(1), 36–55.

Kovandzic, T. V., Sloan, J. J., & Vieraitis, L. M. (2002). Unintended consequences of politically popular sentencing policy: The homicide promoting effects of "Three Strikes" in U.S. cities (1980–1999). *Criminology and Public Policy, 1*(3), 399–424.

Kravets, D. (2004, November 3). Schwarzenegger, 'angel' who defeated Prop 66 sentencing reform. *Sacramento Bee.* Retrieved from http://www.nlada.org/DMS/Documents/1099585138.19/11305250p-12220095c.html

Krejci, M. (1993). People of Illinois vs. Montañez Cook County Circuit Court, 92 CR 13088.

Krisberg, B., & Taylor-Nicholson, E. (2011). *Realignment: A bold new era in California corrections.* Berkeley: The Chief Justice Earl Warren Institute on Law and Social Policy, University of California. Retrieved from http://www.law.berkeley.edu/files/REALIGNMENT_FINAL9.28.11.pdf

Krivo, L. J., & Peterson, R. D. (1996). Extremely disadvantaged neighborhoods and urban crime. *Social Forces, 75*(2), 619–648.

Kruttschnitt, C., Gartner, R., & Miller, A. (2000). Doing her own time? Women's responses to prison in the context of the old and new penology. *Criminology, 38*(3), 681–717.

Kubrin, C. E., & Stewart, E. A. (2006). Predicting who reoffends: The neglected role of neighborhood context in recidivism studies. *Criminology, 44,* 165–197.

Kupchik, A. (2006). *Judging juveniles: Prosecuting adolescents in adult and juvenile courts.* New York: NYU Press.

Kupchik, A. (2007). The correctional experiences of youth in adult and juvenile prisons. *Justice Quarterly, 24,* 247–270.

Kupchik, A., Fagan, J., & Liberman, A. (2003). Punishment, proportionality and jurisdictional waiver of adolescent offenders: A test of the leniency gap hypothesis. *Stanford Law & Policy Review, 14,* 57–83.

Kupers, T. A. (1996). Trauma and its sequelae in male prisoners: Effects of confinement, overcrowding, and diminished services. *Journal of Orthopsychiatry, 66,* 189–196.

Kupers, T. A., Dronet, T., Winter, M., Austin, J., Kelly, L., Morris, T. J., ...McBride, J. (2009). Beyond supermax administrative segregation: Mississippi's experience rethinking prison classification and creating alternative mental health programs. *Criminal Justice and Behavior Online First.* doi:10.1177/0093854809341938

Kurki, L., & Morris, N. (2001). The purposes, practices, and problems of supermax prisons. *Crime and Justice, 28,* 385–424.

Kurlychek, M. C., & Johnson, B. D. (2004). The juvenile penalty: A comparison of juvenile and young adult sentencing outcomes in criminal court. *Criminology, 42,* 485–517.

Kurlychek, M. C., &. Johnson, B. D. (2010). Juvenility and punishment: Sentencing juveniles in adult criminal court. *Criminology, 48,* 725–758.

Laglagaron, L., Rodriguez, C., Silver, A., & Thanasombat, S. (2008, October). *Regulating immigration at the state level: Highlights from the database of 2007 state immigration legislation.* Washington, DC: Migration Policy Institute and the National Center on Immigrant Integration Policy.

Lagos, M. (2010, October 2). State downgrades pot possession. *San Francisco Chronicle.* Retrieved from http://www.sfgate.com

Lain, C. B. (2007). Furman fundamentals. *Washington Law Review, 82,* 1–74.

Lakshmi, R. (2012). India faces flood of counterfeit cash from Pakistan. *The Washington Post.* Retrieved from http://www.washington-post.com/world/asia_pacific/india-cracks-down-on-counterfeit-cash/2012/02/24/gIQA3T0DuR_story.html

Lamb, H. R., & Lamb, D. (1990). Factors contributing to homelessness among the chronically and severely mentally ill. *Hospital and Community Psychiatry, 41,* 301–305.

Landenberger, N. A., & Lipsey, M. W. (2005). The positive effects of cognitive-behavioral programs for offenders: A meta-analysis of factors associated with effective treatment. *Journal of Experimental Criminology, 1*(4), 451–477.

Lane, J., Gover, A. R., & Dahod, S. (2009). Fear of violent crime among men and women on campus: The impact of perceived risk and fear of sexual assault. *Violence and Victims, 24*(2), 172–192.

Lane, R. (1971). *Policing the city: Boston, 1822–1885.* New York: Atheneum.

Langan, P., & Levin, D. (2002). *Recidivism of prisoners released in 1994.* (Special report). Washington, DC: U.S. Department of Justice, Office of Justice Programs.

Langevin, R. (2003). A study of the psychosexual characteristics of sex killers: Can we identify them before it is too late? *International Journal of Offender Therapy and Comparative Criminology, 47*(4), 366–382.

Lanza-Kaduce, L., Frazier, C. E., Lane, J., & Bishop, D. M. (2002). *Juvenile transfer to criminal court study: Final report.* Tallahassee: Florida Department of Juvenile Justice.

Lapidus, L., Luthra, N., Verma, A., Small, D., Allard, P., & Levingston, K. (2005). *Caught in the net: The impact of drug policies on women and families.* New York: American Civil Liberties Union, The Brennan Center, Break the Chains.

Larson, R. C. (1972). *Urban police patrol analysis.* Cambridge: MIT Press.

Lasley, J. (1998). *"Designing out" gang homicides and street assaults.* (Research in brief). Washington, DC: U.S. Department of Justice.

Latessa, E., Travis, L., Fulton, B., & Stichman, A. (1998). *Evaluating the prototypical ISP.* (Research in brief). Washington, DC: National Institute of Justice.

Latessa, E. J., Cullen, F. T., & Gendreau, P. (2002). Beyond correctional quackery: Professionalism and the possibility of effective treatment. *Federal Probation, 66*(2), 43–49.

Latimer, J., Dowden, C., & Muise, D. (2005). The effectiveness of restorative justice practices: A meta-analysis. *The Prison Journal, 85,* 127–144.

Lattimore, P. K., Visher, C. A., & Lindquist, C. (2005). Implementation of prisoner reentry programs: Findings from the Serious and Violent Offender Reentry Initiative multi-site evaluation. *Justice Research and Policy, 7*(2), 87–109.

Laufer, W. S. (2006). *Corporate bodies and guilty minds: The failure of corporate criminal liability.* Chicago, IL: University of Chicago Press.

Law Enforcement Assistance Agency. (1978). *National Institute of Law Enforcement and Criminal Justice annual report, FY 1978.* (NCJRS-59147). Washington, DC: National Institute of Justice. Retrieved from https://www.ncjrs.gov/app/publications/abstract.aspx?ID=59147

Lawrence, R., & Hesse, M. (2012). *Juvenile justice: The essentials.* Thousand Oaks, CA: Sage.

Lawrence, S., Mears, D. P., Dubin, G., & Travis, J. (2002). *The practice and promise of prison programming.* Washington, DC: Urban Institute, Justice Policy Center.

League of Women Voters California Education Fund. (2010). *Easy voter guide: Fast facts: State ballot measures.* Retrieved from http://www.easyvoterguide.org/wp-content/pdf/FastFacts-BallotMeasures.pdf

Lee, E. (2006). A nation of immigrants and a gatekeeping nation: American immigration law and policy. In R. Ueda (Ed.), *A companion to American immigration* (pp. 5–35). Malden, MA: Blackwell.

Lee, H. K. (2013, January 29). Many more '3rd strikes' in some counties. *San Francisco Chronicle,* p. 1.

Lee, N., & Vukich, E. M. (2001). *Representation and equity in Washington state: An assessment of disproportionality and disparity in adult felony sentencing—fiscal year 2000.* Olympia, WA: State of Washington Sentencing Guidelines Commission.

Lee, R. (2002). *Terrorist financing: The U.S. and international response.* Washington, DC: Congressional Research Service.

Legislative Analyst Office. (2008–2009). *How much does it cost to incarcerate an inmate in prison?* Sacramento, CA: Author. Retrieved from http://www.lao.ca.gov/laoapp/laomenus/sections/crim_justice/6_cj_inmatecost.aspx?catid=3

Lehman, J. D., & Labecki, L. A. (1998). Myth versus reality: The politics of crime and punishment and its impact on correctional administration in the 1990s. In T. Allman & R. Gido (Eds.), *Turnstyle justice: Issues in American corrections* (pp. 42–70). Upper Saddle River, NJ: Prentice Hall.

Lejeune, C. (2009). Immigrants in the United States: "Illegal aliens" on their way to becoming emergent "possible subjects." (Special issue: Immigration). *European Journal of American Studies, 4.*

Lelyveld, J. (2012). *Great soul: Mahatma Ghandi and his struggle with India.* New York: Knopf.

Lemmon, J. H., Fetzer, M. D., Austin, T. L., Whitman, T. K., Cookus, J., Bishop, S. P., . . . Gladfelter, A. S. (2012). *An examination of BARJ services in four Pennsylvania counties* (Report to the Pennsylvania Commission on Crime and Delinquency). Washington, DC: U.S. Office of Justice Programs. Retrieved from http://www.portal.state.pa.us/portal/server.pt?parentname=SearchResult&space=SearchResult&in_tx_query=An+Examination+of+BARJ+Services&parentid=9&in_hi_userid=2&control=bannerstart&cached=false

Leon, C. S. (2011a). *Sex fiends, perverts and pedophiles: Understanding sex crime in America.* New York: New York University Press.

Leon, C. S. (2011b). Policy essay: The contexts and politics of evidence-based sex offender policy. *Criminology and Public Policy, 10*(2), 421–430.

Leon, C. S., Burton, D. L., & Alvare, D. (2011). The overuse of registration and residential treatment for youth who commit sex offenses. *Widener Law Review, 17*(1), 127–158.

Leonard, J. (2012, October 28). Three strikes reform not so simple: Two inmates' stories illustrate contrasting views on Prop. 36's easing of the law. *Los Angeles Times,* p. 37.

Leonard, J., & Dolan, M. (2012a, September 30). Californians back change on three strikes, but not on death penalty. *Los Angeles Times.* Retrieved from http://articles.latimes.com/2012/sep/30/local/la-me-poll-three-strikes-20120930

Leonard, J., & Dolan, M. (2012b, November 8). Priming cases for 3-strikes review. *Los Angeles Times,* p. 1.

Leshner, A. (1999). Science-based views of drug addiction and its treatment. *Journal of the American Medical Association, 282,* 1314–1316.

Lessard v. Schmidt, 349 F. Supp. 1078 (E. D. Wis. 1972), *vacated and remanded,* 414 U.S. 473, *on remand,* 379 F. Supp. 1376 (E. D. Wis. 1974), *vacated and remanded,* 421 U.S. 957 (1975), *reinstated,* 413 F. Supp. 1318 (E. D. Wis. 1976).

Letourneau, E. J., & Miner, M. H. (2005). Juvenile sex Offenders: A case against the legal and clinical status quo. *Sexual abuse: A journal of research and treatment, 17*(3), 293–312.

Levenson, J. S. (2006). Sex offender residence restrictions. *Sex Offender Law Report, 7*(3), 46–47.

Levenson, J. S., & Cotter, L. P. (2005). The impact of sex offender residence restrictions: 1,000 feet from danger, or one step from absurd? *International Journal of Offender Therapy and Comparative Criminology, 49*(1), 168–178.

Levenson, J. S., & Hern, A. L. (2007). Sex offender residence restrictions: Unintended consequences and community reentry. *Justice Research and Policy 9*(1), 59–74.

Leverentz, A. (2006). People, places, and things: The social process of reentry for female ex-offenders. (Document No. 215178). Washington, DC: U.S. Department of Justice.

Lewis, O. (1938). *The big four: The story of Huntington, Stanford, Hopkins, and Crocker and the building of the Central Pacific.* New York: Knopf.

Liebman, J. S., Fagan, J., & West, V. (2000). *A broken system: Error rates in capital cases, 1973–1995* (Public Law Research Paper No. 15). New York: Columbia Law School. Retrieved from http://papers.ssrn.com/s013/papers.cfm?abstract_id=232712

Ling, L. (Writer). (2000). *The world's most dangerous gang* [DVD]. Washington, DC: National Geographic.

Linn, L. (1961). *Frontiers in general hospital psychiatry.* New York: International University Press.

Lipsey, M. W., Chapman, G. L., & Landenberger, N. A. (2001). Cognitive-behavioral programs for offenders. *Annals of the American Academy of Political and Social Science, 578,* 144–157.

Lipsky, M. (2010). *Street-level bureaucracy: Dilemmas of the individual in public services* (30th Anniversary ed.). New York: Russell Sage Foundation.

Liptak, A. (2011, April 18). Judges see sentencing injustice. *New York Times*. Retrieved from http://www.nytimes.com

Lira v. California Director of Corrections, 2007 U.S. Dist. LEXIS 116727 (N.D. Cal. 2008).

Litschge, C. M., & Vaughn, M. G. (2009). The mentally ill offender treatment and crime reduction act of 2004: Problems and prospects. *The Journal of Forensic Psychiatry & Psychology, 20*(4), 542–558.

Listwan, S. J., Colvin, M., Hanley, D., & Flannery, D. (2010). Victimization, social support, and psychological well-being: A study of recently released prisoners. *Criminal Justice and Behavior, 37*, 1140–1159.

Loeber, R., & Stouthamer-Loeber, M. (1986). Family factors as correlates and predictors of juvenile conduct problems and delinquency. In M. Tonry & N. Morris (Eds.), *Crime and Justice* (Vol. 7). Chicago, IL: University of Chicago Press.

Lofstrom, M., Petersilia, J., & Raphael, S. (2012). *Evaluating the effects of California's corrections realignment on public safety*. San Francisco, CA: Public Policy Institute of California. Retrieved from http://www.ppic.org/content/pubs/report/R_812MLR.pdf

Logan, T. K., Walker, R., & Hoyt, W. (2012). The economic costs of partner violence and the cost-benefit of civil protective orders. *Journal of Interpersonal Violence, 27*, 1137–1154.

Logan, W. A. (2009). *Knowledge as power: Criminal registration and community notification laws in America*. Stanford, CA: Stanford University Press.

Looney, R. (2006). The mirage of terrorist financing: The case of Islamic charities. *Strategic Insights, 5*(3).

Lopez, M., & Minushkin, S. (2008, July). *2008 national survey of Latinos: Hispanic voter attitudes*. Washington, DC: Pew Research Hispanic Center.

Lord, E. A. (2008). The challenges of mentally ill female offenders in prison. *Criminal Justice and Behavior, 35*(8), 928–942.

Loughran, T. A., Mulvey, E. P., Schubert, C. A., Chassin, L. A., Steinberg, L., Piquero, A. R., ... Losoya, S. (2010). Differential effects of adults court transfer on juvenile offender recidivism. *Law and Human Behavior, 34*, 476–488.

Louw, D. J. (2006). The African concept of Ubuntu and restorative justice. In D. Sullivan & L. Tifft (Eds.), *Handbook of restorative justice: A global perspective* (pp. 161–173). New York: Taylor & Francis.

Lovell, D., Cloyes, K., Allen, D., & Rhodes, L. (2000). Who lives in supermaximum custody? A Washington state study. *Federal Probation, 64*(2), 33–38.

Lovell, D., Gagliardi, G. J., & Peterson, P. D. (2002). Recidivism and use of services among persons with mental illness after release from prison. *Psychiatric Services, 53*(1), 1290–1296.

Lovell, D., Johnson, L. C., & Cain, K. C. (2007). Recidivism of supermax prisoners in Washington state. *Crime and Delinquency, 53*, 633–656.

Lowen, M., & Isaacs, C. (2012). *Lifetime lockdown: How isolation conditions impact prisoner reentry*. Tucson, AZ: American Friends Service Committee.

Lowenkamp, C. T., Latessa, E. J., & Holsinger, A. M. (2006). The risk principle in action: What we learned from 13,676 offenders and 97 correctional programs? *Crime & Delinquency, 52*, 77–93.

Lowenkamp, C. T., Latessa, E. J., & Smith, P. (2006). Does correctional program quality really matter? The impact of adhering to the principles of effective interventions. *Criminology and Public Policy, 5*(3), 575–594.

Lowenkamp, C. T., Hubbard, D., Makarios, M. D., & Latessa, E. J. (2012). A quasi-experimental evaluation of thinking for a change: A real world application. In *Community-based corrections: A text/reader* (pp. 158–164). Thousand Oaks, CA: Sage.

Lucas, W. (2008). Parents' perceptions of the Drug Abuse Resistance Education program (DARE). *Journal of Child & Adolescent Substance Abuse, 17*(4), 99–114.

Lundy, S. E. (1993). Abuse that dare not speak its name: Assisting victims of lesbian and gay domestic violence in Massachusetts. *New England Law Review, 28*, 273–312.

Lurigio, A. J. (2011). Examining prevailing beliefs about people with serious mental illness in the criminal justice system. *Federal Probation, 75*(1), 11–18.

Lurigio, A. J., Snowden, J., & Watson, A. (2006). Police handling of the mentally ill: Historical and research perspectives. *Law Enforcement Executive Forum, 6*, 87–110.

Luskin, M. L. (2001). Who is diverted? Case selection for court-monitored mental health treatment. *Law & Policy, 23*(2), 217–236.

Luskin, M. L. (2012, December 3). More of the same? Treatment in mental health courts. *Law & Human Behavior*. Washington, DC: American Psychological Association. Advance online publication. doi: 10.1037/lhb0000016

Lutze, F. E. (2006). Boot camp prisons and corrections policy: Moving from militarism to an ethic of care. *Journal of Criminology and Public Policy, 5*(2), 389–400.

Lutze, F. E., Hamilton, Z., & Rosky, J. (2012). *Housing and reentry: An outcome evaluation of the Washington State Housing Reentry Pilot Program*. A paper presented at the annual meetings of the Academy of Criminal Justice Sciences. New York, NY.

Lutze, F. E., Johnson, W., Clear, T., Latessa, E., & Slate, R. (2012). The future of community corrections is now: Stop dreaming and take action. *Journal of Contemporary Criminal Justice, 28*(1), 42–49.

Lutze, F. E., & Kigerl, A. (2013). The psychology of prisoner reentry. In J. Helfgott (Ed.), *Criminal Psychology* (Vols. 1–4). Westport, CT: Praeger.

Lutze, F. E., & van Wormer, J. (2007). The nexus between drug and alcohol treatment program integrity and drug court effectiveness: Policy recommendations for pursuing success. *Criminal Justice Policy Review, 18*(3), 226–245.

Lyon, W. (2002). Partnerships, information, and public safety. *Policing, 25*, 530–543.

MacCharles, T. (2002, December 9). Safe sites urged for hard drug users. *Toronto Star*. Retrieved from http://www.thestar.com

MacCoun, R. (2011). What can we learn from the Dutch cannabis coffeeshop system? *Addiction 106*(11), 1988–2910.

MacCoun, R., & Reuter, P. (1997). Interpreting Dutch cannabis policy: Reasoning by analogy in the drug legalization debate. *Science, 278*, 47–52.

MacDonald, J., & Saunders, J. (2012). Are immigrant youth less violent? Specifying the reasons and mechanisms. *The Annals of the American Academy of Political and Social Science, 641*, 125–147.

MacKenzie, D. (2006). *What works in corrections: Reducing the criminal activities of offenders and delinquents.* Cambridge, UK: Cambridge University Press.

MacKenzie, D. L. (2000). Evidence-based corrections: Identifying what works. *Crime and Delinquency, 46*(6), 457–471.

MacKinzie-Mulvey, E. (2007). United States announces arrest of Taliban-linked Afghan heroin trafficker on charges of conspiring to import millions of dollars' worth of heroin. *DEA News Release.* Retrieved from http://www.usdoj-gov/dea/pubs/states/newsrel/ny0051107a.html

MacQueen, R. (2010, September 7). Jailhouse nation. *Macleans.* Retrieved from http://www2.macleans.ca

MacRae, A., & Zehr, H. (2004). *The little book of family group conferences: New Zealand style.* Intercourse, PA: Good Books.

Madensen, T. D., & Knutsson, J. (Eds.). (2011). Preventing crowd violence. *Crime Prevention Studies, 26.*

Madrid v. Gomez, 889 F. Supp. 1146 (N.D. Cal. 1995).

Maguire, B. (1988). Image vs. reality: An analysis of prime-time television crime and police programs. *Crime and Justice, 11*, 165–188.

Maier, P. (1980). *The old revolutionaries: Political lives in the age of Samuel Adams.* New York: Knopf.

Main, F. (2011, June 22). Police unleash war on Maniac Latin Disciples gang, arrest 120. *Chicago Sun-Times.* Retrieved from http://www.suntimes.com/news/crime/6123366-418/police-unleash-war-on-maniac-latin-disciples-gang-arrest-120.html

Malcolm, J. G., & Slattery, E. (2012, June 25). Juvenile life without parole: Constitutionality depends on sentencing discretion. *The Foundry.* Washington, DC: The Heritage Foundation. Retrieved from http://blog.heritage.org/2012/06/25/juvenile-life-without-parole-constitutionality-depends-on-sentencing-discretion/

Mallicoat, S. L., & Ireland, C. E. (2013). *Women and crime: The essentials.* Thousand Oaks, CA: Sage.

Mallik-Kane, K., Parthasarathy, B., & Adams, W. (2012). *Examining growth in the federal prison population, 1998–2010.* Washington, DC: The Urban Institute. Retrieved from http://www.urban.org/UploadedPDF/412720-Examining-Growth-in-the-Federal-Prison-Population.pdf

Mann, J. (2011). Delivering justice to the mentally ill: Characteristics of mental health courts. *Southwest Journal of Criminal Justice, 8*(1), 44–58.

Mann, K. (1985). *Defending white collar crime: A portrait of attorneys at work.* New Haven, CT: Yale University Press.

Markovitz, J. (2011). *Racial spectacles: Explorations in media, race, and justice.* New York: Routledge.

Marsch, L. (1998). The efficacy of methadone maintenance interventions in reducing illicit opiate use, HIV risk behavior and criminality: A meta-analysis. *Addiction, 93*, 515–532.

Marshall, B., Milloy, M-. J., Wood, E., Montaner, J. SG., & Kerr, T. (2011). Reduction in overdose mortality after the opening of North America's first medically supervised injecting facility: A retrospective population-based study. *Lancet, 377*(9775), 1429–1437.

Marshall, W. L. (2007). Diagnostic issues, multiple paraphilias, and comorbid disorders in sexual offenders: Their incidence and treatment. *Aggression and Violent Behavior, 12*(1), 16–35.

Martin, J. (2011, December 1). Gregoire to DEA: Make marijuana a legal drug. *Seattle Times.* Retrieved from http://www.seattletimes.com

Martin, J. (2012, September 10). Children's Alliance backs pot measure on ballot. *Seattle Times.* Retrieved from http://nwsource.com

Martin, M. (2004, November 4). Proposition 66: Efforts to reform 'three strikes' law likely to be on ballot again. *San Francisco Chronicle.* Retrieved from http://www.sfgate.com/politics/article/PROPOSITION-66-Efforts-to-reform-three-2638541.php#ixzz2JgyResqY

Martin, M. E. (1997). Double your trouble: Dual arrest in family violence. *Journal of Family Violence, 12*, 139–157.

Martinez, R., Jr., Stowell, J. I., & Lee, M. T. (2010). Immigration and crime in an era of transformation: A longitudinal analysis of homicides in San Diego neighborhoods, 1980–2000. *Criminology, 48*, 797–829.

Martinson, R. (1974). What works? Questions and answers about prison reform. *The Public Interest, 35*, 22–54.

Martinson, R. (1979). New findings, new views: A note of caution regarding sentencing reform. *Hofsra Law Review, 7*(2), 243–258.

Marvell, T. B., & Moody, C. E. (2001). The lethal effects of three-strikes laws. *Journal of Legal Studies, 30*(1), 89–106.

Maryland v. King, 569 U.S. ___ (2013).

Mason, C. (2012). *Dollars and detainees: The growth of for-profit detention.* Washington, DC: The Sentencing Project. Retrieved from http://sentencingproject.org/doc/publications/inc_Dollars_and_Detainees.pdf

Mathews, J. (2004, November 7). How prospects for Prop. 66 fell so far, so fast. *Los Angeles Times.* Retrieved from http://articles.latimes.com/2004/nov/07/local/me-pete7

Mathews, R. (1997). Developing more effective strategies for curbing prostitution. In R. Clarke (Ed.), *Situational crime prevention: Successful case studies* (2nd ed.). Guilderland, NY: Harrow and Heston.

Matthews, W. (2010). *ACLU strikes deal to shutter notorious unit 32 at Mississippi state penitentiary.* Jackson, MS: ACLU of Mississippi. Retrieved from http://www.aclu-ms.org/news/2010/06/11/aclu-strikes-deal-to-shutter-notorious-unit-32-at-mississippi-state-penitentiary

Mauer, M. (2009). *The changing racial dynamics of the war on drugs.* Washington, DC: The Sentencing Project.

Mauer, M., & King, R. S. (2007). *Uneven justice: State rates of incarceration by race and ethnicity.* Washington, DC: The Sentencing Project. Retrieved from http://www.sentencingproject.org/doc/publications/rd_stateratesofincbyraceandethnicity.pdf

Mauer, M., & King, R. S. (2007). *A 25-year quagmire: The war on drugs and its impact on American society.* Washington, DC: The Sentencing Project.

Mauer, M., Potler, C., & Wolf, R. (1999). *Gender and justice: Women, drugs, and sentencing policy.* Washington, DC: The Sentencing Project.

Maxfield, M., & Widom, C. (1996). The cycle of violence: Revisited six years later. *Archives of Pediatrics and Adolescent Medicine, 150,* 390–395.

Maxson, C. (2011). Street gangs. In J. Q. Wilson & J. Petersilia (Eds.), *Crime and public policy.* New York: Oxford University Press.

Maxwell, C. D., Garner, J. H., & Fagan, J. A. (2001). *The effects of arrest on intimate partner violence: New evidence from the Spouse Assault Replication Program* (Research in Brief, NCJ 188199). Washington, DC: National Institute of Justice.

Maxwell, G., Morris, A., & Hayes, H. (2008). Conferencing and restorative justice. In D. Sullivan & L. Tifft (Eds.), *Handbook of restorative justice.* New York: Routledge.

Maynard-Moody, S., & Musheno, M. (2003). Cops, teachers, counselors: Stories from the front lines of public service. Ann Arbor: The University of Michigan Press.

Mayors Against Illegal Guns. (2013, January). *Access denied: How the gun lobby is depriving police, policy makers, and the public of the data we need to prevent gun violence.* New York: Author. Retrieved from http://www.demandaction.org/detail/2013–01-access-denied-how-the-gun-lobby-is-depriving-police

McAdam, D. (1986). Recruitment to high-risk activism: The case of freedom summer. *American Journal of Sociology, 92,* 64–90.

McCabe, K., & Meissner, D. (2010, January). *Immigration and the United States: Recession affects flows, prospects for reform.* Washington, DC: Migration Information Source. Retrieved from http://www.migrationinformation.org/usfocus/display.cfm?ID=766

McCauley, C., & Segal, M. (1987). Social psychology of terrorist groups. In C. Hendrick (Ed.), *Group processes and intergroup relations: Review of personality and social psychology* (Vol. 9, pp. 231–256). Newbury Park, CA: Sage.

McClellan, D. S., Farabee, D., & Crouch, B. M. (1997). Early victimization, drug use, and criminality: A comparison of male and female prisoners. *Criminal Justice and Behavior, 24*(4), 455–476.

McCold, P. (2008). The recent history of restorative justice: Mediation, circles, and conferencing. In D. Sullivan & L. Tifft (Eds.), *Handbook of restorative justice.* London, UK: Routledge.

McCord, J. (1982). A longitudinal view of the relationship between paternal absence and crime. In J. Gunn & D. Farrington (Eds.), *Abnormal offenders, delinquency, and the criminal justice system.* Chichester, England: Wiley.

McCord, J. (1997). On discipline. *Psychological Inquiry, 8,* 215–217.

McCormick, J. S., Maric, A., Seto, M. C., & Barbaree, H. E. (1977). Relationship to victim predicts sentence length in sexual assault cases. *Journal of Interpersonal Violence, 13*(3), 413–420.

McDonald, L. G., & Robinson, P. (2009). *A colossal failure of common sense and the collapse of Lehman Brothers.* New York: Crown.

McDonald v. Chicago, 561 U.S. (2010).

McGarrell, E. F., & Chermak, S. (2004). Strategic approaches to reducing firearms violence: Final report on the Indianapolis violence reduction partnership. National Institute of Justice. Washington, DC: U.S. Department of Justice.

McGarrell, E. F., & Hipple, N. K. (2007). Family group conferencing and re-offending among first-time juvenile offenders: The Indianapolis experiment. *Justice Quarterly, 24*(2), 221–246.

McGowan, A., Hahn, R., Liberman, A., Crosby, A., Fullilove, M., Johnson, R., . . . Stone, G. (2007). Effects on violence of laws and policies facilitating the waiver of juveniles from the juvenile justice system to the adult system. *American Journal of Preventive Medicine,* I, S7–S28.

McKean, J., & Warren-Gordon, K. (2011). Racial differences in graduation rates from adult drug treatment courts. *Journal of Ethnicity in Criminal Justice, 9*(1), 41–55.

McKinley, J. (2010, March 25). Legal-marijuana advocates focus on a new green. *New York Times.* Retrieved from http://www.nytimes.com

McManus, J. H. (1994). *Market-driven journalism: Let the citizen beware.* Thousand Oaks, CA: Sage.

McNiel, D. E., & Binder, R. L. (2007). Effectiveness of a mental health court in reducing criminal recidivism and violence. *American Journal of Psychiatry, 164*(9), 1395–1403.

Me, A., Bisogno, E., & Malby, S. (2011). *2011 global study on homicide: Trends, context, data.* Vienna, Austria: United Nations Office on Drugs and Crime.

Mears, D. P. (2006). *Evaluating the effectiveness of supermax prisons.* Washington, DC: Urban Institute Justice Policy Center.

Mears, D. P., & Bales, W. D. (2009). Supermax incarceration and recidivism. *Criminology, 47,* 1131–1166.

Mears, D. P., & Bales, W. D. (2010). Supermax housing: Placement, duration, and time to reentry. *Journal of Criminal Justice, 38,* 545–554.

Mears, D. P., & Castro, J. L. (2006). Wardens' views on the wisdom of supermax prisons. *Crime and Delinquency, 52,* 398–431.

Mears, D. P., & Reisig, M. D. (2006). The theory and practice of supermax prisons. *Punishment and Society, 8,* 33–57.

Mears, D. P., & Watson, J. (2006). Towards a fair and balanced assessment of supermax prisons. *Justice Quarterly, 23,* 232–270.

Megan's Law (n.d.). Retrieved from http://www.meganslaw.com

Mele, C., & Miller, T. A. (Eds.). (2005). *Civil penalties, social consequences.* New York: Routledge.

Mello, M., & Perkins, P. J. (1998). Closing the circle: The illusion of lawyers for people litigating for their lives at the fin de siecle (pp. 245–284). In J. R. Acker, R. M. Bohm, & C. S. Lanier (Eds.), *America's experiment with capital punishment: Reflections on the past, present, and future of the ultimate penal sanction.* Durham, NC: Carolina Academic Press.

Meloy, M. L., Miller, S. L., & Curtis, K. M. (2008). Making sense out of nonsense: The deconstruction of state-level sex offender residence restrictions. *American Journal of Criminal Justice, 33*(2), 209–222.

Mendelson, M., Strom, S., & Wishnae, M. (2009). *Collateral damage: An examination of ICE's fugitive operations program.* Washington, DC: Migration Policy Institute.

Menjívar, C., & Salcido, O. (2002). Immigrant women and domestic violence: Common experiences in different countries. *Gender & Society, 16,* 898–920.

Mentally Ill Offender Treatment and Crime Reduction Act, 118 Stat. 2327, Pub. L. 108–414 (2004), *reauthorized by* 122 Stat. 4352, Pub. L. 110–416 (2008).

Mercado, C. C., Alverez, S., & Levenson, J. (2008). The impact of specialized sex offender legislation on community re-entry. *Sexual Abuse: A Journal of Research and Treatment, 20*(2), 188–205.

Messina, N., Burdon, W., Hagopian, G., & Prendergast, M. (2004). One year return to custody rates among co-disordered offenders. *Behavioral Sciences and the Law, 22,* 503–518.

Metraux, S., & Culhane, D. P. (2004). Homeless shelter use and reincarceration following prison release. *Criminology and Public Policy, 3*(2), 139–160.

Metraux, S., & Culhane, D. P. (2006). Recent incarceration history among a sheltered homeless population. *Crime & Delinquency, 52*(3), 504–517.

Michaelson, A. (2009). *The foreclosure of America: The rise and fall of Countrywide, home loans, the mortgage crisis and the defeat of the American dream.* New York: Berkley Books.

Miccio, G. K. (2005). A house divided: Mandatory arrest, domestic violence, and the conservatization of the battered women's movement. *Houston Law Review, 42,* 237–323.

Michel, L., & Herbeck, D. (2001). *American terrorist: Timothy McVeigh & the Oklahoma City bombing.* New York: Regan Books.

Miethe, T. D., Olson, J., & Mitchell, O. (2006). Specialization and persistence in the arrest histories of sex offenders: A comparative analysis of alternative measures and offense types. *Journal of Research in Crime and Delinquency, 43*(3), 204–229.

Mignon, S. I., & Holmes, W. M. (1995). Police response to mandatory arrest laws. *Crime & Delinquency, 41,* 430–442.

Mihm, S. (2006). No ordinary counterfeit. *New York Times.* Retrieved from http://www.nytimes.com/2006/07/23/magazine/23counterfeit .html?pagewanted=all

Miller, Evan, Petitioner v. Alabama. 567 US ____ (2012). No. 10-9646. Supreme Court of the United States.

Miller, J. (2002). Young women in street gangs: Risk factors, delinquency, and victimization risk. In W. Reed & S. Decker (Eds.), *Responding to gangs: Evaluation and research.* Washington, DC: National Institute of Justice.

Miller, J., &. Gerth, J. (2001, October 11). Trade in honey is said to provide money and cover for bin Laden. *New York Times,* p. A1.

Miller, J. L., & Sloan, J. J., III. (1994). A study of criminal justice discretion. *Journal of Criminal Justice, 22*(2), 107–123.

Miller, M., & Ngugi, I. (2009). *Impacts of housing supports: Persons with mental illness and ex-offenders.* Olympia: Washington State Institute for Public Policy.

Miller, S. L. (2005). *Victims as offenders: The paradox of women's violence in relationships.* New Brunswick, NJ: Rutgers University Press.

Miller v. Alabama, 567 U.S. ___ (2012).

Miller, W. (1958). Lower class culture as a generating milieu of gang delinquency. *Journal of Social Issues, 14,* 5–19.

Miller, W. (1975). *Violence by youth gangs and youth groups as a crime problem in major American cities.* Washington, DC: U.S. Department of Justice.

Mills, Linda (2003). *Insult to Injury: Rethinking Our Responses to Intimate Abuse.* Princeton University Press.

Miner, M. H. (2002). Factors associated with recidivism in juveniles: An analysis of serious juvenile sex offenders. *Journal of Research in Crime and Delinquency, 39*(4), 421–436.

Mintz, H. (2013, January 8). Governor: Drop California prisons from court orders to shed inmates. *San Jose Mercury News.*

Mitchell, O. (2009). Is the war on drugs racially biased? *Journal of Crime and Justice, 32*(2), 49–75.

Mitchell, O., Wilson, D. B., Eggers, A., & Mackenzie, D. L. (2012). Assessing the effectiveness of drug courts on recidivism. A meta-analytic review of traditional and non-traditional drug courts. *Journal of Criminal Justice, 40,* 60–71.

Mitnik, P. A., & Halpern-Finnerty, J. (2010). Immigration and local governments: Inclusionary local policies in the era of state rescaling. In M. W. Varsanyi (Ed.), *Taking local control: Immigration policy activism in U.S. cities and states* (pp. 51–72). Stanford, CA: Stanford University Press.

Mittelstadt, M., Speaker, B., Meissner, D., & Chishti, M. (2011). *Through the prism of national security: Major immigration policy and program changes in the decade since 9/11.* Washington, DC: Migration Policy Institute. Retrieved from http://www.migrationpolicy.org/pubs/FS23_Post-9-11policy.pdf

Modestin, J., Nussbaumer, C., Angst, K., Scheidegger, P., & Hell, D. (1997). Use of potentially abusive psychotropic substances in psychiatric in-patients. *European Archives of Psychiatry and Clinical Neuroscience, 247,* 146–153.

Moffitt, T. (1993). Adolescence-limited and life-course-persistent antisocial behavior: A developmental taxonomy. *Psychological Review, 100*(4), 674–701.

Moffitt, T., Ross, S., & Raine, A. (2011). Crime and biology. In J. Q. Wilson & J. Petersilia (Eds.), *Crime and public policy.* New York: Oxford University Press.

Monahan, T., & Palmer, N. (2009). The emerging politics of DHS fusion centers. *Security Dialogue, 40,* 617–636.

Monkkonen, E. (1981). *Police in urban America, 1860–1920.* Cambridge, MA: Cambridge University Press.

Moody, C. E., Marvell, T. B., & Kaminski, R. J. (2002). *Unintended consequences: Three-strikes laws and the murders of police officers* [NCJRS# 203649]. Rockville, MD: National Institute of Justice/National Criminal Justice Reference Service.

Moore, D. B., & McDonald, J. M. (2002). Community conferencing as conflict transformation. In J. G. Perry (Ed.), *Repairing communities through restorative justice* (pp. 107–122). Lanham, MD: American Correctional Association.

Moore, L. (2012, June 14). Governor Quinn and Mayor Emanuel on same page with new RICO law. *Examiner.* Retrieved from http://www.examiner.com/article/governor-quinn-and-mayor-emanuel-on-same-page-with-new-rico-law

Moore, M. E., & Hiday, V. A. (2006). Mental health court outcomes: A comparison of re-arrest and re-arrest severity between mental health court and treatment court participants. *Law and Human Behavior, 30,* 659–674.

Moore, M. H., & Trojanowicz, R. C. (1988). Policing and the fear of crime. National Institute of Justice and Harvard University. *Perspectives on Policing, 3.*

Moore, M. J. (Writer, Producer, Director). (1999). *The legacy: Murder & media, politics & prisons* [videorecording]. Princeton, NJ : Films for the Humanities.

Moore N., & Williams, L. (2010). *The almighty Black P. Stone nation.* Chicago, IL: Lawrence Hill Books.

Morabito, A., & Greenberg, S. (2005). *Engaging the private sector to promote homeland security: Law enforcement-private security partnerships.* Washington, DC: Bureau of Justice Assistance.

Morash, M. (2009). Editorial introduction: A great debate over using the Level of Service Inventory-Revised (LSI-R) with women offenders. *Criminology & Public Policy, 8*(1), 173–181.

Morash, M., Bynum, T. S., & Koons, B. A. (1998). Women offenders: Programming needs and promising approaches. Washington, DC: U.S. Department of Justice, National Institute of Justice.

Morash, M., & Schram, P. J. (2002). *The prison experience: Special issues of women in prison.* Prospect Heights, IL: Waveland Press.

Moreno, I. (2013, March 20). Colorado Gov. John Hickenlooper signs landmark gun control bills into law. *Huffington Post.* Retrieved from http://www.huffingtonpost.com/2013/03/20/colo-governor-to-sign-lan_n_2914925.html

Morenoff, J. D., & Astor, A. (2006). Immigrant assimilation and crime: Generational differences in youth violence in Chicago. In R. M. Martinez, Jr. & A. Valenzuela, Jr. (Eds.), *Immigration and crime: Race, ethnicity, and violence* (pp. 36–63). New York: New York University Press.

Morgenson, G., & Story, L. (2011, April 14). In financial crisis, no prosecution of top figures. *New York Times,* pp. A1, A12.

Morris, R. G., Longmire, D. R., Buffington-Vollum, J., & Vollum, S. (2010). Institutional misconduct and differential parole eligibility among capital inmates. *Criminal Justice and Behavior, 37,* 413–438.

Morrissey, J. P. (1982). Deinstitutionalizing the mentally ill: Process, outcomes, and new directions. In W. Gove (Ed.), *Deviance and mental illness* (pp. 147–176). Beverly Hills, CA: Sage.

Morrissey, J. P., & Goldman, H. H. (1986). Care and treatment of the mentally ill in the United States: Historical developments and reforms. *Annals of the American Academy of Political and Social Science, 484,* 12–27.

Mosher, C. (1999). Imperialism, irrationality, and illegality: The first 90 years of Canadian drug policy. *New Scholars, New Visions, 3,* 1–40.

Mosher, C., & Akins, S. (2007). *Drugs and drug policy.* Thousand Oaks, CA: Sage.

Mossman, D., Schwartz, A. H., & Elam, E. R. (2012). Risky business versus overt acts: What relevance do "actuarial," probabilistic risk assessments have for judicial decisions on involuntary psychiatric hospitalization? *Houston Journal of Health Law and Policy, 11,* 365–453.

Moteff, J. (2007). *Critical infrastructure: The national asset database.* CRS Report for Congress. Washington, DC: Congressional Research Service, Library of Congress.

Mounts, S. E. (1982). Public defender programs, professional responsibility, and competent representation. *Wisconsin Law Review, 4,* 473–533.

Mueller, J., & Stewart, M. G. (2011, April 1). *Terror, security, and money: Balancing the risks, benefits, and costs of homeland security.* Paper presented at the Annual Convention of the Midwest Political Science Association, Chicago, IL.

Mulgrew, I. (2007, October 10). City drug policy at odds with Harper's announced plans. *Vancouver Sun.* Retrieved from http://www.canada.com

Mumola, C. J. (2000, August). *Incarcerated parents and their children* (Special report, NCJ 182335). Washington, DC: U.S. Department of Justice, Bureau of Justice Statistics.

Munetz, M. R., Grande, T., Kleist, J., & Peterson, G. A. (1996). The effectiveness of outpatient civil commitment. *Psychiatric Services, 47,* 1251–1253.

Murphy, C. M., Musser, P. H., & Maton, K. I. (1998). Coordinated community intervention for domestic abusers: Intervention system involvement and criminal recidivism. *Journal of Family Violence, 13,* 263–284.

Mustaine, E. E., Tewksbury, R., & Stengel, K. M. (2006). Social disorganization and residential locations of registered sex offenders: Is this a collateral consequence? *Deviant Behavior, 27*(3), 329–350.

Musto, D. F. (1999). *The American disease: Origins of narcotic control* (3rd ed.). New York: Oxford University Press.

Muwakkil, S. (1989, May 24–June 6). The death penalty and the illusion of justice. *In These Times, 13*(26), 6.

Myers, D. L. (2001). *Excluding violent youths from juvenile court: The effectiveness of legislative waiver.* New York: LFB Scholarly Press.

Nadelmann, E. (1996). Doing methadone right. *Public Interest, 123,* 83–93.

Nadelmann, E. (2011, November 6). Reefer madness. *New York Times.* Retrieved from http://www.nytimes.com

National Association For Community Mediation (NAFCM). (2012). *Community mediation history.* Walnut Creek, CA: Author. Retrieved from http://www.nafcm.org

National Association of Drug Court Professionals (NADCP). (2012). *Facts and figures.* Retrieved from http://www.nadcp.org

National Association of School Psychologists (NASP). (2001). *Zero tolerance and alternative strategies: A fact sheet for educators and policymakers.* Bethesda, MD: Author. Retrieved from http://www.nasponline.org/resources/factsheets/zt_fs.aspx

National Center for Injury Prevention and Control. (2003). *Costs of intimate partner violence against women in the United States.* Retrieved from http://www.cdc.gov/violenceprevention/pdf/IPVBook-a.pdf

National Center for State Courts. (2012). *Indigent defense.* Williamsburg, VA: Author. Retrieved from http://www.ncsc.org/topics-access-and-fairness/indigent-defense/state-links.aspx?cat=Capital%20Case%20Representation

National Center on Addiction and Substance Abuse. (2009). *Shoveling up II: The impact of substance abuse on federal, state, and local budgets.* New York: Columbia University.

National Clearinghouse for the Defense of Battered Women. (2010). *Collateral consequences of arrest, conviction, & incarceration.* Retrieved from http://www.biscmi.org/wshh/NCDBW_Collateral_Consequences_Internet_Resources.pdf

National Coalition Against Domestic Violence. (2012). *Domestic violence and lesbian, gay, bisexual and transgender relationships.* Retrieved from http://www.uncfsp.org/projects/userfiles/File/DCE-STOP_NOW/NCADV_LGBT_Fact_Sheet.pdf

National Commission on Terrorist Attacks Upon the United States. (2004). *The 9/11 commission report.* London, UK: W.W. Norton.

National Conference of State Legislatures. (1996). *"Three Strikes" legislation update.* Denver, CO: Author.

National Conference of State Legislatures. (2007, November 29). *2007 enacted state legislation related to immigrants and immigration* [Policy report]. Washington, DC: Author.

National Conference of State Legislatures. (2008, January–March). *Overview of state legislation related to immigrants and immigration* [Policy report]. Washington, DC: Author.

National Conference of State Legislatures. (2010). *Arizona's immigration enforcement laws* [Policy report]. Washington, DC: Author. Retrieved from http://www.ncsl.org/issues-research/immig/analysis-of-arizonas-immigration-law.aspx

National Conference of State Legislatures. (2011, Jan. 1–Dec. 7). *Immigration-related laws and resolutions in the* States [Policy Report]. Washington, DC: Author. Retrieved from http://www.ncsl.org/issues-research/immig/state-immigration-legislation-report-dec-2011.aspx

National Conference of State Legislatures. (2012, June 25). *U.S. Supreme Court rules on Arizona's immigration enforcement law* [Policy report]. Washington, DC: Author. Retrieved from http://www.ncsl.org/issues-research/immig/us-supreme-court-rules-on-arizona-immigration-laws.aspx

National Day Laborer Organizing Network (NDLON). (2012). *Newly obtained documents reveal Secure Communities Program leads to deportations of people who have never been arrested* [Press release]. Washington, DC: Author. Retrieved from http://ndlon.org/en/pressroom/press-releases/item/532-scomm-foia-doj-objects

National Drug Court Resource Center. (2012). *FAQ: How many drug courts are there?* Retrieved from http://www.ndcrc.org

National Gang Center. (2009). *National gang survey analysis.* Retrieved from http://www.nationalgangcenter.gov/Survey-Analysis/Defining-Gangs

National Immigration Forum. (2007, August). Immigration law enforcement by state and local police. *Backgrounder.* Washington, DC: Author.

National Immigration Forum. (2011). *The math of immigration detention: Runaway costs for immigration detention do not add up to sensible policies.* Washington, DC: Author. Retrieved from http://www.immigrationforum.org/images/uploads/MathofImmigrationDetention.pdf

National Institute of Corrections (NIC). (n.d.). *Gender-informed practices assessment.* Washington, DC: Author. Retrieved from http://community.nicic.gov/cfs-file.ashx/_key/CommunityServer.Components.PostAttachments/00.00.06.30.83/About-the-GIPA-final_5F00_3.pdf

National Institute of Corrections. (1997). *Supermax housing: A survey of current practice.* Washington, DC: U.S. Department of Justice.

National Institute on Money in State Politics. (2004). *Proposition 66: Revision of the three strikes law.* Retrieved from http://www.followthemoney.org/database/StateGlance/ballot.phtml?s=CA&y=2004&m=249

National Institutes of Health. (1997). *Workshop on the medical utility of marijuana.* Retrieved from http://www.nigh.gov

Needels, K. E. (1996). Go directly to jail and do not collect? A long-term study of recidivism, employment, and earnings patterns among prison releases. *Journal of Research in Crime and Delinquency, 33,* 471–496.

Negroponte, M. (Director). (2005). *Methadonia.* [Documentary]. United States: Home Box Office and Roco Films.

Nellis, A. M., & Savage, J. (2012). Does watching the news affect fear of terrorism? The importance of media exposure on terrorism fear. *Crime and Delinquency, 58*(5), 748–768.

Netherlands Ministry of Health. (2003). Drug policy in the Netherlands: Basic principles and enforcement in practice. *International Publication Series, Health, Welfare and Sport, 18.* The Hague, Netherlands: Author. Retrieved from http://www.jaapvanderstel.nl/Boeken_en_rapporten_files/Drugpolicy_vws_2003.pdf

New Jersey Commission to Review Criminal Sentencing. (2005). *Report on New Jersey's drug free zone crimes and proposal for reform.* Trenton, NJ: Author.

Newman, A., & Moynihan, C. (2010, May 18). Faisal Shahzad arraigned on terror charges. *New York Times.*

Newport, F. (2007, July 13). Americans have become more negative on impact of immigrants. *Gallup News Service.* Retrieved from http://www.gallup.com/poll/28132/americans-become-more-negative-impact-immigrants.aspx

Newton, L. (2005). It is not a question of being anti-immigration: Categories of deservedness in immigration policy making. In A. L. Schneider & H. M. Ingram (Eds.), *Deserving and entitled: Social constructions and public policy.* Albany, NY: SUNY Press.

New York Central and Hudson River Railroad v. United States. (1908). 212 U.S 481.

New York City Youth Board. (1960). *Reaching the fighting gang.* New York: Author.

New York State Office of Mental Health. (2005). *Kendra's law: Final report on the status of assisted outpatient treatment.* Albany, NY: Author. Retrieved from http://bi.omh.ny.gov/aot/files/AOTFina12005.pdf

New York Times. (1900, July 16). The first insane asylum: To Virginia belongs the credit in this country. *New York Times.* Retrieved from http://query.nytimes.com/mem/archive-free/pdf?res=F00A10F73D5B11738DDDAF0994DF405B808CF1D3

Nicholl, C. G. (1999). *Community policing, community justice, and restorative justice: Exploring the links for the delivery of a balanced approach to public safety.* Washington, DC: U.S Department of Justice, Office of Community Oriented Policing Services.

Nicholls, T. L., Brink, J., Greaves, C., Lussier, P., & Verdun-Jones, S. (2009). Forensic psychiatric inpatients and aggression: An exploration of incidence, prevalence, severity, and interventions by gender. *International Journal of Law and Psychiatry, 32,* 23–30.

NJADP-New Jerseyans for Alternatives to the Death Penalty. (2005, November 21). Death penalty has cost New Jersey taxpayers $253 Million [Press release]. *Newsday.* Retrieved from http://www.deathpenaltyifo.org/node/1574

Nugent, W., Umbreit, M., Wiinamaki, L., & Paddock, J. (2001). Participation in victim-offender mediation and re-offense: Successful replications? *Research on Social Work Practice, 11*(1).

O'Brien, C. (1997). A range of research-based pharmacotherapies for addiction. *Science, 278,* 66–70.

Office of Criminal Justice Services. (2006). *Report to the Ohio criminal justice sentencing commission: Sex offenders.* Columbus, OH: Ohio Public Safety.

Office of Justice Programs (n.d.). Jacob Wetterling Crimes Against Children and Sexually Violent Offender Registration Act. Retrieved from http://www.ojp.usdoj.gov/BJA/ what/02ajwactcontents.html

Office of Juvenile Justice and Delinquency Prevention. (2006). *Juvenile offenders and victims: 2006 national report.* Washington, DC: U.S. Department of Justice. Retrieved from http://www.ojjdp.gov/ojstatbb/nr2006/downloads/nr2006.pdf

Office of National Drug Control Policy (ONDCP). (1997). *ONDCP statement on medical marijuana.* Washington, DC: Author.

Office of National Drug Control Policy (ONDCP). (2000). *Fact sheet. Methadone.* Rockville, MD: Author.

Office of National Drug Control Policy (ONDCP). (2012). *National drug control strategy.* Washington, DC: Author.

Office of the Assistant Secretary for Planning and Evaluation (ASPE). (2011, October). *Drug testing welfare recipients: Recent proposals and continuing controversies* (ASPE Issue Brief). Washington, DC: U.S. Department of Health and Human Services. Retrieved from http://aspe.hhs.gov/hsp/11/DrugTesting/ib.pdf

Ohio Department of Rehabilitation and Correction. (2007). Best practices tool-kit: Sex offender registration and notification. London, OH: Author.

O'Keefe, E. (2013, April 2). What are the states doing about gun control? *Washington Post.* Retrieved from http://www.washingtonpost.com/blogs/the-fix/wp/2013/04/02/what-are-the-states-doing-about-gun-control/

O'Keefe, M. L. (2008). Administrative segregation from within: A corrections perspective. *The Prison Journal, 88*(1), 123–143.

Oliver, M. B., & Armstrong, B. G. (1995). Predictors of viewing and enjoyment of reality based and fictional crime shows. *Journalism and Mass Communication Quarterly, 72,* 559–570.

Oliver, W. M. (2003). The power to persuade: Presidential influence over Congress on crime control policy. *Criminal Justice Review, 28*(1), 113–132.

Orbis Partners, Inc. (2009). *Outcome evaluation of the women offender case management model in Connecticut probation.* Washington, DC: National Institute of Corrections. Retrieved from http://nicic.gov/Library/025927

Owen, B. (1998). *"In the Mix": Struggle and survival in a women's prison.* Albany: State University of New York Press.

Owen, B. (2001). Perspectives on women in prison. In C. M. Renzetti & L. Goodstein (Eds.), *Women, crime, and criminal justice: Original feminist readings* (pp. 243–254). Los Angeles, CA: Roxbury.

Packer, H. (1968). *The limits of the criminal sanction.* Stanford, CA: Stanford University Press.

Pager, Devah. (2007). *MARKED: Race, crime, and finding work in an era of mass incarceration.* Chicago, IL: University of Chicago Press.

Palmer, T. (1975). Martinson revisited. *Journal of Research in Crime and Delinquency, 12,* 133–152.

Papachristros, A. W. (2008). The impact of CeaseFire on gang homicide networks: Appendix C evaluation of CeaseFire-Chicago. Chicago, IL: Northwestern University. Retrieved from http://www.chicago-justice.org/foi/relevant-documents-of-interest/ceasefire/Northwestern-CeaseFire-Evaluation-Appendices.pdf

Paparozzi, M., & Gendreau, P. (2005). An intensive supervision program that worked: Service delivery, professional orientation and organizational supportiveness. *The Prison Journal, 85,* 445–466.

Papua New Guinea Law and Justice Sector. (2000). *Law and justice policy.* Retrieved from http://www.lawandjustice.gov.pg/www/html/50-overview.asp

Parry-Jones, W. L. (1988). Asylum for the mentally ill in historical perspective. *The Psychiatrist/Psychiatric Bulletin, 12,* 407–410.

Pate, A. M., & Hamilton, E. E. (1992). Formal and informal deterrents to domestic violence: The Dade County Spouse Assault Experiment. *American Sociological Review, 57,* 691–697.

Pate, T., Bowers, R. A., & Parks, R. (1976). *Three approaches to criminal apprehension in Kansas City: An evaluation report.* Washington, DC: Police Foundation.

Paternoster, R., & Brame, R. (2003). *An empirical analysis of Maryland's death sentencing system with respect to the influence of race and legal jurisdiction* (Report commissioned by the Maryland governor). Annapolis, MD: Department of Public Safety and Correctional Services. Retrieved from http://www.newsdesk.umd.edu/pdf/finalrep.pdf

Pattavina, A., Buzawa, E., Hirschel, D., & Faggiani, D. (2007). Policy, place, and perpetrators: Using NIBRS to explain arrest practices in intimate partner violence. *Justice Research and Policy, 9,* 31–51.

Pattavina, A., Hirschel, D., Buzawa, E., Faggiani, D., & Bentley, H. (2007). A comparison of the police response to heterosexual versus same-sex intimate partner violence. *Violence Against Women, 13,* 374–394.

Peachy, D. E. (1989). The Kitchener experiment. In M. Wright & B. Galaway (Eds.), *Mediation and criminal justice: Victims, offenders and community.* London, UK: Sage.

Pelikan, C., & Trenczek, T. (2008). Victim offender mediation and restorative justice: The European landscape. In D. Sullivan & L. Tifft (Eds.), *Handbook of restorative justice.* New York: Routledge.

People v. Fuhrman, 16 Cal. 4th 930 (1997).

People v. Superior Court (Romero), 13 Cal. 4th 497 (1996).

Peralta, E. (2013, March 26). In new poll, support for stricter gun control law drops since Newtown shootings. *National Public Radio.* Retrieved from http://www.npr.org/blogs/thetwo-way/2013/03/26/175377122/in-new-poll-support-for-stricter-gun-control-law-drops-since-newtown-shootings

Perkins, U. E. (1987). *Explosion of Chicago's Black street gangs.* Chicago, IL: Third World Press.

Perrow, C. (2002). Using organizations: The case of FEMA. *Homeland Security Journal, 1*(2), 1–8.

Perry, J. (2002). Challenging the assumptions. In J. Perry (Ed.), *Restorative justice: Repairing communities through restorative justice* (pp. 1–17). Lanham, MD: American Correctional Association.

Perry, J. L., & Recascino Wise, L. (1990). The motivational bases of public service. *Public Administration Review, 50*, 367–373.

Peters, R. H., Bartoi, M. G., & Sherman, P. B. (2008). *Screening and assessment of co-occurring disorders in the justice system*. Delmar, NY: Center for Mental Health Services, National GAINS Center.

Petersilia, J. (1990). Death penalty resolution debated and endorsed. *The Criminologist, 15*, 1.

Petersilia, J. (1999). Parole and prisoner reentry in the United States. *Crime and Justice*, 479–529.

Petersilia, J. (2002). Community corrections. In J. Q. Wilson & J. Petersilia (Eds.), *Crime: Public policies for crime control* (pp. 483–508). Oakland, CA: Institute for Contemporary Studies.

Petersilia, J. (2003). *When prisoners come home: Parole and prisoner reentry*. New York: Oxford University Press.

Petersilia, J., & Turner, S. (1993). Intensive probation and parole. *Crime and Justice, 17*, 281–335.

Peterson, D., Miller, J., & Esbensen, F. A. (2001). The impact of sex composition on gang member attitudes and behavior. *Criminology, 39*, 411–440.

Peterson, J., Skeem, J., Hart, E., Vidal, S., & Keith, F. (2010). Analyzing offense patterns as a function of mental illness to test the criminalization hypothesis. *Psychiatric Services, 61*, 1217–1222.

Pew Center on the States. (2011). *State of recidivism: The revolving door of America's prisons*. Washington, DC: The Pew Charitable Trusts. Retrieved from http://www.pewtrusts.org/uploadedFiles/wwwpewtrustsorg/Reports/sentencing_and_corrections/State_Recidivism_Revolving_Door_America_Prisons%20.pdf

Phelan, J. C., Sinkewicz, M., Castille, D. M., Huz, S., Muenzenmaier, K., & Link, B. G. (2010). Effectiveness and outcomes of assisted outpatient treatment in New York State. *Psychiatric Services, 61*, 137–143.

Phillips, S. (2008). Racial disparities in the capital of capital punishment. *Houston Law Review, 45*, 807–840.

Phillips, S. (2009). Legal disparities in the capital of capital punishment. *Journal of Criminal Law and Criminology, 99*, 717–755.

Phillips, S. (2010). Status disparities in the capital of capital punishment. *Law and Society Review, 43*, 807–837. Retrieved from http://onlinelibrary.wiley.com/doi/10.1111/j.1540-5893.2009.00389.x/abstract?userIsAuthenticated=false&deniedAccessCustomisedMessage= ()

Phillips, S. A. (2012). *Operation Fly Trap: L. A. gangs, drugs, and the law*. Chicago, IL: University of Chicago Press.

Pierce, G. L., Spaar, S., & Briggs, L. (1986). *The character of police work: Strategic and tactical implications*. Boston, MA: Center for Applied Social Research, Northeastern University.

Pignal, S. (2010, October 8). Amsterdam's cannabis-selling coffee shops face crackdown. *Washington Post*. Retrieved from http://www.washingtonpost.com

Pinkerton, S. (2010). Is Vancouver, Canada's supervised injection facility cost-saving? *Addiction, 105*, 1429–1436.

Pisciotta, A. (1994). *Benevolent repression: Social control and the American reformatory prison movement*. New York: New York University Press.

Piven, F., & Cloward, R. (1977). *Poor people's movements: Why they succeed, how they fail*. New York: Pantheon Books.

Pizarro, J. M., & Narag, R. E. (2008). Supermax prisons: What we know, what we do not know, and where we are going. *Prison Journal, 88*, 23–42.

Pizarro, J., & Stenius, V. M. K. (2013). Supermax prisons: Their rise, current practices, and effect on inmates. In M. Stohr, A. Walsh, & C. Hemmens (Eds.), *Corrections: A text reader* (2nd ed., pp. 238–248). Thousand Oaks, CA: Sage.

Pizzaro, J. M., Stenius, V. M. K., & Pratt, T. (2006). Supermax prisons: Myths, realities, and the politics of punishment in American society. *Criminal Justice Policy Review, 17*, 6–21.

Pizzo, S., Fricker, M., & Muolo, P. (1989). *Inside job: The looting of America's savings and loans*. New York: McGraw-Hill.

Platt, A. M. (2009). *The child savers: The invention of delinquency* (40th Anniversary ed.). New Brunswick, NJ: Rutgers University Press.

Plumer, B. (2013, January 17). Gun research is allowed again. So what will we find out? *Washington Post*. Retrieved from http://www.washingtonpost.com/blogs/wonkblog/wp/2013/01/17/gun-research-is-allowed-again-so-what-will-we-find-out/

Policy. (n.d.). Merriam-Webster's online dictionary. Retrieved from http://www.m-w.com/dictionary

Pollock, J. M. (1984). Women will be women: Correctional officers' perceptions of the emotionality of women inmates. *The Prison Journal, 64*, 84–91.

Pollock, J. M. (1986). *Sex and supervision: Guarding male and female inmates*. New York: Greenwood Press.

Pollock, J. M. (1995). Women in corrections: Custody and the "caring ethic." In M. V. Merlo & J. M. Pollock (Eds.), *Women, law & social change* (pp. 97–116). Boston, MA: Allyn & Bacon.

Pollock, J. M. (2004). *Prisons and prison life: Costs and consequences*. Los Angeles, CA: Roxbury Publishing.

Pontell, H. N. (1984). *Capacity to punish: The ecology of crime and punishment*. Bloomington: Indiana University Press.

Pontell, H. N., Calavita, K., & Tillman, R. (1994). Corporate crime and the criminal justice system capacity: Government response to financial institution fraud. *Justice Quarterly, 11*, 383–410.

Pope, C. (2003, June 27). White House to tap Seattle in drug war. *Seattle Post-Intelligencer*. Retrieved from http://www.seattlepi.nwsource.com

Portes, A., Fernández-Kelly, P., & Haller, W. (2005). Segmented assimilation on the ground: The new second generation in early adulthood. *Ethnic and Racial Studies, 28*(6), 1000–1040.

Posner, R. (2011). A failure of capitalism: The crisis of '08 and the descent into depression. Cambridge, MA: Harvard University Press.

Post, L. (2004). ABA death penalty guidelines languish. *The National Law Journal, 26*. Retrieved from http://www.law.com/jsp/nlj/PubArticleNLJ.jsp?id=900005398645&slreturn=1

Pranis, K. (2005). *The little book of circle processes: A new/old approach to peacemaking*. Intercourse, PA: Good Books.

Pranis, K., & Bazemore, G. (1999). *Engaging the community in the response to youth crime: A restorative justice approach*. Washington, DC: Office of Juvenile Justice and Delinquency Prevention.

Prendergast, M. L., & Burdon, W. M. (2002). Integrated systems of care for substance-abusing offenders. In C. Leukefeld, F. Tims, & D. Farabee (Eds.), *Treatment of drug offenders: Policies and issues* (pp. 111–162). New York: Springer.

Prendergast, M. L., Podus, D., Chang, E., & Urada, D. (2002). The effectiveness of drug abuse treatment: A meta-analysis of comparison group studies. *Drug and Alcohol Dependence, 67*, 53–72.

Preston, J. (2012, June 6). Deportations continue despite U.S. review of backlog. *The New York Times.* Retrieved from http://www.nytimes.com/2012/06/07/us/politics/deportations-continue-despite-us-review-of-backlog.html?pagewanted=all

Prins, S. J., Osher, F. C., Steadman, H. J., Robbins, P. C., & Case, B. (2012). Exploring racial disparities in the Brief Jail Mental Health Screen. *Criminal Justice & Behavior, 39*(5), 635–645.

PrisonPolicy.org. (2011). *From prisons to hospitals and back: The criminalization of mental illness.* Retrieved from http://www.prisonpolicy.org/scans/menbrief.html

Proffitt v. Florida, 428 U.S. 153 (1976).

Proposition 19. (2010, November 3). Marijuana initiative drew strongest support in Bay Area but failed in "Emerald Triangle." *Los Angeles Times.* Retrieved from http://www.latimes.com

Ptacek, J. (1999). *Battered women in the courtroom: The power of judicial response.* Boston, MA: Northeastern University Press.

Quicker, J. C. (1983). *Homegirls: Characterizing Chicano gangs.* San Pedro, CA: International University Press.

Radelet, M. L. (1981). Racial characteristics and the imposition of the death penalty. *American Sociological Review, 46*, 918–927.

Radelet, M. L., & Akers, R. L. (1996). Deterrence and the death penalty: The view of the experts. *Journal of Criminal Law and Criminology, 87*, 1–16.

Radelet, M. L., & Pierce, G. L. (1985). Race and prosecutorial discretion in homicide cases. *Law and Society Review, 19*, 587–621.

Radin, M. J. (1980). Cruel punishment and respect for persons: Super due process for death. *Southern California Law Review, 53*, 1143–1185.

Rafter, N. H. (1990). *Partial justice: Women, prisons, and social control.* New Brunswick, NJ: Transaction.

Rainville, G. A., & Smith, S. K. (2003). *Juvenile felony defendants in criminal courts.* Washington, DC: U.S. Department of Justice, Office of Justice Programs, Office of Juvenile Justice and Delinquency Prevention.

Ramakrishnan, K., & Wong, T. (2007, November). *Immigration policies go local: The varying responses of local governments to undocumented immigration.* Unpublished paper, University of California, Riverside. Retrieved from http://www.law.berkeley.edu

Rank, M. R. (2004). *One nation, underprivileged: Why American poverty affects us all.* New York: Oxford University Press.

Rapaport, E. (1993). The death penalty and gender discrimination. In V. L. Streib (Ed.), *A capital punishment anthology* (pp. 145–152). Cincinnati, OH: Anderson.

Raphael, J. (2000). *Saving Bernice: Battered women, welfare, and poverty.* Boston, MA: Northeastern University Press.

Raphael, J. (2004). Rethinking criminal justice responses to intimate partner violence. *Violence Against Women, 10*, 1354–1366.

Rawls, J. (1971/1999). *A theory of justice.* Cambridge, MA: Harvard University Press.

Raye, B. E., & Roberts, A. W. (2007). Restorative processes. In G. Johnstone & D. W. Van Ness (Eds.), *Handbook of restorative justice* (pp. 211–227). Portland, OR: Willan.

Raymond, J., & Hughes, D. (2001). *Sex trafficking of women in the United States.* Coalition Against Trafficking in Women. Washington, DC: National Institute of Justice. Retrieved from http://www.uri.edu/artsci/wms/hughes/sex_traff_us.pdf

Reaves, B. (2010). *Local police departments, 2007.* Washington DC: Bureau of Justice Statistics. Retrieved from http://www.bjs.gov/index.cfm?ty=pbdetail&iid=1750

Redding, R. E. (2003). The effects of adjudicating and sentencing juveniles as adults: Research and policy implications. *Youth Violence and Juvenile Justice, 1*, 128–155.

Redding, R. E. (2010). *Juvenile waiver laws: An effective deterrent to delinquency?* Washington, DC: U.S. Department of Justice, Office of Justice Programs, Office of Juvenile Justice and Delinquency Prevention.

Redlich, A. D., Hoover, S., Summers, A., & Steadman, H. J. (2010). Enrollment in mental health courts: Voluntariness, knowingness, and adjudicative competence. *Law and Human Behavior, 34*, 91–104.

Reentry Court Solutions. (2013, Feb. 10). *The easy part of prison reform.* Albany, CA: Author. Retrieved from http://www.reentrycourtsolutions.com/tag/ab109/

Regoli, R., Hewitt, J., & DeLisi, M. (2009). *Delinquency in society* (8th ed.). Upper Saddle River, NJ: Prentice Hall.

Regoli, R., Hewitt, J., & DeLisi, M. (2011). *Delinquency in society: The essentials.* Sudbury, MA: Jones & Bartlett.

Reid, L. W., Weis, H. E., Adelman, R. M., & Jaret, C. (2005). The immigration–crime relationship: Evidence across U.S. metropolitan areas. *Social Science Research, 34*(4), 757–780.

Reid, T. (2002, May 3). Europe moves drug war from prisons to cities. *Washington Post.* Retrieved from http://www.washingtonpost.com

Reiman, J. (1998). *The rich get richer and the poor get prison: Ideology, crime, and criminal justice.* Boston, MA: Allyn & Bacon.

Reiman, J. (2004). *The rich get richer and the poor get prison: Ideolgy, class, and criminal justice* (7th ed.). Boston, MA: Allyn & Bacon.

Reinarman, C., & Levine, H. G. (1997). The crack attack: Politics and media in the crack scare. In C. Reinarman & H. G. Levine (Eds.), *Crack in America: Demon drugs and social justice.* Berkeley, CA: University of California Press.

Reinhold, M., & Alessi, P. T. (Eds.). (1978). *The golden age of Augustus.* Toronto, Canada: University of Toronto Press.

Reisig, M. D., Holtfreter, K., & Morash, M. (2006). Assessing recidivism risk across female pathways to crime. *Justice Quarterly, 23*(3), 384–405.

Reiss, A. J., & Tonry, M. (Eds.). (1986). *Communities and crime.* Chicago, IL: University of Chicago Press.

Reiter, K. A. (2012). Parole, snitch, or die: California's supermax prisons and prisoners, 1997–2007. *Punishment & Society, 14*(5), 530–563.

Rennison, C. M., & Welchans, S. (2000). *Intimate partner violence* (Special Report, NCJ 178247). Washington, DC: Bureau of Justice Statistics.

Repetto, T. (1976). Crime prevention and the displacement phenomenon. *Crime & Delinquency, 22*, 166–177.

Reynolds, D. (2012, June 12). *Gang wars at the root of Chicago's high murder rate* [Television program]. Washington, DC: CBS News. Retrieved from http://www.cbsnews.com/8301–18563_162–57451996/gang-wars-at-the-root-of-chicagos-high-murder-rate/

Rhodes, L. A. (2005). Pathological effects of the supermaximum prison. *American Journal of Public Health, 95,* 1692–1695.

Richards, S. C. (2008). USP Marion: The first federal supermax. *Prison Journal, 88,* 6–22.

Richards, S. C., & Jones, R. (2004). Beating the perpetual incarceration machine: Overcoming structural impediments to re-entry. In S. Maruna & R. Immarigeon (Eds.), *After crime and punishment: Pathways to offender reintegration* (pp. 201–232). Portland, OR: Willan.

Richburg, K. (2001, April 15). Pragmatic Dutch tolerate ecstasy use. *Washington Post.* Retrieved from http://www.washingtonpost.com

Ridgeway, G. (2007). *Analysis of racial disparities in the New York Police Department's stop, question, and frisk practices.* New York: RAND.

Ritchie, B. E. (1996). *Compelled to crime: The gender entrapment of Black women.* New York: Routledge.

Ritchie, B. E. (2001). Challenges incarcerated women face as they return to their communities: Findings from life history interviews. *Crime & Delinquency, 47*(3), 368–389.

Rivas, O. (2010, August 8). War on drugs: Why the U.S. and Latin America could be ready to end a fruitless 40-year struggle. *Reuters.* Retrieved from http://www.guardian.co.uk

Riveland, C. (1999). *Supermax prisons: Overview and general considerations.* Washington, DC: U.S. Department of Justice.

Robbers, M. L. (2009). Lifers on the outside: Sex offenders and disintegrative shaming. *International Journal of Offender Therapy and Comparative Criminology, 53*(1), 5–28.

Robbins, C. A., Martin, S. S., & Surratt, H. L. (2009). Substance abuse treatment, anticipated maternal roles, and reentry success of drug-involved women prisoners. *Crime & Delinquency, 55*(3), 388–411.

Robertiello, G., & Terry, K. J. (2007). Can we profile sex offenders? A review of sex offender typologies. *Aggression and Violent Behavior, 12,* 508–518.

Roberts, A. R. (1990). *Helping crime victims: Research, policy, and practice.* Newbury Park, CA: Sage.

Roberts v. Louisiana, 428 U.S. 325 (1976).

Robinson, G. (2009). *A tragedy of democracy: Japanese confinement in North America.* New York: Columbia University Press.

Robinson, J., Sareen, J., Cox, B. J., & Bolton, J. (2009). Self-medication of anxiety disorders with alcohol and drugs: Results from a nationally representative sample. *Journal of Anxiety Disorders, 23,* 38–45.

Roche, D. (2006). Dimensions of restorative justice. *Journal of Social Issues, 62*(2), 217–238.

Rodríguez, C., Chishti, M., Capps, R., & St. John, L. (2010). *A program in flux: New priorities and implementation challenges for 287(g).* Washington, DC: Migration Policy Institute. Retrieved from http://www.migrationpolicy.org/pubs/287g-March2010.pdf

Rodriguez, N. (2007). Restorative justice at work: Examining the impact of restorative justice resolutions on juvenile recidivism. *Crime & Delinquency, 53*(3), 355–379.

Rohland, B. M. (1998). *The role of outpatient commitment in the management of persons with schizophrenia.* Iowa City: Iowa Consortium for Mental Health, Services, Training, and Research.

Roman, C. G., Moore, G. E., Jenkins, S., & Small, K. M. (2002). *Understanding community justice partnerships: Assessing the capacity to partner.* Washington, DC: Final Report by the Urban Institute, Justice Policy Center prepared for National Institute of Justice.

Roman, C. G., & Travis, J. (2006). Where will I sleep tomorrow? Housing, homelessness, and the returning prisoner. *Housing Policy Debate, 17*(2), 389–418.

Roman, J. K., Chalfin, A. J., & Knight, C. R. (2009). Reassessing the cost of the death penalty using quasi-experimental methods: Evidence from Maryland. *American Law and Economics Review, 11,* 530–574. Retrieved from http://aler.oxfordjournals.org/content/11/2/530.abstract

Romer, D., Jamieson, K. H., & Aday, S. (2003). Television news and the cultivation of fear of crime. *Journal of Communication, 53*(1), 88–104.

Romer, D., Jamieson, K. H., & DeCoteau, N. (1998). The treatment of persons of color in local television news: Ethnic blame discourse or realistic group conflict. *Communications Research, 25*(3), 286–305.

Roper, Superintendent, Potosi Correctional Center v. Simmons. 543 U.S. 551 (2005). No. 03-633.

Rose, D., & Clear, T. (1998). Incarceration, social capital, and crime: Implications for social disorganization theory. *Criminology, 36*(2), 441–479.

Rose, V. M. (1977). Rape as a social problem: A byproduct of the feminist movement. *Social Problems, 25*(1), 75–89.

Rosenbaum, D. (2006). The limits of hot spots policing. In D. L. Weisburd & A. A. Braga (Eds.), *Police innovation: Contrasting perspectives.* New York: Cambridge University Press.

Rosenfeld, R. (2000). Patterns in adult homicide 1980–1995. In A. Blumstein (Ed.), *The crime drop in America.* Cambridge, MA: University of Cambridge Press.

Rosoff, S. M., Pontell, H. N., & Tillman, R. (2004). *Profit without honor: White-collar crime and the looting of America* (3rd ed.). Upper Saddle River, NJ: Prentice Hall.

Ross, C. E., & Jang, S. J. (2000). Neighborhood disorder, fear, and mistrust: The buffering role of social ties with neighbors. *American Journal of Community Psychology, 28*(4), 401–420.

Ross, L. (1998). *Inventing the savage: The social construction of Native American criminality.* Austin: University of Texas Press.

Rothman, D. (1970). *The discovery of the asylum.* Boston, MA: Little, Brown.

Rothman, D. (1980). *Conscience and convenience: The asylum and its alternatives in progressive America.* Boston, MA: Little, Brown.

Rothman, D. J. (2002). *Conscience and convenience: The asylum and its alternatives in progressive America* (2nd ed.). New York: Aldine.

Rucker, P., & O'Keefe, E. (2013, April 1). Gun measures may be in jeopardy in Congress. *Washington Post.* Retrieved from http://www.washingtonpost.com/politics/firearms-advocates-target-gun-control-measures/2013/04/01/07d3a29a-9afa-11e2-9a79-eb5280c81c63_story.html

Ruiz v. Johnson, 178 F 3d. 385 (5th Circuit, 1999).

Rumbaut, R. G. (2008, August 21–22). *Undocumented immigration and rates of crime and imprisonment: Popular myths and empirical realities.* Paper presented to the Police Foundation National Conference, Washington, DC.

Rumbaut, R. G., Gonzales, R. G., Komaie, G., Morgan, C. V., & Tafoya-Estrada, R. (2006). Immigration and incarceration: Patterns and predictors of imprisonment among first- and second-generation young adults. In R. Martinez, Jr. & A. Valenzuela, Jr. (Eds.), *Immigration and crime: Race, ethnicity and violence* (pp. 64–89). New York: New York University Press.

Russakoff, D., & Eggen, D. (2007, May 9). Six charged in plot to attack Fort Dix. *The Washington Post.* Retrieved from http://www.washingtonpost.com/wp-dyn/content/article/2007/05/08/AR2007050800465.html

Russo, G. (2001). *The outfit: The role of Chicago's underworld in the shaping of modern America.* New York: Bloomsbury.

Rutgers School of Law—Newark. (2012). *Freed but not free: A report examining the current use of alternatives to immigration detention.* Newark, NJ: Immigrant Rights Clinic and American Friends Service Committee. Retrieved from http://www.law.newark.rutgers.edu/files/FreedbutnotFree.pdf

Ruth, H. S., & Reitz, K. R. (2003). *The challenge of crime: Rethinking our response.* Cambridge, MA: Harvard University Press.

Ruttenberg, M. H. (1994). A feminist critique of mandatory arrest: An analysis of race and gender in domestic violence policy. *American University Journal of Gender & the Law, 2,* 171–200.

Sabol, W. J., West, H. C., & Cooper, M. (2009). *Prisoners in 2008.* Washington, DC: U.S. Department of Justice, Bureau of Justice Statistics.

Sacks, S., Chaple, M., Sacks, J. Y., McKendrick, K., & Cleland, C. (2012). Randomized trial of a reentry modified therapeutic community for offenders with co-occurring disorders: Crime outcomes. *Journal of Substance Abuse Treatment, 42*(3), 247–259.

Sacks, S., Sacks, J., McKendrick, K., Banks, S., & Stommel, J. (2004). Modified therapeutic community for MICA offenders: Crime outcomes. *Behavioral Sciences and the Law, 22,* 477–501.

Salisbury, E. J., & Van Voorhis, P. (2009). Gendered pathways: A quantitative investigation of women probationers' path to incarceration. *Criminal Justice Behavior, 36*(6), 541–566.

Sample, L. L., & Bray, T. M. (2006). Are sex offenders different? An examination of rearrest patterns. *Criminal Justice Policy Review, 17*(1), 83–102.

Sample, L. L., & Kadleck, C. (2008). Sex offender laws: Legislator's accounts of the need for policy. *Criminal Justice Policy Review, 19*(1), 40–62.

Sampson, R. (2011). The community. In J. Q. Wilson & J. Petersilia (Eds.), *Crime and public policy.* New York: Oxford University Press.

Sampson, R., Morenoff, J., & Gannon-Rowley, T. (2002). Assessing neighborhood effects: Social processes and new directions in research. *Annual Review of Sociology, 28,* 443–478.

Sampson, R. J., & Bean, L. (2006). Cultural mechanisms and killing fields: A revised theory of community-level racial inequality. In R. Peterson, L. Krivo, & J. Hagan (Eds.), *The many colors of crime: Inequalities of race, ethnicity, and crime in America* (pp. 8–36). New York: New York University Press.

Sampson, R. J., & Loeffler, C. (2010). Punishment's place: The local concentration of mass incarceration. *Daedalus, 139*(3), 20–31.

Sampson, R. J., Morenoff, J. D., & Raudenbush, S. (2005). Social anatomy of racial and ethnic disparities in violence. *American Journal of Public Health, 95,* 224–232.

Sampson, R., & Raudenbush, S. (1999). Systematic social observation of public spaces: A new look at disorder in urban neighborhoods. *American Journal of Sociology, 105*(3), 603–651.

San Bernardino County. (2012). County probation prepared for AB 109. San Bernardino, CA: *The Rutherford Report.* Retrieved from http://www.sbcounty.gov/rutherford/report/issues/2012_aug/probation.html

Sandler, J. C., Freeman, N. J., & Socia, K. M. (2008). Does a watched pot boil? A time-series analysis of New York State's sex offender registration and notification law. *Psychology, Public Policy, and Law, 14*(4), 284–302.

Sandwick, T., Tamis, K., Parsons, J., & Arauz-Cuadra, C. (2013). *Making the transition: Rethinking jail reentry in Los Angeles County.* Los Angeles, CA: Vera Institute of Justice. Retrieved from http://www.vera.org/pubs/making-the-transition-rethinking-jail-reentry-in-los-angeles-county

Sanger, D. (2012). Obama order sped up wave of cyberattacks against Iran. *New York Times.* Retrieved from http://www.nytimes.com/2012/06/01/world/middleeast/obama-ordered-wave-of-cyberattacks-against-iran.html?pagewanted=all

Santana, A. (2002, September 20). Court blocks D.C. vote on medical use of marijuana. *Washington Post.* Retrieved from http://www.washingtonpost.com

Savings, Accountability and Full Enforcement (SAFE) Act. (2012). Retrieved from http://www.safecalifornia.org

Scheck, B., Neufeld, P., & Dwyer, J. (2001). *Actual innocence: When justice goes wrong and how to make it right.* New York: Penguin Putnam.

Schlanger, M. (2013). *Plata v. Brown* and realignment: Jails, prisons, courts, and politics. *Harvard Civil Rights-Civil Liberties Law Review, 48*(1).

Schneider, E. M. (2000). *Battered women and feminist lawmaking.* New Haven, CT: Yale University Press.

Schneider, V., & Smykla, J. O. (1991). A summary analysis of executions in the United States, 1608–1987: The Espy file (pp. 1–19). In R. M. Bohm (Ed.), *The death penalty in America: Current research.* Cincinnati, OH: Anderson.

Schram, D. D., & Milloy, C. D. (1995). Community notification: A study of offender characteristics and recidivism. Retrieved from http://www.wsipp.wa.gov/rptfiles/chrrec.pdf

Schram, P. J. (2003). Stereotypes and vocational programming for women prisoners. In S. F. Sharp (Ed.), *The incarcerated woman: Rehabilitative programming in women's prisons* (pp. 17–28). Upper Saddle River, NJ: Prentice Hall.

Schram, P. J., Koons-Witt, B. A., & Morash, M. (2004). Management strategies when working with female offenders. *Women & Criminal Justice, 15*(2), 25–50.

Schram, P. J., Koons-Witt, B. A., Williams, F. P., & McShane, M. D. (2006). Supervision strategies and approaches for female parolees: Examining the link between unmet needs and parole outcome. *Crime & Delinquency, 52*(3), 450–471.

Schug, R. A., & Fradella, H. F. (2014). *Mental illness and crime.* Thousand Oaks, CA: Sage.

Schulhofer, S. (1993). Rethinking mandatory minimums. *Wake Forest Law Review, 28*, 199–222.

Schultz, P. D. (2005). *Not monsters: Analyzing the stories of child molesters.* Lanham, MD: Rowman & Littlefield.

Schwartz, H. (2002, March 21). Out of jail and out of food. *New York Times.* Retrieved from http://www.nytimes.com

Schwartz, J. (2011, June 20). Thousands of prison terms in crack cocaine cases could be erased. *New York Times.* Retrieved from http://www.nytimes.com

Schweigert, F. J. (2002a). Solidarity and subsidiarity: Complementary principles of community development. *Journal of Social Philosophy, 33*(1), 33–44.

Schweigert, F. J. (2002b). Moral and philosophical foundations of restorative justice. In J. Perry (Ed.), *Restorative justice: Repairing communities through restorative justice* (pp. 19–37). Lanham, MD: American Correctional Association.

SCJS, Sourcebook of Criminal Justice Statistics. (2006). *Direct expenditures for correctional activities of state governments.* Washington, DC: U.S. Department of Justice. Retrieved from http://www.albany.edu/sourcebook/pdf/t1112006.pdf

SCJS. (2008). *Number and rate of female prisoners under jurisdiction of state and federal correctional authorities.* Washington, DC: U.S. Department of Justice. Retrieved from http://www.albany.edu/sourcebook/pdf/t6412008.pdf

Scull, A. (1991). Psychiatry and social control in the nineteenth and twentieth centuries. *History of Psychiatry, 2*, 149–169.

Seiter, R. P. (2005). *Corrections: An introduction.* Upper Saddle River, NJ: Pearson.

Seiter, R. P., & Kadela, K. R. (2003). Prisoner reentry: What works, what does not, and what is promising. *Crime & Delinquency, 49*(3), 360–388.

Seligman, K. (2012, January). *Fourth Amendment issues in the digital age: Cell phone and computer searches.* San Francisco, CA: First District Appellate Project training seminar packet. Retrieved from http://www.fdap.org/downloads/articles_and_outlines/Seminar2012-Digital-4th-Amend.pdf

Seltzer, T. (2005). Mental health courts. *Psychology, Public Policy, and Law, 11*, 570–586.

Senate Bill No. 1058, 7-306.1. (2013). *Education–The reasonable school discipline act of 2013.* Annapolis, MD.

Sengupta, S. (2013, February 15). Rise of drones in U.S. drives efforts to limit police use. *New York Times.* Retrieved from http://www.nytimes.com/2013/02/16/technology/rise-of-drones-in-us-spurs-efforts-to-limit-uses.html?pagewanted=all&_r=0

Serrano, R., Savage, D., & Williams, C. (2011, June 1). Early release proposed for crack cocaine offenders. *Los Angeles Times.* Retrieved from http://www.latimes.com

Shader, M. (2003). *Risk factors for delinquency: An overview.* Washington, DC: Office of Juvenile Justice and Delinquency Prevention.

Shaffer, D. (2011). Looking inside the black box of drug courts: A meta-analytic review. *Justice Quarterly, 28*, 493–521.

Shapiro, J. (2007). Managing homeland security: Developing a threat-based strategy. In M. O'Hanlon (Ed.), *Opportunity 08: Independent ideas for America's next president.* Washington DC: Brookings Institute.

Sharp, C., Aldridge, J., & Medina, J. (2006). *Delinquent youth groups and offending behaviour. Findings from the 2004 offending, crime and justice survey.* London, UK: Research Development and Statistics Directorate, Home Office. Retrieved from http://www.homeoffice.gov.uk/rds/pdfs06/rdsolr1406.pdf

Sharp, S. F. (2003). Mothers in prison: Issues in parent-child contact. In S. F. Sharp (Ed.), *The incarcerated woman: Rehabilitative programming in women's prisons* (pp. 151–166). Upper Saddle River, NJ: Prentice Hall.

Sharkey, P. (2008). The intergenerational transmission of context. *American Journal of Sociology, 113*(4), 931–969.

Shaw, C. R., & McKay, H. D. (1969). *Juvenile delinquency and urban areas* (Rev. ed.). Chicago, IL: University of Chicago.

Shearer R. A. (2003). Identifying the special needs of female offenders. *Federal Probation, 67*, 46–51.

Shelden, R. G. (n.d.). *Conservative, liberal and radical views of crime.* Retrieved from http://www.sheldensays.com/conserli-brad.htm

Shelden, R. G., Tracy, S. K., & Brown, W. B. (2004). *Youth gangs in American society* (3rd ed.). Belmont, CA: Wadsworth.

Shelp, R., & Ehbar, A. (2009). *Fallen giant: The amazing story of Hank Greenberg.* Hoboken, NJ: Wiley.

Shepard, M. F., Falk, D. R., & Elliott, B. A. (2002). Enhancing coordinated community responses to reduce recidivism in cases of domestic violence. *Journal of Interpersonal Violence, 17*, 551–569.

Sherman, L., Gottfredson, D., MacKenzie, D., Eck, J., Reuter, P., & Bushway, S. (1997, February). *Preventing crime: What works, what doesn't, what's promising.* (Report to the United States Congress. NCJ 165366). Washington, DC: National Institute of Justice.

Sherman, L., Gottfredson, D., MacKenzie, D., Eck, J., Reuter, P., & Bushway, S. (1998, July). *Preventing crime: What works, what doesn't, what's promising* (National Institute of Justice Research in Brief, NCJ 165366). Washington, DC: National Institute of Justice.

Sherman, L. W. (1971). *Youth workers, police, and the gangs: Chicago 1956–70.* (Master's thesis). University of Chicago, Chicago, IL.

Sherman, L. W. (1989). Violent stranger crime at a large hotel: A case study in risk assessment. *Security Journal, 1,* 40–46.

Sherman, L. W. (1992a). Influence of criminology on criminal law: Evaluating arrests for misdemeanor domestic violence. *Journal of Criminal Law and Criminology, 83,* 1–45.

Sherman, L. W. (1992b). *Policing domestic violence: Experiments and dilemmas.* New York: Maxwell Macmillan.

Sherman, L. W. (1995). Hot spots of crime and criminal careers of places. In J. E. Eck and D. Weisburd (Eds.), *Crime and Place (Vol. 4).* Washington, DC: Police Executive Research Forum, Criminal Justice Press.

Sherman, L. W., & Berk, R. A. (1984). *The Minneapolis domestic violence experiment.* Washington, DC: Police Foundation. Retrieved from http://www.policefoundation.org/pdf/minneapolisdve.pdf

Sherman, L. W., Gartin, P. R., Buerger, M. E. (1989). Hot spots of predatory crime: Routine activities and the criminology of place. *Criminology, 27,* 27–55.

Sherman, L. W., & Eck, J. E. (2002). Policing for prevention. In L. W. Sherman, D. Farrington, & B. Welsh (Eds.). In *Evidence-based crime prevention.* New York: Routledge.

Sherman, L. W., & Weisburd, D. (1995). General deterrent effects of police patrol in crime "hot spots": A randomized, controlled trial. *Justice Quarterly,* 12(4), 625–648.

Sherman, L. W., Schmidt, J. D., Rogan, D. P., & Smith, D. A. (1992). Variable effects of arrest on criminal careers: The Milwaukee domestic violence experiment. *Journal of Criminal Law and Criminology, 83,* 137–169.

Shields, P. J. (2008, April 9). Emotions high over murderer's future— Longmont (CO) Times Call [web blog post]. *Mental Health News from North Carolina Mental Hope.* Asheville, NC: North Carolina Mental Hope. Retrieved from http://mentalhopenews.blogspot.com/2008/04/emotions-high-over-murderers-future.html

Siegel, R. B. (1996). Rule of love: Wife beating as prerogative and privacy. *Yale Law Journal, 105,* 2117–2207.

Silbert, R. S. (2012). *Thinking critically about realignment.* Berkeley, CA: Chief Justice Earl Warren Institute on Law and Social Policy.

Silver, E., Mulvey, E. P., & Monahan, J. (1999). Assessing violence risk among discharged psychiatric patients: Toward an ecological approach. *Law and Human Behavior, 23,* 235–253.

Simon, J. (2007). *Governing through crime: How the war on crime transformed American democracy and created a culture of fear.* Oxford, UK: Oxford University Press.

Simon, J., & Leon, C. (2007). The third wave: American sex offender policies since the 1990s. *International handbook of penology and criminal justice.* Tel Aviv, Israel: CRC Press, Taylor and Francis Group.

Simon, R. J., & Ahn-Redding, H. (2005). *The crimes women commit: The punishments they receive* (3rd ed.). Lanham, MD: Lexington Books.

Sinclair, U. (1906). *The jungle.* New York: Doubleday, Page.

Singer, S. I. (1996). *Recriminalizing delinquency: Violent juvenile crime and juvenile justice reform.* New York: Cambridge University Press.

Singer, S. I., & MacDowall, D. (1988). Criminalizing delinquency: The deterrent effects of the juvenile offender law. *Law & Society Review, 22,* 521–535.

Siskin, A. (2012). *Immigration-related detention: Current legislative issues.* (CRS Report RL32369). Washington, DC: Congressional Research Service.

Skeem, J. L., Manchak, S., & Peterson, J. K. (2010). Correctional policy for offenders with mental illness: Creating a new paradigm for recidivism reduction. *Law and Human Behavior, 35,* 110–126.

Skelton, G. (1993, December 9). A father's crusade born from pain. *Los Angeles Times,* p. A3.

Skelton, G. (2013, January 10). Brown the master tactician: Governor's tough-talking stance on prisons and the budget shows his political prowess; he scores points for good politics and good policy. *Los Angeles Times,* p. 2.

Sklansky, D. (1995). Cocaine, race, and equal protection. *Stanford Law Review, 47,* 1283–1322.

Skogan, W. (1990). *Disorder and decline: Crime and the spiral of decay in American neighborhoods.* Berkeley, CA: University of California Press.

Skogan, W., & Maxfield, M. (1981). *Coping with crime: Individual and neighborhood reactions.* Beverly Hills, CA: Sage.

Slate, R. N. (2009). Seeking alternatives to the criminalization of mental illness. *American Jails, 23*(1), 20–28.

Slate, R. N., & Johnson, W. W. (2008). *Criminalization of mental illness: Crisis and opportunity for the justice system.* Durham, NC: Carolina Academic Press.

Sloan-Howitt, M., & Kelling, G. (1997). Subway graffiti in New York City: 'Getting up' vs. 'meaning it'. *Security Journal,* 1(3), 131–136.

Smith, A. (2001). Domestic violence laws: The voices of battered women. *Violence and Victims, 16,* 91–111.

Smith, B. (1994). *Terrorism in America: Pipe bombs and pipe dreams.* Albany, NY: New York University Press.

Smith, G. (2012, March 14). Why I am leaving Goldman Sachs. *New York Times,* p. A21.

Smith, P. (2009, June 5). Canada: New heroin maintenance pilot program to get underway later this year. *Drug War Chronicle, 588.* Retrieved from http://stopthedrugwar.org/chronicle/2009/jun/05/canada_new_heroin_maintenance_pi

Smith, R. (2010). Arbitrariness as ever: Only 10% of counties in the country have imposed a death sentence in the last 6 years [Web log post]. *Second Class Justice.* Retrieved from http://www.secondclassjustice.com/?p=116

Smude, L. (2012). Realignment: A new frontier for California criminal justice. In C. Gardiner & S. Mallicoat (Eds.), *California's criminal justice system.* Durham, NC: Carolina Academic Press.

Socia, K. M. (2011). The policy implications of residence restrictions on sex offender housing in Upstate NY. *Criminology & Public Policy, 10*(2), 351–389.

Sokoloff, N. J. (2005). Women prisoners at the dawn of the 21st century. *Women & Criminal Justice, 16*(1/2), 127–137.

Solomon, A., Osborne, J., LoBuglio, S., Mellow, J., & Mukamal, D. (2008, May). *Life after lockup: Improving reentry from jail to the community.* Washington, DC: Urban Institute, Justice Policy Center. Retrieved from http://www.ncjrs.gov/pdffiles1/bja/220095.pdf

Sorensen, J., & Wallace, D. H. (1999). Prosecutorial discretion in seeking death: An analysis of racial disparity in the pretrial stages of case processing in a Midwestern county. *Justice Quarterly, 16,* 559–578.

Sorensen, J., Wrinkle, R., Brewer, V., & Marquart, J. (1999). Capital punishment and deterrence: Examining the effects of executions in Texas. *Crime & Delinquency, 45*(4), 481–493.

Sorensen, J., Wrinkle, R., & Gutierrez, A. (1998). Patterns of rule-violating behaviors and adjustment to incarceration among murderers. *The Prison Journal, 78*(3), 222–231.

Sorensen, J. R., Cunningham, M. D., Vigen, M. P., & Woods, S. O. (2011). Correlates and actuarial models of assaultive prison misconduct among violence-predicted capital offenders. *Criminal Justice and Behavior, 38*, 5–25.

Soulliere, D. M. (2003). Prime time crime: Presentations of crime and its participants on popular television justice programs. *Journal of Crime and Justice, 26*(2), 47–75.

Sousa, W. H., & Kelling, G. L. (2006). Of 'broken windows,' criminology, and criminal justice. In D. Weisburd & A. A. Braga (Eds.), *Police innovation: Contrasting perspectives* (pp. 77–97). Cambridge: Cambridge University Press.

Sousa, W. H., & Kelling, G. L. (2010). Police and the reclamation of public places: A study of MacArthur Park in Los Angeles. *International journal of police science and management, 12*(1), 41–54.

South African Department of Welfare. (1997). *White paper for social welfare: Principles, guidelines, recommendations, proposed policies and programmes for developmental social welfare in South Africa.* Pretoria, South Africa: Author. Retrieved from http://www.info.gov.za/view/DownloadFileAction?id=127937

Spangenberg, R. L., & Walsh, E. R. (1989). Capital punishment or life imprisonment? Some cost considerations. *Loyola of Los Angeles Law Review, 23*, 45–58.

Specter, M. (2011, October 12). Getting a fix. *New Yorker.* Retrieved from http://wwwnewyorker.com

Spelman, W. (1995). The severity of intermediate sanctions. *Journal of Research in Crime and Delinquency, 32*, 107–135.

Spelman, W., & Eck, J. (1989). Sitting ducks, ravenous wolves, and helping hands: New approaches to urban policing. *Public Affairs Comment, 35*(2), 1–9.

Spergel, I. A., Wa, K. M., Grossman, S., Jacob, A., Choi, S. E., Sosa, R. V., . . . Lyndes, K. (2003). The Little Village gang violence reduction project in Chicago. Washington, DC: Illinois Criminal Justice Information Authority, U. S. Department of Justice. Retrieved from http://www.icjia.state.il.us/public/pdf/ResearchReports/LittleVillageGVRP.pdf

Spiegel, J., & Grinker, R. (1945). *Men under stress.* Philadelphia, PA: Blakiston.

Spiro, P. (2002). Federalism and immigration: Models and trends. *International Social Science Journal, 53*(167), 67–73. Retrieved from http://www3.interscience.wiley.com/journal/118970711/abstract

Spohn, C., & Cederblom, J. (1991). Race and disparities in sentencing: A test of the liberation hypothesis. *Justice Quarterly, 8*(3), 305–327.

Stachelberg, W., Gerney, A., & Parsons, C. (2013, March 19). *Blindfolded, and with one hand tied behind the back: How the gun lobby has debilitated federal action on firearms and what President Obama can do about it.* Washington, DC: Center for American Progress. Retrieved from http://www.americanprogress.org/issues/civil-liberties/report/2013/03/19/56928/blindfolded-and-with-one-hand-tied-behind-the-back/

Stambough, S. J. (2012). Direct democracy and crime policies. In C. L. Gardiner & S. L. Mallicoat (Eds.), *California's Criminal Justice System* (pp. 37–46). Durham, NC: Carolina Academic Press.

Stanford v. Kentucky, 492 U.S. 361 (1989).

State of Illinois. (2002). *Governor's commission on capital punishment.* Springfield, IL: Author. Retrieved from http://www.chicagojustice.org/foi/relevant-documents-of-interest/illinois-govenor-george-ryans-commission-on-capital-punishment/Report_of_the_Commission_on_Capital_Punishment_Com.pdf

State of Maryland v. Raines. (2004)—857 A.2d 19, 33.

Steadman, H. J., Cocozza, J. J., & Melick, M. E. (1978). Explaining the increased arrest rates among mental patients. *American Journal of Psychiatry, 135*, 816–820.

Steadman, H. J., Osher, F. C., Robbins, P. C., Case, B., & Samuels, S. (2009). Prevalence of serious mental illness among jail inmates. *Psychiatric Services, 60*, 761–765.

Steffens, L. (1904). *The shame of the cities.* New York: McClure, Phillips.

Steinberg, L. (2009). Adolescent development and juvenile justice. *Annual Review of Clinical Psychology, 5*, 47–73.

Steiner, B. (2009). The effects of juvenile transfer to criminal court on incarceration decisions. *Justice Quarterly, 26*, 77–106.

Steiner, B., Hemmens, C., & Bell, V. (2006). Legislative waiver reconsidered: General deterrent effects of statutory exclusion laws enacted post-1979. *Justice Quarterly, 23*, 34–59.

Steiner, B., & Wooldredge, J. (2009a). Individual and environmental effects on assaults and nonviolent rule-breaking by women in prison. *Journal of Research in Crime and Delinquency, 46*(4), 437–467.

Steiner, B., & Wooldredge, J. (2009b). The relevance of inmate race/ethnicity versus population composition for understanding prison rule violations. *Punishment & Society, 11*(4), 459–489.

Steiner, B., & Wright, E. (2006). Assessing the relative effects of state direct file waiver laws on violent juvenile crime: Deterrence or irrelevance? *Journal of Criminal Law and Criminology, 96*, 1451–1477.

Stephey, M. J. (2007, August 16). De-criminalizing mental illness. *Time.* Retrieved from http://www.time.com/time/health/article/0,8599,1651002,00.html

Stevenson, B. (2004). Close to death: Reflections on race and capital punishment in America. In H. A. Bedau & P. G. Cassell (Eds.), *Debating the death penalty: Should America have capital punishment? The experts on both sides make their best case* (pp. 76–116). New York: Oxford.

Stickrath, T. J., & Bucholtz, G. A. (2003). Supermax prisons: Why? In D. Neal (Ed.), *Supermax prisons: Beyond the rock* (pp. 1–14). Lanham, MD: American Correctional Association.

Stowell, J. I., Messner, S. F., McGeever, K. F., & Raffalovich, L. E. (2009). Immigration and the recent violent crime drop in the United States: A pooled, cross-sectional time-series analysis of metropolitan areas. *Criminology, 47*, 889–928.

Strakowski, S. M., & DelBello, M. P. (2000). The co-occurrence of bipolar and substance use disorders. *Clinical Psychological Review, 20*(2), 191–206.

Strang, H. (2004). Is restorative justice imposing its agenda on victims? In H. Zehr & B. Toews (Eds.), *Critical issues in restorative justice.* Monsey, NY: Criminal Justice Press.

Strassberg, D. S., Eastvold, A., Kenney, J. W., & Suchy, Y. (2012). Psychopathy among pedophilic and nonpedophilic child molesters. *Child Abuse & Neglect: The International Journal, 36*(4), 379–382.

Strathdee, S., & Pollini, S. (2007). A 21st century Lazarus: The role of safer injection sites in harm reduction and recovery. *Addiction, 102*, 848–849.

Straus, M. A., & Gelles, R. J. (Eds.). (1990). *Physical violence in American families.* New Brunswick, NJ: Transaction.

Streib, V. L. (1993). Death penalty for female offenders. In V. L. Streib (Ed.), *A capital punishment anthology* (pp. 142–145). Cincinnati, OH: Anderson.

Streib, V. L. (2010). *Death penalty for female offenders, January 1, 1973, through October 31, 2010.* Washington, DC: Death Penalty Information Center. Retrieved from http://www.death-penaltyinfo.org/documents/femaledeathrow.pdf

Strickland v. Washington, 466 U.S. 668, 1984.

Strobel, T. (2009). *CDCR's supervision of Parolee Phillip Garrido* (Special report). Sacramento, CA: California Coalition Against Sexual Assault.

Students for Sensible Drug Policy. (2006). *Harmful drug law hits home.* Washington, DC: Author. Retrieved from http://www.ssdp.org

Su, R. (2009). *Local fragmentation as immigration regulation.* Legal Studies Research Paper Series. University of Buffalo Law School, Baldy Center for Law and Social Policy. Retrieved from http://ssrn.com/abstract=1416107

Suarez-Orozco, M. (2002). *Children of immigration.* Cambridge, MA: Harvard University Press.

Sullivan, M. (2005). Maybe we shouldn't study "gangs": Does reification obscure youth violence? *Journal of Contemporary Criminal Justice, 21*, 170–190.

Surette, R. (1992). *Media, crime, and criminal justice: Images and realities.* Pacific Grove, CA: Brooks/Cole.

Surette, R. (2010). *Media, crime, and criminal justice: Images and realities* (3rd ed.). Belmont, CA: West/Wadsworth.

Surette, R. (2011). *The media, crime, and criminal justice: Images and realities* (4th ed.). Belmont, CA: Thompson Wadsworth.

Swanson, J. W., Swartz, M. S., Borum, R., Hiday, V. A., Wagner, H. R., & Burns, B. J. (2000). Involuntary out-patient commitment and reduction of violent behaviour in persons with severe mental illness. *The British Journal of Psychiatry, 176*, 324–331.

Swartz, M. S., Wilder, C. M., Swanson, J. W., Van Dorn, R. A., Robbins, P. C., Steadman, H. J., . . . Monahan, J. (2010). Assessing outcomes for consumers in New York's assisted outpatient treatment program. *Psychiatric Services, 61*(10), 976–981.

Swift, J. (1707). *A critical essay upon the facilities of the mind.* London, UK: E. Curil.

Swift, J. (2013, February 11). Proposed Neb. Bill replaces juvenile LWOP with 20-year minimum sentence. *Juvenile Justice Information Exchange.* Kennesaw, GA: JJIE, Center for Sustainable Journalism. Retrieved from http://jjie.org/proposed-neb-bill-replaces-juvenile-lwop-year-minimum-sentence/104339

Sykes, G. (1958). *The society of captives: A study of maximum security prison.* Princeton, NJ: Princeton University Press.

Syrett, H. C., & Cooke, J. E. (Eds.). (1961). *Papers of Hamilton* (Vol. 5). New York: Columbia University Press.

Szalavitz, M. (2009, April 26). Drugs in Portugal: Did decriminalization work? *Time.* Retrieved from http://www.time.com

Tabichnick, C. (2012, September 25). Straight talk from a judge. *The Crime Report.* Retrieved from http://www.crimereport.org

Taifa v. Bayh, 846 F. Supp. 723 (Dist. Court, ND Indiana)1994.

Talbott, J. A. (1982). Twentieth-century developments in American psychiatry. *Psychiatric Quarterly, 54*, 207–219.

Tanenhaus, D. S. (2004). *Juvenile justice in the making.* New York: Oxford University Press.

Tarbell, I. (1904). *The history of the Standard Oil Company.* New York: McClure, Phillips.

Taxman, F. S. (2002). Supervision: Exploring the dimensions of effectiveness. *Federal Probation, 66*(2), 14–27.

Taxman, F. S., & Bouffard, J. A. (2000). The importance of systems in improving offender outcomes: New frontiers in treatment integrity. *Justice Research and Policy, 2*(2), 37–58.

Taxman, F. S., Shepardson, E. S., & Byrne, J. M. (2004). *Tools of the trade: A guide to incorporating science into practice.* Washington, DC: Community Corrections Division, National Institute of Corrections.

Taylor, K. N., & Blanchette, K. (2009). The women are not wrong: It is the approach that is debatable. *Criminology and Public Policy, 8*, 221–229.

Taylor, R. B. (2001). *Breaking away from broken windows.* Boulder, CO: Westview Press.

Teff, H., & Munro, C. R. (1976). *Thalidomide: The legal aftermath.* Farnborough, UK: Saxon House.

Teji, S. (2011). CA policy: Three strikes reform: What happened last time? Retrieved from http://www.cjcj.org/post/adult/corrections/three/strikes/reform/what/happened/last/time

Telsavaara, T.V.T., & Arrigo, B. A. (2006). DNA evidence in rape cases and the Debbie Smith Act. *International Journal of Offender Therapy and Comparative Criminology, 50*(5), 487–505.

Teplin, L. A. (1984). Managing disorder: Police handling of the persons with mental illnesses. In L. Teplin (Ed.), *Mental health and criminal justice* (pp. 157–175). Beverly Hills, CA: Sage.

Teplin, L. A. (1990). Criminalizing mental disorder: The comparative arrest rate of the mentally ill. *American Psychologist, 39*, 794–803.

Teplin, L., & Pruett, N. (1992). Police as street corner psychiatrist: Managing the mentally ill. *International Journal of Law and Psychiatry, 15*, 139–156.

Tewksbury, R., & Zgoba, K. M. (2010). Perceptions and coping with punishment: How registered sex offenders respond to stress, Internet restrictions, and the collateral consequences of registration. *International Journal of Offender Therapy and Comparative Criminology, 54*(4), 537–551.

Thacher, D. (2004). Order maintenance reconsidered: Moving beyond strong causal reasoning. *The Journal of Criminal Law & Criminology, 94*(2), 101–133.

The Constitution Project. (2005). *Mandatory justice: The death penalty revisited.* Washington, DC: Author. Retrieved from http://www.constitutionproject.org/pdf/30.pdf

The Economist. (2010, July 22). Rough justice in America: Too many laws, too many prisoners: Never in the civilized world have so many been locked up for so little. *The Economist.* Retrieved from http://www.economist.com/node/16636027

The Pew Center on the States. (2009). *One in 31: The long reach of American corrections.* Washington, DC: The Pew Charitable Trusts.

The Sentencing Project. (2002). *Mentally ill offenders in the criminal justice system: An analysis and prescription.* Washington, DC: Author.

The Sentencing Project. (2007). *Racial disparities in criminal court processing in the United States.* Washington, DC: Author. Retrieved from http://www.sentencingproject.org/doc/publications/CERD%20December%202007.pdf

The Sentencing Project. (2010, March). *Felony disenfranchisement laws in the United States.* Washington, DC: Author. Retrieved from http://www.sentencingproject.org/doc/publications/fd_bs_fdlawsinusMarch2

Theurer, G., & Lovell, D. (2008). Recidivism of offenders with mental illness released from prison to an intensive community treatment program. *Journal of Offender Rehabilitation, 47*(4), 385–406.

Thompson, D. (2010, December 18). U.S. spending millions to see if herbs really work. *USA Today.* Retrieved from http://www.usatoday.com

Thompson, M. D., Reuland, M., & Souweine, D. (2003). Criminal justice/mental health consensus: Improving responses to people with mental illness. *Crime & Delinquency, 49*(1), 31–50.

Thompson II, R. (2012, September). *Drones in domestic surveillance operations: Fourth Amendment implications and legislative responses.* Washington, DC: Congressional Research Service Report. Retrieved from http://www.fas.org/sgp/crs/natsec/R42701.pdf

Thrasher, F. (1927). *The gang: A study of 1313 gangs in Chicago.* Chicago, IL: University of Chicago.

Tibbetts, S. G. (2012). *Criminological theory: The essentials.* Thousand Oaks, CA: Sage.

Tillyer, R., & Klahm, C. (2011). Searching for contraband: Assessing the use of discretion by police officers. *Police Quarterly, 14*(2), 166–185.

Tillyer, R., Klahm, C., & Engel, R. S. (2012). The discretion to search: A multilevel examination of driver demographics and officer characteristics. *Journal of Contemporary Criminal Justice, 28*(2), 185–205.

Tirman, J. (2010). Security and antiterror policies in America and Europe. In A. C. D'Appollonia & S. Reich (Eds.), *Managing ethnic diversity after 9/11* (pp. 59–78). New Brunswick, NJ: Rutgers University Press.

Tjaden, P., & Thoennes, N. (2000). *Extent, nature, and consequences of intimate partner violence.* Washington, DC: National Institute of Justice and Centers for Disease Control.

Tjaden, P., & Thoennes, N. (2006). *Extent, nature, and consequences of rape victimization: Findings from the National Violence Against Women survey.* Washington, DC: U.S. Department of Justice.

Tobolowsky, P. M., Gaboury, M. T., Jackson, A. L., & Blackburn, A. G. (2010). *Crime victim rights and remedies* (2nd ed.). Durham, NC: Carolina Academic Press.

Toch, H. (2001). The future of supermax confinement. *The Prison Journal, 81*, 376–388.

Toch, H. (2003). The contemporary relevance of early experiments with supermax reform. *The Prison Journal, 83*, 221–228.

Tofler, B. L., & Reingold, J. (2003). *Final accounting: American greed and the fall of Arthur Andersen.* New York: Broadway Books.

Tonry, M. (2009). The mostly unintended effects of mandatory penalties: Two centuries of consistent findings. *Crime and Justice, 38*(1), 65–114.

Toobin, J. (2003, February 3). Lunch at Martha's: Problems with the perfect life. *The New Yorker, 78*, 38–43.

Torrey, E. F. (2011). *Criminalization of individuals with severe psychiatric disorders.* Retrieved from http://mentalillnesspolicy.org/consequences/criminalization.html

Torrey, E. F., Kennard, A. D., Eslinger, D., Lamb, R., & Pavle, J. (2010). *More mentally ill persons are in jails and prisons than hospitals: A survey of the states.* Arlington, VA: National Sheriffs' Association, Treatment Advocacy Center. Retrieved from http://treatmentadvocacycenter.org/storage/documents/final_jails_v_hospitals_study.pdf

Torrey, E. F., Stieber, J., Ezekiel, J., Wolfe, S. M., Sharfstein, J., Noble, J. H., & Flynn, L. M. (1992). *Criminalizing the seriously mentally ill.* Washington, DC: National Alliance for the Mentally Ill and Public Citizen Health Research.

TRAC, Transactional Records Access Clearinghouse. (2011, June). Illegal reentry becomes top criminal charge. *Trac Reports, Inc.* Syracuse, NY: Author.

TRAC, Transactional Records Access Clearinghouse. (2012a, January 26). DHS referred most federal criminal prosecutions in October, 2011. *Trac Reports, Inc.* Syracuse, NY: Author.

TRAC, Transactional Records Access Clearinghouse. (2012b, July 30). Drop in ICE deportation filings in immigration court. *Trac Reports, Inc.* Syracuse, NY.

Tramonte, L. (2011). *Debunking the myth of "sanctuary cities": Community policing policies protect American communities.* Retrieved from http://immigrationpolicy.org/sites/default/files/docs/Community_Policing_Policies_Protect_American_042611_update.pdf

Trautman, T. C. (2004). Concerns about crime and local television news. *Communication Research Reports, 21*(3), 310–315.

Travis, J. (2005). *But they all come back: Facing the challenges of prisoner reentry.* Washington, DC: The Urban Institute Press.

Travis, J., Solomon, A. L., & Waul, M. (2001). *From prison to home: The dimensions and consequences of prisoner reentry.* Washington, DC: Urban Institute, Justice Policy Center.

Treatment Advocacy Center. (2012). *Assisted outpatient treatment laws.* Retrieved from http://www.treatmentadvocacycenter.org/solution/assisted-outpatient-treatment-laws

Treble, P. (2008, December 8). Amsterdam orders pot cafes to close. *Macleans.* Retrieved from http://www.macleans.ca

Trotter, C. (2000). Social work education, pro-social orientation and effective probation practice. *Probation Journal, 47*, 256–261.

Trupin, E., & Richards, H. (2003). Seattle's mental health courts: Early indicators of effectiveness. *International Journal of Law and Psychiatry, 26*(1), 33–53.

Tummino v. Hamburg, 2013 No. 12-CV-763 (ERK)(VVP).

Tummino v. Torti. (2009). 05-CV 366 (ERK) (VVP). U.S. District Court, Eastern District, New York.

Turner, D. (2012, October 24). An odd conservative split on Propositions 34 and 36. *Los Angeles Times.* Retrieved from http://articles.latimes.com/2012/oct/24/news/la-ol-prop-34-prop-36-20121024

Turner, F. (1985). *John Muir: Rediscovering America.* Cambridge, MA: Perseus.

Turner, S., Fain, T., Greenwood, P. W., Chen, E., & Chiesa, J. (2001). *National evaluation of the violent offender incarceration/truth-in-sentencing incentive grant program, 1996–1999.* Washington, DC: U.S. Department of Justice, National Institute of Justice.

Tyler, T. R. (2006). *Why people obey the law.* Princeton, NJ: Princeton University Press.

Uelmen, G., Abrahamson, D., Appel, J., Cox, A., & Taylor, W. (2002). *Substance abuse and crime prevention act of 2000.* Sacramento, CA: Drug Policy Alliance.

Ulmer, J. T., Kurlychek, M., & Kramer, J. (2007). Prosecutorial discretion and the imposition of mandatory minimums. *Journal of Research in Crime and Delinquency, 44*(4), 427–458.

Umbreit, M. S. (2001). *The handbook of victim offender mediation: An essential guide to practice and research.* San Francisco, CA: Jossey-Bass.

Umbreit, M. S., Coates, R. B., Kalanj, B., Lipkin, R., & Petros, G. (1995). *Mediation of criminal conflict: An assessment of programs in four Canadian provinces* (Executive summary report). Minneapolis: University of Minnesota, Center for Restorative Justice & Peacemaking. Retrieved from http://www.cehd.umn.edu/ssw/rjp/Resources/Research/Mediation_Criminal_Confilct_4_Canadian_Prov.pdf

Umbreit, M. S., Coates, R. B., & Vos, B. (2001). The impact of victim offender mediation: Two decades of research. *Federal Probation, 65*(3), 29–35.

Umbreit, M. S., Coates, R. B., & Vos, B. (2008). Victim offender mediation: An evolving evidence-based practice. In D. Sullivan & L. Tifft (Eds.), *Handbook of restorative justice.* New York: Routledge.

Umbreit, M. S., & Greenwood, J. (1999). National survey of victim-offender mediation programs in the United States. *Mediation Quarterly, 16*(3), 235–251.

Umbreit, M. S., Vos, B., Coates, R. B., & Lightfoot, E. (2007). Restorative justice: An empirically grounded movement facing many opportunities and pitfalls. *Cardozo Journal of Conflict Resolution, 8*, 511–564.

United Nations Congress on Crime. (2005). *Bangkok declaration* (11th congress). Retrieved from http://www.un.org/events/11thcongress/declaration.htm

United Nations Office on Drugs and Crimes. (2006). *Handbook on restorative justice programs.* New York: Author.

United Nations Office on Drugs and Crime (UNODC). (2011). *World Drug Report.* Retrieved from http://www.unodc.org

United States Department of Justice. (2012). *The federal budget: Fiscal year 2012.* Retrieved from http://www.whitehouse.gov/omb/factsheet_department_justice/

United States v. E. C. Knight Co. (1895). 156 U.S. 1.

United States v. Jones. (2012)—565 US ___, 132 S. Ct. 945.

United States v. Paramount Pictures. (1948). 334 U.S. 131.

United States v. Paramount Pictures. (1949). 85 Fed. Supp. 881 (So. Dist., NY).

United States v. Pineda-Moreno, 591 F.3d 1212, 1214-15 (9th Cir. 2010).

United States v. Skinner. (2012)—09–6497.

University of Albany. (2007). *Sourcebook of criminal justice statistics.* Washington, DC: Bureau of Justice Statistics.

University of Albany. (2012). *Sourcebook of criminal justice statistics.* Washington, DC: Bureau of Justice Statistics. Retrieved from http://www.albany.edu/sourcebook/pdf/t2392011.pdf

Unnever, J. D., & Cullen, F. T. (2010). The social sources of Americans' punitiveness: A test of three competing models. *Criminology, 48*(1), 99–129.

Urbina, M. G. (2005). Transferring juveniles to adult court in Wisconsin: Practitioners voice their views. *Criminal Justice Studies, 18*, 147–172.

U.S. Census Bureau. (2012). *The foreign-born population in the United States: 2010.* Retrieved from http://www.census.gov/prod/2012pubs/acs-19.pdf

U.S. Census Bureau. (2013). *Population profile of the United States: Dynamic version.* Retrieved from http://www.census.gov/population/pop-profile/dynamic/RACEHO.pdf

U.S. Chamber of Commerce and Immigration Policy Center. (2012). *Immigrant entrepreneurs: Creating jobs and strengthening the economy.* Retrieved from http://www.uschamber.com/sites/default/files/reports/Immigrant%20Entrepreneur%20final%201-22-2012.pdf

U.S. Citizenship and Immigration Services. (2012, August 3). *Consideration of deferred action for childhood arrivals process.* Retrieved from http://www.uscis.gov/

U.S. Congress. (1994). H.R.3355– *Violent crime control and law enforcement act of 1994.* Retrieved from http://thomas.loc.gov/cgi-bin/query/z?c103:H.R.3355.ENR

U.S. Customs and Border Protection. (2012). *Snapshot: A summary of CBP facts and figures.* Retrieved from http://www.cbp.gov/linkhandler/cgov/about/accomplish/cbp_snapshot.ctt/snapshot

U.S. Department of Health and Human Services. (2001). *Mental health: Culture, race and ethnicity: A supplement to mental health: A report of the surgeon general.* Rockville, MD: Author. Retrieved from http://www.ncbi.nlm.nih.gov/books/NBK44243/

U.S. Department of Justice. (2012). *Overview.* Washington, DC: Author. Retrieved from http://www.justice.gov/jmd/2012summary/pdf/fy12-bud-summary-request-performance.pdf

U.S. Department of Justice—Federal Bureau of Investigation. (1993). *Crime in the United States: Uniform crime reports.* Washington, DC: Author.

U.S. Department of Justice, Office of Justice Programs. (1985–1996). *Sourcebook of criminal justice statistics.* Washington, DC: Author.

Useem, B., & Kimball, P. (1989). *States of siege: U.S. prison riots, 1971–1986.* New York: Oxford University Press.

U.S. General Accounting Office. (1990). *Death penalty sentencing: Research indicates pattern of racial disparities.* Report to Senate and House Committees on the Judiciary. Washington, DC: Author.

U.S. PATRIOT Act. (2001). 42 USC § 5195c(e). Retrieved from http://www.law.cornell.edu/uscode/text/42/5195c

Van Derbeken, J. (2004, January 9). New D.A. promises to be 'smart on crime'; Harris speaks well of Hallinan, will continue some of his policies. The San Francisco Chronicle, p. A10.

Van Dorn, R. A., Swanson, J. W., Swartz, M. S., Wilder, C. M., Moser, L. L., Gilbert, A. R., . . . Robbins, P. C. (2010). Continuing medication and hospitalization outcomes after assisted outpatient treatment in New York. Psychiatric Services, 61(10), 982–987.

van het Loo, M., van Beusekom, I., & Kahan, J. (2002). Decriminalization of drug use in Portugal: The development of a policy. Annals, 582, 49–63.

Van Ness, D. (2005, April 22). An overview of restorative justice around the world. Paper presented to the 11th UN Congress on Crime Prevention and Criminal Justice. Bangkok, Thailand. Retrieved from http://www.neighbourhoodjustice.vic.gov.au/webdata/resources/files/An_Overview_of_Restorative_Justice.pdf

Van Ness, D., & Strong, K. H. (2010), Restoring justice: An introduction to restorative justice (3rd ed.). Cincinnati, OH: Anderson.

Van Voorhis, P., & Presser, L. (2001). Classification of women offenders: A national assessment of current practices. Washington, DC: U.S. Department of Justice, National Institute of Corrections.

Van Voorhis, P., Salisbury, E., Wright, E., & Bauman, A. (2008). Achieving accurate pictures of risk and identifying gender responsive needs: Two new assessments for women offenders. Washington, DC: Department of Justice, National Institute of Corrections.

Van Voorhis, P., Wright, E. M., Salisbury, E., & Bauman, A. (2010). Women's risk factors and their contributions to existing risk/needs assessment: The current status of a gender-responsive supplement. Criminal Justice and Behavior, 37(3), 261–288.

van Wormer, K. (2010). Working with female offenders: A gender-sensitive approach. Hoboken, NJ: Wiley.

van Wormer, K., & Kaplan, L. E. (2006). Results of a national survey of wardens in women's prisons: The case for gender specific treatment. Women & Therapy, 29(1/2), 133–151.

Veysey, B. M., & Bichler-Robertson, G. (2002). Prevalence estimates of psychiatric disorders in correctional settings. In The health status of soon-to-be-released inmates: A report to Congress (Vol. 2, pp. 57–80). Chicago, IL: National Commission on Correctional Health Care. Retrieved from http://www.ncchc.org/stbr/volume2/health%20status%20(vol%202).pdf

Viney, W., & Zorich, S. (1982). Contributions to the history of psychology XXIX: Dorothea Dix. Psychological Reports, 50, 211–218.

Violence Against Women Act. (1994). Title IV, sec. 40001-40703 of the Violent Crime Control and Law Enforcement Act. (1994). H.R. 3355, Pub. L. 103–322. (Commonly referred to as the Assault Weapons Ban)

Vitiello, M. (1997a). Three strikes and the Romero case: The Supreme Court restores democracy. Loyola of Los Angeles Law Review, 30, 1643–1708.

Vitiello, M. (1997b). Three strikes: Can we return to rationality? Journal of Criminal Law & Criminology, 87(2), 395–481.

Vitiello, M. (2003). California's three strikes and we're out: Was judicial activism California's best hope. UC Davis Law Review, 37, 1025.

Vitiello, M. (2010). Addressing the special problems of mentally ill prisoners: A small piece of the solution to our nation's prison crisis. Denver University Law Review, 88, 57–71.

Vuong, L., Hartney, C., Krisberg, B., & Marchionna, S. (2010). The extravagance of imprisonment revisited. Judicature, 94(2), 70–81.

Wacquant, L. J. D. (2009). Punishing the poor: The neoliberal government of social insecurity. Durham, NC: Duke University Press.

Wadsworth, T. (2010). Is immigration responsible for the crime drop? An assessment of the influence of immigration on changes in violent crime between 1990 and 2000. Social Science Quarterly, 91, 531–553.

Wakefield, H. (2006). The vilification of sex offenders: Do laws targeting sex offenders increase recidivism and sexual violence? Journal of Sex Offender Civil Commitment: Science and the Law, 1, 141–149.

Walgrave, L. (2004). Has restorative justice appropriately responded to retributive theory and impulses? In H. Zehr & B. Toews (Eds.), Critical issues in restorative justice. Monsey, NY: Criminal Justice Press.

Walker, D. F., McGovern, S. K., Poey, E. L., & Otis, K. E. (2005). Treatment effectiveness for male adolescent sexual offenders: A meta-analysis and review. Journal of Child Sexual Abuse, 13(3–4), 281–293.

Walker, S. (2011). Sense and nonsense about crime, drugs, and communities (7th ed.). Belmont, CA: Wadsworth.

Wal-Mart Drug Stores v. American Drugs. (1995). 891 S.W. 2nd. 30 (Arkansas).

Walters, S. T., Vader, A. M., Nguyen, N., Harris, T. R., & Eells, J. (2011). Motivational interviewing as a supervision strategy in probation: A randomized effectiveness trial. Journal of Offender Rehabilitation, 49, 309–323.

Ward, D. A., & Werlich, T. G. (2003). Alcatraz and Marion: Evaluating super-maximum custody. Punishment and Society, 5, 53–75.

Ward, V. (2010). The devil's casino: Friendship, betrayal, and the high stakes game played within Lehman Brothers. Hoboken, NJ: Wiley.

Washington State Institute for Public Policy. (n.d.). Retrieved from http://www.wsip.wa.gov

Washington State Institute for Public Policy. (2002). Washington State's drug courts for adult defendants: Outcome evaluation and cost-benefit analysis. Olympia, WA: Author.

Watanabe, T. (2012, September 3). L.A. schools moving away from zero tolerance policies. Los Angeles Times. Retrieved from http://articles.latimes.com/2012/sep/03/local/la-me-citations-20120904

Waters, M. (1999). Crime and immigrant youth. Thousand Oaks, CA: Sage.

Watson, A. C., Ottati, V. C., Morabito, M. S., Draine, J., Kerr, A. N., & Angell, B. (2010). Outcomes of police contacts with persons with mental illness: The impact of CIT. Administration & Policy in Mental Health & Mental Health Services Research, 37(4), 302–317.

Watts, J., & Hutchinson, A. (2008, February 12). Reforming crack-cocaine law. Washington Post. Retrieved from http://www.washingtonpost.com

Webb, J. (2009, March 29). Why we must fix our prisons. *Parade Magazine.* Retrieved from http://www.parade.com/news/2009/03/why-we-must-fix-our-prisons.html?index=2

Weber, M. (1964). *Essays in sociology.* H. H. Gerth & C. Wright Mills (Eds. & Trans.). New York: Oxford University Press.

Weiner, R. (2012, December 14). Obama: I've got 'bigger fish to fry' than pot smokers. *Washington Post.* Retrieved from http://www.washingtonpost.com

Weisburd, D., & Eck, J. (2004). What can police do to reduce crime, disorder, and fear? *The Annals of the American Academy of Political and Social Science, 593,* 42–65.

Weisburd, D., Hinkle, J. C., Famega, C., & Ready, J. (2011). The possible 'backfire' effects of hot spots policing: An experimental assessment of impacts on legitimacy, fear and collective efficacy. *Journal of Experimental Criminology, 7,* 297–320.

Weiser, B. (2012, March 16). Man says gifts to lawmaker were for love. *New York Times,* p. A20.

Weitzer, R. (1996). Racial discrimination in the criminal justice system: Findings and problems in the literature. *Journal of Criminal Justice, 24*(4), 309–322.

Weitzer, R. (2002). Incidents of police misconduct and public opinion. *Journal of Criminal Justice, 30,* 397–408.

Welch, M., Fenwick, M., & Roberts, M. (1998). State managers, intellectuals, and the media: A content analysis of ideology in experts' quotes in feature newspaper articles on crime. *Justice Quarterly, 15*(2), 219–241.

Wellford, C., Chemers, B., & Schuck, J. (2010). *Strengthening the National Institute of Justice.* Washington, DC: National Academies Press. Retrieved from http://www.nap.edu

Wells, T. L., Johnson, W. W., & Henningsen, R. J. (2002). Attitudes of prison wardens toward administrative segregation and supermax prisons. In L. F. Alarid & P. F. Cromwell (Eds.), *Correctional perspectives: Views from academics, practitioners, and prisoners* (pp. 171–180). Los Angeles, CA: Roxbury.

Wells, W., & Schafer, J. A. (2007). Police skepticism of citizen oversight: Officer attitudes toward specific processes, and outcomes. *Journal of Crime and Justice, 30*(2), 1–25.

Welytok, J. G. (2008). *Sarbanes-Oxley for dummies.* Hoboken, NJ: Wiley.

West, D., & Farrington, D. (1973). *Who becomes delinquent?* London, UK: Heinemann.

Western, B., Kling, J. R., & Weiman, D. F. (2001). The labor market consequences of incarceration. *Crime and Delinquency, 47,* 410–427.

Westneat, D. (2012, October 2). King County sheriff makes case for pot. *Seattle Times.* Retrieved from http://www.seattletimes.com

Whitaker, B. (2000, November 10). Rocky tenure ends for Los Angeles prosecutor. *New York Times,* p. 18.

White House (2009, May 29). *Cybersecurity: Remarks by the President on securing our nation's cyber infrastructure.* Washington, DC: National Security Council. Retrieved from http://www.whitehouse.gov/cybersecurity

White House. (2011). *Building a 21st century immigration system.* Washington, DC: Government Printing Office. Retrieved from http://www.whitehouse.gov/sites/default/files/rss_viewer/immigration_blueprint.pdf

White, R. (1996). Racism, policing, and ethnic youth gangs. *Current Issues in Criminal Justice, 7*(3), 302–313.

Whittier, N. (2009). *The politics of child sexual abuse.* New York: Oxford University Press.

Wikström, P., & Loeber, R. (2000). Do disadvantaged neighborhoods cause well-adjusted children to become adolescent delinquents? A study of male juvenile serious offending, individual risk and protective factors, and neighborhood context. *Criminology, 38,* 1109–1142.

Wilkins, W., Newton, P., & Steer, J. (1993). Competing sentencing policies in a "war on drugs" era. *Wake Forest Law Review, 28,* 305–327.

Wilkinson v. Austin, 545 U.S. 209 (2005).

Williams, K. (2005). Ensuring the capital defendant's right to competent counsel: It's time for some standards. *The Wayne Law Review, 51,* 129–161. Retrieved from http://web.lexis-nexis.com

Williams, K. G., Curry, D., & Cohen, M. (2002). Gang prevention programs for female adolescents: An evaluation. In S. H. Decker (Ed.), *Responding to gangs: Evaluation and research.* Washington, DC: National Institute of Justice.

Wilson, A. (2013, February 14). County-wide effort addresses re-entry plan for California's realignment proposal. *San Jose Mercury News.* Retrieved from http://www.mercurynews.com/cupertino/ci_22594743/county-wide-effort-addresses-re-entry-plan-californias

Wilson, D. B., Bouffard, L. A., & MacKenzie, D. L. (2005). A quantitative review of structured, group-oriented, cognitive-behavioral programs for offenders. *Criminal Justice and Behavior, 32*(2), 172–204.

Wilson, D. B., Gallagher, C. A., & MacKenzie, D. L. (2000). A meta-analysis of corrections-based education, vocation, and work programs for adult offenders. *Journal of Research in Crime and Delinquency, 37,* 347–368.

Wilson, J. Q. (1975). *Thinking about crime.* New York: Basic Books.

Wilson, J. Q. (1993). *The moral sense.* New York: Free Press.

Wilson J. Q. (1995). Crime and public policy. In J. Q. Wilson and J. Peterson (Eds.), *Crime.* San Francisco: Institute for Contemporary Studies Press.

Wilson, J. Q., & Kelling, G. L. (1982, March). Broken windows: The police and neighborhood safety. *The Atlantic Monthly, 249,* 29–38.

Wilson, O. W., & McLaren, R. C. (1972). *Police administration* (3rd ed.). New York: McGraw-Hill.

Wilson v. Seiter, 111 S. Ct. 2321 (1991).

Wilson, W. J. (1987). *The truly disadvantaged.* Chicago, IL: University of Chicago.

Wilson, W. J. (2010). Why both social structure and culture matter in a holistic analysis of inner-city poverty. *The Annals of the American Academy of Political and Social Science, 629,* 200–219.

Winner, L., Lanza-Kaduce, L., Bishop, D. M., & Frazier, C. E. (1997). The waiver of juveniles to criminal court: Reexamining recidivism over the long term. *Crime & Delinquency, 43,* 548–563.

Winterfield, L., Lattimore, P. K., Seffey, D. M., Brumbaugh, S., & Lindquist, C. (2006). The serious and violent reentry initiative: Measuring the effects on service delivery. *Western Criminology Review, 7*(2), 3–19.

Wodahl, E. J., Garland, B., Culhane, S. E., & McCarty, W. P. (2011). Utilizing behavioral interventions to improve supervision outcomes in community-based corrections. *Criminal Justice & Behavior, 38*(4), 386–405.

Wohlsen, M. (2010, September 26). California measure shows state's conflicted link to pot. *Associated Press*. Retrieved from http://www.ap.org

Wojkowska, E. (2006, December). *Doing justice: How informal justice systems can contribute*. United Nations Development Program, Oslo Governance Centre, the Democratic Governance Fellowship Program. Retrieved from http://www.democraciaejusticia.org/cienciapolitica3/sites/default/files/doingjusticeewa-wojkowska130307.pdf

Wolff, N., Bjerklie, J. R., & Maschi, T. (2005). Reentry planning for mentally disordered inmates: A social investment perspective. *Journal of Offender Rehabilitation, 41*(2), 21–42.

Wolfgang, B. (2013, February 15). Drone privacy scare: Feds don't know who is responsible for oversight, GAO reveals. *Washington Times*. Retrieved from http://www.washingtontimes.com/news/2013/feb/15/drone-privacy-scare-nobody-federal-government-know/

Wolfgang, M. E., Figlio, R. M., & Sellin, T. (1972). *Delinquency in a birth cohort*. Chicago, IL: University of Chicago Press.

Wolverton II, J. (2012, June 5). First American arrested by aid of drone argues 4th Amendment violation. *The New American*. Retrieved from http://www.thenewamerican.com/usnews/crime/item/11613-first-american-arrested-by-aid-of-drone-argues-4th-amendment-violation

Wood, E., Kerr, T., Spittal, P. M., Tyndall, M. W., O'Shaughnessy, M. V., & Schechter, M. T. (2003, April). The health care and fiscal costs of the illicit drug use epidemic: The impact of conventional drug control strategies, and the potential of a comprehensive approach. *BC Medical Journal, 45*(3), 128–134.

Wood, E., Tyndall, M., Zhang, R., Montaner, J., & Kerr, T. (2007). Rate of detoxification service use and its impact among a cohort of supervised injection facility users. *Addiction, 102*, 916–919.

Wood, G. S. (2011). *The idea of America: Reflections on the birth of the United States*. New York: Penguin Press.

Woodson v. North Carolina, 428 U.S. 280 (1976).

Wooldredge, J. (1991). Correlates of deviant behavior among inmates of U.S. correctional facilities. *Journal of Crime and Justice, 14*(1), 1–25.

Wooldredge, J. (1994). Inmate crime and victimization in a southwestern correctional facility. *Journal of Criminal Justice, 22*(4), 367–381.

Woodward, B., & Armstrong, S. (1979). *The brethren: Inside the Supreme Court*. New York: Simon & Schuster.

Worcel, S. D., Burrus, S. W., Finigan, M. W., Sanders, M. B., & Allen, T. L. (2009). *A study of substance-free transitional housing and community corrections in Washington County, Oregon*. Portland, OR: NPC Research.

Wright, B. E. (2007). Public service and motivation: Does mission matter? *Public Administration Review 67*(1), 54–64.

Wright, E. M., Salisbury, E. J., & Van Voorhis, P. (2007). Predicting the prison misconducts of women offenders: The importance of gender-responsive needs. *Journal of Contemporary Criminal Justice 23*, 310–340.

Wright, E. M., Van Voorhis, P., Salisbury, E. J., & Bauman, A. (2009, October/November). Gender-responsive prisons: Lessons from the NIC/UC gender-responsive classification project. *Women, Girls & Criminal Justice*, 85–96.

Wright, E. M., Van Voorhis, P., Salisbury, E. J., & Bauman, A. (2012). Gender-responsive lessons learned and policy implications for women in prison. *Criminal Justice and Behavior, 39*, 1612–1632.

Wright, K., & Goodstein, L. (1989). Correctional environments. In L. Goodstein & D. L. MacKenzie (Eds.), *The American prison: Issues in research and policy*. New York: Plenum Press.

Wright, K. N., Clear, T. R., & Dickson, P. (1984). Universal applicability of probation risk assessment instruments. *Criminology, 22*, 113–134.

Wright, R. G. (2009). *Sex offender laws: Failed policies, new directions*. New York: Springer.

Wright, R. T., & Decker, S. H. (1994). *Burglars on the job: Streetlife residential break-ins*. Boston, MA: Northeastern University Press.

Wright, R. T., & Decker, S. H. (1997). *Armed robbers in action: Stickups and street culture*. Boston, MA: Northeastern University Press.

Wright, V. (2010). *Deterrence in criminal justice: Evaluating certainty versus severity of punishment*. Washington, DC: The Sentencing Project.

Wyatt, E. (2012, March 16). Ruling gives edge to U.S. in its appeal of Citi case. *New York Times*, pp. B1, B7.

Wyatt, K. (2012, December 10). Marijuana legalized in Colorado with Hickenlooper proclamation. *Huffington Post*. Retrieved from http://www.huffingtonpost.com/2012/12/10/pot-legalized-in-colorado_0_n_2272678.html

Yang, B., & Lester, D. (2008). The deterrent effect of executions: A meta-analysis thirty years after Ehrlich. *Journal of Criminal Justice, 36*, 453–460. Retrieved from http://www.mendeley.com/research/the-deterrent-effect-of-executions-a-metaanalysis-thirty-years-after-ehrlich/

Young, M. A. (1995). *Restorative community justice: A call to action*. Washington, DC: National Organization for Victim Assistance.

Young, M. C., & Gainsborough, J. (2000). *Prosecuting juveniles in adult court: An assessment of trends and consequences*. Washington, DC: The Sentencing Project.

Young, V. D. (1992). Fear of victimization and victimization rates among women: A paradox? *Justice Quarterly, 9*(3), 419–441.

Zahn, M. A. (1989). Homicide in the twentieth century: Trends, types, and causes. In T. R. Gurr (Ed.), *Violence in America: The history of crime* (Vol. 1, pp. 216–234). Newbury Park, CA: Sage.

Zanni, G., & deVeau, L. (1986). Inpatient stays before and after outpatient commitment. *Hospital and Community Psychiatry, 37*, 941–942.

Zehr, H. (1995). *Changing lenses* (Rev. ed.). Scottsdale, PA: Herald.

Zehr, H. (2002). *The little book of restorative justice*. Intercourse, PA: Good Books.

Zelizer, V. A. (1985). *Pricing the priceless child: The changing social value of children*. Princeton, NJ: Princeton University Press.

Zevitz, R. G. (2004). Sex offender placement and neighborhood social integration: The making of a scarlet letter community. *Criminal Justice Studies, 17*(2), 203–222.

Ziff, K. (2004). *Asylum and community: Connections between the Athens lunatic asylum and the village of Athens, 1867–1893.* Unpublished dissertation, Ohio University, Athens, Ohio.

Zimmer, L., & Morgan, J. (1997). *Marijuana myths, marijuana facts.* New York: The Lindesmith Center.

Zimring, F. E., & Hawkins, G. (1995). *Incapacitation: Penal confinement and the restraint of crime.* New York: Oxford University Press.

Zimring, F. E., Hawkins, G., & Kamin, S. (2001). *Punishment and democracy: Three strikes and you're out in California.* New York: Oxford University Press.

Zimring, F. E., Jennings, W. G., Piquero, A. R., & Hays, S. (2009). Investigating the continuity of sex offending: Evidence from the second Philadelphia birth cohort. *Justice Quarterly, 26*(1), 58–76.

Zimring, F. E., & Leon, C. S. (2008). A cite-checker's guide to sexual dangerousness: Reply to Ruby Andrew. *Berkeley Journal of Criminal Law, 13*(1), 65–76.

Zion, J. W., & Yazzie, R. (2008). Navajo peacemaking: Original dispute resolution and a life way. In D. Sullivan & L. Tifft (Eds.), *Handbook of restorative justice: A global perspective* (pp. 151–160). New York: Taylor & Francis.

Zolberg, A. R. (2006). *A nation by design: Immigration policy in the fashioning of America.* New York: Russell Sage.

Zorza, J. (1991). Woman battering: A major cause of homelessness. *Clearinghouse Review, 25,* 421–430.

Zorza, J. (1992). Criminal law of misdemeanor domestic violence, 1970–1990. *Journal of Criminal Law and Criminology, 83,* 46–72.

Index

Abrahamse, A. F., 264, 266
   see also Greenwood, P. W.
Abrahamson, D., 141
Abramson, M. F., 211
Abuse Prevention Act (1977), 105
Abusive behaviors, 103–105, 231
   see also Intimate partner violence
Academy of Criminal Justice Sciences, 298
Accountability, 41, 47–49, 146, 155
Achilles, M., 245, 253
Acker, J. R., 294
Active agents, 243
Adams, B., 96, 184
   see also Griffin, P.
Adams, L., 228
Adams, S., 230
Adams, Samuel, 160
Adams, W., 4
Adam Walsh Child Protection and Safety
   Act (2006), 4 (table), 148–149, 156
Aday, S., 178
Addams, J., 177
Addie, S., 184
   see also Griffin, P.
Addington v. Texas (1979), 205
Adelman, R. M., 95
Adelphia, 166
Adjudicated delinquents, 155–156, 194
Adjudicative competency, 209
Adolescent Coping with Depression, 27
   (table)
Adolescent-limited (AL) offenders, 19
Adolescents
   see Youth
African Americans
   California incarceration and realignment
      practices, 325

capital punishment, 299, 300–301
delinquency, 20
disadvantaged neighborhoods, 283
disenfranchisement, 136
drug court programs, 134
drug use, 196
drug use and arrests, 125, 129, 130,
   135, 142
gang violence, 176, 178, 180, 183, 186,
   188, 189
gender responsive practices, 237
incarceration rates, 5, 134, 237, 253–254,
   282, 313
intimate partner violence, 111–112, 118
juvenile waiver policies, 193, 196–197
mass incarceration, 256
mentally ill offenders, 215–216
parolees, 312
state control policies, 313
supermax confinement, 283–284
Three Strikes Law, 266–267, 273
unemployment rates, 186
white-collar/corporate crime, 170
Aftercare programs, reentry and, 214, 222
   see also Community corrections
Aggravating factors, 294–295, 299–300
Agnew, R., 19, 20, 23
Aguayo, T., 329
Aguilar, J., 329
Ahn-Redding, H., 226, 234
Akers, R. L., 298
Akins, S., 122, 139
Alabama
   DNA collection, 336
   tough-on-crime policies, 263
Alabama, Miller v. (2012), 181, 184, 329
Alaska, 106, 336

Albonetti, C. A., 216
Alcatraz penitentiary, 276, 281
Alcohol, Drug Abuse and Mental Health
   Administration (ADAMHA), 124
   (table), 125 (table)
Aldridge, J., 179
Alessi, P. T., 160
Alexander, B., 141
Alexander, M., 143, 181, 183, 254, 256, 282
Alito, Samuel, 337
Allard, J., 330
Allard, P., 135, 136
   see also Lapidus, L.
Allen, D. G., 281
   see also Cloyes, K. G.
Allen, T. L., 316
   see also Worcel, S. D.
All hazards, 68
Almquist, L., 213
Almsgiving, 78
al Qaeda terrorists, 68, 78–79
Alvare, D., 148
Alverez, S., 145
Ama, S. M., 213
   see also Herinckx, H. A.
Amendment 64 (Colorado), 132
American Bar Association (ABA), 245,
   300, 302
American Bar Association Commission on
   Immigration, 91
American Civil Liberties Union (ACLU),
   91, 293
*American Drugs, Wal-Mart Drug
   Stores v.* (1995), 161
American International Group (AIG), 166,
   167–168
American Law Institute, 171

American Psychological Association (APA), 330
American Public Health Association, 130
American Society of Criminology, 298
Ammonium nitrate, 70
Ammunition magazines, 331, 332
Amnesty International, 89, 90, 181, 306
Amphetamines, 138
Amstutz, L. S., 245
Anand, P., 269
Anderson, D. C., 263
Anderson, T. L., 230, 231
Anderson v. Commonwealth of Virginia (2007), 336
Andrade, J. T., 156
Andrade, Lockyer v. (2003), 267
Andrews, D. A., 314–315, 319, 320, 321
Angell, B.
    see Watson, A. C.
Angelton, Robert, 299
Angst, K., 208
Annabi, Sandy, 159
Annan, Kofi, 140
Anti-Alien Contract Labor Law (1885), 88
Anti-Drug Abuse Act (1986), 4 (table), 124 (table)
Anti-Drug Abuse Act (1988), 124 (table), 129, 136
Anti-immigration laws, 75, 88
Antipsychotic drugs, 205
Antisocial behaviors, 20, 21
Antitrust enforcement, 161
Appel, J., 141
Applegate, B. K., 192, 193
Arauz-Cuadra, C., 327
Arbitrariness, 296
Archibald, B., 248
Arendt, H., 188
Arizona
    DNA collection, 336
    mandatory arrest policies, 106, 107
    mass shooting, 202
    medical marijuana laws, 131
    mentally ill offenders, 209, 210–211, 218–219
    supermax confinement, 282
    tough-on-crime policies, 263
Arizona, Clark v. (2006), 209, 210–211, 222
Arizona Senate Bill 1070 (2010), 8, 37, 91, 93, 97

Arizona vs. United States (2012), 8, 93
Armor piercing ammunition, 331
Armstrong, B. G., 12
Armstrong, S., 294
Aromaa, S., 130
Arpaio, Joe, 218–219
Arrigo, B. A., 146, 205
Arthur Andersen, 164, 166
Arthur Andersen, LLP v. United States (2005), 166
Arya, N., 195
Aryan Brotherhood, 278
Asian Americans
    acculturation impacts, 96
    capital punishment, 299
    intimate partner violence, 111
    white-collar/corporate crime, 170
Assault-style weapons, 332
Assault weapons ban, 331, 332
Assembly Bill 109 (California), 272, 326, 327
Assisted outpatient treatment (AOT), 221, 222
Astor, A., 94
Asylums, 203–204
Asylums (Goffman), 205
Athletes Training and Learning to Avoid Steroids (ATLAS), 27 (table)
"Attention to detail" strategy, 187–189
Attorneys, 171–172, 302–303
    see also Defense attorneys; Public defenders
Augmentation model, 256
Aurora, Colorado, 201, 206, 331
Austin, J., 128, 261, 269
    see also Kupers, T. A.
Austin, T. L.
    see Lemmon, J. H.
Austin, Wilkinson v. (2005), 286, 290
Australia, 140, 242 (box), 244, 251, 252
Automatic appellate review, 295
Autonomy, 45–47
Avian influenze, 70

Bachman, R., 112, 146
Bach, R., 74
Bagdikian, B., 178
Bahrampour, T., 74
Bahr, S., 133
Bakalar, J., 130
Baker, A., 63

Baker, E., 31
Baker, M., 131
Balanced and Restorative Justice (BARJ) Project, 242 (box), 245
Baldus, D. C., 300, 301
Bales, W. D., 282, 283
Balingit, M., 194
Ball, R. A., 178, 179
Bangkok Declaration, 248
Bank Holding Act (1956), 69
Bank of America, 163, 168
Banks, D., 75
Bank Secrecy Act (1970), 77
Banks, S., 214
    see also Sacks, S.
Bannister, J., 11
Baptist Foundation of America, 166
Barak, G., 177
Barbaree, H. E., 146
Bardwell, R. A., 11
Barker, R., 134
Barker, T., 16
Barlow M. H., 177
Barnes, J., 21
Barrett, C. J., 195
Barr, W. P., 262
Bartoi, M. G., 215
Basic Principles on the Use of Restorative Justice Programmes in Criminal Matters (U.N. Resolution), 248
Basile, K. C.
    see Black, M. C.
Bassuk, E., 206
Bassuk, S. S., 112
Battered Women's Justice Project, 107
Battered women's movement, 103–104
Bauman, A., 227, 229, 230
    see also Van Voorhis, P.; Wright, E. M.
Bayh, Taifa v. (1994), 285
Bayoumi, A., 139
Bazelon Center for Mental Health Law, 217, 218
Bazemore, G., 243, 245, 249, 250, 256
Bd. of Managers of N.J. State Prison, Ford v. (1969), 285
Bean bags, 335
Bean, L., 283
Bean, M. G., 97
Bear Stearns, 166–170, 167

Beatty, P., 134, 135
Beccaria, C., 280
Beck, A. J., 135, 282
Beck, C., 63
Beck, Charlie, 269
Becker, J. V., 150
Beckett, K., 135
Beckman, M., 311
 see also Grattet, R.
Bedau, H. A., 293, 302
Behavioral Monitoring and Reinforcement
  Program, 27 (table)
Beichner, D., 146
Beittel, J., 188
Belenko, S., 133
Belgium, 137
Belkin, D., 185
Belknap, J., 108, 117, 225, 226, 227, 229,
  231, 238
Bellavita, C., 68, 72
Bell, V., 192, 233
Bennett, B., 93
Benson, E., 9
Benson, J., 130
Bentley, H., 107, 113
 see also Pattavina, A.
Be Proud! Be Responsible!, 27 (table)
Berge, Jones 'El v. (2001), 285
Bergerson, L. E., 318
Berg, M., 284
Bergseth, K. J., 252, 253
Berkes, L. J., 38
Berkowitz, Sean M., 171
Berk, R. A., 105, 117, 298
Bernstein, M., 114
Berton, J., 272
Bettis, P., 110
Beyrer, C., 139
Bichler-Robertson, G., 207
Bidinotto, R. J., 9
Bifurcated trials, 295
Big Brothers Big Sisters of America
  (BBBSA), 27 (table)
Binder, R. L., 213, 220
Bin Laden, Osama, 78
Binsbacher, R., 109
 see also DeLeon-Granados, W.
Biological risk factors, 20–21
Biological vulnerabilities, 20–21
Biological weapons, 70

Biometric recognition software, 335
Bipolar disorder, 207
Birth defects, 162
Bishop, D. M., 193, 196
Bishop, Jackson v. (1968), 285
Bishop, S. P.
 see Lemmon, J. H.
Bisogno, E., 182
 see also Me, A.
Bjerklie, J. R., 214
 see also Wolff, N.
Blackburn, A. G., 244
 see also Tobolowsky, P. M.
Black, M. C., 12, 101, 111
Blackmun, Harry, 302
Black Panther Party, 177
Black population
 Black victims and offenders, 111–112
 California incarceration and realignment
  practices, 325
 capital punishment, 299, 300–301
 delinquency, 20
 disadvantaged neighborhoods, 283
 disenfranchisement, 136
 drug court programs, 134
 drug use and arrests, 125, 129, 130, 135,
  142, 196
 gang violence, 176, 178, 180, 183, 186,
  188, 189
 gender responsive practices, 237
 incarceration rates, 5, 134, 237, 253–254,
  282, 313
 intimate partner violence, 105,
  111–112, 118
 juvenile waiver policies, 193, 196–197
 mass incarceration, 256
 mentally ill offenders, 215–216
 parolees, 312
 state control policies, 313
 supermax confinement, 283–284
 Three Strikes Law, 266–267, 273
 unemployment rates, 186
 white-collar/corporate crime, 170
Black T., 182
Black, W. K., 165
Blanchette, K., 228, 230, 232, 233
Blickman, T., 137
Block, R., 344
Bloom, B., 226, 227, 228, 232, 233, 234, 237,
  238, 239

Bloomberg, Michael, 333
Blueprints for Healthy Youth
  development, 344
Blueprints Model and Promising Programs,
  26, 26–31 (table), 32, 33
Blumstein A., 182
Boardman, F. W., Jr., 160
Boeing Company, 74
Boggs Amendment (1951), 123 (table)
Bogira, S., 186
Bolton, J., 208
Bonczar, T. P., 282
Bonta, J., 248, 251, 314–315, 319, 320, 321
Boodhoo, N., 186
Boos, E. J., 11
Boothroyd, R. A., 213, 220
Border protection, 73–74, 89–90
Bortner, M. A., 192, 196
Borum, R., 208, 209
 see also Swanson, J. W.
Boss, M. S., 171
Boston Marathon Bombers, 71
Bottoms, A., 278, 284
Botvin, G., 31
Botvin, W., 31
Bouffard, J. A., 252, 253, 316, 317, 318
Bouffard, L. A., 315
 see also Wilson, D. B.
Bourgon, G.
 see Bonta, J.
Bowen, D., 268
Bowers, J. E., 266
Bowers, R. A., 55
Bowers, W. J., 294, 301, 302
Boyd, G., 131
Bradshaw, W., 249, 251, 252, 253
Braga, A. A., 56, 59, 60, 61, 62, 63, 318
 see also Kennedy, D. M.
Brain research, 19, 20–21
Braithwaite, J., 165, 241, 247
Brame, R., 301
Branson, Richard, 140
Brantingham, P. J., 56
Brantingham, P. L., 56
Bratton, W. J., 63, 263
Bray, T. M., 147, 148, 152
Breach, S. R., 279
 see also King, K.
Brecher, E., 122, 128

Breeder documents, 76

Brehm, J., 39, 46, 47, 50

Breiding, M. J.
see Black, M. C.

Brewer, V., 263

Brezina, A., 19, 20, 23

Bribery, 159

Brief Alcohol Screening and Intervention for
College Students (BASICS), 26 (table)

Brief Jail Mental Health Screen, 216

Brief psychotic disorder, 207

Briggs, C. S., 282

Briggs, L., 56

Bright Bodies, 27 (table)

Bright, S. B., 300, 301, 303

Brink, J., 216
see also Nicholls, T. L.

British Columbia Center for Excellence in
HIV/AIDS, 139

Brodey, B. B., 209

Broffitt, B., 300

Broken windows theory, 61–62, 164–165,
209, 330

Bromberg, W., 203

Bronner, E., 256

Brossart, Rodney, 335

Brown, B., 82

Brown Berets, 177

Brown, C., 55

Brown, C. A., 214, 215 (figure)
see also Held, M. L.

Browne, A., 112, 226, 230, 231

Brown, Jerry, 269

Brown, Jordan, 194

Brown, M., 226, 232, 233

Brown, R., 134

Brownsberger, W., 130

Brown, T., 256

Brown v. Plata (2011), 272, 326

Brown, W. B., 279
see also Shelden, R. G.

Bruck, C., 168

Brumbaugh, S., 317
see also Winterfield, L.

Brunson, R. K., 254

Bucholtz, G. A., 276, 289

Buck, D. S., 214, 215 (figure)
see also Held, M. L.

Budgets, criminal justice, 218

Buell, M., 230, 235

Buerger, M. E., 56
see also Sherman, L. W.

Buffett, Warren, 168, 169

Buffington-Vollum, J., 284

Bui, H. N., 96

Bullock, J. A., 77

Bulwa, D., 272

Bumiller, K., 109

Bundy, Ted, 297

Buprenorphine, 127

Burchfield, K. B., 155

Burdon, W. M., 211, 316

Bureaucracy, 38–39

Bureau of Alcohol, Tobacco,
and Firearms, 132

Bureau of Justice Statistics, 40, 128

Bureau of Prisons, 134

Burge, Jon, 186, 187

Burgess, M., 67

Burke, M., 329

Burke, P., 228

Burley, L. M., 263

Burns, B. J.
see also Swanson, J. W.

Burrow, J. D.
see Koons, B. A.

Burrus, S. W., 316
see also Worcel, S. D.

Burt, M. R., 146, 155

Burton, D. L., 148

Bush-Baskette, S. R., 237

Bush, George H. W., 9, 125 (table)

Bush, George W., 79, 131, 211

Bush, Jeb, 269

Bushway, S., 17–19 (table)
see also Sherman, L. W.

Bussiere, M. T., 152

Butcher, K. F., 94

Butler, A. M., 225

Butzin, C. A., 316

Buzawa, E., 104, 105, 106, 107, 108, 113
see also Hirschel, D.; Pattavina, A.

Bynum, T. S., 227, 279
see also Decker, S. H.; Koons, B. A.;
Morash, M.

Byrne, J. M., 186, 278, 279, 288, 317
see also Taxman, F. S.

Cadora, E., 243
see also Clear, T. R.

Caeti, T. J., 192
see also Fritsch, E. J.

Cain, K. C., 282
see also Lovell, D.

Calavita, K., 88, 165

California
capital punishment statutes, 297
citizen initiative process, 6
civilly committed sex offenders, 149
crime rates, 262, 265–266, 272–273
DNA collection, 336
drug inmates, 135
federal penitentiaries, 276
gang violence, 184
homicide rates, 298
incarceration and realignment practices,
325–328
juvenile offenders, 329
marijuana legalization measures, 132, 141
medical marijuana laws, 131
prison overcrowding, 325–326
state prisons, 284
supermax confinement, 286
Three Strikes Law, 261–266
tough-on-crime policies, 263

California Common Sense, 269

California Correctional Peace Officers
Association, 263, 268, 270

California Department of Corrections and
Rehabilitation (CDCR), 268, 270, 272,
325, 326–327

*California Director of Corrections,
Lira v.* (2008), 286, 287, 290

California District Attorneys, 266

California District Attorneys Association,
261, 269

California, Ewing v. (2003), 267

California Gun Owners Association, 263

California Healthy Kids Resource Center, 31

California Legislative Analyst's Office, 264,
267, 269, 273

Californians for Safety and Justice, 269, 270

California Organization of Police and
Sheriffs, 268

California Penal Code, 262, 270–271

California Secretary of State, 268

California State Auditor, 265–266

California Supreme Court, 267

California v. Greenwood (1988), 336

Callins v. Collins (1994), 302

Campbell, C., 317
Campbell Collaboration, 32
Camp, C. G., 183, 234, 235
Camp, G. M., 183, 234
    see also Camp, C. G.
Camp, J., 214
Camp, S., 284
Campus Sex Crimes Prevention Act
    (2000), 148
Campus Sexual Assault Victims' Bill of
    Rights, 7
Canada
    drug policies, 139–140
    restorative justice programs, 242 (box),
        246, 247
Canadian Medical Journal, 139
Canfield, D., 142
Cannabis
    see Marijuana
Capital punishment
    arbitrary applications, 296–297
    claims of actual innocence, 305
    clemency process improvements, 305
    constitutionality challenge, 293–294
    cost factors, 296–297
    crime lab technicians, 304
    current policy state, 294–295
    death penalty guidelines, 304
    death penalty restoration, 294
    defense attorneys, 302–303
    disclosure requirements, 305
    DNA testing, 304
    evidentiary research results, 295
    eyewitness testimony, 303
    general deterrence, 297–298
    jailhouse snitches/informants, 304
    judicial veto power, 305
    moratorium calls, 306
    police investigations, 303
    police misconduct, 304
    policy reform, 302–306
    prosecutor misconduct, 305
    race, gender, and class implications,
        298–301
    review guidelines, 295
    super due process, 295, 296–297, 299,
        300, 301
    time constraints, 305
    trial judge training and
        certification, 305

Caplan, J. M., 57
Capone, Al, 185
Capps, R., 92
Cardoso, F., 140
Cardozo Immigration Justice Clinic, 92
Career criminals, 19
Carey, B., 140
Carleton, S., 316
Carlson, D. K., 11
Carlson, D. P., 39, 48
Carpenter, D. P., 161
Carroll, S., 98
Carr, T. R., 2, 5 (figure)
Carson, E. A., 3, 5
Carson, R., 132
Carter, D., 67
Carter, J., 127
Carter, Jimmy, 127
Carter, W., 134
Case, B., 207, 211, 216
    see also Prins, S. J.; Steadman, H. J.
Casella, R., 330
Cassens-Weiss, D., 337
Castellano, T. C., 282
    see also Briggs, C. S.
Castille, D. M.
    see Phelan, J. C.
Castro, J. L., 277, 282
Catalano, S., 110
Catastrophes, 68
Cato Institute, 138
Caulkins, J. P., 264
    see also Greenwood, P. W.
Cavanaugh, M., 329
Cayer, N. J., 2, 5 (figure)
CeaseFire, 175, 176, 185, 186, 188
Cederblom, J., 267
Cell phones, 337–338
Center for Community Alternatives, 198
Center for Constitutional Rights, 92
Center for Court Innovation, 243, 254
Center for Effective Public Policy (CEPP), 236
Center for Justice and Peacebuilding, 247
Center for Sex Offender Management,
    145, 153
Center for the Study and Prevention of
    Violence (CSPV), University of
    Colorado, Boulder, 26, 32
Centers for Disease Control and Prevention
    (CDC), 196, 331, 333

Central America, 140
Chadee, D., 11
Chafee, Lincoln, 132
Chaffin, M., 156
Chaiken, J. M., 55
Chalfin, A. J., 297
Champion, D. J., 40
Chang, E., 316
Chaple, M., 214
Chapman, G. L., 315
Charitable donations, 78–79
Chassin, L. A.
    see Loughran, T. A.
Chavez, L., 93
    see also Kohli, A.
Chemerinsky, E., 337
Chemers, B., 16
    see also Wellford, C.
Chemical Diversion and Trafficking Act
    (1988), 124 (table)
Chemical weapons, 70
Chemie Grünthal, 162
Chen, E. Y., 261, 262–263, 264, 265, 266, 267
    see also Greenwood, P. W.; Turner, S.
Chermak, S., 61
Chesney-Lind, M., 20, 31, 110, 112, 180, 181,
    199, 226, 231
Chettiar, I., 6
Chicago
    gang violence, 175, 183, 184–185
    homicide rates, 185 (table), 185–187
    juvenile court system, 191, 328
Chicago, McDonald v. (2010), 332
Chicago Police Department, 184, 185
Chicago Project for Violence
    Prevention, 176
Chiesa, J., 262–263, 264, 266
    see also Greenwood, P. W.; Turner, S.
Child Protective Services, 111, 113
Child-rearing methods, 21–22
Children
    childhood abilities and vulnerabilities,
        191–192
    incarcerated mothers, 232
    sexual offender legislation, 147
    see also Youth
Children, Young Persons and Their Families
    Act (1989), 246, 255
Chinese Exclusion Act (1882), 88
Chiricos, T., 11, 180, 266

Chishti, M., 91, 92
   see also Mittelstadt, M.
Cho, H., 106
Choi, S. E.
   see Spergel, I. A.
Cho Seung-Hoi, 202, 331
Christy, A., 213
Cioffi, Ralph, 167
Citigroup, 163
Citizen-agent narrative, 42–43, 48
Citizens for Responsibility and Ethics in
   Washington (CREW), 169
Civil commitment, 145, 146, 149, 205,
   220–221
Civilian oversight, 49
Civil Rights Act (1871), 326
Claims of actual innocence, 305
Clark, Eric, 210, 222
Clarke, R. V., 56, 60, 61, 63
Clark, J., 261
Clark, M., 7
Clark v. Arizona (2006), 209, 210–211, 222
Class
   capital punishment, 298–299
   delinquency, 20
   drug policies, 134–135
   female offenders, 237
   gang violence, 180–181
   gender responsive practices, 237
   juvenile waiver policies, 197
   mandatory arrest implications, 112–113
   mentally ill criminal offenders, 217
   problem-prone locations, 62–64
   reentry and rehabilitation programs, 313
   restorative justice programs, 253–255
   sexual offenders, 155
   supermax confinement, 282–284
   Three Strikes Law, 266–267
   white-collar/corporate crime, 170
Claypoole, K., 211
   see also Junginger, J.
Clayton Act (1914), 161
Clear, T. R., 228, 243, 279, 283, 311, 312, 313,
   316, 318
Cleland, C., 214
Clemency process improvements, 305
Clinton, Bill, 125 (table), 131, 142
Closed-circuit cameras, 334
Cloward, R., 279
Cloyes, K. G., 281, 291

Coalition for Evidence-Based Policy, 33
Coates, R. B., 241, 247, 249, 250
   see also Umbreit, M. S.
Cocaine, 122, 125, 129, 138, 140, 142
Cochran, C. E., 2, 5 (figure)
Cochran, S., 209
Cocozza, J. J., 208
Code of silence, 48
Coffee shops, 137–138
Cognitive Behavioral Intervention for
   Trauma in Schools (CBITS), 28 (table)
Cognitive-behavioral treatment (CBT)
   programs, 315
Cohan, W. D., 167
Cohen, A., 177, 180
Cohen, L. E., 56
Cohen, M., 145, 148, 149, 179
Cohen, T., 8
Coker, A. L., 112
Coker, D., 111, 112
Cole, G. F., 228
Coleman v. Wilson (1995), 326
Coles, C. M., 62, 209
Collateral review, 295
Collective efficacy, 23
Collins, Callins v. (1994), 302
Colonial Reality, 166
Colorado
   Aurora movie theater incident, 201,
      206, 331
   Columbine High School shootings,
      330, 331
   DNA collection, 336
   gun control policies, 332
   juvenile offenders, 195, 329
   mandatory arrest policies, 106, 107
   marijuana legalization measures,
      132–133
   supermax confinement, 280, 283,
      284–285
Color, women of, 111–112, 135, 237, 313
Colquhoun, Patrick, 54
Columbine High School (Littleton,
   Colorado), 330, 331
Colvin, M., 312
Combat Methamphetamine Epidemic Act
   (2005), 4 (table), 125 (table)
*Commonwealth of Virginia,
   Anderson v.* (2007), 336
Commonwealth v. McAfee (1871), 103

Communism, 88
Communities That Care (CTC), 28 (table)
Community-based treatment programs,
   205–206, 214
Community corrections
   California incarceration and realignment
      practices, 325–328
   cognitive-behavioral treatment (CBT)
      programs, 315
   community resources, 214, 312–313
   community supervision practices,
      320–321
   coordinated community response,
      317–318, 327
   cultural competency, 317
   current policy state, 312–313
   effective implementation challenges,
      318–321
   evidence-based practices, 314–318
   historical perspective, 310–312
   importance, 309–310
   individual interventions, 315–316
   innovative strategies, 319
   organizational success, 319
   policy reform recommendations,
      321–323
   post-release community supervision
      (PRCS) programs, 326–327
   race, gender, and class implications,
      313–314
   risk assessment tools, 314
   risks, needs, and responsivity (RNR)
      programs, 314–317
   transitioning programs, 214, 222,
      312–313
Community corrections officers, 309,
   319–321, 322
Community justice, 243–244, 257–259
Community Justice Initiatives
   Association, 247
Community mediation centers, 243–244
Community Mental Health (CMH)
   movement, 204–206
Community notification, 148
Community Oriented Policing Services
   (COPS) program, 4 (table)
Community policing, 59, 82–83, 99
Community Protection Act (1990), 147
Community reparative boards, 249
Community supervision practices, 320–321

Compassionate Use Act (1996), 141
Competency to stand trial, 209
Comprehensive Crime Control Act (1984), 4 (table)
Comprehensive Drug Abuse Prevention and Control Act (1970), 4 (table), 123 (table), 128
Comprehensive Methamphetamine Control Act (1996), 125 (table)
Comprehensive National Cybersecurity Initiative, 76–77
Compstat, 176, 185
Computer Crimes Task Forces, 77
Conant, M., 161
Concentrated disadvantage, 20, 23
Congressional Research Service, 93
Connecticut
    drug laws, 129
    juvenile offenders, 195
    mandatory arrest policies, 106, 107
    Newtown Elementary School incident, 201, 206, 331
Conroy, J., 186
Conservative politics, 8
Constantini, C., 331
Consumer Sentinel Network, 76
Controlled Substances Act (1970), 4 (table), 123 (table)
Cook County Jail, 191, 218
Cooke, J. E., 165
Cook, P. J., 297
Cookus, J.
    see Lemmon, J. H.
Cooley, Steve, 269
Cooper, M., 237, 312, 313
Cooper, V. G., 215–216
Cooper v. Pate (1964), 326
Coordinated community response policy, 116, 317–318, 327
Coping Power, 28 (table)
Coppola, D. P., 77
COPS, 12
Cops, D., 10
Cormier, R., 248
    see also Bonta, J.
Cornell Industries, 91
Cornish, D. B., 56, 60
Corporate crime
    American International Group (AIG), 166, 167–168

Arthur Andersen, 166
Bear Stearns, 167
broken windows theory, 164–165
challenges, 159–160
Citizens for Responsibility and Ethics in Washington (CREW) report, 169
consequences, 166–170
control strategies, 170–173
criminal law reforms, 171
current policy state, 163–165
defense attorneys, 171–172
Dodd-Frank Remedial Legislation, 168–169
Enron, 166
evidentiary research results, 165–166
Food and Drug Administration (FDA), 161–163
Great Economic Meltdown, 166–170
historical perspective, 160–163
Lehman Brothers Holdings, 168
medical fraud, 170
race, gender, and class implications, 170
Savings and Loan crisis, 165–166
Correctional programming
    abuse and victimization, 231
    educational and job training, 232–234
    management and supervision policies and practices, 234–237
    mental health issues, 231–232
    parenting programs, 232
    physical health issues, 230–231
    program evaluations, 233–234
    recommended approaches, 230
    restorative justice programs, 250
    substance abuse, 232
Corrections Corporation of America (CCA), 91
Cosden, M., 213
Cost of 'three strikes' law, 265
Cotter, L. P., 154
Council of State Governments, 212, 214, 221
Counterfeiting crimes, 75
Countrywide Financial Corporation, 168
Court-appointed lawyers, 302
Cousin, M., 109
    see also Crager, M.
Couts, A., 335
Covington, S. S., 226, 234, 239
    see also Bloom, B.
Cox, A., 141

Cox, B. J., 208
Coyle, M., 302
Crack cocaine, 124 (table), 129, 142
Crager, M., 109, 110
Craun, S. W., 149, 151
Crawford, A., 243
Crawford, C., 266
Crawley, E., 288
Crawley, P., 288
Crenshaw, K., 109
Crime Control Act (1973), 16
Crime control model, 10, 332–333
Crime displacement, 62–63
Crime dramas, 11–12
Crime lab technicians, 304
Crime mapping, 57
Crime-prone locations
    community policing strategies, 59
    empirical research, 56
    hazards patrols, 54–55
    historical perspective, 54
    hot spots/hot spots policing, 55–56, 59, 62–63
    identification strategies, 57
    index offense reports, 57–58
    management strategies, 64
    proactive policing, 63–64
    problem-oriented policing, 33, 53, 59–62
    race, gender, and class implications, 62–64
    random preventive patrols, 55
    theoretical developments, 56
Crime rates, 2–5, 262–263, 265, 272–273, 310
Crimesolutions.gov, 33
Criminal Alien Program, 92
Criminalization, drug, 126
    see also Drug policy
Criminalization of the mentally ill, 211
Criminal justice budgets, 218
Criminal Justice/Mental Health Consensus Project, 212
Criminal justice policy
    challenges, 33–34
    criminal justice research, 16–17, 17–19 (table), 19
    developmental process, 5 (figure), 5–7
    evidence-based practices, 32–33
    fear of crime, 10–11
    mass media, 11–13

models, 10
needs, 2–5
policy implementation, 37, 40, 49–50
politics, 7–10
presidential influence, 8–9
see also Delinquency
Criminal Justice Policy on Victim Offender Mediation/Dialogue, 245
Criminal Justice Project, 301
Criminal justice research, 16–17, 17–19 (table), 19
Crips, 177
Crisanti, A., 211
see also Junginger, J.
Crisis Intervention Teams (CITs), 218
Critchley, T. A., 54
Critical infrastructure assets, 71
Crosby, A.
see Hahn, R.; McGowan, A.
Cross deputization agreements, 97
Crouch, B. M., 231, 278
see also McClellan, D. S.
Crow, M. S., 266
Cruz, Jimmie, 181
CSI: Crime Scene Investigation, 12
Culhane, D. P., 316, 318
Culhane, S. E., 320
Cullen, F. T., 192, 310, 311, 313, 314, 315, 318, 319, 321
see also Applegate, B. K.
Cultural competency, 317
Cumming, A., 138
Cunningham, M. D., 284
Cure Violence, 176
Curran, D. J., 69
Curry, D., 179
Curry, G. D., 178, 179
Curtilage, 335
Curtis, K. M., 145
Curtis, M. A., 316
Customs and Border Protection Agency (CBP), 74
Cutting college aid, fostering crime, 136
Cyber Action Teams, 77
Cyber assets, 71
Cyber Command, 77
Cybersecurity, 68, 76–77

Daane, D. M., 231
Daemmrich, A., 162

Dahod, S., 11
Daly, M., 185
Dangerousness, 202, 205–206, 220
Danjczek, L. J., 212
D.A.R.E., 32
Dark Knight Rises, The (film), 201, 331
Dasgupta, S.D., 115
Davenport-Hines, R., 130, 136
Davey, M., 185
Davies, G., 63, 94, 95, 96
Davis, D., 142
Davis, Richard Allen, 263, 273
Davis, R. K., 192
see also Applegate, B. K.
Deadman, D., 312
Death penalty
see Capital punishment
Death Penalty Information Center (DPIC), 295, 329
Decertification hearings, 194
Decker, S. H., 172, 183, 279
de Cordoba, J., 140
DeCoteau, N., 178
Decriminalization policies, 124 (table), 126–127
Deegan, M. J., 177
De facto legalization, 126
Defense attorneys, 171–172, 302–303
see also Public defenders
De Groof, S., 11
DeHart, D. D., 226, 231
Deinstitutionalization policies, 205–206
Deitch, D., 316
Delaware, 300, 303
DelBello, M. P., 208
DeLeon-Granados, W., 109
Delgado, R., 248, 249
Delinquency
biological risk factors, 20–21
childhood abilities and vulnerabilities, 191–192
crime-delinquency correlation, 19–20
current knowledge state, 24–33
environmental risk factors, 23–24
evidence-based practices, 32–33
family risk factors, 21–22
juvenile court system, 176, 191–193, 328
juvenile sex offenders, 155–156
prevention programs, 24–26, 26–31 (table), 31–33

psychological risk factors, 20–21
social risk factors, 22–23
see also Gang violence
DeLisi, M., 13, 19, 284, 328
Delusional disorder, 207
DeMichele, M. T., 321
Democratic Party, 333
Demonization, 187
Department of Defense (DOD), 77
Department of Homeland Security (DHS), 68, 71–73, 77, 79, 80, 83–84, 89–93
Department of Justice (DOJ), 2, 33, 131, 161, 183, 184, 194, 196, 207, 242 (box), 245
Depenalization, 126
Deportations, 87–93, 97–99
Depression, 207
Deregulation, 165
Deschenes, E. P., 179
Designer Drug Act (1984), 124 (table)
Deterrence theory
community justice programs, 243
general deterrence, 280, 295, 297–298
juvenile waiver policies, 196
mandatory arrest policies, 105–106, 108, 117
retributive justice model, 311
supermax confinement, 280–281
Three Strikes Law, 261
Detroit, Michigan, 186
Deutsch, A., 204
deVeau, L., 221
Dewey, D., 161
Diallo, Amadou, 48
Diaz, T., 31
Dickey, W. J., 261
Dickson, P., 279
Dieckman, D., 55
Dieter, R. C., 296, 297
Diffusion of benefits, 63
Dillian, J., 168
Dilulio, J., 184, 328
DiMento, J. F. C., 171
Diminished capacity defense, 209, 210
see also Mentally ill criminal offenders
Direct democracy, 6
Direct file laws, 193, 199
Dirks-Linhorst, P. A., 213, 219
Disadvantaged neighborhoods, 23–24
Disaster management strategies, 79–83
Discipline styles, 21–22

Discretion
  bureaucratic discretion, 39–45, 49
  capital punishment, 293–295, 300–301
  community supervision practices, 328
  drug policies, 126
  juvenile offenders, 329, 330
  juvenile waiver policies, 192–193, 199
  mandatory arrest policies, 102, 106–107,
      108, 114–116
  police discretion, 62, 102
  prosecutorial discretion, 99, 301
  reentry and rehabilitation programs,
      310–311
  restorative justice programs, 256
  sexual offenders, 146–147
  super due process, 301
  supermax confinement, 280, 289
  Three Strikes Law, 264, 266–267,
      270–271
Discretionary arrest policies, 102, 106–107,
      108, 114–116
Disenfranchisement statutes, 136
Distinguished Federal Civilian Service
      Award, 162
District Attorneys, 270–271
District of Columbia, 130, 131, 141
District of Columbia v. Heller
      (2008), 332
Ditton, J., 11
Dix, D. L., 203
Dix, Dorothea, 203, 207
Dixon, L., 208
DNA testing, 304, 336–337
Dodd, Christopher, 168
Dodd, E., 213
Dodd-Frank Act (2010), 168–169
Dodd, Thomas, 168
Dodd, Wesley, 147
Dolan, M., 268, 269
Dolezal, C. D., 213
  see also Herinckx, H. A.
Domestic relations courts, 103–104
Domestic violence, 101–103
  see also Intimate partner violence
Donnay, W., 148, 154
Douglas, M., 205
Douglas, W., 142
Douglas, William O., 298
Dowden, C., 232, 233, 249, 320
  see also Latimer, J.

Dow, D. R., 299, 302
Dowler, K., 11
Downey, P., 133
Doyle, C., 69
Draine, J.
  see Watson, A. C.
Drones, 334–336
Dronet, T.
  see Kupers, T. A.
Drug abuse
  see Substance abuse
Drug Abuse Control Amendments (1965),
      123 (table)
Drug Abuse Control Amendments (1968),
      123 (table)
Drug Abuse Office and Treatment Act
      (1972), 124 (table)
Drug Abuse Resistance Education
      (D.A.R.E.), 32
Drug Analogue (Designer Drug) Act (1984),
      124 (table)
Drug courts, 133–134
Drug criminalization, 126
Drug Enforcement Administration (DEA),
      124 (table), 130, 132, 142
Drug legalization, 126
Drug policy
  arrest rates, 128
  background information, 121
  criminalization policies, 135–137, 188
  current policy state, 126–134
  definition, 126
  drug courts, 133–134
  Europe, 137–139
  evidentiary research results, 137–140
  historical perspective, 122, 122–125
      (table), 125–126, 311
  incarceration rates, 128, 133–135, 188
  less punitive drug policies, 137–140
  prevention and treatment strategies,
      141–143
  race, gender, and class implications,
      134–135, 237
  sentence reduction practices,
      141–143
  specific drug policies, 128–134
  state legislation, 129–130
  unintended consequences, 135–137
Drug Policy Alliance, 131, 133, 134
Drug trafficking, 78

Drug use
  see Substance abuse
Dual arrests, 110, 113, 114
Dubin, G., 316
Due process, 10, 220, 257, 286–287, 311, 333
Dugan, L., 108, 117
Duggard, Jaycee Lee, 156
Dukakis, Michael, 9
Dunham, H. W., 217
Dupont, R., 209
Dupuis, S. A., 211
Durham-Humphrey Amendment (1951),
      123 (table)
Dusenbury, L., 31
Dutton, M. A., 115
Duwe, G., 317, 318
Duwe, J., 148, 154
Dwight, Louis, 203
Dwyer, J., 302

Early Literacy and Learning Model, 28 (table)
Eastern Mennonite University, 247
Eastvold, A., 150
Ebola virus, 70
Eckberg, D. L., 182 (figure)
Eck, J. E., 17–19 (table), 56, 59, 62
  see also Sherman, L. W.
E. C. Knight Co., United States v.
      (1895), 161
Ecstasy, 138
Educational training, 232–234, 316
Education laws, 136
Eells, J., 321
EFFEKT, 28 (table)
Egelko, B., 131
Eggen, D., 82
Eggers, A., 134
Ehbar, A., 167
Ehlers, S., 265
Ehrlich, I., 298
Ehrlich, Robert, 131
Eichelberger, E., 8
Eighteenth Amendment (U.S. Constitution),
      122 (table)
Eighth Amendment (U.S. Constitution),
      257, 267, 285, 293, 294, 326, 329
Einstein program, 77
Eitle, D., 108, 117
Elam, E. R., 205
  see also Mossman, D.

Electronic Monitoring (EM) initiative, 91
Elkhardt, Indiana, 247
Ellens, J., 213
Elliott, B. A., 116
Elliott, J. F., 55
El Salvador, 183, 186
Emanuel, R., 186
Emerging issues
    California incarceration and realignment
        practices, 325–328
    gun control policies, 330–333
    search and seizure policies, 334–338
    zero tolerance policies, 328–330
Empathy, 21
Employment opportunities, 136, 198
Engel, John, 329
Engel, K., 278
Engel, R. S., 42, 208, 209
Enhanced Supervision Reporting (ESR), 91
Eno-Louden, J., 211, 214
Enron, 164, 166, 171
Entertainment programming, 11–12
Environmental risk factors, 23–24
Epstein, L. M., 97
Equal protection, 257
Equitable treatment, 227, 238
Esbensen, F.-A., 179, 184
Eschholz, S., 180
Eslinger, D., 203
    see also Torrey, E. F.
Essa, Mohammad, 78
Estelle v. Gamble (1976), 326
Estep, R., 12
Estrich, S., 254
Ethnicity
    drug court programs, 134
    drug use and arrests, 125–126
    female offenders, 237
    gang violence, 177, 283–284
    gender responsive practices, 237
    mandatory arrest implications, 111–112
    mentally ill criminal offenders, 215–216
    reentry and rehabilitation programs,
        310–311
Europe, 244, 251, 252
European Monitoring Centre for Drugs and
    Drug Addiction (EMCDDA), 137,
    138, 139
European School Survey Project on Alcohol
    and Other Drugs (ESPAD), 139

Everingham, S., 266
    see also Greenwood, P. W.
Ewing v. California (2003), 267
Execution costs, 296–297
    see also Capital punishment
Executive Order 9066, 88
Expressed expectation of privacy, 334
Eyewitness testimony, 303
Ezekiel, J.
    see Torrey, E. F.

Facial recognition software, 335
Fagan, J., 63, 94, 95, 96, 97, 104, 106, 113,
    117, 195, 196, 197, 198, 297, 298
    see also Forst, M.; Maxwell, C. D.
Faggiani, D., 106, 107, 108, 113
    see also Hirschel, D.; Pattavina, A.
Fain, T., 262–263
    see also Turner, S.
Fair Sentencing Act (2010), 4 (table), 125
    (table), 142
Faith-based organizations, 247
Falk, D. R., 116
Fallen woman, 226
False identities, 76
Falshaw, L., 312
Famega, C., 63
Familias Unidas, 28 (table)
Family Group Conferencing (FGC), 242
    (box), 249, 252
Family relationships, 232
Family risk factors, 21–22
Family violence courts, 104
Farabee, D., 231
    see also McClellan, D. S.
Faris, R. E., 217
Farkas, M. A., 145
Farrall, S., 11
Farrell, A., 56
Farrell, G., 56
Farrington, D., 21, 22, 25
Farr, K. A., 228, 229
Farwell, J. P., 71
Fear of crime, 10–11
Fears, D., 135
Fedders, B., 111, 112, 113
Federal Assault Weapons Ban (1994), 4 (table)
Federal Aviation Administration (FAA), 335
Federal Bureau of Investigation (FBI), 2, 77,
    82–83, 188, 262, 299, 301, 328

Federal Bureau of Prisons, 276
Federal criminal justice policies, 4 (table)
Federal Death Penalty Act (1994), 4 (table)
Federal Emergency Management Agency
    (FEMA), 72–73, 79
Federal financial aid eligibility, 136
Federal incarceration rates, 2–5
Federal penitentiaries
    see Supermax confinement
Federal Reserve Bank of San Francisco, 75
Federal Trade Commission (FTC),
    76, 161
Federation for American Immigration
    Reform (FAIR), 93
Federation of American Scientists, 130
Feeley, M. M., 277
Feld, B. C., 176, 191
Felson, M., 56
Female offenders
    see Gender responsive practices
Fennelly, K., 96, 97
Fenwick, M., 180
Ferdinand, T. N., 328
Fernandez, G. A., 221
Fernández-Kelly, P., 95
Ferrara, A., 55
Ferraro, K. J., 104
Ferrell, J., 187
Ferrini, R., 127
Fetzer, M. D.
    see Lemmon, J. H.
Fidelity, program, 31
Fifth Amendment (U.S. Constitution),
    171, 333
Figlio, R. M., 56
Filindra, A., 96
Financial Action Task Force, 77
Financial crime, 75–76
Finckenauer, J. O., 319
Finigan, M. W., 316
    see also Worcel, S. D.
Finn, M. A., 110
Firestine, K.
    see Griffin, P.
Firmin, C., 187
First Amendment (U.S. Constitution), 326
First Nations/First Peoples, 245–247
Fischer, L., 172
Fischman, M., 129
Fish, Albert, 149

Fisher, B. S., 11
Fisher, D., 220
Fisher, W. H., 206, 211, 217
Fiss, O. M., 257
Flagstaff, Arizona, 210–211
Flannery, D., 312
Fleisher, M. S., 183, 280
Fletcher, W. H., 165
Flint Foot Patrol Experiment, 16
Florida
    capital punishment statutes, 297, 300,
        301, 306
    DNA collection, 336
    juvenile justice system, 193, 194
    mentally ill inmates, 218
    supermax confinement, 282, 283
    Three Strikes Law, 266
Florida, Graham v. (2010), 257
Florida, Proffitt v. (1976), 294
Flygare, C., 320
Flynn, L. M.
    see Torrey, E. F.
Foley, H. A., 205
Food and Drug Administration (FDA),
    161–163
Food, Drug, and Cosmetic Act (1938),
    123 (table)
Forbes, D., 131
Ford, D. A., 104
*Ford v. Bd. of Managers of N.J. State
    Prison* (1969), 285
Forensic Assertive Community Treatment
    (F-ACT) programs, 212
Forensic Files, 12
Forensic Intensive Case Management
    (FICM) programs, 212
Formal sanctions, 117
Forman, M., 205
Forst, M., 197, 198
Fort Dix conspiracy, 82
Foucault, M., 204
Fourteenth Amendment (U.S. Constitution),
    286, 293, 326, 329, 332
Fourth Amendment (U.S. Constitution),
    326, 333, 334, 335, 338
Fox, J. A., 182
Fox, J. G., 226, 238
Fox, R. J., 178, 179
Fradella, H. F., 202, 205, 206, 209,
    210–211, 222

France, 137
Franklin, D., 263
Frank, S. A., 46
Fraud Enforcement and Recovery Act
    (2009), 4 (table)
Fraudulent identities, 76
Frazier, C. E., 193, 196
Freedman, E. B., 146
Freeman, N. J., 153–154, 156
    see also Sandler, J. C.
Freiburger, T. L., 197
Fricker, M., 165
Friedman, N., 285
Frisman, L. K., 214
Fritsch, E. J., 192
Frohmann, L., 146, 155
Frost, L. E., 214, 215 (figure)
    see also Held, M. L.
Frost, N. A., 12
Fry, L. W., 39
    see also Jermier, J. M.
Fugitive aliens, 90
Fuhrman, People v. (1997), 267
Fuld, L. F., 54
Fuld, Richard, 168
Fuller, D. A., 219
Fullilove, M.
    see Hahn, R.; McGowan, A.
Fully automatic firearms, 331
Fulton, B., 320
Functional Family Therapy (FFT), 26
    (table)
Furillo, A., 269, 270
Furman v. Georgia (1972), 293–294, 295,
    298, 299
Fusion centers, 82–83

Gaarder, E., 254
Gaboury, M. T., 244, 249, 250
    see also Tobolowsky, P. M.
Gaes, G. G., 284
    see also Camp, S.
Gagliardi, G. J., 211
    see also Lovell, D.
Gahlinger, P., 127
Gaines, J., 39
    see also Jermier, J. M.
Gaines, L. K., 70, 71, 72
Gainsborough, J., 196, 198
Gajewski, F.

    see Braga, A. A.
Galinsky, K., 160
Gallagher, C. A., 316
    see also Wilson, D. B.
Gamble, Estelle v. (1976), 326
Gandhi, Mohandas (Mahatma), 172
Gang injunctions, 179, 263
Gang Resistance Education and Training
    (G.R.E.A.T.), 175, 177, 179, 184
Gang violence
    "attention to detail" strategy, 187–189
    current policy state, 178–179
    evidentiary research results, 183–187
    historical perspective, 177–178
    juvenile delinquency, 22–23
    key factors, 176–177
    membership estimates, 178–179
    policy reform, 187–189
    prison inmates, 178, 183, 278–280,
        283–284, 287–289
    race, gender, and class implications, 176,
        177, 179, 180–181, 283–284
    social reform efforts, 177–178
    unintended consequences, 181–183
Gannon-Rowley, T., 23
Garber, A., 133
Garcia, M., 183
Gardiner, C. L., 8, 134
Garland, B., 278, 320
Garland, D., 178, 310, 311
Garner, B. A., 294
Garner, J. H., 106, 113, 117
    see also Maxwell, C. D.
Garner, Tennessee v. (1985), 37
Garofalo, J., 11
Garrido, Phillip, 156
Gartin, P. R., 56
    see also Sherman, L. W.
Gartner, R., 229
Gascón, George, 269
Gassman, M., 134
Gates, S., 39, 46, 47, 50
Gateway drugs, 138
Gau, J. M., 254
Gavett, G., 90
Gaviria, C., 140
Gay men, 113–114
Geary Act (1892), 88
Gehring, K., 233
Geis, G., 165, 166, 170, 171

Geis, R., 170
Geithner, Timothy, 163
Gelacak, M., 129
Geller, A., 63, 316
Geller, J. L., 206
Gelles, R. J., 112
Gender
    capital punishment, 299–300
    delinquency, 19–20
    drug court programs, 134
    drug policies, 134–135, 237
    fear of crime, 10–11
    gang violence, 176, 177, 179, 180–181
    juvenile waiver policies, 197
    mandatory arrest implications, 109–111
    mentally ill criminal offenders, 216–217
    problem-prone locations, 62–64
    reentry and rehabilitation programs, 313
    restorative justice programs, 252–255
    supermax confinement, 282–284
    Three Strikes Law, 266–267
    white-collar/corporate crime, 170
Gender-Informed Practices Assessment
    (GIPA) tool, 236, 238, 239
Gender-neutral classifications, 227,
    229–230
Gender responsive practices
    correctional programming, 230–237
    current policy state, 228–237
    gender-responsive guidelines, 227–228
    historical perspective, 225–228
    mentally ill offenders, 216–217
    offender characteristics, 226
    policy reform, 238–240
    race, ethnicity, gender, and class
        implications, 237
    risk and needs assessments, 228–230
    supermax confinement, 282–284
    treatment and program background,
        226–228
Gender-specific practices, 227, 229–230
Gendreau, P., 284, 319, 320
General Accounting Office (GAO)
    see Government Accountability
        Office (GAO)
General deterrence, 280, 295, 297–298
General Educational Development (GED)
    programs, 233
General Electric (GE), 165
General Re, 166

Geographic Information Systems (GIS), 57
Geo Group, 91
George, B. C., 171
Georgia, 301, 329
Georgia, Furman v. (1972), 293–294, 295,
    298, 299
Georgia, Gregg v. (1976), 294–295, 298
Gerber, E. R., 44
Gerbner, G., 11
Germany, 137, 140
Gerney, A., 333
Gerson, S., 206
Gerth, J., 79
Gertz, M., 11
Gfroerer, J. C., 96
Gibeaut, J., 263
Gideon, L., 315
Giffords, Gabrielle, 202, 331
Gilbert, A. R.
    see Van Dorn, R. A.
Gilbert, L., 93, 94
Gilbert, M. J., 243
Gilchrist, E., 11
Gilfus, M. E., 226, 231
Gilliam, F. D., 180
Gilman, E., 284
    see also Gaes, G. G.
Gilmore, Gary, 294
Gingrich, Newt, 269
Giwargis, R., 327
Gladfelter, A. S.
    see Lemmon, J. H.
Glaze, L. E., 207, 219, 225, 226, 231, 232, 234,
    248, 253
Glesmann, C., 91
Glionna, J., 139
Global Commission on Drugs, 140
Global Crossing, 166
Global positioning system (GPS), 337
Glober, R. W., 206
Goffman, E., 180, 205
Goff, P. A., 97
Goggin, C. E., 284
Golash-Boza, T. M., 90
Goldenson, R. M., 203
Goldfarb, S. F., 103, 117
Goldman, H. H., 203, 204, 205, 206
Goldman Sachs, 173
Goldstein, H., 60
Gomez, Madrid v. (1995), 285

Gonzales, R. G., 95, 97
Good Behavior Game (GBG), 28 (table)
Good, D., 325
Goode, E., 127, 285
Goodman, P., 284
Goodmark, L., 112
Goodstein, L., 284
Good woman, 226
Gorman, A., 8, 40
Goss, J. R., 209
Gottfredson, D., 17–19 (table)
    see also Sherman, L. W.
Gover, A. R., 11
Government Accountability Office (GAO),
    165, 300–301, 312
Graber, D., 11
Graffiti, 164, 180, 330
Graham v. Florida (2010), 257
Grana, S. J., 226, 238
Grande, T., 221
Grassian, S., 281, 285
Grattet, R., 37, 39, 45, 311, 321
Gray, J., 129
Gray, M., 138
Great American Meltdown, 161
Great Britain, 137, 140
Great Economic Meltdown, 164, 166–170
G.R.E.A.T. (Gang Resistance Education and
    Training), 175, 177, 179, 184
Greaves, C., 216
    see also Nicholls, T. L.
Greenberg, Maurice Raymond, 167–168
Greenberg, S., 82
Greene, J., 179
Greene, J. R., 39, 48, 49
Greenfeld, L., 135, 232, 233, 234
Green-Mazerolle, L.
    see Braga, A. A.
Green River Killer, 296
Greenwald, G., 138, 139
Greenwood, California v. (1988), 336
Greenwood, J., 241
Greenwood, P. W., 25, 34, 262–263, 264, 266
    see also Turner, S.
Gregg v. Georgia (1976), 294–295, 298
Gregoire, Christine, 132
Grekin, P. M., 216
Griffin, M., 284
Griffin, P., 193, 194
Grimshaw, R., 42

Grinker, R., 204
Grinspoon, L., 130
Grob, G. N., 203, 204
Gross, L., 11
Grossman, S.
      see also Spergel, I. A.
Gross, S. R., 301
Guerette, R. T., 62
Guerino, P., 134, 248, 282, 283
Guided discretion death penalty statutes, 294
Guiding Good Choices, 28 (table)
Gun control policies, 330–333
Gun-Free Schools Act (1994), 330
Gur, O. M., 218, 219
Gutierrez, A., 284

H5N1 influenza, 70
Haake, J., 141
Haddow, G. D., 77
Hadley, M. L., 247
Hadley, T., 316
      see also Culhane, D. P.
Hagedorn, J. M., 178, 180, 186, 188
Hagopian, G., 211
Hahn, R., 196
      see also McGowan, A.
Hails, J., 209
Haines, H. H., 293, 297
Hakiaha, M., 253
Haller, W., 95
Halpern-Finnerty, J., 92
Hamas, 78
Hamburg, Tummino v. (2013), 163
Hamilton, Alexander, 165
Hamilton, E. E., 117
Hamilton, J. R., Jr., 243
      see also Clear, T. R.
Hamilton, J. T., 178
Hamilton, Z., 316, 317, 318
      see also Lutze, F. E.
Handbook on Restorative Justice
      Programs (U.N.), 248
Haney, C., 275, 281, 285, 287, 290
Hanley, D., 312, 317, 318, 319
Hanson, R. K., 152
Harcourt, B. E., 63, 206
Hard drugs, 126–127, 128, 137–138
Harding, W., 172
Hardyman, P. L., 228, 229, 234
      see also Camp, C. G.

Hardy, T., 109
      see also Crager, M.
Harer, M., 284
Harlow, C. W., 40, 231
Harmelin v. Michigan (1991), 297
Harm reduction strategies, 126–128, 138
Harris County, Texas, 299, 300
Harris, Eric, 331
Harris, Kamala D., 266
Harrison Narcotics Act (1914), 122 (table),
      125, 128
Harrison, P. M., 134, 135, 248, 282
      see also Guerino, P.
Harris, P. E., 133
Harris, T. R., 321
Hart, B. J., 47
Hart, E., 211
Hartney, C., 91, 328
Hartocollis, A., 170
Hart, Scott v. (1979), 113
Hartwell, S., 216–217
Hass, G. S., 115
Hastings, D., 142
Hatch Act (1939), 131
Hatsukami, D., 129
Hawaii, 135
Hawkins, D. F., 196
Hawkins, G., 265, 278
      see also Zimring, F. E.
Hayden, T., 183
Hayes, H., 252
Hays, S., 156
Hazards patrols, 54–55
Health care services, 230–231
Held, M. L., 214, 215 (figure)
Hell, D., 208
Heller, District of Columbia v.
      (2008), 332
Hemmens, C., 192
      see also Fritsch, E. J.
Henderson, M. L., 317, 318, 319
Henningsen, R. J., 277
Henretta, J. C., 193
Henriques, Z. W., 231, 237
Henry, D. A., 261
Hepatitis, 70, 139
Hepburn, J. R., 216, 284
Herbeck, D., 297
Herinckx, H. A., 213, 219
Herman, S., 245

Hern, A. L., 154
Hernández, D. M., 88, 91
Heroin, 122, 127, 138, 139, 140
Heroin Act (1924), 122 (table)
Heroin Trafficking Act (1973), 124 (table)
Hesse, M., 328
Hewitt, J., 13, 19, 328
Hezbollah, 78
Hickenlooper, John, 332
Hickey, J. S., 214, 215 (figure)
      see also Held, M. L.
Hiday, V. A., 208, 213, 220
      see also Swanson, J. W.
Higher Education Act (1998), 136
High-rate offenders, 19–20
High-risk inmates, 276–277, 287–288
      see also Supermax confinement
High-risk policing
      community acceptance, 63–64
      community policing strategies, 59
      empirical research, 56
      hazards patrols, 54–55
      historical perspective, 54
      hot spots/hot spots policing, 55–56, 59,
            62–63
      management strategies, 64
      proactive policing, 63–64
      problem-oriented policing, 33, 53, 59–62
      problem-prone locations, 57–64
      race, gender, and class implications, 62–64
      random preventive patrols, 55
      theoretical developments, 56
HighScope Preschool, 28 (table)
Hill, M., 42, 44, 47
Hilts, P. J., 161
Hinckley, John, Jr., 201, 209, 222
Hing, J., 330
Hinkle, J. C., 63
Hipple, N. K., 250, 252, 253
Hirschel, D., 104, 105, 106, 107, 108, 110,
      113, 117
      see also Pattavina, A.
Hispanic population
      acculturation impacts, 96
      California incarceration and realignment
            practices, 325
      capital punishment, 299
      disadvantaged neighborhoods, 283
      drug use and arrests, 129, 130, 134
      gang violence, 188, 189, 283

gender responsive practices, 237
immigration enforcement, 75, 96–97
incarceration rates, 5, 134, 142, 237, 254,
    282, 313
intimate partner violence, 111, 112
juvenile waiver policies, 197
mentally ill offenders, 216
parolees, 312
state control policies, 313
supermax confinement, 282–284
Three Strikes Law, 266
Hitt, J., 131
HIV/AIDS, 70, 139
Hoffman, M., 134
Holder, Eric, 142
Holmes, James, 201–202, 206, 331
Holmes, W. M., 108, 110, 117
Holsinger, A. M., 315, 319
Holtfreter, K., 228
Holy Land Foundation, 78–79
Homeland security
    border protection, 73–74, 89–90
    challenges, 72–73
    core mission and functional role, 68–69
    critical infrastructure and key resources
        (CI/KR), 71–72, 82
    current state, 69–72
    cybersecurity, 76–77
    financial and identification crime, 75–76
    immigration enforcement, 74–75, 89–94,
        96–99
    money laundering, 77–79
    police response, 81–83
    response strategies, 79–84
    terrorist attacks, 67
    terrorist financing, 77–79
    transportation protection, 73
    USA PATRIOT Act (2001), 69–70
    weapons of mass destruction, 70–71
Homelessness
    mentally ill patients, 206, 209, 217
    women, 112–113
Home life quality, 21–22
Homicide rates
    capital punishment deterrent effect, 298
    Chicago, 185 (table), 185–187
    Detroit, 186
    New York City, 186
    United States, 181–183, 182 (figure), 185
        (table)

Hoover, Herbert, 8
Hoover, S., 213
    see also Redlich, A. D.
Horn, D., 267
Horney, J., 146
Horton, Willie, 9
Horwitz, S., 77, 132
Hospitalization
    see Civil commitment
Hot spots/hot spots policing, 55–56, 59, 62–63
Houghtalin, M., 192
Housing instability, 316
Houston Post, 300
Howell, J. C., 177, 184, 195
Howley, P., 246
Hoyt, W., 101
H.R. 4472—109th Congress: Adam Walsh
        Child Protection and Safety Act (2006)
    see Adam Walsh Child Protection and
        Safety Act (2006)
Hubbard, D., 315
Huebner, B., 284
Hueston, John E., 171
Huffington, Michael, 263
Hughes, C., 138, 139
Hughes, D., 75
Hughes, K. A., 311
Hughes, L. A., 155
Huizinga, D., 179
Human assets, 71
Human Rights Watch, 90, 91, 218
Human trafficking, 75
Hummer, D., 278, 279, 288
Huntington, Collis, 160
Huntington, S., 176
Hunt, N., 143
Hupe, P., 42, 44, 47
Hureau, D. M., 59, 60, 318
    see also Braga, A. A.
Hurricane Katrina, 79, 81
Hutchinson, A., 77, 142, 333
Huz, S.
    see Phelan, J. C.
Hylton, J. H., 208

Ianni, F., 180
ICE
    see Immigration and Customs
        Enforcement Agency (ICE)
Identify fraud, 76

Identity theft, 76
Illegal drug use
    see Drug policy; Substance abuse
Illegal Immigrant Reform and Immigrant
        Responsibility Act (1996), 91, 92, 94
Illinois
    capital punishment statutes, 296
    drug laws, 129
    federal penitentiaries, 276, 284
    gang violence, 178, 184
    juvenile justice system, 193
    sexual offenders, 150
    supermax confinement, 282
    see also Chicago
ImClone, 166
Immigrant Rights Clinic and American
        Friends Service Committee, 91
Immigrants
    acculturation impacts, 96
    Arizona Senate Bill 1070 (2010), 8, 37,
        91, 93, 97
    border protection, 73–74
    crime rates, 87, 94–96
    current policy state, 89–94
    detention and deportation, 87–93, 97–99
    drug use, 122
    drug use and arrests, 126
    evidentiary research results, 94–96
    federal policies, 89–92
    federal-state immigration partnerships,
        92–93
    generational differences, 95–96
    historical perspective, 88
    immigration enforcement, 74–75, 89–94,
        96–99
    immigration policy reform, 98–99
    intimate partner violence, 114–115
    mandatory arrest implications, 114–115
    policy consequences, 96–98
    al Qaeda terrorists, 68
    state and local initiatives, 93–94
Immigration and Customs Enforcement
        Agency (ICE), 74–75, 89, 90–93, 96
Immigration and Nationality Act (1952), 91
Immigration and Naturalization Service
        (INS), 89
Immigration enforcement, 74–75, 89–94,
        96–99
Immigration Reform and Control Act
        (1986), 88

Impoverished women, 112–113
Incairdi, J. A., 316
  see also Butzin, C. A.
Incapacitation, 261, 265, 278–280
Incarceration rates, 2–5
Incredible Years (IY)
  Child Treatment, 28 (table)
  Parent, 29 (table)
  Teacher Classroom Management, 29
    (table)
Index crimes, 58
Index offense reports, 57–58
Indiana
  DNA collection, 336
  restorative justice programs, 242 (box),
    247, 252
Indicated prevention programs, 25
Indigenous cultures, 245–247
Individual interventions, 315–316
Informants, 304
Initiative process, 6
Innocence claims, 305
Insanity defense, 209, 210
  see also Mentally ill criminal offenders
InShape, 29 (table)
Insite, 139
Institute for Mediation and Conflict Resolu-
    tion, 243
Institute of Medicine, 130
Institutional segregation, 276
Intelligence, 21
Intensive Supervision Appearance Program
    (ISAP), 91
Intensive supervision programs (ISPs), 320
Interception patrol model, 55
International Association of Chiefs of Police
    (IACP), 98, 104
International Monetary Fund (IMF), 77
Internet security, 68
Interrupters, The (documentary), 176, 185
Intimate partner violence
  arrest rates, 108, 117
  coordinated community response
    policy, 116
  current policy state, 106–107
  definition, 101
  deterrence theory, 105–106, 108, 117
  evidentiary research results, 108–109
  formal sanctions, 117
  gender, 109–111

historical perspective, 103–106
  immigration status, 114–115
  local and state policies, 106–107
  policy consequences, 117–118
  policy reform, 115–117
  prevalence and consequences, 101–103
  primary aggressor statutes, 116–117
  race and ethnicity, 111–112
  same-sex relationships, 113–114
  social class, 112–113
  Violence Against Women Act (1994), 8
  see also Mandatory arrest
Intravenous drug users, 139
Invisible population, 225
Involuntary commitment, 205,
    215–216, 220
Iowa, 106, 107, 219
Ireland, C. E., 122–125 (table)
Irell & Manelle (law firm), 171
Irritability, 21
Irwin, J., 128
Irwin, K., 180, 199
Isaacs, C., 283
Italian Mafia, 177–178, 180
Iyengar, S., 180

Jackall, R., 39, 49
Jackson, A., 187
Jackson, A. L., 244
  see also Tobolowsky, P. M.
Jackson, D., 331–332
Jackson v. Bishop (1968), 285
Jacob, A.
  see Spergel, I. A.
Jacobs, J., 178, 183
Jacob Wetterling Crimes Against Children and
    Sexually Violent Offender Registration
    Act (1994), 4 (table), 147, 148
Jailhouse snitches/informants, 304
Jalbert, S. K., 320
James, D. J., 207, 219, 226, 231
James, N., 109
James, William, 204
Jamieson, K. H., 178
Jang, S. J., 58
Jankowski, M. S., 279
Janofsky, M., 131
Janus, E. S., 155
Japanese-American confinement camps, 88
Jaret, C., 95

Jaycee Lee Duggard/Phillip Garrido
    case, 156
Jefferson, T., 42
Jeglic, E., 145, 148, 149
Jelsma, M., 137
Jemelka, R., 216
Jenkins, M., 253, 254
Jenkins, S., 243
Jenness, V., 37, 39, 45
Jennings, J. B., 330
Jennings, W. G., 156
Jensen, E. L., 133, 196
Jermier, J. M., 38, 39
Jesilow, P. D., 170
Jesseman, R., 248, 251
Jessica's Law, 6
Jesus, Zehy, 159
Jimmy Ryce State Civil Commitment Program
    for Sexually Dangerous Persons, 149
Job training, 232–234
Johnson, B. D., 192, 195
Johnson, G., 6
Johnson, K. A., 266
Johnson, L. C., 282
  see also Lovell, D.
Johnson, Lyndon, 8
Johnson, M. P., 101, 116
Johnson, R., 278, 280
  see also Hahn, R.; McGowan, A.
Johnson, Ruiz v. (1999), 285
Johnson, W. W., 211, 218, 219, 277, 318
Johnston, D., 232
Joint Terrorism Task Force (JTTF), 83
Jonaitis, A., 172
Jones, Bill, 263
Jones-Correa, M., 90, 94, 96, 97
Jones, D. A., 108, 117
Jones 'El v. Berge (2001), 285
Jones, N., 312, 313
Jones, R., 318
Jones, United States v. (2012), 335, 337
Jonson, C., 310, 311, 314, 315, 318, 319, 321
Jordan, C. E., 108
Jordan, K. L., 195, 197
Josephson, M., 160
*Journal of the American Medical
    Association (JAMA)*, 130, 162
Joy, J., 130
Juarez, Mexico, 182
Judicial veto power, 305

Judicial waiver, 192
Junginger, J., 211
Jurek v. Texas (1976), 294
Jurisdictional hazards, 68
Jury nullification, 294
Justice and Mental Health Collaboration Program (JMHCP), 211–212
Justice Department, 2, 33, 131, 161, 183, 184, 194, 196, 207, 242 (box), 245
Justice Policy Institute, 3 (figure), 91, 134, 265
Just Say No campaign, 124 (table)
Juvenile Justice and Delinquency Prevention Act (1974), 4 (table)
Juvenile justice system, 176, 191–193, 328
Juvenile Law Center, 194
Juvenile sex offenders, 155–156
Juvenile waiver policies
    capital punishment statutes, 329
    current policy state, 193–195
    estimated number of offenders, 193–195
    evidentiary research results, 195–196
    gang members, 184
    historical perspective, 191–192, 328
    policy reform, 198–199
    race, gender, and class implications, 196–197
    unintended consequences, 195–198
    youth versus adult correctional facilities, 197–198

Kadela, K. R., 316
Kadleck, C., 150, 155
Kafauver-Harris Amendments (1962), 123 (table)
Kagan, Elena, 329
Kahan, J., 138
Kalanj, B., 247
    see also Umbreit, M. S.
Kalb, K., 209
Kalven, H., 267
Kamin, S., 265
    see also Zimring, F. E.
Kaminski, R. J., 265
Kane, J., 76
Kane, M., 320
Kanka, Megan, 7, 147–148
Kansas
    capital punishment statutes, 306
    defense counsel performance guidelines, 302

DNA collection, 336
    mandatory arrest policies, 106, 107
Kansas City Preventive Patrol Experiment, 16, 55
Kaplan, L. E., 237
Kaplan, T., 269, 270, 272
Kaplan, W. J., 196
Kappeler, V. E., 70, 71, 72
Karp, D. R., 243
Katz v. United States (1967), 334
Kazmierczak, Stephen, 331
KCET, 270
Keenan, Jerry, 268
Keith, F., 211
Kelley, R. B., 161
Kelling, G. L., 55, 58, 59, 61, 62, 63–64, 164, 209, 263, 330
Kelly, L.
    see Kupers, T. A.
Kelsey, Frances, 162
Kendall, K., 233
Kennard, A. D., 203
    see also Torrey, E. F.
Kennard, D., 316
Kennedy, Anthony, 93–94, 222
Kennedy, D. M., 61, 185
Kennedy, John F., 162
Kennedy, L. W., 57
Kenney, J. W., 150
Kennon, S. S., 233
Kentucky, 302
Kentucky, Stanford v. (1989), 329
Kerlikowske, Gil, 142
Kerner Commission, 8
Kerr, A. N.
    see Watson, A. C.
Kerr, T., 128, 139
    see also Wood, E.
Kerry, John, 124 (table)
Kerwin, D., 89, 91
Kessler, D. P., 41
Kesten, K. L., 214, 221
Khantzian, E. J., 208
Kiewiet, D. R., 44
Kigerl, A., 312, 316
Killebrew, R., 183–184
Kilmer, A., 154
Kimball, P., 278, 280
Kimisopa, B., 258
Kingdon, J. W., 262, 270
King, K., 279, 281, 284, 285, 287

King, Maryland v. (2013), 337
King, R. D., 276, 277, 280, 281, 288, 290
King, Rodney, 48
King, R. S., 135, 253, 254
King, S., 213
    see also Herinckx, H. A.
Kingsbury, A., 183
Kirk, D. S., 97, 316
Kirkorian, G., 135
Kitchener experiment, 242 (box), 247
Klaas, Polly, 263, 267, 273
Klahm, C., 42
Klebold, Dylan, 331
Kleck, G., 266
Kleiman, M., 328
Klein-Saffran, J., 284
    see also Gaes, G. G.
Klein, S. P., 264
    see also Greenwood, P. W.
Kleist, J., 221
Kling, J. R., 198
Klite, P., 11
Knight, C. R., 297
Knouss, R., 81
Know Nothing Party, 94
Knutsson, J., 61
Koebler, J., 335
Kohli, A., 93, 97
Komaie, G., 95
Koons, B. A., 225, 227, 230, 236, 238
    see also Morash, M.
Koons-Witt, B. A., 233
    see also Schram, P. J.
Kort-Butler, L. A., 12
Kostelac, C., 114
Koutsenok, I. B., 316
Kovandzic, T. V., 265
Kramer, J., 266
Kravets, D., 268
Krejci, M., 181
Krienert, J. L., 280
Krisberg, B., 327, 328
Krivo, L. J., 283
Kruttschnitt, C., 229
Kubrin, C. E., 316
Kupchik, A., 192, 195, 196, 197, 198
Kupers, T. A., 281, 286
Kurki, L., 278, 284, 287
Kurlychek, M. C., 192, 195, 266
Kyckelhahn, T., 75

Labecki, L. A., 311
Laglagaron, L., 96
Lagos, M., 132
Lain, C. B., 294
Lakshmi, R., 76
Lamb, D., 361
Lambert, S., 21
Lamb, H. R., 361
Lamb, R., 203
    see also Torrey, E. F.
Landa, Adam, 13
Landenberger, N. A., 315
Lane, J., 11, 196
Lane, R., 177
Langan, N., 284
    see also Camp, S.
Langan, P., 152
Langevin, R., 148
Lanza, Adam, 201, 206, 331
Lanza-Kaduce, L., 196
Lapidus, L., 135
Larson, R. C., 55
Laser radar (LIDAR), 335
Lasley, J., 61
Las Vegas Boulevard (the Strip), 58
Las Vegas Police Department, 82
Latessa, E. J., 315, 318, 319, 320
Latham & Watkins (law firm), 171
Latimer, J., 249, 251, 253
Latin American Commission on Drugs and
    Democracy, 140
Latino Americans
    acculturation impacts, 96
    California incarceration and realignment
        practices, 325
    capital punishment, 299
    disadvantaged neighborhoods, 283
    drug use and arrests, 129, 130, 134
    gang violence, 188, 189, 283
    gender responsive practices, 237
    immigration enforcement, 75, 96–97
    incarceration rates, 5, 134, 142, 237, 254,
        282, 313
    intimate partner violence, 111, 112
    juvenile waiver policies, 197
    mentally ill offenders, 216
    parolees, 312
    state control policies, 313
    supermax confinement, 282–284
    Three Strikes Law, 266

Lattimore, P. K., 317, 318, 319
    see also Winterfield, L.
Laufer, W. S., 166
Lavelle, M., 302
Law and Society Association, 298
Law Enforcement Assistance Agency
    (LEAA), 16
Law-in-action, 37, 45
Lawless, M. W., 55
Law, M. A., 284
Law-on-the-books, 37, 45
Lawrence, R., 328
Lawrence, S., 316
Laygo, R., 211
    see also Junginger, J.
Lay, Kenneth, 171
League of Women Voters California
    Education Fund, 264
Leavenworth Federal Penitentiary, 281
Leavitt-Smith, E., 214
    see also Kesten, K. L.
Lee, E., 88
Lee, H. K., 271
Lee, M. T., 95
Lee, N., 135
Lee, R., 77
Legalization, drug, 126
Legislative Analyst Office, 273, 326
Lehman Brothers Holdings, 168
Lehman, J. D., 311
Lejeune, C., 89
Lelyveld, J., 172
Lemmon, J. H., 253
Leonard, J., 268, 269, 272
Leon, C. S., 145, 146, 148, 149, 152, 155, 156
Lesbian population, 113–114
Leshner, A., 127
Lessard v. Schmidt (1972), 205
Less punitive drug policies, 137–140
Lester, D., 298
Letourneau, E. J., 156
Leukefeld, C. G., 230
    see also Adams, S.
Level of Service Inventory-Revised (LSI-R), 230
Levenson, J. S., 145, 154
Leverentz, A., 226
Levin, D., 152
Levine, H. G., 129
Levingston, K.
    see Lapidus, L.

Lewis, G. B., 46
Lewis, O., 160
Lewis, Peter, 133
Liberal politics, 7–8
Liberation hypothesis, 267
Liberman, A., 195, 196
    see also Hahn, R.; McGowan, A.
Libertarian Party, 333
License plate readers, 335
Liebman, J. S., 297
Life-course-persistent offenders, 19
Life imprisonment without opportunity of
    parole (LWOP), 295, 297–298, 329
LifeSkills Training (LST), 26 (table), 31
Lifestyle choices, 172
Lightfoot, E., 241
    see also Umbreit, M. S.
Lindquist, C., 317
    see also Lattimore, P. K.; Winterfield, L.
Ling, L., 184
Linhorst, D. M., 213, 219
Lin, J., 311
    see also Grattet, R.
Link, B. G.
    see Phelan, J. C.
Linn, L., 205
Lipkin, R., 247
    see also Umbreit, M. S.
Lipsey, M. W., 315
Lipsky, M., 39, 40, 42, 43, 44–45, 46, 47, 48, 49
Liptak, A., 142
*Lira v. California Director of
    Corrections* (2008), 286, 287, 290
Listwan, S. J., 312
Litschge, C. M., 207, 220
Little Village Gang Violence Reduction
    Project, 184
Llewellyn, J., 248
Lobbyists, 159
LoBuglio, S., 209
Location-oriented interventions, 56
Lockdown prisons
    see Supermax confinement
Lockyer v. Andrade (2003), 267
Loeber, R., 20, 21, 24
Loeffler, C., 283
Lofstrom, M., 327
Logan, T. K., 101
Logan, W. A., 148
Longmire, D. R., 284

Long-term tracking, 335
Looney, R., 79
Lopez, M., 97
Lord, E. A., 226, 231, 232, 234, 283
Los Angeles County, California, 266, 269
Los Angeles County Jail, 218, 327
Los Angeles Police Department, 48, 187
Los Angeles Times, 268
Losoya, S.
    see also Loughran, T. A.
Loughner, Jared, 202, 331
Loughran, T. A., 363
Louisiana
    capital punishment statutes, 329
    DNA collection, 336
    mandatory arrest policies, 106, 107
Louisiana, Roberts v. (1976), 294
Louw, D. J., 245, 246
Lovell, D., 211, 214, 221, 281, 282, 283
    see also Cloyes, K. G.
Lowenkamp, C. T., 315, 319
Lowen, M., 283
Low-income women, 112–113
Low-rate offenders, 19
Loyalties, 39
Lucas, W., 32
Ludwig, J., 63
Lundy, S. E., 113, 114
Lupia, A., 44
Lurigio, A. J., 209, 217, 221, 222
Luskin, M. L., 213, 216
Lussier, P., 216
    see also Nicholls, T. L.
Luthra, N.
    see Lapidus, L.
Lutze, F. E., 312, 313, 316, 317, 318, 320
Lychner, Pam, 148
Lymphoma Association of America, 130
Lyndes, K.
    see Spergel, I. A.
Lyon, W., 82

MacCharles, T., 140
MacCoun, R., 126, 138
MacDonald, J., 94, 95
MacDonald, P. T., 12
MacDonald, Z., 312
MacDowall, D., 196
MacKenzie, D. L., 17–19 (table), 134, 314, 315, 316

    see also Sherman, L. W.; Wilson, D. B.
Mackintosh, V. H., 233
MacKinzie-Mulvey, E., 77
MacLean, B. A., 180
MacQueen, R., 140
MacRae, A., 247, 249, 255
Madensen, T. D., 61
Madhani, A., 331–332
Madison, Bruce, 132
Madoff, Bernie, 173
Madrid v. Gomez (1995), 285
"Magic bullet" programs, 176, 185, 187, 188
Maguin, E., 226
    see also Browne, A.
Maguire, B., 11
Maier, P., 160
Maine, 106
Main, F., 186
Major Cities Chiefs Association (MCCA), 98
Makarios, M. D., 315
Malby, S., 182
    see also Me, A.
Malcolm, J. G., 329
Mallicoat, S. L., 122–125 (table)
Mallik-Kane, K., 4
Malvo, John Lee, 82
Manatu-Rupert, N., 231, 237
Manchak, S., 207, 212
    see also Skeem, J. L.
Mandatory arrest
    arrest rates, 108, 117
    coordinated community response
        policy, 116
    current policy state, 106–107
    definition, 102
    deterrence theory, 105–106, 108, 117
    evidentiary research results, 108–109
    formal sanctions, 117
    gender, 109–111
    historical perspective, 103–106
    immigration status, 114–115
    local and state policies, 106–107
    mandatory action policies, 115–117
    policy consequences, 117–118
    policy reform, 115–117
    primary aggressor statutes, 116–117
    race and ethnicity, 111–112
    recidivism, 105–106, 108, 117
    same-sex relationships, 113–114
    social class, 112–113

    see also Intimate partner violence
Mandatory death penaly statutes, 294
Mandatory minimum sentencing policies,
        121, 128–130, 141–143, 329
Maniac Latin Disciples, 186
Mann, J., 212, 213, 222
Mann, K., 171–172
MAOA gene, 20
Maori population, 245, 255
Marchionna, S., 328
Maric, A., 146
Marihuana Tax Act (1937), 123 (table), 125
Marijuana
    arrest rates, 128
    Canada, 139
    decriminalization policies, 124
        (table), 188
    Europe, 137–139
    federal enforcement and control
        legislation, 123 (table), 125–127
    legalization measures, 132–133, 141
    medical marijuana laws, 130–132
    Netherlands, 137–138
    racial and ethnic perceived use, 125–126
Marín, M. C., 214
Marion penitentiary, 276–277, 281
Markovitz, J., 187
Markowitz, P. L., 93
    see also Kohli, A.
Marquart, J. W., 263, 278
Marsch, L., 127
Marshall, B., 139
Marshall, W. L., 150
Marsolais, K., 316
Martinez, R., Jr., 95
Martin, J., 131, 132
Martin, M., 268
Martin, M. E., 110
Martinson, R., 310–311
Martinson Report, 310–311
Martin, S. S., 233, 316
    see also Butzin, C. A.; Robbins, C. A.
Martin, Trayvon, 7
Maruschak, L. M., 225, 226, 231, 232, 234
Marvell, T. B., 265
Maryland
    capital punishment statutes, 297, 301
    DNA collection, 336
    juvenile justice system, 193, 330
    medical marijuana laws, 131

Maryland v. King (2013), 337
Maschi, T., 214
    see also Wolff, N.
Mason, C., 91
Massachusetts
    drug laws, 129–130
    mental illness reforms, 202–203, 220
Massachusetts Supreme Court, 103
Mass incarceration, 176, 178, 179, 183, 184
Mass media
    fear of crime, 11–13
    gang violence coverage, 176, 178, 187
    undocumented immigrants, 94
Mass shootings, 13, 201–202, 330–331
Mathews, J., 268
Mathews, R., 61
Maton, K. I., 117
Matthews, W., 285
Mauer, M., 134, 135, 237, 253, 254
Mauro, R., 301
Maxfield, M., 22, 58
Maxson, C., 22
Maxwell, C. D., 106, 108–109, 113, 117
Maxwell, G., 252
May, D., 11
Mayer, L. C., 2, 5 (figure)
Maynard-Moody, S., 39, 42–45, 46, 48
Mayors Against Illegal Guns, 333
May, R., 234
    see also Camp, C. G.
Mays, G. L., 192
McAdam, D., 279
McAfee, Commonwealth v. (1871), 103
McBride, J.
    see Kupers, T. A.
McCabe, K., 89, 93
McCaffrey, Barry, 131
McCarthy, Garry, 185–186
McCarty, W. P., 320
McCauley, C., 279
McClellan, D. S., 231, 232
McCold, P., 242, 244, 245, 247
McCord, J., 22
McCormick, J. S., 146
McCubbins, M. D., 44
McDevitt, J. F., 344
McDonald, J. M., 250
McDonald, L. G., 168
McDonald v. Chicago (2010), 332
McGaha, A., 220

McGarrell, E. F., 61, 250, 252, 253
McGeever, K. F., 87
    see also Stowell, J. I.
McGill University, 162
McGovern, S. K., 380
McGowan, A., 196
    see also Hahn, R.
McGuire, Jerome, 272
McKay, H. D., 177
McKay, John, 132
McKean, J., 134
McKendrick, K., 214
    see also Sacks, S.
McKenzie, M., 2, 5 (figure)
McKinley, J., 132
McLaren, R. C., 54–55
McLearen, A. M., 215–216
McManus, J. H., 178
McNiel, D. E., 213, 220
McShane, M. D., 233
McVeigh, Timothy, 297
Me, A., 182, 183, 185, 186
Mead, Margaret, 255
Mears, D. P., 277, 278, 279, 280, 281, 282,
    283, 287, 288, 290, 316
Media consumption, 11–13
Medical drugs, 122
Medical fraud, 170
Medical marijuana laws, 130–132
Medicare/Medicaid, 206
Medillín, Colombia, 182
Medina, J., 179
Megan's Law (1996), 7, 148
Mehra, S., 213
Meissner, D., 89, 91, 93
    see also Mittelstadt, M.
Mele, C., 311, 313
Melick, M. E., 208
Mello, M., 302
Mellow, J., 209
Meloy, M. L., 145
Mendelson, M., 90
Menjívar, C., 115
Mennonite Central Committee, 247
Mental health courts, 212–213, 219–220,
    221, 222
Mental hospitals, 202, 203, 204–206
Mentally ill criminal offenders
    arrest factors, 208–209
    civil commitment laws, 220–221

    Community Mental Health (CMH)
        movement, 204–206
    evidentiary research results, 212–214
    female offenders, 227, 231–232
    historical perspective, 202–206
    incarceration rates, 203–204, 207–209,
        208 (figure), 211, 218–219, 222, 256
    jails, prisons, and asylums, 203–204
    juvenile offenders, 198
    legislative reforms, 219, 220–221
    mental health courts, 212–213, 219–220,
        221, 222
    offender treatment, 211–212
    policy reform, 219–223
    prisoner reentry and aftercare programs,
        214, 222
    psychiatric and psychological
        approaches, 204
    psychiatric care programs, 205–208, 211,
        215–216, 218–223
    race, ethnicity, gender, and class
        implications, 215–217
    recent cases, 201–202
    recidivism, 211, 212–214, 215 (figure),
        221, 222
    reform efforts, 203–206, 219–221
    sexual offenders, 149
    specialty mental health probation, 214
    supermax confinement, 280–281, 285,
        290–291
    unintended consequences, 217–219
Mentally Ill Offender Treatment and Crime
    Reduction Act (2004), 211–212, 219
Mercado, C. C., 145
Merced County, California, 327
Mercy bookings, 209, 217
Merriam-Webster Dictionary, 1
Merrick, M. T.
    see Black, M. C.
Merrill Lynch, 163
Merritt, N., 266
    see also Greenwood, P. W.
Mesh-tightening, 134
Mesloh, Debbie, 266
Messer, G., 150
Messina, N., 211
Messner, S. F., 87
    see also Stowell, J. I.
Meta hazards, 68
Methadone Control Act (1973), 124 (table)

Methadone Maintenance (1963), 123 (table)
Methadone maintenance programs, 123 (table), 127, 138, 140
Methylenedioxymethamphetamine (MDMA), 138
Metraux, S., 316
    see also Culhane, D. P.
Metsger, L. K., 196
Mexican Mafia, 278
Mexico, 186
Meyer, Adolf, 204
Miccio, G. K., 104
Michaelson, A., 168
Michel, L., 297
Michigan, 336
Michigan, Harmelin v. (1991), 297
Miethe, T. D., 151
Mignon, S. I., 108, 110, 117
Migration Policy Institute, 90
Mihm, S., 76
Miletich, S., 133
Miller, A., 229
Miller, B., 226
    see also Browne, A.
Miller, J., 79, 179
Miller, J. E., 206
Miller, J. L., 40
Miller, M., 316
Miller, S. L., 110, 111, 145
Miller, T. A., 311, 313
Miller v. Alabama (2012), 181, 184, 329
Miller, W., 177, 178, 180
Milloy, C. D., 153
Milloy, M-. J., 139
Mills, David, 270
Mills, Linda, 109
Miner, M. H., 156
Minneapolis Domestic Violence Experiment (MDVE), 105–106
Minneapolis Police Department, 105
Minnesota
    DNA collection, 336
    restorative justice programs, 242 (box), 248
    sexual offender legislation, 147
    supermax confinement, 280, 282
Minnesota Restitution Center, 243
Minority neighborhoods, 23–24
Minority offenders
    see Ethnicity; Race

Minority women, 111–112, 135, 237, 313
    see also Ethnicity; Gender responsive practices; Race
Mintz, H., 272
Minushkin, S., 97
Mississippi, 106, 107, 303
Mississippi Department of Corrections, 286
Mississippi State Penitentiary, 286
Missouri
    capital punishment statutes, 296, 306, 329
    DNA collection, 336
    mandatory arrest policies, 106, 107
Mitchell, O., 125, 134, 151
Mitigating factors, 294–295, 299–300
Mitnik, P. A., 92
Mittelstadt, M., 91, 92
Mobile phones, 337
Model, K. E., 264
    see also Greenwood, P. W.
Modestin, J., 208
Moffitt, T., 19, 20
Monahan, J., 217
    see also Swartz, M. S.
Monahan, T., 83
Money laundering, 77–79
Monkkonen, E., 177
Monopolies, 160–161
Montana, 135
Montaner, J. SG., 128, 139
    see also Wood, E.
Montañez, Jacqueline, 180–181
Moody, C. E., 265
Moore, D. B., 250
Moore, G. E., 243
Moore, L., 186
Moore, M. E., 213, 220
Moore, M. H., 58, 59
Moore, M. J., 263
Moore N., 183, 186
Morabito, A., 82
Morabito, M. S.
    see Watson, A. C.
Morash, M., 20, 225, 226, 227, 228, 229, 230, 231, 232, 233, 235, 237
    see also Chesney-Lind, M.; Koons, B. A.; Schram, P. J.
Moratorium on executions, 306
Morenoff, J. D., 23, 94
    see also Sampson, R. J.
Moreno, I., 332

Morgan, C. V., 95
Morgan, J., 130, 138
Morgan, M., 11
Morgenson, G., 163
Moritz, Jeffrey, 210
Morning-after birth control medicine, 162–163
Morphine, 122
Morris, A., 252
Morris, L. S., 211
Morris, N., 278, 284, 287
Morris, R. G., 284
Morrissey, J. P., 203, 204, 205, 206
Morris, T. J.
    see Kupers, T. A.
Morton-Bourgon, K., 152
Moser, L. L.
    see Van Dorn, R. A.
Mosher, C., 122, 126, 133, 139
Mossman, D., 205
Moteff, J., 72
Motion picture industry, 161
Mounts, S. E., 40
Moynihan, C., 82
Mozilo, Angelo, 168
MS-13 (gang), 184
Muckrackers, 160
Mueller, J., 84
Muenzenmaier, K.
    see Phelan, J. C.
Muhammad, John Allen, 82
Muise, D., 249
    see also Latimer, J.
Mukamal, D., 209
Mulgrew, I., 139
Multidimensional Treatment Foster Care (MTFC), 26 (table)
Multisystemic Therapy (MST), 27 (table)
Mulvey, E. P., 217
    see also Loughran, T. A.
Mumola, C. J., 135, 225, 226, 232, 233
Munetz, M. R., 221
Munro, C. R., 162
Muolo, P., 165
Murphy, C. M., 117
Musheno, M., 39, 42–45, 46, 48
Musser, P. H., 117
Mustaine, E. E., 155
Musto, D. F., 128
Muwakkil, S., 297

Myers, B. J., 233
Myers, D. L., 195, 196

NAACP Legal Defense and Educational
    Fund (LDF), 293
Naat'aanii, 245
Nadelmann, E., 127, 131
Nagin, D. S., 108
Nahat'a, 246
Napolitano, J., 90
Narag, R. E., 287
Narcotic Addict Rehabilitation Act (1966),
    123 (table)
Narcotic Drug Import & Export Act (1922),
    122 (table)
Narcotics Control Act (1956), 123 (table)
National Academy Press, 130
National Association For Community Medi-
    ation (NAFCM), 244
National Association for the Advancement
    of Colored People (NAACP), 293
National Association of Drug Court Profes-
    sionals (NADCP), 134
National Association of Prosecutors and
    Criminal Defense Attorneys, 130
National Association of School Psycholo-
    gists (NASP), 330
National Center for Injury Prevention and
    Control, 101
National Center for State Courts, 302, 303
National Center on Addiction and
    Substance Abuse, 141
National Clearinghouse for the Defense of
    Battered Women, 111
National Coalition Against Domestic
    Violence (NCADV), 107
National Commission on Terrorist Attacks
    Upon the United States, 77
National Conference of State Legislatures,
    93, 96, 261
National Crime Victimization Survey, 262
National Cybersecurity and Communications
    Integration Center, 77
National Day Laborer Organizing Network
    (NDLON), 92
National Disaster Medical System, 81
National Drug Court Resource Center, 133
National Family Violence Survey, 112
National Fugitive Operations Program
    (NFOP), 90

National Gang Center, 178, 179
National Immigration Forum, 89, 91
National Incident Based Reporting System
    (NIBRS), 108
National Incident Management System
    (NIMS), 80–81
National Institute of Corrections (NIC), 229,
    236, 238, 275, 277, 291
National Institute of Justice (NIJ), 16,
    17, 105
National Institute of Law Enforcement and
    Criminal Justice (NILECJ), 16
National Institute of Mental Health, 205
National Institute on Drug Abuse
    (NIDA), 129
National Institute on Money in State
    Politics, 268
National Institutes of Health (NIH), 130
National Intimate Partner and Sexual
    Violence Survey, 111
National Opinion Research Center, 94
National Organization for Victim Assistance
    (NOVA), 245
National Response Framework, 79–80
National Rifle Association, 13
National Rifle Association (NRA), 263,
    332, 333
National security, 68
National Security Entry-Exit Registration
    System (NSEERS), 90
National Survey of Latinos, 97
National Violence Against Women Survey
    (NVAWS), 108
National Vital Statistics, 182 (figure)
Native Americans
    incarceration rates, 134–135
    intimate partner violence, 111
    mentally ill offenders, 216
    restorative justice programs, 245
    virtue ethics, 172
Nature-nurture debate, 20
Navajo Peacemaker Courts, 242 (box),
    245, 246
Nebraska, 329
Needels, K. E., 198
Needle exchange programs, 127, 138, 140
Negroponte, M., 127
Nellis, A. M., 11, 13
Netherlands, 137–138
Netherlands Ministry of Health, 137

Net-widening, 134, 288
Neufeld, P., 302
Nevada, 106, 131
Newark Foot Patrol Experiment, 16, 55
New England Journal of Medicine, 130
New Hampshire, 303, 306
New Jersey
    capital punishment statutes, 297
    drug laws, 129, 130
    intensive supervision programs
        (ISP), 320
    mandatory arrest policies, 106
New Jerseyans for Alternatives to the Death
    Penalty (NJADP), 297
New Jersey Commission to Review
    Criminal Sentencing, 130
New Jim Crow practices, 254, 256
Newman, A., 82
New Mexico
    capital punishment statutes, 297
    DNA collection, 336
New penology, 277
Newport, F., 94
News programming, 11
Newton, L., 94, 96
Newton, P., 129
Newtown, Connecticut, 201, 206, 331
New York
    community justice programs,
        243–244, 254
    drug policies, 142
    homicide rates, 186, 298
    juvenile waiver policies, 194, 199
    mandatory arrest policies, 106, 107
    mentally ill offenders, 220
    restorative justice programs, 242 (box), 248
    sexual offender legislation, 153–154
    tough-on-crime policies, 263
*New York Central and Hudson River
    Railroad v. United States*
    (1908), 171
New York City Police Department, 82
New York City Youth Board, 177
New York Police Department, 48
New York State Office of Mental Health,
    220, 221
New York subway, 55
New York Times, 131, 136, 203
New Zealand
    drug policies, 140

restorative justice programs, 245,
246–247, 251, 252, 255
Ngugi, I., 316
Nguyen, N., 321
Nicholas, Henry T., III, 268
Nicholl, C. G., 243
Nicholls, T. L., 216
Night Prosecutor Program, 243–244
9/11 terrorist attacks, 67
Nixon, Richard, 9, 123 (table)
Noble, J. H.
see Torrey, E. F.
No-drop prosecution policies, 104
Norquist, Grover, 269–270
North America, 251
North Carolina, 194
North Carolina Supreme Court, 103
North Carolina, Woodson v. (1976), 294
North Dakota, 336
Northern Illinois University, 331
"Nothing works" concept, 310–311
Nova Scotia Restorative Justice Program,
242 (box)
Nuclear materials, 70
Nugent, W., 251
Nuisance crimes, 206, 208, 220, 330
Nurse-Family Partnerships (NFP), 27
(table)
Nussbaumer, C., 208
Nygard, S., 221

Oakland Police Department, 104, 111
Obama administration, 91–92, 142
Obama, Barack, 71, 76, 131, 133, 331, 333
O'Brien, C., 127
Occupational common sense, 42
O'Connell, D. J., 316
see also Butzin, C. A.
Office of Criminal Justice Services, 153
Office of Justice Programs, 147, 148
Office of Juvenile Justice and Delinquency
Prevention (OJJDP), 33, 242 (box)
Office of National Drug Control Policy
(ONDCP), 127, 143
Office of the Assistant Secretary for
Planning and Evaluation (ASPE), 136
Ohio
capital punishment, 303
defense counsel performance
guidelines, 303

mandatory arrest policies, 106, 107
mentally ill offenders, 218
restorative justice programs, 242 (box),
244, 248
sexual offenders, 153
state prisons, 286
supermax confinement, 284, 285, 286
Ohio Department of Rehabilitation and
Correction, 145, 147, 148, 149, 154,
284, 286
Ohio Sentencing Commission, 152–153
Ohio State Penitentiary, 286
O'Keefe, E., 332
O'Keefe, M. L., 283
Oklahoma
capital punishment statutes, 306, 329
Oklahoma City bombing, 70
Oliver, M. B., 12
Oliver, W. M., 9
Olson, J., 151
Olweus Bullying Prevention Program, 29
(table)
Omnibus Crime Control and Safe Streets
Act (1968), 16–17
Omnibus Drug Act (1988), 124 (table)
"Once waived, always waived" rule, 192, 193
One Flew Over the Cuckoo's Nest
(film), 205
Operation Ceasefire, 61
Opiate replacement therapy, 127
Opinion polls, 262–263, 268, 269
Opium, 122, 127, 138
Opium and Narcotic Drug Act (1908), 139
Opium Exclusion Act (1909), 122 (table)
Opium Poppy Control Act (1942), 123
(table)
Orbis Partners, Inc., 236
Order maintenance policing, 61–62
Oregon
defense counsel performance
guidelines, 302
mandatory arrest policies, 106
marijuana legalization measures,
132–133
Organizational cultures, 39
Organized crime, 177–178, 180
Orloff, L. E., 115
Ornuma, T., 96
Orsagh, T., 182
Osborne, J., 209

O'Shaughnessy, M. V.
see also Wood, E.
Osher, F. C., 207, 216
see also Prins, S. J.; Steadman, H. J.
Otis, K. E., 380
Outcome evaluation, 2
Outpatient civil commitment, 221, 222
Over-classification, 229
Overt acts, 205
Owen, B., 225, 226, 229, 232, 239
see also Bloom, B.

Pacific Islanders, 111
Packer, H., 10
Packer, Herbert, 10, 332
Paddock, J., 251
Padgett, K., 11
Pager, Devah, 197
Palmer, N., 83
Palmer, T., 310
Pam Lychner Sexual Offender Tracking and
Identification Act (1996), 148
Pandiani, J. A., 206
Papachristos, A. V., 59, 60, 97
see also Braga, A. A.
Paparozzi, M., 320
Papua New Guinea, 257–259
Papua New Guinea Law and Justice
Sector, 258
Paramount Pictures, United States v.
(1948), 161
Paramount Pictures, United States v.
(1949), 161
Paranoid schizophrenia, 210, 222
parens patriae, 328
Parent-Child Interaction Therapy (PCIT),
29 (table)
Parenting programs, 232
Parenting skills, 21–22
Parks, R., 55
Parry-Jones, W. L., 203–204
Parsons, C., 333
Parsons, J., 327
Parthasarathy, B., 4
Participatory accountability, 47
Pasko, L., 181
Pate, A. M., 55, 117
Pate, Cooper v. (1964), 326
Paternoster, R., 146, 301
Paterson, David, 142

Pate, T., 55

Pathways Perspective, 231

Pattavina, A., 106, 107, 108, 113, 114, 117
    see also Hirschel, D.

Paul, Ron, 169

Pavle, J., 203
    see also Torrey, E. F.

Peacemaker Courts, 242 (box), 245, 246

Peacemaking circles, 242 (box), 249

Peachy, D. E., 247

Peden, A. R., 230
    see also Adams, S.

Peer Assisted Learning Strategies (PALS),
    29 (table)

Pelican Bay State prison, 284

Pelikan, C., 249, 252

Penal systems
    see Prison industry; Supermax
        confinement

Penitentiaries
    see Prison industry; Supermax
        confinement

Pennsylvania, 194, 300

Pentagon terrorist attacks, 67

People v. Fuhrman (1997), 267

People v. Superior Court (Romero)
    (1996), 264, 267

Peralta, E., 331

Perceived worthiness, 43–44, 46

Perkins, P. J., 302

Perkins, U. E., 177

Permissive drug policies, 137–140

Perpetrator-oriented interventions, 56

Perrow, C., 73

Perry, J., 241

Perry, J. L., 46

Personal Responsibility and Work Opportu-
    nities Reconciliation Act (1996), 135

Personal victimization, 10–11

Petaluma, California, 263

Petersilia, J., 263, 272, 298, 311, 312, 313,
    316, 317, 318, 320, 321, 327
    see also Grattet, R.

Peterson, D., 179

Peterson, G. A., 221

Peterson, J. K., 207, 211, 212, 214
    see also Skeem, J. L.

Peterson, K., 209

Peterson, P. D., 211
    see also Lovell, D.

Peterson, R. D., 283

Peters, R. H., 215

Petrila, J., 213, 220

Petros, G., 247
    see also Umbreit, M. S.

Petrosino, C., 228

Petteruti, A., 134
    see also Beatty, P.

Pew Center on the States, 248, 311, 312,
    313, 327

Pew Hispanic Center, 74

Phelan, J. C., 221

Philadelphia, Pennsylvania, 300

Phillips, N. D., 12

Phillips, S. A., 183, 299, 300

Phocomelia, 162

Physical disorder, 58

Physicians' Association for AIDS Care, 130

Piehl, A. M., 41, 61, 94, 318
    see also Braga, A. A.; Kennedy, D. M.

Pierce, G. L., 56, 301

Pignal, S., 138

Pineda-Moreno, United States v. (2010), 337

Pinkerton, J., 98

Pinkerton, S., 139

Pin maps, 54

Piquero, A. R., 156
    see also Loughran, T. A.

Pisciotta, A., 310, 318

Piven, F., 279

Pizarro, J. M., 40, 276, 277, 281, 285, 287

Pizzo, S., 165

Plan B (morning-after pill), 163

Plata, Brown v. (2011), 272, 326

Platt, A. M., 191

Pled and proved provision, 264, 270–271

Plett, T. N., 165

Pleysier, S., 10

Plumer, B., 333

Podus, D., 316

Poey, E. L., 380

Police
    community policing, 59, 82–83, 99
    homeland security, 81–83
    immigration enforcement, 96–99
    intimate partner violence, 113
    investigation and interrogation
        guidelines, 303
    mentally ill offenders, 208–209, 215–218
    misconduct, 48, 304

police brutality, 46, 48

police culture, 39
    see also Gang violence; Intimate partner
        violence

Police Foundation, 98

Policy implementation, 37, 40, 49–50

Policy process, stages of, 1–2

Political accountability, 47–48

Pollini, S., 139

Pollock, J. M., 233, 234, 235–236

Pontell, H. N., 163, 165, 166, 170

Ponzi schemes, 166

Poor neighborhoods, 23–24

Poor women, 112–113

Pope, C., 142

Portes, A., 95

Portugal, 138–139

Positive Family Support-Family Check Up,
    29 (table)

Posner, R., 164

Post, L., 302

Post-release community supervision
    (PRCS) programs, 326–327

Posttraumatic stress disorder (PTSD),
    197, 198

Potler, C., 237
    see also Mauer, M.

Poverty, 112–113, 135, 217, 227, 313
    see also Socioeconomic status

Powder cocaine, 129, 142

Poythress, N. G., 213, 220

Pranis, K., 179, 245, 246

Pratt, T., 40, 276
    see also Pizarro, J. M.

Predatory street crimes, 164

Prendergast, M. L., 211, 316

President's Commission on Law
    Enforcement, 8

Presser, L., 229, 254

Prestige, 172

Preston, J., 90

Prevention programs, 24–33

Primary aggressor statutes, 107, 110,
    116–117

Primary prevention programs, 24

Principal-agent theory, 45–47

Prins, S. J., 216

Prisoner reentry and aftercare programs,
    214, 222
    see also Community corrections

Prison Fellowship International, 247
PrisonPolicy.org, 211, 218
Prison system
    "attention to detail" strategy, 188
    California incarceration and realignment
        practices, 325–328
    disciplinary systems, 280
    drug inmates, 128, 133–135, 188, 237
    economic burden, 311–312, 313, 326
    female offenders, 226–240
    gang culture, 178, 183, 278–280,
        283–284, 287–289
    immigration detainees, 91–93, 98–99
    incapacitation, 261, 265, 278–280
    incarceration rates, 2–5, 128, 253–254
    inmate code of conduct, 278
    juvenile offenders, 196–197
    mentally ill inmates, 203–204, 207–209,
        208 (figure), 211, 218–219,
        222, 256
    minority offenders, 253–254,
        283–284, 311
    overcrowding issues, 325–326
    physical victimization, 312
    population growth, 311–312
    post-release community supervision
        (PRCS) programs, 326–327
    prisoners' constitutional rights, 326
    prisoner security classification systems,
        228–230, 286–287, 289–290
    realignment legislation, 272
    reentry and rehabilitation programs,
        214, 222, 250, 309–323
    restorative justice programs, 250
    Three Strikes Law, 265–266
    youth versus adult correctional facilities,
        197–198
    see also Supermax confinement
Privacy rights, 334–338
Private asylums, 204
Private prisons, 91
Proactive policing, 63–64
Pro-arrest policies, 102, 106–107
Probable cause, 334
Probation and parole officers
    see Community corrections officers
Problem locations, 54
Problem-oriented policing, 33, 53, 59–62
Problem-prone locations, 57–64
Process evaluation, 2

Professional accountability, 47
Proffitt v. Florida (1976), 294
Program fidelity, 31
Progressive Era, 310
Progressive Insurance, 133
Project Northland, 29 (table)
Project Toward No Drug Abuse (TND), 27
    (table)
Promoting Alternative Thinking Strategies
    (PATHS), 27 (table)
Proper woman, 226
Proportionality review, 295
Proposition 19 (California), 132
Proposition 34 (California), 270
Proposition 36 (California), 141, 262, 266,
    267, 268, 269–273
Proposition 66 (California), 262, 267–268,
    269, 270
Proposition 184 (California), 264
Proposition 187 (California), 88
Proposition 215 (California), 141
Prosecuting attorneys, 271, 299, 300–301,
    304, 305
Prosecutorial waiver, 193
Prostitution, 75
Protection orders, 107
Protective factors, 20
Pruett, N., 209
Psychiatric care programs, 205–208, 211,
    215–216, 218–223
Psychological punishment
    see Supermax confinement
Psychological risk factors, 20–21
Psychopathic hospitals, 204
Psychotic disorder not otherwise specified,
    207
Psychotropic medications, 205
Ptacek, J., 111
Public accountability, 41
Public asylums, 204
Public Company Reform and Investor Pro-
    tection Act (2002), 164
Public defenders, 40, 271, 299, 302
Public housing eligibility, 136
Public Policy Institute of California, 269
Public Safety Realignment Act (2011), 326
Public service motivation, 46
Pulaski, C., 301
    see also Baldus, D. C.
Pulling levers interventions, 61

Punishments
    juvenile offenders, 195
    prisons, 280
Pure Food & Drug Act (1906), 122
    (table), 125
Pyschiatric hospitals, 205–206

al Qaeda terrorists, 68, 78–79
Quasi-military organizations, 38
Quicker, J. C., 179
Quick Reads, 29 (table)

Race
    capital punishment, 300–301
    delinquency, 20
    drug court programs, 134
    drug policies, 134–135, 237
    drug use and arrests, 125–126, 129
    female offenders, 237
    gang violence, 176, 177, 180–181,
        283–284
    gender responsive practices, 237
    juvenile waiver policies, 196–197
    mandatory arrest implications, 111–112
    mentally ill criminal offenders, 215–216
    problem-prone locations, 62–64
    racial profiling, 75, 97
    reentry and rehabilitation programs,
        310–311, 313
    restorative justice programs, 253–255
    stop-and-frisk practices, 63
    supermax confinement, 282–284
    Three Strikes Law, 266–267
    white-collar/corporate crime, 170
Racketeer Influenced and Corrupt
    Organizations Act (RICO), 183, 186
Radelet, M. L., 298, 301
Radin, M. J., 295
Radiological weapons, 70
Raffalovich, L. E., 87
    see also Stowell, J. I.
Rafter, N. H., 226, 229, 238
Railroad construction, 160
Raine, A., 20
    see also Moffitt, T.
Raines, State of Maryland v. (2004), 336
Rainville, G. A., 194
Raising Healthy Children, 30 (table)
Ramakrishnan, K., 96
Random preventive patrols, 55

Rank, M. R., 312, 313
Rapaport, E., 299
Raphael, J., 109, 312, 313
Raphael, S., 327
Raudenbush, S., 24, 94
    see also Sampson, R. J.
Rau, D. R.
    see Kesten, K. L.
Rawls, J., 254, 256
Raye, B. E., 248
Raymond, J., 75
Ready, J., 63
Reagan, Ronald, 9, 165, 201, 209
Real ID Act (2005), 76, 93
Realignment, 326
Reality-based crime programming, 11–12
Rearrest rates
    see Recidivism
Reasonable School Discipline Act
    (2013), 330
Reaves, B., 57
Recascino Wise, L., 46
Recidivism
    California prison inmates, 326
    crime reduction strategies, 34
    drug court programs, 133–134
    female offenders, 233–234, 253
    intimate partner violence, 105–106, 108,
        116, 117
    juvenile offenders, 251–253
    juvenile sex offenders, 156
    juvenile waiver policies, 196, 198
    mentally ill criminal offenders, 211,
        212–214, 215 (figure), 221, 222
    parolees, 248
    public perceptions, 12
    restorative justice programs, 244–245,
        250, 251–254
    sexual offenders, 145, 150–155, 152
        (figure)
    supermax confinement, 282
    Three Strikes Law, 261
    victim impact panels, 250
    victim-offender mediation
        programs, 251
    see also Community corrections
Redding, R. E., 196, 198
Red Hook Community Justice Center,
    New York, 243, 254
Redlich, A. D., 213

Reentry and rehabilitation
    California incarceration and realignment
        practices, 325–328
    cognitive-behavioral treatment (CBT)
        programs, 315
    community corrections, 309–310
    community resources, 214, 312–313
    community supervision practices,
        320–321
    coordinated community response,
        317–318, 327
    cultural competency, 317
    current policy state, 312–313
    effective implementation challenges,
        318–321
    evidence-based practices, 314–318
    historical perspective, 310–312
    individual interventions, 315–316
    innovative strategies, 319
    organizational success, 319
    policy reform recommendations,
        321–323
    post-release community supervision
        (PRCS) programs, 326–327
    race, gender, and class implications,
        313–314
    restorative justice programs, 250
    risk assessment tools, 314
    risks, needs, and responsivity (RNR)
        programs, 314–317
    transitioning programs, 222, 312–313
Reentry Court Solutions, 327
Regoli, R., 13, 19, 328
Rehabilitation programs, 195–196, 198
Reid, L. W., 95
Reid, T., 137
Reiman, J., 135, 313
Reinarman, C., 129
Reingold, J., 166
Reinhold, M., 160
Reisig, M. D., 228, 278, 279, 280
Reiss, A. J., 53
Reiter, K. A., 283
Reitz, K. R., 262, 273
Rennison, C. M., 112
Renzetti, C. M., 69
Reoffending rates
    see Recidivism
Repeat crimes
    see Recidivism

Repetto, T., 62
Republican Party, 263, 269–270, 333
Restitution, 244
Restorative Community Justice: A Call
    to Action, 245
Restorative justice
    basic principles, 248–250
    best-practices approach, 255–259
    characteristics, 241
    common themes, 247
    community justice, 243–244, 257–259
    current policy state, 247–250
    drug courts, 133–134
    evidentiary research results, 251–253
    faith-based influences, 247
    First Nations/First Peoples, 245–247
    historical perspective, 241–247, 248
    international programs, 248
    juvenile offenders, 251–253
    Papua New Guinea, 257–259
    policy reform, 255–259
    race, gender, and class implications,
        252–255
    timeline, 242 (box)
    victims' rights movements, 7, 244–245
    village-based cultural philosophies,
        245–247
Restoring Financial Stability Act
    (2010), 169
Retributive justice model, 249, 256, 311, 328
Reuland, M., 209
Reuter, P., 17–19 (table), 126
    see also Sherman, L. W.
Reverse waivers, 193
Reyes, Hector, 181
Reynolds, D., 185
Reynolds, Kimber, 263
Reynolds, Mike, 263, 272
Rhode Island, 106
Rhodes, L. A., 281
    see also Cloyes, K. G.
Rhodes, State v. (1868), 103
Rhodes, W., 320
Riccardi, N., 8
Richards, H., 213, 220
Richards, S. C., 275, 276, 277, 318
Richburg, K., 138
RICO (Racketeer Influenced and Corrupt
    Organizations Act), 183, 186
Ridgeway, G., 63

Ridgway, Gary, 296
Right on Crime, 269
Right to bear arms, 332–333
Rikers Island, 207, 218
Risk assessment tools, 314
Risk factors, 15
Risks, needs, and responsivity (RNR)
   model, 314–317
Ritchie, B. E., 112, 233
Rivas, O., 132
Riveland, C., 275, 276, 280, 284, 287, 288,
   289–290
Rivera, R., 63
Robber Barons, 160
Robbers, M. L., 155
Robbins, C. A., 233, 234
Robbins, P. C., 207, 216
   see also Prins, S. J.; Steadman, H. J.;
      Swartz, M. S.; Van Dorn, R. A.
Robertiello, G., 150
Roberts, A. R., 244
Roberts, A. W., 248
Roberts, J., 316
Roberts, M., 180
Roberts v. Louisiana (1976), 294
Robinson, G., 88
Robinson, J., 208
Robinson, P., 168
Robinson-Patman Act (1936), 161
Roche, D., 241
Rockefeller drug laws, 142
Rodríguez, C., 92, 96
Rodriguez, N., 252, 253, 254
Rogan, D. P., 104
   see also Sherman, L. W.
Rohland, B. M., 221
Rohozinski, R., 71
Rolleston Committee (1926), 122 (table)
Roman, C. G., 243, 312, 316
Roman, J., 133
Roman, J. K., 297
Romer, D., 178
Romney, Mitt, 169
Roosevelt, Franklin D., 88
*Roper, Superintendent, Potosi Correctional
   Center v. Simmons* (2005), 184, 329
Roseborough, D., 249, 251, 252, 253
   see also Bradshaw, W.
Rose, D., 283
Rosenbaum, D., 59, 63

Rosenfeld, R., 108, 182
Rosen, Jeff, 269
Rose, V. M., 146
Rosky, J., 316, 318
   see also Lutze, F. E.
Rosoff, S. M., 166
Ross, C. E., 58
Ross, L., 135
Rossman, D., 196
Ross, S., 20
   see also Moffitt, T.
Rothman, D. J., 191, 204, 318
Rothman, S., 278
Rouse, J., 325
RU-426, 162
Rucker, P., 331
Rugge, T., 248, 320, 321
   see also Bonta, J.
Ruiz v. Johnson (1999), 285
Rule of law, 257
Rumbaut, R. G., 89, 95
Russakoff, D., 82
Russo, G., 178
Rutgers School of Law (Newark), 91
Ruth-Heffelbower, D., 249, 250
Ruth, H. S., 262, 273
Ruttenberg, M. H., 112
Rydell, C. P., 264

Sabol, W. J., 3, 5, 134, 237, 248, 312, 313
   see also Guerino, P.
Sabotage, 45–47
Sacks, J. Y., 214
   see also Sacks, S.
Sacks, S., 214, 221
Sadowski, S. R., 206
Safe Dates, 30 (table)
Safe injection facilities, 139
Safety net model, 256
Safety valves, 264
Salcido, O., 115
Saleh, F. M., 156
   see also Andrade, J. T.
Salisbury, E. J., 225, 227, 228, 229, 230
   see also Van Voorhis, P.; Wright, E. M.
Salzman, J., 11
Same-sex partners
   immigrant women, 115
   intimate partner violence, 107, 113–114
   mandatory arrest implications, 113–114

Sample, L. L., 147, 148, 150, 152
Sampson, R. J., 23, 24, 94, 95, 283
Samuels, S., 207
   see also Steadman, H. J.
San Bernardino County, California, 327
Sanctuary cities, 98
Sanders, M. B., 316
   see also Worcel, S. D.
Sandler, J. C., 153–154, 156
Sandwick, T., 327
Sandy Hook Elementary School tragedy, 13,
   201, 206, 330, 331
San Francisco County, California, 266, 269
Sanger, D., 71
Santa Clara County, California, 266, 269, 327
Santana, A., 131
Sarbanes-Oxley Act (2002), 164
Sareen, J., 208
Saunders, J., 94, 95
Savage, D., 142
Savage, J., 11, 13
Savings, Accountability and Full Enforce-
   ment (SAFE) Act (2012), 6
Savings and Loan crisis, 165–166
Saylor, W., 284
   see also Camp, S.
SB 1070
   see Arizona Senate Bill 1070 (2010)
Scalia, Antonin, 332
Scared Straight, 32
Schafer, J. A., 49
Schechter, M. T.
   see also Wood, E.
Scheck, B., 302
Scheidegger, P., 208
Schiff, M., 243, 256
Schiraldi, V., 265
Schizoaffective disorder, 207
Schizophrenia, 201, 202, 207, 210, 217, 222
Schizophrenia spectrum disorder, 207
Schlanger, M., 272
Schmidt, J. D., 104
   see also Sherman, L. W.
Schmidt, Lessard v. (1972), 205
Schneider, E. M., 102, 104, 105, 109
Schneider, V., 299
Schnell, J., 213
School-related risk factors, 23
School safety, 329–330
School zone drug policies, 129–130

Schram, D. D., 153
Schram, P. J., 225, 226, 229, 231, 232, 233, 234, 235, 237, 239
Schubert, C. A.
    see also Loughran, T. A.
Schuck, J., 16
    see also Wellford, C.
Schug, M. C., 210–211
Schug, R. A., 209
Schulhofer, S., 128
Schultz, George, 140
Schultz, P. D., 155
Schwartz, A. H., 205
    see also Mossman, D.
Schwartz, H., 135
Schwartz, J., 142
Schwarzenegger, Arnold, 132, 268, 269
Schweigert, F. J., 245, 250
SCJS
    see Sourcebook of Criminal Justice Statistics (SCJS)
Scott, T.-L.
    see Bonta, J.
Scott v. Hart (1979), 113
Scull, A., 204
Search and seizure policies
    constitutionality, 334
    DNA testing, 336–337
    drones, 334–336
    emerging technologies, 334
Search warrants, 334–338
Seattle Police Department, 110
Seattle, Washington, 142
Second Amendment (U.S. Constitution), 332–333
Secondary prevention programs, 24–25
Second strike provision, 262, 268, 270
Secure Border Initiative (SBInet), 74, 90
Secure Communities program, 92–93, 97
Securities and Exchange Commission (SEC), 163, 167
Security Uber Alles, 68
Seffey, D. M., 317
    see also Winterfield, L.
Segal, M., 279
Segregation units, 276, 287–288
Seiter, R. P., 278, 316
Seiter, Wilson v. (1991), 285
Selective prevention programs, 24–25

Self-medication, 231
Self-regulation policies, 165
Seligman, K., 337
Sellin, T., 56
Seltzer, T., 218
    see also Watson, A. C.
Semi-automatic firearms, 331
Senate Banking Committee, 168
Senate Bill 9 (California), 329
Senate Bill 1058 (Maryland), 330
Senate Ethics Committee, 168
Sengupta, S., 336
Sensible gun policies, 333
Sentencing circles, 242 (box), 246, 249
Sentencing enhancements, 179
Sentencing Project, 40, 49, 136, 206
Sentencing Reform Act (1984), 4 (table)
September 11, 2001 terrorist attacks, 67
Serious and Violent Offender Reentry Initiatives (SVORI), 318
Serious mental illnesses (SMIs)
    arrest factors, 208–209
    civil commitment laws, 220–221
    current policy state, 207–209
    evidentiary research results, 212–214
    female offenders, 227, 231–232
    historical perspective, 202–206
    incarceration rates, 203–204, 207–209, 208 (figure), 211, 218–219, 222
    legislative reforms, 219, 220–221
    mental health courts, 212–213, 219–220, 221, 222
    offender treatment, 211–212
    policy reform, 219–223
    prisoner reentry and aftercare programs, 214, 222
    psychiatric care programs, 205–208, 211, 215–216, 218–223
    race, ethnicity, gender, and class implications, 215–217
    recidivism, 211, 212–214, 215 (figure), 221, 222
    reform efforts, 203–206, 219–221
    specialty mental health probation, 214
    unintended consequences, 217–219
Serrano, R., 142
Seto, M. C., 146
Settles, T. L., 243
Severe acute respiratory syndrome (SARS), 70

Sex Offender (Jacob Wetterling) Act (1994), 4 (table), 147, 148
Sex Offender Registration Act (1996, New York), 154
Sex Offender Registration and Notification Act (SORNA), 148–149
    see also Adam Walsh Child Protection and Safety Act (2006)
Sex trafficking, 75
Sexual assaults, 198
Sexual offenders
    characteristics, 150–151
    civil commitment laws, 145, 146, 149
    criminal records, 150–151
    current policy state, 147–150
    evidentiary research results, 150–155, 151 (figure)
    historical perspective, 145–147
    legal impacts, 153–155
    policy reform, 156
    race, gender, and class implications, 155–156
    recidivism, 145, 150–155, 152 (figure)
    registration and notification requirements, 147–149, 153–155
    residency restrictions, 148, 153–155
    unintended policy consequences, 153–155
    victim advocacy, 146, 148
    victim-offender relationship, 151
Sexual psychopaths, 149
Shader, M., 19, 20
Shaffer, D., 133, 134
Shalom, 247
Shapiro, J., 72
Sharfstein, J.
    see Torrey, E. F.
Sharfstein, S. S., 205
Sharkey, P., 283
Sharp, C., 179
Sharp, S. F., 232
Shaw, C. R., 177
Shearer R. A., 232
Shelden, R. G., 8, 279
Shelp, R., 167
Shelton, D.
    see Kesten, K. L.
Shepard, M. F., 116
Shepardson, E. S., 317
    see also Taxman, F. S.

Sherman Antitrust Act (1890), 161
Sherman, L. W., 17, 17–19 (table), 19, 56, 59,
    104, 105, 108, 113, 117, 118, 178
Sherman, P. B., 215
Shields, P. J., 329
Shirking, 45–47
"Show me your papers" provision, 37, 49,
    94, 97
Shriner, Earl, 147
Siegel, R. B., 103, 105, 111
Signorielli, N., 11
Silbert, R. S., 272
Silver, A., 96
Silver, E., 208, 209, 211, 217
    see also Fisher, W. H.
Simmons, Roper, Superintendent,
    Potosi Correctional Center v.
    (2005), 184, 329
Simon, J., 145, 146, 277
Simon, R. J., 226, 234
Simple living, 172
Sinclair, U., 160
Singer, S. I., 196, 197–198
Sinkewicz, M.
    see Phelan, J. C.
Siskin, A., 91
Sittner Hartshorn, K. J., 12
Situational crime prevention (SCP), 60–61
Sixth Amendment (U.S. Constitution), 326
Sixth Circuit Court, 286
Skeem, J. L., 207, 211, 212, 214, 220,
    221, 222
Skelton, G., 263, 269
Skilling, Jeffrey, 171
Skinner, United States v. (2012), 337
Sklansky, D., 129
Skogan, W., 24, 58, 63
Slate, R. N., 211, 218, 221, 318
Slattery, E., 329
Slawson, D. B., 297
Sloan-Howitt, M., 61
Sloan, J. J., 265
Sloan, J. J., III, 40
Slocum, J. W., Jr., 39
    see also Jermier, J. M.
Small, D.
    see Lapidus, L.
Small, K. M., 243
Smallpox, 70
Smith, A., 112

Smith, B., 279
Smith, D. A., 104
    see also Sherman, L. W.
Smith, G., 173
Smith, Greg, 173
Smith, L. W., 209
Smith, P., 140, 315, 319
Smith, R., 296
Smith, S. G.
    see Black, M. C.
Smith, S. K., 194
Smude, L., 326
Smykla, J. O., 299
Snell, T., 135, 232, 233, 234
Snowden, J., 209
Socia, K. M., 153–154, 155
    see also Sandler, J. C.
Social control theory, 154
Social disorder, 58
Social disorganization theory, 177
Social justice, 243
Social media, 337, 338
Social risk factors, 22–23
Socioeconomic status
    capital punishment, 298–299
    delinquency, 20
    drug court programs, 134
    drug policies, 134–135
    female offenders, 237
    gang violence, 180–181
    gender responsive practices, 237
    intimate partner violence, 112–113
    juvenile waiver policies, 197
    mandatory arrest implications, 112–113
    mentally ill criminal offenders, 217
    problem-prone locations, 62–64
    reentry and rehabilitation programs, 313
    restorative justice programs, 253–255
    sexual offenders, 155
    supermax confinement, 282–284
    Three Strikes Law, 266–267
    white-collar/corporate crime, 170
Soft drugs, 126–127, 137
Sokoloff, N. J., 226
Solitary confinement, 276, 280–281
    see also Supermax confinement
Solomon, A., 209
Solomon, A. L., 313
Sorensen, J., 263, 284, 301
Soros, George, 270

Sosa, R. V.
    see Spergel, I. A.
Soulliere, D. M., 12
Sourcebook of Criminal Justice Statistics
    (SCJS), 311, 313
Sousa, W. H., 56, 61, 62, 63–64
South African Department of Welfare, 246
South America, 140
South Carolina, 106, 107, 336
South Dakota
    capital punishment, 303
    defense counsel performance
      guidelines, 303
    DNA collection, 336
    mandatory arrest policies, 106, 107
Southern Pacific Railroad, 160
Souweine, D., 209
Spaar, S., 56
Spain, 137, 140
Spangenberg, R. L., 297
Speaker, B., 91
    see also Mittelstadt, M.
Specialization, 151
Specialty mental health probation, 214
Specific deterrence, 280
Specter, M., 138
Spelman, W., 56
Spergel, I. A., 184
Spiegel, J., 204
Spiro, P., 96
Spittal, P. M.
    see also Wood, E.
Spohn, C., 146, 267
SPORT, 30 (table)
Spot maps, 54
Spouse Assault Replication Program
    (SARP), 104, 105, 108, 113
Stachelberg, W., 333
Stafford Act (1988), 79
Stambough, S. J., 6
"Stand your ground" laws, 7
Stanford v. Kentucky (1989), 329
State-agent narrative, 42–43, 48
State Lunatic Asylum, Worcester,
    Massachusetts, 203
State of Illinois, 302
State of Maryland v. Raines (2004), 336
Stateville Penitentiary, Illinois, 178
State v. Rhodes (1868), 103
Statutory exclusion, 192

Steadman, H. J., 207, 208, 211, 213, 216, 218
    see also Prins, S. J.; Redlich, A. D.;
        Swartz, M. S.
Steer, J., 129
Steffens, L., 160
Steffensmeier, D., 284
Steinberg, L., 198
    see also Loughran, T. A.
Steiner, B., 192, 195, 196, 279, 284, 294
    see also King, K.
Stengel, K. M., 155
Stenius, V. M. K., 40, 276, 281, 285
    see also Pizarro, J. M.
Stephey, M. J., 207, 218
Steps to Respect, 30 (table)
Stevens, A., 138, 139
Stevens, M. R.
    see Black, M. C.
Stevenson, B., 299
Stevenson, K. A., 55
Stevens, T., 20
    see also Chesney-Lind, M.
Steves, Rick, 133
Stewart, E. A., 316
Stewart, Martha, 170–171
Stewart, M. G., 84
Stewart, Potter, 294
Stichman, A., 145, 320
Stickrath, T. J., 276, 289
Stieber, J.
    see Torrey, E. F.
Stinson, J., 150
St. John, L., 92
Stommel, J., 214
    see also Sacks, S.
Stone, D., 178
Stone, G.
    see Hahn, R.; McGowan, A.
Stone, J., 97
Stop-and-frisk practices, 63
Story, L., 163
Story-Talk – Interactive Book Reading
    Program, 30 (table)
Stouthamer-Loeber, M., 21
Stowell, J. I., 87, 94, 95
Strachan, Steve, 133
Strakowski, S. M., 208
Strang, H., 245, 253
Strassberg, D. S., 150
Strasser, F., 302

Strathdee, S., 139
Straus, M. A., 112
Street-level bureaucracy
    accountability, 47–49
    autonomy, 45–47
    bureaucratic structures, 38–39
    characteristics, 39–41
    discretion, 42–45
    funding challenges, 40
    professional norms, 41–42, 49–50
    public policy actions and
        implementation, 37, 40, 49–50
    rules and regulations, 41–42
    standard operating procedures, 41–42
Street-level policy implementation, 37, 40
Street-level realism, 42
Streib, V. L., 299–300
Strengthening Families 10-14 (SF10-14),
    30 (table)
Strickland v. Washington (1984), 302
Strip, the, 58
Strobel, J. H., 133, 156
Strobel, T., 156
Strom, S., 90
Strong African American Families Program,
    30 (table)
Strong, K. H., 241, 242, 244, 246, 247, 248,
    255, 256
Students for Sensible Drug Policy, 136
Stutzman-Amstutz, L., 245
Stuxnet, 71
Suarez-Orozco, M., 95
Subprime mortgage scandal, 164
Sub-Sahara Africa, 182
Substance abuse
    ex-offenders, 316
    female offenders, 227, 228, 232
    mentally ill offenders, 207–208, 216–217
Substance Use and Crime Prevention Act
    (2000), 141
Success for All, 30 (table)
Suchy, Y., 150
Suicide, 198
Sullivan, M., 180
Summers, A., 213
    see also Redlich, A. D.
Sunbeam, 166
Sundt, J. L., 282
    see also Briggs, C. S.
Sung, H., 315

Super due process, 295, 296–297, 299, 300, 301
Superior Court (Romero), People v.
    (1996), 264, 267
Supermax confinement
    admission requirements, 286
    basic concepts, 275–276
    constitutionality, 285–287
    current policy state, 277–281
    deterrence, 280–281
    evidentiary research results, 281–282
    financial costs, 284–285
    future outlook, 287–291
    goals/performance measures, 277,
        288–289
    historical perspective, 276–277
    impacts, 281–282
    incapacitation, 278–280
    inmate-on-inmate/inmate-on-staff
        violence, 282
    legal issues, 285–287
    mental health assessments, 290–291
    needs assessments, 287–288
    placement and confinement policies and
        procedures, 289–290
    policy implications, 284–287
    policy reform recommendations,
        287–291
    prisoner security classification systems,
        286–287, 289–290
    qualified and well-trained staff, 290
    race, gender, and class implications,
        282–284
Supermax prisons, 276
Superpredators, 328
Suppa, S., 284
    see also Gaes, G. G.
Support our Law Enforcement and
    Safe Neighborhoods Act (SB 1070),
    8, 37
Supreme Court
    see U.S. Supreme Court decisions
Supreme Court, Arizona v. (2012), 342
Su, R., 96
Surette, R., 11, 177, 202
Surratt, H. L., 233
    see also Robbins, C. A.
Surveillance
    see Search and seizure policies
Surveillance and monitoring programs,
    87–92, 99

Survival crimes, 217
Swanson, J. W., 208, 214, 221
see also Swartz, M. S.; Van Dorn, R. A.
Swart, S. C., 213
see also Herinckx, H. A.
Swartz, M. S., 208, 221
see also Swanson, J. W.; Van Dorn, R. A.
Swift, J., 329
Swift, Jonathan, 159
Sykes, G., 280
Syrett, H. C., 165
Szalavitz, M., 139

Tabichnick, C., 129
Tafoya-Estrada, R., 95
Taifa v. Bayh (1994), 285
Talbott, J. A., 205
Taliban, 78
Tamis, K., 327
Tamms Penitentiary, 284, 287
Tanenhaus, D. S., 192
Tan, L. L., 96
Tarbell, I., 161
Targeted Reading Intervention, 30 (table)
Target hardening, 60–61
Tasers, 335
Tate, Lionel, 329
Taxman, F. S., 288, 316, 317, 319, 320
Taylor, B. M., 133
Taylor, K. N., 228, 230
Taylor-Nicholson, E., 327, 328
Taylor, R. B., 58
Taylor, W., 141
Teamsters Pension Fund, 177
Teen Outreach Program®, 31 (table)
Teff, H., 162
Teji, S., 268
Television programming, 11–12
Telsavaara, T.V.T., 146
Temperance movement, 103
Temporary Assistance for Needy Families (TANF), 24
Tennessee
capital punishment statutes, 300
DNA collection, 336
Tennessee v. Garner (1985), 37
Teplin, L. A., 208, 209
Terrorism
definition, 68

homeland security, 67
National Incident Management System (NIMS), 80–81
National Response Framework, 79–80
response strategies, 79–84
September 11, 2001 terrorist attacks, 67
terrorist financing, 77–79
Terry, K. J., 150
Tertiary prevention programs, 25
Tewksbury, R., 148, 154, 155
Texas
capital punishment statutes, 296, 299, 300, 306, 329
DNA collection, 336
homicide rates, 298
tough-on-crime policies, 263
Texas, Addington v. (1979), 205
Texas, Jurek v. (1976), 294
Thacher, D., 61
Thalidomide, 162
Thanasombat, S., 96
The Constitution Project, 302
The Economist, 214
Therapeutic communities, 316
Theriot, M. T., 149, 151
The Sentencing Project, 40, 49, 136, 206
Theurer, G., 211, 214, 221
Thoennes, N., 108, 112, 117, 146
Thompson, C. B., 203
Thompson, D., 135
Thompson, M. D., 209
Thompson, R., II, 334–335, 336
Thoreau, Henry David, 172
Thrasher, F., 177
Threats, 68
Three Strikes Law
conviction rates, 261–262
current policy state, 264
developmental process, 6
discretionary practices, 44
evidentiary research results, 264–266
future outlook, 270–273
historical perspective, 262–264
impacts, 273–274
implementation, 264, 270
legal challenges and modifications, 267–270, 272–274
policy reform, 267–270
race, gender, and class implications, 266–267

resentencing provision, 270–273
second strike provision, 262, 268, 270
Thrift industry
see Savings and Loan crisis
Tibbetts, S. G., 69
Tichenor, D., 96
Tillman, R. H., 165, 166
Tillyer, R., 42
Times Square bomber, 82
Timmendequas, Jesse, 147–148
Tirman, J., 90
Tjaden, P., 108, 112, 117, 146
Tobolowsky, P. M., 244
Toch, H., 276, 285
Tofler, B. L., 166
Tonry, M., 53, 265, 269
Toobin, J., 171
Torrey, E. F., 203, 207, 208, 208 (figure), 209, 211, 214, 219, 220, 221
Torti, Tummino v. (2009), 163
Tough-on-crime policies
background information, 3, 6, 9
California incarceration and realignment practices, 325
drug sentencing practices, 141
gang violence, 186
juvenile offenders, 192, 328–330
mentally ill offenders, 211
political aspects, 12, 40
reentry and rehabilitation programs, 311
supermax confinement, 287
Three Strikes Law, 261, 262–263, 270, 273
Tracking length, 335
Tracy, S. K., 279
see also Shelden, R. G.
Tramonte, L., 97, 98
Transactional Records Access Clearinghouse (TRAC), 89, 90
Transparency, 41
Transportation Security Administration (TSA), 73
Trautman, T. C., 12
Travis, J., 282, 311, 312, 313, 316
Travis, L., 320
Treatment Advocacy Center, 221
Treble, P., 137
Trenczek, T., 249, 252
Trestman, R. L.
see Kesten, K. L.

Trial judge training and certification, 305
Triple P System, 30 (table)
Trojanowicz, R. C., 58
Tromp, S., 150
Trotter, C., 320
Trupin, E. W., 213, 216, 220
Tsarnaev, Dzhokhar, 71
Tsarnaev, Tamerlan, 71
Tucson, Arizona, 202, 331
Tummin, Matthew, 167
Tummino v. Hamburg (2013), 163
Tummino v. Torti (2009), 163
Turner, D., 269, 270
Turner, F., 160
Turner, S., 25, 34, 262–263, 320
Twenty-first Amendment (U.S. Constitution),
    123 (table)
287(g) cooperation agreements, 92–93
Tyco International, 166
Tyler, T. R., 97, 254
Tyndall, M. W., 128
    see also Wood, E.

Ubuntu, 246
Uelmen, G., 141
Ulmer, J. T., 266
Umbreit, M. S., 241, 242, 245, 247, 248, 249,
    250, 251, 252, 255
    see also Bradshaw, W.
Undocumented immigrants, 88, 89–94,
    96–99, 114–115
Unemployment, 233
Uniform Crime Report, 2, 182 (figure), 262
United Kingdom, 244, 251
United Nations Congress on Crime
    Prevention and Criminal Justice, 242
    (box), 248
United Nations Economic and Social
    Council, 242 (box), 248
United Nations Global Study on Homicide,
    182, 185
United Nations Office on Drugs and Crime
    (UNODC), 139, 248
United States, Arizona vs. (2012), 8, 93
United States, Arthur Andersen, LLP v.
    (2005), 166
United States homicide rates, 181–183, 182
    (figure)
United States, Katz v. (1967), 334
United States, New York Central and

Hudson River Railroad v.
    (1908), 171
United States Pharmacopeia, 130
United States v. E. C. Knight Co. (1895),
    161
United States v. Jones (2012), 335, 337
United States v. Paramount Pictures
    (1948), 161
United States v. Paramount Pictures
    (1949), 161
United States v. Pineda-Moreno
    (2010), 337
United States v. Skinner (2012), 337
Universal background checks, 332
Universal prevention programs, 24
University of Albany, 67
University of Maryland Report, 17–19
    (table)
Unmanned Aerial Vehicles (UAVs), 334–336
Unnever, J. D., 313
Unreasonable searches, 334, 335–336
Upper-class violators
    see White-collar crime
Urada, D., 316
Urban terrorists
    see Gang violence
Urbina, M. G., 192
USA PATRIOT Act (2001), 4 (table), 69–70,
    71, 77–78, 91
U.S. Census Bureau, 89, 253
U.S. Chamber of Commerce, 164
U.S. Chamber of Commerce and Immigra-
    tion Policy Center, 95
U.S. Citizenship and Immigration Services
    (USCIS), 98–99
U.S. Coast Guard, 73–74
U.S. Congress, 263
U.S. Customs and Border Protection
    see Customs and Border Protection
    Agency (CBP)
U.S. Cyber Command, 77
U.S. Department of Health and Human Ser-
    vices, 215
U.S. Department of Justice, 2, 33, 131, 161,
    183, 184, 194, 196, 207, 242 (box), 245
U.S. Department of Justice—Federal
    Bureau of Investigation, 262
U.S. Department of Justice, Office of Justice
    Programs, 262
Useem, B., 278, 280

U.S. Government Accountability Office
    (GAO)
    see Government Accountability Office
    (GAO)
U.S. military, 296, 306
U.S. Secret Service, 75
U.S. Sentencing Commission, 125 (table),
    129, 142
U.S. Supreme Court decisions
    capital punishment, 293–295, 298,
        302, 329
    deadly force, 37
    defense counsel performance
        guidelines, 302
    DNA collection, 337
    gun control policies, 332–333
    immigration enforcement, 8, 37, 49, 88,
        93, 97
    juvenile death penalty, 329
    juvenile life without parole sentencing,
        181, 184, 257
    mentally ill offenders, 209, 210, 222, 285
    prison inmate constitutional rights, 326
    prison overcrowding, 272, 326
    search warrants, 334, 337
    supermax confinement, 285, 286
    Three Strikes Law, 267
    white-collar/corporate crime, 161, 166
Utah, 106, 107
Utne, M., 55

Vader, A. M., 321
van Beusekom, I., 138
Vancouver, British Columbia, Canada, 139
Vandalism, 164
Van Derbeken, J., 266
Van Dorn, R. A., 221
    see also Swartz, M. S.
van het Loo, M., 138
Van Ness, D., 241, 242, 244, 246, 247, 248,
    255, 256
Van Voorhis, P., 225, 227, 228, 229, 230,
    233, 238
    see also Wright, E. M.
van Wormer, J., 316, 317
van Wormer, K., 226, 231, 237
Vaughn, M. G., 207, 220
VAWA
    see Violence Against Women Act (1994)
Vera Institute of Justice, 327

Verdun-Jones, S., 216
    see also Nicholls, T. L.
Verma, A.
    see Lapidus, L.
Vermont
    DNA collection, 336
    restorative justice programs, 242 (box)
Vertical prosecution programs, 179
Veysey, B. M., 207
Vice Lords, 177
Victim-based racial discrimination,
    300–301
Victim-defendants, 110, 111, 113, 114
Victim impact panels, 250
Victim impact statements, 244
Victimization, 226, 227, 231, 254, 312
Victim-Offender Mediation model, 242
    (box), 249–250, 251–252
Victim Offender Reconciliation Programs
    (VORPs), 242 (box), 244–245,
    247, 250
Victimology studies, 244
Victims' rights movements, 7, 244–245
Vidal, S., 211, 214
Vieraitis, L. M., 265
Vigen, M. P., 284
Village-based cultural philosophies,
    245–247
Village Courts Act (1973), 258
Village Courts Act (1989), 258
Village Courts (Papua New Guinea),
    257–259
Vincent, G. M., 156
    see also Andrade, J. T.
Viney, W., 203
Violence Against Women Act (1994), 4
    (table), 8, 106, 115
Violence Reduction Strategy, 185
Violent Crime Control and Law
    Enforcement Act (1994), 4 (table), 69,
    125 (table), 147, 148, 263
Virginia
    capital punishment statutes, 306, 329
    DNA collection, 336
    mandatory arrest policies, 106, 107
    school shooting, 202, 330, 331
Virginia Tech University, 202, 330, 331
Visher, C. A., 317
    see also Lattimore, P. K.
Vitiello, M., 219, 263, 267

Vivona, T. S., 197
    see also Forst, M.
Vocational programs, 233, 316
Vollmer, August, 54
Vollum, S., 284
Volstead Act (1919), 122 (table)
Vos, B., 241, 249, 250
    see also Umbreit, M. S.
Vukich, E. M., 135
Vuong, L., 328

Wadsworth, T., 87, 94
Wagner, H. R.
    see also Swanson, J. W.
Wagner, J.
    see Kesten, K. L.
Wakefield, H., 154
Wa, K. M.
    see Spergel, I. A.
Walgrave, L., 249
Walker, D. F., 380
Walker, R., 101
Walker, S., 278, 280
Wall, A., 76
Wallace, D. H., 301
Wallace, S., 284
    see also Gaes, G. G.
Wallman J., 182
Wall Street Journal, 140
Wall Street Reform and Consumer
    Protection Act (2010), 168–169
Wal-Mart, 161
*Wal-Mart Drug Stores v. American
    Drugs* (1995), 161
Walsh, E. R., 297
Walters, Barbara, 133
Walters, John, 131, 142
Walters, M. L.
    see Black, M. C.
Walters, S. T., 321
Ward, D. A., 276, 277, 278, 281, 282
Ward, V., 168
Waring, E. J., 61
War on crime, 311
    see also Community corrections
War on drugs
    arrest rates, 128
    background information, 121
    criminalization policies, 135–137, 188
    current policy state, 126–134

drug courts, 133–134
Europe, 137–139
evidentiary research results, 137–140
historical perspective, 122, 122–125
    (table), 125–126, 311
incarceration rates, 128, 133–135, 188
less punitive drug policies, 137–140
prevention and treatment strategies,
    141–143
race, gender, and class implications,
    134–135, 237
sentence reduction practices, 141–143
specific drug policies, 128–134
state legislation, 129–130
unintended consequences, 135–137
War on gangs
    "attention to detail" strategy, 187–189
    current policy state, 178–179
    evidentiary research results, 183–187
    historical perspective, 177–178
    key factors, 176–177
    membership estimates, 178–179
    policy reform, 187–189
    prison inmates, 178, 183, 278–280,
        283–284, 287–289
    race, gender, and class implications, 176,
        177, 179, 180–181, 283–284
    social reform efforts, 177–178
    unintended consequences, 181–183
War on terror, 89
Warrants, search, 334–338
Warren-Gordon, K., 134
Wartell, J., 148
Washington
    mandatory arrest policies, 106
    marijuana legalization measures,
        132–133, 141–142
    Native Americans, 135
    sexual offender legislation, 147, 153
    supermax confinement, 281, 282, 283
    Three Strikes Law, 261
Washington Post, 142
Washington State Institute for Public Policy
    (WSIPP), 32, 133
Washington, Strickland v. (1984), 302
Waste Management, 166
Watanabe, T., 330
Waters, M., 95
Watson, A., 209
Watson, A. C., 218

Watson, J., 277, 281, 283, 288, 290
Watson, S., 130
Watts, J., 142
Watts, J. C., 142
Waul, M., 313
Weapons of mass destruction (WMDs),
    70–71
Webb, J., 188
Weber, M., 38, 39
Weiman, D. F., 198
Weiner, N. A., 300
Weiner, R., 133
Weisburd, D. L., 56, 59, 62, 63
Weisel, D. L., 279
    see also Decker, S. H.
Weiser, B., 159
Weis, H. E., 95
Weitzer, R., 40, 48
Welchans, S., 112
Welch, M., 180
Welfare benefits, 135–136
Welfare Reform Act (1996), 135
Wellford, C., 16
Wells, T. L., 277
Wells, W., 49, 109
    see also DeLeon-Granados, W.
Welsh, B., 22, 25
Welytok, J. G., 165
Werlich, T. G., 276, 277, 278, 281, 282
West, D., 22
Western, B., 135, 198
West Germany, 162
West, H. C., 237, 312, 313
Westneat, D., 133
West, V., 63, 297
Wetterling, Jacob, 147
Wetterling, Patty, 147
"What works" websites, 33
Whitaker, B., 266
White-collar crime
    American International Group (AIG),
        166, 167–168
    Arthur Andersen, 166
    Bear Stearns, 167
    broken windows theory, 164–165
    challenges, 159–160
    Citizens for Responsibility and Ethics in
        Washington (CREW) report, 169
    consequences, 166–170
    control strategies, 170–173

criminal law reforms, 171
current policy state, 163–165
defense attorneys, 171–172
Dodd-Frank Remedial Legislation,
    168–169
Enron, 166
evidentiary research results, 165–166
Food and Drug Administration (FDA),
    161–163
Great Economic Meltdown, 166–170
historical perspective, 160–163
Lehman Brothers Holdings, 168
medical fraud, 170
race, gender, and class implications, 170
Savings and Loan crisis, 165–166
White House, 76, 91
White population
    California incarceration and realignment
        practices, 325
    capital punishment, 299, 300–301
    crime reports, 97
    disadvantaged neighborhoods, 283
    drug court programs, 134
    drug use and arrests, 129, 196
    gang violence, 175
    gender responsive practices, 237
    incarceration rates, 5, 134–135, 237,
        253–254, 282, 313
    intimate partner violence, 105, 108,
        111, 112
    juvenile waiver policies, 196–197
    mentally ill offenders, 215–216
    sexual assaults, 125
    state control policies, 313
    supermax confinement, 283
    Three Strikes Law, 266–267, 273
    white-collar/corporate crime, 170
    White victims and offenders, 111–112
White, R., 180
Whitman, T. K.
    see Lemmon, J. H.
Whittier, N., 146
Wickersham Commission, 8
Widom, C., 22
Wiinamaki, L., 251
Wikström, P., 20, 24
Wilder, C. M.
    see Swartz, M. S.; Van Dorn, R. A.
Wilke, D. J., 106
Wilkinson v. Austin (2005), 286, 290

Wilkins, W., 129
Williamsburg, Virginia, 203
Williams, C., 142
Williams, F. P., 233
Williams, K., 302
Williams, K. G., 179
Williams, L., 183, 186
Wilson, A., 327
Wilson, Coleman v. (1995), 326
Wilson, D. B., 134, 315, 316
Wilson, J. Q., 58, 61, 63, 164, 172, 328, 330
Wilson, O. W., 54–55
Wilson, Pete, 263
Wilson v. Seiter (1991), 285
Wilson, W. J., 183, 283
Winfree, L. T., Jr., 179
Winner, L., 196
Winnicott, D. W., 181
Winship, C., 61
Winterfield, L., 317, 318
Winter, M.
    see Kupers, T. A.
Wiretaps, 334
Wire, The (HBO show), 185
Wisconsin, 106, 107
Wishnae, M., 90
Wobbler offenses, 262, 264
Wodahl, E. J., 320
Wohlsen, M., 132
Wojkowska, E., 257, 259
Wolfe, S. M.
    see Torrey, E. F.
Wolff, N., 211, 214, 221
    see also Fisher, W. H.
Wolfgang, B., 335
Wolfgang, M. E., 56
Wolf, R., 237
    see also Mauer, M.
Wolverton, J., II, 335
Women
    abuse and victimization, 231
    capital punishment statutes, 299–300
    domestic violence arrests, 109–111
    drug inmates, 135
    fear of crime, 10–11
    health care services, 230–231
    immigrant women, 114–115
    incarceration rates, 313
    mentally ill offenders, 216–217
    supermax confinement, 282–284

women of color, 111–112, 135, 237, 313
see also Gender responsive practices
Women Offender Case Management Model
  (WOCMM), 236, 239
Women's rights movement, 103
Women's Risk and Needs Assessments
  (WRNA), 230
Wong, T., 96
Wood, E., 128, 139
Wood, G. S., 160
Woodson v. North Carolina (1976), 294
Woods, S. O., 284
Woodward, B., 294
Woodworth, G. G., 300, 301
  see also Baldus, D. C.
Wooldredge, J., 284
Worcel, S. D., 316, 318
Workplace raids and arrests, 90
World Com, 166
World Trade Center terrorist attacks, 67
Worthiness, 43–44, 46
Wright, B. E., 46
Wright, E. M., 192, 196, 227, 228, 229, 230,
  234, 235, 236, 238
  see also Van Voorhis, P.
Wright, K. N., 279, 284
Wright, R. G., 145, 147, 148, 149
Wright, R. T., 172
Wright, V., 280
Wrinkle, R., 263, 284
Wyatt, E., 163
Wyatt, K., 6

Wycoff Medical Center, 170
Wyman's Teen Outreach Program, 31 (table)
Wyoming, 303

Yamini-Diouf, Y., 213
Yang, B., 298
Yates, Andrea, 202
Yazzie, R., 245, 246
Yessine, A. K.
  see Bonta, J.
Yi-Ying Lin, S., 89, 91
Young, Francis L., 130
Young Lords, 177
Young, M. A., 245
Young, M. C., 196, 198
Young, V. D., 10
Youth
  capital punishment statutes, 329
  criminal conviction impacts, 196–197
  delinquency, 19
  foreign-born youth, 95–96
  gang violence, 177, 179, 184, 187–189
  juvenile court system, 328
  juvenile versus adult correctional
    facilities, 197–198
  mentally ill offenders, 216
  sexual offenders, 155–156
  see also Juvenile waiver policies
Yukon Territory, Canada, 242 (box), 246

Zaentz, S., 205
Zahn, M. A., 301

Zakat, 78
Zanni, G., 221
Zapf, P. A., 215–216
Zaric, G., 139
Zatz, M. S., 196
Zawitz, M. W., 182
Zedillo, E., 140
Zehr, H., 241, 247, 248, 249, 253,
  255, 256
Zeisel, H., 267
Zelizer, V. A., 191
Zero tolerance policies, 62, 176, 188, 263,
  328–330
Zevitz, R. G., 155
Zgoba, K. M., 154
Zhang, R., 128
  see also Wood, E.
Zhang, W.
  see Kesten, K. L.
Ziedenberg, J., 134, 265
  see also Beatty, P.
Ziff, K., 204
Zimmer, L., 130, 138
Zimmerman, George, 7
Zimring, F. E., 148, 152, 156, 265,
  266, 278
Zion, J. W., 245, 246
Zolberg, A. R., 88
Zorich, S., 203
Zorza, J., 104, 105, 111, 112
Zuckerman, D., 300
Zuelsdorff, M., 134

About the Editors and Contributors

 Editors

Stacy L. Mallicoat is currently an associate professor of criminal justice in the Division of Politics, Administration, and Justice at California State University, Fullerton. She earned her BA in legal studies and sociology, with a concentration in crime and deviance from Pacific Lutheran University (Tacoma, WA) in 1997, and received her PhD in sociology from the University of Colorado at Boulder in 2003. Her primary research interests include feminist criminology and public opinion on the death penalty. She is the author of three books, including *Women and Crime: A Text/Reader, Women and Crime: The Essentials* with Connie Estrada Ireland, and *California's Criminal Justice System* with Christine L. Gardiner. Her work also appears in a number of journals, such as *Feminist Criminology, Journal of Criminal Justice, Journal of Ethnicity and Criminal Justice,* and *Southwestern Journal of Criminal Justice* as well as a number of edited volumes. She is an active member of the American Society of Criminology, the ASC's Division on Women and Crime (where she currently serves as an executive counselor), Western Society of Criminology, and the Academy of Criminal Justice Sciences.

Christine L. Gardiner is an assistant professor of criminal justice at California State University, Fullerton. She received her PhD in criminology, law, and society from the University of California, Irvine. She was awarded a prestigious National Institute of Justice Dissertation Fellowship to support her research on the effects of Proposition 36 on Orange County practitioners. Her areas of expertise include crime policy, policing, and juvenile delinquency. Her research has been published in *Criminal Justice Policy Review* and *Journal of Drug Issues.* She is the editor of *California's Criminal Justice System* (with Stacy L. Mallicoat). Prior to her academic career, she worked as a police explorer, dispatcher, crime analyst, and intern-probation officer.

 Contributors

Scott Akins is an associate professor in the Public Policy Program, Sociology Department at Oregon State University. His research interests include drug use and policy, the epidemiology of drug use and the intersection of disadvantage, ethnicity, and crime. His recent work has been published in *Homicide Studies, Justice Quarterly,* and the *Journal of Drug Issues.*

Shelly Arsneault received her PhD from Michigan State University and is a professor of political science at California State University, Fullerton. Her research interests include public administration and policy, with a special interest in welfare and poverty policies, and nonprofit organizations. Her most recent publication, with Shannon K. Vaughan, is *Managing Nonprofit Organizations in a Policy World.*

Robert M. Bohm is a professor of criminal justice at the University of Central Florida. He has published extensively in the areas of criminal justice and criminology, most notably on the subject of capital punishment. His most recent books include *Capital Punishment's Collateral Damage, The Past as Prologue: The Supreme Court's Pre-Modern Death Penalty Jurisprudence and Its Influence on the Supreme Court's Modern Death Penalty Decisions,* and *Deathquest: An Introduction to the Theory and Practice of Capital Punishment in the United States,* 4th ed.

H. Daniel Butler is a doctoral student at the University of Nebraska at Omaha. He earned his master of arts in criminal justice from the University of Southern Mississippi. His primary research interests are institutional corrections and the application of threat assessments to terrorist organizations. He recently published articles in the *Rutgers Journal of Law and Public Policy* on the constitutionality of super-maximum security prisons, and an article in *Criminal Justice Policy Review* that examines the admission criteria of supermax facilities.

Elsa Chen is an associate professor of political science at Santa Clara University. Her research is primarily on sentencing and corrections policy, focusing on empirical analysis of prosecutorial and judicial discretion, the implementation and effects of Three Strikes, and racial and ethnic disparities in criminal justice outcomes. Her work has been published in *Justice Quarterly, Social Science Quarterly,* the *Journal of Contemporary Criminal Justice,* the *Journal of Ethnicity in Criminal Justice,* and other journals. She earned a PhD in political science from UCLA, a Master's in public policy from Harvard, and an AB in public and international affairs from Princeton.

Meda Chesney-Lind is a professor of women's studies at the University of Hawaii. Nationally recognized for her work on women and crime, her testimony before Congress resulted in national support of gender responsive programming for girls in the juvenile justice system. Her most recent book on girls' use of violence, *Fighting for Girls* with co-editor Nikki Jones, won an award from the National Council on Crime and Delinquency for "focusing America's attention on the complex problems of the criminal and juvenile justice systems."

Courtney Crittenden is an assistant professor at East Tennessee State University in the Department of Criminal Justice and Criminology. She is currently working on her PhD from the Department of Criminology and Criminal Justice at the University of South Carolina. Her research interests include correctional programming, women in prison, and violence against women.

Alesha Durfee is an associate professor in the School of Social Transformation at Arizona State University. Her research and teaching focus on social policy and domestic violence, including mandatory arrest policies and civil protection orders. Her work has been published in journals such as *Gender & Society, Violence Against Women, Journal of Marriage and Family,* and *Feminist Criminology.* Her current research includes legal mobilization among domestic violence survivors, the arrest decision in cases of domestic violence reported to law enforcement, the social construction of domestic violence victimization, and how gender influences the way that narratives of violence are interpreted in the justice system. She has also volunteered as a domestic violence victim advocate for law enforcement.

Katherine Fennelly is professor of public affairs at the Hubert H. Humphrey School, University of Minnesota. Her research and outreach interests include the human rights of immigrants and refugees in the United States, and the preparedness of individuals, communities, and public institutions to adapt to demographic changes. She was dean of the University of Minnesota Extension Service, a faculty member and department head at Pennsylvania State University, and a faculty member at Columbia University School of Public Health. She holds a certificate of studies from the University of Madrid, and a doctorate in adult education and a master's of philosophy from Columbia University

Henry F. Fradella earned a BA in psychology from Clark University, a master's in forensic science and a law degree from The George Washington University, and a PhD in interdisciplinary justice studies from Arizona State University. His professional experience includes working in the Office of the Chief Medical Examiner of Washington, DC, practicing law with a large firm and as a sole-practitioner, and serving as a federal judicial law clerk. He is currently a professor of law and criminal justice at California State University, Long Beach. His area of specialization is the social scientific study of courts and law. This includes research and teaching on the historical development of substantive, procedural, and evidentiary criminal law (including courtroom acceptability of forensic and social scientific evidence, especially forensic psychological/psychiatric testimony); evaluation of law's effects on human behavior; the dynamics of legal decision making; and the nature, sources, and consequences of variations and changes in legal institutions or processes. Dr. Fradella is the author of eight books and more than 75 articles, book chapters, reviews, and scholarly commentaries. He serves as a reviewer for numerous journals, was a guest editor for two volumes of the *Journal of Contemporary Criminal Justice,* and has served three terms as the legal literature editor for West's *Criminal Law Bulletin.*

Larry K. Gaines is a professor and chair of the criminal justice department at California State University in San Bernardino. He received his doctorate in criminal justice from Sam Houston State University. He also has experience with the Lexington, Kentucky Police Department and the Kentucky State Police and has served as the executive director of the Kentucky Association of Chiefs of Police. He has published 13 books; his most recent book is *Homeland Security and Terrorism.* His other books address a wide range of topics, including community policing, police administration, police supervision, gangs, and drugs. He also has published approximately 50 scholarly journal articles on a broad array of criminal justice related subjects. His current interests include homeland security and terrorism, police tactical operations, and community policing.

Brett Garland is an associate professor and graduate program director in the Department of Criminology and Criminal Justice at Missouri State University. He received his PhD from the School of Criminology and Criminal Justice at the University of Nebraska, Omaha in 2007. His current research focuses on criminal justice management and staff, prisoner reeentry, and public opinion regarding correctional policy and practice. He has written over two dozen academic and professional publications and worked as a pre-release coordinator in the Indiana Department of Correction prior to entering academia.

Gilbert Geis was professor emeritus of criminology, law, and society at the University of California, Irvine. A prolific writer in a number of areas of criminology and criminal justice, he is best known for his seminal contributions to the subjects of white-collar and corporate crime. He served as president of the American Society of Criminology and was a recipient of its Edwin H. Sutherland award for outstanding research.

John Hagedorn is professor of criminology, law, and justice at the University of Illinois-Chicago. He has written two books on gangs, the most recent *A World of Gangs: Armed Young Men and Gangsta Culture.* He has edited two other books, including *Female Gangs in America* with co-editor Meda Chesney-Lind, which is still the only edited volume on female gangs. He is currently writing a book on the gang wars in Chicago of the 1990s. He has served as an expert witness in more than 50 gang-related court cases.

Megan Gosse is a Masters student studying criminology at the University of Delaware. She received her bachelor's degree in sociology and criminal justice from the University of Wisconsin-La Crosse. Her main areas of study include juvenile delinquency and drug use, and juvenile justice, and she is currently writing her thesis on prisoner reentry.

Ashley Kilmer is a graduate student pursuing a PhD in criminology from the Department of Sociology and Criminal Justice at the University of Delaware. She earned a master's degree in criminal justice at Youngstown State University. She worked as a co-facilitator of an intervention program aimed at helping sex offenders identify and address behaviors and thoughts that may increase their risk for recidivism. Her current research interests include examination of the unintended consequences of criminal justice related legislation and policy and political participation of marginalized groups, such as inmates and ex-offenders.

Barbara Koons-Witt is an associate professor at the University of South Carolina in the Department of Criminology and Criminal Justice. She received her PhD from the School of Criminal Justice at Michigan State University in 2000. Her primary research interests are in the area of women and offending, incarcerated women, and the influence of gender on sentencing decisions. Her work has appeared in journals, such as *Criminology, Punishment & Society, Feminist Criminology, Crime & Delinquency,* and *Women & Criminal Justice.* She currently serves as co-chair for the South Carolina Task Force on Female Offenders in the state of South Carolina.

Aaron Kupchik is an associate professor in the Department of Sociology and Criminal Justice at the University of Delaware. His work focuses on the punishment of youth in courts, correctional facilities, and schools. He is the author of *Homeroom Security: School Discipline in An Age of Fear,* and *Judging Juvenile: Prosecuting Adolescents in Adult and Juvenile Courts* (winner of the 2007 American Society of Criminology Michael J. Hindelang Award).

Chrysanthi Leon is an associate professor of sociology and criminal justice at University of Delaware. She received her JD and PhD from UC Berkeley and is a research fellow at the Criminal Justice Research Program, Institute for Legal Research at the Boalt Hall School of Law. She is an interdisciplinary scholar in the area of penology, law, and society. Her book, *Sex Fiends, Perverts, and Pedophiles: Understanding Sex Crime Policy in America,* is available from NYU Press. In addition to other publications regarding sex offenders, her recent research gives voice to women in prostitution and more generally examines the inclusion of public health values in justice systems.

Faith E. Lutze is an associate professor in the Department of Criminal Justice and Criminology at Washington State University. She received her MA in criminal justice from the University of Cincinnati in 1988 and her PhD in the administration of justice from the Pennsylvania State University in 1996. Her current research interests include drug courts, the professional role of community corrections officers, offender adjustment to community corrections supervision, and gender and justice with an emphasis on masculinity in prisons. Dr. Lutze has published her research related to boot camp prisons, masculine prison environments, community corrections officers, and drug courts in various journals, including *Justice Quarterly, Crime & Delinquency, Criminology and Public Policy,* and *The Journal of Criminal Justice.*

Donna Decker Morris is an associate professor in the Henry C. Lee College of Criminal Justice and Forensic Sciences, Director of the Legal Studies Program, and Director of the Center for Dispute Resolution at the University of New Haven. She received her BS in psychology from Tufts University (1972) and her JD from Yale Law School (1979). Before joining the UNH faculty in 1999, she was an attorney in the New Haven area focusing on civil litigation, civil rights, employment law, and appellate advocacy. Her research interests include studying the utilization of mediation and restorative justice practices, their impact on participants and the justice system, and international conflict resolution practices.

Clayton J. Mosher earned his PhD in sociology at the University of Toronto and is currently a professor in the Department of Sociology at Washington State University, Vancouver. His research focuses on criminal justice system policies with specific interests in racial profiling and inequality in criminal justice system processing and juvenile justice.

Nicole Palasz is a program coordinator at the Institute of World Affairs in the University of Wisconsin-Milwaukee's Center for International Education. She develops educational programs for public and K-12 audiences on human rights, sustainability, and other global issues. Previously, she worked with the New Tactics in Human Rights project at the Center for Victims of Torture, where she coordinated research on the use of innovative approaches to address human rights violations around the world. She holds master's degrees from the Fletcher School of Law and Diplomacy at Tufts University and the Humphrey Institute of Public Affairs at the University of Minnesota.

Henry N. Pontell is professor of criminology, law, and society and of sociology at the University of California, Irvine. He has written extensively on white-collar and corporate crime. Among other awards and honors, he received the Albert J. Reiss, Jr. Distinguished Scholarship Award from the American Sociological Association, the Herbert Bloch Award from the American Society of Criminology, and the Paul Tappan Award from the Western Society of Criminology. He is a past vice-president of the American Society of Criminology.

Roger L. Schaefer is a doctoral candidate at Washington State University in the Department of Criminal Justice and Criminology. He completed his master of science degree at Indiana State University in criminology and criminal justice. Roger has served as an editor's assistant for the *Journal of Theoretical and Philosophical Criminology* since its beginning in 2009. His research interests include sex offender reintegration, correctional therapeutic interventions, the evolution of criminological theory, and issues of race in the criminal justice context.

Rebecca Smith-Casey is a graduate of The College of New Jersey, where she completed a double major in psychology and criminal justice. She earned a master's degree in clinical psychology at Drexel University and a law degree from Villanova School of Law. For the past six years, she has worked as a consultant doing forensic psychological evaluations for criminal and civil court matters at Associates in Forensic Psychology in Bound Brook, New Jersey. Rebecca is currently enrolled in the combined school and clinical psychology program at Kean University, which she expects to complete in 2016. Rebecca's main research interests currently involve anger management treatment of court mandated domestic violence offenders, and the use of personality assessment measures with forensic populations.

William H. Sousa is an associate professor in the Department of Criminal Justice at the University of Nevada, Las Vegas. His past research projects include evaluations of crime reduction policies in New York City, Los Angeles, and Las Vegas. He is currently involved in studies of police order maintenance practices and community crime prevention in Las Vegas neighborhoods. His most recent publications appear in *The Journal of Experimental Criminology* and *Police Practice and Research.*

Benjamin Steiner is an assistant professor in the School of Criminology and Criminal Justice at the University of Nebraska, Omaha. He received his PhD from the University of Cincinnati. His research interests focus on issues related to juvenile justice, institutional, and community corrections. He has published over 50 journal articles and book entries related to these topics. Some of his most recent work appeared in *Journal of Research in Crime and Delinquency, Law and Society Review, Justice Quarterly,* and *Crime and Delinquency.* He is currently the co-principal investigator on a study funded by the National Institute of Justice that examines the effects of exposure to different types of violence on inmate maladjustment. His other current projects involve examining the causes and correlates of inmate victimization and rule breaking, along with the official responses to inmate rule violations.

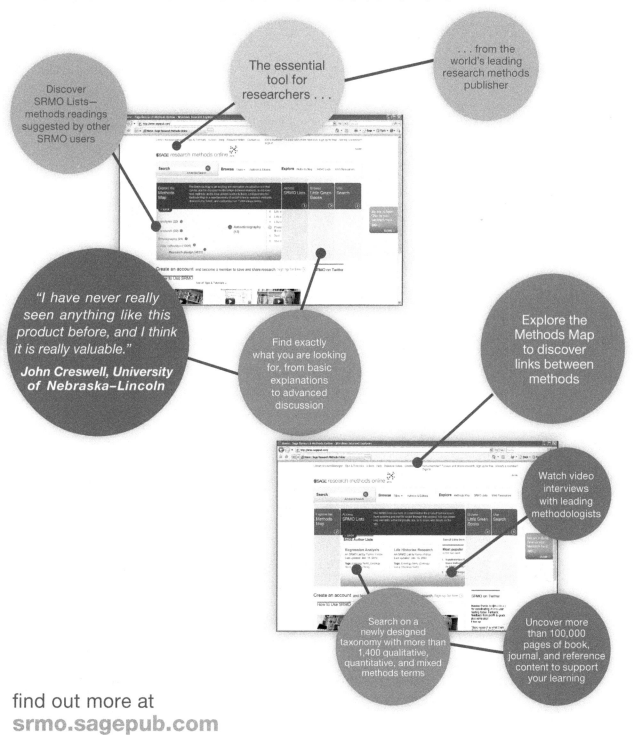

CPSIA information can be obtained
at www.ICGtesting.com
Printed in the USA
FFHW012152190719
53713219-59427FF

9 781452 242248